THE
MOZART
HANDBOOK

Books by LOUIS BIANCOLLI

THE MOZART HANDBOOK

THE BOOK OF GREAT CONVERSATIONS

MARY GARDEN'S STORY

THE FLAGSTAD MANUSCRIPT

THE ANALYTICAL CONCERT GUIDE

THE OPERA READER

with Robert Bagar

THE CONCERT COMPANION

THE VICTOR BOOK OF OPERAS

with Herbert F. Peyser

MASTERS OF THE ORCHESTRA

WOLFGANG AMADEUS MOZART

An unfinished portrait (about 1783) by his brother-in-law Joseph Lange.
In the Mozarteum, Salzburg.

THE

Mozart

HANDBOOK

A GUIDE TO THE MAN AND HIS MUSIC

COMPILED AND EDITED BY

Louis Biancolli

CLEVELAND AND NEW YORK

THE WORLD PUBLISHING COMPANY

LIBRARY OF CONGRESS CATALOG CARD NUMBER: 54-8174

FIRST EDITION

HC 854

COPYRIGHT ACKNOWLEDGMENTS

The editor and The World Publishing Company herewith render thanks to the following authors, publishers and agents whose interest, cooperation and permission to reprint have made possible the preparation of *The Mozart Handbook*. All possible care has been taken to trace the ownership of every selection included and to make full acknowledgment for its use. If any errors have accidentally occurred they will be corrected in subsequent editions, provided notification is sent to the publisher.

APPLETON-CENTURY-CROFTS, INC., for a selection from *Mozart,* by Sacheverell Sitwell, copyright, Appleton-Century-Crofts, Inc.

A. L. BACHARACH, for a selection by Edwin Evans from *The Musical Companion,* edited by A. L. Bacharach, published by Victor Gollancz, Ltd., copyright, 1934, A. L. Bacharach; and for a selection by Dyneley Hussey from *Lives of the Great Composers,* edited by A. L. Bacharach, published by E. P. Dutton & Co., Inc., copyright, A. L. Bacharach.

ERNEST BENN LIMITED, for selections from *Mozart on the Stage,* by Christopher Benn, copyright, Ernest Benn Limited.

BOSTON SYMPHONY ORCHESTRA, for selections by William Foster Apthorp, John N. Burk, and Philip Hale, from the Boston Symphony program notes, copyright, Boston Symphony Orchestra.

CHICAGO SYMPHONY ORCHESTRA, for selections by Felix Borowski, from the Chicago Symphony program notes, copyright, Chicago Symphony Orchestra.

CINCINNATI SYMPHONY ORCHESTRA, for selections by James G. Heller, from the Cincinnati Symphony Orchestra program notes, copyright, Cincinnati Symphony Orchestra.

COLUMBIA UNIVERSITY PRESS, for selections from *Chamber Music,* by Homer Ulrich, copyright, 1948, Columbia University Press.

DOUBLEDAY & COMPANY, INC., for selections from *The Concerto,* by Abraham Veinus, copyright, 1944, Abraham Veinus.

E. P. DUTTON & CO., INC., for selections by Phoebe Rogoff Cave and Otto Zoff from *Great Composers,* edited by Otto Zoff, copyright, 1951, E. P. Dutton & Co., Inc.

FARRAR, STRAUS & YOUNG, INC., for selections from *Mozart,* by Eric Blom, copyright, 1935, J. M. Dent & Sons, Ltd.

HENRY HOLT AND COMPANY, INC., for selections from *Mozart: Genius of Harmony,* by Ann M. Lingg, copyright, 1946, Henry Holt and Company, Inc.

ALFRED A. KNOPF, INC., for selections from *Mozart: The Man and His Works,* by W. J. Turner, copyright, 1938, Alfred A. Knopf, Inc.; for selections from *The Literature of the Piano,* by Ernest Hutcheson, copyright, 1949, Alfred A. Knopf, Inc.; and for selections from *The Symphonies of Mozart,* by Georges de Saint-Foix, translated by Leslie Orrey, copyright, 1949, Alfred A. Knopf, Inc.

JOHN LANE THE BODLEY HEAD LIMITED, for a selection from *Mozart's 'Cosi fan tutte',* by Edward J. Dent, copyright, 1946, John Lane The Bodley Head Limited.

J. B. LIPPINCOTT COMPANY, for a selection from *Memoirs of Lorenzo Da Ponte,* translated by Elisabeth Abbott, copyright, 1929, J. B. Lippincott Company.

MACMILLAN & CO. LTD., for selections from *The Letters of Mozart and His Family,* translated and edited by Emily Anderson, copyright, 1938, Macmillan & Co. Ltd.

THE METROPOLITAN OPERA GUILD, INC., for selections by William S. Ashbrook and Herbert F. Peyser from *Opera Lover's Companion,* edited by Mary Ellis Peltz, copyright, 1948, The Metropolitan Opera Guild, Inc.; and for a selection by Paul Nettl from *The Metropolitan Opera News,* copyright, The Metropolitan Opera Guild, Inc.

MINNEAPOLIS SYMPHONY ORCHESTRA, for a selection by Donald Ferguson from the Minneapolis Symphony Orchestra program notes, copyright, Minneapolis Symphony Orchestra.

NEW YORK HERALD TRIBUNE, for a selection by Peter Bowdoin, copyright, 1938, *New York Herald Tribune.*

New York Philharmonic-Symphony Society, for selections by Louis Biancolli and Herbert F. Peyser from the New York Philharmonic-Symphony Society program notes, copyright, New York Philharmonic-Symphony Society.

The New York Times, for a selection by Meyer Berger, copyright, 1953, *The New York Times;* and for a selection by Noel Straus, copyright, 1937, *The New York Times.*

W. W. Norton & Company, Inc., for a selection from *Composer and Critic,* by Max Graf, copyright, 1946, W. W. Norton & Company, Inc.

Oxford University Press, Inc., for selections from *Mozart: His Character, His Work,* by Alfred Einstein, translated by Arthur Mandel and Nathan Broder, copyright, 1945, Oxford University Press, Inc.

Oxford University Press, London, for selections from *Mozart's Operas,* by Edward J. Dent, copyright, 1947, Oxford University Press, London.

Penguin Books Ltd., for selections by A. Hyatt King from *The Concerto,* edited by Ralph Hill, copyright, 1952, Penguin Books Ltd.; and for selections by Eric Blom from *The Symphony,* edited by Ralph Hill, copyright, 1950, Penguin Books Ltd.

Philosophical Library, Inc., for a selection from *The Book of Musical Documents,* by Paul Nettl, copyright, 1948, Philosophical Library, Inc.

G. P. Putnam's Sons, for selections by Lord Harewood from *The Complete Opera Book,* by Gustave Kobbe, edited by Lord Harewood, copyright, 1954, G. P. Putnam's Sons.

Routledge & Kegan Paul Ltd, for selections from *Wolfgang Amade Mozart,* by Dyneley Hussey, copyright, Routledge & Kegan Paul Ltd; and for selections from *Some Musicians of Former Days,* by Romain Rolland, copyright, Routledge & Kegan Paul Ltd.

Saint Louis Symphony Orchestra, for selections by Bateman Edwards from the Saint Louis Symphony Orchestra program notes, copyright, Saint Louis Symphony Orchestra.

Sheed and Ward, Incorporated, for a selection from *In Search of Mozart,* by Henri Ghéon, copyright, 1934, Sheed and Ward, Inc.

Simon and Schuster, Inc., for a selection from *The Victor Book of Operas,* edited by Louis Biancolli and Robert Bagar, copyright, 1949, Simon and Schuster, Inc.; for a selection from *A Treasury of Grand Opera,* edited by Henry W. Simon, copyright, 1946, Simon and Schuster, Inc.; for selections from *The Metropolitan Book of the Opera,* edited by Pitts Sanborn, copyright, 1937, Simon and Schuster, Inc.; and for selections from *The Victor Book of Concertos,* by Abraham Veinus, copyright, 1948, Abraham Veinus.

George H. L. Smith, for a selection by him from The Cleveland Orchestra program notes, copyright, The Cleveland Orchestra.

For my daughter

MARGARET

on her 17th birthday

KEY TO CONTRIBUTORS

(The following list identifies every set of initials appearing in this volume. Where material was taken from more than one book, or other source, by the same author, the initials are usually followed by numerals. In the editor's case, no such distinguishing mark was thought necessary. What is not from The Victor Book of Operas *or the New York Philharmonic-Symphony program notes will be readily identified as his own editorial commentary for this book. Nor were numerals needed after the initials of William Foster Apthorp, whose two sources are easily differentiated. This is also true in one or two other instances. Where supplementary material appears in brackets it is always the editor's.)*

E.A.   .... Emily Anderson, translator and editor, *The Letters of Mozart and His Family,* three volumes, Macmillan and Co., Ltd., London, 1938.

W.F.A.   ... William Foster Apthorp, *The Opera Past and Present,* Charles Scribner's Sons, New York, 1905. Also, Boston Symphony program notes.

W.S.A. .... William S. Ashbrook, from the *Opera Lover's Companion,* edited by Mary Ellis Peltz, Ziff-Davis Publishing Co., Chicago, 1948.

C.B.   ..... Christopher Benn, *Mozart on the Stage,* Coward-McCann, Inc., New York, 1947.

M.B.   ..... Meyer Berger, *The New York Times,* August 21, 1953.

L.B.   ..... Louis Biancolli, New York Philharmonic-Symphony Society program notes. Also, *The Victor Book of Operas* (with Robert Bagar), Simon and Schuster, Inc., New York, 1949.

E.B.   ..... Eric Blom, *Mozart,* J. M. Dent & Sons, Ltd., London, 1935 (Pellegrini & Cudahy, Farrar, Straus & Young, Inc., New York). Also, "Wolfgang Amadeus Mozart," in *The Symphony,* edited by Ralph Hill, Penguin Books. London, 1950.

F.B.   .... Felix Borowski, Chicago Symphony program notes.

W.B.   .... Wallace Brockway (and Herbert Weinstock), *The Opera,* Simon and Schuster, Inc., New York, 1941.

J.N.B. .... John N. Burk, Boston Symphony program notes.

P.R.C. ....   Phoebe Rogoff Cave, translator and assistant editor of Otto Zoff's *Great Composers,* E. P. Dutton & Co., Inc., New York, 1951.

E.J.D. ....   Edward J. Dent (1) *Mozart's Operas,* second edition, Oxford University Press, New York, 1947; (2) *Mozart's 'Così fan tutte',* John Lane, The Bodley Head, Ltd., London, 1946.

B.E. ......   Bateman Edwards, St. Louis Symphony Orchestra program notes.

A.E. ......   Alfred Einstein, *Mozart: His Character, His Work,* translated by Arthur Mendel and Nathan Broder, Oxford University Press, London, 1945.

E.E. ......   Edwin Evans, *The Musical Companion,* edited by A . L. Bacharach, Victor Gollancz, Ltd., London, 1934.

D.F. .....   Donald Ferguson, Minneapolis Symphony Orchestra program notes.

H.G. .....   Henri Ghéon, *In Search of Mozart,* translated by Alexander Dru, Sheed & Ward, Inc., New York, 1934.

L.G. .....   Lawrence Gilman, New York Philharmonic-Symphony and Philadelphia Orchestra program notes.

M.G. .....   Max Graf, *Composer and Critic,* W. W. Norton & Co., Inc., New York, 1946.

P.H. .....   Philip Hale, Boston Symphony program notes.

L.H. .....   Lord Harewood, editor of new edition of Gustave Kobbe's *The Complete Opera Book,* G. P. Putnam's Sons, New York, 1954.

J.G.H. ....   James G. Heller, Cincinnati Symphony Orchestra program notes.

D.H. ....   Dyneley Hussey (1) *Lives of the Great Composers,* edited by A. L. Bacharach, E. P. Dutton & Co., Inc., New York, 1936; (2) *Wolfgang Amade Mozart,* Harper and Brothers, New York, 1928.

E.H. .....   Ernest Hutcheson, *The Literature of the Piano,* second edition, Alfred A. Knopf, Inc., New York, 1949.

O.J. .....   Otto Jahn, *Life of Mozart,* translated by Pauline D. Townsend, 3 volumes, Novello, Ewer & Co., London, 1882.

M.K. .....   Michael Kelly, *Reminiscences,* Henry Colburn, London, 1826.

A.H.K. ...   A. Hyatt King, from *The Concerto,* edited by Ralph Hill, Penguin Books, London, 1952.

E.C.M. ...   Elizabeth C. Moore, two appendices, chronological table, and list of Mozart's works, from *Mozart: Genius of Harmony,* by Ann M. Lingg, Henry Holt and Co., Inc., New York, 1946.

P.N. .....   Paul Nettl (1) from the Metropolitan *Opera News;* (2) from

The Book of Musical Documents, Philosophical Library, New York, 1948.

H.F.P. .... Herbert F. Peyser, from the *Opera Lover's Companion,* edited by Mary Ellis Peltz, Ziff-Davis Publishing Co., Chicago, 1948. Also, New York Philharmonic-Symphony program notes.

L. Da P. .. Lorenzo Da Ponte, *Memoirs,* translated by Elizabeth Abbott, edited and annotated by Arthur Livingston, J. B. Lippincott Company, Philadelphia and London, 1929.

R.R. ..... Romain Rolland, *Some Musicians of Former Days,* Henry Holt and Co., Inc., New York, 1915.

G. de St.-F. Georges de Saint-Foix, *The Symphonies of Mozart,* translated by Leslie Orrey, Alfred A. Knopf, Inc., New York, 1949.

P.S. ..... Pitts Sanborn, *The Metropolitan Book of the Opera,* Simon and Schuster, Inc., New York, 1937.

H.W.S. ... Henry W. Simon, *A Treasury of Grand Opera,* Simon and Schuster, Inc., New York, 1937.

S.S. ...... Sacheverell Sitwell, *Mozart,* Peter Davies, Ltd., London, 1932.

G.H.L.S. .. George H. L. Smith, Cleveland Orchestra program notes.

N.S. ..... Noel Straus, *The New York Times,* August 8, 1937.

P.D.T. .... Pauline D. Townsend, translator of Otto Jahn's *Life of Mozart,* London, 1891.

W.J.T. .... W. J. Turner, *Mozart: The Man and His Works,* Alfred A. Knopf, Inc., New York, 1938.

H.U. ...... Homer Ulrich, *Chamber Music,* Columbia University Press, New York, 1948.

A.V. ..... Abraham Veinus (1) *The Victor Book of Concertos,* Simon and Schuster, Inc., New York, 1948; (2) *The Concerto,* Doubleday, Doran and Co., New York, 1944.

H.W. .... Herbert Weinstock (and Wallace Brockway), *The Opera,* Simon and Schuster, Inc., New York, 1941.

O.Z. ..... Otto Zoff, editor, *Great Composers,* E. P. Dutton & Co., Inc., New York, 1951.

Introduction

FOR A COMPOSER whose life was as pathetically brief as Mozart's, it is astonishing how many books and articles have been written about him. But, then, everything is astonishing about this little man who, at thirty-six, had burned himself out in a fever of unremitting work. So much music was crowded into this young life that the bare monument of this achievement—Köchel's thematic catalogue—remains the most awesome record of creative output in the whole realm of music. Dead at just less than thirty-six, Mozart bequeathed a deathless and plenteous legacy of art, the full wealth of which the world has yet to assess. It is safe to say that of all composers only Beethoven and Wagner have had more written about their music—its quality, its place in the stream of musical history, its interpretation. It is at least likely that no opera has had so much said about it, both nonsense and wisdom, as *The Magic Flute,* and no opera has been more frequently hailed in book and article as the "perfect," or at any rate, the "greatest," opera than *Don Giovanni.*

What of Mozart the man? There, too, the bookshelf is ample, if not overloaded. His was not a life of spectacular outward drama, of momentous encounters, of flamboyant romance and exotic adventure. To be sure, the personal chronicle of so short a life is rich in episodes of childhood tours, home life, marriage, and fatherhood. It is the abundant life of a son, brother, husband, father, and friend. It is not, however, a "life of action." It is that other life of Mozart the creative genius—the solitary life of the study wherein this fabulous youth dwelt with the enchantment of his art—that lights up with blinding drama. Only there does one find the supreme exultation and frenzy, the lone ecstasy before the miracle of his gift, and the profoundest tragedy too. For Mozart, in the long years of neglect and impoverishment, must have known that his was the finest mind to cross the path of music, must have known, as we know it, that he was Mozart. That he was alone in that final knowledge, amid a blandly unconcerned world, was his deepest despair, and his solitary glory.

It is that Mozart—Mozart with pen in hand—who has inspired perhaps the best and certainly the greater part of the Mozart bibliography. There is little that can be added to the biographical shelf that has not already been refined over and over again from one book to the next. For the small circle that became Mozart's daily life we have his letters to guide us in retracing his brief earthly passage. Each of the biographies in English has its merits, but none of them springs any surprises on the student. We of the English-speaking world have no elaborate and detailed study in several volumes such as the French have in the work of Wyzewa and Saint-Foix and the Germans in Abert's edition of Jahn's century-old biography. These are the masterworks in the Mozart bibliography, woven together out of music and life with monumental thoroughness. Nor—to our shame and inconvenience—have we yet in English the Köchel catalogue (brilliantly revised and edited by the late Alfred Einstein), an indispensable companion of every toiler in the Mozart vineyard. We do have Einstein's own book on Mozart, and that is a priceless possession of every true devotee of Mozart, as is Eric Blom's compact and perceptive life. From both these excellent volumes I have culled freely and gratefully in compiling this *Handbook*.

Yet, it is amazing how the music, in number of pages allotted, far outweighs the man in all these volumes. Perhaps that is inevitable. It is, after all, the music that speaks for Mozart. In any large sense, we can know Mozart only through his music. Subtract the music from the man, and you confront, in all essentials, a rather conventional life. But we cannot subtract the music, and thus, by a paradox, every tiny detail, trivial or commonplace, that we salvage from this brief and distant interlude becomes doubly precious. Mozart is such a universal legend, so overwhelming a phenomenon in the story of human accomplishment, that we want to know everything. Even the knowledge that he played billiards takes on a singular magic.

When I set out on the journey that has ended in *The Mozart Handbook* I had certain objectives in mind. My primary aim was to bring together as many of the most helpful writings on Mozart and his music as were available in English (original or translated). I resolved at the outset not to employ musical illustrations. In a book of this kind there is a beginning, but no end, to the application of such a device. In any case, there was always Köchel for those seeking themes, and the score for those needing more. I preferred to envision a lover of Mozart who would not be troubled by the absence of musical quotations. To make up for this absence, I was determined to provide as much "technical" analysis of at least the instrumental music as a book of this kind could accommodate, short of textual sampling of the score.

For the operas, I wanted a clear and detailed synopsis of each of the seven major works, in addition to a background essay narrating the circumstances of its composition, and a short paragraph or two of statistical interest. For each of the music sections, I also wanted prefatory material that would in some way or other set the scene for the arrival of Mozart in that particular field of composition. For the piano sonatas, I sought a pianist who could write, who could analyze, who could teach. I found him, I believe, in Ernest Hutcheson.

The *Handbook,* I felt, should cover every important aspect of Mozart's creative activity. The Mozart legacy is, of course, colossal. Outside of the comprehensive pages of the Köchel catalogue, there is no hope, and perhaps little point, in attempting to name and outline every single work of Mozart's or even every single category of composition. I limited myself to what the average Mozart enthusiast was likely to hear in the course of several seasons in the way of operas, symphonies, concertos, sonatas, chamber music, religious music, and miscellaneous concert numbers like overtures and "divertimenti." In each instance, I wanted the reader to find background material, a movement-by-movement analysis (wherever useful), and again a quick glimpse of Mozart's predecessors.

For a handbook of this kind I thought, too, that the reader I had in mind would be best served by a short, compact biography to launch the portion of the book devoted to Mozart the man. There it was necessary to have the main themes of Mozart's life and career strongly, if succinctly, expounded. Many of these themes I wanted expanded and more sharply scrutinized in later sections. Having long ago discovered that one biographer will treat a certain phase of Mozart in fuller detail and sharper perspective than another, I went to different sources for such "expansion." I found what I wanted about Mozart's father in Einstein's book. For a vivid record of the *Wunderkind* tour (the very first of its kind) that brought Mozart and his sister before the great sovereigns of Europe, I helped myself to a chapter in Blom's biography. Again, the question of Mozart and Love I thought best documented in the pages of Einstein. For a selection of the letters, I went to Emily Anderson's superb translation, where, needless to say, everyone should go who wishes to know Mozart the son and lover and husband and sometimes shocking commentator on the smaller crudities of life.

Before I was finished with my exploratory work, I knew there were two other chapters I wanted, two complementary approaches to Mozart without which the title *Handbook* would have been a misnomer. There were people who knew Mozart and were thoughtful— or braggart—enough to leave a record of the little fellow at the billiard table, in company, at home, in the opera house, at the piano, in his deathbed. These reminiscences of Kelly and Grimm and Da Ponte and Schachtner, for what varying authenticity they contain, have been put together as a contemporary "close-up" of Mozart. They should bring us as close as we can get to the man, always apart from the letters, which are themselves a portrait of almost reckless and random revelation. The other thing I wanted was a parallel survey of the critics' view of Mozart in his own day. That, I found, had been handsomely done by the Viennese musicologist Max Graf.

To introduce the *Handbook* I sought a word-picture of Mozart's birthplace—the legendary Salzburg. I believe I found the answer in a chapter of Henri Ghéon's book on Mozart. To complete it, I needed a chronological table showing parallel events in Mozart's life and the world he lived in. This Elizabeth C. Moore had skillfully compiled for Miss Lingg's book on Mozart. Miss Moore's too, was the catalogue of works I chose because of its handy arrangement and meticulous accuracy. From that I omitted only the references to available recordings. Mozart "discography" moves much too fast for any "handbook" to keep abreast of it for long, and there is always the danger of personal preference in making what must be a selection, however generous. The final portion of the book deals with three aspects of Mozart's death—ending on a note of speculation.

Mozart's life and music weave inevitably into one pattern. Since my *Handbook* is divided into sections, each concerned with a separate aspect of Mozart's life or music, it is understandable that certain details of personal background will reappear, in one guise or another, as one consults other places in the book. They are leitmotivs that are often part of the personal fabric surrounding an opera, a symphony, a bassoon concerto, or only a letter. Their recurrence constitutes duplication only because a book of this kind cannot safely escape repetition without the clumsy device of continual cross reference. In a sense each section of *The Mozart Handbook* speaks for itself. All of it, I trust, speaks for Mozart.

LOUIS BIANCOLLI

Contents

PART III
Mozart in His Death

APPENDICES

List of Illustrations

 PART I

Mozart

IN HIS LIFE

 PRELUDE

The Birthplace: SALZBURG

THOSE WHO LOVE Salzburg love Mozart. Those who understand his town must understand him. And Mozart, who perhaps did not love it, little knew how much it resembled him!

If the country explains the man, there is no truer case than this. Neither Schobert nor Paris, nor even Italy, where he was to spend months, towards which his love of light was always to draw him, went so deep. Whatever he thought, I cannot imagine him born or centered anywhere else.

Mozart is explained by Salzburg. To tell the truth I never doubted it for a moment.

Those who go to Salzburg in the summer go there meaning to gorge themselves with music. Nor will they be disappointed: the best orchestra of Vienna, its best singers, the most famous conductors, some unique voices, an excellent Conservatoire, serenades in the open air. . . . One closes one's eyes almost, to hear better or, like the God of Love who is a little Mozart's God, goes blindfold.

"A town in the Austrian Tyrol, 400 metres above sea level, situated on the banks of the Salzach, with four bridges, and dominated on the left bank by the castle of Hohen-Salzburg; 40,000 inhabitants; no industry . . ."

So much for the guide book.

A small town of bourgeois that becomes a tourist centre as soon as the season opens. A few monuments left over from the days of the prince-bishops. Hardly anything worth visiting except the surrounding country; fields, woods and mountains with Tyrolese chalets. . . .

3

I was told that it rained often. As I never carry an umbrella I was prepared to rush from the theatre to the concert, and between times shelter in a café, ignoring the outside world.

Well, I was deceived! The morning of my arrival the weather was brilliantly fine. The modern town, near the station, has no charm, but my hotel was a real palace painted ochre colour, with a superb courtyard, vaulted passages, and to the south a miracle of a garden.

What a beautiful garden! But I put off visiting it for the present. The first item on my list was to get tickets for the concerts. So I imprisoned myself in a queue of Austrians, Bavarians, Americans and English, Swedes, Italians, and Dalmatians. After an hour's wait I was told there was not even standing room.

I went out cursing. Had I gone to Salzburg to see the town?— I was forgetting that Mozart was born there. He even lived for a time in the house opposite the office where I had been waiting. An ordinary looking house that is not visited: a placard politely asks you not to disturb the new owner and I took care not to.

Yet the small gently sloping square with its flower-beds leading up to a 17th century church at one end, all yellow, with green copper cupolas—in spite of its new hotel, new theatre, and post office— is laid out with great moderation: the church is its centre point. An old town that is not spoilt by the present is so rare nowadays that it is worth noting and appreciating.

An iron bridge leads to the old town on the other side of the Salzach. Perched up on a rock stands the castle, a Walhalla without heaviness or severity; above and beyond the high Italian roofs of the houses bordering the river, innumerable spires and domes, gay and light, are bathed in sunshine . . . Where in the world are we?

I crossed the river that seemed suddenly to have become the Arno or the Tiber, and plunged into the streets, so narrow as to be mere lanes, full of a southern shade. Vaulted passages, little balconied courtyards, and everywhere magnificent wrought-iron work . . . lost one moment and back again the next. The general effect is bourgeois and sympathetic, though not without a certain distinction. . . . There is his house! Wolfgang must have walked about here . . . and to think that this evening I shall be missing his music. I tried to console myself by humming the incomparable adagio of the Concerto in A that I was not to hear . . . At any rate I could go to the Festspielhaus where Max Reinhardt was giving Goldoni's play—*The Servant and Two Masters*—that Mozart ought to have put to music.

I wandered about the town—there must be any number of small towns in Germany with the same charm, the same appearance— when suddenly without any warning—though contrast is a preparation as Mozart knew well—the narrow street I was in opened on to a square.

I stood still, dazzled. Not dazzled perhaps, because I saw everything, the very shade was transparent, and everything perfectly clear. . . . Here was the highest peak of Mozart's art. Leaving his humility behind me I stepped out into his light, into the sphere of his gentleness, grandeur, and perfection.

The quadrangle, with almost equal sides, is composed of three adjoining palaces, and on the fourth side is a church. Though it really is big it looks enormous and the proportions take one's breath away. It is built in the grand Roman style of the 16th and 17th centuries that began with Palladio and ended with Bernini, not to everyone's taste though at last receiving its due. Fault may be found with it for excessive decoration but no one can deny its solidity, power, and purity of line. At any rate it is the last style that really lived and that presented a new form of grandeur independent of Romanesque, Gothic, or Classical models (in the sense in which David understood it). Under the names of Jesuit, Baroque, and Rococo it took root in all countries, and particularly in Austria where it was really understood.

And here perhaps is its masterpiece: the cathedral square, a square that is both cathedral close and palace courtyard opening out on to yet others. . . . Were it alone, lost in the midst of lanes and bye-streets, it would only be an incongruous or happy accident, according to the visitor's mood. But hardly has one had time to enjoy the beauty of the square and its silence (for it seems shut in and motors rarely pass that way) than through two porticos one sees two other squares, even more open and built in the same grand style. The porticos themselves are such as are only found in the Vatican, with rounded arcades and long windows, surmounted by a balustrade, joining the two palaces to the Cathedral on a level with the third floor. On the right is the square of the chapter, and on the left the square of the Residence: the spiritual and the temporal.

Nor are those the only ones. The cathedral square is prolific. It was the model and inspiration of an entire town that sprang up at about the same time. Only one enclave has survived: the Romanesque and Gothic church of the Franciscans and their monastery buildings. Everywhere else churches, palaces, and abbeys planned on the geometrical idea of the square, but at the same time lifting up to heaven the craziest of shapes, imitate one another and form a single domain both monastic and princely. And the tripper going from court to court, from cloister to cloister, is astonished by the repetition that is never without novelty and by passing a dozen times along the same road perpetually renews and increases his own delight.

The mark of a chef d'oeuvre is that it may be viewed in any light and from any angle, and though always the same is yet always different. Let me enjoy the calm of noon during which the happiest of chances revealed such marvels. Here are the Residence where Mozart gave concerts to the prince, the cathedral with its two towers and St. Peter's Abbey where between his tenth and twentieth year he conducted so many Masses; the wonderful fountains in which perhaps he bathed his hands. Enormous fountains whose florid and serried basins rise up and seem to top the houses. Their curving dolphins and rampant horses of marble, blackened and polished by the water, shine like seals. As in Venice flights of coloured pigeons settle in hundreds. The campaniles with their bulbous tops look as though they were ringing. The copper green domes add a delicate shade of colouring to the ochre walls, even those of the little café with its Virginia creeper terrace hiding under a tiny chapel with an ingeniously complicated little bell tower. An ochre wash reigns everywhere, renewed each year for our delight: on the palaces, on the monasteries, on the houses: from orange to red, from yellow to green; the whole scale of ochres of gold almost, as it shines from Naples to Genoa. The cathedral alone has a façade of marble, gilded by time, thrown into relief by the dark grey stone of the rest of the fabric. Once again I ask myself: where are we?

There are two recognizable factors.

Salzburg is a little Rome. Salzburg is a composition.

Like a Roman palace or a Mozart masterpiece.

Here is the story as I was told it:—

The prince-bishops had reigned for centuries, but in time had become more princes than bishops. On the Mönchsberg, the rock beneath which lies the old Salzburg, they had built the "Festung," the castle that dominates the whole valley. One can still see in it the traces of their former luxury: magnificent halls with gilded beams, cloisonnés, and painted ceilings supported on gigantic spiral pillars of wine-coloured marble. For a long time they were semi-barbarous overlords, more occupied with the chase than with art: the Lutheran crisis gave them back their Roman feelings. They withstood the Reformation; the Renaissance swallowed them at a gulp.

Of them all, the one most soaked in Italian taste was Wolfgang Dietrich von Raitenau, for he was related both to the Medici and the Borromei. He had something of each of them in him. Such portraits as we have of him do not exactly breathe forth sanctity. Hard and severe in his surtout or bright-eyed and smiling with his biretta over one ear, he alternates between brutality and cunning, between the cultivated politeness of a humanist and avidity. Elected in 1587 and not yet twenty when he ascended the double throne, this remarkable man, equipped with as many defects as with qualities, scandalized his people and his flock, opposed the Pope and the Emperor in a quarrel with his Bavarian neighbour over salt, and was finally deposed and imprisoned (in 1612) in his own castle. There he became, so his chronicler tells us, "a mirror of virtue and penitence"—it only remained for him to die.

Arriving in the little town of twisted streets and unsymmetrical façades, of enclosed squares and dark churches, Wolfgang Dietrich grew indignant. "What barbarism!" For him there was only Rome. From one day to the next he calmly tore down the confusion of mediaeval buildings, Romanesque, Gothic, post-Gothic—masterpieces perhaps—so as to rebuild his capital according to his own taste. And thus there sprang up, as though by magic, a miniature Rome of the Popes in a green valley of the Tyrol. And, intrigued no doubt by the game, the Italian sun followed the architecture: but on that point history is silent.

It is only a story, but like so many stories it rings true. The truth is that Wolfgang Dietrich could not bear having a Residence that did not conform to the fashion of the day, that he pulled down everything he could, straightened the streets, enlarged the squares, built himself a palace worthy of Julius II and Leo X, ordered enormous monasteries for his monks, sumptuous stables for his horses, and could never resign himself to pontificating in a Romanesque basilica. Fortunately it was burnt and he was accused of setting fire to it; but that would have been too much. He sent at once for his Italian architect Scamozzi and ordered him to reproduce, on a smaller scale, the plan of St. Peter's—which was done. God, however, did not let him triumph with his chef d'oeuvre; it was his successor who finished it. But Wolfgang Dietrich consoled himself by building for his mistress, Salome Alt, the daughter of a Salzburg merchant, the magnificent palace of Altenau, afterwards called Mirabelle, the very one, somewhat shorn of its magnificence, in which fate had lodged me. But in order that morality shall be half-saved we should add that Salome bore the prelate twelve children.

His immediate successors imitated him in almost everything; at any rate in his magnificence and his mania for building. The first was his nephew, Mark Sittich von Hohenems—Marcus Sitticus in the latinized form—to whom we owe the palace of Hellbrunn; the second, Paris, Count Lodron, who embellished the Mirabelle; then come the two Count Thuns, the counts of Harrach, Firmian and Lichtenstein, whose portraits may be seen in the cathedral, ranged along the walls of the transept, each different in the same purple: pious, sceptical, formidable, or florid, with coats-of-arms in beautiful stone bulging on every pediment.

The abbey church restored, the churches of the University and St. Sebastian built, the castles of Aigen and Leopoldskron . . . that is their title to glory. And so on down to Graf Schrattenbach, Sigismund III, Mozart's protector until 1772—a man of prayer—who drove a tunnel, over a hundred yards long, through the Mönchsberg so as to give Salzburg a replica of the Pausilippo. The inscription engraved under his effigy applies to the whole line, of which he was the last but one: "Te saxa loquuntur." The stones will indeed talk long of those strange prince-bishops! If for lack of a prison they did not all make amends like Wolfgang Dietrich, perhaps the stones will have pleaded for them in heaven and a merciful God have accounted them as good works.

The merit of all of them was to have respected the initial idea of the builder, submitting to his plan, modifying only the decorative detail according to changing fashion. And thus the fantasy, the affectations, the pathos and contortions, all that goes to make the charm and ridiculousness of Austrian baroque or rococo, fell obediently into the original plan without destroying or even altering it. And in point of fact it is wonderful to see how cheap and gaudy the stucco, the garlands of cupids, cascades of clouds, shells, and volutes, for all their superfluity, are swallowed up and absorbed by the broad lines. We should miss them if they weren't there. Like the arpeggios and "gruppettos" of the period they weigh no more on the cornice or the vaulting than the flourishes on a Mozart melody. Even if all the ornaments of Salzburg seemed to us laughable and odious, the Salzburg of the prince-bishops would remain as pure and great as the day it was born.

Such is the strength of order and style.

How can one think that the young musician passing daily through the streets, courts, and squares, short-sighted though he was, blind to all arts but his own, should not have felt one day—or indeed every day—the power of rhythm, the infallible power of true proportion, engrave itself upon him? He could hardly take a step without something being added to his formation. The prince-bishop was sent from Rome with the express purpose of building a classical town . . . for Mozart.

H. G.

1

Wolfgang Amadeus Mozart

Born January 27, 1756, at Salzburg
Died December 5, 1791, at Vienna

WITH THE POSSIBLE exception of Schubert, no composer has suffered more from the attentions of sentimental biographers than Mozart. Even in recent years books have appeared, representing the composer as a divinely inspired child who never grew up, a musical Peter Pan too dearly beloved by the gods. This view of Mozart would matter less, did it not encourage the damnable heresy that his music is so much innocent lollipoppery, the blameless confections of an infant mind endowed with extraordinary musical gifts. With the object of correcting this misconception, I propose to allot as little space as is consistent with a complete sketch to the often told story of his childhood, and to attempt a portrait, however summary, of the composer as a man.

The extraordinary musical gifts were there, indeed, and made themselves evident at an early age. At three the child was taking an interest in the music-lessons of his sister, four and a half years older than himself. Like any other child, he delighted in the sounds produced by hitting the keyboard with his fingers; but, unlike other children, he discriminated between concords and discords. His ear was so keen that he was soon able to detect a slight variation in the pitch of a violin. At four he began his musical studies in earnest, and at five he was composing little pieces which were copied by the proud father, not perhaps without correction, into his sister's exercise-book.

There is no accounting for genius, but at least Wolfgang Amadeus

Mozart was no exception among composers in being the son of a musician. His father, Georg Leopold, was a violinist in the Archbishop's band at Salzburg, where Wolfgang was born. Georg Leopold's fame as a musician rested upon his treatise on violin-technique, published at Augsburg, actually in the year of his son's birth, rather than upon his competent mediocrity as a composer. The book became a standard work and was translated into several languages.

The better side of Leopold's nature is indicated in the general principles he laid down for his pupils. He demands of them unselfishness and patient application. Virtuosity for its own sake is frowned upon and the honest orchestral player is preferred to the brilliant soloist. Further, the musician must be a sound Christian (which may be translated into modern terms as a man of good morals apart from any orthodoxy in religious belief) and be possessed of a general acquaintance with the other arts, so that he may play with intelligence. Such enlightened principles of education are not unimportant qualifications for a tutor of young genius.

Leopold's character had another side. He was not free from the narrow prejudices of middle-class society in a provincial town. His letters reveal too often a man without humour, obstinate and too little charitable. His pusillanimity was displayed alike in harshness towards subordinates and sycophancy towards the great. Always ready to suspect the worst motives in others, he attributed to hostile intrigues any disappointment of his hopes. These faults arose in part out of his genuine love and concern for his family. He was ambitious for their success, transferring to them the hopes of great achievement which he had failed to realise in himself. In his attitude towards his son he was not unlike the Victorian father of convention, guiding his footsteps with tender care, but unwilling to allow them to make any independent explorations. Until long after he had reached manhood, Wolfgang was not allowed without a conflict to make any decisions on his own responsibility. The wonder is that the inevitable breach was not irreparable. Wolfgang's affectionate nature was able in the end to span it, and Leopold seems to have mellowed in his later years. His tenderness towards his children and his self-sacrifice in their interests, as he conceived them, are the redeeming features of an unlovable character.

As a music-teacher Leopold had little trouble with his son, who was obedient and docile. The difficulty, indeed, was to get the boy away from the keyboard, at which he played as other boys play with soldiers or railway-trains. Wolfgang's only other interest was in arithmetic, often the counterpart of musical talent, and he covered every available surface with his sums. At the age of thirteen we find him writing to his sister, Maria Anna, to ask for the rules of arithmetic and adding to his signature the high-flown title of "Friend of the League of Numbers."

If Wolfgang was in some things an abnormal child, many well authenticated anecdotes are evidence of a healthy mind. In spite of his acute sensitiveness, he was lively and full of not always innocent fun. In stature he was small, but he was not particularly delicate. Indeed, his physique must have been wiry to withstand the severe illness and nervous strain to which he was subjected in boyhood. He was deeply affectionate and craved in return expressions of the love he lavished upon those around him. Herein lay the source of that charm which never deserted him, even though hard circumstance was to sharpen his tongue and a blind faith in friends was to lead him into unjust prejudices. There was, indeed, in his nature a genuine core of sweetness upon which the sentimentalists have fashioned their icing-sugar statuettes.

Leopold Mozart was quick to perceive that the precocious talents of his children—for "Nannerl" also showed an astonishing facility—might be turned to account, and in 1762 the family started out on a "celebrity tour" of Europe. The performances of the apple-cheeked boy, so pretty in his lilac coat, so lively in his intelligence, and yet so unaffected in his manner, enchanted in turn the Courts of Vienna, Munich, Paris, and London. The father's letters to his landlord, Lorenz Hagenauer, at Salzburg, are a series of exclamations, in which wonder is mingled with pride, at their triumphal progress, varied only by occasional attacks upon those who are supposed to have put in their way some obstacle to success. Now "Wolferl" has astonished everyone by playing on an organ with pedals, without previous experience, and standing up; now he has fiddled their baggage through the Viennese customs; now he has told the Archduchess Marie-Antoinette that he will marry her, or been kissed by a Prussian Princess—though kisses will not pay hotel-bills—or has rebuked Mme. de Pompadour for refusing a like salutation.

It is possible that Leopold's fond imagination exaggerated the musical and social success of his son, but there is plenty of independent evidence to show that wherever they appeared the children excited uncommon interest. In London, where they were announced as "Miss Mozart of Eleven and Master Mozart of Seven years of age, Prodigies of Nature," the boy was subjected to scientific tests by the Hon. Daines Barrington, the results of whose investigation proved that the boy's extraordinary powers were genuine enough. Some of his feats were, indeed, astonishing. At St. James's Palace he played pieces by J. C. Bach and Handel at sight, accompanied Queen Charlotte in an air, and then improvised a beautiful melody upon the figured bass of a piece by Handel. His public appearances in London were an immense success, even though the attraction to the audience may have been sensational and sentimental rather than musical. Nevertheless it would be a mistake to suppose that at this early stage Wolfgang was already a creative genius. The pieces published in Paris and in London are no sure criterion of his ability as a composer, for they were certainly revised and corrected by the experienced hand of his father. The only authentic document of this period is a sketch-book, which shows that at the age of eight the boy was by no means a skilled musician. There are many mistakes and no signs of a real control over his material.

The Mozarts returned to Salzburg in November, 1766, after an absence of nearly four years in all. They were delayed by the illness, first of the father in England, then of Nannerl in Holland. But Leopold was, in any case, never too scrupulous about the performance of his duties to the Archbishop when they conflicted with the interests of his son's career. He has been blamed, not without justice, for his exploitation of the boy's talent at so early an age. To modern educationists the spectacle of a child being subjected to the fatigue of travelling under the conditions then existing, to the excitement of public appearances, and to the adulation of sentimentalists, must indeed seem appalling. The marvel is that, whatever grave effects they may have had upon his physical strength, his temperament remained so remarkably unspoilt. Yet it is difficult to believe that his character was entirely unaffected by the attentions paid to him both by great personages and by the ordinary public. For the contrast between his easy successes as a child and the harsh difficulties that he encountered as a man may well have aroused in him the bitterness which embroiled him with authority.

From these early tours the Mozarts brought back no tangible gains, except the usual souvenirs presented by the great to musicians. Such money as they received—and Leopold was always grumbling at the smallness of their rewards—was swallowed up in expenses. But travelling in foreign lands and contacts with musicians like J. C. Bach undoubtedly had a great effect upon the mind of even so young a boy and developed his precocious talent. He was soon kept busy on his return to Salzburg by commissions from the Archbishop and others who wished to make use of the now celebrated young genius. It was recorded that the Archbishop, sceptical of his powers, had him shut up by himself while he composed a cantata. In the meantime he was set to study composition in earnest, his chief models being P. E. Bach, Hasse, and Handel.

In the autumn of 1767, a year after their return to Salzburg, the family again visited Vienna, where the wedding-festivities of the Archduchess Maria Josepha held out prospects of a profitable season. These hopes were not realised, for an epidemic of smallpox carried off the bride among its victims, and the Mozart children contracted the disease at Olmütz, whither they had retired to avoid it. With singular generosity, the Dean of Olmütz took them into his house, and though Wolfgang was seriously ill both he and his sister recovered. The boy had some years before had a severe attack of scarlet fever, and it may well be that these illnesses caused that lack of lustre in his eyes so noticeable in later life.

The Mozarts returned to Vienna in January, 1768, and, with the approval of the Emperor Joseph, who had succeeded to the throne four years before, Leopold obtained for his son a commission to write an opera. Gluck looked with favour upon the project, but Afflisio, the manager of the Opera, was not convinced of the wisdom of producing a work by a boy of twelve, and the project fell through. As a result of a petition from the aggrieved Leopold, the Emperor ordered 100 ducats (about £45 [$225]) to be paid by way of compensation. The young composer was further consoled by the performance at the house of Dr. Anton Mesmer of *Bastien und Bastienne,* a little piece of considerable charm though of no outstanding genius, and the earliest of Mozart's dramatic works to retain its place in the modern theatre.

In the eighteenth century, music meant, first and foremost, Italian opera, and it was to Italy that composers looked for their education, just as, a hundred years later, students flocked to Leipzig and Dresden in order to study German symphony. Handel served his apprenticeship in Italy; Bach based much of his music upon Italian models. It was natural that Leopold Mozart should wish his son to drink at the living source of current musical practice, and to exhibit his powers in the capital of the artistic world. He had intended to proceed to Italy from Vienna before "Wolfgangerl should have reached the age and stature which would deprive his accomplishments of all that was marvellous." He saw in the boy nothing more than a precocious talent, which must be exploited to the full before he grew to manhood and settled down as a respectable musician like his father.

Leopold had, however, to return to Salzburg at the beginning of 1769, and was unable to obtain further leave of absence until the end of that year. In the meantime Wolfgang had been appointed Concert-master. The post carried at first no salary, and it is not known when he began to receive the £14 [some $70] a year which was his stipend eight years later. The shades of the prison-house were beginning to close about the growing boy, who had basked in the sunshine of royal smiles and popular admiration.

At this time begin those letters of Mozart, which are the most revealing documents that any composer has left for historians. The boy's character is plainly to be seen even in these early letters from Italy, most of them no more than postscripts to Leopold's correspondence with his wife and daughter, who remained on this occasion at Salzburg. Already there are signs of that keen dramatic sense, of that ability to draw a character in a phrase, which was to place him in the front rank of operatic composers. There is an immense sense of fun, which was later to develop into a less pleasant form of jesting, but, where music is concerned, there is already a complete seriousness. Even to the boy of thirteen, music was the central fact of existence, a matter to be treated with the same seriousness and reverence as religion. Other subjects were matters for puns, jingles, and rigmaroles in three or four languages. It is as if the boy were cutting his literary teeth upon the hard bones of words, and his mature letters are, not least in their idiosyncrasy of style, very remarkable literary efforts and unique among the records of musicians.

His achievement is the more extraordinary in that his education seems to have been rudimentary in everything except music. He displayed no particular interest in literature. His taste lay in the direction of fantastic tales. *The Arabian Nights,* presented to him by an Italian admirer, particularly delighted him. The works of Metastasio, the great Italian poet and librettist, appealed to him rather as a young opera-composer learning his trade than as a student of poetry. Here it may be added that there is not a single reference in his letters to the masterpieces of painting, which he can hardly have failed to see during his travels, nor to the natural beauties of the Italian scene. Music was what he had come to study, and it engaged the whole of his mind, provoking comments that are astonishingly acute as well as wholly serious.

This Italian visit was completely successful. In Milan he secured a commission to write an *opera seria.* In Bologna he made a deep impression alike upon Padre Martini, the *doyen* of Italian musicians, and upon Farinelli, the great singer, who was living there in retirement. In Rome he performed the astonishing feat of writing out from memory after a single hearing the famous "Miserere" by Allegri, the exclusive property of the Papal Choir which no one was allowed to copy under penalty of excommunication. The Pope, however, bestowed upon the boy the Order of the Golden Spur and he was able to add to the collection of whimsical signatures at the end of his letters, "Chevalier de Mozart." At Naples, where he was entertained by Sir William Hamilton, the English Ambassador, he was suspected by the superstitious Neapolitans of black magic and had to prove to them that he could play as well without as with the ring which was supposed to be the source of his extraordinary powers.

On his way back to Milan for the production of his opera, he was admitted after a severe examination to membership of the Philharmonic Society of Bologna, at the unprecedented age of fourteen. In spite of the misgivings aroused by the age of the composer, the opera, *Mithridates, King of Pontus,* pleased both the singers and the public, and the "Cavaliere Filarmonico" was hailed with cries of "Viva il Maestrino!" *Mitridate* was given twenty performances during the season, after its production in December, 1770. The membership of the Philharmonic Society of Verona was added to Mozart's honours and he received a commission to compose a dramatic serenade for the approaching marriage of the Archduke Ferdinand. Here was the climax of his infant fame, and amid this blaze of glory the boy passed into manhood.

To the fond Leopold it seemed that his son was made for life. He could not see that in composing *Mitridate* the boy had shown nothing more, though that was astonishing enough, than a facility for pouring music into an existing mould. There was still no individual creative imagination in his music. One of Burney's correspondents, writing from Salzburg a few months later, summed up the true position, as it appeared to an impartial witness: "If I may judge of the music which I have heard of his composition, in the orchestra, he is one further instance of the early fruit being more extraordinary than excellent." A second shrewd observer, the composer Hasse, had other fears. "Young Mozart," he wrote, "is certainly a prodigy for his age and I am extremely fond of him. The father . . . adores his son overmuch and does all he can to spoil him; but I have so good an opinion of the innate goodness of the boy that I hope that, despite his father's adulation, he will not allow himself to be spoilt, but will turn out an honourable man."

The Archiepiscopal Court at Salzburg, in which he occupied so insignificant a place, must have appeared doubly dreary to the boy after the freedom and the excitements of Italy. Salzburg was a city without any important industry, in which everyone from the impoverished nobles downwards lived on pickings from the Court, and the Prince-Archbishop was no longer the wealthy and powerful figure of a hundred years before. The people spoke a clipped dialect of German with narrowed vowels and dropped consonants, which affords parallels with certain American corruptions of English. Salzburg becomes Soisburg as girl becomes "goil" or work "woik." Besides this dialect, which Mozart often uses for fun in his letters, the Soisburgers had their own brand of humour, which was embodied in the figure of Hanswurst, a character in the German marionette plays. This personage, whose name may be rendered as "Jack-Pudding," made jokes in "poor" taste or worse. We shall have occasion to see that in some respects Mozart was a true member of the Salzburg middle class, and that he was not unjust to himself in signing some of his letters with the name of Hanswurst.

The Archbishop, under whose rule he was born, was Sigismund

Schrattenbach, an old-fashioned disciplinarian, who seems to have allowed his musical establishment to deteriorate in quality, if not in numbers. There were nearly 100 musicians at his Court, but, according to Burney, they were "more remarkable for coarseness and noise than for delicacy and high-finishing." It is small wonder that the boy was deeply impressed when he heard the famous Mannheim orchestra at Schwetzingen on the way to Paris and London. Sigismund died in 1771 on the day of Mozart's return from a second visit to Milan for the reproduction of *Lucio Silla,* an opera which failed to repeat the success of *Mitridate,* and Hieronymus von Colloredo, Bishop of Gurk, was translated to the Archbishopric.

Hieronymus has been represented as the evil genius of Mozart, and, in the light of subsequent history, it is easy to accuse him of harshness and lack of imagination. He was, in fact, a man of considerable distinction in the Church and State, independent, enlightened, and tolerant. He was interested in music to the extent of reforming his establishment and improving its standards and, if he preferred Italian music to German, that was not unnatural in view of his own origin and the fashions of the time. He was not inclined, therefore, to further the ambitions of his touchy German Vice-Kapellmeister, Leopold Mozart, and infuriated him by importing an Italian to take command of his musicians when the post fell vacant.

The failure of *Lucio Silla* was due to several causes. It had a poor libretto; its impressionable composer, who readily adapted himself to his musical environment, had been out of touch with Italy for nearly two years; and he had passed the age at which everything he did was certain to provoke the astonishment and win the sympathy of his audience. It was an important turning-point in Mozart's career, for it ruled out the possibility of his developing into an Italian composer, like Handel and Hasse. A visit to Vienna, whither the Archbishop went in 1773, renewed Wolfgang's contact with German music, this time in the compositions, if not the person, of Joseph Haydn. Haydn's was the most powerful single influence upon Mozart's development as a composer, and from this time he began to speak of the older man as his "master." The visit to Vienna was, therefore, fruitful, though it failed of its immediate object, which was to obtain for Wolfgang a post in the capital.

A year later, in December, 1774, Mozart again left Salzburg for a visit to Munich, whence he had received a commission to write a comic opera. *La finta giardiniera,* which was produced in the following January, had a great success and its composer was once more spoken of as a "wonderful genius." Yet he received no tangible reward in the way of an appointment. On his return to Salzburg, Leopold set him to work harder than ever at violin-playing. His father (no mean judge) was of the opinion that, if he would do himself justice, he would be "the first violinist in Europe." The results of his application are embodied in the five violin concertos, all written at this time. But although he worked at the instrument to please his father, Wolfgang had no great love for it, and turned his attention to the newly invented pianoforte as soon as he cut his apron-strings.

The year 1776 was busily spent in composition. Pianoforte concertos, organ sonatas, Masses and divertimenti, including the well-known "Haffner Serenade," composed for the wedding of the Burgomaster's daughter, came tumbling from Mozart's prolific pen. But discontent with his position was growing. He was disgusted with the lack of any real interest in art, with the company he had to keep at the Archbishop's table, and above all with the attitude of the Archbishop himself, who would neither recognize his merits nor let him seek fame elsewhere. For when Leopold, who was becoming anxious at the growing strain in the relations between his son and his master, applied for leave to go on yet another tour, it was refused. Wolfgang called the Archbishop's bluff by applying for his discharge; and that dignitary, who had no wish to lose him, retorted with an ill grace that both father and son might seek their fortunes where they pleased—which in less archiepiscopal language meant that they were free to go to the devil. Leopold was, in the event, not allowed to leave Salzburg, and with great reluctance he dispatched his son in the company of his wife and with more paternal admonitions than those that sped Laertes upon his travels.

Paris was the ultimate objective of this tour. Leopold hoped, on the strength of Wolfgang's success in the French capital as a child, that all doors would be open to the young man of one-and-twenty, and that some lucrative post at Court would quickly be offered to him. Not that the travellers were to miss any opportunities that might offer themselves on the way to Paris. So mother and son, setting off in their new carriage, bought at great self-sacrifice, first visited Munich, where on 30th September, 1777, the young composer humbly offered his services to the Elector of Bavaria, only to receive the reply, "Yes, yes, my dear child, but there is no vacancy, I am sorry to say. If only there were a vacancy!"

At Augsburg, Mozart found more congenial company. He divided his time between Andreas Stein, whose new pianofortes aroused his keen interest, and his cousin, Maria Anna Thekla Mozart, of whom he writes, "We suit one another very well, for like me she is rather naughty; we laugh at everybody and have great fun!" This remarkably plain young woman, the daughter of Leopold's brother, brought out the Hanswurst in Wolfgang and the fun they had seems to have consisted mainly of jokes connected with that humble part of the human body upon which men sit. That Wolfgang was really in love with his "Bäsle" (cousin), as he always calls the girl, is psychologically improbable. He certainly flirted with her, as he had flirted with any girl who came within his reach for some years past. To his father he writes about the Bäsle with a mocking rapture, which rules out of question a serious entanglement, though not a genuine affection. So much has been made of the indecency of Mozart's conversations and correspondence with his cousin, that it is as well to state frankly that, for the most part, they consisted of nothing worse than, for example, singing in a part-song, in place of the proper words, "Padre Emilian, you booby, you may kiss my a——!" If this seems impolite language to use in the presence of a young girl, the difference of eighteenth-century manners from those of the recent past must be taken into account. Such expressions . . . hardly argue a base morality in the young man and their importance has been grossly exaggerated by writers who have reacted against the view of Mozart as an innocent child. Mozart was neither innocent nor a profligate. He was, as he says in one of the most dignified defences of his conduct against his father's misconstruction of his actions, a man like other men, and one in whom "perhaps nature speaks more strongly than in many big and vigorous louts." In an age of loose morals Mozart stands out, on the evidence of his letters and his actions, as a man, not always impeccable, but controlled by that idealism in his relations with women that is one of the marks of a noble character. Whatever the shortcomings of Leopold's education of his son in other practical matters, he must at least be credited with fostering, in his somewhat narrow and puritanical way, this side of Wolfgang's nature.

From Augsburg the travellers went to Mannheim, the seat of Prince Karl Theodor, one of those German princes who sought to emulate the glories and the vices of Versailles. The vices have passed away, but the glories remain in one of the finest pieces of town-planning in the world, whose severity of ordered outline is made warm and beautiful by the rosy stone of which the houses are built. Here Wolfgang fell seriously in love. Among the musicians in the town was Fridolin Weber, a copyist, who had four daughters, of whom the eldest, Josepha, was the possessor of a remarkable voice and has her place in musical history as the creator of the part of the Queen of the Night in *The Magic Flute*. The second daughter, Aloysia, was also a singer, and Wolfgang soon began to write of her to his father with a discreet enthusiasm, while the lively correspondence with the Bäsle at Augsburg temporarily ceased. Finally the young man proposed that he should abandon his visit to Paris and accompany the Weber family on a tour in Italy. Leopold received this hare-brained project "with amazement and horror" and ordered his son to be off to Paris. For the first time Wolfgang showed signs of revolt against his father's oppressive guardianship. He is no longer a child, he writes, and, though his love and respect are undiminished, he will not tolerate accusations about his conduct with Aloysia. "There are some people," he says scornfully, "who think it impossible to love a girl without evil designs and this pretty word *mistress* is indeed a fine one!"

Leopold was adamant and Wolfgang eventually departed for Paris in the middle of March, 1778. The visit was completely unfruitful. Melchior Grimm, who had helped the infant prodigies fifteen years before, was less interested in a young man without the social attractions of a resounding success and was frankly bored by Leopold's tedious screeds about his son's marvellous gifts. Grimm was a lion-hunter, to whom genius was synonymous with success. Le Gros, the director of the Concert Spirituel, was no more helpful. Projects for an opera came to nothing and the only work that Mozart composed for the Parisian stage was the ballet, *Les Petits Riens*. He was, indeed, offered the post of organist at Versailles with a salary of

2,000 livres (about £90 [$400]), which Leopold urged him to accept. But Mozart rightly felt that Versailles was a backwater and Paris, pre-occupied with the rivalry of Gluck and Piccinni, no place for an unknown German composer. Possibly, too, he was influenced by thoughts of the separation from Aloysia, which acceptance would involve. While he was still undecided, his mother fell ill and on 3rd July she died.

For the first time in his life, Mozart was alone in the world. He remained in Paris until the end of September, seemingly stunned and incapable of action. His father now urged him to return to Salzburg, where there were prospects of his advancement owing to the deaths of the organist and the Kapellmeister. Wolfgang was appointed on his return to the former of these posts with a salary of about £40 [some $200] but the latter was given, as I have related, to an Italian. Salzburg held no attractions for the young man and he made no haste to reach home. His first objective was, not unnaturally, Mannheim, but the Court and with it the Weber family had moved to Munich. At Mannheim he received peremptory orders to return at once. So he left—for Munich. A sorry figure in his mourning clothes, he presented himself to Aloysia. But she had become in the meantime a successful singer and thought she could do better for herself than link her fortunes with a composer of little outward favour and less worldly success. Wolfgang, the story goes, sat down at the pianoforte and sang, with a mixture of bitterness and humour, to the melody of "Ich lass das Mädel gern, dass mich nicht will," words in the vein of his letters to the Bäsle. That young person, by the way, had been cajoled into coming to Munich "to play a great *rôle*," which was apparently to be bridesmaid at her fickle cousin's wedding. Aloysia's idea of bettering herself was to marry a travelling actor named Lange, whose sole distinction is that some years later he painted the best portrait of Mozart.

In spite of Leopold's entreaties and commands Wolfgang could not tear himself away from Munich. He found consolation in the company of his spritely cousin, with whom he concocted joint epistles to Salzburg full of jibes and puns. A blot is turned into a portrait "of my cousin writing in her shirt-sleeves" and the word "cousin" before her signature is altered to "cochon." Such fooling infuriated Leopold, and he commanded Wolfgang peremptorily to return home. At last in the middle of January, 1779, Wolfgang obeyed, but he took his "dear little Bäsle" with him.

It was a sad and disillusioned young man who took his place at the Archbishop's table between Ceccarelli, the male soprano, and the disreputable violinist, Brunetti. Their company and the whole atmosphere of Salzburg were more than ever repugnant to his sensitive nature. He settled down to his duties as organist, composing music for the Cathedral as well as symphonies and divertimenti. He also tried his hand at a German opera to a libretto by his friend Schachtner, the horn-player. This was interrupted by a commission to write an *opera seria* for the Munich Carnival of 1781. He was given a long-winded and ineffective libretto concocted, in poor imitation of Metastasio, by the Archbishop's chaplain. The theme was the story of the return from Troy of Idomeneo, King of Crete, who made the same rash vow as Jephthah.

Mozart's letters from Munich concerning his troubles with Raaf, the elderly tenor, who was only too willing to give the composer the benefit of his experience, and the juvenile dal Prato (*"mio molto amato castrato dal Prato"*), a boy of sixteen who had no experience at all, make amusing reading. They contain, too, the only considerable record of Mozart's views upon opera. Mozart was never a conscious theorist, and rarely expressed his ideas about music as an art. The grasp of the principles of operatic, as of symphonic, composition was intuitive rather than intellectual. It is fortunate for us, therefore, that circumstances compelled him to put down on paper his reasons for altering the libretto of *Idomeneo,* so that Leopold might pacify the author. . . .

Idomeneo, a classical *opera seria* in the manner of Gluck, had a momentary success, but its production led to no advancement for the composer. Wolfgang was summoned from Munich to join the Archbishop at Vienna, whither he had moved with part of his musical staff, Leopold being left behind at Salzburg. Wolfgang's letters to his father reveal his ever growing discontent with his position. Sarcastically he congratulates himself upon having the honour to sit above the cooks at table, and grumbles at the allowance of three ducats paid when no meal was provided. "The Archbishop is glad enough to get credit from his people; he takes their services and does not pay for them."

The storm was brewing and in vain Leopold counselled his son to have patience. With incredible meanness the Archbishop at first refused to allow his organist to arrange a charity concert, and, although he had to yield on this point, Wolfgang was not permitted to give a concert for his own benefit. When to these injuries there were added insults, Mozart decided that, despite his father's entreaties, he would endure such indignities no longer. The Archbishop, who was unpopular with the Emperor and the nobility, took offence at not receiving an invitation to the summer residence of the Court at Laxenburg, and decided to return at once to Salzburg. Mozart was told to clear out of the house at short notice with several "grossly impertinent" terms of abuse added to the order. He did not leave town, but went to lodge with his friends, the Webers, who had moved to Vienna. After a further stormy interview with his master, Mozart sent in his resignation. It was ignored. After an interval he wrote out his application for a discharge once more, and presented it in person on 8th June. For answer he was kicked out of the Archbishop's house by Count Arco, the high steward. Smarting from this insult, Wolfgang wrote to his father: "No more Salzburg for me! I hate the Archbishop almost to fury." He further threatened that, if he met Count Arco in the street, he would return the assault with interest.

Reading between the lines of Wolfgang's letters, it is not difficult to see that, besides his indignation at his treatment by "this man of God," he had other motives when he seized the opportunity to gain his freedom. He clearly hoped to make a career in Vienna and even urged his father to cut himself free from Salzburg and join him in the capital. And there were the Webers. Wolfgang, having lost Aloysia, fell in love with her next sister, Constanze, a plain girl eight years younger than himself. When he realised the position, Leopold, who had a poor opinion of the Webers, was horrified, but Wolfgang knew what he wanted and this time was determined to get it, with his father's consent if possible, otherwise, without it. To Leopold's letters, which put the worst construction on his conduct, he replied with a dignity that only a cynic could dismiss as insincere. Indeed, in view of Constanze's subsequent series of annual confinements, there is, at least, negative evidence that she was not Wolfgang's mistress at this time. Their first child, Raimund Leopold, was born nine months after their wedding on 4th August, 1782.

Wolfgang could, indeed, be as prudish as his father, and during the engagement he took Constanze to task for allowing her leg to be measured during a game of forfeits. Although Wolfgang compares her favourably with the once-adored Aloysia, Constanze had something of her elder sister's capriciousness and love of pleasure. Coming from what we may call a "Bohemian" household where nothing was ever in order, she was hardly the person to manage the affairs of a young man who had never been allowed by his father any responsibility in money-matters and had persistently been shielded from the practical difficulties of life. Leopold had good cause to be anxious about his son's marriage, but he cannot be absolved from all blame for its disastrous consequences. He had educated Wolfgang admirably as a musician, but he had wholly neglected to prepare him to face life as a man.

The newly married couple were happy enough at the start. They were undoubtedly deeply in love and, if we want a picture of them settling into their home, the first scene in *The Marriage of Figaro* is probably as truthful a portrait as we could find. In spite of the success of his German comic opera, *Die Entführung aus dem Serail,* produced in July, 1782, which was patronised by the Emperor, Wolfgang had practically no income and the expected appointment at Court failed to materialise. Within six months they were already in difficulties and Constanze was pregnant. In judging her as a housewife, we must not forget that, for the greater part of her married life, Constanze was either pregnant or recovering from the difficult births of her children, of whom only two survived, one to become an official in the Austrian service at Milan and the other an insignificant conductor and pianist.

There is no reason to suppose that Constanze encouraged her husband in his work or appreciated his genius—at least until after his death, when she developed for his music in retrospect a sentiment never manifested in his lifetime. In spite, therefore, of his happy companionship with his wife, Mozart suffered from the loneliness that

is possibly the invariable lot of great men. It may be that this personal loneliness—and in this connection Haydn and Beethoven come
to mind—is one of the driving forces that compel an artist to create.

As a wedding-present for Constanze and as an act of piety Mozart
set to work on the composition of a large-scale Mass in C minor, but
he failed to complete it. He was always temperamentally incapable
of writing without the stimulus of a definite performance in view,
but in this instance a profound change in his religious convictions
made it impossible for him to complete the work. Hitherto Mozart
had shown a childlike faith in religion; but in Vienna he came into
contact with a number of musicians and literary men who belonged
to the secret Society of Freemasons. In Germany and Austria, Freemasonry had not the exclusively charitable objects which character-
ise it in England to-day. . . . It gained the accession . . . of men
like Frederick the Great, Goethe, and Herder, while in Austria
the Emperor Joseph joined the Society, whose leader in Vienna
was Ignaz von Born. Although, therefore, Freemasonry was driven
underground by oppressive measures and the disapproval of the
Roman Catholic Church, which has never tolerated secret societies,
it was a potent force in Vienna at this time. Wolfgang persuaded his
father to join the Society, and hereafter his letters are full of cryptic
allusions to Masonic ideas. Among other musicians, Gluck and, surprisingly, that good churchman, Joseph Haydn, were Freemasons.

The year of Mozart's marriage (1782) was prolific in compositions,
the most important being the set of six quartets dedicated to Haydn.
For a livelihood he took pupils, a task always distasteful to him, and
supplied them with music to play. After the birth of their first child,
the couple paid a visit to Salzburg in the hope that Leopold might
be reconciled to the marriage. Constanze failed to remove the deep-
seated prejudices of her father-in-law, which were shared by
Nannerl. The visit was uncomfortable and the parting cold.

On returning to Vienna, Wolfgang proceeded to give concerts at
the Augarten, with meagre financial results but with great artistic
success. Gluck praised his music and the Emperor stayed "to the
very end until the encores were finished." When it is remembered
that these programmes included the "Haffner" symphony and a series
of pianoforte concertos played by the composer, it is easy to share
Haydn's indignation at the failure of the Court to recognise his

worth by finding him some employment. It was not until the end of 1787, after he had written *The Marriage of Figaro* and *Don Giovanni,* that he was appointed chamber-musician and Court-composer to the Emperor with a salary that barely paid his rent.

Several minor operatic projects were occupying Mozart's mind at this time, but they came to nothing. Then, as the result of an amateur performance of *Idomeneo,* he was brought into contact with an ideal collaborator. Lorenzo da Ponte was an Italian Jew by birth, a priest by profession, and a poet by inclination. After a series of adventures not unworthy of Casanova himself—if we may believe the autobiography he published in his old age—he arrived in Vienna in 1783 and wrote librettos for Salieri and Martin. Mozart suggested that da Ponte should adapt for him Beaumarchais' *Les Noces de Figaro*. This play had been banned in Vienna, and its predecessor, *Le Barbier de Séville,* had just been successfully staged as an opera with music by Paisiello. There was, therefore, a double incentive for the choice. Da Ponte approached the Emperor and obtained permission for the production of the opera, from whose libretto the more biting passages of Beaumarchais' satire were removed.

Figaro was produced on 1st May, 1786, after many difficulties and intrigues. Michael Kelly, the English tenor who created the parts of Basilio and Curzio, records that Mozart was "as touchy as gunpowder and swore he would put the score in the fire" if his work were not produced before that of the rival, who was trying to forestall him. The opera was most favourably received by the audience, while, after Figaro's air at the end of Act I, singers and orchestra combined with the spectators to acclaim the composer. "I shall never forget," writes Kelly, "his little animated countenance when lighted up with the glowing rays of genius; it is as impossible to describe as it would be to paint sunbeams."

Yet still nothing was done for Mozart in Vienna. But from Prague, where *Figaro* was given with immense success, came a commission for a new opera, for which he was to receive 100 ducats. So it was in Prague and not in Vienna that his greatest Italian opera, *Don Giovanni,* was produced in October, 1787. Da Ponte again provided him with an excellent libretto and the opera achieved a triumphant success.

In the meantime, Leopold, who had come to Vienna for the production of *Figaro* and joyfully witnessed the fulfilment of his most extravagant hopes, fell ill. In spite of the coldness of their relations at the time of his marriage, Wolfgang's affection for his father had never faltered and their common interest in Freemasonry had drawn them closer together during these last years. He wrote to his father:

> ... I need not tell you with what anxiety I await better news from yourself. I count upon that with certainty, although I am wont in all things to anticipate the worst. Since death (take my words literally) is the true goal of our lives, I have made myself so well acquainted during the past two years with this true and best friend of mankind that the idea of it no longer holds any terror for me, but rather much that is tranquil and comforting. And I thank God that He has granted me the good fortune to obtain the opportunity (you understand my meaning) of regarding death as the key to our true happiness. I never lie down in bed without considering that, young as I am, perhaps I may on the morrow be no more. Yet not one of those who know me could say that I am morose or melancholy, and for this I thank my Creator daily and wish heartily that the same happiness may be given to my fellow men. ... I clearly explained my way of looking at the matter on the occasion of the death of my very dear, my best friend, Count von Hatzfeld. He was just 31, like myself. I do not grieve for him—but from the bottom of my heart for myself and for all who knew him as well as I.

Herein stand revealed Mozart's mature philosophy and the innate nobility of his mind. Beneath the gay frivolity of his nature, which is so charmingly displayed in his letters to his sister and his wife, there lay a fundamentally serious attitude toward the broad issues of moral conduct and religion in the widest sense. The apparent paradox of his character—the combination of the strictest intellectual discipline, that alone could have produced the perfect union of form and feeling in his music, with a complete lack of discipline in practical affairs—is resolved if we regard it as the sign of a sense of proportion which perceived, more clearly than most of us do, the true essentials of our life. There is no real opposition between his music and his life. Both were ruled by this same sense of proportion, and although it entailed a disregard for all those petty affairs which occupy so much time in the life of the average man, and which are always irksome to men, in Wordsworth's phrase, "of more than ordinary organic sensibility," there is never a suggestion of meanness or pusillanimity in his conduct. No sensitive ear can fail to perceive the workings of this mind, at once so deeply emotional and so well-controlled, in the two string quintets, which he wrote after his father's death in May, 1787, or in *The Magic Flute,* which contains in its fantastic pantomime his whole philosophy of love and death.

The disadvantages of Mozart's philosophy, combined with Constanze's equal incapacity for the practical management of money, are only too plainly to be seen in the following year (1788). It is, indeed, impossible to approach this final phase of Mozart's career without something like a personal sense of sorrow. The story has, apart from its sordidness, every element of tragedy. The catastrophe, inescapable and yet not inevitable, overwhelms the hero owing to a flaw in his essentially fine character. There is even the touch of irony in the offers of help that came just too late to save him, and of supernatural horror in the queer story of the Requiem Mass.

The letters of this period include a number addressed to Michael Puchberg, a rich Viennese merchant, an amateur of music and a fellow Freemason. In them Mozart asks for loans in language that grows ever more pitiable in its despairing appeal. Puchberg was generous, but he could not entirely support the Mozart family. Yet when financial worries were most acute, Mozart was able to write within the space of two months the three symphonies in E flat, G minor, and C major, which are his highest achievements in that form. The speed with which he composed is astonishing, but it is well to remember that his was a mind that could think out a whole movement and retain it until the time came to commit it on paper. Herein lies the explanation of the legend that the overture to *Don Giovanni* was composed on the night before its first performance.

In May of this year *Don Giovanni* was given in Vienna, but failed to please the audience. The Emperor thought it "divine, but not meat for my Viennese," to which Mozart retorted: "We must give them time to chew it." Disappointment and neglect discouraged him and his output fell off. The period of virtuosity was over, and, although he was still to write some of his finest pianoforte concertos, music no longer poured out in such abundance. In his capacity as Court-composer, he wrote, indeed, a quantity of dance-music, for which he received a salary of £80 [about $400]—"Too much for what I produce; too little for what I could produce."

In 1789 there was a diversion. He accompanied Prince Lichnowsky on a visit to Berlin. On the way he played before the Court at Dresden, and at Leipzig he seized the chance of enlarging his knowledge of Bach. King Frederick William II received him favourably, commissioned some quartets, for which he received 100 Friedrichs d'or [about $500], and offered him, it is said, the post of Kapellmeister with a salary of about £600 [nearly $3,000]. It is difficult to believe that he refused such an offer out of loyalty to the Emperor and the Viennese, who had done so little for him, and the story is probably apocryphal. To his wife he wrote, "You must be glad to have *me* back, and not think of money." The tour did nothing to alleviate his financial position and its musical outcome was negligible.

Doctor's bills were now added to his other liabilities, for Constanze fell ill and had to go to Baden for a cure. A successful revival of *Figaro* brought him a commission for another opera, and for the third time he collaborated with da Ponte. *Così fan tutte* was produced in January, 1790, but the illness and death of the Emperor interrupted its career. On the accession of the new Emperor, Leopold II, Mozart applied for the post of Kapellmeister and was refused. Later, in May, 1791, he was appointed assistant, with the right of succession to the post, "without pay for the present." But before the office fell vacant he was dead.

The coronation of the Emperor at Frankfurt seemed to offer the chance of making money, but, in order to get there, Mozart had to pledge such valuables as he possessed and borrow money at usurious rates. Characteristically he paid also for the expenses of Hofer, the violinist who had married Josepha Weber, and agreed to share with his brother-in-law any profits that might accrue from the tour. Mozart was ever willing to give away his last shilling to a friend who seemed in need, and his generosity was sometimes shamefully abused. We do not know what money he made during this tour to Frankfurt, where two new pianoforte concertos were produced, but it is improbable that it did more than cover the expenses and the interest on the loan.

The year 1790 had been barren and at its end Mozart's situation was desperate. Yet he declined an offer to go to England. He had been considering such a visit for many years past and, when Kelly, Nancy Storace, and his pupil, Attwood, left Vienna after the production of *Figaro,* he had asked them to arrange matters for him in London. His refusal of a not unreasonable offer is only explicable on the grounds of his own ill-health and Constanze's. Perhaps he felt too weary to seize this opportunity which might well have saved his life. It was Haydn who went to London and made a fortune. Da Ponte, too, had left Vienna, in disgrace, and, having married an Englishwoman, went to London. It is tantalising to imagine what the two might have added as an operatic counterpart to the glory of Haydn's "London" Symphonies.

Although Mozart was ill, worn out with anxiety, undernourishment, and the strain of hard work since childhood, he was soon producing music again with astonishing fertility. Nothing could be more false than the suggestion, sometimes made, that, when he died, he had exhausted his genius. It was his body that gave out, not his mind. There was still plenty of pure metal in the mine that produced during this last year the two strong quintets in D major and E flat, the pianoforte concerto in B flat, and *The Magic Flute.*

It was in March, 1791, that he received the commission to compose what was to be his last and most imaginative opera. Schickaneder, the author of the libretto, ranks with da Ponte as one of the most remarkable men with whom Mozart came in contact. An impresario and a comic actor, he was the creator, in every sense of the word, of Papageno. Mozart had met him and composed music for one of his plays years before in Salzburg. Now Schickaneder, who knew his man, lodged Mozart near his theatre on Prince Stahremberg's estate, and set him to work on writing music for the most curious pantomime ever offered to a great composer. In a summerhouse in the garden Mozart by some magic transmuted this childish fairy-tale into one of the eternal allegories of man's ideal endeavour. He put into it all his most profound religious convictions, all his sense of "the mystery of things." It is the very counterpart in music of *Everyman* and *Faust*. Here in the garden Mozart spent his last happy days, perhaps the happiest of all his life.

Work on *The Magic Flute* was interrupted by a command from

the Emperor to write a serious opera for the coronation festivities at Prague. Hurriedly written against time to a frigid classical libretto in a now old-fashioned style, Mozart's imagination was not fired by *La clemenza di Tito*. Like all he wrote, it was a piece of good craftsmanship, but not one of his masterpieces.

At the very moment of his departure for Prague in September, there occurred an incident that was to have a profound effect upon Mozart. He had been asked by a mysterious stranger, "dressed from head to foot in grey," to compose for a patron, whose identity he must not seek to discover, a Requiem Mass. Now, as he entered his carriage, the stranger, whose manner and costume gave him every appearance of weirdness, had come to demand the fulfilment of the contract. Mozart had been unable to write the Mass and promised to do so on his return to Vienna, but the vision of this stranger took on in his fancy a supernatural aspect, which so affected him that he came to believe that his visitant was none other than the messenger of Death.

That Mozart was at this time in an extremely despondent state is proved by a letter, written apparently to da Ponte, just after this incident. It seems that da Ponte had urged Mozart to come to England.

> I wish I could follow your advice, but how can I do so? I feel stunned, I reason with difficulty, and cannot get rid of the vision of this unknown man. I see him perpetually; he entreats me, he presses me, and impatiently demands the work. I go on writing, because composition tires me less than resting. Otherwise I have nothing more to fear. I know from what I suffer that the hour is come; I am at the point of death; I have come to an end before having had the enjoyment of my talent.

By how little he missed his enjoyment! *The Magic Flute* was enormously successful and established at a stroke the future of German opera. A group of Hungarian nobles and admirers in Holland were independently setting in motion schemes to provide him by subscription with a stable income. But it was all too late. He had come to an end, and was unable even to make good his determination, expressed at the end of the letter just quoted, to complete his "death-song," the commission for which was a terrible, though

unintended, practical joke played upon him by an eccentric nobleman who had lost his wife and desired to commemorate her
worthily.

In November his exhausted body began to give way completely
and his mind was affected. He imagined himself poisoned by Salieri.
At the end of the month he took to his bed, and there, watch in
hand, followed in imagination the triumphal progress of *The Magic
Flute*. He worked spasmodically at the Requiem, giving directions
to his pupil, Süssmayer, who eventually completed the score. On
4th December, after singing the first strain of the "Lacrymosa," he
burst into tears and soon lapsed into unconsciousness. Music, the
mainspring of his life, was the last faculty left to him, and still as he
lay dying he continued to puff out his cheeks as though sounding
the trumpets.

Early next morning he was dead and in a few weeks' time no
one knew where his body lay. Constanze was prostrated with grief
and unable to attend the funeral. A few friends gathered at St.
Stephen's Church for the brief service, but not one faced the bitter
cold to follow the greatest composer of his time to a pauper's grave.
Very lonely he was in life, and lonely in death, but his spirit lives
in the companionship of all who love his music. Alas! for Mozart;
alas! for us: he had indeed come to an end before having had enjoyment of his genius.

D. H. (1)

2

Child Prodigy and
The Grand Tour

AT THE AGE of six Wolfgang had learnt so much that there was no
holding Leopold's pride in any longer. After all, the younger the
gifted child, the greater the miracle: and so his incredible gifts had to
be shown the world as soon as might be. Besides, Nannerl was getting
on for eleven: it was quite time she too was exhibited before her own
precocity began to look too normal. Thus in January, 1762, the children were dragged off to Munich. Leopold for the first time obtained
leave from the archbishop, as he was to do with such frequency
during the next few years that this may well be the reason why, good
musician and conscientious servant though he was, he never advanced
to the post of musical director at the *Residenz*. In this very year it
passed from Johann Ernst Eberlin to Joseph Franz Lolli, Leopold
being overlooked and obtaining merely a vice musical directorship
the following year. He knew, no doubt, that more was not to be
expected if he absented himself too frequently, knew too that he was
making a sacrifice for Wolfgang—by no means the only one.

Of the visit to the Bavarian capital we only know that it lasted
three weeks and that the children played to the Elector Maximilian
Joseph. He must have been duly astonished. But Munich never took
more than passing notice of Mozart all his life. Leopold came back to
Salzburg with his two bewildered little freaks, who had not seen a
court before, for they do not appear ever to have been taken to the

34

archbishop at so early a stage. Perhaps he did not believe in local miracles.

For a while the Mozarts lay low, crouching to leap the better next time. For by September Leopold was ready to tackle Vienna and the empress. He left with the two young victims of their own genius on 18th September, and this time they made an impression such as he had scarcely dared to hope for. The Bishop of Passau first delayed them for five days, anxious to hear Wolfgang and kind enough to bestow a ducat on him. Then, accompanied by Canon Count Herberstein, they proceeded to Linz, where Count Schlick induced them to give a concert under his patronage. Next, at the monastery of Ips, Wolfgang lured the monks from their dinner by his organ playing, and on their arrival in Vienna he saved his father the toll by making friends, in his confiding, childish way, with the customs official.

The Austrian capital, not yet at the height of musical glory which was to reach its climax in the next century, nevertheless vied with Paris and London for the honour of being the world's chief musical centre. No Italian city was quite so alive even with Italian musical culture, of which Vienna was the central seat. No Italian operas achieved fame without sooner or later coming to Vienna, and many of them were actually produced there. Naturally enough there was also a German element. Gassmann had just been invited to set up as a composer of ballets, Wagenseil produced serious instrumental music, and Reutter, as chapel master at St. Stephen's Cathedral, turned out his famous showy masses. Reutter's former pupil, Haydn, now aged thirty, was no longer anything but a visitor to the capital, and his services were confined to the house of the Esterházy for a long time to come. Still, he existed and was making his great name. Gluck was still writing French comic operas for the court, for performance at Schönbrunn or at Laxenburg.

That court was musical. Maria Theresa sang well and had appeared in an opera by Fux at the age of seven. Francis I was fond of music too, and the archduchesses, including Marie Antoinette, sang in that very year of the Mozarts' visit in a private performance of a setting of Metastasio's *Il Trionfo di Clelia*.[1] The empress heard of the remarkable children, probably from Count Herberstein or Count Schlick, or

---

[1] Probably Hasse's setting, produced at Dresden that year.

possibly from young Count Palffy, who had been astonished by them during the visit to Linz. The nobility also seem to have been prepared for the wonders to come. At all events Leopold received a command to reveal them at Schönbrunn on 13th October. They stayed at the splendid yet domesticated palace for three hours in the afternoon. The emperor called Wolfgang a little conjurer and made him play various tricks on the keyboard; Marie Antoinette, who was only two months older than Wolfgang, helped him up, so the story goes, when he slipped on the polished floor, and received an offer of marriage in return; the empress, into whose lap he jumped, kissed him. He asked to see Wagenseil, one of whose concertos he played and whom he allowed to turn over the pages. Nannerl was less of a success only in so far as she was less of a sensation. Leopold received an honorarium and the children various presents, including the court dresses, pink and silver for the girl, lilac and gold for the boy, in which they were afterwards painted.[2]

Now the Viennese aristocracy began to take notice. The family were called for to go here, there, and everywhere by carriage. They were well rewarded for showing off their tricks. The ladies were enchanted with the self-possessed little artist and innocent little boy. But suddenly he went down with scarlet fever, and though the attentions did not cease, they became markedly less personal. An invitation to some nobles at Pressburg came as a welcome change after Wolfgang's recovery, and on 11th December a journey in terrible weather and over atrocious roads was made to the Hungarian border. Back in Vienna, the children played at a feast given by Countess Kinsky in honour of Field-Marshal Daun. Early in January they returned home. Their mother's ears must have ached from all the excited talk poured into them.

Before long it was her heart that was made to ache again. She was rooted to her home, but Leopold had tasted success and wanted more. Level-headed as he was, and careful about his children's welfare, he could not resist trying a grand tour. After a short spell at home, during which Wolfgang perfected himself on the violin, which he was found one day to be able to play without any tuition whatever, the four of them were off on 9th June 1763.

At Wasserburg, on the way to Munich, the diligence broke down,

---

[2] The portraits, by an unknown and indifferent artist, are in the Mozart house.

and they had to wait a day; but as Wolfgang for the first time came across a pedal organ there, time was not wasted. Leopold showed him the instrument, and of course he could play at once, standing on the pedals which he could not reach when seated on the bench. The Elector of Bavaria was at Nymphenburg, where Wolfgang played both the clavier and the violin, producing a concerto on the latter and improvising the cadenzas.

At Augsburg, Leopold's native town, they stayed a fortnight. There were relatives to be visited, though they put up at the inn of the "Three Moors," and three concerts were given. On 6th July they departed for Ludwigsburg, the luxurious country residence of Duke Carl Eugen of Württemberg, who, however, did not consent to hear them. Leopold, always ready to suspect jealousy and intrigue, especially on the part of Italian musicians, who indeed were not as a tribe above using questionable means to maintain their supremacy in foreign countries, had no doubt that Niccolò Jommelli, the duke's musical director, was responsible for the rebuff. That Jommelli had himself listened to Wolfgang with astonishment and interest carried no weight with Leopold, who thought that the Italian master was merely dissembling. There is no reason, however, to suspect Jommelli, who was a serious composer of noble music and an honourable man, not to mention that he was perfectly secure in his fame, happily unaware that he would be unfairly forgotten by later generations. He had no reason for wishing to stand in the way of a small boy whose genius, spirit, and fire he, like a true Italian, thought to be almost incredible in a child of Germanic race. It is quite possible that the duke maintained a musical establishment merely because it was expected of him, but that he was not interested in itinerant musicians, whether recommended by his *Capellmeister* or not. He may also have been busy with more important or agreeable matters, as such people often were at their summer residences.

Other triumphs soon compensated for this one failure. The Elector Palatine Carl Theodor, who spent his summer at the palace of Schwetzingen, received the family graciously and arranged a concert for them that lasted four hours. The orchestra was that of Mannheim, "without contradiction the best in Germany," says Leopold in a letter to his landlord Hagenauer, a band in connection with which the historically important school of early German symphonists had arisen, and which Mozart was to meet again later, to make his first acquaintance with the clarinet as an orchestral instrument in its midst. Just as in the Stuttgart band at Ludwigsburg the Mozarts had met the famous violinist Nardini, a pupil of Tartini's, so here they first came across the flute player J. B. Wendling, who was to become a friend later on.

Passing through Heidelberg, Wolfgang played the organ at the church of the Holy Ghost and amazed the hearers to such an extent that the dean had a description of the event inscribed on the instrument. At Mainz the elector was ill and could not hear them, but they gave two concerts at the "King of Rome" and made two hundred florins. At Frankfort a concert held on 18th August was so successful that three more were given. Among the audience was Goethe, aged fourteen. The poet never forgot the impression made on him by "the little man with wig and sword," as he told Eckermann, his Boswell, a great many years later. Marianne and Wolfgang were now celebrities, and no mistake. They had to behave accordingly; Leopold saw to that. He loved music, but he loved honour more, and honour was not to be had in such large quantities as his rapidly growing appetite for fame demanded except by satisfying not merely the good taste of the few, but the curiosity and love of sensation of the many. The announcement of the last Frankfort concert, to be given on 30th August, shows what was expected of that little freak Wolfgang. He would not only play a concerto on the violin and accompany symphonies on the clavier, but cover up the keyboard with a cloth and play as well as if he saw the keys. Moreover, he would tell the intervals of all notes played singly or in chords on the clavier or any imaginable instrument, such as bells, glasses, clocks, etc. And finally he would play, on the organ as well as on the clavier, for as long as the public would care to listen, and extemporize in all keys, even the most difficult, that people would choose to name.

On they went, to Coblenz, Bonn, Cologne, Aix-la-Chapelle; but they played only at the first and the last. At Aix it was before Princess Amalia of Prussia, the sister of Frederick the Great, who was taking the waters. She was a genuine music lover, and, falling in love with little Wolfgang, tried to persuade his father to visit Berlin; but the astute Leopold saw no profit in such a modification of his plans. As he wrote to Hagenauer:

She has no money, and her whole equipage and retinue as much resemble the suite of a doctor as one drop of water does another. If the kisses she gave to my children, and Master Wolfgang in particular, were as many new-coined *louis d'or,* we should be fortunate enough; howbeit, neither mine host nor the postmaster are to be contented with kisses.

Thus they continued to Brussels. Leopold wrote on 17th October showing some interest in the Flemish and Dutch painters whose pictures he had seen, and speaking of the fairly assiduous religious observances he had noticed, which showed, to his mind, that they were in Maria Theresa's territory. That part of the Netherlands, indeed, was under Austrian rule, Prince Charles of Lorraine, brother of the Emperor Francis I, being governor-general. He was in no great hurry to hear the Mozart children. Leopold complained on 4th November:

We have now been nearly three weeks in Brussels . . . and nothing has happened. Indeed, it looks as though all were in vain, for his highness the prince does nothing but hunt, gobble, and swill, and we may in the end discover that he has no money. . . . I own, we have received sundry valuable presents here, but do not wish to convert them into cash. . . . What with snuff-boxes and leather cases and such-like gewgaws, we shall soon be able to open a stall.

At last they succeeded in giving a grand concert, which the prince condescended to suspend his more urgent pleasures to attend, and on 15th November they left for Paris, where they arrived on the 18th. The Bavarian ambassador von Eyck, whose wife was a daughter of the Salzburg chamberlain Count Arco, invited them to stay at the Hôtel Beauvais in the Rue Saint-Antoine.[3]

The Mozarts, even the fairly worldly Leopold, must have opened their eyes wide when first they set them on the French capital, which was then less regularly beautiful than it is to-day, but no doubt far more fascinating, varied, and picturesque. Indeed the district of the Marais in which they stayed, much less changed than any other part of Paris, still shows the kind of place the city as a whole must have

---

[3] To-day the house is 68 Rue François-Miron.

been before the Revolution and before the artificial face-lifting which its beauty has been undergoing ever since that upheaval.

The house to which they were invited had formerly belonged to Madame de Beauvais, lady-in-waiting to Anne of Austria, who, with Henrietta Maria of England, Turenne, and Mazarin, had watched the entry into Paris of her son, Louis XIV, and the Infanta Maria Theresa, on 26th August, 1660, from the balcony. Narrow and irregular streets, ill-paved and ill-lighted, but with houses that matched stateliness with comfort, the lovely backwater of the Place des Vosges close by, and drawn straight through it all the Rue Saint-Antoine with its marketing and merchandise, its beggars and loafers, with cartloads streaming endlessly towards the Bastille and away from it—any one who knows the district may still imagine it all very nearly as the Mozarts saw it.

They had various letters of recommendation from and to nobles and diplomats, but found that the cold shoulder was turned on them everywhere. Only Friedrich Melchior Grimm, who had been settled in Paris for fifteen years, become almost wholly frenchified, contributed to the *Encyclopédie* of Diderot and d'Alembert, and learnt the art of advancement by wire-pulling and log-rolling to perfection, was found willing enough to help his fellow-countrymen. (He was born at Ratisbon.) Perhaps he felt that by being the first to introduce the wonder-children to a people that has ever been quick to pounce on a new interest and quick to relinquish it for one newer still, he would earn some temporary credit. At least he seems to have been clever enough to see that there was matter for credit. Be that as it may, the Mozarts were asked to appear at court.

On Christmas Eve they were at Versailles, invited to stay a fortnight. The arrangements for their appearance before the royal family, elaborately made by the courtiers charged with the *menus plaisirs,* who had to justify their decorative existence, went forward, as Leopold said, "even more than those at other courts, by the snail's post." But by degrees things happened—exciting things for the good provincials. They paid a visit to the quarters of Madame de Pompadour, whom Leopold describes as if she were the chief sight of France; the children were smiled upon and hugged by the king's three musical daughters, Madame Adélaïde, Madame Henriette, and Madame Victoire, pleasant, friendly creatures who played the violin, the *viola da gamba,* and the clavier; Wolfgang was made to stand on a chair to be examined by the Pompadour, who would not let him kiss her, whereupon, as his sister remembered later—and one hopes correctly—he audibly made unfavourable comparisons with his own empress, who did allow herself to be kissed; then, on New Year's Day, the four of them were graciously allowed to attend the royal dinner, not, of course, to eat at the table, but at any rate to stand behind the chairs of the king and queen. The latter, Marie Leczinska, spoke in German to Wolfgang and passed him various dainty morsels from the table, as to a lapdog. They felt honoured, it appears, to stand about with the lackeys. At any rate they were near the royal fire and had not to shiver with the fur-clad court ladies farther down the table in the icy gallery of that sumptuous and comfortless palace, where the dishes had to be chafed on their endless journey up from the kitchens and where it was no unknown occurrence for the wine to freeze on the board.

The nobility now began to take notice of the little royal favourites. They were invited to play at various aristocratic houses, including that of Prince Conti, where, as Ollivier's picture in the Louvre shows, Wolfgang played to a brilliant assembly. The British and Russian ambassadors, the Duke of Bedford and Prince Galitsin, took a great fancy to them, and Madame de Clermont, who lived in the Hôtel Beauvais, procured them an invitation to appear twice at the house of a M. Félix in the Rue Saint-Honoré, where there was a small private theatre. It was only through powerful influences that permission was to be had to give these two concerts, on 10th March and 9th April, 1764, all rights of performance being vested by patent in the Opéra, the Théâtre Italien, and the Concert Spirituel. Marianne performed the most difficult keyboard music that could be found. Wolfgang did everything: played the clavier, the violin, the organ, accompanied at sight, transposing, amplifying thorough-bass, and even inventing new accompaniments at various repetitions of the same air or piece without any indication of the bass. What is more, he improvised astonishingly, according to Grimm and Suard, from whom one gathers the usual impression of all the great masters in their youth—that they must have played far more mature music extempore than they ever wrote down at the same period.

The unanimity of such reports, which always compare more than favourably with one's own criticism of such contemporary music by their heroes as may have been preserved in manuscript or print, is so persistent that one feels bound to seek for an explanation of these wonders of improvisation other than the witness's enthusiasm, exaggerated though that is sure to be by reminiscent sentiment and pride. It is very probable, all things considered, that when the performer was surrounded by an admiring crowd, a more than normal heat of inspiration may have infused itself into his invention, a heat that could not fail to cool down considerably in the merely mechanical and delaying act of committing the notions to paper.

Wolfgang did write down some music during these Paris days, and Leopold had four Sonatas for piano with violin accompaniment (K. 6-9) engraved, the first two being dedicated to one of the kindly princesses, Madame Victoire, the other pair to the Comtesse de Tessé. Grimm undertook the writing of the dedications, but the countess, who was lady-in-waiting to the dauphine, surprisingly declined the first version of this document as being too flattering. It must have been fulsome indeed if a lady of the French court could not bear it, and it was replaced, much to Leopold's regret, by a more moderately polite epistle.

Wolfgang underwent various influences in Paris, especially that of two German musicians who had settled in the French capital as clavier players and composers: Johann Schobert, a Silesian, who was in the service of Prince Conti, and Johann Gottfried Eckhardt, born, like Leopold, at Augsburg. Schobert seems to have behaved far from well: he was ambitious and jealous. But there is no doubt that the susceptible young genius came under the sway of his music, an influence far more powerful than that of the French operas, some of which he may have heard at the theatres and separate pieces from which he must have come across all over Paris, from the street-corner to the drawing-room. Italian opera held the field, for the *guerre des bouffons* of a decade or so ago had been decided in its favour. Such composers as Galuppi, Jommelli, Pergolesi, Piccinni, Sarti, and Traetta were fashionable. French comic opera, too, with less verve and spirit, but more grace and gentleness, was popular, and the Mozarts might well have heard pieces by Monsigny and Philidor, or by the Franco-Italian Duni. What is more immediately significant is that Wolfgang may have been present at a performance of the ballad opera, *Les Amours de Bastien et Bastienne,* which the charming and virtuous actress, Madame Favart, had put together for herself from Rousseau's little opera, *Le Devin du Village,* which might also have been revived during their stay in Paris, either this time or on their return in 1766. It is pleasant to think that the boy may have known the prototypes of a little opera of his own that musically made an immense improvement on both.

Leopold had not been sure about venturing so far as England when the family left Salzburg; but in Paris every one urged him to try London. They took coach to Calais on 10th April, 1764, stayed there more expensively than Leopold liked, dined with the Procureur du Roy et de l'Admirauté, and arrived in London, after an unpleasant crossing in a specially hired boat—the packet boat being full—on 22nd April. The address was given to Hagenauer in Leopold's letter of 25th April:

à Monsieur

Monsieur Mozart at Mr. Couzin

Hare cutter in cecil court

St Martinslane

att

London.

As early as the 27th they obtained permission to present themselves at court. George III and Queen Charlotte both had a great liking for music, and the Mozarts' reception at St. James's was so friendly and unceremonious that it warmed their hearts. Leopold is full of enthusiasm, for all that their reward was "only twenty-four guineas," which were handed them immediately on their departure. A few days later they met the royal carriage in St. James's Park, and although they "all wore different clothes," they received the most affable greeting from the king and queen. On 19th May they were invited again, to play to a small gathering from six until ten in the evening. The king made Wolfgang play pieces by Handel, Wagenseil, and others at sight, the boy went from the clavier to the organ, accompanied the queen in an aria, then played with a flautist, and finally improvised a new melody and harmony on the bass of a Handel air.

Handel had been dead five years, but he dominated music in London still. Half a dozen at least of his oratorios were to be heard during the Mozarts' stay in London, and everywhere Wolfgang met with his music, which made impressions on him that he never forgot. Not that a Handelian influence became at all conspicuous in his music at any time, except in fleeting glimpses, but it would have been strange if the solidity of Handel's noble workmanship had not made its mark on his receptive young mind. He must have affectionately recalled his early acquaintance with the musical circle of Handel's declining years later on, when Baron van Swieten engaged him to provide additional accompaniments to four of the master's oratorios.

There were more immediate influences at work on him in London. Here again, as in Paris, two German musicians taught him most. The less important of the two was Carl Friedrich Abel, a former pupil of Bach's in Leipzig, a famous *viola da gamba* player and a composer of some reputation. Then there was Bach's own youngest son, Johann Christian, aged twenty-nine, who had lived in Milan and transferred himself to England in 1762, to remain in London until his death. He had turned Roman Catholic in Italy and composed a good deal of church music; but he brought several Italian operas to London with him; in fact he was wholly italianized, and finding no musical outlet for his faith in a Protestant country he became more and more secularized as a composer. With his great father he had nothing in common as an artist. His music does not sound like Bach; it sounds much more like Mozart. The truth is that he influenced Mozart to a great extent.

Apart from J. C. Bach and Abel, not to mention Handel again, Wolfgang must have heard some English music, by Arne and Boyce, for example, as well as Italian operas and pasticcios at the King's Theatre in the Haymarket, if his strict and solicitous father did not consider it a place unfit for a little boy of eight to visit. However that may be, they made the acquaintance of the two famous male sopranos Manzuoli and Tenducci, and the former, from pure friendship and astonishment at Wolfgang's gifts, undertook to teach him singing. The boy had a poor little voice, but picked up that branch of his art, like every other, as though he had always known all about it.

The season was not favourable to a public concert. The nobility and gentry were out of town. Still, Leopold was clever enough to realize that many of them would pour into London for the king's birthday on 4th June. He accordingly arranged a performance on the 5th. It was a success. The grandees turned up in masses, and Leopold had "the shock of taking a hundred guineas in the space of three hours." There were counter-shocks, it is to be feared, for he found that the expenses were heavy: five guineas for the hall, without lights or music stands, half a guinea for each clavier (the children played a double concerto), five or six guineas for each of the singers, three for the leader—and then the orchestra, at half a guinea a head. However, he found in the end that most of the musicians would take nothing. Who would charge children a fee for the privilege of playing with them? And such children!

Having made a profit, Leopold was not averse to doing a little advertising. He let Wolfgang play at a charity concert at Ranelagh for the benefit of the new maternity hospital on 29th June, "a way to earn the love of this very special nation." A planned visit to Tunbridge Wells, where many fashionable people were taking the waters, fell through, but a private performance at Lord Thanet's was doubtless profitable. From this Leopold returned with an inflammation of the throat that worried him terribly. Poor little chicks, what would they do if anything happened to him in a strange country? Friends were kind, the mother very capable—but still . . . He writes apprehensively to his landlord friend, preparing him for the worst. His handwriting alone will show good Hagenauer how ill he is; clysters, purges, blood-letting have been tried; he cannot eat, scarcely think. A day or two later he is well enough to be taken into the country—the idyllic riverside village of Chelsea. On 9th August it still depends on the will of God whether he will recover or not. But on 13th September he is sufficiently restored to endeavour to convert the son of a Dutch Jew, who has abandoned his faith and not yet embraced a new one, to Catholicism.

During their father's illness the children were not allowed to touch an instrument for some time. Wolfgang therefore amused himself by writing two Symphonies (K. 16 and 19),[4] urging his sister to remind him now and again to give plenty of interesting work to the horns for the exceptionally good London players. Here, then, is Mozart at the age of eight, a fully fledged composer. An instrumental composer, too —this genius of whom it has so often been said that all his music sings, and whose vocal writing would entice musically minded people with the voices of rooks, crows, and ravens to sing mellifluously. He was a symphonist before he became a conjurer with song. His first vocal work, so far as we know,[5] was not produced until the end of the visit

---

[4] But not, as Jahn-Abert have it, K. 17, which is spurious. So too is K. 18, which is included in the complete Mozart edition, but is now known to be by Abel.
[5] Unless the tenor aria, "Va, dal furor portata" (K. 21), came first. The point is of no great importance, and Köchel did give this work a later number.

to England, when, in July 1765, he presented the so-called madrigal, "God is our refuge" to the British Museum. Curious, is it not? This Austrian boy of German descent with an Italian veneer and some quickly acquired French manners first sings to us in English. Truly, he began his career in the very way in which he was to gain immortality. For Mozart among all great musicians is the most universal, the least locally rooted.

Towards the end of September, 1764, Leopold was well again, and the family returned to town. They played at court once more on 25th October, the fourth anniversary of the accession of George III. There is a great deal for royalty to do on such occasions; that they had time to think of making the Mozarts take part in the celebrations shows in what esteem the Salzburg family—and music—were held by them. It was high time something were done in return. Leopold therefore had six Sonatas for clavier with violin or flute[6] (K. 10–15) engraved at his own expense and dedicated to the queen, who returned fifty guineas for the compliment. The dedication is dated 18th January, 1765, and on 20th March the Sonatas were on sale.

On 21st February the Mozarts gave another concert on their own account, with the usual artistic success, but with small profit. The king was ill, politics were inauspicious, and other entertainments interfered. The notorious Mrs. Cornelys was just beginning her subscription concerts under the direction of Abel and J. C. Bach, Samuel Arnold brought out his first opera, *The Maid of the Mill,* Dibdin appeared in it, Bach produced his *Adriano in Siria,* and Burney brought out his adaptation of Rousseau's *Devin du Village* under the title of *The Cunning Man.* Several times the Mozarts' reappearance was announced, but it did not take place until 13th May, when reduced prices combined with a hint that the wonder-children were about to leave England produced a revival of interest. A novelty at this concert was Wolfgang's playing on Shudi's new harpsichord with two manuals and a set of pedals. But fickle London had had its sensation, and its

---

[6] Those who still persist in thinking of the piano part in a sonata as an accompaniment will receive a wholesome shock on discovering that in the eighteenth century the opposite if equally erroneous view prevailed: the clavier was generally regarded as the principal instrument, and it played the outstanding part. Alternative flute parts were the rule in London, where the German flute was much cultivated. Arrangements for it of the popular music of the day flooded the market.

busy life held other things. It was time to make an end of this long and on the whole prosperous visit. Before the family's departure, however, Leopold undertook to let his son be privately examined by any one who chose to do so, first at the lodgings in Frith (then Thrift) Street, Soho, to which they had moved from St. Martin's Lane, then at one of the rather obscure inns in the neighborhood. But a severer and at the same time more flattering test yet awaited the boy. The Hon. Daines Barrington subjected him to a thorough scientific examination, a detailed report of which is preserved in the *Philosophical Transactions* for the year 1770[7] and which not only confirms all the rumours of Wolfgang's incredible capabilities, but makes them appear the more marvellous because the report is free from exaggerations.

In actual composition, however, as Abert shows,[8] Wolfgang still had very much to learn. A manuscript book[9] of the time contains forty-three small pieces which are far from mature and sometimes positively faulty. There can thus be no doubt that the sonatas and symphonies of this period were extensively revised by Leopold, and some possibly by J. C. Bach. It does not, surely, detract from the miracle of the genius of a child approaching his ninth birthday to admit that he must have been helped in committing his ideas tidily to paper. What matters is that he did have ideas, and as to his skill, Barrington's testimony, if no other, is beyond suspicion. To reconcile the wonders he performed at the keyboard with the comparative helplessness of the work which we know him to have written down unaided we need only remember once again that there is a great difference between the immediately if transitorily creative process of improvisation and the slowed-down and mechanical act of setting down such inspirations on paper; and we need not regard the interference of Leopold, or J. C. Bach, or anyone else, in the act of composing with the aid of the pen as anything more than the effort of a finished technician to give shape to what a child of genius was plainly striving after but could not force his hand to fix in black and white.

London, huge but friendly, dirty and haphazard, yet gay and sympathetic, was left at last on 24th July. Nannerl's diary shows, in the spidery writing of a child and the spelling of a little foreigner doing

[7] Vol. xl. Also in Barrington's *Miscellanies on Various Subjects* (London, 1781).
[8] Jahn-Abert, *W. A. Mozart,* i. 66.
[9] Published in 1908 by Breitkopf & Härtel, edited by Dr. G. Schünemann.

her best to wrestle with an erratic language, some of the places they saw in London:

> London bridge, St. Paul kirch, Soudwark, Monument, foundling hospital, enchange, Lincolnsin fiels garten Tempel bar, Soumerset hauss.[10]

Then, "zu Canterbury, die haupt kirch": they spent a day there and saw the cathedral, evidently. Thence they went to the country seat of Sir Horace Mann, "very beautiful," according to Nannerl, where they saw a horse-race and remained as guests until the end of the month.

Leopold had meant to return home by way of Milan and Venice. A grand tour without Italy, forsooth, was unthinkable. But it was not to be. The Dutch ambassador had let him know that the Princess Caroline of Nassau-Weilburg was anxious to hear the children at The Hague. The invitation was not to be refused—"you cannot deny a pregnant woman anything," Leopold said—much as the archbishop was by that time fretting to have his servant back and sending out impatient summonses. They left Dover for Calais on 1st August, visited Dunkirk, and got as far as Lille, where Wolfgang fell ill with catarrh and Leopold with fits of dizziness. A month had to be wasted there.

On the way to Holland the boy tried the new organ at a church in Ghent. At Antwerp he played in the cathedral. On 11th September, 1765, The Hague was reached at last. How tired and battered these brave travellers must have been—and the "Ville de Paris," an inn much frequented by artists, was far from comfortable. But the Prince of Orange, William V, and his sister, Princess Caroline, received them very graciously at the Stadtholder's court. A public concert was arranged for 30th September, but Wolfgang must have played alone, as on the 12th it was Nannerl's turn to be taken ill—so ill that on 21st October she was given extreme unction. Patience, patience! We think of mere flying visits; but how the weeks must have dragged in these strange towns when one or another was not well; how often the Mozarts must have felt the archbishop's nagging reminders of home to be sweetly reasonable after all; what a blessed shelter the cool white-

---

[10] Leopold reported to Hagenauer: "I shall describe the Tower (i.e., the fortress) to you by word of mouth and tell you that the roaring lions there frightened our Master Wolfgang exceedingly."

washed walls at the back of the Löchelplatz must have seemed from afar. Now what could Salzburg do? Leopold, frantic with anxiety, had masses read there for his daughter's recovery.

Wolfgang had the kind of success to which he was used by this time. He played with an orchestra of resident musicians, he extemporized, he undertook to read anything at sight that might be put before him. At home—such a home as could be found for a time—he practised and composed while Nannerl lay in the next room, alternately raving and meekly discussing with her parents the blessedness of leaving a world of whose wickedness she as yet knew only by hearsay.

The princess sent the court physician, Professor Thomas Schwencke, who saved Nannerl. She had scarcely recovered when Wolfgang was seized with a fever. So time crept on wearily until January, 1766, when he was well enough again to write a soprano aria, "Conservati fedele" (K. 23), with string accompaniment, for the princess. The words were from the *Artaserse* of Metastasio, the eighteenth century's universal librettist and—hard to credit in a librettist—a poet to boot. A second concert took place on the 22nd, and towards the end of the month they all went to Amsterdam for four weeks. On 29th January and 26th February they gave concerts there, a Symphony in B-flat major (K. 22), which Wolfgang had finished at The Hague, being performed for the first time. The story goes that a special dispensation was necessary to allow the children to perform in Lent. To make known such wonderful specimens of humanity was an act in praise of God, they said, and all was well.

From quiet, middle-class Amsterdam, where trade prospered on a metropolitan scale and its traffic went on vastly but mutely on the silent canals, the family returned to The Hague, with its courtly, fashionable life and its more cosmopolitan setting. The Prince of Orange came of age on 8th March, and on the 11th the little Mozarts again played at court, to provide not the least of the fireworks let off for the occasion. Wolfgang wrote six more Sonatas for clavier with violin (K. 26–31), which were engraved and dedicated to the Princess of Nassau-Weilburg; he also wrote variations for clavier on an air which the local conductor, Christian Ernst Graaf, had written for the festivities (K. 24) and another set on the national song, *Wilhelmus van Nassouwe* (K. 25), which Wolfgang had known from his earliest childhood in some form or another and had already varied in his own babyish way. For the celebration itself he wrote, clearly with Leopold's help, a kind of quodlibet or potpourri on popular airs, beginning with a quotation from Handel and closing with a fugue, a work he called a *Galimathias musicum* (K. 32). It was a comic piece frankly calculated to be entertaining, and much of it is in the vein of Leopold's descriptive pieces illustrating peasants' weddings, hunts, sleigh-parties, village bands, and so forth. The subject of the fugue, as might be expected, is the *Wilhelmus* song.

Some time in the middle of March came a visit to Haarlem, where Wolfgang played the famous organ. After another lengthy stay at The Hague, during which Leopold's treatise on the violin was published in Dutch to his immense gratification, they gave a last concert at Amsterdam on 16th April, followed by one at Utrecht. Then, by way of Mechlin and Brussels, they returned to Paris, where some of their belongings had been sent straight from Calais. 10th May, 1766, saw them once more in the French capital, where Grimm had procured a lodging for them. Both Marianne and Wolfgang were considered to have made great progress, and they were several times asked to appear at Versailles again. It was at this time that Mozart composed his first piece of Catholic church music, a *Kyrie* in F major (K. 33), based on a French song and dated 12th June.

Paris was left on 9th July. An invitation from the Prince de Condé brought them to Dijon. Four weeks were spent at Lyons. Switzerland came next: three weeks at Geneva, five days at Lausanne, a week in Berne, and a fortnight at Zürich, where they were the guests of the painter and poet Solomon Gessner and gave a concert with the Musical Society. After a very brief call at Winterthur and Schaffhausen, they re-entered Germany, being eagerly awaited by Prince Joseph Wenzeslaus von Fürstenberg at Donaueschingen, with whom they spent twelve days and played nine times from five o'clock until nine in the evening. At Biberach Wolfgang met another boy prodigy two years older than himself, Sixtus Bachmann, and they engaged in a friendly contest on the organ. Ulm, Günzburg, Dillingen, and Augsburg were the stages that brought them nearer Munich, where they arrived on 8th November and appeared before the elector during dinner the following day.

Towards the end of November, 1766, they were back home at Salzburg, after an absence of three and a half years. Wolfgang was now nearly eleven; the Hagenauers and other good Salzburgers no doubt exclaimed, with the usual innocent astonishment of grown-ups at nature's persistence in her old habits, how little Wolfgangerl had grown. The change that had wrought itself upon Nannerl while they were not looking was more amazing still. Indeed, she was quite a young lady. These familiar voices must have been pleasant, like the bells of the Collegiate Church behind, the clanging buckets and clacking of the servant-wenches at the fountain in front, like the colour-washed rococo houses in the better streets, the eternal smell of beer and dinner issuing from the inns that stuck their wrought and gaudy signs across the Getreidegasse.

Thus ended the grand tour—grand even without Italy.

E. B.

 3

Leopold Mozart

BORN NOVEMBER 14, 1719, AT AUGSBURG

DIED MAY 28, 1787, AT SALZBURG

LEOPOLD MOZART IS REMEMBERED by posterity as the father of his son. If he had not been connected with Wolfgang Amadeus, his name would be no more significant than that of any one of the hundred other honest musicians of the eighteenth century, pursuing their goals at the many little ecclesiastical and secular courts of South Germany; and his name would not even have been the first within his own narrow circle, since he never even became first Kapellmeister.

But he was the father of his son, and as the father of such a genius, he understood his mission. Without the influence of the father, reflected both in the son's submission and resistance to it, Wolfgang would never have achieved the character and the greatness that he did. Leopold stands in the circle illuminated by his son, and without that illumination he would have remained in obscurity. But the light of his son's genius and fame does reveal him: not always a completely attractive personality, often a very questionable one, but clearly outlined as a plastic and living figure. Although his talent does not lift him far above his many contemporaries, his ambition, his will, and his energy do. He was no mere *Musikant*. The literary evidence he left—the *School of Violin-Playing*—assures him in any case of a small place in every history of instrumental music. Even without Wolfgang's fame, Leopold would always have been known as the author of this *Versuch einer gründlichen Violinschule,* which he was writing at about the time of the birth of his son.

52

During the first year of Wolfgang's life, Leopold wrote a short auto-biography for F. W. Marpurg's *Historisch-kritische Beyträge zur Aufnahme der Musik*, which contains a "report on the present state of the music of His Princely Grace, the Archbishop of Salzburg, in the year 1757." In it is a sketch of the life and works of the 38-year-old musician:

Mr. Leopold Mozart of the Imperial city of Augspurg. First violinist and leader of the orchestra. He composes both sacred and secular music. He was born 14 November, 1719, and, soon after finishing his studies in philosophy and law, entered the Princely service in the year 1743. He has made himself known in all forms of composition, but has not yet printed any music, although in the year 1740 he himself engraved on copper 6 sonatas *à 3*—mostly in order to study the art of engraving. In June, 1756, he published his School of Violin-Playing.

Of the manuscript works of Mr. Mozart which have become known, the ones principally to be noted are many contrapuntal and other sacred pieces; also a large number of symphonies, some only *à 4*, and some with all the usual instruments; further, more than 30 grand serenades, in which solos for various instruments occur. He has also written many concertos, especially for transverse flute, oboe, bassoon, horn, trumpet, etc., innumerable trios and divertimenti for various instruments; also 12 oratorios and a great number of theatrical pieces, including pantomimes; and especially occasional compositions such as: military music for trumpets, timpani, drums, and fifes in addition to the usual instruments; a Turkish music; a piece including a steel clavier [a kind of celesta]; and finally a sleigh-ride piece with 5 sleigh bells; not to speak of marches, so-called *Nachtstücke,* and many hundred minuets, opera dances, and similar pieces.

We may amplify this information somewhat. Leopold Mozart was the eldest of six sons of the Augsburg bookbinder Johann Georg Mozart, whose paternal ancestors can be traced back to the seventeenth and perhaps to the sixteenth century. The name, which has become a symbol of grace, sometimes took on rougher forms (e.g. Motzert) and rough doubtless were those who bore it—artisans and peasants. Leopold's mother, *née* Anna Maria Sulzer, the bookbinder's second wife, was also a native of Augsburg. She outlived her husband, who died at the age of fifty-seven on 19 February, 1736, by more than thirty years. She seems to have been in comfortable circumstances, for at the time of the creation of the *School of Violin-Playing* Leopold was active in an effort not to receive less than his many brothers and sisters from the estate; each of them had already received an advance of 300 gulden.

Leopold did not become an artisan like his brothers Joseph Ignaz and Franz Aloys, who were both bookbinders. His godfather, the canon Johann Georg Grabher, got him appointed as *discantist* in the choir of the church of the Holy Cross and St. Ulrich—and of course a church singer could easily become a clerygman. He learned not only singing but also organ-playing. In 1777 Wolfgang made the acquaintance in Munich of a former fellow pupil of Leopold's who clearly remembered the forceful and individual organ-playing of the young musician in the monastery of Wessobrunn.

Upon the death of his father, Leopold was sent to Salzburg and received financial support on the assumption that it would be used for theological studies. But he was already a young diplomatist. Secretly, he cherished quite other plans and meanwhile he "hoodwinked the clerics about becoming a priest." After two years at the university of Salzburg he was no longer studying theology at all, but logic instead, and, as he claimed, jurisprudence. Consequently the financial help from Augsburg presumably stopped, and Leopold was forced to give up his studies. He became a domestic in the service of the President of the Chapter of the Salzburg Cathedral—Count Johann Baptist Thurn, Valsassina, und Taxis (the name Thurn und Taxis is world famous as that of the hereditary postmasters of the Holy Roman Empire).

That is about all we know concerning the first twenty years of Leopold's life. Who his teachers in organ playing and in composition were remains obscure; what he sang as a member of the Augsburg cathedral choir, on the other hand, is easier to establish. The music consisted of the *concertante* church works of South-German and Italian masters, of whom the most brilliant and historically most influential was the Imperial Kapellmeister J. J. Fux. The free city of Augsburg, which included both Roman Catholics and Protestants within its walls, contributed to Leopold's personality a certain tolerance, perhaps, or more accurately, a certain critical attitude towards everything clerical, which kept him from becoming a priest. Further, it made his taste in church music solid and somewhat provincial, and in secular music gave it a typically South-German sturdiness. The clearest documentary evidence we have of this South-German taste is contained in Valentin Rathgeber's *Augsburger Tafel-Confect*—a lengthy collection in four volumes, containing folksongs, songs of the peasants and burghers, choruses, quodlibets, and instrumental pieces, all published in the years 1733 to 1746 by Leopold's Augsburg publisher, Lotter, and all full of the broad, easy, often rough humor typical of Bavaria and Swabia. These pieces played a great role in the Mozart family, and without them neither Leopold's *Sleigh-Ride* and *Peasant Wedding* nor Wolfgang's youthful *Galimathias musicum* would have been conceivable. Leopold had a very poor opinion of the people of his native Augsburg, and Wolfgang a much poorer one still; nevertheless, this South-German heredity was in their blood.

We do not know what led Leopold to Salzburg and why he should have passed over, on his way from Augsburg, a cultural center like Munich. Ingolstadt, the Electoral University of Bavaria, was much closer to the people of Augsburg, and would have offered just as much as Salzburg a strictly orthodox education for the young theologian. Perhaps the canons of St. Ulrich recommended that Leopold go to Salzburg, for St. Ulrich was one of the Benedictine monasteries that had once contributed to the founding of the University there, and some of the canons of St. Ulrich (e.g. Dietrichstein and Waldstein) were also canons of Salzburg. However that may be, fate led Leopold to the Salzach—a circumstance that was not without consequences either for Leopold or for Salzburg. His study of *Logica* had important effects upon his thinking, both good and bad. He became an "educated" musician, who had ideas not only about the world and his fellow-men, but also about the rules of his art. He interested himself in Rubens's pictures, in literature, and in all phases of the politics of the princes of his time, both great and small. He understood Latin fairly well, and knew how to handle his own language—handled it, in fact, with extraordinary skill and liveliness, employing many robust, South-German folk-expressions, which give his style a particular charm. Anyone who has read the descriptions in his letters from Paris and London, or in those to his son in Mannheim, knows how vividly and graphically Leopold Mozart could write. When he describes his feelings on the morning of the departure of his wife and son for Paris—

a fateful moment, for he was never to see his wife again—the truth and realism of his description rise to the level of the unconsciously poetic (letter of 25 September, 1777):

> After you both had left, I walked up our steps very wearily and threw myself down on a chair. When we said good-bye, I made great efforts to restrain myself in order not to make our parting too painful; and in the rush and flurry I forgot to give my son a father's blessing. I ran to the window and sent my blessing after you: but I did not see you driving out through the gate and so came to the conclusion that you were gone already, as I had sat for a long time without thinking of anything. Nannerl wept bitterly and I had to use every effort to console her. She complained of headache and a sick stomach and in the end she retched and vomited; and putting a cloth round her head she went off to bed and had the shutters closed. Poor Bimbes [the Mozarts' little dog] lay down beside her. For my own part, I went to my room and said my morning prayers. I then lay down on my bed at half past eight and read a book and thus becoming calmer fell asleep. The dog came to my bedside and I awoke. As she made signs to me to take her for a run, I gathered that it must be nearly noon and that she wanted to be let out. I got up, took my fur cloak, and saw that Nannerl was fast asleep. The clock then showed half past twelve. When I came in with the dog, I waked Nannerl and ordered lunch. But she had no appetite, she would eat nothing and went to bed immediately afterwards, so that, when Bullinger had left, I passed the time lying on my bed, praying and reading. In the evening she felt better and was hungry. We played piquet and then had supper in my room. After that we had a few more games and, with God's blessing, went off to bed. That is how we spent that sad day which I never thought I should have to face...

There is no harm in the fact that Leopold, ever the diplomat, wished in writing this naive description to make an impression upon his son, who for his part was in the best of moods. "...All will yet be well," he had written two days earlier. "I hope that Papa is well and as happy as I am..."

The intellectual superiority of Leopold enhanced, in the course of the many journeys he made, by experience and increased knowledge of the world, was not an unmixed blessing. For it made him feel superior to his colleagues, and critical of those placed above him. It isolated him professionally and contributed greatly to his unpopularity. His "diplomatic sense" caused him to suspect behind the words and actions of his fellow-men even more hidden malice than was actually there, and led him not only into keen observations but also into mistakes of decisive importance. But who could blame him for warning Wolfgang, in a letter dated 18 October, 1777: "Hold fast to God, I beg you, who will see to everything. For all men are villains! The older you become and the more you associate with people, the more will you realize this sad truth." Had Leopold read Machiavelli's *Il Principe?*

> For of men it may generally be affirmed that they are thankless, fickle, false, studious to avoid danger, greedy of gain, devoted to you while you are able to confer benefits upon them, and ready ... while danger is distant, to shed their blood, and sacrifice their property, their loves, and their children for you; but in the hour of need they turn against you.

This pessimism is balanced by Leopold's affection for his family and his care for them in all details of daily life, a care that showed itself strikingly on journeys. For in 1760 it was an adventurous undertaking to travel all over Europe with a wife and two delicate children, and to act as travel agent and impresario combined. And to the favorable side of the scales we must also add his uprightness as a citizen and as a professional musician. It is true that he considered his colleagues mere hacks and drunkards, and that he saw in his archiepiscopal patron not only the patron but also the cruel tyrant, and accordingly felt there was no harm in occasionally pulling the wool over his eyes. (Unfortunately, the Archbishop did not relish being taken in.) But all Leopold's weaknesses were atoned for in the tragic bitterness of his fate, which he keenly felt. He saw in his child the sun and light of his life, and he believed that under his direction Wolfgang would attain the peak of human success. Yet he had to watch his son slip away from him; and he died a lonely man to whom nothing remained but his correspondence with his daughter and his joy in a little grandson, whose first apparent musical stirrings he observed with delight—although actually this grandson did not inherit even the palest reflection of the brilliance of his family.

A. E.

4

The Women in Mozart's Life

NO BIOGRAPHY of Mozart would be complete without a chapter on "Women in Mozart's Life," any more than a biography of Goethe, or Byron, or Wagner could pass over this *punctum puncti*. This aspect of life may not be important when the subject is a philosopher like Kant, or some other great man in the field of abstract knowledge, but it is of the essence with a great dramatist. The dramatist Mozart—who created figures like Constanze and Blonde; Susanna and the Countess; Donna Anna, Donna Elvira, and Zerlina; Fiordiligi and Dorabella; Pamina and Papagena—knew as much about women as Shakespeare, and his achievement in opera can in fact be compared only with that of Shakespeare, who gave his characters the reality of living human beings: eternal types, and yet completely living embodiments of those types. Just as Olivia, Rosalind, and Katharina, although they still have something to do with the stock comedy figures of the virtuous lady, the disguised shepherdess, and the shrew, live in Shakespeare's comedies as real women—so although Susanna has something of Colombina in her, she is wholly herself, a living and individual being, and we know every fiber of her heart.

Mozart's knowledge of woman was not derived from any actual success with women. Casanova had considerable success with women, but his knowledge of woman, astute as it sometimes is, is one-sided. Byron may have had great success with women, despite his club-foot, but he was a romantic poet, a romantic hero, extraordinarily rich, and a peer—and in Italy especially peers were held in great respect in those days. Mozart had no club-foot, but he was small, delicate, unprepossessing, and poor. Thus his relations with women formed a

59

chain of inadequacies, and in them we have further evidence that he was not fitted to deal with the actualities of life.

As a child-prodigy in Vienna, Paris, and London, he was naturally pampered by women. As a boy, whose senses were already awakened, he was often rewarded for his playing or for a composition by a kiss from a lovely lady. While he was in Italy or in Vienna, he always had a flame back in Salzburg to whom he sent messages and greetings through his sister, who acted as his confidante and *postillon d'amour*. Salzburg, where as in all of southern Bavaria the erotic has always been treated more lightly and more naturally than in the Protestant north, was the right place for flirtations by the score, and Mozart himself once declared in later years that he would have been a husband a hundred times over if he had had to marry every girl with whom he had flirted on occasion. The most grateful object of these flirtations he found in Augsburg in 1777—his cousin, Maria Anna Thekla Mozart, the daughter of Leopold's younger brother Franz Alois. His "Bäsle" dressed up for him once in French style, and then of course she was a thousand times prettier than in her native Augsburg costume. The flirtation of the two cousins was continued in the notorious "Bäsle" letters, which with their indecencies and double meanings were intended to call forth blushes. These may very well be called disguised love letters, for bantering and love-making are very closely allied. No doubt "Bäsle" also set certain hopes upon her cousin. But after the experience with Aloysia, although Mozart did indeed take "Bäsle" along from Munich to his parents' house in Salzburg, the tone of his letters to her became steadily more serious. Maria Anna consoled herself in thoroughly South-German fashion. Leopold Mozart, who from the first judged the character of his niece better than Wolfgang, refers to it in a letter to his daughter (dated Vienna, 21 February, 1785):

> The story of your cousin in Augsburg you can easily imagine— a gentleman of the cathedral has made her happy. As soon as I have time I will write the devil of a letter from here to Augsburg, as if I had heard about it in Vienna. The funniest part of it is that all the presents she received, which the whole world admired, came from her uncle in Salzburg. What an honor for me!

But why "the devil of a letter"? A contemporary observer, Professor August Ludwig Schlözer of Göttingen, who passed through Augsburg on a trip to Italy in 1781–82, explained what Leopold knew better than many another: "The freedom of most of the citizens of Augsburg is as cheap as the virginity of their daughters, who are bought in dozens every year by the gentlemen of the cathedral here." In the year 1793 "Bäsle" bore a natural daughter, christened Maria Anna Victoria, who in 1822 married the bookbinder and night-watchman Franz Fidelio Pümpel, resident in Feldkirch in Vorarlberg, and died in 1857.

If "Bäsle" ever had hopes of Wolfgang, they were lost the instant he set eyes on Aloysia Weber, in Mannheim. Aloysia possessed every quality needed to capture him: youth—she was barely sixteen years old; beauty—she was of the slender, proud, queenly type; and musical gifts—her voice and her singing were of excellent quality, although she never became what Mozart in his lover's blindness expected of her. True coquette that she was, she encouraged Mozart only as far as her mother permitted, and only as long as he seemed a good matrimonial prospect. We may learn something about her from the fact that she did not consider it worth while to save the letters Mozart wrote her from Paris; chance has preserved one, in Italian, containing the most loving suggestions for her development as a singer. When he passed through Munich in December, on his way home from Paris, Aloysia, now that her father was engaged at a salary of 600 florin, and she herself at 1,000 florin, made it unmistakably clear to Mozart that he had become superfluous. He kept his outward composure— it is related that he went to the clavier and relieved his feelings with a rough, South-German expression whose equivalent can hardly be printed in English. But in his heart he was a broken man.

Later he saw through Aloysia and was even unjust to her—and he had opportunity enough to observe her from close by. For, to his misfortune, the Weber family had preceded him to Vienna by a year and a quarter, arriving in September, 1779—Aloysia as a singer in the Deutsche Oper, and her father Fridolin as a box-office employee in the National Theater. The father died a few weeks after their arrival, leaving nothing but a small chest with a little linen in it. At least that is what his widow managed to tell the probate court. Aloysia was the support of the family. And she became so in even greater degree when, on the last day of October, 1780, in the Stefanskirche, she became the wife of Joseph Lange (1751–1831), painter and actor in the Court Theater. Mozart was completely wrong when he wrote to his father as follows (9 June, 1781; Leopold had apparently reproached him for leaving his family in the lurch, like Aloysia, although he owed his entire education to them):

> Your comparison of me to Madame Lange positively amazed me and made me feel distressed for the rest of the day. That girl lived on her parents as long as she could earn nothing for herself. But as soon as the time came when she could show them her gratitude (remember that her father died before she had earned anything in Vienna), she deserted her poor mother, attached herself to an actor, and married him—and her mother has never had a *farthing* from her.

This was Mother Weber speaking through him, and Mother Weber was lying, because her evil and hysterical nature was such that she could not help lying. In actual fact, Aloysia was not taken from the Weber household without compensation. Lange had obligated himself to contribute 600 florin annually to the Weber household, as long as he and Aloysia should both be earning. This did not prevent Mother Weber from intriguing against their marriage, or from attempting to separate the couple. Lange had to appeal to the office of the Chief Court-Marshal for consent to the marriage. At the hearing in this office, he raised his offer of support from 600 to 700 gulden, and he obligated himself to pay that amount annually to his mother-in-law throughout her life. But he never found happiness with Aloysia. He was "a jealous fool"—at least so Mozart terms him—and he doubtless had reason enough to be jealous, for Aloysia seems to have made eyes even at Mozart again:

> Even now I feel that she is not a matter of indifference to me; it is, therefore, a good thing for me that her husband is a jealous fool and lets her go nowhere, so that I seldom have an opportunity of seeing her . . . [letter of 16 May, 1781]

An opportunity did present itself, however, in the first Vienna years: in 1782 and 1783 Mozart wrote four big arias for her. Then there came a pause, and not until April, 1788, did he again supply her with a brilliant aria, the last one. It is possible from the arias he wrote for her between 1778 and 1788 to obtain a picture of her voice and ability, or rather to see what picture Mozart had of them. The arias he wrote in Mannheim are full of warmth; in the ones that date from the Vienna period, Mozart was thinking chiefly of how best to exhibit her exceptional vocal technique—for by now he knew how cold was the heart of Aloysia Lange, his sister-in-law.

Yes, Aloysia Lange, *née* Weber, was his sister-in-law. For on 4 August, 1782, Mozart had married Aloysia's younger sister Constanze, and the events that led up to this fatal step are too characteristic to be passed over. The relation of the Weber family to Mozart, of which Carl Maria von Weber was so proud, cost Mozart very dear. We have hinted above that in Mozart's life Maria Cäcilie Weber was the evil genius. There is, as we have said, an evil genius that shadows many men's lives, which they can no more escape than a fly can keep out of the spider's web.

Mother Weber, after the death of her husband, had quite purposefully taken the rudder of the family into her own hands. There were four daughters to be taken care of, and the younger ones were just reaching marriageable age. Maria Cäcilie decided to rent rooms. She abandoned the little dwelling on the Kohlmarkt, from which her husband had been buried, and moved to the *Auge Gottes,* taking a fairly large apartment on the third floor, where she rented rooms to young men. Aloysia very soon left her mother's home, and there remained Josefa (the eldest daughter), Constanze, and Sophie. The first lodger to walk into the spider's web, on 2 May, 1781, was Wolfgang Amadeus Mozart, who was in the midst of his quarrel with the Archbishop. A week later he reported quite naively to his father:

> . . . old Madame Weber has been good enough to take me into her house, where I have a pretty room. Moreover, I am living with people who are obliging and who supply me with all the things which one often requires in a hurry and which one cannot have when one is living alone . . .

His father smelled a rat at once, and must have written warning after warning, in letters which, it goes without saying, were later destroyed by Mozart's widow. But they did not help:

Believe me when I say that old Madame Weber is a very obliging woman and that I cannot do enough for her in return for her kindness, as unfortunately I have no time to do so.

But he had time enough to joke and banter with the second of the three remaining daughters, Constanze. Josefa was already a little too old for him and Sophie a little too young. Meanwhile, Mother Weber took care that there should be talk in Vienna—which in those days and for a long time afterwards remained a small town as far as gossip and slander were concerned—about the fact that Wolfgang and Constanze were in love and were going to be married. Too late she gave him the insincere advice to move out, in order to silence such talk. Mozart took the advice and left the Weber apartment in September, 1781, but only to return for daily visits. And it was only a few months later that he had to ask his father, to whom he had so long painted his relations with the Weber family as quite harmless, for permission to marry Constanze Weber.

For in the meantime Mother Weber, believing that she had taken sufficient steps to compromise her second daughter with Mozart, had been pulling other strings. In doing so, she hid behind an accomplice, an accomplice thoroughly worthy of her, Johann Thorwart, the man appointed by the Court Marshal as guardian of her four daughters. This Thorwart had pushed his way up from the position of house-servant and hair-dresser to Prince Lambert, to that of auditor in the National Theater. He was a crude climber, who, as the factotum of the Gentleman-Intendant, Prince Franz von Orsini-Rosenberg, had his chief in his pocket; and it was with Thorwart that Mozart had to reckon when he wanted to accomplish anything in the theater. Thorwart had become rich, obviously through adroit peculations that could never be definitely traced to him, or at least never were. How much Maria Cäcilie gave him or promised him is not known. At any rate, he played his part well, and acted as if Mother Weber had had nothing to do with the whole affair. Mozart quite unjustly suspected others, such as the composer Peter Winter (letter of 22 December, 1781):

Certain busybodies and impudent gentlemen like Herr Winter must have shouted in the ears of this person [Thorwart] (who doesn't know me at all) all sorts of stories about me as, for example, that he should beware of me—that I have no settled income—that I was far too intimate with her—that I would probably jilt her—and that the girl would then be ruined, and so forth. All this made him smell a rat—for the mother, who knows that I am honorable, let things take their course and said nothing to him about the matter. For my whole association with her consisted in my lodging with the family and later in my going to their house every day. No one ever saw me with her outside the house. But the guardian kept pestering the mother with his representations until she told me about them and asked me to speak to him myself, adding that he would come some day to her house. He came—and we had a talk—with the result (as I did not explain myself as clearly as he desired) that he told the mother to forbid me to associate with her daughter until I had come to a written agreement with him. The mother replied: "Why, his whole association with her consists in his coming to my house, and—I cannot forbid him my house. He is too good a friend—and one to whom I owe a great deal. I am quite satisfied. I trust him. You must settle it with him yourself." So he forbade me to have anything more to do with Constanze, unless I would give him a written undertaking. What other course was open to me? I had either to give him a written contract or—to desert the girl. What man who loves sincerely and honestly can forsake his beloved? Would not the mother, would not my loved one herself place the worst interpretation upon such conduct? That was my predicament. So I drew up a document to the effect *that I bound myself to marry Mlle. Constanze Weber within the space of three years and that if it should prove impossible for me to do so, owing to my changing my mind, she should be entitled to claim from me three hundred gulden a year.* Nothing in the world could have been easier for me to write. For I knew that I should never have to pay these three hundred gulden, because I should never forsake her, and that even should I be so unfortunate as to change my mind, I should only be too glad to get rid of her for three hundred gulden, while Constanze, if I know her, would be too proud to let herself be sold. But what did the angelic girl do when the guardian was gone? She asked her mother for the document, and said to me: *"Dear Mozart! I need no written assurance from you. I believe what you say,"* and tore up the paper.

With which noble gesture Constanze only enmeshed the fly more securely in the web. Thorwart had given his word of honor never to breathe a word of the whole story, not even on his deathbed, but (letter of 16 January, 1782) "notwithstanding his word of honor he has told the story to the whole town of Vienna, which has very much shaken the good opinion I once had of him . . ." Mozart goes on to defend, though a bit weakly, the blackmailer and her accomplice:

> Herr von Thorwart did not behave well, but not so badly that [as the enraged Leopold seems to have proposed] he and Madame Weber "should be put in chains, made to sweep streets, and have boards hung around their necks with the words *seducers of youth."*

But soon his eyes were opened to the true nature of his future mother-in-law and sisters-in-law. Mother Weber's next attempt was to induce her daughter and future son-in-law to lodge with her. In her eyes, Mozart must have taken on more and more the character of a very promising object for exploitation. When both Mozart and Constanze declined the invitation, she began to make life miserable for her daughter, in order to get her out of the house, being ably assisted in this project by her other daughters. Only Constanze was an angel (letter of 15 December, 1781):

> In no other family have I ever come across such difference of character. The eldest is a lazy, gross, perfidious woman, and as cunning as a fox. Mme. Lange is a false, malicious person, and a coquette. The youngest—is still too young to be anything in particular—she is just a good-natured, but feather-headed crea-ture. May God protect her from seduction! But the middle one, my good, dear Constanze, is the martyr of the family and, prob-ably for that very reason, is the kindest-hearted, the cleverest, and, in short, the best of them all . . .

Things came to a point where Constanze left her mother's dwelling and moved to the home of a patroness of Mozart, Baroness von Waldstätten—which was little help to Constanze's reputation, for the Baroness was a very broad-minded woman, and her own reputation was none too good. Mother Weber then wanted to have her daughter brought home by the police. Nothing was left but to marry quickly. The fourth of August, 1782, was the fateful day; symbolically enough, Leopold's consent did not arrive until the day after.

When one looks back upon the whole dreary story of Mozart's marriage, his inability to break out of the web that was spun around him is very hard to understand. For Mozart could be very rough in dealing with women who had designs upon him. For example, there was the daughter of the court baker in Salzburg, the one with the lovely big eyes, "who danced with him at the Stern, who often paid him friendly compliments, and who ended by entering the convent at Loreto" (letter of Leopold, 23 October, 1777). When she heard that Wolfgang planned to quit Salzburg, she left the convent, hoping to keep him from going. It is a story of hopeless love, which one cannot hear without being touched. Mozart's reply to Leopold (25 October) was embarrassed but at the same time flippant. It is clear that he felt badly about the affair, but he tried to get it out of his head.

During his first years in Vienna, Mozart became the object of another one-sided love affair, with the pianist Josephine Aurnhammer. In a letter dated 22 August, 1781, he describes her with gruesome realism:

> If a painter wanted to portray the devil to the life, he would have to choose her face. She is as fat as a farm-wench, perspires so that you feel inclined to vomit, and goes about so scantily clad that really you can read as plain as print: *"Pray, do look here."* True, there is enough to see, in fact, quite enough to strike one blind; but—one is thoroughly well punished for the rest of the day if one is unlucky enough to let one's eyes wander in that direction—tartar is the only remedy! so loathsome, dirty, and horrible! Faugh, the devil!

The fact is that Constanze had just won her game.

What sort of woman was Constanze Weber? She owes her fame to the fact that Wolfgang Amadeus Mozart loved her, and in so doing preserved her name for eternity, as a fly is preserved in amber. But this does not mean that she deserved either his love or the fame it brought her. Schlichtegroll's necrology has this to say of her:

> In Vienna he married Constanze Weber and found in her a good mother for the two children she bore him, who sought to restrain him from many follies and dissipations . . .

Was it shame at such a perversion of the truth that impelled Constanze to make this passage illegible in the Graz edition of the necrology?

Mozart—follies and dissipations! Mozart died in his thirty-sixth year; yet he went through all the stages of human life, simply passing through them faster than ordinary mortals. At thirty he was both childlike and wise; he combined the highest creative power with the highest understanding of his art; he observed the affairs of life and he saw behind them; and he experienced before his end that feeling of imminent completion that consists in the loss of all love for life (letter from Frankfurt, dated 30 September, 1790):

> If people could see into my heart, I should almost feel ashamed. To me everything is cold—cold as ice. Perhaps if you were with me I might possibly take more pleasure in the kindness of those I meet here. But, as it is, everything seems so empty . . .

And even more unmistakably five months before his death (7 July, 1791):

> I can't describe what I have been feeling—a kind of emptiness, which hurts me dreadfully—a kind of longing, which is never satisfied, which never ceases, and which persists, nay, rather increases daily . . .

It was certainly not longing for his wife—as he tried to make her believe, and perhaps believed himself—that made him feel "a kind of emptiness," "a kind of longing." It was the presentiment of death. Did Constanze understand this? No—she was not fitted to follow Mozart into such regions. She was not even a good housewife. She never looked ahead, and instead of making her husband's life and work easier by providing him with external comforts she thoughtlessly shared the bohemianism of his way of living. Mozart, on the other hand, tried to make her life as pleasant as possible by his tender care for her—care that, with her numerous confinements, she certainly needed. She bore six children between June, 1783, and July, 1791, four boys and two girls, of whom only the second and fourth sons survived. Mozart was tied to her by a physical attraction to which a few of his last letters give striking testimony; other such bits of evidence have been destroyed or made illegible.

From her father, Constanze had inherited a slight musicality. Mother Weber was completely unmusical; Mozart once remarked, when he was taking her to a performance of *Die Zauberflöte* (October, 1791): "In her case what will probably happen will be that she will see the opera, but not *hear* it." Constanze's musical gifts were not very considerable as expressed either in her singing or in her understanding of music, and the fact that Mozart never finished any of the compositions intended for her is significant.

She was wholly uneducated, and had no sense of the fitness of things. To try to gain the affections of her future father-in-law and sister-in-law, she sat down on 20 April, 1782, and wrote the following postscript to a letter of her betrothed, which must be reproduced in the German original[1] in order to indicate the intellectual and cultural level of the writer:

> Wertheste und schätzbahreste freundin! Niemals würde ich so kühn gewesen seyn, mich so ganz gerade meinem triebe und Verlangen, an sie, wertheste freindin, zu schreiben, zu überlassen, wenn mich dero Hr. bruder nicht Versichert hätte dass sie mir

---

[1] It contains awkwardnesses and mistakes in orthography impossible to reproduce in translation.

Dearest and most precious friend! Never would I have been so bold as to abandon myself wholly to my impulse and longing to write to you, dearest friend, if your esteemed brother had not assured me that you would not take amiss such a step, which results from too great a desire to converse at least in writing with a person still unknown to me but made very precious by the name of Mozart. Would you be angry if I dared to tell you that I prize you above everything, just as the sister of so worthy a brother, even without knowing you in person and—love you—and dare to ask for your friendship. Without being proud I may say that I have half earned it, and to earn it wholly will be the object of my striving! May I offer you mine in return (in my heart I have long since given it to you)? Oh, yes! Indeed I hope so. And in this hope I remain, dearest and most precious friend,

your most obedient servant and friend
Constanze Weber

Please give my greeting to your esteemed papa!

diesen schritt, welcher aus zu grosser begierde mich mit einer obschon unbekannten, doch durch den namen Mozart mir sehr schätzbahren Person wenigestens schriftlich zu besprechen, geschieht, nicht übel nehmen werden.—sollten sie böse werden wenn ich mich ihnen zu sagen unterstehe, dass ich sie, ohne die Ehre zu haben sie von Personn zu Kennen, nur ganz allein als schwester eines—ihrer so würdigen bruders, überalles Hochschätze und—liebe—und es wage—sie um Ihre freundschaft zu bitten.—ohne stolz zu seyn darf ich sagen dass ich sie halb Verdiene, ganz—werde ich mich sie zu Verdienen bestreben!— darf ich ihnen die meinige (welche ich ihnen schon längst heimlich in meinem Herzen geschenkt habe) entgegen anbieten?—o ja! ich Hoffe es.—und in dieser hofnung Verharre ich

werteste und schätzbahreste freundin

dero

gehorsamste dienerin

und freundin

Constanze Weber

bitte meinen handkuss an dero herren papa!—

It is easy to picture the shrug of the shoulders with which Leopold must have read this diplomatic message. The superficiality that Mozart saw in the youngest sister was present to a quite sufficient extent in Constanze herself. A letter is well known in which Mozart, on 29 April, 1782, three months before the wedding, made Constanze the gentlest and at the same time most serious reproaches about her thoughtless behavior in playing a game of forfeits:

> . . . the least acknowledgment of your somewhat thoughtless behavior on that occasion would have made everything all right again; and if you will not make a grievance of it, dearest friend, everything will still be all right. You realize now how much I love you. *I do not fly into a passion as you do.* I think, I reflect, and I feel. *If you will but surrender to your feelings,* then I know that this very day I shall be able to say with absolute confidence that Constanze is the virtuous, honorable, prudent, and loyal sweetheart of her honest and devoted

Mozart

A passage in a letter written from Dresden on 16 April, 1789, suffices in itself to document fully all Mozart's care and concern:

> DEAR LITTLE WIFE, I have a number of requests to make. I beg you
> 1) not to be melancholy,
> 2) *to take care of your health and to beware of the spring breezes,*
> 3) not to go out walking alone—and preferably not to *go out walking at all,*
> 4) to feel absolutely assured of my love. Up to the present I have not written a single letter to you without placing your dear portrait before me.
> 5) I beg you in your conduct not only to be careful of *your honor and mine,* but also to consider *appearances.* Do not be angry with me for asking this. You ought to love me even more for thus valuing our honor.
> 6) and lastly I beg you to send me more details in your letters. I should very much like to know whether our brother-in-law Hofer came to see us the day after my departure? Whether he comes very often, as he promised me he would? Whether the Langes come sometimes? Whether progress is being made with the portrait? What sort of life you are leading? All these things are naturally of great interest to me.

In nothing could Mozart really rely upon Constanze. Even in the very last period, he had to warn her, whose behavior was all-important to him, against bad company (summer of 1791):

> . . . please do not go to the Casino.
> *Primo,* the company is—*you understand what I mean*—
> *Secondo,* you can't dance, as things are—and to look on . . . ?
> Why, you can do that more easily when your little husband is with you.

He was not at all sure of her fidelity, and in this connection an anecdote that has come down to us deserves to be believed, and to be taken as not altogether harmless:

> In the summer of 1791 the young lieutenant von Malfatti was taking the cure near by in Baden, in order to recover fully from wounds received in the last Turkish war; and, since he limped,

he had to spend the greater part of his time in his ground-floor room. He sat in his window reading, and often enough raised his eyes from his book to glance across the way to the slender, dark-haired young woman who occupied another one of the rented lodgings on the ground floor. One day, towards evening, he saw a little man creep up to the house, look around carefully in all directions, and act as if he were going to climb in the lady's window. The lieutenant quickly hobbled over to the defense of his pretty neighbor and grasped the little man by the shoulder:

"What do you want here, Sir, that is not the door!"

"Well, I guess I may climb in my wife's window!" was the answer. It was Mozart himself, who had returned, no doubt unexpectedly, from Vienna to visit his "Stanzerl" [as he nicknamed Constanze], and who wanted, in characteristic fashion, to surprise her doubly by letting her find him sitting in her room in the evening, when she returned from her evening "constitutional," before any one knew he was there.

We may read a good deal between the lines when he writes to Constanze at the spa (25 June, 1791): "Beware of the baths! And do sleep more—and not so irregularly, or I shall worry—I am a little anxious as it is . . ."

But Constanze knew how to turn things around to make it appear that *she* had had to overlook her husband's little escapades and affairs with chambermaids. There is not the slightest evidence to justify any such insinuation. Not even the so-called Hofdemel affair offers any testimony against Mozart. The Court-Attaché Franz Hofdemel, formerly private secretary of one Count Seiler, was a lodge-brother of Mozart's. He was married to the daughter of the Kapellmeister Gotthard Pokorny, Magdalene, to whom Mozart gave lessons. Hofdemel was one of Mozart's creditors. Mozart had asked him several times for loans, as is evidenced by a letter (April, 1789) in which Mozart alludes to the approaching reception of Hofdemel into the lodge. Five days after Mozart's death, Hofdemel attempted to kill his wife, who was expecting a child, slashing at her face and throat with a razor, and then committed suicide. The deed was attributed to a fit of jealousy—but cases of unwarranted jealousy are not unknown. The widow received a pension of 560 gulden from the Emperor Leopold.

The public scandal impelled her to leave Vienna for her father's home in Brünn, where she gave birth to a son, Johann Alexander Franz. Whether the boy was Mozart's or Hofdemel's we cannot know; he bore the first names of both.[2]

The only woman of whom Constanze would really have had a right to be jealous, a woman who had more than a mere physical attraction for Mozart, was Anna (Nancy) Selina Storace, his first Susanna. She was born in 1766 in London, of an Italian father, the contrabass player Stefano Storace, and an English mother. Her brother Stephen was a composition pupil of Mozart's, and by no means an unworthy one, as his most popular *opere buffe* show. She studied singing under Rauzzini and then went to Italy where she completed her vocal studies at the Ospedaletto in Venice. From 1780 on, she appeared in public in Florence, Parma, and Milan, and in 1783 she came to Vienna. Her marital history, like Mozart's, was not very happy. In 1784 she was stupid enough to marry her countryman John Abraham Fisher, twenty-two years her senior, a violinist, composer, and bachelor and doctor of music of Oxford, who was passing through Vienna on a concert tour. He so mistreated her that the indignant Emperor banished him from the Imperial domains. Anna Selina resumed her maiden-name, and always kept her marriage a secret in her native country.

Between Mozart and her there must have been a deep and sympathetic understanding. She was beautiful, attractive, an artist, and a finished singer, whose salary at the Italian opera in Vienna attained a figure at that time unheard of. The scena and aria *Ch'io mi scordi di te* (K. 505) for soprano, obbligato clavier, and orchestra, is dedicated to her. In Mozart's thematic catalogue it is labelled "Für Mselle Storace und mich"; the autograph reads: "Composto per la Sig^{ra}. Storace dal suo servo ed amico W. A. Mozart Vienna li 26 di dec^{bre} 1786." It is an accompanied duet for voice and clavier, a declaration of love in music, the transfiguration of a relation that could not be realized except in this ideal sphere. Fortunately, Constanze had no ear for such things. It was with Miss Storace, her brother, and the tenor Michael Kelly that Mozart planned in 1787 to visit London— a plan his father upset. But he remained in correspondence with Anna

---

[2] Mozart was christened Johann Wolfgang Amadeus.

Selina. What happened to these letters is a mystery. Anna Selina certainly treasured them, but perhaps before her death, which occurred in Dulwich in 1817, she destroyed them as not intended for the eyes of an outsider.

Constanze's behavior upon the death of Mozart, and after it, has been criticized with varying degrees of severity. She was ill and beside herself, and she could not prevent Mozart's "patron," the Imperial Court Librarian Gottfried van Swieten, from having Mozart's body buried in a pauper's grave, for reasons of economy. Later, she could not visit the grave, or bedeck it with flowers, or erect a tombstone—and this has also been the basis of stupid reproaches—simply because the grave could not be found. Not until years later (1808 or 1809) did she ride out to the graveyard of St. Mark's in search of the spot. But she was told that paupers' graves were left intact for only seven years. Under the date of her husband's death she wrote in his album, beneath an entry which Mozart had written for his friend Dr. Sigmund Barisani:

> What once thou hast written upon this page for thy friend, that do I now, deeply bowed in sorrow, write for thee, dearly beloved husband! O Mozart, whom neither I nor all Europe can ever forget, now is it well with thee—forever well.
>
> At one o'clock in the morning between the fourth and fifth of December of this year he departed, in his thirty-sixth year—alas, all too soon!—this good but ungrateful world. O God—for eight years we were joined by the tenderest bond, on earth unbreakable! Oh! could I but soon be joined with thee forever, thy most deeply troubled wife,
>
> *Constanze Mozart, née Weber.*

I see no reason to doubt that this entry was made on 5 December, but it seems very unlikely that the year was 1791. In 1791 Constanze had no idea that "all Europe could never forget" her husband. Only the growing world-fame of Mozart awakened her gradually to the realization of the nature of the man who had once led her forth from the Auge Gottes, and with whom she had lived for nine or ten years. What contributed most to this realization was the growing material value of his unpublished manuscripts, of which she still possessed a great number (not more than 70 of his more than 600 works had been published during his lifetime), and which she accordingly kept together very carefully.

Now we are almost ready to take leave of Constanze Weber—almost, because there are still a few words in her favor left to say. For after Mozart's death she exhibited certain better qualities, among which, ironically, we find even a marked native business sense, which she had lacked completely during his lifetime. A few weeks after his death she sold eight manuscripts to the King of Prussia for 800 ducats, i.e. about $1500; she produced concerts in memory of Mozart as benefits for herself; and she carried on negotiations concerning a few of his works. Like her mother before her, she began to rent rooms. The counselor of the Danish legation, Georg Nikolaus von Nissen, born in 1761, an admirer of Mozart, took lodgings with her. He became her friend and adviser: all the letters she wrote to the publisher André in Offenbach about the sale of Mozart's manuscript remains show Nissen's influence, in both thought and style. When Nissen was called back to Copenhagen in 1809, he legitimized his relation with Constanze, and from that time on she signed herself in letters as *"Constanze Etatsräthin von Nissen, gewesene Witwe Mozart"* (Constanze, wife of the State Counselor von Nissen, formerly Widow Mozart). Under Nissen's influence she even became a good mother to her two sons, Karl Thomas and Franz Xaver Wolfgang. For ten years, from 1810 to 1820, she lived with Nissen in Copenhagen; then, strangely enough, the couple moved to Mozart's birthplace, since Nissen wished to settle near Bad Gastein, and doubtless also wished to be near the sources for the story of Mozart's early life. Constanze remained in Salzburg even after Nissen's death in 1826, and thus there lived in Salzburg two old women who in their youth had been the closest companions of Wolfgang Amadeus—his sister Marianne and his wife Constanze; but they had very little to do with each other. In 1828, Constanze published the first big biography of Mozart, prepared by Nissen. This gives only a conventional idea of Mozart's greatness, and limits itself mainly to biographical matter; and even here, there are omissions, suppressions, and even misrepresentations. But it was the first biography, and even today it is not without a certain value, since it reproduces many documents which have since disappeared. After Nissen's death, Constanze took into her house her younger sister, Sophie Haibel, who had also lost her husband; and eventually Aloysia Lange, too, came to spend her last days in Salzburg. Constanze departed from this group of ghosts in 1842, having outlived Mozart by fifty years. A series of her letters, principally to her sons, are preserved, as well as a diary of the years 1824–37. The letters are chiefly a reflection of Nissen's views. They are conventional and insignificant, with never a word of wit, magnanimity, or humor. In the diary platitudes alternate with observations that show a sense of business. Constanze is taking the baths in Gastein, as once she took them in Baden-bei-Wien:

Today, being the 19th of December, 1829, I had the good fortune to take my seventh bath, I took my coffee as usual at half past five, after I had washed my face and my mouth I went to visit Mr. Rösiger at the baths, but found instead of him a stranger, who had just come from London and told me much about it, and who will take some letters there for me. I do not know his name yet. A very nice man. Then I went to my room, got my bath linen, and when the bath was free I went in with Mona and let her bathe for a good quarter of an hour with me, but I stayed a whole hour, after which I went to bed again to rest a little, and then took half a cup of camomile tea and then I sat here to write all this down, and now Dr. Storck has just come and praise God has found me well—so much till 11 o'clock, the rest will follow—at half past eleven I went out to take a little walk in front of the house.

A. E.

5

The Letters

I HAVE just been reading Mozart's letters for the second time (in the French translation by Henri de Curzon), and I think they ought to be included among the books of every library, for they are not only of interest to artists but instructive for other people as well. If you read these letters, Mozart will be your friend for life; his kind face will show itself in moments of trouble, and when you are miserable you will hear his merry boyish laugh and blush to give way to dark moods as you think of what he himself so courageously endured. Let us recall his memory; it is fast slipping into shadow.

The first thing that strikes us is his wonderful moral health. This is the more surprising because physically he was far from strong. All his faculties seem extraordinarily well balanced: his soul was full of feeling and yet master of itself; his mind was wonderfully calm, even in events like his mother's death and his love for Constance Weber; his intellect was clear and instinctively grasped what people liked and the best way to achieve success; and he was able to bring his proud genius to conquer the world's affections without hurt to himself.

This moral balance is rare in passionate natures; for all passion is excess of feeling. Mozart had every kind of feeling, but he had no passion—except his terrible pride and a strong consciousness of his genius.

"The archbishop of Salzburg thinks you are steeped in pride," said a friend to him one day.

Mozart did not seek to conceal this pride, and to those who hurt

77

it he replied with an arrogance worthy of one of Rousseau's republican contemporaries. "It is the heart that gives a man nobility," he said, "and if I am not a count, I have perhaps more honor in me than many a count. And whether it is a valet or a count, he becomes a low scoundrel from the moment he insults me." In 1777, when he was twenty-one years old, he said to two would-be jokers who laughed at his Cross of the Golden Spur, "It would be easier for me to get all the decorations that you could possibly receive than for you to become what I am now, even if you died and were born again twice over." "I was boiling with rage," he added.

He carefully used to keep and sometimes calmly quote all the flattering things that were said about him. In 1782 he said to a friend, "Prince Kaunitz told the archduke that people like myself came into the world only once in a hundred years."

He was capable of intense hate when his pride was wounded. He suffered greatly at the idea of being in the service of a prince: "The thought is intolerable," he said (October 15, 1778). After he had heard the archbishop of Salzburg's remark, "he trembled all over and reeled in the street like a drunken man. He was obliged to go home and get to bed, and he was still not himself on the following morning." (May 12, 1781.) "I hate the archbishop with all my soul," he said. Later on he remarked, "If anyone offends me I must revenge myself, and unless I revenge myself with interest I consider I have only repaid my enemy and not corrected him."

When his pride was at stake, or rather when his inclination was likely to be thwarted, this respectful and obedient son owned only the authority of his own desires.

"I did not recognize my father in a single line of your letter. It was certainly a letter from a father; but it was not from *my* father." (May 19, 1781.)

And he got married before he had received his father's consent (August 7, 1782).

If you take away Mozart's great passion for pride, you will find him a pleasant and cheerful soul. He had quick sympathies and the gentleness of a woman—or rather of a child, for he was given to tears and laughter, to teasing, and all the tricks of a warm-hearted boy.

Usually he was very lively, and amused at nothing in particular;

he had difficulty in keeping still and was always singing and jumping about, nearly killing himself with laughter over anything funny, or even over things that were not funny. He loved good jokes and bad ones (especially the bad ones, and sometimes the coarse ones), was without malice or *arrière pensée,* and enjoyed the sound of words without any sense in them: "Stru! Stri! . . . Knaller paller . . . Schnip. . . . Schnap. . . . Schnur. . . . Schnepeperl! . . . Snai!" is what we find in the letter of July 6, 1791. In 1769 he writes:

"I am simply bursting with joy because this journey amuses me so much . . . because it is so hot in the carriage . . . and because our coachman is a good lad and drives like the wind when the road allows it!"

One may find hundreds of examples of his merriment at nothing at all, and of the laughter that comes from good health. The blood flowed freely in his veins, and his feelings were not oversensitive.

"I saw four rogues hung today on the square by the cathedral. *They hang them here as they do at Lyons.*" (November 30, 1770.)

He had not very wide sympathy—that "humanity" of modern artists. He loved those he knew—his father, his wife, and his friends; and he loved them tenderly and spoke of them with ardent affection, so that one's heart is warmed as it is by his music.

"When my wife and I were married, we burst into tears, and everyone else was so affected by our emotion that they wept too." (August 7, 1782.)

He had a splendid capacity for friendship, as only those who have been poor understand friendship. He himself says:

"Our best and truest friends are those who are poor. Rich people know nothing of friendship." (August 7, 1778.)

"Friend?" (he says elsewhere), "I call only that man a friend who, whatever the occasion, thinks of nothing but his friend's welfare and does all he can to make him happy." (December 18, 1778.)

His letters to his wife, especially those written between 1789 and 1791, are full of loving affection and mad gaiety; and he seems unaffected by the illness, cares, and terrible distress that went to make up this most cruel portion of his life. *"Immer zwischen Angst und Hoffung"* (Always between anxiety and hope), he says; but he does not say it, as you might think, in a kind of valiant effort to reassure his wife and deceive her as to his true circumstances; the words come from an irresistible desire to laugh, which he cannot conquer and which he had to satisfy even in the midst of the worst of his troubles. His laughter is very near to tears—those happy tears that well up from a loving nature.

He was very happy though no life could have been harder than his. It was a perpetual fight against sickness and misery. Death put an end to it—when he was thirty-five years old. Where could his happiness come from?

Well, first of all, from his religion, which was sound and free from all superstition, a firm, strong kind of faith which doubt had never injured though it may have touched it. It was also a calm and peaceful faith, without passion or mysticism: *Credo quia verum*. To his dying father he wrote:

"I am counting on good news although I make a practice of always imagining the worst. As death is the true purpose of life, I have, for many years, made myself familiar with that best friend of man; and his face has now no longer any terror for me, but is, if anything, calm and consoling to look upon. I thank God for this blessing . . . and I never go to bed without thinking that perhaps on the morrow I may no longer be alive. And yet no one who knows me could say that I am sad or discontented. I give thanks to my Creator for this happiness and hope with all my heart my fellow-creatures may share it." (April 4, 1787.)

So he found happiness in the thought of eternity. His happiness on earth was in the love of those about him and especially in his love for them. In writing to his wife, he says:

"If I may only feel that you lack nothing, all my troubles will be precious to me and even pleasant. Yes! the most painful and complicated of difficulties would seem nothing but a trifle if I were sure that you were happy and in good health." (July 6, 1791.)

R. R.

The letters shed their light on every part of this singularly eventful career and help mightily toward an understanding of Mozart's elusive and, as far as surface values go, contradictory character. One need not hesitate to pronounce this correspondence one of the great collections of letters, engrossing reading not only for the musician in general and the student of Mozart in particular, but for every one who feels the fascination of the second half of the eighteenth century and finds a family of surpassing genius a subject of compelling curiosity.

Mozart, though one of the most meticulously trained of musicians, thanks to his father as well as to his own instinct and desire for perfection, was by no means a highly literate person; still less so his good-humored, competent mother. Therefore, these letters are not great literature in the sense that those of Madame de Sévigné, Horace Walpole, and Cowper are. On the other hand, as human documents, to employ the hard driven but still serviceable phrase, they are vivid and vital to the highest degree.

In Mozart, as in many other geniuses, there was always something of the child, and both the abounding gayety and humor and the searching pathos of these letters partake of the endearing quality of the child speaking from his heart. Here, however, we encounter a problem by no means easy of solution.

The candid and childlike Mozart was not wholly the angelic being that we infer from the "divine" music, to borrow Rossini's adoring word, that makes of him (though such identifications are always dangerous and never quite exact) the Raphael of composers. At times Mozart may seem to us the most guileless of men, quite unable to manage well his own affairs, and yet some recent critics, scrutinizing the facts of his life, have decided that he really was shrewd in business, though less successful in applying his shrewdness than his father had been, and inclined eventually not only toward good fellowship in liberal quantity, but toward downright dissipation. And certain of the letters leave no doubt as to coarseness in his words, if not in the deeper strata of his character.

His youthful letters to his cousin, Maria Anna Thekla Mozart (the "Bäslebriefe"), have long provoked mirth and mild wonder, but there are letters in this collection, notably a doggerel epistle to his mother written when he was twenty-three, and some of the letters of the mother herself, which are of a grossness rarely duplicated outside of Martial and Rabelais, and, as the true Martialist or Rabelaisian would not fail to remark, each of those worthies is something else again! We should bear in mind, however, the prevailing condition of manners in the eighteenth century, and especially the manners of the Salzburg countryside, which apparently have not suffered an undue softening since!

In spite of the letters, in their wide diversity and the light they shed, some of us must agree with W. J. Turner that Mozart in the last analysis remains a mystery; with Artur Schnabel, that he is the most inaccessible of the great masters. Certainly in the generality of his work he is the most idealizing of composers. The duality which exists in us all may well have been the most pronounced of all in Mozart. He seems to have lived a second life which had only a tenuous connection with his obvious life of this earth. The present fashion likes to call that part of thing compensation or escape; yet in Mozart's case it may have been simply the reality.

                                                                    P. S.[1]

As to the value of Mozart's letters, their spontaneousness, their wit, their extreme gaiety, their profound poignancy, their humanity and timelessness, there is nothing fresh to say. But long association with Mozart as a letter-writer has not failed to open up certain trains of thought which it may be of interest to indicate. In the first place, there is the strange fact that, with few exceptions, nearly all Mozart's letters are addressed to members of his family, and that, as far as we know, he never wrote to any composer or musician. Then, singular as the comparison may seem, in many of his letters Mozart, while expressing himself in words, seems in reality to be thinking in terms of music. Thus when we come upon passages which are curiously involved, words written backwards, phrases reversed, and other similar oddities of expression, we remember his description of how on a certain occasion he extemporised fugues on a given theme in a minor key, playing all kinds of tricks with it, reversing it, turning it into the major and so forth. Again, when we take up one of Mozart's autograph letters, many of which are untidily written, larded with erasures and splashed with ink-blots, and suddenly find him weaving delicate scrolls and fantastic flourishes round a capital, we remember certain themes, upon which he has embroidered a wealth of variations, deliciously interlaced and flawless in texture. Then again when he describes in such masterly fashion the Langenmantels, the Aurn-hammers, Wieland, Grimm, and gives us the long gallery of pen-

---

[1] Pitts Sanborn, in the New York *Herald-Tribune,* Dec. 18, 1938, under the assumed name "Peter Bowdoin."

portraits with which we are familiar, we remember that these are only the rough sketches for the Don Alfonsos, the Basilios, and the Marcellinas which later on will be immortalised by his music. Indeed, though the letters we possess only make us wish for more, we have here the substance of what Mozart thought about music, his ideas on the training of a pianist, his profound knowledge of the art of the singer, and, if we collect the relevant passages, some indication of his own method of composition. As an autobiography their value is, if anything, greater than that of the letters of other composers, such as Beethoven, Schumann, and Wagner. Lastly, it is no exaggeration to say that from a psychological and personal point of view, Mozart's letters bear comparison with those of the great letter-writers of the world.

E. A.

(71a) MOZART TO HIS MOTHER[2]
(Autograph in the Pierpont Morgan Library, New York City)
Wörgl, December 13th, 1769

Dearest Mamma!

My heart is completely enchanted with all these pleasures, because it is so jolly on this journey, because it is so warm in the carriage and because our coachman is a fine fellow who, when the road gives him the slightest chance, drives so fast. Papa will have already described the journey to Mamma. The reason why I am writing to Mamma is to show her that I know my duty and that I am with the deepest respect her devoted son

Wolfgang Mozart

(88a) MOZART TO HIS SISTER
(Autograph in the possession of D. Salomon, Berlin)
Rome, April 21st, 1770

Cara Sorella Mia!

I am delighted that you liked the minuet I sent you from Bologna, I mean, the one which Signor Pick danced at Milan. I hope that you have received the contredanse which I enclosed in my first letter from Rome. Do tell me quite frankly how you like it.

---

[2] This whole section of letters is taken from the three volumes of *The Letters of Mozart & His Family,* translated and edited by Emily Anderson (Macmillan and Co., London, 1938).

Please try to find the arithmetical tables. You know that you wrote
them down yourself. I have lost my copy and so have quite forgotten
them. So I beg you to copy them out for me with some other examples
in arithmetic and send them to me here.

Manzuoli is negotiating with the Milanese to sing in my opera.
With that in view he sang four or five arias to me in Florence, including some which I had to compose in Milan, in order that the Milanese,
who had heard none of my dramatic music, should see that I am
capable of writing an opera. Manzuoli is demanding a thousand
ducats. It is not known for certain whether Gabrielli will come. Some
say that De Amicis will sing. We are to meet her in Naples. I should
like her and Manzuoli to take the parts. Then we should have two
good acquaintances and friends. The libretto has not yet been chosen.
I recommended to Don Ferdinando and Herr von Troger a text by
Metastasio.

At the moment I am working at the aria: Se ardire, e speranza.

(205) MOZART TO PADRE MARTINI, BOLOGNA
(Autograph in the Nationalbibliothek, Vienna)
Salzburg, September 4th, 1776
Most Reverend Padre Maestro, my esteemed Patron,

The regard, the esteem and the respect which I cherish for your
illustrious person have prompted me to trouble you with this letter
and to send you a humble specimen of my music, which I submit
to your masterly judgment. I composed for last year's carnival at
Munich an opera buffa, "La finta giardiniera." A few days before
my departure the Elector expressed a desire to hear some of my contrapuntal compositions. I was therefore obliged to write this motet
in a great hurry, in order to have time to have the score copied for
His Highness and to have the parts written out and thus enable it to
be performed during the Offertory at High Mass on the following
Sunday. Most beloved and esteemed Signor Padre Maestro! I beg
you most earnestly to tell me, frankly and without reserve, what
you think of it. We live in this world in order to learn zealously and,
by interchanging our ideas, to enlighten one another and thus endeavour to promote science and art. Oh, how often have I longed
to be near you, most Reverend Father, so that I might be able to
talk to and reason with you. For I live in a country where music leads

a struggling existence, though indeed apart from those who have left us, we still have excellent teachers and particularly composers of great wisdom, learning and taste. As for the theatre, we are in a bad way for lack of singers. We have no castrati, and we shall never have them, as they insist on being handsomely paid; and generosity is not one of our faults. Meanwhile I am amusing myself by writing chamber music and music for the church, in which branches of composition we have two other excellent masters of counterpoint, Signori Haydn and Adlgasser. My father is in the service of the Cathedral and this gives me an opportunity of writing as much church music as I like. He has already served this court for thirty-six years and as he knows that the present Archbishop cannot and will not have anything to do with people who are getting on in years, he no longer puts his whole heart into his work, but has taken up literature, which was always a favourite study of his. Our church music is very different from that of Italy, since a mass with the whole Kyrie, the Gloria, the Credo, the Epistle sonata, the Offertory or Motet, the Sanctus and the Agnus Dei must not last longer than three quarters of an hour. This applies even to the most solemn mass said by the Archbishop himself. So you see that a special study is required for this kind of composition. At the same time, the mass must have all the instruments—trumpets, drums and so forth. Alas, that we are so far apart, my very dear Signor Padre Maestro! If we were together, I should have so many things to tell you! I send my devoted remembrances to all the members of the Accademia Filarmonica. I long to win your favour and I never cease to grieve that I am far away from that one person in the world whom I love, revere and esteem most of all and whose most humble and devoted servant, most

Reverend Father, I shall always be.
Wolfgango Amadeo Mozart

If you condescend to write to me, please address your letter to Salzburg via Trento.

(273) MOZART TO HIS FATHER

(From Nissen, pp. 342–345)
Mannheim, January 17th, 1778

Next Wednesday I am going for a few days to Kirchheim-Bolanden to visit the Princess of Orange. People here have said such nice things to me about her that I have at last decided to go. A Dutch officer, a good friend of mine, got a terrible scolding from her for not bringing me with him when he went to offer her his New Year wishes. I shall get eight louis d'or at least, for, as she is passionately fond of singing, I have had four arias copied for her and, as she has a nice little orchestra and gives a concert every day, I shall also present her with a symphony. Moreover the copying of the arias will not cost me much, for it has been done by a certain Herr Weber,[3] who is accompanying me there. He has a daughter[4] who sings admirably and has a lovely, pure voice; she is only fifteen. The only thing she lacks is dramatic action; were it not for that, she might be the prima donna on any stage. Her father is a thoroughly honest German, who is bringing up his children well, and for that very reason the girl is persecuted with attentions here. He has six children, five girls and one son.[5] He and his wife and children have been obliged to live for fourteen years on an income of 200 gulden and, because he has always attended carefully to his duties and has provided the Elector with a very talented singer, he now gets in all—400 gulden. She sings most excellently my aria written for De Amicis with those horribly difficult passages, and she is to sing it at Kircheim-Bolanden.

Now for something else. Last Wednesday there was a big party at our house to which I was invited. There were fifteen guests and in the evening the young lady of the house was to play the concerto I had taught her. About eleven in the morning the Privy Councillor came to see me and brought Herr Vogler, who wanted absolument to make my closer acquaintance; he had so often bothered me to go to him, and at last he had overcome his pride and paid me the first visit. Besides, people tell me that he is now quite different, as he is no longer so much admired; for at first they made an idol of him. So we at once went upstairs together, the guests began to arrive by

---

[3] Fridolin Weber (1733–79), uncle of Karl Maria von Weber, composer of *Der Freischütz,* was first a notary. In 1765 he accepted a post as bass singer at the Mannheim court. He and his family followed the Electoral Court to Munich in 1778, but soon moved to Vienna, where his second daughter, Aloysia, had obtained an appointment at the opera. He died in October, 1779.

[4] Aloysia (c. 1760–1839), Weber's second daughter.

[5] We only know of four daughters, Josefa Hofer, Aloysia Lange, Konstanze Mozart, and Sophie Haibel.

degrees and we did nothing but chatter. After dinner, however, he sent to his house for two claviers, tuned to the same pitch, and also for his tedious engraved sonatas. I had to play them, while he accompanied me on the other clavier. At his urgent request I had to send for my sonatas also. I should mention that before dinner he had scrambled through my concerto at sight (the one which the daughter of the house plays—written for Countess Lutzow). He took the first movement prestissimo—the Andante allegro and the Rondo even more prestissimo. He generally played the bass differently from the way it was written, inventing now and then quite another harmony and melody. Nothing else is possible at that pace, for the eyes cannot see the music nor the hands perform it. Well, what good is it?—that kind of sight-reading—and shitting are all one to me. The listeners (I mean those who deserve the name) can only say that they have seen music and piano-playing. They hear, think and—feel as little during the performance as the player himself. Well, you may easily imagine that it was unendurable. At the same time I could not bring myself to say to him, *Far too quick!* Besides, it is much easier to play a thing quickly than slowly: in difficult passages you can leave out a few notes without anyone noticing it. But is that beautiful music? In rapid playing the right and left hands can be changed without anyone seeing or hearing it; but is that beautiful? And wherein consists the art of playing prima vista? In this; in playing the piece in the time in which it ought to be played and in playing all the notes, appoggiaturas and so forth, exactly as they are written and with the appropriate expression and taste, so that you might suppose that the performer had composed it himself. Vogler's fingering too is wretched; his left thumb is just like that of the late Adlgasser and he does all the treble runs downwards with the thumb and first finger of his right hand.

(288) MOZART TO HIS FATHER
(Autograph in the Mozarteum, Salzburg)
Mannheim, February 19th, 1778

Monsieur
    mon très cher Père!

I hope you received my last two letters safely. In the last one I discussed my mother's journey home, but I now see from your letter of the 12th that this was quite unnecessary. I always thought that you would disapprove of my undertaking a journey (with the Webers,) but I never had any such intention—I mean, of course in our present circumstances. I gave them my word of honour, however, to write to you about it. Herr Weber does not know how we stand—and I shall certainly never tell anyone. I wish my position was such that I had no cause to consider anyone else and that we were all comfortably off. In the intoxication of the moment I forgot how impossible it is at present to carry out my plan, and therefore also—to tell you what I have now done. The reasons why I have not gone off to Paris must be sufficiently evident to you from my last two letters. If my mother had not first raised the point, I should certainly have gone with my friends, but when I saw that she did not like the scheme, then I began to dislike it myself. For as soon as people lose confidence in me, I am apt to lose confidence in myself. Those days when, standing on a chair, I used to sing to you *Oragna fiagata fa* and finish by kissing you on the tip of your nose, are gone indeed; but do I honour, love and obey you any the less on that account? I will say no more. As for your reproach about the little singer in Munich, I must confess that I was an ass to tell you such a palpable lie. Why, she does not yet know what *singing* means. It is true that for a person who had only been studying for three months she sang surprisingly well, and she had, in addition, a very pleasing and pure voice. Why I praised her so much may well have been because I was hearing people say from morning to night "There is no better singer in all Europe" and "Who has not heard her has heard nothing." I did not dare to contradict them, partly because I wanted to make some good friends, and partly because I had come straight from Salzburg, where we are not in the habit of contradicting anyone; but as soon as I was alone, I never could help laughing. Why then did I not laugh at her when writing to you? I really cannot tell.

What you say so cuttingly about my merry intercourse with your brother's daughter has hurt me very much; but since matters are not as you think, it is not necessary for me to reply. I don't know what to say about Wallerstein. I was very grave and reserved at Beecke's and at the officers' table also I maintained a very serious demeanour and did not say a word to anyone. Let us forget all that; you only wrote it in a temper.

What you say about Mlle. Weber is all perfectly true; and at the time I wrote that letter I knew quite as well as you do that she is still too young and that she must first learn how to act and make frequent appearances on the stage. But with some people one must proceed—by degrees. These good people are as tired of being here as—you know whom and where;[6] and they think that every scheme is practicable. I promised them to write everything to my father; but when the letter was on its way to Salzburg, I kept on telling them: "She must be patient a little longer, she is a bit too young yet, etc." They do not mind what I say to them, for they have a high opinion of me. On my advice the father has engaged Madame Toscani (an actress) to give his daughter lessons in acting. Everything you say about Mlle. Weber is true, except one thing—that "she sings like a Gabrielli"; for I should not at all like her to sing in that style. Those who have heard Gabrielli are forced to admit that she was an adept only in runs and roulades; she adopted, however, such an unusual interpretation that she won admiration; but it never survived the fourth time of hearing. In the long run she could not please, as people soon get tired of coloratura passages. Moreover, she had the misfortune of not being able to sing. She was not capable of *sustaining* a breve properly, and, as she had no *messa di voce,* she could not dwell on her notes; in short, she sang with skill but without understanding. Mlle. Weber's singing, on the other hand, goes to the heart, and she prefers to sing cantabile. Lately I have made her practise the passages in my grand aria,[7] because, if she goes to Italy, she will have to sing bravura arias. Undoubtedly she will never forget how to sing cantabile, for that is her natural bent. Raaff himself (who is certainly no flatterer), when asked to give his candid opinion, said "She sang, not like a student, but like a master." So now you know all. I still commend her to your interest with all my heart; and please don't forget about the arias, cadenzas and the rest. Farewell. I kiss your hands 100000 times and remain your most obedient son

Wolfgang Amadé Mozart

I can't write any more for sheer hunger. My mother will display the contents of our large cash-box. I embrace my sister with all my heart. Tell her that she must not cry over every silly trifle, or I shall

[6] Mozart and his father in Salzburg.

[7] From *Lucio Silla.*

never go home again. My greetings to all our good friends, especially to Herr Bullinger.

(293) MOZART TO HIS COUSIN, MARIA ANNA THEKLA MOZART, AUGSBURG
(Autograph in the possession [1938] *of Stefan Zweig)*
Mannheim, February 28th, 1778

Mademoiselle ma Très Chère Cousine!

Perhaps you think or are even convinced that I am dead? That I have pegged out? Or hopped a twig? Not at all. Don't believe it, I implore you. For believing and shitting are two very different things! Now how could I be writing such a beautiful hand if I were dead? How could that be possible? I shan't apologise for my very long silence, for you would never believe me. Yet what is true is true. I have had so many things to do that I had time indeed to think of my little cousin, but not to write, you see. So I just had to let things be. But now I have the honour to inquire how you are and whether you perspire? Whether your stomach is still in good order? Whether indeed you have no disorder? Whether you still can like me at all? Whether with chalk you often scrawl? Whether now and then you have me in mind? Whether to hang yourself you sometimes feel inclined? Whether you have been wild? With this poor foolish child? Whether to make peace with me you'll be so kind? If not, I swear I'll let off one behind! Ah, you're laughing! Victoria! Our arses shall be the symbol of our peacemaking! I knew that you wouldn't be able to resist me much longer. Why, of course, I'm sure of success, even if to-day I should make a mess, though to Paris I go in a fortnight or less. So if you want to send a reply to me from that town of Augsburg yonder, you see, then write at once, the sooner the better, so that I may be sure to receive your letter, or else if I'm gone I'll have the bad luck, instead of a letter to get some muck. Muck!—Muck!—Ah, muck! Sweet word! Muck! chuck! That too is fine. Muck, chuck!—muck!—suck—o charmante! muck, suck! That's what I like! Muck, chuck and suck! Chuck muck and suck muck!

Now for something else. When the carnival was on, did you have some good fun? One can have far more fun at this time in Augsburg than here. How I wish I were with you so that we could run about together. Mamma and I send our greetings to your father and mother and to you, little cousin, and we trust all three of you are well and in good spirits. Praise and thanks be to God, we are in good health. Don't believe it. All the better, better the all. A propos, how are you getting on with your French? May I send you a whole letter in French? You would like one from Paris, would you not? Do tell me whether you still have that Spuni Cuni business? I'm sure you have. Well, I must tell you something before I close, for I must really stop soon, as I am in a hurry, for just at the moment I have nothing whatever to do; and also because I have no more room, as you see; the paper will soon be at an end; and besides I am tired and my fingers are twitching from so much writing; and finally even if I had room, I really don't know what I could tell you, apart from this story which I am proposing to relate. Now listen, it happened not very long ago, it all took place here and it made a great sensation too, for it seemed almost unbelievable; and, between ourselves, no one knows how the affair is going to turn out. Well, to make a long story short, about four hours from here—I have forgotten the name of the place— at some village or other—and indeed it is all one, whether the village was Tribsterill, where muck runs into the sea, or Burmesquik, where the crooked arse-holes are manufactured—in short, it was a village. Now in that village there was a peasant or shepherd, who was well advanced in years but was still hale and hearty. He was unmarried and very comfortably off and led a jolly life. But, before I finish my story, I must tell you that when he spoke he had a dreadful voice, so that whenever he said anything, people were always terrified of him. Well, to make a long story short, you must know that he had a dog called Bellot, a very fine large dog, white with black spots. Now one day the shepherd was walking along with his sheep, of which he had eleven thousand, and was carrying in his hand a stick with a beautiful rose-coloured ribbon. For he always carried a stick. It was his habit to do this. Well, let's get on. After he had walked for a good hour or so, he got tired and sat down near a river and fell asleep, and dreamt that he had lost his sheep. He awoke in terror, but to his great joy found all his sheep beside him. So he got up and walked on, but not for very long; for he had hardly walked for half an hour before he came to a bridge, which was very long but well protected on both sides in order to prevent people from falling into the river. Well, he looked at his flock and, as he was obliged to cross the river, he began to drive his eleven thousand sheep over the bridge. Now please be so kind as to wait until the eleven thousand sheep have reached the other side and then I shall finish my story. I have already told you that no one knows how the affair is going to turn out. But I hope that before I send you my next letter the sheep will have crossed the river. If not, I really don't care very much; as far as I am concerned, they could have remained this side of the water. So you must just be content with this instalment. I have told you all I know; and it is much better to stop than to make up the rest. If I did so, you would not believe any of the story; but as it is, you will surely believe—not even half of it. Well, I must close, though it makes me morose. Whoever begins must cease, or else he gives people no peace. My greetings to every single friend, and whoever doesn't believe me, may lick me world without end, from now to all eternity, until I cease to be a nonentity. He can go on licking for ever, in truth, why, even I am alarmed, forsooth, for I fear that my muck will soon dry up and that he won't have enough if he wants to sup. Adieu, little cousin. I am, I was, I should be, I have been, I had been, I should have been, oh that I were, oh that I might be, would to God I were, I shall be, if I should be, oh that I should be, I shall have been, oh that I had been, would to God that I had been, what?—a duffer. Adieu, ma chère cousine, where have you been? I am your same old faithful cousin

Wolfgang Amadé Mozart

Mannheim, February 28th, 1778.

(299) MOZART TO HIS FATHER
(Autograph in the Mozarteum, Salzburg)
Paris, le 24 mars, 1778

Mon très cher Père,

Yesterday, Monday the 23rd, at four o'clock in the afternoon we arrived here, thank God, both safe and sound, having been nine and a half days on our journey. We really thought that we should not be able to hold out; for never in all my life have I been so bored. You can easily imagine what it meant for us to leave Mannheim and so many dear, kind friends and then to have to spend nine and a half days, not only without these good friends, but without anyone, without a single soul with whom we could associate or converse. Well, thank Heaven! we are at our journey's end and I trust that with the help of God all will go well. To-day we are going to take a fiacre and look up Grimm and Wendling. To-morrow morning, however, I intend to call on the Minister of the Palatinate, Herr von Sickingen (a great connoisseur and passionate lover of music, for whom I have two letters from Herr von Gemmingen[8] and Mr. Cannabich). Before leaving Mannheim I had copies made for Herr von Gemmingen of the quartet[9] which I composed one evening at the inn at Lodi, and also of the quintet[10] and the variations on a theme by Fischer.[11] On receiving them he sent a most polite note, expressing his pleasure at the souvenir which I was leaving him and enclosing a letter for his intimate friend Herr von Sickingen with the words: "I feel sure that you will be a greater recommendation for the letter than it can possibly be for you." To cover the expenses of copying he sent me three louis d'or. He assured me of his friendship and asked for mine. I must say that all the courtiers who knew me, Court Councillors, Chamberlains and other worthy people, as well as all the court musicians, were very reluctant and sorry to see me go. There is no doubt about that. We left on Saturday, the 14th, and on the previous Thursday there was an afternoon concert at Cannabich's, where my concerto for three claviers[12] was played. Mlle. Rosa Cannabich played the first, Mlle. Weber the second and Mlle. Pierron Serrarius, our house nymph, the third. We had three rehearsals of the concerto and it went off very well. Mlle. Weber sang two arias of mine the "Aer tranquillo" from *Il Rè pastore*[13] and my new one, "Non so d'onde viene."[14] With the latter my dear Mlle. Weber did herself and me indescribable honour, for everyone said that no aria had ever affected them as did this one; but then she sang it as it ought to be

---

[8] Otto Heinrich Freiherr von Gemmingen-Homberg (1753–1836), who held a government post in Mannheim, and was a dramatist. It is thought that he encouraged Mozart to become a Freemason.

[9] K. 80, composed 1770–1773 or 1774.

[10] K. 174, composed in 1773.

[11] K. 179, composed in 1774.

[12] K. 242, composed in 1776.

[13] K. 208, composed in 1775.

[14] K. 294, composed in 1778.

sung. As soon as it was over, Cannabich called out loudly: "Bravo! Bravissimo, maestro! Veramente scritta da maestro!" It was the first time I had heard it with orchestral accompaniment and I wish you also could have heard it, exactly as it was performed and sung there with that accuracy in interpretation, piano and forte. Who knows, perhaps you may hear it yet—I hope so. The members of the orchestra never ceased praising the aria and talking about it. I have many good friends in Mannheim (people of position and means), who wished very much to keep me there. Well, if they pay me decently, they can have me. Who knows, perhaps it will come off. I wish it would. And I still have a feeling and I still cherish the hope that it will. Cannabich is an honest, worthy man and my very good friend, but he has just one failing, which is, that, although no longer young, he is rather careless and absent-minded. If you are not perpetually after him, he forgets everything. But when it's a matter of helping a *real friend,* he roars like a bull and takes the deepest interest in him; and that means a great deal, for he has influence. But on the whole I can't say much of his courtesy and gratitude, for I must confess that, in spite of their poverty and obscurity, and although I did much less for them, the Webers have shown themselves far more grateful. For M. and Mme. Cannabich did not say a word to me, nor did they even offer me the smallest keepsake, not even a bagatelle, to show their kindly feeling. They gave me nothing at all, they didn't even thank me, after I had spent so much time and trouble on their daughter. She can now perform before anyone, and for a girl of fourteen and an amateur she plays quite well; and it is thanks to me, as all Mannheim knows. She now has taste and can play trills; her time is good and her fingering is much better; formerly she had nothing of this. So in three months' time they will miss me sorely; for I fear she will soon be spoiled again and will spoil herself, because, unless she has a master constantly beside her, and one who knows his job, she will be no good, as she is still too childish and careless to practise seriously and to any purpose by herself. Mlle. Weber out of the goodness of her heart has knitted me two pairs of mittens in filet, which she has given me as a remembrance and a small token of her gratitude. And Herr Weber copied out gratis whatever I required, supplied me with music paper and also made me a present of Molière's comedies (as he knew that I had not yet read them) with this inscription:

Ricevi, amico, le opere del Molière in segno di gratitudine, e qualche volta ricordati di me. And once, when alone with Mamma, he said: "Indeed our best friend, our benefactor is about to leave us. Yes, that is certain, we owe everything to your son. He has done a great deal for my daughter and has taken an interest in her and she can never be grateful enough to him." The day before I left they wanted me to have supper with them, but I could not do so, as I had to be at home. All the same I had to spend two hours before supper at their house. They thanked me repeatedly, saying that they only wished they were in a position to show their gratitude, and when I left, they all wept. Forgive me, but my eyes fill with tears when I recall the scene. Herr Weber came downstairs with me, and remained standing at the door until I had turned the corner and called out after me— Adieu! The expenses of our journey, food and drink, lodging and tips, amounted to over four louis d'or, for the farther we penetrated into France, the dearer things became. This very moment I have received your letter of the 16th. Please don't worry, I will certainly make good. And I have one request to make, which is, to show in your letters a cheerful spirit. If war breaks out near Salzburg, come and join us. My greetings to all our good friends. I kiss your hands a thousand times and embrace my sister with all my heart and remain your most obedient son

Wolfgang Amadé Mozart

(305a) MOZART TO HIS FATHER
(Autograph in the Mozarteum, Salzburg)
Paris, May 14th, 1778

I have so much to do already, that I wonder what it will be like in winter! I think I told you in my last letter that the Duc de Guines, whose daughter is my pupil in composition, plays the flute extremely well, and that she plays the harp magnifique. She has a great deal of talent and genius, and in particular a marvellous memory, so that she can play all her pieces, actually about two hundred, by heart. She is, however, extremely doubtful as to whether she has any talent for composition, especially as regards invention or ideas. But her father, who, between ourselves, is somewhat too infatuated with her, declares that she certainly has ideas and that it is only that she is too bashful and has too little self-confidence. Well, we shall see. If she gets no inspirations or ideas (for at present she really has none whatever), then it is to no purpose, for—God knows—I can't give her any. Her father's intention is not to make a great composer of her. "She is not," he said, "to compose operas, arias, concertos, symphonies, but only grand sonatas for her instrument and mine." I gave her her fourth lesson to-day, and, so far as the rules of composition and harmony are concerned, I am fairly well satisfied with her. She filled in quite a good bass for the first minuet, the melody of which I had given her, and she has already begun to write in three parts. But she very soon gets bored, and I am unable to help her, for as yet I cannot proceed more quickly. It is too soon, even if there really were genius there, but unfortunately there is none. Everything has to be done by rule. She has no ideas whatever—nothing comes. I have tried her in every possible way. Among other things, I hit on the idea of writing down a very simple minuet, in order to see whether she could not compose a variation on it. It was useless. "Well," I thought, "she probably does not know how she ought to begin." So I started to write a variation on the first bar and told her to go on in the same way and to keep to the idea. In the end it went fairly well. When it was finished, I told her to begin something of her own—only the treble part, the melody. Well, she thought and thought for a whole quarter of an hour and nothing came. So I wrote down four bars of a minuet and said to her: "See what an ass I am! I have begun a minuet and cannot even finish the melody. Please be so kind as to finish it for me." She was positive she couldn't, but at last with great difficulty—something came, and indeed I was only too glad to see something for once. I then told her to finish the minuet, I mean, the treble only. But for *home work* all I asked her to do was to alter my four bars and compose something of her own. She was to find a new beginning, use, if necessary, the same harmony, provided that the melody should be different. Well, I shall see tomorrow what she has done. I shall soon, I believe, get the libretto for my opera en deux actes. Then I must first present it to the Director M. de Vismes,[15] to see if he will accept it, though there is no doubt about that, for Noverre suggested it and De Vismes owes his appointment to him. Noverre is also going to arrange a new ballet for which I am going to compose

---

[15] Director-General of the Paris Academie Royale de Musique.

the music.[16] Rodolphe[17] (who plays the French horn) is in the Royal service here and is a very good friend of mine; he understands composition thoroughly and writes well. He has offered me the post of organist at Versailles, if I will accept it. The salary is 2000 livres a year, but I should have to spend six months at Versailles and the other six in Paris, or wherever I like. I do not think that I shall accept it, but I have yet to hear the advice of some good friends on the subject. After all, 2000 livres is not such a big sum. It would be so in German money, I admit, but here it is not. It amounts to 83 louis d'or, 8 livres a year—that is, to 915 gulden, 45 kreutzer in our money (a considerable sum, I admit), but here worth only 333 thalers, 2 livres—which is not much. It is frightful how quickly a thaler disappears here. I am not at all surprised that so little is thought of a louis d'or in Paris, for it really does not go far. Four of these thalers or one louis d'or, which is the same thing, are spent in no time. Well, adieu. Farewell. I kiss your hands a thousand times and embrace my sister with all my heart and remain your most obedient son

Wolfgang Amadé Mozart

My greetings to all our good friends, and especially to Herr Bullinger.

(311) MOZART TO HIS FATHER
(Autograph in the Mozarteum, Salzburg)
Paris, le 3 de juillet, 1778

Monsieur
  mon très cher Père!

I have very sad and distressing news to give you, which is, indeed, the reason why I have been unable to reply sooner to your letter of June 11th. My dear mother is very ill.[18] She has been bled, as in the

---

[16] Mozart's ballet music *Les Petits Riens,* K. Anh. 10, performed on June 11, 1778.

[17] Jean Joseph Rodolphe (1730–1812), born in Strassburg, studied the horn and violin in France and Italy. In 1767 he entered the service of Prince Conti, became solo horn at the Opera in 1769 and member of the Royal Chapel in 1770. He composed operas and ballets and wrote two valuable works on the theory of music.

[18] Mozart's mother had died at ten o'clock that night. He wrote this letter afterwards.

past, and it was very necessary too. She felt quite well afterwards, but a few days later she complained of shivering and feverishness accompanied by diarrhoea and headache. At first we only used our home remedies—antispasmodic powders; we would gladly have tried a black powder, too, but we had none and could not get it here, where it is not known even by the name of *pulvis epilepticus*. As she got worse and worse (she could hardly speak and had lost her hearing, so that I had to shout to make myself understood), Baron Grimm sent us his doctor. But she is still very weak and is feverish and delirious. They give me hope—but I have not much. For a long time now I have been hovering day and night between hope and fear—but I have resigned myself wholly to the will of God—and trust that you and my dear sister will do the same. How else can we manage to be calm or, I should say, calmer, for we cannot be perfectly calm! Come what may, I am resigned—for I know that God, who orders all things for our good, however strange they may seem to us, wills it thus. Moreover I believe (and no one will persuade me to the contrary) that no doctor, no man living, no misfortune and no chance can give a man his life or take it away. None can do so but God alone. These are only the instruments which he usually employs, though not always. For we see people around us swoon, fall down and die. Once our hour has come, all means are useless; they rather hasten death than delay it. This we saw in the case of our late friend Hefner. I do not mean to say that my mother will and must die, or that all hope is lost. She may recover health and strength, but only if God wills it. After praying to Him with all my might for health and life for my dear mother, I like to indulge in these consoling thoughts, because they hearten, soothe and comfort me; and you may easily imagine that I need comfort. Now let us turn to something else. Let us banish these sad thoughts: let us hope, but not too much; let us put our trust in God and console ourselves with the thought that all is well, if it is in accordance with the will of the Almighty, as He best knows what is profitable and beneficial to our temporal happiness and our eternal salvation.

I have had to compose a symphony[19] for the opening of the Concert Spirituel. It was performed on Corpus Christi day with great applause,

---

[19] K. 297.

and I hear, too, that there was a notice about it in the *Courier de L'Europe,*—so it has given great satisfaction. I was very nervous at the rehearsal, for never in my life have I heard a worse performance. You have no idea how they twice scraped and scrambled through it. I was really in a terrible way and would gladly have had it rehearsed again, but as there was so much else to rehearse, there was no time left. So I had to go to bed with an aching heart and in a discontented and angry frame of mind. I decided next morning not to go to the concert at all; but in the evening, the weather being fine, I at last made up my mind to go, determined that if my symphony went as badly as it did at the rehearsal, I would certainly make my way into the orchestra, snatch the fiddle out of the hands of Lahoussaye, the first violin, and conduct myself! I prayed God that it might go well, for it is all to His greater honour and glory; and behold—the symphony began. Raaff was standing beside me, and just in the middle of the first Allegro there was a passage which I felt sure must please. The audience were quite carried away—and there was a tremendous burst of applause. But as I knew, when I wrote it, what effect it would surely produce, I had introduced the passage again at the close—when there were shouts of "Da capo." The Andante also found favour, but particularly the last Allegro, because, having observed that all last as well as first Allegros begin here with all the instruments playing together and generally unisono, I began mine with two violins only, piano for the first eight bars—followed instantly by a forte; the audience, as I expected, said "hush" at the soft beginning, and when they heard the forte, began at once to clap their hands. I was so happy that as soon as the symphony was over, I went off to the Palais Royal, where I had a large ice, said the rosary as I had vowed to do—and went home—for I always am and always will be happiest there, or else in the company of some good, true, honest German who, if he is a bachelor, lives alone like a good Christian, or, if married, loves his wife and brings up his children properly. Now I have a piece of news for you which you may have heard already, namely, that that godless arch-rascal Voltaire has pegged out like a dog, like a beast! That is his reward! You are quite right, we owe Theresa wages for five quarters. That I do not like being here, you must long ago have noticed. I have very many reasons, but, as I am here, it is useless to go into them. It is not my fault, however, that I dislike Paris and it never shall be, for I will do my very best. Well,

God will make all things right! I have a project in my mind for the success of which I daily pray to Him. If it is His divine will, it will succeed, and if not, then I am content also—at least I shall have done my part. When all this has been set going and if all turns out as I wish, you too must do your part, or the whole work would be incomplete—I trust to your kindness to do so. Only don't indulge in unnecessary conjectures now. I only wanted to beg one favour of you beforehand, which is, not to ask me to reveal my thoughts more clearly, until it is time to do so.

As for the opera, matters are as follows. It is very difficult to find a good libretto. The old ones, which are the best, are not adapted to the modern style and the new ones are all quite useless. For poetry, the only thing of which the French have had reason to be proud, becomes worse every day—and yet the poetry is the one thing which must be good here, as they do not understand music. There are now two operas in aria which I might compose. One en deux actes and the other en trois. The one en deux is "Alexandre et Roxane"—but the poet who is writing the libretto is still in the country; the one en trois is a translation of Demofoonte (by Metastasio) interlarded with choruses and dances and altogether adapted to the French stage. Of this one too I have not yet been able to get a glimpse.

Write and tell me whether you have Schröter's concertos in Salzburg—and Hüllmandel's sonatas? If not, I should like to buy them and send them to you. Both works are very fine. As for Versailles, I never thought of going there. I asked Baron Grimm and some other good friends for their advice and they all thought as I did. The salary is small and I should have to pine for six months of the year in a place where nothing else can be earned and where my talent would be buried. Whoever enters the king's service, is forgotten in Paris—and then, to be an organist! I should very much like a good appointment, but it must be a Kapellmeister's and a well-paid one too. Now, farewell. Take care of your health; put your trust in God—it is there you will find consolation. My dear mother is in the hands of the Almighty. If He still spares her, as I hope He will, we shall thank Him for this blessing. But if it is His will to take her to Himself, all our fears and sorrows and all our despair can be of no avail. Let us rather resign ourselves with fortitude to His divine will, fully convinced that it will be for our good—for He does nothing without a cause. Farewell, then, dearest Papa, take care of your health for my sake. I kiss your hands a thousand times and embrace my sister with all my heart and remain your most obedient son

Wolfgang Amadé Mozart

(312) MOZART TO THE ABBÉ BULLINGER, SALZBURG
(Autograph in the Mozarteum, Salzburg)
Paris, le 3 juillet, 1778

Most Beloved Friend!
For you alone.

Mourn with me, my friend! This has been the saddest day of my life—I am writing this at two o'clock in the morning. I have to tell you that my mother, my dear mother, is no more! God has called her to Himself. It was His will to take her, that I saw clearly—so I resigned myself to His will. He gave her to me, so He was able to take her away from me. Only think of all my anxiety, the fears and sorrows I have had to endure for the last fortnight. She was quite unconscious at the time of her death—her life flickered out like a candle. Three days before her death she made her confession, partook of the Sacrament, and received extreme unction. During the last three days, however, she was constantly delirious, and to-day at twenty-one minutes past five o'clock the death agony began and she lost all sensation and consciousness. I pressed her hand and spoke to her—but she did not see me, she did not hear me and all feeling was gone. She lay thus until she expired five hours later at twenty-one minutes past ten. No one was present but myself, Herr Heina (a kind friend whom my father knows) and the nurse. It is quite impossible for me to describe to-day the whole course of her illness, but I am firmly convinced that she was bound to die and that God had so ordained it. All I ask of you at present is to act the part of a true friend, by preparing my poor father very gently for this sad news. I have written to him by this post, but only to say that she is seriously ill; and now I shall wait for his answer and be guided by it. May God give him strength and courage! O my friend! Not only am I now comforted, but I have been comforted for some time. By the mercy of God I have borne it all with fortitude and composure. When her illness became dangerous, I prayed to God for two things only—a happy death for her, and strength and courage for myself; and God in His goodness heard my prayer and gave me those two blessings in the richest measure. I beg you, therefore, most beloved friend, watch over my father for me and try to give him courage so that, when he hears the worst, he may not take it too hardly. I commend my sister to you also with all my heart. Go to them both at once, I implore you—but do not tell them yet that she is dead—just prepare them for it. Do what you think best—use every means to comfort them —but so act that my mind may be relieved—and that I may not have to dread another blow. Watch over my dear father and my dear sister for me. Send me a reply at once, I entreat you. Adieu. I remain your most obedient and grateful servant

Wolfgang Amadé Mozart

As a precaution I send you my address:
rue du Gros Chenet
vis-à-vis celle du Croissant,
à l'Hôtel des quatre fils Aymon.

(335) MOZART TO HIS FATHER
(Autograph in the Mozarteum, Salzburg)
Nancy, ce 3 octob:, 1778

Mon très cher Père,

Please forgive me for not having informed you of my departure before leaving Paris, but I simply cannot describe it to you, on account of the way in which the whole business was hurried up, contrary to my plans, hopes and wishes. At the last moment I wanted to send my luggage to Count Sickingen's instead of to the Bureau des Diligences, and stay on in Paris for a few days longer—and on my honour I would have done so, had I not—thought of you—for I did not wish to cause you any anxiety. We shall be able to go into all this more satisfactorily in Salzburg. But one thing more. Just imagine, M. Grimm actually deceived me, when he said that if I went by the diligence I should arrive in Strassburg in five days. It was not until the last day that I found out that it was quite another coach, which goes at a snail's pace, never changes horses and takes ten days! So you may easily conceive my rage; but I only expressed my feelings to my intimate friends —to him I pretended to be quite happy and contented. When I got into the carriage, I heard the pleasant news that we should be twelve days on the road. So you can see the great wisdom of Herr Baron von Grimm. He sent me off by this slow conveyance simply to save money, without ever considering that, as I should have continually to be making use of inns, my expenses would be just the same. Well, it is all over now; but what annoyed me most in the whole affair was his not being straightforward with me. Of course it was his own money which he saved, and not mine, as he paid for my journey, but not for my keep; whereas, had I stayed eight or ten days longer in Paris, I should have been able to arrange for my journey myself and much more comfortably. Well, I endured a week in that carriage, but any longer I could not stand—not on account of fatigue, for the carriage was well sprung, but for want of sleep. We were off every morning at four o'clock, so we had to get up at three; and twice I had the honour of getting up at one o'clock, as the carriage was to leave at two. You know that I cannot sleep in a coach; so it was impossible for me to go on in this way without endangering my health. Moreover, one of our fellow-travellers was badly afflicted with the French disease—and didn't deny it either—which in itself was enough to make me prefer, should it come to the point, to travel by post-chaise. But that is not necessary, for I have had the good fortune to fall in with a man whom I like—a German merchant who lives in Paris and deals in English wares. Before getting into the coach we exchanged a few words, and from that moment we remained together. We did not take our meals with the other passengers, but in our own room, where we also slept. I am glad I met this man, for he has travelled a great deal and therefore understands the business. As he too has got bored with that coach, we have both left it and to-morrow we are proceeding to Strassburg by a good conveyance which does not cost us much. There I hope to find a letter from you and to learn from it something about my further journey. I hope you have received all my letters. Yours have reached me safely. Please forgive me for not writing much, but I am never in a good humour when I am in a town where I am quite unknown; though I believe that, if I had friends here, I should like to stay on, for it is indeed a charming place with handsome houses, fine broad streets and superb squares. I have one thing more to ask you, which is to put a large chest in my room, so that I may have all my belongings beside me. I should also like to have beside my writing-desk the little clavier which Fischietti and Rust had, as it suits me better than Stein's small one. I am not bringing you many new compositions, for I haven't composed very much. I have not got the three quartets[20] and the flute concerto[21] for M. De Jean, for, when he went to Paris, he packed them into the wrong trunk and so they remained in Mannheim. But he has promised to send them to me as soon as he returns to Mannheim and I shall ask Wendling to forward them. I am therefore bringing no finished work with me except my sonatas[22]—for Le Gros purchased from me the two ouvertures[23] and the sinfonia concertante.[24] He thinks that he alone has them, but he is wrong, for they are still fresh in my mind, and, as soon as I get home, I shall write them down again. The Munich players must now be giving performances. Are they popular? Do people go to see them? I suppose that Piccinni's *Fishermaiden (La pescatrice)* or Sacchini's *Peasant girl at court (La contadina in corte)* will be the first of the singspiele to be given. The prima donna will be Mlle. Kaiser, the girl I wrote to you about from Munich. I do not know her—I have only heard her sing. It was then her third appearance on the stage and she had only been learning music for three weeks. Well, good-bye. I shall not have one quiet hour until I see again all those I love in this world. I embrace my dear sister with all my heart and I kiss your hands a thousand times and remain your most obedient son

Wolfgang Amadé Mozart

My greetings to all my good friends, and especially to our true, dear friend Bullinger.

---

[20] K. 285, 285a, and K. Anh. 171.
[21] K. 313.
[22] K. 301–306, or K. 330–333.
[23] K. 297, K. Anh. 8.
[24] K. Anh. 9.

(342) MOZART TO HERIBERT VON DALBERG[25]
(Autograph in the Staatsbibliothek, Munich)
Mannheim, November 24th, 1778

Monsieur le Baron!

I have called on you twice to pay my respects, but have not had the good fortune to find you at home. Yesterday you were in the house, it seems, but I could not see you! So I hope that you will forgive me for troubling you with these few lines, as it is very important to me to explain myself fully. Herr Baron, you are well aware that I am not a self-interested person, particularly when I know that it is in my power to render a service to so great a lover and so true a connoisseur of music as yourself. At the same time I am convinced that certainly you would not wish that I should be a loser here. I therefore take the liberty of stating my final conditions, as it is quite impossible for me to remain here any longer in uncertainty. I undertake to compose a monodrama for the sum of twenty-five louis d'or, to stay on here for another two months, to make all the arrangements which will be necessary in connection with it, to attend all the rehearsals and so forth, but on this condition that, whatever happens, I shall be paid by the end of January. In addition I shall of course expect free admission to the theatre. You see, my dear Baron, that this is all I can do! If you consider it carefully, you will admit that I am certainly acting with great discretion. In regard to your opera I assure you that I should be delighted to compose the music for it; but you yourself must agree that I could not undertake this work for twenty-five louis d'or, as (reckoned at its lowest) it would be twice the labour of writing a monodrama. Again, what would deter me most would be the fact that Gluck and Schweitzer, as you yourself told me, are already composing the music. Yet, even assuming that you were willing to give me fifty louis d'or, I should still as an honest man most certainly dissuade you from the undertaking. An opera without male and female singers! What an extraordinary idea! Still, if in the meantime there is a prospect of its being performed, I shall not refuse to undertake the work to oblige you—but it would be no

---

[25] Baron Heribert von Dalberg (1750–1806) had obtained from the Elector a charter dated Sept. 1, 1778, allowing the establishment of a Mannheim National Theatre under the management of Dalberg and with a subsidy of 500 gulden from the court.

light task, that I swear to you on my honour. Well, I have now set forth my ideas clearly and candidly and I request your decision as soon as possible. If I might have it today, I should be the better pleased, as I hear that someone is travelling alone to Munich next Thursday and I should very much like to take advantage of this opportunity. Meanwhile I have the honour to remain with the greatest respect—

Monsieur le Baron!
your most obedient servant
Wolfgang Amadé Mozart
ce mercredi le 24 novembre
1778

(409) MOZART TO HIS FATHER
(Autograph in the Mozarteum, Salzburg)
Vienne, ce 9 de juin, 1781

Mon très cher Père!

Well, Count Arco has made a nice mess of things! So that is the way to persuade people and to attract them! To refuse petitions from innate stupidity, not to say a word to your master from lack of courage and love of toadyism, to keep a fellow dangling about for four weeks, and finally, when he is obliged to present the petition in person, instead of *at least* granting him admittance, to throw him out of the room and give him a kick on his behind—that is the Count, who, according to your last letter, has my interest so much at heart—and that is the court where I ought to go on serving—the place where whoever wants to make a written application, instead of having its delivery facilitated, is treated in this fashion! The scene took place in the antechamber. So the only thing to do was to decamp and take to my heels—for, although Arco had already done so, I did not wish to show disrespect to the Prince's apartments. I have written three memoranda, which I have handed in five times; and each time they have been thrown back at me. I have carefully preserved them, and whoever wishes to read them may do so and convince himself that they do not contain the slightest personal remark. When at last I was handed back my memorandum in the evening through Herr von Kleinmayr (for that is his office), I was beside myself with rage, as the Archbishop's departure was fixed for the following day. I could not let him leave thus and, as I had heard from Arco (or so at least he had told me) that the Prince knew nothing about it, I realized how angry he would be for staying on so long and then at the very last moment appearing with a petition of this kind. I therefore wrote another memorandum, in which I explained to the Archbishop that it was now four weeks since I had drawn up a petition, but, finding myself for some unknown reason always put off, I was now obliged to present it to him in person, though at the very last moment. This memorandum procured me my dismissal from his service in the most pleasant way imaginable. For who knows whether the whole thing was not done at the command of the Archbishop himself? If Herr von Kleinmayr still wishes to maintain the character of an honest man, he can testify, as can also the Archbishop's servants, that his command was carried out. So now I need not send in any petition, for the affair is at an end. I do not want to write anything more on the subject, and if the Archbishop were to offer me a salary of 1200 gulden, I would not accept it after such treatment. How easy it would have been to persuade me to remain! By kindness, but not by insolence and rudeness. I sent a message to Count Arco saying *that I had nothing more to say to him*. For he went for me so rudely when I first saw him and treated me as if I were a rogue, which he had no right to do. And—by Heaven! as I have already told you, I would not have gone to him the last time, if in his message he had not added that he had had a letter from you. Well, that will be the last time. What is it to him if I wish to get my discharge? And if he was really so well disposed towards me, he ought to have reasoned quietly with me—or have let things take their course, rather than throw such words about as "clown" and "knave" and hoof a fellow out of the room with a kick on his arse; but I am forgetting that this was probably done by order of our worthy Prince Archbishop.

I shall reply very briefly to your letter, for I am so sick of the whole affair that I never want to hear anything more about it. In view of the original *cause* of my leaving (which you know well), no father would dream of being angry with his son; on the contrary, he would be angry if his son *had not left*. Still less ought you to have been angry, [*as you knew that even without any particular cause I definitely wanted to leave*. Really, you cannot be in earnest;] and I am therefore led to suppose that [you are driven to adopt this attitude on account of the court.] But I beg you, most beloved father, [not to cringe too much; for the Archbishop cannot do you any harm.] Let him try! I almost wish he would; for that would be a deed, a fresh deed, [which would ruin him completely with the Emperor, who, as it is, not only does not like him, but positively detests him.] If after [such treatment you were to come to Vienna and tell the story to the Emperor,] you would at all events receive [from him the salary you are drawing at present,] for in such cases [the Emperor] behaves most admirably. Your comparison of me to Madame Lange[26] positively amazed me and made me feel distressed for the rest of the day. That girl lived on her parents as long as she could earn nothing for herself. But as soon as the time came when she could show them her gratitude (remember that her father died before she had earned anything in Vienna), she deserted her poor mother, attached herself to an actor and married him—and her mother had never had *a farthing* from her. Good God! *He* knows that my sole aim is to help you and to help us all. Must I repeat it a hundred times that I can be of more use to you here than in Salzburg? I implore you, dearest, most beloved father, for the future to spare me such letters. I entreat you to do so, for they only irritate my mind and disturb my heart and spirit; and I, who must now keep on composing, need a cheerful mind and a calm disposition. The Emperor is not here, nor is Count Rosenberg. The latter has commissioned Schröder (the eminent actor) to look around for a good libretto and to give it to me to compose.

Herr von Zetti has had to leave unexpectedly by command and has set off so very early that I can neither send the portrait, nor the ribbons for my sister, nor the *other thing you know of* until to-morrow week by the mail coach.

Now farewell, dearest, most beloved father! I kiss your hands a thousand times and embrace my dear sister most cordially and am ever your most obedient son

Wolfgang Amadé Mozart

---

[26] Aloysia Weber.

(436) MOZART TO HIS FATHER
(Autograph in the Mozarteum, Salzburg)
Vienne, ce 15 *de Dec*^{bre}, 1781

Mon très cher Père!

I have this moment received your letter of the 12th. Herr von Daubrawaick will bring you this letter, the watch, the Munich opera,[27] the six engraved sonatas, the sonata for two claviers[28] and the cadenzas. As for the Princess of Wurtemberg and myself, all is over. The Emperor has spoilt everything, for he cares for no one but Salieri. The Archduke Maximilian recommended *me* to her and she replied that had it rested with her, she would never have engaged anyone else, but that on account of her singing the Emperor had suggested Salieri. She added that she was extremely sorry. What you tell me about the House of Wurtemberg and yourself may possibly prove useful to me.

Dearest father! You demand an explanation of the words in the closing sentence of my last letter! Oh, how gladly would I have opened my heart to you long ago, but I was deterred by the reproaches you might have made to me for *thinking of such a thing at an unseasonable time*—although indeed thinking can never be unseasonable. Meanwhile I am very anxious to secure here a small but *certain* income, which, together with what chance may provide, will enable me to live here quite comfortably—and then—to marry! You are horrified at the idea? But I entreat you, dearest, most beloved father, to listen to me. I have been obliged to reveal my intentions to you. You must, therefore, allow me to disclose to you my reasons, which, moreover, are very well founded. The voice of nature speaks as loud in me as in others, louder, perhaps, than in many a big strong lout of a fellow. I simply cannot live as most young men do in these days. In the first place, I have too much religion; in the second place, I have too great a love of my neighbour and too high a feeling of honour to seduce an innocent girl; and, in the third place, I have too much horror and disgust, too much dread and fear of diseases and too much care for my health to fool about with whores. So I can

---

[27] *Idomeneo.*

[28] K. 448, composed in November, 1781.

swear that I have never had relations of that sort with any woman. Besides, if such a thing had occurred, I should not have concealed it from you; for, after all, to err is natural enough in a man, and to err *once* would be mere weakness—although indeed I should not undertake to promise that if I had erred once in this way, I should stop short at one slip. However, I stake my life on the truth of what I have told you. I am well aware that this reason (powerful as it is) is not urgent enough. But owing to my disposition, which is more inclined to a peaceful and domesticated existence than to revelry, I who from my youth up have never been accustomed to look after my own belongings, linen, clothes and so forth, cannot think of anything more necessary to me than a wife. I assure you that I am often obliged to spend unnecessarily, simply because I do not pay attention to things. I am absolutely convinced that I should manage better with a wife (on the same income which I have now) than I do by myself. And how many useless expenses would be avoided! True, other expenses would have to be met, but—one knows what they are, and can be prepared for them—in short, one leads a well-ordered existence. A bachelor, in my opinion, is only half alive. Such are my views and I cannot help it. I have thought the matter over and reflected sufficiently, and I shall not change my mind. But who is the object of my love? Do not be horrified again, I entreat you. Surely not one of the Webers? Yes, one of the Webers—but not Josefa,[29] nor Sophie,[30] but Constanze,[31] the middle one. In no other family have I ever come across such differences of character. The eldest is a lazy, gross, perfidious woman, and as cunning as a fox. Mme. Lange is a false, malicious person and a coquette. The youngest—is still too young to be anything in particular—she is just a good-natured, but feather-headed creature! May God protect her from seduction! But the middle one, my good, dear Constanze, is the martyr of the family and, probably for that very reason, is the kindest-hearted, the cleverest and, in short, the best of them all. She makes herself respon-

---

[29] Josefa Weber (1758–1819), the eldest daughter. She became a singer and took the part of the "Konigin der Nacht" in the first performances of *Zauberflote* in Vienna.
[30] Maria Sophie Weber (1767–1846), the youngest daughter.
[31] Constanze Weber (1763–1842), the third daughter.

sible for the whole household and yet in their opinion she does nothing right. Oh, my most beloved father, I could fill whole sheets with descriptions of all the scenes that I have witnessed in that house. If you want to read them, I shall do so in my next letter. But before I cease to plague you with my chatter, I must make you better acquainted with the character of my dear Constanze. She is not ugly, but at the same time far from beautiful. Her whole beauty consists in two little black eyes and a pretty figure. She has no wit, but she has enough common sense to enable her to fulfil her duties as a wife and mother. It is a downright lie that she is inclined to be extravagant. On the contrary, she is accustomed to be shabbily dressed, for the little that her mother has been able to do for her children, she has done for the two others, but never for Constanze. True, she would like to be neatly and cleanly dressed, but not smartly, and most things that a woman needs she is able to make for herself; and she dresses her own hair every day. Moreover she understands house-keeping and has the kindest heart in the world. I love her and she loves me with all her heart. Tell me whether I could wish myself a better wife?

One thing more I must tell you, which is that when I resigned the Archbishop's service, our love had not yet begun. It was born of her tender care and attentions when I was living in their house.

Accordingly, all that I desire is to have a small assured income (of which, thank God, I have good hopes), and then I shall never cease entreating you to allow me to save this poor girl—and to make myself and her—and, if I may say so, all of us very happy. For you surely are happy when I am? And you are to enjoy one half of *my fixed income*. My dearest father, I have opened my heart to you and explained my remarks. It is now my turn to beg you to explain yours in your last letter. You say that I cannot imagine that you were aware of *a proposal which had been made to me and to which I, at the time when you heard of it, had not yet replied.* I do not understand one word of this—I know of no such proposal. Please take pity on your son! I kiss your hands a thousand times and am ever your most obedient son

W. A. Mozart

(448) MOZART TO CONSTANZE WEBER
(Autograph in the possession of Frau Jahns, Berlin)
Vienna, April 29th, 1782

Dearest, most beloved Friend!

Surely you will still allow me to address you by this name? Surely you do not hate me so much that I may be your friend no longer, and you—no longer mine? And even if you will not be my friend any longer, yet you cannot forbid me to wish you well, my friend, since it has become very natural for me to do so. Do think over what you said to me to-day. In spite of all my entreaties you have thrown me over three times and told me to my face that you intend to have nothing more to do with me. I (to whom it means more than it does to you to lose the object of my love) am not so hot-tempered, so rash and so senseless as to accept my dismissal. I love you far too well to do so. I entreat you, therefore, to ponder and reflect upon the cause of all this unpleasantness, which arose from my being annoyed that you were so impudently inconsiderate as to say to your sisters—and, be it noted, in my presence—that you had let a *chapeau*[32] measure the calves of your legs. No woman who cares for her honour can do such a thing. It is quite a good maxim to do as one's company does. At the same time there are many other factors to be considered— as, for example, whether only intimate friends and acquaintances are present—whether I am a child or a *marriageable* girl—more particularly, whether I am already betrothed—but, above all, whether only people of my own social standing or my social inferiors—or, what is even more important, my social superiors are in the company? If it be true that the Baroness[33] herself allowed it to be done to her, the case is still quite different, for she is already past her prime and cannot possibly attract any longer—and besides, she is inclined to be promiscuous with her favours. I hope, dearest friend, that, even if you do not wish to become my wife, you will never lead a life like hers. If it was quite impossible for you to resist the desire to take part in the game (although it is not always wise for a man to do so, and still less for a woman), then why in the name of Heaven did you not take the ribbon and measure your own calves *yourself* (as

---

[32] A young gallant.
[33] The Baroness von Waldstädten.

all self-respecting women have done on similar occasions in my presence) and not allow a *chapeau* to do so?—Why, I myself *in the presence of others* would never have done such a thing to you. I should have handed you the ribbon myself. Still less, then, should you have allowed it to be done to you by a stranger—a man about whom I know nothing. But it is all over now; and the least acknowledgment of your somewhat thoughtless behaviour on that occasion would have made everything all right again; and if you will not make a grievance of it, dearest friend, everything will still be all right. You realise now how much I love you. *I do not fly into a passion as you do.* I think, I reflect, and I feel. *If you will but surrender to your feelings,* then I know that this very day I shall be able to say with absolute confidence that Constanze is the virtuous, honourable, prudent and loyal sweetheart of her honest and devoted

Mozart

(467) MOZART TO BARONESS VON WALDSTÄDTEN
(*Copy in the Preussische Staatsbibliothek, Berlin*)
Vienna, October 2nd, 1782

Dearest, best and loveliest of all,
gilt, silvered and sugared,
most valued and honoured
Gracious Lady
Baroness!

Herewith I have the honour to send your Ladyship the rondo[34] in question, the two volumes of plays and the little book of stories. I committed a terrible blunder yesterday! I felt all the time that I had something more to say and yet I could cudgel nothing out of my stupid skull. But it was to thank your Ladyship for having at once taken so much trouble about the beautiful coat, and for your goodness in promising to give me one like it. But it never occurred to me, which is what usually happens with me. It is my constant regret that I did not study architecture instead of music, for I have often heard it said that he is the best architect to whom nothing ever occurs.[35]

---

[34] Probably K. 382.
[35] Mozart is punning on the word "einfallen," which means "to collapse" and "to occur."

I can say with truth that I am a very happy and a very unhappy man —unhappy since the night when I saw your Ladyship at the ball with your hair so beautifully dressed—for—gone is my peace of mind! Nothing but sighs and groans! During the rest of the time I spent at the ball I did not dance—I skipped. Supper was already ordered, but I did not eat—I gobbled. During the night instead of slumbering softly and sweetly—I slept like a dormouse and snored like a bear and (without undue presumption) I should almost be prepared to wager that your Ladyship had the same experience *à proportion!* You smile! you blush! Ah, yes—I am indeed happy. My fortune is made! But alas! Who taps me on the shoulder? Who peeps into my letter? Alas, alas, alas! My wife! Well, well, in the name of Heaven, I have taken her and must keep her! What is to be done? I must praise her—and imagine that what I say is true! How happy I am that I need no Fraulein Aurnhammer as a pretext for writing to your Ladyship, like Herr von Taisen or whatever his name is! (how I wish he had no name!), for I myself had something to send to your Ladyship. Moreover, apart from this, I should have had occasion to write to your Ladyship, though indeed I do not dare to mention it. Yet why not? Well then, courage! I should like to ask your Ladyship to— Faugh, the devil—that would be too gross! A propos. Does not your Ladyship know the little rhyme?

> *A woman and a jug of beer,*
> *How can they rhyme together?*
> *The woman has a cask of beer*
> *Of which she sends a jugful here.*
> *Why, then they rhyme together.*

I brought that in very neatly, didn't I? But now, *senza burle.* If your Ladyship could send me a jugful this evening, you would be doing me a great favour. For my wife is—is—is—and has longings— but only for beer prepared in the English way! Well done, little wife! I see at last that you are really good for something. My wife, who is an angel of a woman, and I, who am a model husband, both kiss your Ladyship's hands a thousand times and are ever your

faithful vassals,
MOZART *magnus, corpore parvus,*
et
CONSTANTIA, *omnium uxorum pulcherrima*
et prudentissima.

Vienna, October 2nd, 1782.
Please give my kind regards to that Aurnhammer girl.

(495) MOZART TO HIS FATHER
(Autograph in the possession of Frau Floersheim-Koch, Florence)
Vienne, ce 5 de Juillet, 1783

Mon très cher Père,

We both thank you for the prayer you made to God for the safe delivery of my wife. Little Raimund is so like me that everyone immediately remarks it. It is just as if my face had been copied. My dear little wife is absolutely delighted, as this is what she had always desired. He will be three weeks old next Tuesday and he has grown in an astonishing manner. As for the opera[36] you have given me a piece of advice which I had already given myself. But as I prefer to work slowly and with deliberation, I thought that I could not begin too soon. An Italian poet here has now brought me a libretto[37] which I shall perhaps adopt, if he agrees to trim and adjust it in accordance with my wishes. I feel sure that we shall be able to set out in September; and indeed you can well imagine that our most ardent longing is to embrace you both. Yet I cannot conceal from you, but must confess quite frankly that many people here are alarming me to such an extent that I cannot describe it. *You already know what it is all about.* However much I protest I am told: *"Well, you will see, you will [never get away again.] You have no idea of what [that wicked malevolent Prince is capable of!] And you [cannot] conceive what [low tricks] are resorted to in affairs of this kind. Take my advice and [meet your father] in some third place."* This, you see, is what has been worrying my wife and me up to the present and what is still perturbing us. I often say to myself: "Nonsense, it's quite impossible!"

---

[36] *L'oca del Cairo.*
[37] Undoubtedly the Italian poet is Da Ponte and the libretto that of *Lo sposo deluso,* Mozart's unfinished opera buffa.

But the next moment it occurs to me that after all it might be possible and that it would not be the [first injustice] which he has [committed.] Basta! In this matter no one can comfort me but you, my most beloved father! And so far as I am concerned, whatever happened would not worry me very much, for I can now adapt myself to any circumstances. But when I think of my wife and my little Raimund, then my indifference ceases. Think it over. If you can give me an assurance that I shall be [running no risk,] we shall both be overjoyed. If not, then we must hit on some plan; and there is one which I should prefer above all others! As soon as I receive your reply, I shall tell you about it. I am convinced that if one is to enjoy a great pleasure, one must forego something. Why! In the greatest happiness there is always something lacking. Meanwhile, farewell. Take care of your health. We both kiss your hands and embrace our dear sister with all our hearts and are ever your most obedient children

W: C: Mozart

P.S.—This does not mean that you are to give up prodding Varesco. Who knows whether I shall like the opera of the Italian poet?

Adieu

(526) MOZART TO PROFESSOR ANTON KLEIN,[38] MANNHEIM

(Autograph in the possession [1938] *of Stefan Zweig)*
Vienna, March 21st, 1785

Most highly esteemed Privy Councillor!

It was very wrong of me, I must confess, not to have informed you at once of the safe arrival of your letter and the parcel which you sent along with it. You presume that in the meantime I have received two more letters from you; but this is not the case. The first would have instantly aroused me from my slumber and I should have replied, as I am now doing. No, I received last post-day your two letters together. Well, I have already acknowledged my guilt in not replying immediately. But as for the opera, I should have been able to say as little then as I can now. Dear Privy Councillor! My hands are so full that I scarcely ever find a minute I can call my own. A man of such

---

[38] Professor Anton Klein (1748–1810), an ex-Jesuit, was a lecturer on philosophy and a popular dramatist. In 1780 he wrote a drama, which he sent to Mozart with the suggestion that the latter should set it to music.

great insight and experience as yourself will know even better than I that a libretto of this kind has to be read through with all possible attention and deliberation, and not once only, but several times. So far I have not had time to read it through even once without interruption. All that I can say at the moment is that I should not like to part with it yet. So I beg you to leave the play with me for a little longer. If I should feel inclined to set it to music, I should like to know beforehand whether its production has actually been arranged for at a particular place; for a work of this kind, from the point of view both of the poetry and of the music, deserves a better fate than to be composed to no purpose. I trust that you will clear up this point.

At the moment I cannot send you any news about the coming German operatic stage, as at present, apart from the building operations at the Kärntherthor theatre, which has been set apart for this purpose, things are progressing very slowly. They say that it is to be opened early in October. I for my part have no great hopes of its success. To judge by the preparations which have been made up to the present, it looks as if they were trying altogether to ruin German opera, which is probably only suffering a temporary eclipse, rather than to help to put it on its legs again and keep it going. My sister-in-law Madame Lange is the only singer who is to join the German opera. Madame Cavalieri, Adamberger, Mlle. Teiber, all Germans of whom Germany may well be proud, have to stay at the Italian opera—and compete against their own countrymen! At present it is easy to count up the German singers, male and female; and even if there really are as good singers as the ones I have mentioned, or even better ones, which I very much doubt, yet I am inclined to think that the directors of our theatre are too parsimonious and too little patriotically-minded to offer large sums of money to strangers when they have on the spot better singers, or at least equally good ones, whom they can rope in for nothing. For the Italian company does not need them—so far as numbers go. The company can fill all the parts themselves. The idea at present is to carry on the German opera with actors and actresses, who only sing when they must. Most unfortunately the directors of the theatre and those of the orchestra have all been retained, and it is they who owing to their ignorance and slackness are chiefly responsible for the failure of their own enterprise. Were there but one good patriot in charge—things would take a different turn. But then, perhaps, the German national theatre which is sprouting so vigorously would actually begin to flower; and of course that would be an everlasting blot on Germany, if we Germans were seriously to begin to think as Germans, to act as Germans, to speak German, and, Heaven help us, to sing in German!!

Dear Privy Councillor, do not take it amiss if in my zeal I have perhaps gone too far! Completely convinced as I am that I am talking to a *true German,* I have given rein to my tongue, a thing which unfortunately is so seldom possible in these days that after such an outpouring of my heart I might boldly drink myself tipsy without running the risk of endangering my health.

I remain, with the deepest respect, most esteemed Privy Councillor, your most obedient servant

W. A. Mozart

Vienna, March 21st, 1785

(529) MOZART TO JOSEPH HAYDN, EISENSTADT
(Autograph in the possession of Frau Iselin-Merian, Basle)
Vienna, September 1st, 1785

To my dear friend Haydn.

A father who had decided to send out his sons into the great world, thought it his duty to entrust them to the protection and guidance of a man who was very celebrated at the time and who, moreover, happened to be his best friend.

In like manner I send my six sons to you, most celebrated and very dear friend. They are, indeed, the fruit of a long and laborious study; but the hope which many friends have given me that this toil will be in some degree rewarded, encourages me and flatters me with the thought that these children may one day prove a source of consolation to me.

During your last stay in this capital you yourself, my very dear friend, expressed to me your approval of these compositions. Your good opinion encourages me to offer them to you and leads me to hope that you will not consider them wholly unworthy of your favour. Please then receive them kindly and be to them a father, guide and friend! From this moment I surrender to you all my rights over them. I entreat you, however, to be indulgent to those faults which may have escaped a father's partial eye, and, in spite of them, to continue your generous friendship towards one who so highly appreciates it. Meanwhile I remain with all my heart, dearest friend, your most sincere friend

W. A. Mozart

Vienna, September 1st, 1785

(544) MOZART TO BARON GOTTFRIED VON JACQUIN,[39] VIENNA
(Copy in the Preussiche Staatsbibliothek, Berlin)
Prague, January 14th, 1787

Dearest Friend!

At last I have found a moment to write to you. I resolved immediately after my arrival to write four letters to Vienna, but in vain! I was only able to manage one (to my mother-in-law) and then only half of it. My wife and Hofer had to finish it. Immediately after our arrival at noon on Thursday, the 11th, we had a dreadful rush to get ready for lunch at one o'clock. After the meal old Count Thun entertained us with some music, performed by his own people, which lasted about an hour and a half. This kind of *real entertainment* I could enjoy every day. At six o'clock I drove with Count Canal[40] to the so-called Bretfeld[41] ball where the cream of the beauties of Prague are wont to gather. Why—you ought to have been there, my friend! I fancy I see you running, or rather, limping after all those pretty women, married and unmarried! I neither danced nor flirted with any of them, the former, because I was too tired, and the latter owing to my natural bashfulness. I looked on, however, with the greatest pleasure while all these people flew about in sheer delight to the music of my *Figaro,* arranged for quadrilles and waltzes. For here they talk about nothing but *Figaro.* Nothing is played, sung or whistled but *Figaro.* No opera is drawing like *Figaro.* Nothing, nothing but *Figaro.* Certainly a great honour for me! Well, to return to my

---

[39] Gottfried von Jacquin (1763–92) was the second son of the famous botanist, Professor Nicolaus Josef, Baron von Jacquin. He and his sister Franziska were pupils of Mozart.

[40] Josef Emanuel, Count Canal von Malabaila (1745–1826), botanist and lover of music, lived in Prague and had a private orchestra.

[41] Baron Bretfeld, a wealthy member of the Bohemian aristocracy, gave famous balls.

order of the day. As I got home very late from the ball and moreover was tired and sleepy after my journey, nothing in the world could be more natural than that I should sleep it out the next morning; which was just what I did. So the whole of the next morning was spent *sine linea*. After lunch the Count's music must always be listened to, and as on that very day an excellent pianoforte had been put in my room, you may readily suppose that I did not leave it unused and untouched for the whole evening; so as a matter of course we performed amongst ourselves a little *Quatuor in caritatis camera* ("und das schöne Bandl hammera")[42] and in this way the whole evening was again spent *sine linea;* and so it actually was. Well, you must scold not me but Morpheus, for that deity is very attentive to us in Prague. What the cause may have been I know not; at any rate we slept it out. Still, we managed to be at Father Unger's at eleven o'clock and made a *thorough* inspection of the Imperial Library and the General Theological Seminary. When we had almost stared our eyes out, we thought that we heard a little stomach-aria in our insides and that it would be just as well to drive to Count Canal's for lunch. The evening surprised us sooner than you might perhaps believe. Well, it was soon time to go to the opera. We heard *Le gare generose*. In regard to the performance of this opera I can give no definite opinion because I talked a lot; but that quite contrary to my usual custom I chattered so much may have been due to . . . Well, never mind! that evening too was frittered away *al solito*. To-day I have at last been so fortunate as to find a moment to enquire after the health of your dear parents and the whole Jacquin family. I hope and trust with all my heart that you are all as well as we are. I must frankly admit that, although I meet with all possible courtesies and honours here and although Prague is indeed a very beautiful and pleasant place, I long most ardently to be back in Vienna; and be-

---

[42] K. 441, called the Bandl-Terzett, a humorous three-part song for soprano, tenor and bass, which Mozart composed in 1783, and dedicated to Gottfried von Jacquin. Mozart and his wife and Jacquin were out walking one day when Constanze happened to lose a ribbon which her husband had given her and exclaimed, using the Viennese dialect: "Liebes Mandl, wo is's Bandl?" Jacquin, a tall fellow, picked up the ribbon and refused to let her have it until she or her little husband should catch it. Upon which Mozart wrote the poem which he afterward set to music.

lieve me, the chief cause of this homesickness is certainly *your* family. When I remember that after my return I shall enjoy only for a short while the pleasure of your valued society and shall then have to forgo this happiness for such a long time, perhaps for ever, then indeed I realise the extent of the friendship and regard which I cherish for your whole family. Now farewell, dearest friend, dearest Hikkiti Horky! That is your name, as you must know. We all invented names for ourselves on the journey. Here they are. I am Punkititi. My wife is Schabla Pumfa. Hofer is Rozka Pumpa. Stadler is Notschibikitschibi. My servant Joseph is Sagadarata. My dog Goukerl is Schomanntzky. Madame Quallenberg is Runzifunzi. Mlle. Crux is Ramlo Schurimuri. Freistädtler is Gaulimauli. Be so kind as to tell him his name. Well, adieu. My concert is to take place in the theatre on Friday, the 19th, and I shall probably have to give a second one, which unfortunately will prolong my stay here. Please give my kind regards to your worthy parents and embrace your brother (who, by the way, could be christened Blatterrizzi) a thousand times for me; and I kiss your sister's hands (her name is Signora Dini Mini Niri) a hundred thousand times and urge her to practice hard on her new pianoforte. But this admonition is really unnecessary, for I must confess that I have never yet had a pupil who was so diligent and who showed so much zeal—and indeed I am looking forward to giving her lessons again according to my small ability. A propos. If she wants to come to-morrow, I shall certainly be at home at eleven o'clock. But surely it is high time to close, is it not? You will have been thinking so for a long time. Farewell, beloved friend! Keep me in your precious friendship. Write to me soon—very very soon—and if perchance you are too lazy to do so, send for Satmann and dictate a letter to him, though indeed no letter comes as much from the heart as it does when one writes oneself. Well, I shall see whether you are as truly my friend as I am entirely yours and ever shall be.

Mozart

P.S.—Address the letter which you will possibly write to me "At Count Thun's palace."

My wife sends her love to the whole Jacquin family, and so does Hofer.

P.S.—On Wednesday I am to see and hear *Figaro* in Prague, if I

have not become deaf and blind before then. Possibly I may not
become so until after the opera.

(562) MOZART TO HIS WIFE

(Copy in the Preussiche Staatsbibliothek, Berlin)

Dresden, April 16th, 1789

Half past eleven at night

Dearest, most beloved little Wife!

What? Still in Dresden? Yes, my love. Well, I shall tell you everything as minutely as possible. On Monday, April 13th, after break-
fasting with the Neumanns we all went to the Court chapel. The
mass was by Naumann, who conducted it himself, and very poor
stuff it was. We were in an oratory opposite the orchestra. All of a
sudden Neumann nudged me and introduced me to Herr von König,
who is the Directeur des Plaisirs (of the melancholy plaisirs of the
Elector). He was extremely nice and when he asked me whether I
should like His Highness to hear me, I replied that it would indeed
be a great privilege, but that, as I was not travelling alone, I could
not prolong my stay. So we left it at that. My princely travelling companion invited the Neumanns and Madame Duschek to lunch. While
we were at table a message came that I was to play at court on the
following day, Tuesday, April 14th, at half past five in the evening.
That is something quite out of the ordinary for Dresden, for it is
usually very difficult to get a hearing, and you know that I never
thought of performing at court here. We had arranged a quartet
among ourselves at the Hôtel de Pologne. So we performed it in
the Chapel with Anton Teiber (who, as you know, is organist here)
and with Herr Kraft, Prince Esterhazy's violoncellist, who is here
with his son. At this little concert I introduced the trio which I wrote
for Herr von Puchberg and it was played quite decently. Madame
Duschek sang a number of arias from *Figaro* and *Don Giovanni*. The
next day I played at court my new concerto in D,[43] and on the following morning, Wednesday, April 15th, I received a very handsome
snuff-box. Then we lunched with the Russian Ambassador, to whom
I played a great deal. After lunch we agreed to have some organ

---

[43] K. 537, Clavier concerto in D major, composed in 1788.

playing and drove to the church at four o'clock—Naumann was there, too. At this point you must know that a certain Hässler, who is organist at Erfurt, is in Dresden. Well, he too was there. He was a pupil of a pupil of Bach's. His forte is the organ and the clavier (clavichord). Now people here think that because I come from Vienna, I am quite unacquainted with this style and mode of playing. Well, I sat down at the organ and played. Prince Lichnowsky, who knows Hässler very well, after some difficulty persuaded him to play also. This Hässler's chief excellence on the organ consists in his foot-work, which, since the pedals are graded here, is not so very wonderful. Moreover, he has done no more than commit to memory the harmony and modulations of old Sebastien Bach and is not capable of executing a fugue properly; and his playing is not thorough. Thus he is far from being an Albrechtsberger.[44] After that we decided to go back to the Russian Ambassador's, so that Hässler might hear me on the fortepiano. He played too. I consider Mlle. Aurnhammer as good a player on the fortepiano as he is, so you can imagine that he has begun to sink very considerably in my estimation. After that we went to the opera, which is truly wretched. Do you know who is one of the singers? Why—Rosa Manservisi.[45] You can picture her delight at seeing me. But the leading woman singer, Madame Allegranti, is far better than Madame Ferraresi,[46] which, I admit, is not saying very much. When the opera was over we went home. Then came the happiest of all moments for me. I found a letter from you, that letter which I had longed for so ardently, my darling, my beloved! Madame Duschek and the Neumanns were with me as usual. But I immediately went off in triumph to my room, kissed the letter countless times before breaking the seal, and then devoured it rather than read it. I stayed in my room a long time; for I could not read it or kiss it often enough. When I rejoined the company, the Neumanns asked me whether I had had a letter from you, and

---

[44] Johann Georg Albrechtsberger (1736–1809), organist and composer.

[45] Rosa Manservisi took the part of Sandrina in Mozart's *La finta giardiniera,* which was performed at Munich in 1775.

[46] Adriana Ferraresi del Bene first appeared in Vienna in 1788. For the revival of *Figaro* in August 1789, Mozart composed for her the aria "Al desio di chi t'adora."

when I said that I had, they all congratulated me most heartily—
as every day I had been lamenting that I had not yet heard from you.
They are delightful people. Now for your dear letter. You shall receive by the next post an account of what will have taken place here
up to the time of our departure.

Dear little wife, I have a number of requests to make. I beg you

(1) not to be melancholy,

(2) *to take care of your health and to beware of the spring breezes,*

(3) not to go out walking alone—and preferably not to *go out walking at all,*

(4) to feel absolutely assured of my love. Up to the present I have not written a single letter to you without placing your dear portrait before me,

(5) I beg you in your conduct not only to be careful of *your honour and mine,* but also to consider *appearances.* Do not be angry with me for asking this. You ought to love me even more for thus valuing our honour.

(6) and lastly I beg you to send me more details in your letters. I should very much like to know whether our brother-in-law Hofer came to see us the day after my departure? Whether he comes very often, as he promised me he would? Whether the Langes come sometimes? Whether progress is being made with the portrait? What sort of life you are leading? All these things are naturally of great interest to me.

Now farewell, dearest, most beloved! Please remember that every
night before going to bed I talk to your portrait for a good half hour
and do the same when I awake. We are leaving on the 18th, the day
after to-morrow. *So continue to write to Berlin, Poste Restante.*

O Stru! Stri! I kiss and squeeze you 1095060437082 times (now you
can practise your pronunciation) and am ever your most faithful
husband and friend

W. A. Mozart

The account of the rest of our Dresden visit will follow in my next
letter. Good night!

(615) MOZART TO HIS WIFE AT BADEN
(Autograph in the Zavertal Collection, University of Glasgow)
Vienna, [? October 8th–9th], 1791
Saturday night at half past ten o'clock

Dearest, most beloved little Wife,

I was exceedingly delighted and overjoyed to find your letter on my return from the opera. Although Saturday, as it is post-day, is always a bad night, the opera was performed to a full house and with the usual applause and repetition of numbers. It will be given again tomorrow, but there will be no performance on Monday. So Süssmayr must bring Stoll in on *Tuesday* when it will be given again *for the first time*. I say *for the first time,* because it will probably be performed several times in succession. I have just swallowed a delicious slice of sturgeon which Don Primus (who is my faithful valet) has brought me; and as I have a rather voracious appetite to-day, I have sent him off again to fetch some more if he can. So during this interval I shall go on writing to you. This morning I worked so hard at my composition that I went on until half past one. So I dashed off in great haste to Hofer, simply in order not to lunch alone, where I found Mamma too. After lunch I went home at once and composed again until it was time to go to the opera. Leutgeb begged me to take him a second time, and I did so. I am taking Mamma[47] tomorrow. Hofer has already given her the libretto to read. In her case what will probably happen is that she will *see* the opera but not *hear it*. The N.Ns. had a box this evening and applauded *everything* most heartily. But he, the know-all, showed himself to be such a thorough Bavarian that I could not remain or I should have had to call him an ass. Unfortunately I was there just when the second act began, that is, at the solemn scene. He made fun of everything. At first I was patient enough to draw his attention to a few passages. But he laughed at everything. Well, I could stand it no longer. I called him a Papageno and cleared out. But I don't think that the idiot understood my remark. So I went into another box where *Flamm* and his wife happened to be. There everything was very pleasant and I stayed to the end. But during Papageno's aria with the glockenspiel I went behind the scenes, as I felt a sort of impulse to-day to play it

---

[47] Frau Weber.

myself. Well, just for fun, at the point where Schikaneder has a pause, I played an arpeggio. He was startled, looked behind the wings and saw me. When he had his next pause, I played no arpeggio. This time he stopped and refused to go on. I guessed what he was thinking and again played a chord. He then struck the glockenspiel and said *"Shut up."* Whereupon everyone laughed. I am inclined to think that this joke taught many of the audience for the first time that Papageno does not play the instrument himself. By the way, you have no idea how charming the music sounds when you hear it from a box close to the orchestra—it sounds much better than from the gallery. As soon as you return—you must try this for yourself.

Sunday, at seven o'clock in the morning. I have slept very well and hope that you too have done the same. I have just enjoyed thoroughly my half of a capon which friend Primus has brought back with him. I am going to the service at the Piarists at ten o'clock, as Leutgeb has told me that I can then have a word with the Director, and I shall stay to lunch.

Primus told me last night that a great many people in Baden are ill. Is this true? Do take care and don't trust the weather. Well, Primus has just returned with the tiresome news that the coach left to-day before seven o'clock and that there won't be another one until the afternoon. So all my writing at night and in the early morning has been to no purpose and you will not get my letter until this evening, which is very annoying. I shall certainly go to you next Sunday, when we shall all visit the Casino and come home together on Monday. Lechleitner was again at the opera. Though he is no connoisseur, he is at any rate a genuine lover of music, which N.N. is not. N.N. is really a nonentity and much prefers a dinée. Farewell, my love—I kiss you millions of times and am ever your

Mozart

P.S.—Kiss Sophie for me. I send Süssmayr a few good *nose-pulls* and a proper *hair-tug* and Stoll a thousand greetings. Adieu. The hour is striking—Farewell—We shall meet again.

N.B.—You probably sent the two pairs of yellow winter trousers along with the boots to the laundry, for Joseph and I have hunted for them in vain! *Adieu.*

(616) MOZART TO HIS WIFE AT BADEN
(Copy in the Preussiche Staatsbibliothek, Berlin)
Vienna, October 14th, 1791

Dearest, most beloved little Wife,

Hofer drove out with me yesterday, Thursday the 13th, to see our Karl. We lunched there and then we all drove back to Vienna. At six o'clock I called in the carriage for Salieri and Madame Cavalieri— and drove them to my box. Then I drove back quickly to fetch Mamma and Karl, whom I had left at Hofer's. You can hardly imagine how charming they were and how much they liked not only my music but the libretto and everything. They both said that it was an *operone,* worthy to be performed for the grandest festival and before the greatest monarch, and that they would often go to see it, as they had never seen a more beautiful or delightful show. Salieri listened and watched most attentively and from the ouverture to the last chorus there was not a single number that did not call forth from him a bravo! or bello! It seemed as if they could not thank me enough for my kindness. They had intended in any case to go to the opera yesterday. But they would have had to be in their places by four o'clock. As it was, they saw and heard everything in comfort in my box. When it was over I drove them home and then had supper at Hofer's with Karl. Then I drove him home and we both slept soundly. Karl was absolutely delighted at being taken to the opera. He is looking splendid. As far as health is concerned, he could not be in a better place, but everything else there is wretched, alas! All they can do is turn out a good peasant into the world. But enough of this. As his serious studies (God help them!) do not begin until Monday, I have arranged to keep him until after lunch on Sunday. I told them that you would like to see him. So to-morrow, Saturday, I shall drive out with Karl to see you. You can then keep him, or I shall take him back to Heeger's after lunch. Think it over. A month can hardly do him much harm. In the meantime the arrangement with the Piarists, which is now under discussion, may come to something. On the whole, Karl is no worse; but at the same time he is not one whit better than he was. He still has his old bad manners; he never stops chattering just as he used to do in the past; and he is, if anything, *less inclined to learn than before,* as out at Perchtholdsdorf all he does is to run about in the garden for five hours in the morning and five hours in the afternoon, as he has himself confessed. In short, the children do nothing but eat, drink, sleep and run wild. Leutgeb and Hofer are with me at the moment. The former is staying to supper with me. I have sent out my faithful comrade Primus to fetch some food from the Bürgerspital. I am quite satisfied with the fellow. He has only let me down once, when I was obliged to sleep at Hofer's, which annoyed me intensely, as they sleep far too long there. I am happiest at home, for I am accustomed to my own hours. This one occasion put me in a very bad humour. Yesterday the whole day was taken up with that trip to Perchtholdsdorf, so I could not write to you. But that you have not written to me for two days, is really unforgivable. I hope that I shall certainly have a letter from you to-day, and that to-morrow I shall talk to you and embrace you with all my heart.

Farewell. Ever your
Mozart

October 14th, 1791.

I kiss Sophie a thousand times. Do what you like with N.N. Adieu.

6

A Close-Up of Mozart

(FROM CONTEMPORARY SOURCES)

IN THE *pages that follow an attempt has been made to introduce Mozart through the eyes of those who actually knew him, sang for him, lived with him, served him in one capacity or other, in short, watched and heard the living reality of the angel in their midst. If we omit the letters of Leopold Mozart, what exists of this material makes up a tidy little volume. It has, in fact, made up two volumes— one in German, compiled by Albert Leitzmann, the other in French, compiled by J.-G. Prod'homme. A skillful selection of this material was edited by Otto Zoff for a volume entitled* Great Composers: Through the Eyes of Their Contemporaries (*New York: E. P. Dutton & Co., 1951). The assistant editor of that book, Phoebe Rogoff Cave, provided the three translations which appear with her initials here and in the final section on Mozart's death. I have used Mr. Zoff's brief introductory remarks about one or two of those blessed mortals who knew Mozart plain* ...   L. B.

BARON FRIEDRICH MELCHIOR VON GRIMM
(1723–1807)

(*German littérateur and patron of the arts, who lived in Paris from 1750 on and befriended the Mozarts on their great tour. He left a voluminous* Correspondance Littéraire, *from which the following passages are extracted.*)

TRUE MIRACLES are rare, but how wonderful it is when we have the opportunity to see one. A Salzburg Kapellmeister by the name of

129

Mozart has just come here with two of the prettiest children in the world. His daughter, aged eleven, plays piano in the most brilliant fashion, performs the longest and most difficult pieces with astounding precision. Her brother, who will be seven next February, is such an extraordinary phenomenon that you can hardly believe what you see with your own eyes and hear with your own ears. It is easy for the child to play the hardest pieces with perfect accuracy, although his hands are scarcely big enough to take a sixth. You watch him, incredulous, while he improvises for the space of an hour, yielding himself to the inspiration of his genius and a wealth of delightful ideas; what is more, he orders these ideas, playing them in tasteful succession without confusion. The most consummate Kapellmeister cannot possibly have so deep a knowledge of harmony and modulation as this child, and he knows how to do unusual things that are nevertheless always right things. He is so dexterous on the keyboard that you can cover the keys with a napkin and he will go on playing on the napkin with the same velocity and accuracy. It is nothing for him to decipher whatever you put before him; he writes and composes with marvelous ease, does not find it necessary to go to the piano and look for his chords. I wrote out a minuet for him by hand and asked him to put a bass to it. The child seized a pen and without going to the piano he wrote the bass to my minuet. You can well imagine that without the slightest effort he can transpose and play any aria set before him in whatever key requested. But what I now describe, a thing I saw, is not less inconceivable. A lady asked him recently whether, without looking at it, he could accompany an Italian Kavatine that she knew by heart. She began to sing. The child tried a bass that was not entirely correct, for it is impossible to accompany with complete accuracy a song one does not know. But as soon as the song was ended he begged the lady to start over again from the beginning, and now he played not only the whole vocal part with his right hand but simultaneously added the bass with his left, showing not the least hesitation. Then he requested her ten times in succession to begin again and at each repetition he changed the character of his accompaniment. He would have had her repeat it twenty times if they had not begged him to stop. I absolutely predict that this child will turn my head if I listen to him much more. He makes it clear to me how hard it is to keep yourself from madness when you see miracles. I am no longer astonished that St. Paul lost his wits after his wondrous vision. Mozart's children have aroused the admiration of all who have seen them. The Emperor and Empress have overwhelmed them with kindness and they have met with a similar reception at the courts in Munich and Mannheim. A pity that so little is understood of music in this country! The father plans to go from here to England and then to take his children to north Germany.

Translated by P. R. C.

We have just now seen the two charming children of Herr Mozart, Kapellmeister to the Prince-Bishop of Salzburg, who during their stay in Paris, in 1764, had so great a success. Their father has been in England eighteen months, and six months in Holland, and has of late brought them back here, on their way to Salzburg. All over, where these children have visited, there has been but one opinion, and they have astonished all connoisseurs. Mademoiselle Mozart, now thirteen years old, by the way, grown very pretty, has the most brilliant and beautiful way of playing the piano, and her brother alone can steal the applause from her. And this curious boy is now nine years old. He has grown hardly at all, but he has made wonderful progress in music. As early as two years ago he has composed and edited sonatas; and since then, he has had six sonatas printed for the Queen of England; six for the Princess of Nassau-Weilburg; he has composed Symphonies for a large orchestra, that have been performed and were acclaimed with great praise. He has even written several Italian arias, and I am not giving up hope, that he will have written an opera for some Italian theatre before he is twelve years old. He heard Manzuoli in London all winter long, and has made such good use of this, that he, although his voice is very small, sings with both feeling and taste. But the most unbelievable of all is his profound knowledge of harmony and its intricate ways, so that the Prince of Brunswick, truest judge in these matters, has said that many a superior Kapellmeister would die without ever having learned what this nine-year-old boy already knows. We have seen him for an hour and a half under the impact storm of musicians from whose brows the perspiration ran down in streams, and who had all the trouble in the world, to withdraw, creditably, from this struggle with a boy who left the battle field without the least sign of fatigue.

I have seen him confuse and bring to silence organists who considered themselves most proficient. In London (J. Chr.) Bach took him between his knees, and both played alternately on the same piano, uninterruptedly for two hours, in the presence of the King and the Queen. Here he has stood the same test under Raupach, a clever musician, who has been in St. Petersburg for a long while, and who improvises in a very superior manner. There would be a great deal more to tell about this unique phenomenon. And, by the way, he is one of the most charming creatures that you want to see: everything he says and does is full of life and soul, combined with the natural charm and loveliness of his youth. By his gaiety he even removes the fear that one may have, that so ripe a fruit might fall before its full maturity. If these children live, they will not stay in Salzburg. Soon the sovereigns will quarrel over possessing them. The father (Leopold Mozart) is not only a fine musician, but he is also a man of good sense and intelligence, and never yet have I seen a man of his profession combine such a capacity for earning money with talent.

Translated by P. N. (1)

LEOPOLD MOZART

(In a letter from Salzburg in 1778 to Paris, where a restless and dissatisfied young man of 22 was recalling bitterly how much more ecstatically Parisians had greeted a Wunderkind *many years earlier.)*

MY SON! YOU ARE hot-tempered and impulsive in all your ways! Since your childhood and boyhood your whole character has changed. As a child and a boy you were serious rather than childish and when you sat at the clavier or were otherwise intent on music, no one dared to make the slightest jest. Why, even your expression was so solemn that, observing the early efflorescence of your talent and your ever grave and thoughtful little face, many discerning people of different countries sadly doubted whether your life would be a long one. But now, as far as I can see, you are much too ready to retort in a bantering tone to the first challenge—and that, of course, is the first step toward undue familiarity, which anyone who wants to preserve his self-respect will try to avoid in this world. A goodhearted fellow is inclined, it is true, to express himself freely and naturally; nonetheless it is a mistake to do so. And it is just your good heart which prevents you from detecting any shortcomings in a person who showers praises on you, has a great opinion of you and flatters you to the skies, and who makes you give him all your confidence and affection; whereas as a boy you were so extraordinarily modest that you used to weep when people praised you overmuch. The greatest art of all is *to know oneself* and then, my dear son, to do as I do, that is, *to endeavour to get to know others through and through*. This, as you know, has always been my study; and certainly it is a fine, useful and indeed most necessary one. As for your giving lessons in Paris, you need not bother your head about it. *In the first place,* no one is going to dismiss his master at once and engage you. *In the second place,* no one would dare to ask you, and you yourself would certainly not take on anyone except possibly some lady who is already a good player and wants to take lessons in interpretation, which would be easy work for good pay. For instance, would you not have gladly undertaken to give Countess von Lützow and Countess Lodron two or three lessons a week at a fee of two or three louis d'or a month, the more so as such ladies also put themselves to much trouble to collect subscribers for the engraving of your compositions? In Paris everything is done by these great ladies, many of whom are devoted lovers of the clavier and in some cases excellent performers. These are the people who can help you. As for composition, why, you could make money and gain a great reputation by publishing *works for the clavier, string quartets and so forth, symphonies* and possibly a collection of *melodious French arias* with clavier accompaniment like the one you sent me, and finally operas. Well, what objection have you to raise now? But you want everything to be done at once, before people have even seen you or heard any of your works. Read my long list of the acquaintances we had in Paris at that time. All, or at least most of them, are the leading people in that city and they will all be both delighted and interested to see you again. Even if only six of them take you up (and indeed one single one of the most influential of them would be enough), you would be able to do whatever you pleased.

Translated by E. A.

MICHAEL KELLY
1762–1826

(Irish tenor, actor, and composer; friend of Haydn and Mozart, in whose The Marriage of Figaro *he appeared as the first Basilio in Vienna,* 1786, *being billed as "Signor Ochelly." His* Reminiscences, *published in London in* 1825, *offer a lively picture of his composer-friend.)*

I WENT ONE evening to a concert of the celebrated Kozeluch's, a great composer for the pianoforte, as well as a fine performer on that instrument. I saw there the composers Vanhall and Baron Dittersdorf, and, what was to me one of the greatest gratifications of my musical life, was there introduced to that prodigy of genius—Mozart. He favored the company by performing fantasias and *capriccios* on the pianoforte. His feeling, the rapidity of his fingers, the great execution and strength of his left hand, particularly, and the apparent inspiration of his modulations, astounded me. After this splendid performance we sat down to supper, and I had the pleasure to be placed at table between him and his wife, Madame Constance Weber, a German lady of whom he was passionately fond, and by whom he had three children. He conversed with me a good deal about Thomas Linley, the first Mrs. Sheridan's brother, with whom he was intimate at Florence, and spoke of him with great affection. He said that Linley was a true genius, and he felt that, had he lived, he would have been one of the greatest ornaments of the musical world. After supper the young scions of our host had a dance, and Mozart joined them. Madame Mozart told me, that great as his genius was, he was an enthusiast in dancing, and often said that his taste lay in that art, rather than in music.

He was a remarkably small man, very thin and pale, with a profusion of fine fair hair, of which he was rather vain. He gave me a cordial invitation to his house, of which I availed myself, and passed a great part of my time there. He always received me with kindness and hospitality. He was remarkably fond of punch, of which beverage I have seen him take copious draughts. He was also fond of billiards, and had an excellent billiard table in his house. Many and many a game have I played with him, but always came off second best. He gave Sunday concerts, which I always attended. He was kind-hearted, and always ready to oblige, but so very particular when he played that, if the slightest noise were made, he instantly left off. He one day made me sit down to the piano, and gave credit to my first master, who had taught me to place my hand well on the instrument. . . . He conferred on me what I considered a high compliment. I had composed a little melody to a canzonetta of Metastasio which was a great favourite wherever I sang it. It was very simple, but had the good fortune to please Mozart. He took it and composed variations upon it, which were truly beautiful; and had the further kindness and condescension to play them wherever he had an opportunity.

Encouraged by his flattering approbation, I attempted several little airs, which I showed him, and which he kindly approved of, so much indeed, that I determined to devote myself to the study of counterpoint and consulted with him, by whom I ought to be instructed. He said, "My good lad, you ask my advice, and I will give it you candidly; had you studied composition when you were at Naples and when your mind was not devoted to other pursuits, you would perhaps have done wisely; but now that your profession of the stage must, and ought, to occupy all your attention, it would be an unwise measure to enter into a dry study. You may take my word for it, nature has made you a melodist, and you would only disturb and perplex yourself. Reflect, 'a little knowledge is a dangerous thing'; should there be errors in what you write, you will find hundreds of musicians, in all parts of the world, capable of correcting them, therefore do not disturb your natural gift."

"Melody is the essence of music," continued he; "I compare a good melodist to a fine racer, and counterpointists to hack post horses, therefore be advised, let well alone, and remember the old Italian proverb— '*Chi sa più, meno sa*'—'Who knows most, knows least.' " The opinion of this great man made on me a lasting impression.

There were three operas now on the tapis, one by Regini, another by Salieri (the *Grotto of Trophonius*), and one by Mozart, by special command of the Emperor. Mozart chose to have Beaumarchais' French comedy, *Le Mariage de Figaro,* made into an Italian opera, which was done with great ability by Da Ponte. These three pieces were nearly ready for representation at the same time, and each composer claimed the right of producing his opera as the first. The contest raised much discord, and parties were formed. The characters of the three men were all very different. Mozart was as touchy as gunpowder, and swore he would put the score of his opera into the fire if it was not produced first; his claim was backed by a strong party: on the other hand, Regini was working like a mole in the dark to get precedence.

The third candidate was *maestro di cappella* to the court, a clever, shrewd man, possessed of what Bacon called crooked wisdom, and his claims were backed by three of the principal performers, who formed a cabal not easily put down. Every one of the opera company took part in the contest. I alone was a stickler for Mozart, and naturally enough, for he had a claim on my warmest wishes, from my adoration of his powerful genius, and the debt of gratitude I owed him, for many personal favors.

The mighty contest was put an end to by His Majesty issuing a mandate for Mozart's *Nozze di Figaro,* to be instantly put into rehearsal; and none more than Michael O'Kelly enjoyed the little great man's triumph over his rivals.

Of all the performers in this opera at that time but one survives—myself. It was allowed that never was opera stronger cast. I have seen it performed at different periods in other countries, and well too, but no more to compare with its original performance than light is to darkness. All the original performers had the advantage of the instruction of the composer, who transfused into their minds his inspired meaning. I never shall forget his little animated countenance, when lighted up with the glowing rays of genius; it is as impossible to describe it, as it would be to paint sunbeams.

I called on him one evening; he said to me, "I have just finished a little duet for my opera, you shall hear it." He sat down to the piano, and we sang it. I was delighted with it, and the musical world will give me credit for being so, when I mention the duet, sung by Count Almaviva and Susan, "Crudel perche finora farmi languire cosi." A more delicious *morceau* never was penned by man, and it has often been a source of pleasure to me, to have been the first who heard it, and to have sung it with its greatly gifted composer. I remember at the first rehearsal of the full band, Mozart was on the stage with his crimson pelisse and gold-laced cocked hat, giving the time of the music to the orchestra. Figaro's song, "Non più andrai farfallone amoroso," Bennuci gave with the greatest animation and power of voice.

I was standing close to Mozart who, sotto voce, was repeating, Bravo! Bravo! Bennuci! and when Bennuci came to the fine passage, "Cherubino, alla vittoria, alla gloria militar," which he gave out with stentorian lungs, the effect was electricity itself, for the whole of the performers on the stage, and those in the orchestra, as if actuated by one feeling of delight, vociferated, "Bravo! Bravo! *Maestro! Viva, viva grande* Mozart!" Those in the orchestra I thought would never have ceased applauding, by beating the bows of their violins against the music desks. The little man acknowledged, by repeated obeisances, his thanks for the enthusiastic applause bestowed upon him.

The same meed of approbation was given to the finale at the end of the first act; that piece of music alone, in my humble opinion, if he had never composed anything else good, would have stamped him as the greatest master of his art. In the *sestetto,* in the second act (which was Mozart's favorite piece of the whole opera) I had a very conspicuous part, as the Stuttering Judge. All through the piece I was to stutter; but in the *sestetto,* Mozart requested I would not, for if I did, I should spoil his music. I told him that although it might appear very presumptuous in a lad like me to differ with him on this point, I did, and was sure the way in which I intended to introduce the stuttering would not interfere with the other parts, but produce an effect; besides, it certainly was not in nature that I should stutter all through the part, and when I came to the *sestetto* speak plain; and after that piece of music was over, return to stuttering; and, I added (apologizing at the same time, for my apparent want of deference and respect in placing my opinion in opposition to that of the great Mozart), that unless I was allowed to perform the part as I wished, I would not perform it at all.

Mozart at last consented that I should have my own way, but doubted the success of the experiment. Crowded houses proved that nothing ever on the stage produced a more powerful effect; the audience were convulsed with laughter, in which Mozart himself joined. The Emperor repeatedly cried out Bravo! and the piece was loudly applauded and encored. When the opera was over, Mozart came on the stage to me, and shaking me by both hands, said, "Bravo, young man, I feel obliged to you; and acknowledge you to have been in the right, and myself in the wrong." There was certainly a risk run, but I felt within myself I could give the effect I wished, and the event proved that I was not mistaken.

I have seen the opera in London, and elsewhere, and never saw the Judge portrayed as a stutterer, and the scene was often totally omitted. I played it as a stupid old man, though at the time I was a beardless stripling. At the end of the opera, I thought the audience would never have done applauding and calling for Mozart; almost every piece was encored, which prolonged it nearly to the length of two operas, and induced the Emperor to issue an order on the second representation that no piece of music should be encored. Never was anything more complete than the triumph of Mozart and his *Nozze di Figaro,* to which numerous overflowing audiences bore witness.

M. K.

LORENZO DA PONTE
(1749–1838)

(*Poet, adventurer, linguist, teacher, and librettist of* The Marriage of Figaro, Don Giovanni *and* Così fan Tutte. *The following is extracted from his cele-brated* Memoirs. *See biography on p.* 310.)

IT WASN'T long before several composers came to me for li-brettos, but at that time, there were only two deserving of my respect: Martini, at that time favorite composer of Emperor Jos-eph [II], and Mozart, whom I had the occasion to meet at the home of Baron Wetzlar[1], his great friend and admirer. Wolfgang Mozart, although endowed with talents surpassing those of any com-poser of past, present, and future, had not been able as yet, owing to the intrigues of his enemies, to utilize his divine genius here in Vienna. He had remained in the dark, as a precious gem, hidden in the depths of the earth, must hide its glowing brilliance and worth. It is with pride and satisfaction that I can reflect on the fact, that it was to a large degree thanks to my perseverance and firmness that Europe and the world now possess the superior, excellent vocal compositions of

---

[1] Baron Raimund Wetzlar was a Jewish banker, friend and protector of Mozart, in whose home the great composer lived for some time.

this marvelous genius. The injustice and the envy of the journalists, the newspaper reporters, and still more the biographers of Mozart, denied the credit for all this to an Italian, but all Vienna and all who have known him and me in Germany, Bohemia, and Saxony, his family and—more than all others—Baron Wetzlar, under whose roof emanated the first spark of that noble flame, will bear testimony to the truth of my assertions.

And, gracious Baron, of whose friendly consideration I recently received new proof, you, who love and revere this divine man so deeply, and who also have a part in his fame, please acknowledge me, before your age, should these memoirs ever fall into your hands (I shall see to it that they do), and do me the justice which two prejudiced Germans have tried to withold from me: see to it that in public newspapers some truth-loving writer may proclaim what the malevolence of others has covered up. Then will a beam of light, be it ever so small, fall on the honored memory of your friend Da Ponte.

After the great success of *Burbero,* I went to Mozart, told him what had happened to me with Casti, Rosenberg, and the Emperor, and asked him whether he would care to put into music a drama of mine. "That I would gladly do," he answered, "but I do not know whether I will get the permission to perform it." "Let that," I answered, "be my care." And so I went about happily, thinking of the plays I was to write for my two good friends, Mozart and Martini. The immeasurable genius of the former, I realized, demanded a subject wide, manifold, and lofty. When I was at one time conversing with him on the subject, he spoke to me of making an opera text of the Beaumarchais comedy *Le Mariage de Figaro.* I approved entirely of the idea, and promised to do it; but there were great difficulties to overcome.

Not so long ago, the Emperor had forbidden the Deutsche Theatergesellschaft to perform that comedy, which, he said, was too liberal for a well-bred audience: how would it be with an opera text? Baron Wetzlar, with great generosity, offered to pay me a good price for the opera, and, should it prove impossible to have it given in Vienna, to have it performed in London or Paris. Yet I refused his offer and proposed to write the text and the music secretly, awaiting a favorable opportunity to present it to the theatre directors and to the Emperor. I would use the utmost discretion in presenting it. Martini was the

only one to hear my beautiful secret, and, because of his great esteem
for Mozart, he agreed with me, not to write to the latter until the
Figaro had been finished.

So I went to work on it while he wrote the music. It was all ready
in six weeks. Mozart's good luck would have it that there was a scar-
city of scores at the theatre. At the first suitable opportunity, without
telling anyone about it, I took the *Figaro,* to hand it, in person, to the
Emperor. What did he say? "You know that Mozart, so superior in
the field of instrumental music, has written but one opera, and that
not an important one, to be sure." "I, too," I replied, "had it not been
for Your Majesty, would have written but one drama in Vienna."
"That is right," the Emperor said, "but I have forbidden this *Mariage
de Figaro* to be played by the German troupe." "Yes," I answered,
"but since I have written an opera and not a comedy, I have had to
suppress many scenes, and have had to condense still more, and I
have done this to those scenes that might offend the delicacy of feeling
and decorum of a theatre which is Your Majesty's. As far as the music
is concerned, I think it is a work of great and wonderful beauty."
"Very well, if that is the case, I shall depend on your taste for the
music, and on your intelligence for the decorum. Let the copyist have
the score."

I ran to see Mozart, but had not yet finished giving him the good
news when a messenger from the Emperor arrived, bringing a note
which ordered him to appear at the palace at once. He obeyed the
imperial order. The Emperor had him play some of the parts, which
pleased him extremely, and—without exaggerating—of which not
one aroused his displeasure. He had, in musical matters, exquisite
taste, and, be it said, in all the fine arts as well. The great success which
the work has had the world over, proves clearly that he was not
wrong in his judgement. To learn that the Emperor found delight
in Mozart's new composition, did, however, not please the other
Viennese composers and Count Rosenberg who no more liked Mozart
than did Casti . . .

We were, therefore, Mozart as well as I, not without a justified fear
that we might again have to suffer from the cabals of these, our not
too good friends. They were not able to do much against us, but they
did what they could. A certain [Francesco] Bussani, inspector of
scenery and wardrobe, who was proficient in all professions except

that of an honorable man, ran to Count Rosenberg when he heard that I had inserted a ballet into *Figaro,* and told him in tones of astonishment and disapproval: "Your Excellency, the poet has introduced a ballet into his opera!" The Count immediately sent for me, and now began the grim little dialogue here following: "So Signore Poeta has introduced a ballet into his opera, is that right?" "Yes, Your Excellency." "Perhaps Signore Poeta is ignorant of the fact that the Emperor does not wish to see ballets in his theatre?" "No, Your Excellency." "Well, I am now telling you so, and furthermore I declare that you will have to suppress the ballet." Bussani repeatedly said this "Signore Poeta" and he said it in a tone really implying "Sir Jackass" or something similar. But my "Your Excellency" also had the required flavor! So, I answered again: "No, Your Excellency." "Do you have the libretto with you?" "Yes, Your Excellency." "Where is the ballet?" "Here, Your Excellency." "And this is how that is done"— saying which, he tore out two pages of the drama, threw them into the fire, and, with a courtly air, returned the book, with the words: "You see, Signore Poeta, that I can do anything I please."

I, at once repaired to see Mozart who, at hearing this bad news, was in despair. He wanted to see the Count at once, to rate Bussani, to run to the Emperor, and to withdraw his score. I had great pain to soothe him. Finally I begged him to give me just two days and to let me go ahead.

The dress rehearsal of the opera was to take place that same day. I went, in person, to the Emperor, in order to report this to him, and he promised to be there promptly. And, indeed, he did appear and with him half the nobility of Vienna. The Abbate Casti too came with him. The first act was received with general applause. At the close, there is a pantomimic scene between Susanna and the Count [Count Almaviva], during which the orchestra plays and the dance goes on. But when his almighty excellency, Rosenberg, tore out this scene, he had failed to realize one thing, namely, that this mute by-play of Susanna and the Count would, without the orchestra part that he had destroyed, give the impression of a marionette stage.

"What does this mean?" said the Emperor to Casti, who was sitting right behind him. "We must ask the poet," the Abbate answered, maliciously. So I was sent for at once but, instead of answering the question put to me, I just presented my manuscript in which I had restored the scene. The Emperor read it and asked me why the dance that he saw in notation there, had been omitted? My silence led him to realize that there had been a little swindle somewhere. He turned to Count Rosenberg and questioned him on the matter. Rosenberg murmured that the dance had been omitted because there was no ballet personnel at the theatre. "Are there none in the other theatres?" the monarch asked. He was told there were some. "Very well, then raise as many as Da Ponte requires."

In less than half an hour the ballet personnel had been brought together. At the end of the second act, the suppressed scene was repeated and this time the Emperor called out: "Now, that is good." This further evidence of the Emperor's favor doubled the hatred and desire for revenge in the soul of my powerful persecutor . . .

In the meantime Mozart's opera was performed, which, putting to shame all doubters, all other composers, Count Rosenberg and Casti, and a hundred other devils—was generally well received and was judged to be (by the Emperor himself and by other true connoisseurs) something lofty and almost divine.

I now felt that the time had come to bring into flow my poetic vein, which seemed completely dried out. The opportunity soon offered. The three superior masters: Martini, Mozart, and Salieri, applied to me for librettos. I loved and valued all three of them, and hoped from all three compensation for the past failures, and an increase of my small theatrical renown. I meditated whether it wouldn't be possible to satisfy all three and to write three operas at once. Salieri was not asking me for an original drama. In Paris he had written *Tarare*. He wished to change it to an opera in the Italian style, and asked me for such a transposition. Mozart and Martini left the choice entirely to me. I chose *Don Giovanni* for Mozart, which subject pleased him immensely. For Martini I chose *The Tree of Diana*. When I had found these three subjects, I went to the Emperor informing him of my intention to produce the three operas at once. "You won't succeed," said the Emperor. "Perhaps not," I replied, "but I am going to try. I shall write and think for Mozart at night, while reading Dante's *Inferno;* in the morning for Martini, with my imagination dwelling on Petrarca; and in the evening for Salieri, with my Tasso at hand."

I found my metaphor a very beautiful one and, arrived at home, immediately got to work. I went to my writing desk and sat down for twelve unbroken hours, a bottle of Tokay wine to my right, an ink-well in the middle, and a box of Sevilla tobacco to my left. A beautiful sixteen-year-old girl whom I should have loved as my daughter only—but—, lived in the same house with me, with her mother. She took care of the household and had permission to enter my room when I rang (which I very often did)—(particularly when my inspiration began to cool off). She used to bring a biscuit or a cup of coffee for me, and her beautiful ever-smiling face seemed made for bringing poetic inspiration and witty ideas. I continued, for two months, to work twelve hours a day with few interruptions, and during all this time she remained in the adjoining room, either with a book in her hand, or with a needle and embroidery, to be ready, at the ringing of the bell to come to me. She would then sit beside me, without moving, without opening her mouth, gazing at me firmly and smiling very alluringly. At times she sighed and seemed inclined to grieve. This child was my Calliope for those three operas, and for all the verses I wrote in the following six years. At first, I permitted frequent visits, but later I had to see less of her, so as not to lose too much time in making love, of which art she had complete mastery. In the meantime, I wrote, on the first day, between the Tokay, the Sevilla tobacco, the coffee, the bell, and the youthful muse, the first two scenes of *Don Giovanni,* two of the *Tree of Diana,* and more than half the first act of *Tarare,* the name of which I had changed to *Axur.* The next morning I brought these scenes to the three composers who could hardly trust their eyes. In sixty-eight days, however, the first two operas were completely finished; and the third, by two-thirds. *The Tree of Diana* was the first of the operas to be performed.

The first performance had not yet taken place, when I was obliged to go to Prague, where Mozart's *Don Giovanni* was to have its première. The occasion was the arrival of the Duchess of Toscana. I stayed in Prague for a week to coach the actors who were to take part, but hardly had I stepped on the stage, when I was recalled to Vienna to hear that *Axur* was to be staged at once. This time the occasion being the wedding of the Archduke Franz. The Emperor himself had ordered me back, thus I had no chance to witness the performance of *Don Giovanni* in Prague, but Mozart notified me at once of its wonderful success, and Guardassoni [the Prague opera director] wrote to me: "Viva Da Ponte, viva Mozart. Performers as well as directors must count themselves fortunate. As long as they are alive, there will be no more thought of failures." The Emperor sent for me and graciously overwhelmed me with words of praise, made me a present of a hundred zechines, and told me that he ardently desired to see *Don Giovanni*.

Mozart returned and gave the score to the copyist at once, telling him to hurry on with it as the Emperor was obliged to leave soon. The performance took place and—dare I say it?—*Don Giovanni* was *not* a success! Every one except Mozart thought that something was missing. We made changes, added arias—and yet *Don Giovanni* was no success. And what did the Emperor say? "The opera is divine," he said, "perhaps even more beautiful than *Figaro,* but it is not food for the teeth of my Viennese." I told Mozart what the Emperor had said, but he retorted coolly: "All right, give them time to chew." He was not mistaken. I saw to it that his wishes that the opera be frequently given, were carried out. And really—the applause increased with each performance, and gradually the Viennese with the bad teeth, got the taste, learned to recognize its beauty, and counted *Don Giovanni* among the finest works ever performed on the stage.

I tried to persuade Mozart to go to London with me. But he had recently, as a compensation for his divine operas, received an annuity for life, and was busy writing a German opera, *The Magic Flute,* from which he expected great fame. He demanded six months to think it over, and I, in the meantime, underwent all kinds of changes, which forced my life into quite a different channel.

L. Da P.

FRANZ NĚMETSCHEK

Franz Němetschek was a high-school teacher in Prague. He knew Mozart personally, and after his death he went from one member of the Mozart family to the other, inquiring and making notes. The data given him by the widow turned out to be more exact and detailed than friends of the composer had expected. His book Leben des k.k. Kapellmeisters Wolfgang Gottlieb Mozart, nach Originalquellen beschrieben, *was published in Prague in 1798.*

The great monarch of whose death Němetschek speaks is Joseph II, who died in 1790.

O. Z.

BUT HIS END too was approaching. He was not long to survive the great monarch. The year 1791, tragically filled with great men's deaths, was destined to snatch away also the pride of music. But before he died Mozart had drawn prodigally upon the treasures of his spirit and lavished them upon posterity. The year is as memorable for the creation of his most wonderful works as it is painful for his unexpected death. In that year, it may be said as he approached the consummation of his life, he conceived the music for the *Zauberflöte,* for the tragic opera *La Clemenza di Tito,* and for the noble *Requiem,* which he could not even finish. There is no doubt that these three works alone would have assured him a place among the great composers of his age, would have assured him immortality. Hearing them, our longing for the lost genius deepens; upon the sensitive listener, even in the midst of his enjoyment, the thought urges itself irresistibly: "How much more the man could still have achieved, what harmonies he could still have created!"

He put the *Magic Flute* to music for the well-known Schikaneder, an old acquaintance of his. The music for *La Clemenza di Tito* was ordered by the Bohemian patricians for the coronation of Kaiser Leopold. This latter work he began in the post chaise from Vienna and completed in the short space of eighteen days in Prague.

The story of his last composition, the *Requiem* above-mentioned, is as mysterious as it is unusual.

Shortly before the coronation of Kaiser Leopold, before Mozart had even received the order to go to Prague, a letter without signature was delivered to him by an unknown messenger. It contained, among various flattering expressions, an inquiry as to whether Mozart was willing to undertake the composition of a Requiem, what his price would be, and when he would be able to deliver it. Mozart, who never took a step without the knowledge of his wife, told her about the strange commission and at the same time expressed a desire to try what he could do in that line, especially since the more exalted style of church music suited his genius. She advised him to accept the order. He therefore wrote back to his unknown patron that he would write the Requiem for such and such a fee; the exact date of completion, he said, he could not specify, but he would like to know where he was to deliver the work when it was finished. In a short time the same messenger reappeared, bringing not only the stipulated sum but a promise that, since he had set so low a price, he would receive a substantial additional payment when he had dispatched the completed work. He was to write as the spirit moved him but was not to make any effort to find out who his client was, since such effort would assuredly be fruitless.

Meanwhile Mozart had received the honorific and profitable commission to write the opera *Titus* for the coronation of Kaiser Leopold in Prague. To go to Prague, to write for his beloved Bohemians—here was an offer too tempting for him to refuse.

Just as he was getting into the post chaise with his wife, the messenger appeared again and stood there like a specter. He plucked at the lady's skirt and asked "What about the Requiem now?"

Mozart apologized, explained how necessary the trip was, excused himself on the ground that he had been unable to inform the unknown gentleman in advance. He promised that the Requiem would be the first thing he touched on his return; it just depended on whether his unknown client wanted to wait that long. The messenger was entirely satisfied.

Even in Prague Mozart was ailing and taking potions the whole time. His color was pale, his face sad, though in the society of his friends his natural cheerfulness still came out in frequent bursts of gaiety. When he had to leave the circle of his friends he became so melancholy that he shed tears. A presentiment of his approaching end seems to have brought on this melancholy, for even at this time he bore within him the seed of the disease which soon carried him off.

On his return to Vienna he at once commenced his Requiem and worked on it intensively, with lively interest; but his illness worsened visibly and disposed him to the most dismal melancholy. His wife watched him sorrowfully. One day she rode out with him to the Prater to divert and cheer him up a bit. They were sitting there alone together and Mozart started talking about death. He said he was writing the Requiem for himself. Tears stood in his eyes. . . . "I feel myself too much," he said, "I can't last long now. They must have given me poison! I can't get rid of that idea."

The words fell heavy as lead on the heart of his wife; she hardly had the strength to comfort him and prove to him the groundlessness of his gloomy notions. Since she believed he was coming down with some sickness and that the Requiem was too exhausting for his sensitive nerves, she called the doctor and took away the score.

His condition did in fact improve somewhat and he was able to write a little cantata which had been ordered by a society for some celebration. Its first performance and the acclaim it received gave his spirit a new impetus. He became rather more cheerful and repeatedly asked to go on with his Requiem and finish it. His wife now found no objection to giving him back his score.

This hopeful interlude was short, however; in a few days he relapsed into his melancholy, grew more and more languid and feeble, until he finally sank back helpless on his sickbed, never to rise again.

On the day of his death he had the score brought to his bed. "Didn't I prophesy I was writing this Requiem for myself?" So he spoke and looked through the whole thing attentively once more with wet eyes. It was the last anguished look of parting from his beloved art. . . .

Immediately after his death the messenger was announced again. He asked for the Requiem in its uncompleted form and received it. The widow never saw him again and never heard a thing about the Requiem or the client. The reader can well imagine that every effort was made to trace the mysterious messenger, but all in vain.

During his illness Mozart remained fully conscious until the very end; he died calmly but most unwillingly. This is entirely understandable when we consider that he had just been appointed Kapellmeister of St. Stephan's with all the emoluments that traditionally went with the position. Now for the first time he had the cheerful prospect of being able to live a tranquil life, with adequate income, no longer forced to struggle for a livelihood. At almost the same time he received important orders and contracts from Hungary and Amsterdam for periodical deliveries of certain compositions.

Strange, sad combination of circumstances! Harbingers of a happier fate, the while his present financial situation remained miserable; the sight of an inconsolable wife, the thought of two minor children— these were not likely to sweeten the bitterness of death for an admired artist, who had never been a stoic, in the thirty-fifth year of his life. "Why just now," he complained often during his illness, "why must I go now, when I could have begun to live without worry? Why do I have to leave my art now when I'm not the slave of fashion or speculators any more, when I could have followed my perceptions and my visions, when I could have written freely and independently as my heart prompted me! Why must I leave my family now, my poor children, just at the moment when I would have been able to provide better for their well being!"

His death followed in the night of December 5, 1791. The doctors were not agreed on the diagnosis of his illness. It may be said that countless tears flowed for Mozart, not only in Vienna, perhaps even more in Prague, where he was loved and admired. Every connoisseur, every friend of music regarded his loss as an irreparable one.

Translated by P. R. C.

JOHANN ANDREAS SCHACHTNER
(1732–1795)

(Court trumpeter at Salzburg and close friend of the Mozart family. The following letter was addressed to Mozart's sister and is dated April 24, 1792.)

YOUR VERY welcome letter reached me, not at Salzburg, but at Hammerau, where I was visiting my son, who is coadjutor in the office of Oberwestamtmann there.

You may judge from my habitual desire to oblige every one, more especially those of the Mozart family, how much distressed I was at the delay in discharging your commission. To the point therefore!

Your first question is: "What were the favorite amusements of my late lamented brother in his childhood, apart from his passion for his music?" To this question no reply can be made, for as soon as he began to give himself up to music, his mind was as good as dead to all other concerns, and even his childish games and toys had to be accompanied by music. When we, that is, he and I, carried his toys from one room into another, the one of us who went empty-handed had always to sing a march and play the fiddle. But before he began to study music he was so keenly alive to any childish fun that contained a spice of mischief, that even his meals would be forgotten for it. He was so excessively fond of me—I, as you know, being devoted to him—that he used to ask me over and over again whether I loved him; and when in joke I sometimes said "No," great tears would come into his eyes, so tender and affectionate was his dear little heart.

Second question: "How did he behave to great people when they admired his talent and proficiency in music?" In truth he betrayed very little pride or veneration for rank, for, though he could best have shown both by playing before great people who understood little or nothing of music, he would never play unless there were musical connoisseurs among his audience, or unless he could be deceived into thinking that there were.

Third question: "What was his favorite study?" Answer: In this he submitted to the guidance of others. It was much the same to him what he had to learn; he only wanted to learn, and left the choice of a field for his labors to his beloved father. It seemed as if he understood that he could not in all the world find a guide and instructor like his ever memorable father.

Whatever he had to learn he applied himself to so earnestly, that he laid aside everything else, even his music. For instance, when he was learning arithmetic—tables, stools, walls, and even the floor were chalked over with figures.

Fourth question: "What particular qualities, maxims, rules of life, singularities, good or evil propensities had he?" Answer: He was full of fire; his inclinations were easily swayed: I believe that had he been without the advantage of the good education which he received, he might have become a profligate scoundrel—he was so ready to yield to every attraction which offered.

Let me add some trustworthy and astonishing facts relating to his fourth and fifth years, for the accuracy of which I can vouch.

Once I went with your father after the Thursday service to your house, where we found Wolfgangerl ["little Wolfgang"], then four years old, busy with his pen.

Father: What are you doing?

Wolfg.: Writing a concerto for the clavier; it will soon be done.

Father: Let me see it.

Wolfg.: It's not finished yet.

Father: Never mind; let me see it. It must be something very fine.

Your father took it from him and showed me a daub of notes, for the most part written over ink blots. (The little fellow dipped his pen every time down to the very bottom of the ink bottle, so that as soon as it reached the paper, down fell a blot; but that did not disturb him in the least, he rubbed the palm of his hand over it, wiped it off, and went on with his writing.) We laughed at first at this apparent nonsense, but then your father began to note the theme, the notes, the composition; his contemplation of the page became more earnest, and at last tears of wonder and delight fell from his eyes.

"Look, Herr Schachtner," said he, "how correct and how orderly it is; only it could never be of any use, for it is so extraordinarily difficult that no one in the world could play it." Then Wolfgangerl struck in: "That is why it is a concerto; it must be practiced till it is perfect; look! this is how it goes."

He began to play, but could bring out only enough to show us what he meant by it. He had at that time a firm conviction that playing concertos and working miracles were the same thing.

Once more, honored Madame! You will doubtless remember that I have a very good violin which Wolfgangerl used in old times to call "Butterfiddle," on account of its soft, full tone. One day, soon after you came back from Vienna (early in 1763), he played on it, and could not praise my violin enough; a day or two after, I came to see him again, and found him amusing himself with his own little violin. He said directly: "What is your butterfiddle doing?" and went on playing according to his fancy; then he thought a little and said: "Herr Schachtner, your violin is half a quarter of a tone lower than mine, that is, if it is tuned as it was when I played on it last."

I laughed at this, but your father, who knew the wonderful ear and memory of the child, begged me to fetch the violin, and see if he was right. I did, and right he was, sure enough!

Some time before this, immediately after your return from Vienna, Wolfgang having brought home with him a little violin which some one in Vienna had given him, there came in one day our excellent violinist the late Herr Wenzel, who was a dabbler in composition.

He brought six trios with him, composed during the absence of your father, whose opinion on them he came to ask. We played these trios, your father taking the bass part, Wenzel playing first violin, and I second.

Wolfgangerl begged to be allowed to play second violin, but your father reproved him for so silly a request, since he had never had any instruction on the violin, and your father thought he was not in the least capable of playing.

Wolfgang said, "One need not have learned, in order to play second violin," whereupon his father told him to go away at once, and not interrupt us any further.

Wolfgang began to cry bitterly, and slunk away with his little violin. I interceded for him to be allowed to play with me, and at last his father said: "Play with Herr Schachtner then, but not so as to be heard, or you must go away at once." So it was settled, and Wolfgang played with me. I soon remarked with astonishment that I was quite superfluous; I put my violin quietly down, and looked at your father, down whose cheeks tears of wonder and delight were running; and so he played all the six trios. When we had finished, Wolfgang grew so bold from our applause that he declared he could play first violin. We let him try for the sake of the joke, and almost died of laughter to hear him play, with incorrect and uncertain execution, certainly, but never sticking fast altogether.

In conclusion, you ask concerning the delicacy and refinement of his ear:

Until he was almost ten years old, he had an insurmountable horror of the horn when it was sounded alone, without other instruments; merely holding a horn toward him terrified him as much as if it had been a loaded pistol. His father wished to overcome this childish alarm, and ordered me once, in spite of his entreaties, to blow toward him; but, oh! that I had not been induced to do it. Wolfgang no sooner heard the clanging sound than he turned pale, and would have fallen into convulsions, had I not instantly desisted.

This is, I think, all I can say in answer to your questions. Forgive my scrawl, I am too much cast down to do better.

Translated by P. D. T.

ADOLPH HEINRICH VON SCHLICHTEGROLL
(1764–1822)

The obituary written by Schlichtegroll, writer, philologist and librarian, was the first comprehensive biography of Mozart. This little statement is our most important source of facts about Mozart's life; it is reliable because every detail was given to the writer by Mozart's sister, Marianne. It was translated into French by the great novelist Stendhal under the pen name Bombat; shortly afterward the English edition was published.

O. Z.

MOZART NEVER reached his natural growth. During his whole life, his health was delicate. He was thin and pale, and though the form of his face was unusual, there was nothing striking in his physiognomy but its extreme variableness. The expression of his countenance changed every moment, but indicated nothing more than the pleasure or pain which he experienced at the instant. He was remarkable for a habit which is usually the attendant of stupidity. His body was perpetually in motion; he was either playing with his hands, or beating the ground with his foot. There was nothing extraordinary in his other habits, except his extreme fondness for the game of billiards. He had a table in his house, on which he played every day by himself, when he had no one to play with. His hands were so habituated to the piano that he was rather clumsy in everything else. At table he never carved, or if he attempted to do so, it was with much awkwardness and difficulty. His wife usually undertook that office.

The same man, who, from his earliest age, had shown the greatest expansion of mind in what related to his art, in other respects remained a child. He never knew how properly to conduct himself. The management of domestic affairs, the proper use of money, the judicious selection of his pleasures, and temperance in the enjoyment of them, were never virtues to his taste. The gratification of the moment was always uppermost with him. His mind was so absorbed by a crowd of ideas, which rendered him incapable of all serious reflection, that, during his whole life, he stood in need of a guardian to take care of his temporal affairs. His father was well aware of his weakness in this respect, and it was on this account that he persuaded his wife to follow him to Paris, in 1777, his engagements not allowing him to leave Salzburg himself.

But this man, so absent, so devoted to trifling amusements, appeared a being of a superior order as soon as he sat down to a pianoforte. His mind then took wing, and his whole attention was directed to the sole object for which nature designed him, the harmony of sounds. The most numerous orchestra did not prevent him from observing the slightest false note, and he immediately pointed out, with surprising precision, by what instrument the fault had been committed, and the note which should have been played.

When Mozart went to Berlin, he arrived late in the evening. Scarcely had he alighted, when he asked the waiter of the inn whether there was any opera that evening. "Yes, the *Entführung aus dem Serail.*" "That is charming!" He immediately set out for the theater, and placed himself at the entrance of the pit, that he might listen without being observed. But sometimes he was so pleased with the execution of certain passages, and at others so dissatisfied with the manner or the time in which they were performed, or with the embellishments added by the actors, that, continually expressing either his pleasure or disapprobation, he insensibly got up to the bar of the orchestra. The manager had taken the liberty of making some alterations in one of the airs.

When they came to it, Mozart, unable to restrain himself any longer, called out, almost aloud, to the orchestra, in what way it ought to be played. Everybody turned to look at the man in a gray coat who was making all that noise. Some people recognized Mozart, and, in an instant, the musicians and actors were informed that he was in the theater. Some of them, and among the number a very good woman singer, were so agitated at the intelligence, that they refused to come again upon the stage. The manager informed Mozart of the embarrassment he was in. He immediately went behind the scenes, and succeeded, by the compliments which he paid to the actors, in prevailing upon them to go on with the piece.

Music was his constant employment and his most gratifying recreation. Never, even in his earliest childhood, was persuasion required to get him to go to his piano. On the contrary, it was necessary to take care that he did not injure his health by his application. He was particularly fond of playing in the night. If he sat down to the instrument at nine o'clock in the evening, he never left it before midnight, and even then it was necessary to force him away from it, for he would have continued to modulate, and play voluntaries, the whole night. In his general habits he was the gentlest of men, but the least noise during the performance of music offended him violently. He was far above that affected or misplaced modesty which prevents many performers from playing till they have been repeatedly entreated. The nobility of Vienna often reproached him with playing, with equal interest, before any persons that took pleasure in hearing him.

An amateur, in a town through which Mozart passed on one of his journeys, assembled a large party of his friends to give them an opportunity of hearing this celebrated musician. Mozart came, agreeably to his engagement, said very little, and sat down to the pianoforte. Thinking that none but connoisseurs were present, he began a slow movement, the harmony of which was sweet, but extremely simple, intending by it to prepare his auditors for the sentiment which he designed to introduce afterward. The company thought all this very commonplace. The style soon became more lively; they thought it pretty enough. It became severe, and solemn, of a striking, elevated and more difficult harmony. Some of the ladies began to think it quite tiresome, and to whisper a few criticisms to one another; soon half the party were talking. The master of the house was upon thorns, and Mozart himself at least perceived how little his audience was affected by the music. He did not abandon the principal idea with which he commenced, but he developed it with all the fire of which he was capable; still he was not attended to. Without leaving off playing, he began to remonstrate rather sharply with his audience, but as he fortunately expressed himself in Italian, scarcely anybody understood him. They became, however, more quiet. When his anger was a little abated, he could not forbear laughing at his impetuosity himself. He gave a more common turn to his ideas, and concluded by playing a well-known air, of which he gave ten or twelve charming variations. The whole room was delighted, and very few of the company were at all aware of what had passed. Mozart, however, soon took leave, inviting the master of the house, and a few connoisseurs, to spend the evening with him at his inn. He invited them to supper, and upon their intimating a wish to hear him play, he sat down to the instrument, where, to their great pleasure, he played until after midnight.

An old harpsichord tuner came to put some strings to his traveling pianoforte. "Well, my good old fellow," said Mozart to him, "what do I owe you? I leave tomorrow." The poor man, regarding him as a sort of deity, replied, stammering and confounded, "Imperial Majesty ... M. de *Maître de Chapelle* of his Imperial Majesty! ... I cannot. ... It is true that I have waited upon you several times ... You shall give me a crown." "A crown," replied Mozart, "a worthy fellow like you ought not to be put out of his way for a crown"; and he gave him some ducats. The honest man, as he withdrew, continued to repeat, with low bows, "Ah! Imperial Majesty!"

Of his operas, Mozart esteemed most highly the *Idomeneus* and *Don Juan*. He was not fond of talking of his own works; or, if he mentioned them, it was in a few words. Of *Don Juan* he said, one day, "This opera was not composed for the public of Vienna, it is better suited to Prague; but to say the truth, I wrote it only for myself, and my friends."

The time which he most willingly employed in composition was the morning, from six or seven o'clock till ten, when he got up. After this, he did no more for the rest of the day, unless he had to finish a piece that was wanted. He always worked very irregularly. When an idea struck him, he was not to be drawn from it. If he was taken from the pianoforte, he continued to compose in the midst of his friends, and passed whole nights with his pen in his hand. At other times, he had such a disinclination to work that he could not complete a piece till the moment of its performance. It once happened that he put off some music which he had engaged to furnish for a court concert so long that he had not time to write out the part which he was to perform himself. The Emperor Joseph, who was peeping about everywhere, happening to cast his eyes on the sheet which Mozart seemed to be playing from, was surprised to see nothing but empty lines, and said to him: "Where's your part?" "Here," replied Mozart, putting his hand to his forehead.

The same thing nearly occurred with respect to the overture of *Don Juan*. It is generally esteemed the best of his overtures; yet it was only composed the night previous to the first representation, after the general rehearsal had taken place. About eleven o'clock in the evening, when he retired to his apartment, he desired his wife to make him some punch, and to stay with him, in order to keep him awake. She accordingly began to tell him fairy tales, and odd stories, which made him laugh till the tears came. The punch, however, made him so drowsy that he could only go on while his wife was talking, and dropped asleep as soon as she ceased. The efforts which he made to keep himself awake, the continual alternation of sleep and watching, so fatigued him, that his wife persuaded him to take some rest, promising to awake him in an hour's time. He slept so profoundly that she suffered him to repose for two hours. At five o'clock in the morning she awoke him. He had appointed the music copyists to come at seven, and by the time they arrived the overture was finished. They had scarcely time to write out the copies necessary for the orchestra, and the musicians were obliged to play it without a rehearsal. Some persons pretend that they can discover in this overture the passages where Mozart dropped asleep, and those where he suddenly awoke again.[1]

---

[1] From *The Life of Haydn in a series of Letters written at Vienna. Followed by The Life of Mozart with observations on Metastasio by L. A. C. Bombet*. With Notes by William Gardiner. Boston: J. H. Wilkins and R. B. Carter, Philadelphia, 1839.

PART II

Mozart

IN HIS MUSIC

The Music

SEEN IN THE *light of a normal span of years, Mozart lived only half
a lifetime. He had certainly attained the height of his musical powers
in 1791; presumably he would have retained or exceeded those powers
had longer life been granted him. But Mozart began his creative
activity at an age earlier than most composers. Leaving out of account
the half-dozen minuets from his fourth year, his first large compositions—six sonatas for violin and piano—were written about 1763,
when Mozart was seven. From that day until his death he composed;
his activity embraces twenty-nine years. In that sense he was given
almost as full a life as many other composers: thirty-five years elapsed
between Beethoven's Opus 1 and his last work; Brahms had had
scarcely forty years of composing when he died. And Mozart's activity
was continuous during his twenty-nine years of writing.*

*The quantity of his work, while not as great as Haydn's, is con-
siderable. Among the works are some twenty operas, operettas, and
similar works for the stage; fifteen masses, seventeen church sonatas,
and numerous other sacred compositions; more than a hundred airs,
songs, choruses, and vocal canons. The instrumental works include
almost fifty symphonies, more than three dozen serenades, divertimentos, and shorter pieces for orchestral and other ensemble combinations, about fifty concertos (of which more than half are for piano
and orchestra), seventeen piano sonatas, a number of short pieces for
piano, forty-two sonatas and many smaller pieces for violin and piano.
The chamber music consists of twenty-six string quartets, eight string
quintets (two of them with one wind instrument), seven piano trios,*

159

two piano quartets, and almost a dozen larger or smaller works for various combinations.

H. U.

Let us float down the stream of Mozart's music. Here we shall find his soul, and with it his characteristic gentleness and understanding.

These two qualities seem to pervade his whole nature; they surround him and envelop him like a soft radiance. That is why he never succeeded in drawing, or attempted to draw, characters antipathetic to his own. We need only think of the tyrant in *Fidelio,* of the satanic characters in *Freischütz* and *Euryanthe,* and of the monstrous heroes in the *Ring,* to know that through Beethoven, Weber, and Wagner music is capable of expressing and inspiring hate and scorn. But if, as the Duke says in *Twelfth Night,* "music be the food of love," love is also its food. And Mozart's music is truly the food of love, and that is why he has so many friends. And how well he returns their love! How tenderness and affection flow from his heart! As a child he had an almost morbid need of affection. It is recorded that one day he suddenly said to an Austrian princess, "Madame, do you love me?" And the princess, to tease him, said no. The child's heart was wounded and he began to sob.

His heart remained that of a child, and beneath all his music we seem to hear a simple demand: "I love you; please love me."

His compositions constantly sing of love. Warmed by his own feeling, the conventional characters of lyric tragedy, in spite of insipid words and the sameness of love episodes, acquire a personal note and possess a lasting charm for all those who are themselves capable of love. There is nothing extravagant or romantic about Mozart's love; he merely expresses the sweetness or the sadness of affection. As Mozart himself did not suffer from passion, so his heroes are not troubled with broken hearts. The sadness of Anna, or even the jealousy of Elektra in *Idomeneo,* bear no resemblance to the spirit let loose by Beethoven and Wagner. The only passions that Mozart knew well were anger and pride. The greatest of all passions—"the entire Venus"—never appeared in him. It is this lack which gives his whole work a character of ineffable peace. Living as we do in a time when artists tend to show us love only by fleshly excesses or by hypocritical and hysterical "mysticism," Mozart's music charms us quite as much by its ignorance as by its knowledge.

There is, however, some sensuality in Mozart. Though less passionate than Gluck or Beethoven, he is more voluptuous. He is not a German idealist; he is from Salzburg, which is on the road from Venice to Vienna; and there would seem to be something Italian in his nature. His art at times recalls the languid expression of Perugini's beautiful archangels and celestial hermaphrodites, whose mouths are made for everything except prayer. Mozart's canvas is larger than Perugini's, and he finds stirring expressions for the world of religion in quite another way. It is perhaps only in Umbria that we may find comparisons for his both pure and sensual music. Think of those delightful dreamers about love—of Tamino with his freshness of heart and youthful love; of Zerlina; of Constance; of the countess and her gentle melancholy in *Figaro;* of Suzanne's sleepy voluptuousness; of the Quintetto with its tears and laughter; of the Terzetto ("Soave sia il vento") in *Così fan tutte,* which is like "the sweet south, that breathes upon a bank of violets, stealing and giving odor." How much grace and *morbidezza* we have there.

But Mozart's heart is always—or nearly always—artless in its love; his poetry transfigures all it touches; and in the music of *Figaro* it would be difficult to recognize the showy but cold and corrupt characters of the French opera. Rossini's shallow liveliness is nearer Beaumarchais in sentiment. The creation of Cherubino was something almost new in its expression of the disquiet and enchantment of a heart under the mysterious influence of love. Mozart's healthy innocence skated over doubtful situations (such as that of Cherubino with the countess) and saw nothing in them but a subject for merry talk. In reality there is a wide gap between Mozart's Figaros and Don Juans and those of our French authors. With Molière the French mind had something bitter about it when it was not affected, hard, or foolish; and Beaumarchais is cold and bright. Mozart's spirit was quite different and left no aftertaste of bitterness; he was without malice, filled with love and life and activity, and ready for mischief and enjoyment of the world. His characters are delightful creatures who amid laughter and thoughtless jests strive to hide the amorous emotion of their hearts. They make one think of the playful letters Mozart wrote his wife:

"Dear little wife, if I were to tell you all that I do with your dear picture you would laugh a good deal! For instance, when I take it from its cover I say, 'God bless you, little Constance! . . . God bless you, you little rogue! . . . You rufflehead with the pointed nose!' Then when I put it back again I slide it in slowly, coaxing it all the time. I finish by saying very quickly, 'Good night, little mouse, sleep well.' I am afraid I am writing silly things—at least the world would think so. But this is the sixth day I have been parted from you, and it seems as if a year had gone. . . . Well, if other people could look into my heart, I should almost blush . . ." (April 13 and September 30, 1790).

A great lead of gaiety leads to foolery, and Mozart had a share of both. The double influence of Italian opera buffa and Viennese taste encouraged it in him. It is his least interesting side, and one would willingly pass it by if it were not part of him. It is only natural that the body should have its needs as well as the spirit; and when Mozart was overflowing with merriment some pranks were sure to be the result. He amused himself like a child; and one feels that characters like Leporello, Osmin, and Papageno gave him huge diversion.

Occasionally his buffoonery was almost sublime. Think of the character of Don Juan, and, indeed, of the rest of the opera in the hands of this writer of opera buffa. Farce here is mixed with the tragic action; it plays round the commander's statue and Elvira's grief. The serenade scene is a farcical situation; but Mozart's spirit has turned it into a scene of excellent comedy. The whole character of Don Juan is drawn with extraordinary versatility. In truth, it is an exceptional composition, both in Mozart's own work and perhaps even in the musical art of the eighteenth century.

We must go to Wagner to find in musical drama characters that have so true a life and that are as complete and reasonable from one end of the opera to the other. If there is anything surprising in this, it is that Mozart was able to depict so surely the character of a skeptical and aristocratic libertine. But if one studies Don Juan a little closer, one sees in his brilliance, his selfishness, his teasing spirit, his pride, his sensuality, and his anger, the very traits that may be found in Mozart himself, in the obscure depths of his soul where his genius felt the possibilities of the good and bad influences of the whole world.

But what a strange thing! Each of the words we have used to characterize Don Juan has already been used in connection with Mozart's own personality and gifts. We have spoken of the sensuality of his music and his jesting spirit; and we have remarked his pride and his fits of anger, as well as his terrible—and legitimate—egoism.

Thus (strange paradox) Mozart's inner self was a potential Don Juan; and in his art he was able to realize in its entirety, by a different combination of the same elements, the kind of character that was furthest from his own. Even his winning affection is expressed by the fascination of Don Juan's character. And yet, in spite of appearances, this affectionate nature would probably have failed to depict the transports of a Romeo. And so a Don Juan was Mozart's most powerful creation and is an example of the paradoxical qualities of genius.

Mozart is the chosen friend of those who have loved and whose souls are quiet. Those who suffer can seek refuge elsewhere, in that great consoler, the man who suffered so himself and was beyond consolation—I mean Beethoven.

Not that Mozart's lot was an easy one; for fortune treated him even more roughly than she treated Beethoven. Mozart knew sadness in every form; he knew the pangs of mental suffering, the dread of the unknown, and the sadness of a lonely soul. He has told us about some of it in a way that has not been surpassed by either Beethoven or Weber. Among other things, think of his Fantasias and the Adagio in B minor for the piano. In these works a new power appears which I will call genius—if it does not seem an impertinence to imply that there is not genius in his other works. But I use "genius" in the sense of something outside a man's being, something which gives wings to a soul that in other ways may be quite ordinary—some outside power which takes up its dwelling in the soul and is the God in us, the spirit higher than ourselves.

As yet we have only considered a Mozart who was marvelously endowed with life and joy and love; and it was always himself that we found in the characters he created. Here we are on the threshold of a more mysterious world. It is the very essence of the soul that speaks here, a being impersonal and universal—the Being, the common origin of souls, which only genius may express.

Sometimes Mozart's individual self and his inner god engage in sublime discourse, especially at times when his dejected spirit seeks a refuge from the world. This duality of spirit may be seen often in

Beethoven's works; though Beethoven's soul was violent, capricious, passionate, and strange. Mozart's soul, on the other hand, is youthful and gentle, suffering at times from an excess of affection, yet full of peace; and he sings his troubles in rhythmical phrases, in his own charming way, and ends by falling asleep in the midst of his tears with a smile on his face. It is the contrast between his flower-like soul and his supreme genius that forms the charm of his poems in music. One of the fantasias is like a tree with a large trunk, throwing out great branches covered with finely indented leaves and delicately scented flowers. The Concerto in D minor for piano has a breath of heroism about it, and we seem to have lightning flashes alternating with smiles. The famous Fantasia and Sonata in C minor has the majesty of an Olympian god and the delicate sensitivity of one of Racine's heroines. In the Adagio in B minor the god has a graver aspect and is ready to let loose his thunder; there the spirit sighs and does not leave the earth; its thoughts are on human affections, and in the end its plaint grows languorous and it falls asleep.

There are times when Mozart's soul soars higher still and, casting aside his heroic dualism, attains sublime and quiet regions where the stirrings of human passion are unknown. At such times Mozart is equal to the greatest, and even Beethoven himself, in the visions of his old age, did not reach serener heights than these where Mozart is transfigured by his faith.

The unfortunate part is that these occasions are rare, and Mozart's faith seems only to find such expression when he wishes to reassure himself. A man like Beethoven had to reconstruct his faith often and spoke of it constantly. Mozart was a believer from the first; his faith is firm and calm and knows no disquietudes, so he does not talk about it; rather does he speak of the gracious and ephemeral world about him, which he loves so well and which he wishes to love him. But when a dramatic subject opens a way to the expression of religious feeling, or when grave cares and suffering or presentiments of death destroy the joy of life and turn his thoughts to God, then Mozart is himself no longer. (I am speaking of the Mozart the world knows and loves.) He then appears what he might have become if death had not stopped him on the way—an artist fitted to realize Goethe's dream of the union of Christian feeling with pagan beauty, an artist who might have achieved "the reconciliation of the modern world" . . . which was what Goethe tried to do in his second *Faust*.

In three works, particularly, has Mozart expressed the Divine; that is in the Requiem, in *Don Giovanni,* and in *Die Zauberflöte*. The Requiem breathes of Christian faith in all its purity. Mozart there put worldly pleasure away from him, and kept only his heart, which came fearfully and in humble repentance to speak with God. Sorrowful fear and gentle contrition united with a noble faith run through all that work. The touching sadness and personal accent of certain phrases suggest that Mozart was thinking of himself when he asked eternal repose for others.

In the two other works religious feeling also finds an outlet; and through the artist's intuition it breaks away from the confines of an individual faith to show us the essence of all faith. The two works complete each other. *Don Giovanni* gives us the burden of predestination, which Don Juan has to carry as the slave of his vices and the worshiper of outside show. *Die Zauberflöte* sings of the joyous freedom of the Virtuous. Both by their simple strength and calm beauty have a classic character. The fatality in *Don Giovanni* and the serenity of *Die Zauberflöte* form perhaps the nearest approach of modern art to Greek art, not excepting Gluck's tragedies. The perfect purity of certain harmonies in *Die Zauberflöte* soars to heights which are hardly even reached by the mystic zeal of the knights of the Grail. In such work everything is clear and full of light.

In the glow of this light Mozart died on December 5, 1791. The first performance of *Die Zauberflöte* had taken place on September 30 in the same year, and Mozart wrote the Requiem during the two last months of his life. Thus he had scarcely begun to unfold the secret of his being when death took him—at thirty-five years of age. We will not think about that death. Mozart called it "his best friend"; and it was at death's approach and under its inspiration that he first became conscious of the supreme power that had been captive within him—a power to which he yielded himself in his last and highest work. It is only just to remember that at thirty-five Beethoven had not yet written either the *Appassionata* or the Symphony in C minor, and he was a long way from the conception of the Ninth Symphony and the Mass in D.

Death cut short the course of Mozart's life, but such life as he was spared has been to others a never-failing source of peace. In the midst of the turmoil of passion which since the Revolution has entered all art and brought disquiet into music, it is comforting to seek refuge in this serenity, as one might seek it upon the heights of Olympus. From this quiet spot we may look down into the plain below and watch the combats of heroes and gods from other lands and hear the noise of the great world about them like the murmur of ocean billows on a distant shore.

R. R.

In this life that is "so daily," as Jules Laforgue complained, a life of tomorrow rather than of today, we are inclined to patronize the ancient worthies who in their own period were very modern, or to speak jauntily of them as bores, with their works of "only historical interest." Mozart has not escaped. Many concertgoers yawn at his name and wonder why such men as Richard Strauss or Vincent d'Indy could praise him with glowing cheeks. They suspect this attribute of worship to be a pose. Remind them of the fact that to such widely different characters as Rossini, Chopin, Tchaikovsky, Brahms, the musician of musicians was Mozart, and they say lightly, "There's no accounting for tastes; surely you do not pretend to maintain that Mozart is a man of this generation."

No, Mozart was neither a symbolist nor a pessimist. He was not a translator of literature, sculpture, or painting into music. His imagination was not fired by a metaphysical treatise. He simply wrote music that came into his head and disquieted him until it was jotted down on paper. He did not go about nervously seeking for ideas. His music is never the passionate cry, never the wild shriek of a racked soul. His music is never hysterical, it is never morbid. It is seldom emotional as we necessarily and unhappily understand that word today. Perhaps for these reasons it is still modern, immortal, and not merely on account of the long and exquisite melodic line, fitting, inevitable background, delicate coloring. Music that is only the true voice of a particular generation is moribund as soon as it is born.

His music, whether it vitalizes stage characters or is absolute, as in the three famous symphonies, and in the chamber works, is as the music on Prospero's isle: "Sounds and sweet airs that give delight and hurt not." The analyst may find pleasure in praising the unsurpassable workmanship, which is akin to the spontaneity of natural phenomena; he may marvel at the simplicity of plan and expression; the simplicity that is the despair of interpreters, for it is the touchstone of their own art or artificiality—and Mozart himself, when he told his emperor that his opera had just the right number of notes, anticipated the judgment of time—but he is still far from explaining the peculiar and ineffable tenderness of this music that soothes and caresses and comforts.

The serenity, the classic suggestion of emotion without distortion that accompanies passion, would grace a tragedy of Sophocles or a comedy by Congreve. Mozart's music is essentially Grecian, yet now and then it reminds one of Watteau.

Hazlitt said of art that it should seem to come from the air and return to it. But he characterized it with finer appreciation when he said, without mention of Mozart's name, "Music is color without form; a soul without a body; a mistress whose face is veiled; an invisible goddess." And for this reason Debussy is the spiritual brother of Mozart, moderns both, yet classics.

P. H.

It has been for our own century and for the generation of the present day to rediscover Mozart, not as the expression of an imaginary age of innocence, still less as the musical illustrator of an equally imaginary century of rococo artificiality, but as the completely mature creator of music that we can still enjoy as a thing of delight for its own sake.

Italian opera, Italian polyphony, and Italo-German symphony— these three early influences were fundamental and permanent throughout Mozart's life. But to the end of his days he was experimenting, and experimenting with a practical knowledge of his surroundings, so that the course of his development is very different from that of men condemned to a life of solitude and isolation like Beethoven, Domenico Scarlatti, and J. S. Bach. Such men present in some ways a simpler artistic life-story; the foundations of musical character once laid down, the rest is all self-development from the inside. In considering Mozart we are confronted all along by merely external considerations—the exigencies of patrons, the peculiarities of individual executants, as well as the direct influences of other composers' works. What the musician of to-day can learn best from Mozart rather than from any other composer of the past is that pride in craftsmanship which enables him to adapt himself to the conditions of the moment, to rewrite and rewrite again to suit the convenience of a singer or the necessity of the stage, and in every case to preserve and even to intensify his own individuality.

It is absurd to talk of Mozart as a man who remained a child throughout his life, or as a polite composer who never sought to do more than please an aristocratic audience with a succession of graceful frivolities. Only in one sense can he be said to have been a child all his life, and that was in his passionate seriousness, in a complete self-abandonment to emotional impulse which at times (as in the Requiem) becomes positively hysterical.

                                                            E. J. D.

Mr. Bernard Shaw once remarked that nothing could be more uncharacteristic of Mozart than the portraits of the beautiful young man exhibited above his name in all the music-shops of the world today. These portraits show Mozart as the most handsome, the most regular-featured of all great composers. Such "classic" proportions seem at first sight to be peculiarly appropriate to a composer who is universally admired as the classic of classics. Where else in music shall we find those qualities of serenity, limpidity, simplicity, lucidity, which we concentrate in one adjective, "Mozartian"? It is impossible in music to find a parallel to that flawless perfection. Whether we take a whole opera—such as Le Nozze de Figaro—or a mere scrap scribbled impromptu on the page of a visitor's book—such as the Gigue written in 1789 for the Leipzig organist Engel—we are confronted with a completely finished musical composition in which there is not a superfluous bar, not a redundant or meaningless note. There is no "waste" in Mozart—no overlapping, no exaggeration, no strain, no vagueness, no distortion, no suggestion. He is so pure that he seems often meaningless. His music *disappears,* like the air we breathe on a transparent day. All those who have really appreciated

Mozart will admit that at one time or another they have felt certain Mozart masterpieces as one would feel a still, bright, perfect, cloudless day. Such a day has no meaning, none of the suggestiveness, the "atmosphere," the character of a day of cloud or storm, or of any day in which there is a mixture of warring elements whose significance has yet to appear. Such a day does not provoke or in the faintest degree suggest one mood rather than another. It is infinitely protean. It means just what you mean. It is intangible, immaterial—fitting your spirit like a glove. Thus, as Sir Charles Stanford has said, when you are a child, Mozart speaks to you as a child—no music could be more simple, more childlike—but when you are a man, you find to your astonishment that this music which seemed childlike is completely adult and mature. At every age this pure, pellucid day, this intangible transparency, awaits you and envelops you in its unruffled light. Then suddenly there will pass through you a tremor of terror. A moment comes when that tranquility, that perfection, will take on a ghastly ambiguity. That music still suggests nothing, nothing at all; it is just infinitely ambiguous. Then you may remember the phrase of a German critic who wrote of the "demoniacal clang" of Mozart. Then you look at a genuine portrait of Mozart, and instead of that smooth, regular young beauty you see a straight jutting profile with a too prominent nose and an extraordinary salience of the upper lip, and for an instant you feel as if you have had a revelation. But that revelation escapes you as suddenly as it came, and you are left face to face with a mask whose directness and clarity are completely baffling.

One may speak often of a movement of Mozart just as a mathematician might speak of a beautiful proposition. Whereas in the music of most composers it is a case of content *and* structure, it is with Mozart a case of structure only, for there is no perceptible content—*ubi materia ibi geometria*. This is strikingly shown in the overture to *Le Nozze de Figaro*. I would suggest to the reader that he should buy the phonograph records of this overture and of Rossini's overture to *Il Barbiere di Siviglia* and compare them. The difference is astonishing. Rossini was born the year after Mozart's death; he also had the advantage of following instead of preceding Beethoven and he was a composer of striking natural genius. But, after *Figaro,* listen to his *Il Barbiere di Siviglia* overture, with its alluring tunefulness

over its easy *tum-ti, tum-ti, tum-ti* bass, and you will be struck with
its straggling formlessness. Its tunes are very engaging, but you can
carry them away with you and hear them mentally on a penny
whistle, a cornet, or any instrument you like. They are like bright
threads in a commonplace piece of stuff which you can pull out
without compunction as there is no design to spoil. But you can do
nothing of the sort with the *Figaro* overture. There are no bright
threads to pull out. There is no melodic content as such. You cannot
even hear the music in your memory apart from the rush of the
strings and the accents of the woodwind. It cannot be played upon
the piano. Take away a note of it and the whole is completely dis-
integrated. Nor can anyone put his hand upon his heart and say
what feeling that music arouses in his breast. It is completely without expression, as expression is vulgarly understood; but the oftener
you hear it, the more excited you become, the more passionate grow
your asseverations that there was never music like this before or since.
Its effect upon the mind is out of all proportion to its impingement
on the senses. To hear it is as though one had been present at a miracle
and had seen a mountain of matter blown into a transparent bubble
and float vanishing into the sky. Your desire to hear that overture
again and again and again is the simple but intense desire to see the
miracle repeated. It is an astonishing experience, and it is an experience which Mozart is constantly giving us.

W. J. T.

Mozart's true happiness was in creation.

In restless and unhealthy geniuses creation may be a torture—the
bitter seeking after an elusive ideal. But with healthy geniuses like
Mozart creation was a perfect joy and so natural that it seemed
almost a physical enjoyment. Composing was as important for his
health as eating, drinking, and sleeping. It was a need, a necessity—
a happy necessity since he was able continually to satisfy it.

It is well to understand this if one would understand the passages
in the letter about money.

"Rest assured that my sole aim is to get as much money as possible;
for, after health, it is the most precious possession." (April 4, 1781.)

This may seem a low ideal. But one must not forget that Mozart lacked money all his life—and in this way his imagination was hampered and his health suffered in consequence, so that he was always obliged to think of success and of the money that would make him free. Nothing could be more natural. If Beethoven acted differently it was because his idealism carried him to another world and way of living—an unreal world (if we except the rich patrons who made secure his daily bread). But Mozart loved life and the world and the reality of things. He wished to live and conquer; and conquer he did—for living was not exactly under his control.

The most wonderful fact about Mozart was that he directed his art toward success without any sacrifice of himself; and his music was always written with regard to its effect upon the public. Somehow it does not lose by this, and it says exactly what he wishes it to say. In this he was helped by his delicate perceptions, his shrewdness, and his sense of irony. He despised his audience, but he held himself in great esteem. He made no concessions that he need blush for; he deceived the public, but he guided it as well. He gave people the illusion that they understood his ideas; while, as a matter of fact, the applause that greeted his works was excited only by passages which were solely composed for applause. And what matter? So long as there was applause the work was successful, and the composer was free to create new works.

"Composing," said Mozart, "is my one joy and passion." (October 10, 1777.)

This fortunate genius seemed born to create. Few other examples are to be found of such robust artistic health; for one must not confound his extraordinary gift for composition with the indolent imagination of a man like Rossini. Bach worked perseveringly, and he used to say to his friends: "I am obliged to work, and whoever works as hard as I do will succeed quite as well as I." Beethoven had to fight with all his strength when in the throes of composition. If his friends surprised him at work, they often found him in a state of extreme exhaustion. "His features were distorted, sweat ran down his face, and he seemed," said Schindler, "as if he were doing battle with an army of contrapuntists." It is true the reference here is to his Credo and Mass in D. Nevertheless, he was always making sketches of things, thinking them over, erasing or correcting what he had done, beginning all over again, or putting a couple of notes to the adagio of some sonata which he was supposed to have finished long ago and which had perhaps even been printed.

Mozart knew nothing of these torments. He was able to do what he wished, and he never wished to do what was beyond him. His work is like a sweet scent in his life—perhaps like a beautiful flower whose only care is to live. So easy was creation to him that at times it poured from him in a double or triple stream, and he performed incredible feats of mental activity without thinking about them. He would compose a prelude while writing a fugue; and once when he played a sonata for pianoforte and violin at a concert, he composed it the day before, between eleven o'clock and midnight, hurriedly writing the violin part and having no time to write down the piano part or to rehearse it with his partner. The next day he played from memory what he had composed in his head (April 8, 1781). This is only one of many examples.

Such genius was likely to be spread over the whole domain of his art and in equal perfection. He was, however, especially fitted for musical drama. If we recall the chief traits in his nature, we find that he had a sane and well-balanced spirit, dominated by a strong, calm determination, and that he was without excess of passion, yet had fine perceptions and versatility. Such a man, if he has creative gifts, is best able to express life in an objective way. He is not bothered by the unreasonableness of a more passionate nature, which feels it must pour itself out in everything alike. Beethoven remained Beethoven on every page of his work; and it was well, for no other hero could interest us as he did. But Mozart, thanks to the happy mixture of his qualities—sensibility, shrewd perception, gentleness, and self-control—was naturally fitted to understand the differences of character in others, to interest himself in the fashionable world of his time, and to reproduce it with poetic insight in his music. His soul was at peace within him, and no inner voice clamored to be heard. He loved life and was a keen observer of the world he lived in; and it cost him no effort to reproduce what he saw.

R. R.

2

The Operas

THE BACKGROUND

THE CENTURY into which Mozart was born was dominated throughout by the influence of Italian opera. There is no need to quarrel with the consensus of opinion that has placed Handel, Haydn, and Mozart on a higher level of greatness than Leo, Pergolesi, and Jommelli; but it is most important to remember that the great Germans, however sincerely they may have felt that they were

173

bringing about a reaction from the Italian supremacy, were all the time subconsciously expressing themselves in a musical language that was essentially Italian. Vernon Lee has well pointed out that "throughout the eighteenth century the evolution of the musical phrase, the evolution of what I should like to call *melodic form,* took place in Italy.... Musical style, in its musical essentials, was unaltered by Gluck's reforms." But it was not merely the characteristic shape of an eighteenth-century tune that was Italian, but the forms in which all music was written. Composers all over Europe were trying to convey for different surroundings and for various instruments what they had heard sung in the Italian opera. The classical sonata-form was not invented by serious-minded Germans; it was taken over by them from the normal scheme of the operatic aria. The classical symphony, as is well known, was derived from the Italian operatic overtures; and since the early symphonies were composed mostly for the entertainment of German princes and archbishops during dinner, they were based on or imitated from the tunes of the popular comic operas, just as monarchs or prelates of the early twentieth century might dine to selections from the last new musical comedy. The Germans, being a nation of instrumental players rather than of singers, proceeded to develop instrumental, and especially orchestral, music on these lines for its own sake. This symphonic point of view, however, could only be reached by climbing the ladder of Italian opera. The ladder once climbed, young Germany very characteristically kicked it down, and a later generation pretended that there had never been any Italian ladder there at all. But the eighteenth century could not be deceived in this way. Its audiences were enveloped in an atmosphere of perpetual Italian song, just as modern audiences are haunted by the unending strains of Puccini in tea-shops and wherever "light music" is habitually played. It was this subconscious memory of Italian opera that enabled audiences to follow the thought of the symphonic composers; it is a memory that we of to-day have lost, but if we can set ourselves to cultivate it we shall discover new and illuminating lights on the poetry of classical instrumental music. Austria, Germany, and England were swarming with Italian musicians of all kinds; both literally and figuratively Italian was the language of music. Hardly a court was without its Italian opera, and there was hardly a place where Dr. Burney did not find Italian the most convenient medium of conversation. At the same time, the men who were colonizing that "greater Italy" north of the Alps were themselves often susceptible to native influences, and the very fact that Italian was the universal musical language made for a certain cosmopolitanism which became still more marked as the century drew to its end.

Of all cosmopolitan eighteenth-century musicians, Mozart is the chief. . . .

E. J. D. (1)

Musical historians write at length about the genesis of opera and go into great detail on this subject. I prefer to be as brief as possible. The origin of opera is threefold; or we may say that it has a threefold root in Poetry, Dancing, and Music. No matter how opera develops in the future, its seeming changes of form will depend upon the balance and adjustment of these three primary factors. In every good opera, in every opera that is a work of art by a truly creative composer, these three elements are differently combined. We approve of and enjoy all these different combinations according as we are in the mood for this or that proportion of the primary ingredients. The human need for change in order that each element may be freshly experienced is what promotes the so-called new developments; but these new developments are new only in the sense that each opera composed by a musician of genius is a fresh solution of the problem of combining the three primary elements and of making at the same time a creation which is absolutely his. The creative genius not only solves a problem, but his solution is an individual offspring with a life and character of its own.

Instead, therefore, of giving the reader a lengthy description of the development of opera in Italy during the sixteenth and seventeenth centuries, illustrated by the names of Peri (1561–1633), Caccini (1558–c.1616), Cavalieri (c.1550–1600), Monteverde (1567–1643), Legrenzi (1625–90), Stradella (c.1645–82), Carissimi (1604–74), Cesti (1620–69), Cavalli (1602–76), Alessandro Scarlatti (1659–1725), and so on, I shall just present this history, up to Mozart, abbreviated into the following diagram:

THE GENEALOGY OF OPERA

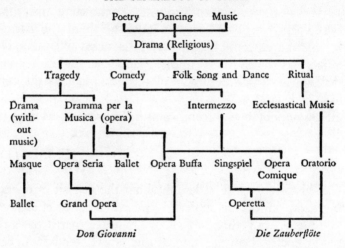

If we take the six best-known operas of Mozart's we shall find that *Idomeneo* is an example of opera seria—that is, an opera in which there is no comedy—springing as it does in my diagrammatic scheme from the "Tragedy" division; that *Die Entführung* is an example of Singspiel—that is, a derivation from Comedy and the more popular sort of Italian variety show known as Intermezzo; that *Figaro* is an example of opera buffa; and that in *Die Zauberflöte* we have a unique example of the combination of Singspiel and Oratorio or Cantata. This leaves us with the two other masterpieces, *Don Giovanni* and *Così fan Tutte*. In these two great works the two forms: (1) Opera Seria and (2) Opera Buffa—that is, of Tragedy and Comedy—are for the first time in the history of opera perfectly united into one, and we may take as a sign that Mozart was aware of this new unity the fact that he described each of them as a *dramma giocoso* instead of *opera buffa*. It is also significant that these two works are precisely those which have most puzzled musicians, musicologists, and music-lovers during the past hundred years.

W. J. T.

MOZART'S OPERAS: GENERAL

A SHARPER contrast than that between Gluck and Mozart—both of them men of surpassing genius, both great in very nearly the same line—can hardly be found in history, which, like melodrama, is rather rich in sharp contrasts. Gluck, warm and impulsive in feeling, was a thinker, a man of ideas, a born champion and espouser of causes; keen of perception and instinct, he was yet well persuaded of the need of weighing his perceptions intellectually and rationally, that his championship might be efficacious. Inconspicuous as the *Alceste* preface is as a documentary statement of art principles, one cannot but see that it represents an immense amount of solid thinking. In short, Gluck was a man who could be truly great only by seconding his native genius with a complete intellectual grasp of the why and wherefore of the business in hand; and, having this grasp, he could claim entire responsibility for everything great he did.

Mozart was his direct antithesis, as irresponsible a person as can be found in the whole tale of opera-composers, Cavalli included. Gifted with vastly superior genius to Gluck's, he had in very truth nothing but his genius, and the unerring accuracy of immediate perception that went therewith. He was decidedly an ordinary man intellectually; outside of his music, without a single intellectual taste. Where Gluck, impelled by a burning sense of the deficiencies of his early education, studied literature and æsthetics, the whole literature, the whole æsthetic movement, of his day left Mozart absolutely untouched; were he alive to-day, he would read nothing but a newspaper. As a boy, he evinced a certain genial brightness of precocious wit and humour; his early letters may be accounted more than ordinarily good boy's letters. But this precocious intellectuality faded out of him with manhood; his later letters show a certain hard-and-fast common sense, but of a quite conventional sort.

What most makes Mozart remarkable is not so much the greatness as the unparalleled self-sufficiency (in a good sense) of his genius. By dint of sheer genius alone—backed up, to be sure, by an exceptionally fine special, technical education; for old Leopold, his father, was the best of musical drill-masters—he did what hardly another man has done with commanding intellect, genius, and culture combined. To be sure, there must have been a profound intellectuality latent in him somewhere, for few men have written music which furnishes the listener and student with a greater wealth of food for thought. No intellectual problem, so to speak, was too high or too deep for him to solve musically; but his unerring dive to the heart of every matter was guided by sheer instinct; he perceived immediately and intuitively what other men had to get at by hard thinking. Pure genius, nothing but genius and an unsurpassed technique, was all he had in his armoury; and with these weapons alone he showed himself fully up to the level of every emergency. His fellow is not to be found in the history of the Opera.

No bad commentary on the man's purely instinctive and unreflective bent is the fact that, with the example of Gluck and his Reform fresh before his very eyes, he went to work with his opera-writing as if Gluck had never existed; he utterly ignored the Gluck movement. It were wholly wrong to suppose that Moazrt began where Gluck left off; he did nothing of the sort, he began where Gluck himself began, and went his own way. Gluck had a formula of his own; Mozart had (consciously) none. Yet he raised the Lyric Drama to a height it had never attained before, which it has reached only once or twice since. For, hazardous as is every comparison between works of utterly different character, it is not too much to say that only Wagner's *Tristan und Isolde* and *Die Meistersinger* can rank with Mozart's *Don Giovanni* as completely great works of art; nothing else in all Lyric Drama maintains itself throughout on quite so high a plane—intellectually, musically, dramatically.

Mozart's position in the history of Opera is so unique that he can hardly be treated historically like other opera-composers. He founded no school, and left no imitators behind him; indeed, there was nothing imitable about him. As has been said, he raised the Lyric Drama to an unprecedented and since unsurpassed height by sheer force of genius, without aparently giving the matter any thought at all—certainly no original thought. It seems never to have entered his head that he might have a "mission"; he was in no sense a reformer, like Gluck. It is not unsignificant that almost the last libretto he set to music was by Metastasio! To be sure, he was no slavish follower of precedent, and wrote exactly as he pleased, often doing quite unprecedented things. The second finale of his *Don Giovanni* shows him with one foot thrust well over the wall of time into Beethoven's *Eroica*. But he evinced no set purpose to be off with the old or on with the new. Like Cavalli, he was by no means fastidious about his libretti, and took them pretty much as they came.

What he did bring to bear upon the operatic problem—little of a

problem, though, to him!—was a wholly new individuality. Two
new items he certainly did introduce into opera-writing. He was the
first composer to strike unmistakably the "modern romantic" note
in Opera; he revived the long-dead art of musical character-drawing.
He did not create it, for there are some rather surprising instances of
sharp musical delineation of character to be found in Monteverde and
Cavalli, especially in the latter; but the "Oratorio" school had pretty
much done away with all that, and Mozart gave it due prominence
again. Gluck cannot compare with him in this matter; as a creator of
"living figures of flesh and blood" in Lyric Drama, Mozart has never
been surpassed, and equalled now and then only by Richard Wagner.

It is not a little remarkable that this power of Mozart's, of putting
thoroughly real-seeming and strongly individualized people upon the
lyric stage, should have gone hand in hand with an unconquerable,
one had almost said, an excessive, bent toward ideality. True as he
was to the core, he absolutely could not help idealizing; *c'était plus
fort que lui!* As Hanslick once said, the rascally little Cherubino in
da Ponte's version of Caron de Beaumarchais's *Figaro* turns into an
actual cherub in his hands; the pert little village coquette, Zerlina,
becomes absolutely angelic. Yet, such is the genius with which it is
done, you accept it all readily; you would not have it otherwise.

Perhaps as characteristic an example as another of this inveterate
ideality of Mozart's, and of the astonishing way he made it go hand
in hand with dramatic truth, is the little quintet, "Di scrivermi ogni
giorno" in *Così fan tutte.* The situation is purely ludicrous: two
young officers, secretly on forbidden pleasure bent, take leave of their
sweethearts, on the pretence of going off to the war; a cynical old
pedagogue, who is quite up to snuff as to the situation, stands by and
can hardly keep his countenance. Here we have sincere pathos on
one side, mock-heroic bathos on the other, with sardonic derision
in the middle. This little scene Mozart has set to just three pages of
music (full score) which, while duly accentuating every emotion
and doing the fullest justice to the humourous side of the situation,
is as divinely angelic as anything ever put upon paper; on hearing it
you simply feel that

> *. . . he on honey-dew hath fed,*
> *And drunk the milk of Paradise.*

"Angelic" is the only word for a good deal in Mozart's music; yet you never feel any lack of a good solid foundation of warm human flesh and blood.

As the due psychical counterpoise to this idealizing bent, Mozart had a practical clearheadedness that almost seeks its fellow in history; and, like most thoroughly clearheaded men, he had a phenomenally retentive and accurate memory. Immediate decision and the consequent retention of a perfectly distinct mental picture of what he had decided upon were perhaps his most prominent mental traits. His peculiar method of composing shows this. When about to compose a movement, he would rule off page after page of score-paper with bars; then he would write down (either completely or sketchily, as the case might be) some sixteen, eighteen, or twenty-four measures of music, then skip a certain number of measures (always carefully counted) and go on from there. His first draft would thus be full of lacunæ; and, in afterwards filling these out, he would seldom have to add or subtract a single measure of this skeleton, nor would the passages already written undergo any alteration. What had been the first draft would become the finished copy; he seldom made another.

The story that he wrote a large part of *Don Giovanni* on a table in a public beer-garden, between turns at bowling, is probably true, certainly characteristic. The fact is that Mozart hardly ever made what other composers would call a preliminary sketch; he would elaborate a whole composition in his head before putting pen to paper at all, so that his actual writing was little more than copying from memory. And this he could very well do under circumstances that would have been utterly unfavourable to thinking out a composition.

This habitual method of composing is a far stronger proof of the power of Mozart's musical memory than the oft-told story of his writing the horn, trumpet, and kettle-drum parts of the overture to *Don Giovanni* after sending off the manuscript score, containing only the string and wood-wind parts, to the copyist. A tolerable feat of memory this certainly was, especially as the whole overture was written in a single night, and so hurriedly that he had no time to look over the first section of the score before sending it off. But it sinks into insignificance beside Wagner's ruling off the bars for his clean copy of the whole first act of the *Meistersinger,* without once referring to his first copy, and finding that he had allowed just the right amount of space for the notes of every measure in the whole act. Neither was Mozart's memory quite so accurate in the case mentioned; for just before the first performance, there having been no time to rehearse the overture, he had to say to the orchestra: "Gentlemen of the brass and drums, at one point you will find in your parts either four measures too many, or four too few, I can't now remember which; but, if you follow my beat, all will come right!"

Mozart wrote, first and last, some twelve Italian and five German operas and operettas. The first performed was *Bastien und Bastienne,* a one-act piece, the text of which was adapted by Anton Schacht from Weiskern's translation of a parody on Jean-Jacques [Rousseau]'s *Devin du village* written by Madame Favart—rather a complicated authorship. This little *Singspiel* was given in Vienna in the summer-house of Mozart's friends, the Missmers, in 1768, the composer being then twelve years old.[1] His last opera, *Die Zauberflöte*—the libretto by Emanuel Schikaneder, manager of the theatre—was brought out at the Theatre an der Wieden on September 30, 1791, the year of the composer's death. Thus Mozart's career as an opera-composer began and ended with German works.

This fact has, however, no real significance; he did his greatest work in Italian Opera. There was, upon the whole, a great deal of the Italian in Mozart, as a musician, even more than in Handel. He had the German depth of *Gemüth,* the Teutonic seriousness and artistic conscientiousness; but in all else he was (musically) Italian to the core. His cast of melody is distinctly Italian; nothing in all Opera is more foreign to what is known as "German singing" than his music—whether to German or Italian words. And what is true of his vocal writing is true of his instrumental compositions.[2] Notably Italian was his complete and facile mastery in *recitativo secco,* that free

---

[1] Curiously enough, the principal theme of the overture is, note for note, the same as the opening theme of Beethoven's *Eroica* symphony—only, in G major instead of E-flat major. Was this a mere coincidence, or had Beethoven seen a score of *Bastien und Bastienne?* At all events, the Thunderer had a way of taking his own wherever he found it.

[2] Hans von Bülow was once heard to say: "I had rather hear an average first-rate Italian or French violinist play the first violin part in a Mozart quartet than any but two or three of my respected fellow-countrymen."

form of colloquial recitative that is accompanied by a 'cello and double-bass, with a few improvised chords struck by the cembalist; no Italian, not even Rossini himself, could beat him in this line. It may have been a keen appreciation of the perfection of this style as a musical medium for familiar dialogue, and of the utter inadaptability of the German language to anything of the sort, that induced him to accept the conventional bastard form of the German *Spieloper* —set musical numbers connected by spoken dialogue—for his German operas. That he made no attempt to develop a corresponding form of German recitative is a fact.

That Mozart came into the world without a manifesto, and quitted it leaving none behind him, that he showed on occasion a singularly easy-going contentedness with even the worst conventions of his day, should not be taken as evidence that he did nothing new; in principle he may have done little, but in fact he did a good deal. His enormous development of the act-finale, the only item in which the Opera in his hands approached the character of the Wagnerian Music-Drama, was in itself something unprecedented. In general, however, what may be called his musical formula was as unlike Wagner's, or that of the old Florentines, as possible; it has been found no little fault with of late years, and people have marvelled at his achievement of such stupendous results with so poor a tool.

But his formula was really not quite so poor as all that; it suited his artistic purpose to a T. And we should not forget that Mozart's task, in other words, the class of libretti he had to deal with, was radically different from Wagner's.

Wagner, notably in his later works, had to deal with the Drama of Continuous Development; the action goes on continuously from the beginning to the end of an act; nothing is omitted, there are no lacunæ in its logic; either it rises by gradual climax to a culminating point at the close of the act, or else this culmination comes earlier, to be followed by a period of subsidence which in turn leads over to the point of departure for a fresh climax. In either came, there is no breach of continuity.

In the texts of Mozart's best operas, on the other hand, we find nothing of the sort. The libretto presents a mere succession of situations the logical connection between any two of which is either but summarily hinted at in the dialogue or else left wholly to the spectator's perception. The dramatic development is nowhere continuous, but proceeds by fits and starts, until we come to a short period of continuity near the end of an act. No doubt the several situations in the above-mentioned succession are culled from an ideal continuous climax, and each one comes in in its proper order; but the logical connection is omitted. Whereas, in the Wagnerian Drama, the account given of the action is fully itemized, like that in a business man's day-book, that given in the Mozart libretti is like the one to be found in the second column of a ledger, consisting of a series of partial results, with most of the separate items omitted. Nevertheless, by supplying the logical connection for himself, the spectator can obtain a certain sense of climax, much as the listener to pianoforte-playing can get a sense of sustained melody from what is really nothing more than a series of well-ordered accents, without sustained musical tone. But, for him to obtain this sense of essential climax, the succession must be rapid; and this indispensable rapidity we surely do find in the Mozart libretti, as we do also in Shakespeare's plays.

Now, Mozart's musical formula—a succession of set musical numbers (solos, duets, ensemble-pieces, etc.), with intervening stretches of *secco* recitative—corresponds exactly to the dramatic formula of his librettists. Such a formula would be ridiculous if applied to texts like *Tristan und Isolde* or the *Meistersinger,* as much out of place as the Wagnerian formula would be with such libretti as *Figaro* or *Don Giovanni;* but with these latter libretti it works to perfection, the sense for artistic fitness is completely satisfied.

Mozart's greatest opera is unquestionably *Don Giovanni* (the text adapted by the abbate Lorenzo Da Ponte from Molière's *Festin de Pierre,* first given, under the composer's personal direction, at Prague on October 29, 1787). *Die Zauberflöte* is pulled down from this high plane by its weak text—of which no one but a Freemason can make head or tail—while *Le Nozze di Figaro* (the libretto also by Da Ponte, after Beaumarchais, brought out at the Vienna Burgtheater on May 1, 1786) lapses nearly as far by reason of a certain failure on the composer's part to enter fully and sympathetically into the "tone" of his subject. Mozart was great, but not quite universal; keen as was his sense of humour, Beaumarchais's spirit of malicious raillery was not in his nature, he could not twist his features into that sardonic, *schadenfrohe* smile.[3]

Curiously enough, *Don Giovanni,* though long one of the most popular,[4] is nowadays one of the least correctly appreciated of operas. Few operas are habitually given so radically and ruinously wrong. Both in Europe and this country *Don Giovanni* is usually given in vast court or metropolitan opera-houses, with orchestras double or treble the size intended by Mozart (a most necessary evil, this last, for Mozart's orchestra would be utterly lost in a large theatre).[5] To counteract these two false conditions, the music is sung, for the most part, with all the stress of voice, all the flamboyant vociferation that belong to "grand" Opera. That certain scenes may be set effectively, the original two acts have been cut up into three and four, and long-ish waits come between some scenes, thus destroying that rapidity of succession which is indispensable to the sense of climax. Indeed, the vast opera-houses, big orchestras, the general style of singing, and the tragic grandeur of the closing statue-scene, have all united to give many, perhaps most, opera-goers the impression that *Don Giovanni* is a grand opera.

This impression is radically wrong; up to the last scene, *Don Giovanni* is an *opera buffa*—it is styled *"dramma giocoso"* on the title-page. It is comedy of the most intimately subtle sort, requiring a very small house and orchestra, that no deft play of feature, no nimbly significant gesture, no delicately expressive shading of the voice may be lost upon the audience. Its gist, as Verlaine would say, lies in the nuance, not in the colour; it is a work of the finest subtlety, not of hammer-and-tongs. Then, the original cut of acts and scenes must be scrupulously preserved, and one scene follows hard upon the heels of another; the iron must never be allowed to cool off, the audi-

---

[3] In this respect, and this respect alone, Rossini's *Barbiere* is far better in tune with the Beaumarchais original than Mozart's *Figaro.*

[4] "Let me tell you that the *Don Giovanni* had the greatest success of any opera which has been brought forward, in my time, in America."—Max Maretzek, *Crotchets and Quavers,* page 102. New York, 1855.

[5] At Covent Garden in London, Sir Michael Costa used to add trombones, tuba, and bass-drum and cymbals in the stretto of the first finale; and doubling the solo voices with a chorus in some portions of this same finale is customary everywhere, save at one theater in Germany.

ence, never be given a moment's breathing-time. Only at the little Residenztheater in Munich is *Don Giovanni* so given nowadays, with all the librettist's and composer's intentions scrupulously carried out —only, what must the singing be?

In *Don Giovanni* Mozart's power of character-drawing shows itself in all its glory. If, in *Figaro,* he has idealized some of the characters out of all semblance to their original selves, in *Don Giovanni* this idealizing process has been carried on on lines exactly parallel with the original bent of the several *dramatis personae,* and serves but more highly to potentize their individuality. Without losing a whit of their identity, without being one jot less sharply individualized, they rise to the stature of universal and eternal types.

To take but one example from out of several, think what it means for a composer to reflect the whole of so profoundly and eternally significant a character as Don Juan—to the very heart of his heart, and to the marrow of his bones—in that elusive mirror we call Music! And this, too, in the jaunty, lightly-tripping dialect of *opera buffa!* This miracle Mozart works through nearly two long acts; then, with sudden flight, he soars up to the loftiest sublime of awful grandeur when, wrong and retribution having met face to face to try conclusions with each other, his hero, long the incarnation of tragedy to fellow-mortals, has at last become tragic to himself.

In this second finale Mozart shows whither his genius could lead him on an emergency; here he suddenly discards his familiar methods and instinctively takes—to be sure, in his own way and style— to the Wagner method. One foot thrust over the wall of the Future into the midst of Beethoven's *Eroica,* is it? Aye, and more than that, into the midst of the Wagnerian Music-Drama.

So far did Mozart bring it in Opera; with a mighty outstretch of his arms, he clasped hands with Handel and Wagner. But, save for the richness of the legacy he left the world, he really affected the history of Opera not a whit. After his death, the opera-writing world went its own way, as if he had not been. After 1787, the year of *Don Giovanni,* nothing so essentially "modern" in conception and style as the statue-scene made its appearance on the lyric stage until 1865, the year of Wagner's *Tristan und Isolde.*

W. F. A.

Let us see how Mozart conceived an opera.

To begin with, he was purely and simply a musician. There is very little trace of literary education or taste in him, such as we find in Beethoven, who taught himself, and did it well. One cannot say Mozart was more of a musician than anything else, for he was really nothing but a musician. He did not long trouble his head about the difficult question of the association of poetry and music in drama. He quickly decided that where music was there could be no rival.

"In an opera, it is absolutely imperative that poetry should be the obedient daughter of music." (October 13, 1781.)

Later he says:

"Music reigns like a king, and the rest is of no account."

But that does not mean Mozart was not interested in his libretto and that music was such a pleasure to him that the poem was only a pretext for the music. Quite the contrary: Mozart was convinced that opera should truthfully express characters and feelings; but he thought that it was the musician's duty to achieve this, and not the poet's. That was because he was more of a musician than a poet, because his genius made him jealous of sharing his work with another artist.

"I cannot express either my feelings or my thoughts in verse, for I am neither a poet nor a painter. But I can do this with sounds, for I am a musician." (November 8, 1777.)

Poetry to Mozart simply furnished "a well-made plan," dramatic situations, "obedient" words, and words written expressly for music. The rest was the composer's affair, and he, according to Mozart, had at his disposal an utterance as exact as poetry and one that was quite as profound in its own way.

When Mozart wrote an opera his intentions were quite clear. He took the trouble to annotate several passages in *Idomeneo* and *Die Entführung aus dem Serail;* and his intelligent care for psychological analysis is clearly shown:

"As Osmin's anger steadily increases and the audience imagines that the air is nearly ended, the allegro assai with its different time and different style should make a good effect; for a man carried away by such violent rage knows no longer what he is about and is bereft of his right senses; so the music should also seem to be beside itself." (September 26, 1781.)

Referring to the air, "O wie ängstlich," in the same opera, Mozart says:

"The beating of the heart is announced beforehand by octaves on the violins. The trembling irresolution and anguish of heart is expressed by a crescendo, and whisperings and sighs are given out by muted first violins and a flute in unison." (September 26, 1781.)

Where will such seeking for truth of expression stop? Will it ever stop? Will music be always like anguish and beating of the heart? Yes, so long as this emotion is harmonious.

Because he was altogether a musician, Mozart did not allow poetry to make demands upon his music; and he would even force a dramatic situation to adapt itself to his music when there was any sign that it would overstep the limits of what he considered good taste.

"Passions, whether violent or not, should never be expressed when they reach an unpleasant stage; and music, even in the most terrible situations, should never offend the ear, but should charm it and always remain music." (September 26, 1781.)

Thus music is a painting of life, but of a refined sort of life. And melodies, though they are the reflection of the spirit, must charm the spirit without wounding the flesh or "offending the ear." So, according to Mozart, music is the harmonious expression of life.

This is not only true of Mozart's operas but of all his work. His music, whatever it may seem to do, is addressed not to the intellect but to the heart and always expresses feeling or passion.

What is most remarkable is that the feelings that Mozart depicts are often not his but those of people he observes. One could hardly believe this, but he says so himself in one of his letters:

"I wished to compose an andante in accordance with Mlle. Rose's character. And it is quite true to say that as Mlle. Cannabich is, so is the andante." (December 6, 1777.)

Mozart's dramatic spirit is so strong that it appears even in works least suited to its expression—in works into which the musician has put most of himself and his dreams.

His gifts shine brightest in his dramatic works; and he seemed to feel this, for his letters tell us of his preference for dramatic composition:

"Simply to hear anyone speak of an opera, or to be in the theater, or to hear singing is enough to make me beside myself!" (October 11, 1777.)

"I have a tremendous desire to write an opera." (*Ibid.*)

"I am jealous of anyone who writes an opera. Tears come to my eyes when I hear an operatic air. . . . My one idea is to write operas." (February 2 and 7, 1778.)

"Opera to me comes before everything else." (August 17, 1782.)

R. R.

Idomeneo, Rè di Creta

[IDOMENEUS, KING OF CRETE]

Opera in three acts.
  Book by Abbé Varesco, after a French opera by Campra and Danchet.
  First performance: Munich, January 29, 1781.

CHARACTERS

Idomeneo, King of Crete, TENOR
Idamante, his son, SOPRANO
Ilia, a Trojan Princess, SOPRANO
Electra, a Greek Princess, SOPRANO
Arbace, confidant of Idomeneo, TENOR
High Priest of Neptune, TENOR
Voice of Neptune, BASS
People of Crete, Trojan Prisoners, Sailors, Soldiers, Priests of Neptune, Dancers
      The action takes place on the island of Crete

THE BACKGROUND

MOZART LEFT Paris in September, 1778, and returned home by way of Mannheim as before. The attraction at Mannheim was, of course, the Weber family; Mozart had fallen violently in love with Aloysia, the eldest daughter, and hoped that the time had now come to make her his wife. But it was a different Mannheim to which he returned in 1778; the electoral court had been transferred to Munich, and with the court went most of the musicians and actors, including the Webers. He found an excuse for going to Munich in January, 1779, and presented Aloysia with the finest of all arias that he wrote for her

—"Popoli di Tessaglia"; but she had changed her mind and would have none of him, although she kept the song and was often associated with him musically in later years. It was a very discontented Mozart that settled down again to the drudgery of a cathedral organist at Salzburg. He hated the Archbishop, he hated the Salzburgers generally, and could find pleasure only in the society of his father and sister, though we may be sure that Leopold got on his nerves fairly often in spite of all his affection. The chance of writing a serious opera seemed further off than ever. The only break in the monotony of Salzburg life was the visit of Schikaneder's theatrical company, which performed Gebler's *Thamos, König in Ägypten*. Mozart took up the music which he had written for Gebler in 1773 and recast it with additions. The principal interest of *Thamos* for us is its connexion with *Die Zauberflöte,* and we must leave to later the story of Mozart's friendship with Schikaneder and his interest in Egyptian mysteries. *Thamos* was not a success. Mozart evidently set some value on the music, for he mentions it again in a letter to his father from Vienna in 1783: "I am very sorry that I shall not be able to make use of the music to *Thamos*. The piece has a bad reputation, since it did not please and is not performed any more. It could only be performed for the sake of the music, and that is hardly likely—it is a pity indeed."

Another dramatic work is an unfinished German opera which appears to have been begun with a view to performance in Salzburg. The libretto was by the Mozarts' old friend Schachtner, to whom posterity is indebted for a good many reminiscences of Wolfgang's earliest childhood. This libretto has for the most part disappeared, and not even the title of it is known. The music has been published under the name of the heroine, *Zaide*. Nothing is known about the circumstances under which it was written, but since it makes no great demand on either singers or orchestra, we may well suppose that Mozart, driven to desperation by the dreariness of life at Salzburg, planned an attempt at organizing some sort of operatic performance with such modest forces as he could raise among his personal friends. The composition was probably interrupted by the invitation which he received in the sumer of 1780 to write a serious opera for Munich.

Here at last, it seemed, was Mozart's great opportunity. The libretto was to be written by the Abbé G. B. Varesco, chaplain to the Archbishop of Salzburg, so that composer and poet might work together with greater facility. Unfortunately, the Archbishop's chaplain had no sense whatever of the stage. Mozart, as usual, left the greater part of the opera to be composed during the last few weeks of rehearsal, and then wrote from Munich to say that various scenes must be altered. Varesco was highly indignant at this mutilation of his masterpiece and insisted that if Mozart cut down his verses his drama should at least appear complete in print.

The general scheme of *Idomeneo, Rè di Creta,* modelled on a French libretto by A. Danchet, set to music by Campra in 1712, might have provided excellent opportunities for a poet who understood the requirements of the theatre. Varesco had no doubt read his Metastasio, but he must have read him with the eyes of a sermon-writer, not those of a dramatist. Metastasio understood better than anyone that an opera libretto, even in the grand manner, must be concise and direct. Varesco is verbose and sententious; he never seems to have imagined for a moment what the effect of his lines would be when set to music and presented on the stage. He seems also to have been a very difficult and disagreeable person to deal with. Wolfgang never corresponded with him directly, but made use of his father as an intermediary; we gather from Leopold's letters that the reverend gentleman not only objected very much to making alterations, but expected to be paid extra for them, like a printer.

There were further difficulties with the singers. The title-part was taken by the tenor Raaff, an excellent singer but no actor; moreover, he was at that time a man of sixty-five. As might be expected, he was only too glad to give Mozart the benefit of his long experience of the stage—in other words, to obstruct the young composer as much as possible whenever his genius led him into unexpected paths of originality. Panzacchi, the other tenor, was a decidedly good actor with some skill in singing, but as he too was of senior standing he had to be given more opportunities for display than were appropriate to the part of a mere confidant. The worst stumbling-block was Dal Prato, who took the youthful part of Idamante. "My *molto amato castrato* Dal Prato," as Mozart called him, could have given no trouble from being too old and experienced, for he was a mere boy and had never been on the stage before. His voice was either badly trained or not trained at all, and he had no intelligence for music or for anything else. Mozart seems to have shown endless patience in teaching him, and we gather from his letters that he could suffer stupidity of this kind better than the conceit of those who professed to be connoisseurs. Luckily, the female parts were taken by Dorothea and Elisabeth Wendling, who were capable singers and gave the composer no trouble. . . .

Mozart's letters to his father show that he at any rate had a thorough sense of the stage. Any musician might have complained when the poet put "asides" into arias or made the sense of one line run over into the next—faults more unpardonable in those days than now, since the normal structure of the eighteenth-century aria would be destroyed by irregular verse construction, and an "aside," if occurring in an aria, might have to be repeated in an inconvenient and undramatic way. But Mozart saw more essential things than these. His technical ingenuity might easily have overcome the problems of musical structure, though probably his elderly and experienced singers would have resented anything that they had not been accustomed to for the last forty years; but Varesco's dramatic blunders had to be corrected without any attempt at compromise. Varesco let Idomeneo make his first entrance scrambling up the rocks at the back of the stage after the shipwreck; Mozart and Quaglio, the scene-painter, saw that this was undignified and ineffective, and caused him to enter with some of his followers, whom he dismisses a few lines later, in order to be alone when he meets his son. This next scene had to be very much cut down (and for modern performance it needs still further cutting), since both Raaff and Dal Prato were such bad actors as to make the long dialogue in *recitativo secco* utterly intolerable. The same applied to the dialogue between Idomeneo and the confidant Arbace at the beginning of the second act. For the chorus "Placido è il mar" Varesco had written several stanzas; Mozart reduced them to one. Between the storm chorus and the final chorus of this act he had put in an aria for Idomeneo; Mozart saw that this would destroy the whole dramatic effect and insisted on having only a short recitative. The same thing had to be done in the third act; Varesco expected that Ilia and Idamante should sing a formal duet when on the point of being sacrificed. Had Raaff's advice been followed, we should have lost the most beautiful number in the whole opera, the quartet in Act III; the worthy tenor considered that its place would be much more effectively filled by an aria for himself. It becomes evident that Varesco's plan was to follow the formal system of Apostolo Zeno and Metastasio—to divide the libretto into what Continental poets call "scenes" and end each "scene" with an aria on which the singer made an exit. This was really a very practical arrangement, because it allowed the audience to applaud as much as they liked without appreciably holding up the progress of the drama. Mozart evidently saw the stage from the standpoint of Gluck and the French librettists. The Italian *opera seria* generally made little or no use of the chorus; for the French the chorus was an indispensable factor in serious opera, and its value was that it allowed the composer to build up a massive climax of sound towards the end of an act. The Italian opera never attempted this; at the very end there is what is marked *coro* in the score (Handel's operas show easily accessible examples), but *coro* in most cases means no more than the principal singers joining for a short movement in block harmony. The elaborate finale which we find in such operas as *Le Nozze di Figaro* and *Don Giovanni* is ultimately derived, not from serious opera, Italian or French, but from Italian comic opera; it begins with the quarrelling scenes for two characters such as we find in the comic episodes of Alessandro Scarlatti's operas, and gradually increases the number of its interlocutors until there may be six or seven of them, with a corresponding increase in length. But it should be noted that this sort of comic finale is practically never choral, any more than it is in the majority of Handel's operas; the dramatic chorus is a purely French invention.[1] Varesco had evidently studied his Greek plays as well as his more recent models; his "dramatic irony" and his "recognition scene" are only too tedious a homage to the classics. But, like the very earliest Italian librettists, he followed classical tradition in assigning a really important dramatic part to the chorus, and Mozart was quick to take advantage of it.

It seems to have been Mozart's invariable practice—probably it was the regular practice of all operatic composers in those days—to com-

---

[1] I am speaking here of opera in the eighteenth century; the functions of the chorus in French, Italian, and English opera of the seventeenth are too complicated a matter to summarize shortly in this place.

pose about half of an opera on receipt of the libretto and to postpone composing the rest until rehearsals had already begun. Indeed, librettists were often dilatory and did not always give their composers a complete book of words at once. Singers, as all composers must have known by sad experience, were more likely to be troublesome than not, and Mozart spent much of his time in accommodating his operas to suit their requirements. The result of this system is that when we come to put Mozart's operas on the modern stage we find that in every one of them the later acts show evidence of alteration and patching, and the modern producer is confronted by the most curious problems in attempting to reduce them to some sort of dramatic unity and continuity. It was the third act of *Idomeneo* that gave Mozart the most trouble. Varesco seems to have been very vague about the changes of scene required. According to the score, there are three separate scenes: the royal garden, for the scene between Ilia and Idamante, the great quartet, and Arbace's soliloquy; then the exterior of the royal palace, for the High Priest's address and the chorus of Cretans; lastly, the exterior of the temple of Neptune, which apparently serves for the interrupted sacrifice, the outburst of Electra (although she ought to have the whole stage to herself) and the abdication of Idomeneo. From Mozart's letters it would appear that there was actually no change of scene at all at the first performance. Arbace sang his aria and in accordance with Italian operatic etiquette left the stage at the end of it; but Varesco directed him to be on the stage with Idomeneo at the beginning of the High Priest's address. "How can he be there again at once?" asks Mozart. "Luckily he can stay away altogether" (he has nothing to say in this scene) "but in order to be on the safe side I have written a rather longer introduction to the High Priest's recitative." The next scene presented a similar difficulty. "After the chorus of mourning, the King, the whole people, and everybody all go away, and in the following scene stands the direction, 'Idomeneo on his knees in the temple.' That cannot possibly be so; he must come with a complete train; so then there must of necessity be a march there, and I have written a quite simple march for strings and two oboes which is played *mezza voce* while the King comes in and the priests prepare the things for the sacrifice; then the King kneels down and begins his prayer." It must be remembered that in *opera seria* great personages were always expected to be accompanied by considerable trains of supers, and the huge size of Italian theatres required a good deal in the way of processions and so forth to fill the stage.

As regards change of scenery, scenes in those days could be changed very quickly and in view of the audience by the system of wings and a backcloth. The front curtain did not fall; it is difficult to establish the exact date at which the main curtain first fell at the end of each act of an opera. It is probable that in *Idomeneo* the main curtain never fell at all until the very end of the opera, judging by what happens on the stage; on the other hand, it seems certain that the act drop must undoubtedly have fallen at the ends of the acts in *Le Nozze di Figaro* and *Don Giovanni,* although one can point to comic operas by Leo and Pergolesi (about 1730–40) in which the elaborate finales are ingeniously planned so as to get the characters gradually *off* the stage (as well as *on*) leaving the chief *basso buffo,* generally the angry old man, to make his effective exit by himself. The wings were shifted by a mechanism under the stage which is still to be seen in a few old German theatres;[2] with one movement of a lever all the wings receded and another set were pushed forward; the backcloth would be drawn up on a roller at the bottom—it was not until about 1800 or later that backcloths could be lifted completely out of sight without rolling. On the English stage there was often no backcloth, but a pair of wide flats joining (or sometimes not joining properly) in the middle. This system of quickly shifting wings no doubt explains the changes of scene in the third act of this opera, changes which become much more difficult under modern conditions.

Idomeneo owes both its failings and its merits to the fact that it is a mixture of two types of opera, Italian and French. Varesco took a French libretto as his foundation and, probably without considering dramatic effects at all, turned it into as close an imitation of Metastasio as his dull brain was capable of conceiving. Mozart in setting it to music was French by deliberate intention, but Italian by natural instinct. Modern audiences, acquainted to some extent with the works of Gluck, are naturally moved most by the French moments of the opera—that is, by the great choruses, the instrumental marches and interludes, and the noble accompanied recitatives, which are closely

---

[2] It is—or was recently—in working order at Ludwigsburg near Stuttgart.

modelled on those of *Alceste*. We require a greater effort to focus our minds on the beauties of the Italian scenes.

THE RECITATIVE

A modern audience has a horror of *recitativo secco,* and well it may, if it knows it only as it is delivered by our orthodox oratorio singers. It is an exclusively Italian method of treating words. Purcell's dramatic recitatives, whether accompanied or not, are always strictly rhythmical and their rhythm is determined more by the normal rhythms of music than by those of English prose or blank verse. Moreover, the varying quantity of English syllables requires the composer to use a variety of time-values, crotchets and semiquavers as well as quavers, whereas Italian recitative seldom employs any unit except the quaver. French recitative, depending on the natural rhythms of French verse, utilizes the three time-values in even more generous mixture than English, and with a style of declamation that is generally more excitable than our own. Italian keeps to the quaver unit, although Italian verse is theoretically more varied in quantity than French; in practice it means that the singer is allowed a great deal more rhythmical latitude. Italian critics always said that French opera consisted entirely of recitative, and it is a fact that the French *air* approximates closely to recitative while the recitative itself tends to approximate to the inflections and rhythms of the *air*. In Italian the contrast was extreme, and it was only in rare moments of accompanied recitative that the Italians approached an *arioso*. As the Italian arias were generally the expression of one single emotion, all the dramatic element, by which I mean the interaction of one character with another, to say nothing of the indispensable moments in which mere information has to be given to the audience, had to be expressed in *recitativo secco;* the more there was of these elements, the more recitative there had to be, and the more necessity there was for getting through it quickly. The Italian recitative, accompanied only by chords on the harpsichord, accomplishes this admirably, provided that the singers deliver it at the normal pace of speech.

The ordinary Englishman of to-day has probably begun his operatic education either with isolated songs from various operas, perhaps heard on gramophone records, or with musical comedies and light operas in which the business of the play, sentimental perhaps, but certainly not poetical, is carried on in spoken dialogue. He probably associates sung recitative exclusively with oratorio. But we must remember that opera originally began with recitative alone; recitative was the main, indeed the only, reason for its creation, and as late as the days of Pepys there was in England a positive craze for "recitative musick." This accounts at once for the survival of recitative in Italy down to our own day; it had become so established a convention that no Italian could conceive of spoken dialogue in opera, however closely the declamation of comic recitative must have approximated to it.[3]

Recitative of any kind, and *secco* all the more, must inevitably be boring in the extreme to audiences which do not understand Italian. It was often boring to the Italians themselves. Rousseau admits this in his *Dictionnaire de Musique,* although he shows his invariable enthusiasm for everything Italian and his contempt for everything French:

> Démosthène parlant tout le jour ennuieroit à la fin; mais il ne s'ensuivroit pas delà que Démosthène fût un Orateur ennuyeux. Ceux qui disent que les Italiens eux-mêmes trouvent leur *Récitatif* mauvais le disent bien gratuitement; pisqu'au contraire il n'y a point de partie dans la Musique dont les Connoisseurs fassent tant de cas et sur laquelle ils soient aussi difficiles. Il suffit même d'exceller dans cette seule partie, fût-on médiocre dans toutes les autres, pour s'élever chez eux au rang des plus illustres Artistes, et le célèbre *Porpora* ne s'est immortalisé que par-là.

Whether Rousseau was well informed as to the last sentence may be doubted, but apart from this exaggeration he probably spoke the truth for his date (1768). Rousseau divided recitative into three categories—*récitatif* (i.e. *recitativo secco*), *récitatif accompagné,* which is much the same as *secco,* but accompanied by held chords played by

---

[3] In the nineteenth century all German operas, such as *Der Freischütz* or *Fidelio,* had to be provided with sung recitatives in place of spoken dialogue, when performed in Italian, whether at Milan, Paris, or London. For Weber's *Oberon,* composed originally to English words, Benedict wrote Italian recitatives for later revivals at Her Majesty's Opera; but to my astonishment, the Rome Opera revived it in 1938 with spoken dialogue. It was the first time that I ever heard spoken dialogue on the stage of an Italian opera house.

the strings, and *récitatif obligé,* which is his name for the sort of accompanied recitative that was being developed about the middle of
the century.

> C'est celui qui, entremêlé de Ritournelles et de traits de Sym-
> phonie, *oblige* pour ainsi dire le Récitant et l'Orchestre l'un envers
> l'autre, en sorte qu'ils doivent être attentifs et s'attendre mutuel-
> lement. L'Acteur agité, transporté d'une passion qui ne lui permet
> pas de tout dire, s'interrompt, s'arrête, fait des réticences, durant
> lesquelles l'Orchestre parle pour lui; et ces silences, ainsi remplis,
> affectent infiniment plus l'Auditeur que si l'Acteur disoit lui-
> même tout ce qui la musique fait entendre.

This is the definition of a Frenchman with a passion for all Italian
ideas; an Italian perhaps would hardly have admitted that an Italian
could become speechless—or songless—with passion. And accompanied recitative (as we and the Italians called it), in the hands of a
second-rate composer, soon became as dull and conventional as *recitativo secco.* In Germany it led to the practice—momentarily fashionable
in Mozart's days—of what was called *Melodram,* an alternation of
instrumental commentary with spoken recitation. German composers,
perhaps influenced by this, and certainly influenced by their habitual
tendency towards an instrumental rather than vocal outlook on music
in general, were tempted to let the orchestra and singer carry on a
sort of *stichomythia,* monotonous in rhythm and really destructive
of the dramatic effect for which it was intended. We see it in such
composers as Holzbauer, but also in Gluck and occasionally even in
Mozart himself.

The aria is another form which modern audiences, especially those
brought up on Wagner, profess to find undramatic. Yet if they would
confess the truth honestly, it is the arias, or the movements of aria
character, which have secured the immortality of all the favourite
operas. Historians reprint and reprint again the preface to Gluck's
Alceste, but what draws the public to hear *Orfeo* is the agreeable
melody of "Che farò" and the dignified grace of the ballet music.
It is naturally difficult for us to put ourselves back into the days of the
Handelian *da capo* aria, but by the time Mozart was a mature composer the *da capo* aria was completely obsolete. The middle section
of the old ternary aria had been dropped and the first part of it had

been extended into something like what is called sonata-form. That form had become the standard form for practically every kind of music, vocal, dance, or symphonic, apart from the strict fugue, and even fugues were often influenced by sonata-form in their construction. And by the time of Mozart the serious opera, thanks to Gluck, had begun to absorb certain features of the comic opera, the most important of which was the *rondo,* exemplified in "Che farò," with its threefold appearance of the initial simple tune. There is another type which we find in the first air of Orpheus, alternating three repetitions of a simple melody in 3/8 with two intermediate *arioso* sections in 4/4; this is almost a throwback to the refrain-recitative-refrain alternation of the well-known "Lamento" in Monteverdi's *Arianna.* The plain *da capo* form is to be seen both in *Orfeo* (Act III; aria of Eurydice) and even in the famous "Divinités du Styx" of *Alceste* itself.

Still more troublesome to a modern audience are the long instrumental introductions to many of Mozart's arias in his early operas, especially those which make a *concertante* display of individual instruments. One has to admit that Mozart sometimes committed errors of judgement in his desire to please his professional friends. In the operas of Gluck the introductions are often intensely expressive, and still more the little instrumental solos, especially for the oboe, which enter into a sort of dialogue with the singer in certain arias. Mozart is aiming at the same type of expression, but he was a much more accomplished composer for the orchestra than Gluck, even at the age of twenty or less, and he had had far more practice in the composition of symphonies and concertos. This fluency and ease in purely symphonic composition tempts him at once to combine the spontaneous and perhaps even crudely expressive instrumental solos of Gluck with the finished elegance of an instrumental concerto, especially as he was often on terms of personal friendship with the players and took a pleasure in showing them off. Add to that Mozart's incomparable "Mozartian" (there is no other possible epithet) grace of pure melody, and the whole aria, the voice framed in its inseparable orchestral setting, becomes a display of serene and exquisite musical beauty that quite eclipses the human passion which it is primarily intended to express. In his later operas Mozart discarded these *concertante* accompaniments; the only later suggestion of them is in *Die*

Zauberflöte, where the magic flute and the magic bells have to be played visibly by the actors on the stage and are integral features of the drama itself. But other composers, notably Méhul and Cherubini, continued systematically to show off the solo instruments in their operas; we find plenty of examples in Spontini and Meyerbeer, and in Donizetti and early Verdi as well; there was no doubt that audiences enjoyed them, as indeed they do still, if the virtuosity is sufficiently obvious.[4]

Lastly, we must in listening to *Idomeneo* try to forget the hurry of modern existence and surrender ourselves to a sense of leisure such as our ancestors were happily able to enjoy. Even at the first performance *Idomeneo* had to be cut down; but I cannot think that that audience was haunted all through the last act by the fear of missing the last public conveyance to Schwabing or the Isarthal. *Idomeneo,* perhaps better than any other opera, illustrates the fact that the course of an opera is like a stream running for long stretches in a narrow channel, hidden perhaps for moments underground, dashing suddenly over a precipice and at frequent intervals broadening out into a vast and tranquil lake. The forms are various which it presents, as are the types of landscape with which it is associated; nevertheless, broad or narrow, shallow or profound, it is always moving onwards and gathering force until it reaches its ultimate goal.

E. J. D.

"Idomeneo," according to available records, was first heard in America at the Berkshire Festival in Tanglewood, Massachusetts, on August 4, 1947. Thomas Scherman brought it into the repertory of his Little Orchestra Society at Town Hall, New York, on April 24, 1951.

THE STORY

ACT I: Idomeneo, King of Crete, has taken part in the Trojan war, and it is many years since he left home. Amongst the prisoners he has sent home is Ilia, daughter of King Priam, who has fallen in love with Idamante, the son of Idomeneo. The overture immediately establishes

---

[4] For the sake of accuracy, I must not forget the *obbligato* for the *corno di bassetto* in *La Clemenza di Tito.*

the character of an opera whose music, without exception, never relaxes its intense seriousness throughout its length; from it, without the need of external evidence as to the conduct of *opera seria,* we may deduce the dignity and stature of the characters involved. Calmly the drama unfolds. In an aria, "Padre, germani addio," Ilia reveals that her hatred for the conquerors of her country is as nothing to her love for Idamante; he enters at its conclusion and in veiled terms states his love for Ilia, at the same time announcing that, in honour of his father's imminent return to Crete, the Trojan prisoners are to be set free. A chorus of rejoicing at this news precedes the entrance of Arbace to say that Idomeneo's ship has been sunk, and the general consternation is given particular expression by Electra, who fears that his death will remove all obstacles to the marriage of Ilia and Idamante, with whom she is herself in love. Seldom if ever before can passionate fury have been given so illuminating an expression as in her aria. She leaves the stage and, at the end of a chorus of intercession, Idomeneo enters with his followers, whom he dismisses before explaining in an aria the nature of the vow which secured Neptune's intervention in quieting the storm: that he will sacrifice the first living creature he meets in return for deliverance from death. It is, of course, Idamante whom he sees, and their dialogue is made the more poignant because it is some time before Idomeneo recognises his son, whom he has not seen since infancy. In horror, the father orders the son from his presence, and Idamante laments his father's apparent displeasure in an aria "Il padre adorato ritrovo e lo perdo." The act ends with a brilliant march and choral *Ciaconna* in honour of Neptune and the returning Cretans.

ACT II: The King tells his secret to his counsellor Arbace, who advises that Idamante be sent to a distant country: let him, suggests the King, escort Electra back to Greece. The whole scene, which was originally included to provide an aria for the tenor Panzacchi, who created the role of Arbace, is usually omitted in modern performance, the act thus beginning with the scene between Idomeneo and Ilia whose aria "Se il padre perdei" is touchingly beautiful. Idomeneo understands that his vow now involves not only disaster for himself and Idamante but for Ilia as well, but he faces the tragedy with courage and dignity in his great aria "Fuor del mar ho un mar in seno." This was written as a show piece for Raaff, the sixty-five-year-old

Leopold Mozart, from the title page of his *Violin-School* (1756), engraved by J. A. Fridrich. In the Carolino-Augusteum State Museum, Salzburg.

Anna Maria Mozart in 1777,
by J. J. Langenhöffel.

Constanze Weber Mozart in 1782/83, lithograph after a painting by Joseph Lange. In the Carolino-Augusteum State Museum, Salzburg.

Das Bäsle, Cousin Maria Anna Thekla Mozart in 1778, from an unsigned pencil drawing in the Mozarteum, Salzburg.

tenor who created the title role in Munich; whatever may be thought about his musical taste (he wanted an aria for himself substituted for the Act III quartet), his technique must have been very considerable indeed. As Professor Dent says: *"Coloratura* for men has gone out of fashion, thanks to Wagner, and, thanks to the late Madame Patti, coloratura for women has become associated with the frail type of heroine rather than the heroic. In the eighteenth century and especially in the early half of it, the grand period of *opera seria,* coloratura was almost invariably heroic in character. . . . Donizetti's Lucia is paired off with a flute. Handel's heroes compete with a trumpet." If the reader doubts whether any twentieth-century singer can overcome the difficulties of such music, I would refer him to a record made by Hermann Jadlowker about the time of the 1914–1918 war, in which this aria is sung with extraordinary fluency.

A beautiful, lyrical aria for Electra, whom the prospect of requited love has turned into a happy woman, leads into a march, and thence to the famous barcarolle chorus of embarcation, "Placido è il mar, andiamo." Idamante and Electra take leave of Idomeneo in a superb trio "Pria di partir" but the music quickens and a storm breaks over the harbour heralding Neptune's vengeance at this attempt to evade the consequences of the vow made to him. Idomeneo admits his guilt but accuses the god of injustice, and the act ends as the crowd disperses in terror.

ACT III: Ilia can think only of her love for Idamante, and her expression of it in her soliloquy "Zefiretti lusinghieri" is one of the most perfect moments of the opera. To her comes Idamante; he is going out to fight the monster Neptune has sent to plague the island, and he may not return. Involuntarily, she confesses her love, which leads to a duet. Idomeneo and Electra interrupt the lovers. Idomeneo still cannot bring himself to explain the exact cause of the disaster which is overtaking them all, and Idamante sadly takes his farewell in the noble quartet "Andrò ramingo e solo." Einstein calls it "the first really great ensemble in the history of the *opera seria"* and Professor Dent does not try to disguise his enthusiasm for it when he describes it as "perhaps the most beautiful ensemble ever composed for the stage." In truth, one has no cause to complain that either is exaggerating; it shows Mozart at his noblest and most expressive, and is the moment in the opera when the spirit of tragedy most completely dominates the music. An elaborate recitative and aria for Arbace, which is found here in the score, is usually omitted in performance, and the scene customarily and appropriately ends with the quartet.

After an introduction, the High Priest exhorts the King to confess his sin to Neptune, and the people are duly horrified to hear that the sacrifice of Idamante is the price they and he will have to pay for deliverance from the god's displeasure. The people are gathered in the Temple of Neptune to witness the sacrifice, the priests enter to a march, and Idomeneo begins the ceremony with a solemn prayer which is answered by the priests. A shout of triumph is heard outside and Arbace announces that Idamante has met the monster in combat and killed it. However, a moment later Idamante, who by now knows the story of his father's vow, enters and offers himself for sacrifice, and Idomeneo cannot but accept him. The ceremony is about to reach its climax when Ilia interrupts and demands to be sacrificed in Idamante's place. The whole situation is resolved by an oracular pronouncement from Neptune, to the effect that the crime can be expiated, the vow fulfilled, if Idomeneo will renounce the throne in favour of his son. In the general rejoicing, only Electra is left with her worst fears realised; in the most furious of her violent utterances, she gives vent to her despair and rushes from the stage, or, as some versions have it, falls dead or commits suicide.

The atmosphere changes to one of peace and fulfilment as Idomeneo in a last recitative and aria, "Torna la pace al core," presents Idamante to the people as their new ruler, and takes his farewell of them. At the first performance, this aria had to be cut, much apparently to Mozart's regret, as anyone who hears it nowadays will readily understand. The opera ends with the people celebrating the accession of Idamante in dance and chorus.

P. N. (2)

Die Entführung aus dem Serail

[The Abduction from the Seraglio]

Comic song-play (singspiel) in three acts.
Book by Gottlob Stephanie, after the play by Christoph Friedrich Bretzner.
First performance: National Theatre, Vienna, July 12, 1782.

CHARACTERS

Selim, Pasha, SPEAKING PART

Constanza (or *Constanze*), beloved of Belmonte, SOPRANO

Blonda (or *Blondchen*), Constanza's maid and beloved of Pedrillo, SOPRANO

Belmonte, a Spanish nobleman, TENOR

Pedrillo, Belmonte's servant, TENOR

Osmin, overseer of the Pasha's country place, BASS

A Mute

Janissaries, Slaves, Guards

The action takes place in Turkey in the sixteenth century

THE BACKGROUND

DURING THE seventeenth and eighteenth centuries the character of the Turk was quite popular in all of Europe. In Vienna little children were frightened by the word "Turk." Persons dressed as Turks sold exotic wares. From the seventeenth century onward, principally after the second siege of Vienna by the Turks in 1687, there was in Vienna a real Turkomania. There was a *Türkencafé,* Turkish candies were sold, and Turkish instruments were introduced into military music. The Turk was for a long time a popular figure at masked balls and *Wirtschaften,* the ball entertainments of the Baroque age. The old *Moresca,* a Moorish dance which was performed with bells worn on the feet and wild gestures, was connected not only with the Moors and the Arabs, but also with the Turks.

In fact, the music of the *Moresca* shows a certain similarity to Turkish music as it has been known in Europe since the seventeenth century. Sharply dotted rhythms and an accompaniment of castanets, cymbals, or bells were typical of the *Moresca,* just as the great drum, cymbals, triangles, and the Turkish crescent were characteristics of the janissary music, played by the bodyguards of the Turkish sultans.

During the Turkish wars in Europe this music had become familiar and left traces not only in the military music of the different nations of Europe, but also in numerous compositions of the classical masters.

Italian opera felt the Turkish imprint from the days of the Venetian School. Cara Mustapha was a popular subject that appeared also in Hamburg in 1682 in an opera of the same name. In this old opera, just as in the *Seraglio,* the Turk is opposed by two Spanish captives, Don Gasparo and Donna Manuela. Later Paisiello in his *Arabo cortese* and *Dardane,* Grétry in his *Caravane du Caire,* Monsigny in his fantastic opera *Isle sonnanate,* used the Turkish milieu. Gluck in his *Rencontre imprévue* treated the material in a manner similar to that in the *Seraglio* in 1764. As is well known, the German text of Mozart's opera is derived from that of the Leipsig merchant Christoph Fr. Bretzner who in 1781 wrote a comedy with the following title: *Belmont und Konstanze oder die Entführung aus dem Serail.* The musical comedy was not set to music by Mozart in its original version, but in an adaptation of the Viennese writer and playwright Stephanie. The arrangement caused Herr Bretzner to write angrily in the *Leipziger Zeitung* in 1782:

> A certain person named Mozart has had the impudence in Vienna to misuse my drama *Belmont und Konstanze* for the text of an opera. I hereby protest solemnly against this invasion of my rights and reserve the right to further action.
>
> CHRISTOPH FRIEDRICH BRETZNER,
> composer of *A Little Tipsy*.

Poor Bretzner! He scarcely imagined that his name would be handed down to posterity not by his "Little Tipsy" but by the impudent misuse of that certain Mozart.

But back to our theme. There was a whole series of Turkish operas in which the subject was handled in almost the same way as in Bretzner's work. The Italian poet Martinelli wrote a semi-serious opera *La schiava liberata* which was composed in 1768 by Jarnelli, and by Josef Schuster in 1777 for Dresden. In this work the two European women are not freed by intrigue and force, but by peaceful arbitration. In Martinelli's version we find two characters, Soliman and Selim, father and son, who in Mozart's opera are combined into one, as Selim, who has Soliman's majesty and dignity and also the hopeless love and magnanimity of Martinelli's Selim.

Bretzner probably saw Schuster's opera in Dresden. Whether he, also, saw the English Turkish plays *The Sultan or a Peep into the Seraglio* by I. Bickerstaffe and *The Captive* (1769) is doubtful. In the English ballad-opera, similar themes were treated. In 1740 *The Generous Freemason* demonstrates the same material, utilized on a Masonic background. Here, too, the generous and noble Turkish prince, who turns out to be a Freemason, is introduced. Presumably Bretzner did not know the English works, but did know *Adelheid von Veltheim* by Grossmann, in which an oriental story of abduction is also treated.

In the opera of the seventeenth century and the first half of the eighteenth century the Turk was for the most part a cruel and unsympathetic fellow, since the Turks and Venetians were bitter enemies, who fought each other up and down the whole Mediterranean. So it happens that the comic opera of all countries presents the Turks as blood-dripping Pashas, thorough scoundrels, stupidly arrogant Kadis, and lascivious harem guards. Osmin belongs to the genus of malicious but easily duped guards, Monostatos in *The Magic Flute* to the lascivious kind. In the course of the eighteenth century, however, the picture of the Turk changes. Above all, this is true of the Pasha, who becomes more and more noble and generous. The unsympathetic Turk turns into a goodhumored noble and aristocratic oriental. Presumably this change went hand in hand with the disappearance of Turkish political power and the fact that the Sublime Porte was forced to live in harmony with the European powers. Perhaps the ideas of Jean-Jacques Rousseau were also partly responsible in that it was felt that the orientals, untouched by the decadent European culture, would be a model for European peoples. Travelers' reports, which often spoke of the sultans in complimentary words, had a definite effect upon the conception of what was Turkish. . . .

In this connection I should like to refer to a figure in the Vienna of Mozart's time, a figure mentioned in the literature of the period again and again. That was Angelo Soliman, a Negro, born in Somaliland or Abyssinia, who had come as a young man to Sicily, had been "bought" by Prince Lobkowitz, and then in Vienna entered the service of Prince Wenzel Liechtenstein. He was a member of the Masonic Lodge *Zur Wahren Eintracht* in which only the elite of the intellectual and social world of Vienna was received. In my book *Mozart und die Königliche Kunst* I have pointed out that Mozart and Angelo Soliman associated together in the lodge, and that in the protocols we often find Angelo's name directly under that of Mozart. Presumably the two entered the lodge arm in arm and there is no doubt that they were close friends. Karoline Pichler, the Viennese writer of memoirs, to whom we owe Angelo's biography, relates how the noble Moor delighted in singing the songs which he had heard in his youth. Angelo was Catholic, but had in his youth been reared as a Mohammedan. I conjecture that even if he didn't know Turkish songs, he at least sang the songs of the Near East, and that Mozart heard such music from him.

Mozart, of course, used oriental coloring in other works. Not only in *Zaide* and *The Magic Flute,* but also in the "Alla Turca" of his A Major sonata, and in the last phrase of his A Major violin concerto in a ballet fragment. There is room for believing that Gluck's *Pilgrime von Mekka* with its oriental coloring had had its influence on him. But back to the *Seraglio.*

Already in the Overture, which from the eighth bar onward has a decided janissary character, we feel that we are in the Orient, the land of contrasting colors and sensual fervor. The minor passages, above all the long statement expressing in minor the sadness and longing of the harem women languishing in their prison, give oriental flavor. The melody is then taken over in Belmonte's aria in C major, a mood in the more familiar manner of the West and expressing the optimism of the lovers. Here Mozart characterizes Orient and Occident through minor and major.

Osmin's song as he picks figs is likewise in the minor. Slowly the melody moves on, indicating the phlegmatic character of Osmin, but the upswing of the "Trallalera" excellently characterizes the fanatical tyrant. Likewise the famous "Drum beim Barte des Propheten" has an oriental character, as does, of course, the chorus of Janissaries, which, according to Mozart himself, was everything one can desire for a janissary chorus and "short and merry and written entirely for the Viennese." But with this short description the *orientalia* of this master opera of Mozart have not been exhausted. One can say that every note in some way or other partakes of the flavor of the Orient. This, of course, is not to mean that Mozart deliberately composed oriental sounding phrases, but during the composition of his opera he lived in such a kind of oriental state of imagination that the fairy-tale coloring of the East impregnated the score.

P. N. (2)

Opera-lovers have every reason to thank the shade of Leopold Mozart, father of the immortal Wolfgang, that the old gentleman did not venture to leave his home in Salzburg to attend the première of *The Abduction from the Seraglio* in Vienna. The composer was thus obliged to write his father full accounts of the various stages of the work in progress, a precious heritage for future generations.

The first of Mozart's letters to Leopold on the subject dates from August, 1781, when he first came in contact with the subject of the article. "The day before yesterday," he wrote, "Stephanie Junior gave me a libretto to compose. I must confess that, however badly he may treat other people, about which I know nothing, he is an excellent friend to me. The libretto is quite good. The subject is Turkish and the title is 'Belmonte und Konstanze,' or 'Die Verführung aus dem Serail.' For the Overture, the Chorus in Act I and the final chorus I will write Turkish music. Mlle. Cavalieri, Mlle. Tieber, Mr. Fischer, Mr. Adamberger, Mr. Dauer, and Mr. Walter are to sing in it. I am so delighted at having to compose this opera that I have already finished Cavalieri's first aria, Adamberger's and the trio which closes Act I. The time is short, it is true, for it is to be performed in the middle of September, but the circumstances connected with the date of the performance, and all my other prospects, generally excite me to such a degree that I rush to my desk with the greatest eagerness and remain seated there with the greatest delight. The Grand Duke of Russia is coming here, and that is why Stephanie entreated me, if possible, to compose the opera in this short space of time."

A week later, Mozart continued his fervent correspondence.

I must write in haste [he told his father], for I have only this very instant finished the Janissary Chorus and it is past twelve o'clock and I have promised to drive out with the Aurnhammers and Mlle. Cavalieri to Mingendorf near Laxenberg where the camp is. Adamberger, Mlle. Cavalieri, and Fischer are exceedingly pleased with their arias. I lunched yesterday with the Countess Thun and am to do so tomorrow. I played what I have finished composing to her and she told me afterwards that she would venture her life that what I have written so far cannot fail to please. But in this matter I pay no attention whatever to anybody's praise or blame, that is until people will have heard the work as a whole. I simply follow my own feelings. All the same you may judge from this how pleased she must have been to express herself so emphatically.

By September Mozart was busied in a hundred fascinating details.

As the original libretto began with a monologue [he wrote his father on the 26th] I asked Herr Stephanie to make a little arietta out of it, and then to put in a duet instead of making the two chatter together after Osmin's short song . . . in the original text Osmin has nothing else to sing except the trio and the finale, so that he will be given an aria in Act I and another in Act II. Osmin's rage becomes comical with its accompaniment of Turkish music. In working out this aria I have occasionally given full scope to Fischer's deep notes. The passage, "Drum beim Barte des Propheten" [by the beard of Allah's prophet] is included in the same tempo, but with quick notes; but as Osmin's rage gradually increases, the *Allegro Assai* comes just when the aria seems to be at an end. This is in a totally different measure and in a different key, which is bound to be very effective.

For just as a man in such a towering rage forgets himself, so must the music too forget itself. But as passions, whether violent or not, must never be expressed in such a way as to excite disgust, and as music, even in the most terrible situations, must never offend the ear, but please the hearer, or in other words, must never cease to be music, so I have gone from F, the original key of the aria, not into a remote key, but into a related one, though not into its most clearly related one, D minor, but into the more distant A minor.

Let me now turn to Belmonte's aria in A major, "O wie ängstlich, o wie feurig." Would you like to know how I have expressed it? And even indicated the throbbing of his heart? By the two violins playing octaves . . . you feel the trembling, the faltering, you see how his throbbing heart begins to swell: this I have expressed by a Crescendo. You hear the whispering and the sighing, which I have indicated by the first violins and the mutes playing in unison.

The Janissary Chorus . . . can be described as lively, short and written to please the Viennese. I have sacrificed Constanza's aria a little to the flexible throat of Mlle. Cavalieri.

Now for the Trio at the close of the first act, it opens quite abruptly, and because the words lend themselves to it, I have made it a fairly respectable piece of three-part writing. Then the major key begins at once pianissimo—it must go very quickly—and I wind up with a great deal of noise, which is always appropriate at the end of an act.[1]

All sorts of procrastinations and intrigues deferred the day of performance again and again, until at last Joseph II commanded that it should be fixed for 16th July, 1782. The house was crammed on this first night, and in spite of an opposing faction that did its best to ruin the composer's chances, the opera was received with rapture. There was frantic applause after every number and many pieces had to be repeated. The music was thought very novel and daring, particularly by the emperor, who prided himself on his solidly conservative tastes and told Mozart that the score was too good for Viennese ears and contained too many notes; to which the composer politely but firmly replied that he had put in exactly as many as were required. The opera was repeated many times during the season and always filled the house.

Although the German *Singspiel* that had been established in 1778 was of a comparatively low and light type, the chief singers engaged for it were artists of distinction, and it so happened that Mozart obtained the services of the best of them. Catharina Cavalieri, a young Viennese in spite of her Italian name, was a soprano of exceptional technical powers, and Therese Teyber, a member of a very musical family, was scarcely less accomplished. Valentin Adamberger was a

---

[1] *Opera News,* Jan. 13, 1947.

tenor who delighted Mozart by his refined, musicianly style, while
Ludwig Fischer was a *buffo* bass of uncommon gifts, among which
was an unusual range of low notes. It was of him that the Archbishop
of Salzburg had said that he sang "too low for a bass." . . .

In *Die Entführung aus dem Serail* Mozart was at last wholly in
his element, not because of any especial liking for the German *Singspiel* or even because he was himself planning an elopement of sorts,
but chiefly because by 1782 he was a fully matured master of his craft
and had learnt a good deal about life. Not that his engagement to
Constanze was entirely without influence, we may be sure. Weber
was not far wrong when he suggested that, although Mozart produced greater works later on, he could never recapture that blithe
bridal tone that pervades this ever youthful and endearing work. It
is impossible for anyone with the least musical sensibility to imagine
a happier evening at a theatre than one spent at a good performance
of *The Elopement*. . . .

[In *Die Entführung,* Mozart] enjoyed donning again that amusing
Turkish fashion he had already worn in the A major piano Sonata
and for which he found plenty of opportunity in the overture, the
janissaries' choruses, and especially the music for that magnificent
figure of fun, the amorous, jealous, cunning, and yet gullible Osmin,
a character that is to opera what Shakespeare's Falstaff—the greater
Falstaff of the historical plays (and incidentally of Elgar's symphonic
masterpiece)—is to drama. It is Osmin especially who gives that
peculiar and unrepeatable flavour of Viennese *turquerie* to this most
delectable of operettas—for that is what *The Elopement* really is,
with its spoken dialogue, its lack of a finale to the first act, and its
conclusion with a mere *vaudeville*. Like Sullivan's pieces, which by
the way almost match its musicianly refinements at times, we can call
it an opera only by a courteous habit.

This is not to say that it is wanting in great music. Indeed one
would not have a note different even where it falls a little short of
greatness, for it never ceases to be as delicious as it is apt to its type
and subject. Constanze's so-called "torture aria," with its brilliant
ornamentation fitted to Cavalieri's "glib gullet," may possibly deserve
that name; at any rate certain singers could easily make one think so.
Her other two songs are heaven-sent things for virtuoso sopranos,

one in the finest bravura style of the concert arias, the other that poignant plaint in G minor.

Blonda's songs are as spritely as Belmonte's are tender. She is a second high soprano (top E) with a part almost as difficult as Constanze's. Pedrillo is a second tenor of the comic servant type, and his aria in which he boasts of his bravery while he trembles at the stirring of every leaf is an admirable piece of *buffo* art. The device of writing high parts for both pairs of lovers yields the most enchantingly airy vocal texture for the quartet in the second act, which is quite extended enough to make an adequate finale for so light a musical play. Adequate, did I say? It is a structure and a collection of tunes of such fascinating grace that one would like to call back every phrase of it to hug it over and over again. But it just flows on happily and will not wait to be loved. That is the worst of music—and the best: it will not be possessed. However, to such a score as that of *The Elopement* you can at least go back for another spell of enticement, and you will never fail to find it fresh.

E. B.

There was a performance of *Die Entführung* in Brooklyn in February, 1860, in Italian, under the title of *Belmonte e Constanze,* which was perhaps the first in America. It was presented in German at the German Opera House, New York, October 10, 1862. In recent years an English version was heard in New York and other cities offered by Vladimir Rosing's Rochester, later American, Opera Company, which gave all of its performances in English. [The Metropolitan *première* occurred on December 18, 1946, in an English translation by Ruth and Thomas Martin, with a cast including Eleanor Steber as Constanza, Pierrette Alarie as Blonda, Charles Kullman as Belmonte, Deszo Ernster as Osmin, Hugh Thompson as Selim, John Carter as Pedrillo, and Ludwig Burgstaller as the Mute; the conductor was Emil Cooper.]

P. S.

THE STORY

ACT I: The overture is mainly concerned with establishing the "Turkish" atmosphere of the piece; Mozart also introduces a reference in the minor to Belmonte's aria, "Hier soll' ich dich denn sehen, Constanze," which is heard in C major when the curtain goes up. Belmonte is outside the Pasha Selim's house, where he believes his beloved Constanze, who has been carried off by pirates, is a captive. Osmin, in charge of the Pasha's harem and also, it seems, of his garden, appears singing a doleful sort of love song, "Wer ein Liebchen hat gefunden," one of the delights of the score. He is questioned by Belmonte: is this not the Pasha Selim's house? It is, and he works for the Pasha, but an enquiry for Pedrillo produces an even surlier answer, as this is his *bête noir,* his rival in love for Blondchen; Pedrillo should, he says, without delay, be hanged, drawn, and quartered. He chases Belmonte away, but is immediately confronted with Pedrillo in person, saucier and more impudent than ever. The situation calls for music and he relieves his pent-up feelings with an aria that is a virtuoso expression of rage and also, in good hands, of the comic bass's art.

Belmonte returns to find his former servant; each is delighted at the other's news, Belmonte to hear that Constanze has remained true to him in spite of the Pasha's persuasive powers, Pedrillo that there is a boat waiting to take them all to safety if they can only spirit the women out of the harem. Belmonte sings a song of love for his absent Constanze: "O wie ängstlich, o wie feurig." It is filled with a romantic feeling that derives in part, we may suppose, from Mozart's own love for his Constanze, whom he married a few weeks after the production of the opera. The orchestral accompaniment, Mozart tells his father in a letter, represents the throbbing of the lover's heart, the heaving of his breast, his sighs and whispers.

Belmonte leaves the stage as Constanze and the Pasha land from a boat to be greeted in a chorus that is very much in the Turkish style. The Pasha once again assures Constanze of his love and of his determination to win hers in return. She sings of the love that she knew before her captivity and protests that she will be true to this memory: "Ach, ich liebte, war so glücklich." It is a coloratura aria, but full of sadness for her past happiness and of determination to resist temptation. She leaves the stage, and Pedrillo takes this opportunity to introduce Belmonte to the Pasha as an architect of high standing; the Pasha intimates that he will not withhold his favour from him, but after he has gone Osmin remains unimpressed and tries to bar their way. It is only after a lively trio, "Marsch, marsch, marsch," that they contrive to outmanœuvre him and enter the palace.

ACT II: Osmin is no match for Blonda in a battle of wits, as she demonstrates in her aria, "Durch Zärtlichkeit und Schmeicheln," and the duet which follows. He knows she will come off best and can do no more than complain at the folly of the English in allowing their women so much liberty (in this story, Blonda is supposed to be English). Constanze unburdens herself to Blonda: "Traurigkeit ward mir zum Loose." It is perhaps the most deeply felt number of the score, and one of Mozart's most sublime expressions of grief (like "Ach, ich fühl's," in the key of G minor). Blonda retires as the Pasha comes once more to urge his suit. Constanze is adamant and launches into one of the most considerable arias Mozart ever wrote for soprano voice: "Martern aller Arten." Laid out on concerto lines, with four solo instruments and a lengthy orchestral introduction, it is the one moment in the opera where Mozart definitely sacrifices the stage situation—the Pasha and Constanze can do little else but glare at each other during the introduction—to the possibilities inherent in his singers, of whom Caterina Cavalieri, the Constanze, was perhaps the most eminent. But the aria that results is musically such a masterpiece that few people will feel disposed to agree with the purists who maintain that it should be cut in performance (unless, that is to say, the singer is going to make a mess of it).

Blonda is wondering if the empty stage signifies that the entreaties of the Pasha have at last been successful when Pedrillo rushes in to tell her that Belmonte is here and a plan afoot for their escape. Osmin is to be drugged to make way for the double elopement. Blonda's joyful song, "Welche Wonne, welche Lust," contrasts with Pedrillo's definitely nervous reaction to the prospect of dealing with Osmin single-handed ("Frisch zum Kampfe"). However, he tackles as to the manner born the business of persuading Osmin that the Mohammedan doctrine of teetotalism is better honoured in the breach than in the observance, and he soon has him tippling with the best and praising wine in one of Mozart's most exquisite inspirations, the duet "Vivat Bacchus." Osmin sinks into a stupor and Pedrillo is able to drag him out of the way and leave the coast clear for a reunion between Belmonte and Constanze. Belmonte in his aria, "Wenn der

Freude Thränen fliessen," is less passionate than Constanze as she begins the quartet which is to end the act. It is a noble piece in spite of the crisis which is contrived to keep it alive—the men ask to be assured again that their lovers were true during captivity—and the musical integrity is unaffected by the dramatic artificiality.

ACT III: With much comic pantomime, Pedrillo organises the disposal of the ladders with the help of the captain of the ship which is to take them to freedom. Belmonte enters and is instructed to sing so that no one will notice that he, Pedrillo, is not serenading his Blonda as usual ("Ich baue ganz auf deine Stärke"). A moment later, Pedrillo is back, and ready to give the signal for escape with his enchanting serenade "Im Mohrenland gefangen war." Nothing in the score is more immediately appealing than this graceful piece, which must be the plum of the whole "second tenor" repertory. Belmonte and Constanze disappear into the darkness, and Pedrillo rushes up the ladder to fetch his Blonda, unaware that his singing has waked up a guard, a mute, who suspects the worst and dashes off to summon Osmin. The latter arrives as the second pair of lovers is on the point of leaving the house, and his suspicions that a double elopement has been planned are confirmed when Constanze and Belmonte are brought back by the guard which has surprised their escape. "Ha! wie will ich triumphieren" he sings in his joy that at last he is to have the chance of settling a hundred and one old scores with Pedrillo, and several new ones as well with Belmonte. Never has one operatic character gloated so convincingly over the misfortunes of others, and Osmin parades his vengeful notions in an orgy of triumph, touching a top E and sustaining a bottom D in his highly satisfactory efforts to give them adequate musical expression.

The Pasha is informed of the intended escape, and arrives to question the prisoners. Constanze pleads her love for Belmonte as justification for the attempted escape, and her lover assures the Pasha that his father, a rich Spaniard of the name of Lostados, will pay a high ransom for his freedom. Lostados? says the Pasha: you are the son of my greatest enemy, the man who stole from me my love, my career, and my right to live in my native country. Belmonte and Constanze are face to face with death and perhaps torture, and their extensive duet, "Welch' ein Geschick," reveals a serious approach to their imminent tragedy. The Pasha returns, and announces that he scorns to return evil for evil, that they are free to return to their native Spain whenever they like. The happy couples return thanks in the form of a *vaudeville,* which Belmonte begins, the others singing a verse each and all joining in the refrain; Blonda cannot resist a final dig at the discomfited Osmin, whose rage overcomes him so that he disrupts the harmony of the ensemble with another furious outburst before rushing defeated from the stage, leaving the others to finish on a note of suitable gratitude. They take their leave while the chorus sings the praises of the Pasha and his clemency.

L. H.

Le Nozze di Figaro

[The Marriage of Figaro]

Opera buffa in two acts.

Book by Lorenzo Da Ponte, after Beaumarchais' comedy *Le Mariage de Figaro.*

First performance: Burgtheater, Vienna, May 1, 1786.

CHARACTERS

Count Almaviva, Grand Corregidor of Andalusia, BARITONE

Figaro, his valet and major-domo of the château, BARITONE

Dr. Bartolo, a physician of Seville, BASS

Don Basilio, music master to the Countess, TENOR

Antonio, gardener of the château and Susanna's uncle, BASS

Don Curzio, counselor-at-law, TENOR

Cherubino, head page to the Count, SOPRANO

Countess Almaviva, SOPRANO

Susanna, head waiting woman to the Countess, betrothed to Figaro, SOPRANO

Marcellina, CONTRALTO

Barbarina, Antonio's daughter, SOPRANO

Servants, Officers of the Court, and Peasants

The action takes place at Count Almaviva's château in the country near Seville

THE BACKGROUND

HAYDN OFTEN came to Mozart's house to play quartets with Dittersdorf as second violinist and Wanhal as cellist, the host playing the viola. It was here that he met Leopold Mozart, who had come to return his son's visit, staying in Vienna from February to April, 1785. (Leopold had made the journey alone, for his daughter had been married in 1784 to a nobleman, Berchthold zu Sonnenberg of St. Gilgen, where she lived in the very house where her mother had been born.) Haydn, who was thirteen years younger than Leopold, warmed his fatherly heart by saying to him, after a home performance of the three new quartets: "I tell you before God, and as an honest man, that your son is the greatest composer I know, either personally or by name; he has taste, and apart from that the greatest science in composition." . . .

The quartet playing did not always take place at the Mozarts', but often at the lodging of Stephen Storace, a promising English composer of twenty-two, who had come to Vienna with his sister Ann Selina, better known as Nancy, who at the age of nineteen was already an opera singer with a reputation in Italy and had just been engaged for the new Italian opera establishment which Vienna had substituted for the unsuccessful German venture. There was almost a musical British colony in the capital, for apart from the Storaces, Thomas Attwood, aged twenty, had come to be, like Stephen Storace, a pupil of Mozart. They soon formed a friendly circle round the Mozart household which was completed by the Irishman Michael Kelly, who, four years older than Nancy Storace, had also made his name as a singer in Italy and was engaged as tenor at the opera. Kelly became a particularly close friend. He visited Mozart almost daily, played billiards with him and received his advice about turning a gift for melodic invention unmatched by technical proficiency to the best advantage. It is to Kelly's attractive *Reminiscences* that we owe one of the best contemporary pen-portraits of Mozart that have been preserved:

He favoured the company by performing fantasias and capriccios on the pianoforte. His feeling, the rapidity of his fingers, the great execution and strength of his left hand particularly, and the apparent inspiration of his modulations, astounded me. After this splendid performance we sat down to supper, and I had the pleasure to be placed at table between him and his wife. . . . After supper the young scions of our host had a dance, and Mozart joined them. Madame Mozart told me, that great as his genius was, he was an enthusiast in dancing, and often said that his taste lay in that art, rather than in music.

He was a remarkably small man, very thin and pale, with a profusion of fine hair, of which he was rather vain. He gave me a cordial invitation to his house, of which I availed myself, and passed a great part of my time there. He always received me with kindness and hospitality. He was remarkably fond of punch, of which beverage I have seen him take copious draughts. He was also fond of billiards, and had an excellent billiard table in his house. Many and many a game have I played with him, but always came off second best. He gave Sunday concerts, at which I never was missing. He was kindhearted, and always ready to oblige; but so very particular when he played that, if the slightest noise were made, he instantly left off.

Before long both Nancy Storace and Kelly, who was also known as O'Kelly and on the Italian stage as Ochelli, were to be artistically associated with Mozart as well as personally. For it was high time for him to tackle another work for the stage, and the German opera having come to grief, he was naturally looking out, without success at first, for an Italian book. Beaumarchais, we know, attracted him, and about the middle of 1786 he found the opportunity to embark on an operatic version of the second comedy in the French author's trilogy—*Le Mariage de Figaro*. He had met the right li-brettist in Lorenzo da Ponte—the right one for him, at any rate, varied success. He was a Venetian Jew by birth, Emanuele Cone-for da Ponte had worked with other composers like Salieri, Gaz-zaniga, Righini, and the italianized Spaniard Martín y Solar with gliano, but had been christened in his fourteenth year by the Bishop of Ceneda, whose name he adopted. He took holy orders, which did not prevent him from being a complete man of both the world and the half-world, a kind of minor Casanova, less abandoned but also less distinguished than that dangerously attractive model. He was no great literary genius, but an adroit craftsman and neat versifier. At any rate the Beaumarchais subject suited him, and he turned it skil-fully into what, but for a weakness in the fourth act, has remained one of the world's best operatic librettos, excising the numerous political allusions in the revolutionary comedy, which did not suit the purposes of the musical stage, but leaving the polished intrigue of the original unimpaired. Moreover, he was shrewd enough to recognize a great composer and saw his advantage in being associated with a genius like Mozart, whose suggestions he knew to be sound and accepted without demur. The book was soon ready to Mozart's hand. He set to work on *Le Nozze di Figaro* with avidity and—who can doubt it?—with none of the misgivings that may have stirred in his breast, almost unknown to himself, at his own wedding.

Joseph II had always, more or less secretly, favoured Italian opera, and when he found that Vienna was not inclined to make a success of the German venture, he was only too glad to convene a new Italian company in 1783, though not disinclined to let the indigenous singers who were conversant with Italian operatic art be transferred to the new enterprise. His favourite composer, Salieri, was given the first chance to appear with a new work, *La Scuola dei gelosi,* and a piece that shared its success was Sarti's *Fra due litiganti il terzo gode,* which we shall meet again in connection with Mozart. By 1786 an excellent company had been assembled. An ideal cast was chosen for *Figaro:* Steffano Mandini, a fine baritone, as Count Almaviva, a soprano named Laschi as the countess, Nancy Storace as Susanna, and a surpassingly good *basso buffo,* Francesco Benucci, as Figaro. It may well have been for the sake of Kelly, who was an accomplished character actor, that Mozart made a tenor part of Basilio.[1] Aloysia Lange was not in the running, although she had gone over to the Italian opera together with Cavalieri, Teyber, and Adamberger; for it was of course for a production of Anfossi's *Il Curioso indiscreto* at the new establishment that her brother-in-law had written the extra arias for her and Adamberger to sing in that work. In 1785 he was asked to contribute a trio and a quartet to Bianchi's *La Villanella rapita,* and only then was he at last invited to supply an Italian opera of his own.

But *Figaro* was not to be produced without trouble. First of all the emperor, who had already forbidden the performance of Beaumarchais's play, would not hear of its presentation as an opera until da Ponte was able to reassure him that all political allusions had been

---

[1] *Figaro* could thus not be performed with the same cast as a sequel to Paisiello's *Barbiere di Siviglia,* where, as in Rossini's later version, Almaviva is a tenor and Basilio a bass.

eliminated. Then the court poet, Giovanni Battista Casti, who was not inclined to tolerate another librettist next to him, began to intrigue against Mozart and da Ponte, with the all too generous support of the intendant, Count Rosenberg, who tried to annoy the composer into withdrawing the work by cutting out the dance in the third act. But the emperor, who attended the rehearsal he had himself ordered, noticed the'omission and commanded that it should be rectified. Mozart also suspected machinations on the part of other composers, notably Salieri and Righini, and he was fully upheld in his misgivings, as usual, by his father, who had spent a lifetime scenting mischief, real and imaginary. Kelly, however, confirms the Mozart's suspicions:

> Mozart was as touchy as gunpowder, and swore he would put the score of his opera into the fire, if it was not produced first; his claim was backed by a strong party: on the contrary Regini [sic] was working like a mole in the dark to get precedence. . . . The third candidate was Maestro di Cappella to the Court, a clever shrewd man, possessed of what Bacon called crooked wisdom.

The story that the singers themselves tried to jeopardize the work by deliberately making mistakes seems to be a pure fabrication of over-zealous biographer-partisans; at any rate the whole company, vocalists and orchestra, broke spontaneously into wild acclamations at one of the rehearsals when Benucci sang "Non più andrai" in the most rousing manner, and the artists did magnificent work on the night of the production of Le Nozze di Figaro (The Marriage of Figaro) on 1st May,[2] 1786. Mozart conducted from the keyboard and, of course, accompanied the secco recitatives, a task which Joseph Weigl took over after the third performance. The house was crammed on the first night, and so many of the numbers had to be repeated that the opera lasted nearly twice its appointed time.[3] For

---

[2] Have socialists ever noticed the date on which this class-subversive opera appeared? If not, a present may here be made them of the observation.

[3] Only those familiar with Gilbert and Sullivan audiences can have some faint conception nowadays of how undisciplined the opera public was in the eighteenth century. Even Mozart, though he wrote the loveliest orchestral perorations to his arias, which must have been ruined again and again by applause, took

all that, the work was withdrawn after the ninth performance on 18th December, the chief cause being Martín's *Una cosa rara,* which proved an immediate and easy success. That Mozart bore the Spanish composer no grudge for this will appear before long.

Figaro did very little to relieve Mozart of the material anxieties that beset him more and more sorely. Only nine performances were given in eight months for which he received nothing, having been paid a lump sum at the beginning. There were debts to settle, and he paid too much rent as it was for the first floor of the comparatively well-set-up house in the Schulerstrasse, and Constanze was once more with child. The third boy, Johann Thomas Leopold, born on 18th October, died on 15th November, so that pecuniary harassments were accompanied by emotional ones. The worried composer worked hard. But then, as soon as he set pen to paper, the usual miracle happened: trouble forsook him, and he turned out one exquisite piece after another. . . .

The perfect *opera buffa.* . . . True, of course; but it is much more than that. Beaumarchais's exposure of a refined but pernicious civilization is here made the pretext for music as sunnily civilized as the world ought to have become if the dreamers of Mozart's age had been right and the French Revolution had not merely replaced one kind of barbarity by another that has not even the merits of elegance and taste. These qualities *Figaro* has to a degree never again attained in music, and it has moreover a profound humanity, a sympathetic penetration into the hearts of men and women—especially women—prompted by the complete artist's understanding of both good and evil, by a kind of sublimated amorality and naïve philosophy based on feelings rather than on principles.

Music dictated by this frame of mind could hardly have been any-

---

this insensitive responsiveness calmly for granted, though he did once say that what he liked most of all was approbation by silence. (But he confessed to Jacquin that he could not tell whether Paisiello's *Le Gare generose* had been well performed in Prague or not, because he had been talking too much.) A characteristic decree was issued after the first *Figaro* performances: it was proclaimed by order that no musical number written for more than one voice would be repeated in future—which amounted to an encouragement to insist on repetition of the arias.

thing but flawless, and the score of *Figaro,* so far as the composer is concerned, really is without a blemish, apart from its pouring forth an incessant stream of the most bewitching and the most perfectly behaved, aristocratic music imaginable. Where there is a fault or so, it is imposed on the music from the outside. The fact that the first and third acts have no finales may pass, for one may regard the work as being conceived in two acts, divided into four scenes, and consider, moreover, that two more such towering structures and incredibly well managed musico-dramatic developments as the two existing finales would have been too much. The serious defect of that set of arias which brings the action of the fourth act to a standstill, and most of which may fortunately be cut without damage to the work, is due partly to the flagging invention of da Ponte and partly to the convention that allowed opera singers to indulge their exhibitionist instincts at some point or other in a comic opera.

Figaro is Italian comic opera in its final stage of perfection. It humanizes and glorifies the traditional figures of the *commedia dell' arte* which are very clearly the ancestry of Beaumarchais's characters. Susanna is not only the daughter of Pergolesi's Serpina and the sister of all the *cameriere* of the Italian musical stage, she is the type of Columbine grown into a lovable individuality, and after having shown many traits of the operatic *servetta* in the course of the first three acts, she assumes a warm and noble womanliness in her aria, "Deh vieni, non tardar," in the garden scene, where she sounds quite a new note.

Cherubino points two ways. He is at once the adolescent Don Juan and the descendant of Leandro, who in the Italian improvised comedy is the disciple of Lelio and kindred more or less dissolute fine gentlemen, who gave Beaumarchais his model for the Count. At the same time Cherubino, being given a soprano part, is a late survivor of the male soprano, though by no means the last, for all through the nineteenth century and beyond (e.g., Octavian in Strauss's *Rose Cavalier*) this convention lingered on. . . .

Figaro himself is a survival of Harlequin, or more exactly a modern compound of Arlecchino and Brighella, two servant types with different traits. Bartolo, of course, is no other than the Bolognese doctor who took his idosyncrasies from Cassandro or Pantalone; Basilio is partly Tartaglia and partly Brighella; Marcellina has the elements of Columbine which are lacking in Susanna; the Countess —the Rosina of *The Barber of Seville*—is the young lady of the Italian comedy, most commonly called Isabella, who is generally the niece or ward, or both, of Pantaloon.

Now all these figures of the *commedia dell' arte* were mere skeletons, as indeed were the plots of their plays, and the actors were expected to improvise on them as the inspiration of the moment dictated. Something of the same kind is done by Mozart with his music. It is true that Beaumarchais had already made these types into personalities, and that da Ponte had by no means spoiled them. But it is Mozart who made them our personal acquaintances, people to be loved or liked or despised, but all of them to be perfectly understood. For he understood them to the last tremor of the heart, the last twinge of conscience. Each is given infallibly the right music, and each keeps to it even when the parts intermingle in those impeccably elegant concerted pieces, of which the two finales and the sextet in the third act are the major miracles, but not one of which can be imagined capable of improvement in the slightest detail. And it is all immaculately beautiful, most of all, perhaps, the wonderful consolatory music lavished on the unhappy Countess, if a choice must be made. But then it should not, for the opera is as great as a whole as it is captivating in detail.

E. B.

With regard to the American *première* of *Le Nozze di Figaro* there is some doubt. Renamed *The Follies of a Day,* it is said to have been presented in New York as early as 1799. Yet a performance of the work at the Park Theater, New York, in English, May 10, 1824, was advertised as a "first time in America." In any event, the opera in English versions was popular in New York throughout the first half of the nineteenth century.

In the original Italian it was produced at the New York Academy of Music November 23, 1858, and in a German translation at the German Opera House, New York, December 18, 1862. It entered the repertory of the Metropolitan Opera House, in Italian, January 31, 1894, with Lillian Nordica as Susanna, Emma Eames as the Countess Almaviva, Sigrid Arnoldson as Cherubino, Mario Ancona as Figaro,

and Édouard de Reszké as Count Almaviva. Emilio Bevignani
conducted.

P. S.

THE STORY

ACT I: When the curtain rises, Susanna is discovered in front of
the looking-glass, and Figaro is measuring out a space on the floor
("Cinque, dieci"). The room, Figaro explains, is to be theirs—"the
most convenient room in the castle, just between milord and milady."
(Not all stage designers have been prepared to admit that, in eighteenth-century castle geography, this is likely to have been a box room
or a curtained-off portion of a passage, not a grand room with a
veranda and a view of the Park.) Susanna astounds him by peremptorily refusing to accept it, but, when he remonstrates ("Se a caso
Madama"—Supposing one evening my lady should want you[1]),
explains that the position may make it easy for her to go to the
Countess, it also makes it easy for the Count to get to her. The
Countess rings, and Figaro is left alone to contemplate a situation
that is by no means to his liking. In the two movements of his duet
with Susanna, the mode has been one of gaiety and light-heartedness,
which is hardly interrupted by the hint of intrigue, as Susanna is
obviously unperturbed by a situation she feels herself quite capable
of dealing with. But "Se vuol ballare" (If you are after a little amusement) shows Figaro in a state of mind in which determination cannot altogether eliminate apprehension. No sooner has he left the
stage than we are shown another aspect of the worry which is to
plague him on his wedding-day. Marcellina comes in with Don
Bartolo, the pair of them hatching a plot which shall compel Figaro
to marry Marcellina as he has defaulted on a debt he owes her. He,
Doctor Bartolo, with his legal knowledge will ensure that there is no
escape for the rascal ("La vendetta"—Now for vengeance)—a splendid example of what such an aria for basso buffo can become in the
hands of a composer of genius. As he goes out of one door, Susanna
enters the room by another and she and Marcellina meet as they
attempt to follow Bartolo; their duet as each offers the other preced-

[1] E. J. Dent's translation.

ence ends in Marcellina's complete discomfiture. Susanna stays behind and is immediately confronted with a disconsolate Cherubino,
who wants to enlist her help in getting the Count to reinstate him
as the Countess's page. No one takes him seriously except himself.
He is just at the wrong age: young enough to be allowed liberties, old
enough to take advantage of them (as has happened over his latest
exploit with Barberina, for which he has been dismissed) in a way
that cannot be tolerated. He is in love with every woman he comes
across, and pours out his adolescent aspirations to Susanna in an
aria, "Non so più cosa son, cosa faccio" (Is it pain, is it pleasure that
fills me?). No sooner has he finished than voices are heard outside
and he has only just time to conceal himself before the Count comes
into Susanna's room and starts to protest his affections. It is not her
lucky day, as the Count is followed a moment or two later by Basilio;
in the scramble for concealment, Cherubino nips into the chair behind which the Count takes refuge. Basilio teases Susanna with
gossip about Cherubino and, when she will not listen, presses her
about the page and the Countess—an intrigue which he says everyone
is talking about. The Count can bear it no longer and emerges from
his hiding-place to demand that the gossip-mongers shall be found
and punished. In the ensuing trio—since "Non so più cosa son" the
action has been carried on in recitative—Susanna faints, but revives
in time to plead the cause of the unhappy Cherubino, a mere boy, she
says. Not so young as you think, says the Count, and describes how
he caught him the previous day hiding in Barberina's room. Suiting
the action to the word, he draws the cover from the chair—and
there is Cherubino again. Only Cherubino's admission that he had
heard what passed between the Count and Susanna ("I did all I
could *not* to hear, my lord") stays the penalty that would otherwise
be his. Led by Figaro, a band of peasants comes in to sing the Count's
praises, and, at its end, the Count yields to the general entreaties, but
only to the extent of giving Cherubino a commission in his regiment,
for which he must leave immediately. Figaro speeds him on his way
with a spirited description of what his future life has in store for him.
Michael Kelly, the Irish tenor who was the Basilio and Curzio in
the original production, tells in his memoirs of the splendid sonority
with which Benucci, the Figaro, sang the martial air "Non più

andrai" (Say good-bye now to pastime and play, lad) at the first
orchestral rehearsal. Mozart, who was on the stage in a crimson
pelisse and cocked hat trimmed with gold lace, kept repeating *Bravo,
bravo, Benucci!* In truth, it is a stirring finale to an act.

ACT II: We are introduced to the Countess in a soliloquy, "Porgia
amor" (God of Love). In this aria, whose simplicity makes it one of
the most taxing entrances for any soprano, we are made aware of her
intense longing for her husband's love and also of the reticence
which her breeding makes natural to her. Susanna explains the situation to her and opens the door to Figaro; his plan is that the Count
shall be given an assignation with Susanna, whose place shall be
taken by Cherubino, and that at the same time he shall be told in an
anonymous letter that the Countess in her turn has made a ren-
dezvous with an unknown man. Cherubino comes in to see if he
can be dressed for the part, but first sings the song he has just composed, "Voi che sapete" (Tell me, fair ladies). Not only has Mozart
got round the difficulty of introducing a song ("words and music by
Cherubino") into a milieu where singing is the natural means of
expression, but he has done so in such a way that this piece has become one of the world's most popular tunes. Cherubino tries on the
dress to the accompaniment of a song with action, Susanna's "Venite
inginocchiatevi" (Come here and kneel before me now). No sooner
is it ended and Cherubino safely buttoned up than a knock is heard
at the door. It is the Count. Consternation. Cherubino dashes into
the Countess's bedroom and Susanna hides behind a curtain. The
Count is suspicious of his wife's all too obvious nervousness, and suspicion that something is being hidden from him becomes certainty
when he hears a noise and finds the door of her room locked ("Susanna, or via sortite"—Come out, come out, Susanna). He takes his
wife with him as he goes off to get tools to break it down with. While
he is away Cherubino slips out of hiding and jumps from the window, leaving Susanna to take his place. The little *allegro assai* duet
for Susanna and Cherubino is a comedy interlude of the greatest
dexterity amidst the ranting and raging of the Count, which re-
doubles in fury when the Countess tries to explain that Cherubino
is in her room without much on because he was being fitted for a
charade. The great finale is begun by the Count in a towering pas-

sion: "Esci omai, garzon malnato" (Out you come, no more concealment). The Countess's pleading seems to be in vain, but both are
struck dumb with amazement when, at the height of the storm, Susanna emerges coolly from the inner room. It is one of those incomparable musico-dramatic strokes which no listener who knows the
opera ever fails to look forward to, and which comes as an anticlimax only in the worst of performances. The Count rushes in to see
if Cherubino is not still there, but, finding he is not, can do nothing
but sue for pardon. With Susanna's aid, this is obtained, but with it
the Count's suspicions begin to take possession of him again. The
anonymous letter? Written by Figaro, delivered by Basilio. He thinks
he has found someone he can safely be angry with, but is told he
must forgive everyone if he himself is to be forgiven for his jealousy.
There is a moment of peace and relaxation which ends as Figaro
bounds in to summon his master and mistress to the wedding dance
which is about to begin. But the Count sees a chance of getting his
own back and questions Figaro about the anonymous letter. In spite
of hints from the Countess and Susanna, Figaro denies all knowledge
of it, and has almost turned the Count's suspicions when Antonio,
the gardener, bursts in, protesting that his life is a perpetual trial but
that to-day they have thrown a man out of the window on to his
flower-beds, and that is too much. Figaro says that it was he who
jumped out, but Antonio thinks it looked more like the page. Figaro
sticks to his story until the Count catechises him about a paper
Antonio says was dropped near the flower bed. Figaro searches his
pockets and racks his brains, and in the nick of time the Countess
recognises it and whispers to Figaro that it is the page's commission.
Why was it left? Again, it is only just in time that the Countess
remembers that it had not been sealed. Figaro's triumph is short-
lived, as Marcellina comes in, supported by Bartolo and Basilio, to
lodge formal complaint before the Count against Figaro for breach
of promise. The act comes to an end in pandemonium.

This finale is one of the greatest single sections in all Mozart's
operas. For variety of motive, tempo, and texture it is unrivalled;
the characterisation is consistent and credible and at no time sub-
ordinated to more general musical needs; the level of invention is
extremely high; and the whole thing is carried on with resources
that make use of the nine principals but involve no chorus or scenic

display. It is a marvel of ingenuity, and at the same time a model
of simplicity.

ACT III: The Count has not yet given up hope of Susanna, and
when she comes to borrow smelling salts for her mistress he seems
within reach of his prize. She agrees to meet him that night in the
garden. Their duet, "Crudel, perchè finora" (Oh, why are you so
cruel), reveals the Count as an ardent lover, Susanna as an inattentive
beloved, but the result is a masterpiece. As Susanna leaves the room,
she meets Figaro and assures him, just a little too loudly, that he is
sure now of winning his case against Marcellina. Sure of winning his
case? repeats the Count, and launches into a superb recitative and aria,
"Vedrò mentr'io sospiro, felice un servo mio" (Must I forgo my
pleasure, whilst serf of mine rejoices?). Professor Dent has observed
that the Count, a man of intense energy, is shown first of all in
ensemble, only later in aria, because, one might almost say, he has not
time to sing an aria until the moment when he has to take stock of
his position. It is an extraordinary piece of self-revelation when it
does come, and takes the Count right out of the category of the unsuccessful lover and erring husband into something much more
sinister. But the balance is redressed when it is discovered, after he
has given judgment for Marcellina, that that lady is in fact none
other than Figaro's mother. In the great sextet which follows, the
Count is reduced to expressions of impotent fury: What can he
do when confronted with this wholly unexpected development? The
sextet is one of the most satisfactory instances in all opera of pure
comedy purveyed in terms of straight-faced music. The scene is left
empty for a moment, and the Countess comes in to sing the most
extended and most moving of her utterances in the opera. "Dove
sono" (I remember days long departed) consists of a lengthy recitative followed by a restrained but highly expressive aria in two sections, *andantino* and later *allegro*. It is her moment of greatest self-
revelation, just as his aria was the Count's; if his thoughts were of
revenge that his desires are not to be satisfied, hers are of the love
he once bore her but which she seems to have lost. His aria grew
out of the situation created by his duet with Susanna, the Countess's
gives audible expression to a situation which can only be resolved
with Susanna's aid and therefore leads to a duet between the two.
Between them they arrange where Susanna is to meet the Count

that evening. The letter duet, "Chè soave zeffiretto" (How delightful 'tis to wander, by the breath of evening fann'd), is one of the most famous numbers in the score; the mistress dictates a letter to the Count, the maid takes it down, and the voices of both blend as they read it back together. But the wedding festivities are about to begin and a crowd of village girls presents flowers to the Countess, who is astonished a moment later, when the Count comes in with Antonio, to see one of them unmasked as Cherubino. A tense situation is saved by Barberina: "My lord, when you kiss me and tell me you love me, you often say you will give me whatever I want. Give me Cherubino for a husband." Figaro announces the beginning of the wedding march, the so-called "fandango," the one Spanish element in the score. Like the march in *Idomeneo* and the minuet in *Don Giovanni* it begins as it were in the middle, and returns to what should properly be the opening section later on. There is a chorus in praise of the generosity and right-mindedness of the Count in having abolished the *droit du seigneur,* and the happy couples—Bartolo and Marcellina as well as Figaro and Susanna—receive their wedding wreaths from the Count and Countess, Susanna taking the opportunity to give the Count the letter she and her mistress have concocted for him. He opens it, pricking his finger on the pin—a comedy which is watched all unknowingly by Figaro and commented on with some relish. The Count announces general festivity—song, dance, feasting, and fireworks—and the act ends with a repetition of the chorus in his honour.

ACT IV: The last act is mainly devoted to clearing up the various situations which have arisen in the course of Figaro's wedding day, but there is one more complication to be added before the process can begin. The atmosphere is highly charged with an almost sinister feeling of foreboding; more perhaps than can be put down to the fact that it is night by the time the act begins. The action takes place in a part of the garden which contains arbours and sheltered walks. Barberina begins it with a little half-finished cavatina; she has been given the pin which sealed the letter to return to Susanna, but has lost it. She tells the story to Figaro, who comes in with Marcellina and is overcome with distress at this apparent indication of his wife's unfaithfulness. Arias for Marcellina and Basilio occur at this point, but both are customarily omitted. Before Basilio's, Figaro watches

Barberina hide in one of the arbours (where she is to meet Cherubino), and tells Bartolo and Basilio that they are to stay near at hand
to witness the seduction of his wife by the Count. Now occurs Figaro's recitative and aria, "Tutto è disposto" (Everything's ready),
and "Aprite un po' quegli occhi" (Yes, fools you are and will be,
fools till your eyes are opened), at the same time his most serious
moment (the recitative is tragic in the extreme) and his most comic
(the horns at the end are surely intended to be illustrative as well
as musical). Susanna asks the Countess (they have by now changed
clothes) to be allowed to walk a little apart from her, and sings
an aria of exquisite sensibility, ostensibly to the lover she is waiting
for, but in reality knowing full well that Figaro is listening to her.
"Deh vieni non tardar" (Then come, my heart's delight). The comedy of mistaken identity begins. Cherubino attempts to flirt with
what he thinks is Susanna, in reality of course the Countess. Susanna,
the Count, and Figaro observe, and the Count interrupts and starts
to make love on his own account to his wife in disguise. Figaro
does not know about the change of clothes and it is his turn to interrupt; with the stage empty he invokes the names of the gods of
antiquity to lend weight to his determination to avenge his honour.
Susanna (still disguised as the Countess) calls to him and he starts
to tell her of the Count's escapade when he recognises that it is in
fact Susanna he is talking to. The dramatic tension which may lead
to tragedy is shattered, and we are once more safely in comedy. Figaro makes love to her as if she were the Countess, and then laughs
at her attempt to disguise herself from him as much as at her indignation. All is forgiven—Susanna does not mind the joke against
herself apparently—and the two combine to make the Count think
their extravagant love-making is in reality that of mistress and valet.
The ruse succeeds, the Count summons anyone within hearing to
bear witness to the unfaithfulness of his wife, and in succession
hauls Cherubino, Barberina, Marcellina, and the supposed culprit
from the arbour in which they have taken refuge. All pleading is
in vain, until the voice of the Countess herself is heard behind them
all: "Almeno io per loro perdono ottero" (May I then for pardon at
last intercede). The dramatic suddenness of her entry combines
with the Count's noble phrase of contrition to make this a moment
that can be set beside that of the emergence of Susanna from the

Countess's room in Act II. The Count begs forgiveness in a swelling phrase, receives it, and the opera ends in general rejoicing, voiced though by the principals alone and unsupported by the chorus.

L. H.

THE CHARACTERS

The Count is an unsympathetic figure. He is not intentionally cruel, but is merely a product of the typical upbringing of a nobleman in the decadent age in which he lived. In England the enjoyment of position and property has always been based upon the rendering of services. The tenure of land and the rights which it involved were, and are, dependent upon duty. This sense of duty has never been wholly lost sight of, with the result that a violent revolution such as occurred in France in 1789 has been avoided. The French aristocracy of the eighteenth century, of whom Almaviva, although nominally translated to Spain, is a typical example, were in a different position. Their regime was one of tyranny, and in consequence their overthrow was ruthless. Almaviva is the victim of his age. Complacent and unimaginative in the extreme, he does not perhaps realize that he is cruel. He thinks of nothing but himself and the subjection of his household to his will. This is a bitter, but no means exaggerated, portrait of the Grand Seigneur.

The Countess is a weak figure, and her very weakness excites pity. She cannot be blamed, as a young and inexperienced girl, for having been swept off her feet by Almaviva's ardent suit. A few years of married life have served to make him tired of her, but it is no fault of hers, if, through inexperience, she has failed to retain his affection. She is still young, for Cherubino would scarcely pay so much attention to her if she were middle-aged, nor for that matter could she convincingly change clothes with Susanna in the last Act. She is more human than her husband, and more sympathetic, perhaps because—a bitter reflection—she is not so well bred. She is entirely dependent upon the support and guidance of Susanna, who directs her every action, and at last wins back for her the love of her husband.

Susanna is the central figure of the opera. Without her sane guidance and moderating influence Figaro would not succeed in overcoming the Count. Her love for Figaro is the basis of her character. This is the firm rock upon which she builds, and she can consequently afford to regard the Count's intentions upon her with dispassionate aloofness. She guides Figaro at every turn, allaying his unfounded suspicions and piloting his ideas into the right channels. She guides the Countess, and above all she knows how to handle the Count, leading him on just far enough to enable her to make him do exactly what she wants. She is in no sense of the word a coquette, far from it. Observe that she never "flirts" with anyone. In the first Act the attentions of Basilio and the Count are terrifying to her. For Cherubino she has the sympathetic regard of an older sister, to whom he turns for advice. Only in the third Act, and then strictly in pursuance of the agreed plan of action, does she approach the Count, and deceive him into thinking that she is as clay in his hands, to mould as he chooses. Her love for Figaro is a factor ignored by the Count in his schemings, but it is a love which proves too powerful for him. Throughout the opera her time is fully taken up in dealing with each situation as it arises. Only at the end, in her Rose aria, is she seen in repose. This aria reveals the genuineness and depth of her character, and must of itself be sufficient to belie a coquettish interpretation of the part.

Figaro himself was the local barber in *Le Barbier de Séville*. Now he is in Almaviva's employ as personal servant. As the barber, his trade gave him the entrée to all the noble houses, including that of Bartolo, and consequently he was a valuable ally of Almaviva in his abduction of Rosina. In the previous play Figaro directed the operations and made the plans. His methods were direct and very crude, but were none the less successful in defeating Bartolo. Here the problem is not so simple. The arrangement of an elopement from the house of a fool was easy, but the defeat of the Count in the delicate matter of his feudal rights is another picture. Figaro approaches the new problem with the same technique as before, and does not appreciate that more subtlety and finesse will be required to defeat the Count. His enthusiasm is the driving force still, but now it is directed by Susanna. Figaro is essentially an honest and straightforward character; a man who gives, and expects to receive, the best from everyone. At once in the opening scene this facet of his character is revealed. He enthusiastically accepts the room which the Count has allotted to him, and Susanna has the utmost difficulty in making him see the Count's sinister motives. In his

Cavatina, Figaro's indignation is boiling over. His fury for the moment is wild, and has not yet been harnessed by Susanna. Figaro is the best of men; his motives are honest, and his intentions good, but he is slow in the uptake and not unnaturally jealous.

In Beaumarchais' play Bartolo was a physician, but in the opera he has become a lawyer. The transformation serves to add point to his support of Marcellina's claims upon Figaro. At the beginning of the opera he still clings to a certain respectability, but he slowly declines, and eventually his past history is revealed in all its disreputable detail. He has to acknowledge Figaro, the servant, as his son, and recognizes Marcellina's right to be his wife. Marcellina must be an old and unattractive woman, for she is Figaro's mother and Bartolo's long-since-discarded mistress.

Cherubino's youth is no longer the excuse that it once was for spending his time pursuing every female in the palace. He realizes this, but makes himself out to be younger and more innocent than he really is, for he is reluctant to relinquish his position as the spoilt baby of the family. The Count deems it necessary to take drastic action to secure his absence, thereby admitting him as a serious rival.

C. B.

Don Giovanni

[*Ossia Il Dissoluto Punito*]

[Don Juan, or The Libertine Punished]

Dramma giocoso in two acts.
Book by Lorenzo Da Ponte.
First performance: National Theater, Prague, October 29, 1787.

CHARACTERS

Don Giovanni, a licentious young nobleman, BARITONE (OR BASS)

Don Pedro, the Commandant, BASS

Don Ottavio, betrothed to Donna Anna, TENOR

Leporello, Don Giovanni's servant, BASS

Masetto, a peasant, BASS (OR BARITONE)

Donna Anna, Don Pedro's daughter, SOPRANO

Donna Elvira, a lady of Burgos, SOPRANO

Zerlina, betrothed to Masetto, SOPRANO

Peasants, Musicians, Dancers, Demons

The action takes place at Seville, in the middle of the seventeenth century

Mozart's baptism. Third entry on a page from the baptismal register at the Domkirche, Salzburg.

Leopold, Wolfgang, and Nannerl at Paris (1763), an engraving by J. B.
Delafosse made in 1764 from a watercolor by Louis Carrogis Carmontelle. In
the Geneva Conservatory of Music.

THE BACKGROUND

MOZART HAD not intended to go [to Prague in January, 1787]; his desire was to revisit England, perhaps to settle there if his prospects proved but a little brighter than those in Vienna, where by this time he despaired of ever making his way. For lessons were irksome as well as insufficiently remunerative, the court continued to be luke-warm, and he had too many enemies, perhaps not altogether without his own fault, for he had a sharp and none too well guarded critical tongue where other people's music was concerned. The English project came to grief because he was apparently unwilling to go without [his wife] Constanze, and they could not take two babies with them. Just before the death of the younger boy[1] he asked his father if he would take care of the children for him, in which case he would send them to Salzburg with the two servant wenches. Leopold's answer, dated 17th November, 1786, must have been cate-gorical, to judge by his account of it given to his daugher on the same day—more so than it would have been had he known that the younger child had just died:

> To-day I was obliged to answer a letter from your brother which has cost me much labour in writing. . . . That I had to write a very emphatical letter, you may well imagine, since he proposed to me nothing less than that I should take care of his two children, as half-way through the carnival he desired to make a journey through Germany to England, &c. . . . Not bad, to be sure!—They could travel in all tranquillity,—they might die,—might remain in England,—and I could run after them with the children &c.: or after payment for the children which he offers me for sluts and children &c.—*Basta!* my excuses are forcible, and instructive, if he will make use thereof.

That was that. Leopold's letter had clearly been both forcible and instructive enough to keep the still obedient son of thirty at home. On the other hand there was no reason to interfere with a visit to

---

[1] Johann Thomas Leopold Mozart, born Oct. 18, 1786; died Nov. 15, 1786.

Prague, indeed no want for Wolfgang to write home about it. He took Constanze with him, feeling perhaps that she could do with some agreeable distraction, poor thing. They found Prague seething with enthusiasm over *Figaro,* which had just been produced there with a positively explosive success. It gave them untold satisfaction to find at a ball that the tunes from the opera had been converted into "nothing but *Contredanses* and *Teutsche,*" as Mozart wrote to his friend Gottfried von Jacquin in Vienna, and he was elated to discover that "here they talk of nothing but *Figaro;* scrape, blow, sing and whistle nothing but *Figaro;* visit no opera but *Figaro,* and eternally *Figaro.*" Not only that, but *The Elopement* had charmed the Bohemians in 1783. When on 17th January they attended a performance of *Figaro,* the rumour of the composer's presence at once went round the house, and after the overture he was accorded a frenzied ovation. On the 20th he conducted the opera himself; but it was the day before, at a concert he gave in the opera house, that the new Symphony, now always called the "Prague" Symphony, received its first performance.

Mozart and Constanze stayed at the house of Count Johann Joseph Thun during their visit [to Prague], but they also saw much of Franz Dušek and his wife Josepha, whom Mozart had already met at Salzburg. Both were influential musicians, and it was largely due to their devoted friendship that Mozart obtained a commission to write a new opera especially for Prague. The impresario who had brought *Figaro* to the Bohemian capital, Pasquale Bondini, was eager to attach so successful a composer to himself, and when the Mozarts left in February Wolfgang had a contract for a hundred ducats in his pocket.

The work was to be produced the following autumn, so that no time was to be lost. Mozart went straight to da Ponte, who suggested, as though a new idea had just struck him, the tremendous subject of Don Juan, probably without in the least realizing its whole import, but taking it merely as an excellent excuse for good comedy, titillating situations and a fine theatrical thrill at the end. How much Mozart himself saw in it just then it is impossible to guess; but if he was unaware that he would make of it one of the few stage works in the world which have a claim to be called the greatest opera ever written, he must at least have felt that the completely new problems raised by this text, so far as he was concerned,[2] would make an engrossing task for weeks to come.

Da Ponte's *Memoirs* give an amusing and characteristic account of how this poetical busybody and worldling set to work, though he does not say that he modelled his libretto very closely on that by Gazzaniga. He at least did not shun concentrated labour, while he knew how to make it highly agreeable for himself, if we may believe the glamorous old-age recollections of an adventurer who, not as abandoned as Casanova, may have been no less mendacious:

> I thought it time . . . to exert my poetic powers again. . . . The opportunity was presented to me by the three above-mentioned composers, Martín, Mozart and Salieri, who all came to me at once asking me for a play. . . .
>
> . . . I went to the emperor, put my ideas before him and informed him that I intended to write these three operas contemporaneously.
>
> "You won't succeed," he replied.
>
> "Perhaps not," I answered, "but I shall make the attempt. At night I shall write for Mozart, and I shall regard it as reading Dante's *Inferno;* in the morning I shall write for Martín, and that will be like reading Petrarch; in the evening for Salieri, and that will be my Tasso." He thought my parallel very good.
>
> Directly I reached home I set to work.
>
> I sat down at my writing table and stayed there for twelve hours on end, with a little bottle of Tokay on my right hand, an inkstand in the middle, and a box of Seville tobacco on the left. A beautiful young girl of sixteen was living in my house with her mother, who looked after the household. (I should have wished to love her only as a daughter—but—.) She came into my room whenever I rang the bell, which in truth was fairly often, and particularly when my inspiration seemed to begin to cool.

---

[2] It was not in itself new. Gluck's *Don Juan* ballet had been produced in Vienna in 1761, and Mozart's music at some points very curiously resembles that of Gazzaniga's opera, *Il Convitato di pietra* (The Stone Guest), produced in Venice early in 1787, though it is impossible to say definitely that he knew this work. He must, on the other hand, have been familiar with Righini's of 1777.

She brought me now a biscuit, now a cup of coffee, or again nothing but her own lovely face, always gay, always smiling and made precisely to inspire poetic fancy and brilliant ideas.

Whether these conditions were the ideal ones in which to tackle Salieri's *Assur* it is hard to decide, and they certainly do not seem to fit Martín's *L'Arbore di Diana;* but it can scarcely be questioned that they suited a Don Juan opera to perfection, always provided that the volatile *abbate* wrote the truth.

Be that as it may, he wrote a sprightly libretto full of well-devised situations which make the spectator quite overlook the fact that his Don Juan, although there is much talk of his amorous escapades, is seen throughout the evening to be notoriously unsuccessful in their pursuit. There is, it must be confessed, an extraordinary confusion about half-way through the second act, which no amount of producer's ingenuity ever succeeds in clearing up satisfactorily; but it must be borne in mind that this may have arisen from subsequent manipulations of the text in which quite possibly Mozart had rather more to say than da Ponte may have liked. What is extremely diverting is that old Casanova himself, who was just about that time writing the recollections of his own Don Juanesque career at the castle of Dux in Bohemia, where he had been charitably offered a librarian's post by an old acquaintance, and who was in Prague in the early autumn of 1787, seems himself to have had a hand in revising, and possibly muddling, da Ponte's libretto at that particular juncture, for a sketch in his handwriting has recently been discovered.

In February, 1787, Mozart lost his English friends all at once. The Storaces, Kelly, and Attwood returned home, paying a visit to his father at Salzburg on the way, and he had a last flicker of desire to join them and try his luck in London. In the end it was cautiously decided that they should first look round for an opening for him, and that he might follow later. Then *Don Giovanni* intervened. It was not the only important composition of that period, though, for the two glorious string Quintets in C major and G minor, the Serenade for strings, "Eine kleine Nachtmusik," and the grand-scale violin Sonata in A major belong to it. Also, two outward events occurred in May, one calculated to shake Mozart personally to his depths and the other a linking-up of musical history, as he had the foresight to discern. It seemed little enough to begin with: merely the visit of a sullen-faced youth of seventeen with a thick Rhenish accent, who was introduced to him by some acquaintance. But Mozart, after a somewhat frigid reception of the unprepossessing lad, soon pricked up his ears on being played to on the pianoforte with a startling power and originality, and said to some other visitors in the next room that this young man had better be watched, for he would make a noise in the world before long. The young man did: his name was Ludwig van Beethoven.

On 29th May Mozart heard that his father had died the day before, at the age of sixty-eight. He had not been quite unprepared, for on 4th April he had written home to say he knew that Leopold had been ill and to ask anxiously for news about his condition. But it was a blow to be suddenly told that the old man was no more. There had been estrangements between father and son; Leopold had been harsh and peremptory enough to cause bitterness in a young man who, while anxious to remain dutiful, chafed under restrictions; and Leopold's admonitions had been none the less disagreeable for being, as Wolfgang well knew, based on common sense and affection. But now the old filial tenderness welled up, and he was genuinely afflicted by his loss.

About the end of August the Mozarts left for Prague a second time, Constanze once again in an interesting situation. How far *Don Giovanni* was finished before their departure is not known, but it is certain that a good deal still remained to be done. They lodged at the "Three Golden Lions," but were half the time the guests of the Dušeks, who lived at a country house in "Bertramka's vineyard." There they enjoyed good food, cheerful company, games of darts and skittles and what not, and Mozart intermittently worked at his score on a stone table in the garden, surrounded by ripening grapes and facing the view from the slope.

There was a good deal of trouble with the singers, who, Mozart wrote to Jacquin, were not as accomplished as those in Vienna in catching hold of a new work quickly. The young baritone Luigi Bassi, who sang the title part, complained that he was given no great display aria, and it is said that Mozart composed the duet, "Là ci darem la mano," five times before Bassi was kind enough to say it pleased him. Then Caterina Bondini, the wife of the impresario, probably from fear of spoiling her voice, could not be persuaded to make Zerlina's cry behind the scenes sufficiently realistic. Mozart's remedy was simple: at a rehearsal he suddenly assailed her roughly from behind at the given moment, whereupon she gave forth a scream which he declared to be a perfect sample of what he wanted at the performance. To complete the traditional complications of opera rehearsals, gossip had it that Mozart, perhaps with a view to still greater realism, indulged in love affairs not only with his Zerlina, but also with his Donna Anna, whose interpreter was Teresa Saporiti, and with his Donna Elvira, sung by Caterina Micelli. Saporiti, it was said, had expressed surprise at Mozart's insignificant appearance, whereupon he transferred his affections in a pique. Some of this may be true; all of it certainly is not, since tittle-tattle always has a way of inflating the facts, if any; and as nobody does know how much is true, let us leave it at that, with a strong suspicion that these rumours emanated from those who can never believe an artist to be capable of creating a dramatic figure without having personally gone through its experiences.

Another set of stories is current, about the composition of the overture to *Don Giovanni,* which is supposed to have been written only the night before the performance and distributed to the players, with the ink still wet, to get through at sight as best they could. But Constanze told Nissen, her second husband, distinctly that it was on the last night but one before the production that Mozart wrote down the overture while she regaled him with punch and kept him awake with stories, so that the sight-reading can only, at the worst, have happened at the dress rehearsal. That the whole piece was fully composed in Mozart's mind, according to his astonishing habit, and only needed writing down, may be taken for granted.

That the music for Don Juan's dinner entertainment in the second finale cannot have been ready until quite late is shown by the original libretto, which does not contain the words sung by Don Juan and Leporello while these little wind octets are played. It appears that they were at first to be left to the players' choice, but in the end Mozart interpolated favourite melodies from three recent popular operas: Martín's *Una cosa rara,* Sarti's *Fra due litiganti* and his own *Figaro.*

At last, on 29th October, 1787, *Il Dissoluto punito, ossia Il Don*

Giovanni (*The Debauchee Punished, or Don Juan*) was produced.
Prague went mad with delight over it, in spite of Mozart's fear lest
the public should be bewildered by the novelty of the music, which
must have astonished even himself as it fell to him with the inevitability that makes genius after its highest flights stand amazed and
ask: "How did I do it?" He conducted the first performance himself, and the artists, anxious to do justice to a work and a composer
of whose greatness they had been given ample opportunity to become
aware, did the utmost in their power to make the production a
success. Those not yet named were Antonio Baglioni as Don Ottavio,
Felice Ponziani as Leporello, and Giuseppe Lolli, who doubled the
parts of the Commendatore and Masetto.

The Mozarts were in no hurry to return to Vienna and their everlasting domestic cares. For once they enjoyed themselves, and their
hosts were reluctant to let them go. The new baby was not due just
yet[3] and little Carl was no doubt taken care of by his grandmother.
On 3rd November Josepha Dušek, who had been promised a concert
aria, locked Mozart into a summer-house at Bertramka and declared
that she would not let him out until he had written it down. He
obeyed, but retaliated by refusing to give up the piece unless she
could sing it at sight. It turned out a grand and extremely difficult
thing, full of strange intervals and harmonies; but Josepha, who
was a bit of a composer herself and a good clavier player, brilliantly
acquitted herself of the task imposed on her by the composer, who
dedicated this aria, "Bella mia fiamme," to her.

Two German songs were also written during the visit to Prague,
but they were less important than one or two of a group composed
earlier that year, among which "Abendempfindung" is particularly
interesting as a true forerunner of the Schubertian *Lied* and only
less so than "Das Veilchen" of two years earlier because that is the
one evidence of Mozart's awareness of Goethe, who as a lad had
attended his infant-prodigy display at Frankfort.

On 12th November the Mozart couple were back in Vienna. Three
days later Gluck died of a stroke at the age of seventy-three, and by
7th December Joseph II, who could not help being rather impressed
by Mozart's successes in Prague, appointed him chamber musician

[3] It was to be a girl this time, Theresia, born 27th December, 1787, died 29th
June, 1788.

to the court in Gluck's place with eight hundred florins a year. The immediate effect seems to have been to drive him to the composition of various dances for the court balls and to inhibit him from writing larger works, the only one being the curiously empty piano Concerto in D major—the last but one. Still, though the new appointment amounted to little enough, it may have given the Mozarts some hope of being relieved of the nagging worries that seemed to plague them the more relentlessly the more the master's creative power grew and the more his fame spread beyond Vienna.

Some time early in 1788 Vienna decided to hear the Prague opera. *Don Giovanni* was put into rehearsal with a notable cast—so notable that what Mozart had written for what they considered a set of provincial singers was not good enough for those in the capital. They cleverly attributed the failure of the work at its first performance, on 7th May, to the fact that they had not been allowed to shine sufficiently with solo displays. With the honourable exception of Aloysia Lange, who sang Donna Anna, Francesco Bussani, who took the Commendatore and Masetto,[4] they all insisted on some extra number or another. Caterina Cavalieri was given Elvira's "Mi tradì," much too lovely a piece to be cut, but rather in the concert-aria style and difficult to fit in logically anywhere;[5] Francesco Morella received a second song for Ottavio, the beautiful though static "Dalla sua pace"; while Luisa Mombelli and Benucci, the original Figaro, were fobbed off with a duet for Zerlina and Leporello that continues deservedly to be neglected as the one inferior number in the whole score.

The opera was given a mere fifteen times in the course of the year and did not reappear in 1789—indeed not until after Mozart's death, when it was revived in a lamentable German translation. Joseph II declared, according to da Ponte, that "the opera is divine, perhaps even more beautiful than *Figaro,* but no food for the teeth of my

---

[4] Masetto's "Ho capito," often indicated as an extra number in old editions, was in the original score; so was Don Juan's "Metà di voi" in the second act, which is too often omitted.

[5] It is a wrong, post-Wagnerian, and anti-musical principle to suggest, as German critics do almost with one accord, that so perfect a piece should be sacrificed because dramatically it is uncalled-for.

Viennese," on which Mozart's comment seems to have been: "Let us give them time to chew it. . . ."

It is impossible to conceive that any notion as here set down by Mozart could have come from the pen of any other composer, then or later. What is more, not a single number in *Don Giovanni* can be imagined to occur in any other opera by Mozart himself. Everything is in character, everything coloured by the particular mood into which this great tragi-comic subject cast him.

Tragi-comic, yes, so much is certain; but nobody knows exactly where comedy ends and tragedy begins in what is formally an opera in D minor with a cheerful coda in D major. It is all inextricably blended, laughter for some and tears for others, and then again both in succession, indeed almost together, for one and the same person. Donna Elvira rampages up and down the stage furiously at her first entry with her E flat major aria, but Don Juan and Leporello laugh behind her back while the orchestra chuckles with kindly understanding of the whole situation. And when in that miraculous trio near the beginning of the second act the same two men plan a cruel jest at Elvira's expense, we feel inclined to weep at the tender loveliness of the music, such music as only Mozart could pour out to comfort a woman whose loving heart is about to break, be she Ilia or Constanze, the Countess Almaviva or Pamina, or indeed that most ill-used of all—foolish, infatuated Elvira, wavering miserably between vengeance and forgiveness.

It may be a too personal impression, but I have come to feel certain that this close sympathy with his women characters was his compensation for his lack of that complete understanding between him and any real woman that was one of the afflictions of his life. He became its supreme poet because he was deprived of it by fate, not through any fault of his, much less of Constanze's. That communion between two beings that needs no words was never his; but he knew an artistic equivalent, and it needed music—his music.

How sharply all the characters in *Don Giovanni* stand out! They do so even—this is Mozart's great dramatic secret—when they sing in concert and weave a piece the shape of which leaves nothing to be desired in a purely musical way. The stony-hearted and domineering Donna Anna; her almost despicably humble wooer Ottavio, who saves himself from our contempt by his tenderness; the minx Zerlina, made more sympathetic than perhaps she deserves by a touch of peasant common sense and simple affection; honest Masetto, too dense to be quite clear about the causes of his jealousy; the Commandant, equally dignified as a man and as a statue: they are all, like Elvira, outlined indelibly by music one can never forget.

Ah, if only one could! If only one might recapture that thrill of first acquaintance! There are times at which one would gladly give up the understanding of a score of which one need never fear to reach the bottom, an understanding that deepens with each new hearing or reading and reveals new secrets, for that first rapture on coming into touch with the *Don Giovanni* music. Not a careless rapture, though; rather a careworn one. This opera oppresses its lover with its beauty and with that sympathy with all aspects of life which is almost unhuman. For Mozart seems to love all his characters impartially, if one may judge from the fact that he lavishes the most wonderful music on all, though vastly different music on each. His Shakespearian indulgence covers Don Juan's vices as well as the weakness of Donna Elvira or the hardness of Donna Anna. Each is for him simply a phase of life to be transmuted into a value of art as good as any other. They or Leporello's garlicky vulgarity and pandering knavery. Before Mozart's overmastering art they are all equal.

E. B.

THE LITERARY GENEALOGY OF DON JUAN

It is generally asserted that the story of Don Juan made its first literary appearance in a Spanish play called *El Burlador de Sevilla,* written by Gabriel Tellez (1571–1641), better known under the name of Tirso de Molina. It has also been asserted that Don Juan Tenorio was an historical personage and that he came of a noble family well known in Spain. There is, however, no very satisfactory evidence for this, and it is even doubtful whether *El Burlador* is really the work of the author to whom it is attributed.

The character of Don Juan falls into two clearly separable aspects, Don Juan the profligate and Don Juan the blasphemer. It is indeed only in the second case that we get a clearly defined story, and this story is in its main outline much older than the seventeenth century and by no means confined to Spain. It was a popular notion in many countries, northern as well as southern, that to insult the dead was a crime which inevitably led to the most awful punishment. The idea of statues coming to life dates back to classical times. The profligate on a grand scale is really quite a different character. There are innumerable legends of passionate and brutal rebels against all moral law, especially in Spain, where the sinner is generally related to have repented at last and to have been converted to a life of piety. Throughout the seventeenth century this story was familiar in Germany through plays of the Jesuits in which the hero is called Leontius. Leontius is almost always described as an Italian, and the play probably came to Germany from Italy, though it may have originated in Spain. But it should be noted that in the Don Juan or Leontius plays the sins committed are not so much of the flesh as of the spirit.

Tirso's play is a long, straggling series of scenes in which Don Juan makes love to various ladies and is finally taken down to Hell. His attempt on Donna Anna, followed by the duel and the death of her father, does not take place until the second act. The play opens, however, with a similar adventure, of which Isabela, the betrothed of Octavio, is the heroine. The other female characters are two peasant girls, each of whom is seduced in turn by Don Juan. Don Octavio, the respectable gentleman, the Commendatore and his statue, the peasant rival and Don Juan's comic servant are all presented in much the same form that they take in later plays. It should be noted too that after the statue has carried Don Juan off to Hell, the comic servant gives a full account of his sad end, and the play ends with the happy nuptials of the other characters.

About the middle of the seventeenth century an Italian version appeared at Naples; this was much influenced by the Comedy of Masks, and Harlequin becomes Don Juan's servant. As in the original play, there is no female character whom we could call a "heroine"; Don Juan proceeds from seduction to seduction until the scene with the statue and the final tableau in which he is seen burning in Hell and tormented by devils. Other Italian versions succeeded this extravaganza and the play can be traced by way of Lyons (1658) to Paris (1659).

In 1665 Molière brought out *Le Festin de Pierre,* a comedy in prose which bears little resemblance to Tirso's poetic drama and presents a social and moral point of view which is entirely different. Molière's Don Juan is a Parisian aristocrat of his own time; his servant Sganarelle says of him: "Voilà de mes esprits forts qui ne veulent rien croire." The murder of the Commendatore does not take place on the stage; it is merely alluded to as having occurred six months before. Molière makes a very important addition to the story—Donna Elvira, whom Don Juan has abducted from a convent and then deserted. In spite of his cruelty, she preserves her devotion for Don Juan up to the end, although when she first appears she is more indignant than affectionate. But in the fourth act she says to him:

> Ce n'est plus cette done Elvire qui faisoit des vœux contre vous, et dont l'âme irritée ne jetoit que menaces, et ne respiroit que vengeance. Le Ciel a banni de mon âme toutes ces indignes ardeurs que je sentois pour vous, tous ces transports tumultueux d'un attachement criminel, tous ces honteux emportements d'un amour terrestre et grossier, et il n'a laissé dans mon cœur, pour vous, qu'une flamme épurée de tout le commerce des sens, une tendresse toute sainte, un amour détaché de tout, qui n'agit point pour soi, et ne se met en peine que de votre intérêt.

This presentation of Donna Elvira is very important, as it helps us to understand her character as it appears in Mozart's opera. There can be no doubt that Da Ponte was well acquainted with Molière's play, for there are many verbal borrowings from it in the recitatives of *Don Giovanni*. Masetto and Zerlina, too, are derived from Molière and not from Tirso. Tirso's peasants belong to a literary Arcadia; Molière's are comically realistic and even talk a peasant dialect. It should be noted that neither Donna Anna nor Don Ottavio come into Molière's play at all.

Le Festin de Pierre had fifteen performances and then disappeared from the stage, except in Thomas Corneille's rearrangement in verse, until 1847. It is altogether an exception among Don Juan's plays, but for all that it is an historic landmark. Molière wrote it with reluctance under pressure from his actors, and was so little satisfied with it that he never printed it in his lifetime. He seems to have thought that he could put an end to the absurdities of the Italian play by transforming it into a satire on contemporary life; but he forgot that the episode of the statue was entirely inappropriate to a realistic comedy. "Votre figure de Don Pedro baisse la tête," said a lady to Molière, "et moi je la secoue." The story was too extravagant to be treated seriously, and it was even considered that the play was dangerous to public morals. The Abbé Terrasson opined that:

> Rien n'est plus funeste à la morale que des pièces de théâtre telle que *Le Festin de Pierre,* où un méchant homme n'est puni qu'après avoir porté le vice et le crime à un point où personne ne veut aller, et auquel même n'arrivent que très peu de scélérats.

In 1676 Don Juan made his appearance in England under the name of *The Libertine,* a play by Thomas Shadwell, derived, not from Molière, but from Dorimon's *Le Festin de Pierre* (1659).[6] Shadwell's preface to it shows us clearly what the general attitude of the day was to the story and to its dramatic treatment:

> The story from which I took the hint of this Play, is famous all over Spain, Italy and France: It was first put into a Spanish play (as I have been told), the Spaniards having a Tradition (which they believe) of such a vicious Spaniard, as is represented in this Play. From them the Italian Comedians took it, and from them the French took it, and four several French plays were made upon the story.
>
> The character of The Libertine, and consequently those of his friends, are borrowed; but all the Plot, till the latter end of the Fourth Act, is new: And all the rest is very much varied from anything which has been done upon the subject.
>
> I hope the Readers will excuse the Irregularities of the Play, when they consider, that the Extravagance of the subject forced me to it: And I had rather try new ways to please, than to write on in the same Road, as too many do. I hope that the severest Reader will not be offended at the Representation of those vices, on which they will see a dreadful punishment inflicted. And I have been told by a worthy gentleman, that many years ago

---

[6] See *The Complete Works of Thomas Shadwell,* edited by the Rev. Montague Summers, London, 1927.

(when first a play was made upon this story in Italy) he has seen it acted there by the name of "Atheisto Fulminato," in Churches, on Sundays, as a part of devotion: and some, not of the least Judgment and Piety here, have thought it rather an useful moral, than an encouragement to vice.

Shadwell's play is of interest to us now only for the fact that Purcell wrote incidental music for it. It is not likely that Da Ponte had read it, and it has no bearing on Mozart's opera. But Shadwell himself is always of interest, as he was devoted to music and a complete unbeliever in matters of religion. His audience for this play would certainly have their full money's worth of murder, blasphemy, and rape, with the pleasing horrors of a fine spectacular effect at the end, heightened by Purcell's very dramatic music. What is noteworthy is that even in England, and as early as 1676, the subject was considered extravagant, and in spite of the success of the piece the same view was held nearly a century later.

> The incidents are so cramm'd together in it, without any consideration of Time or Place, as to make it highly unnatural. The villainy of Don Juan's Character is worked up to such an Height, as to exceed even the Limits of Possibility, and the Catastrophe is so very horrid, as to render it little less than Impiety to represent it on the Stage.[7]

In 1736 Goldoni, who was then not quite thirty, produced a play in verse called *Don Giovanni Tenorio o sia Il Dissoluto*. He tells us in his *Mémoires* that he wrote the play with a definite purpose—to revenge himself on Signora Passalacqua, an actress with whom he had had a *liaison* which ended in her making a fool of him. His plan was to write a Don Juan play in which everybody would recognize under the characters of Don Giovanni, Carino (a shepherd), and Elisa (a shepherdess) his own rival Vitalba, himself, and the lady. It is highly probable that Da Ponte had read this play. The plot is as complicated as any opera-book of Metastasio. The scene is laid in Castile, but Don Giovanni, like most of Goldoni's bad characters, is a Neapolitan, and behaves curiously like the Neapolitans who come into his Venetian comedies, for he has a Harlequin-like readi-

---

[7] David Erskine Baker, *The Companion to the Playhouse*, London, 1764.

ness in making up an entirely untrue story on the spur of the moment. More important for us than the play itself is Goldoni's own criticism of it:

> Everyone knows that wretched Spanish tragicomedy which the Italians call *Il Convitato di Pietra* and the French *Le Festin de Pierre*. I have always regarded it with horror in Italy, and I could never understand why this farce should have maintained itself so long, attracting crowds of spectators and being regarded as the delight of a cultivated nation. Italian actors held the same opinion, and either in jest or in ignorance, some said that the author had made a bargain with the Devil to have it kept on the stage. I never thought that I should have worked on the subject myself; but having learned enough French to read it, and seeing that Molière and Thomas Corneille had treated it, I undertook to present the subject to my own country in order that the Devil's bargain should be kept with a little more decency. I could not give the play the same title, because in my play the statue of the Commendatore does not speak or walk or go out to dinner. I thought I ought not to suppress the thunderbolt which strikes Don Giovanni, because a wicked man ought to be punished; but I managed this event in such a way that it might be considered both as the immediate effect of God's anger, and as the result of a combination of secondary causes. . . .

E. J. D.

"DON JUAN" OPERAS—*Before and After Mozart*

Le Festin de Pierre, vaudeville by Le Tellier at the Foire Saint-Germain, 1713. The final ballet in the infernal regions made such a scandal that the piece was suppressed, but it was afterwards revived.

Don Giovanni, ballet by Gluck (Vienna, 1761). The characters are Don Giovanni, his servant, Donna Anna, her father, and the guests at the feast.

Il Convitato di Pietra, by Righini (Vienna, 1777). In this opera the fisher-maiden was introduced.

Il Convitato di Pietra, by Calegari (Venice, 1777).

Il Convitato di Pietra, by Tritto (Naples, 1783).

Don Giovanni, by Albertini (Venice, 1784).

Don Giovanni Tenorio, by Cazzaniga (Venice, 1787). Goethe saw it at Rome, and described the sensation it made. "It was not possible to live without going to see Don Giovanni roast in flames and to follow the soul of the Commander in its flight toward heaven."

Il Convito di Pietra, by Gardi (Venice, 1787).

Don Giovanni, by Mozart (Prague, October 29, 1787).

Don Giovanni, by Fabrizi (Fano, 1788).

Nuovo Convitato di Pietra, by Gardi (Bologna, 1791).

Il Dissoluto Punito, by Raimondi (Rome, about 1818).

Don Giovanni Tenorio, by Don Ramón Carnicer (Barcelona, 1822).

Il Convitato di Pietra, by Pacini (Viareggio, 1832).

Don Juan de Fantaisie, one-act operetta by Fr. Et. Barbier (Paris, 1866).

The Stone-guest (Kamjennyi Gost), left unfinished by Dargomijsky, orchestrated by Rimsky-Korsakoff, and produced with a prelude by César Cui at St. Petersburg in 1872. The libretto is a poem by Pushkin. The opera is chiefly heightened declamation with orchestral accompaniment. There is no chorus. There are only two songs. The composer, a sick man during the time of composition, strove only after dramatic effect, for he thought that in opera the music should accent only the situation and the dialogue. The commander is characterized by a phrase of five tones that mount and descend diatonically and in whole tones. The opera does not last two hours.

Il Convitato di Pietra, by Manent (Barcelona, 1875).

Il Nuovo Don Giovanni, by Palmieri (Trieste, 1884).

La Statue du Commandeur, pantomime, music by Adolphe David (Paris, 1892). In this amusing piece the Statue loses his dignity at the feast, and becomes the wildest of the guests. He applauds the dancers so heartily that he breaks a finger. He doffs his helmet and joins in a cancan, and forgets to take his place on the pedestal in a square in Seville. Consternation of the passers-by. Suddenly the Statue is seen directing unsteady steps. Don Juan and other revelers assist him to recover his position and his dignity.

Here may be added:

Don Juan et Haydée, cantata by Prince Polognac (St. Quentin, 1877). Founded on the episode in Byron's poem.

Ein kleiner Don Juan, operetta by Ziehrer (Budapest, 1879).

Don Juan Fin de Siècle, ballet by Jacobi (London, 1892).

Don Juan's letztes Abenteuer, music by Paul Gräner (Leipsig, June, 1914).

P. H.

Don Giovanni, ossia Il Dissoluto punito (*Don Juan, or The Libertine Punished*) had its American *première,* in the original Italian, at the Park Theater, New York, May 23, 1826. Manuel Garcia's company presented it, and the cast included Garcia himself (though a tenor) as Don Giovanni, his wife as Donna Elvira, his son, Manuel, Jr., as Leporello, his daughter, Maria Malibran, as Zerlina, Mme. Barberi as Donna Anna, Milon as Don Ottavio, and Carlo Angrisani as both Don Pedro and Masetto.

Such was the success of the work that an English version was speedily put on at the Chatham Theater, with H. Wallack, an uncle of the famous actor Lester Wallack, in the title role. Later on Malibran took part in some of the English performances, and the English version remained current in New York till Max Maretzek revived the Italian original at the Astor Place Opera House in 1850. On April 23, 1863, *Don Giovanni* was given at the New York Academy of Music in German.

The first *Don Giovanni* at New York's Metropolitan Opera House was presented November 29, 1883, with Emmy Fursch-Madi (Donna Anna), Christine Nilsson (Donna Elvira), Marcella Sembrich (Zerlina), Italo Campanini (Don Ottavio), Giuseppe Kaschmann (Don Giovanni), and Mirabella (Leporello).

A distinguished cast on December 31, 1894, offered Lillian Nordica (Donna Anna), Emma Eames, Zélie de Lussan, Giuseppe Russitano, Victor Maurel, and Édouard de Reszké. A still more distinguished cast on January 2, 1899, was adorned by Lilli Lehmann, Nordica (Donna Elvira), Sembrich, Thomas Salignac, Maurel, and Édouard de Reszké. An incomparable Masetto of about this time was Charles Gilibert, who after singing the part at the Metropolitan was heard in it at the Manhattan Opera House in the seasons of 1906–1907 and 1907–1908, together with Maurice Renaud, the most distinguished Don Giovanni New York has had in at least a half century, except only Maurel.

Gustav Mahler conducted a revival of *Don Giovanni* at the Metropolitan on January 23, 1908, with Eames as Donna Anna, Johanna Gadski as Donna Elvira, Sembrich as Zerlina, Alessandro Bonci as Don Ottavio, Feodor Chaliapin as Leporello, and Robert Blass as the Commendatore.

P. S.

THE STORY

ACT I—*Scene* 1: At night, in a handsome garden before a handsome house, lurks Leporello, the humorously surly, heartless, weak-charactered servant and confidant of Don Giovanni. Inside, as he tells us, the Don is at his love-making, while he himself must stand guard. Nobody would like his job. The pay is poor, so is the food provided, and the duties keep you up day and night. Besides, Leporello himself would like to play the gentleman; and so he threatens to leave this bootless service. It is one of his favorite threats. But before he is through singing, he thinks he hears the Don coming out of the house and—quite characteristically—hides behind a bush so that he may at once be safe and also do a bit of eavesdropping.

It is the Don, all right, whom Leporello has heard, and he is engaged in equally characteristic business. He is trying to get away from Donna Anna, after a virtuoso attempt to seduce her without disclosing his identity. At the moment she is hanging on to him, trying to find out who he is while he is attempting three things at once—to hide his face in his cloak, to persuade Donna Anna to remain quiet, and to make his getaway. But in this particular escapade, the virtuoso seducer has misjudged his prey, for Donna Anna, though she fails to identify him, calls for help and swears to pursue him "with desperate fury." All of which, of course, gives Mozart an excellent opportunity for a trio in which the Don and the Donna express their conflicting emotions simultaneously while Leporello, on the other side of the stage, comments sardonically on his libertine master.

The Don manages to free himself from Donna Anna's furious grasp only when she hears her father, the Commandant of Seville, storming out of the house. Dressed in a night robe, he carries a drawn sword in one hand and a lamp in the other. While Donna

Anna rushes into the house for help, the Commandant challenges the Don, who contemptuously warns him that he had better not try to fight. The old gentleman, however, persists, sarcastically suggesting that the Don is trying to run away. According to the Don's ideas about honor, there remains nothing to do but have it out. Efficiently, he first knocks the lamp out of the old gentleman's hand so that he will not be recognized, and then proceeds to kill him in a pathetically brief duel.

Meantime, Leporello, hiding in the bushes, wishes he could get away somehow, and emerges only when the fight is over. The moon slowly rises during the hasty whispers that follow.

"Who's dead?" asks Leporello. "You or the old gent?" And when he finds out, he congratulates his master ironically: "Bravo! a couple of nice jobs—to attack the daughter and murder the father."

"He insisted on it," says the Don in self-defense.

"But Donna Anna. Did she also insist?"

As usual, when he is put in the wrong by Leporello, the Don ends the argument by threatening to beat him, and the two run off—just in time. For Donna Anna has managed to summon help—some servants, who come in with torches, and her fiancé, Don Ottavio. This Don, intended as a noble, tragic character in the classic conventions, strikes modern audiences as one of the most futile lovers in opera; for actually, with the best of intentions, he never accomplishes anything and seldom rises to an occasion with any true romantic feeling. The music Mozart has composed for him, however, has all the beauty and compassion we feel lacking in his actions.

Seeing the body of her father, Donna Anna flings herself on the corpse and bursts into lamentation. Don Ottavio tries to raise her, but overcome by her grief, she repulses him. The unhappy young man can think of nothing better to do than send for smelling salts and wring his hands over her; and then, while the servants carry out the body, she turns furiously upon him almost as though he had been responsible for the tragedy. Little by little, he manages to calm her; and he sings two beautiful phrases, the first of which bears a close resemblance to the comforting music of the Blessed Spirits in Gluck's *Orfeo*.

Solemnly she makes him swear to avenge her dead father, and the scene ends with a duet in which they both take this oath.

Scene 2: Like many other opera librettos, *Don Giovanni* is not very specific about the amount of time supposed to elapse between scenes. The second scene, however, may, as well as not, take place a couple of hours or less after the first. It is early in the morning on a square just outside of Seville, and Don Giovanni is carrying on one of his rapid-fire recitatives with Leporello. (These recitatives, as is usual in eighteenth-century opera, are accompanied only by a harpsichord or, in most modern productions, a piano.)

Leporello is trying to work up enough courage to tell his master something pretty important and asks whether he can be guaranteed freedom from punishment if he speaks freely. "On my honor," promises the Don, "so long as it is not about the Commandant." Still, Leporello hesitates long enough to make sure that there is no one around, and then he utters this profound thought:

"Dear Sir Patron," he says, "the life you are leading"—and he leans over to shout in Sir Patron's ear—"is that of a bum!"

Don Giovanni is—as usual—about to strike Leporello; but, when Leporello promises to shut up, he becomes good-natured again and asks whether his servant knows why they have come to this place. Leporello doesn't have to think very hard to answer that one. "Since it's just about dawn," he says, "what is more likely than some new conquest? I'll have to know her name, though, so that I can put her down in the list."

He has guessed right, of course. The Don says he is in love with a beautiful lady he has seen and spoken to, and he is loved in turn by her. Tonight they are to meet at the casino. Suddenly he stops. "Sh!" he shushes. "It seems to me I sense the odor of femininity."

"What a nose!" murmurs Leporello.

"And out here in the open air, I should say she's beautiful."

"And what an eye!"

And they retire to the back of the stage, while Donna Elvira enters in a traveling dress and proceeds to pour out her heart in an aria ("Ah, chi mi dice mai") full of beautiful Mozartean melodic phrases and broad skips of an octave and more. Elvira, we learn, is searching everywhere for the lover who has seduced her with protestations of love and called her his wife. Her typically feminine reason for wanting to find the man again is simply that she may now spurn him. For the difference in the characters of Donna Anna and Donna

Elvira (not always made clear by the sketchy acting that sopranos give the two roles) lies in Anna's inflexible and practical determination to have bloody vengeance on the Don and Donna Elvira's soft, sentimental determination to ease her own hurt feelings. She is the more futile character of the two, but also the more lovable.

While Donna Elvira sings this aria, Leporello, at the back of the stage, tries to get a look at her (a bit of pantomime that can almost ruin the lovely music), and the Don remarks, with a sort of sardonic pity, that grief becomes this lady very well indeed.

At the close of the number the Don steps politely forward and offers his help. Only then does he discover that he himself is the man of whom she has been complaining, since she is a lady whom he had tired of and abandoned after a three-day elopement to Burgos.[8] Immediately she begins to upbraid him—as she had promised herself she would—while he starts to make excuses and calls on Leporello to witness the validity of the reasons for his hasty departure from Burgos. She, of course, refuses to believe him; and while she has her back turned in contempt, the Don tells Leporello to "tell her all" and manages to slip away before she can catch him again.

Leporello's way of telling Elvira all, and thereby bringing her consolation, is one of the oddest in the world. "Look," he says, "you haven't been the first he has deserted and you won't be the last." And he takes out a book from which a long stretch of paper coils across the stage as he reads her the list of the Don's conquests. This is the "Madamina" patter song. In Italy, he sings, there were 640, in Germany 231, a hundred in France, ninety-one in Turkey, but in Spain— here comes the grand climax—1003! (The total, which Leporello does not bother to tot up, is 2065.) Furthermore, the list includes women of every rank, shape, and complexion—countesses, servant girls, city ladies, baronesses, marchionesses, princesses. The technique

---

[8] The librettist is vague about what actually happened between Donna Elvira and Don Giovanni. Here she says that he declared her his wife and later on she refers to him several times as her husband. Critics seem to assume that this is just the unfortunate lady's delusion, but it may well be that Mozart and Da Ponte thought of the two being legally, if clandestinely, married. The possibility is strengthened by the fact that in Molière's play on the subject (which, of course, antedates the opera) the Don and the Donna were actually married. If they were also married in the opera, Don Giovanni becomes even more of a villain and Donna Elvira less fatuous.

used by the Don, continues Leporello, is to praise blondes for their gentleness and sweetness, brunettes for their constancy. In the winter he likes them a bit on the plump side, in the summer rather thinner. He likes both great, majestic creatures and little minxes, and he has a weakness for getting some of the older ladies down on his list too. However, the predominating passion is for young ones. And, he concludes with the ultimate touch of tactfulness, Donna Elvira herself knows pretty well how successful the Don is! With which Leporello also makes a hasty exit.

Temporarily, at least, Donna Elvira is roused to a more aggressive frame of mind. As the curtain goes down, she says that she now despises the Don and that she will be truly revenged on him.

Scene 3: The next scene—apparently still the same day—takes place in a pretty, rural spot near Don Giovanni's castle on the outskirts of Seville. Villagers are singing and dancing, celebrating the engagement of a pretty girl named Zerlina to her village swain, Masetto, who is usually acted like a much stupider young fellow than he seems to be after one has read the libretto. The sweet little chorus the villagers sing ends as the two young lovers are surrounded by a ring of their friends.

The Don and Leporello, reunited after their successive escapes from Donna Elvira, come upon this rustic scene, and the Don almost at once picks out the just-engaged Zerlina for his next attempt at amorous conquest. With the most gallant condescension, he congratulates the happy young couple and invites the entire company to come into his castle, where Leporello is to show them his gardens, his rooms, his pictures. His plan, of course, is to send the others upstairs and keep Zerlina in the garden with him. He pokes Leporello in the ribs as he gives him instructions to take particular care of Masetto. That young man is at once suspicious and protests that he cannot leave Zerlina. Nor is he in the least reassured when Leporello, the Don, and Zerlina herself all point out that she is in the hands of a nobleman. Even when the Don warns him by tapping the hilt of his sword, Masetto continues to protest bitterly. "Always trust a gentleman," he ironically repeats over and over again. His resentment of the eighteenth-century aristocrat's attitude toward the sanctity of a lower-class marriage is quite as great as Figaro's in *The Marriage of Figaro*. Unfortunately, his fiancée is more dangerously flirtatious than Figaro's, and all that Masetto can do for the moment is to continue to protest as Leporello hustles him off.

With Masetto out of the way, the Don goes to work at once. It is obvious, he says, that nature never meant Zerlina to be married to such a low fellow as that Masetto. She was meant to marry a noble. Zerlina points out that she has promised to marry Masetto the next day—a promise that is worth, says the Don, exactly zero. Zerlina is still resistant (in a very artful way, of course) and suggests that the reputation of noblemen, when it comes to ladies, is not noted for honesty and sincerity. "A plebeian slander," says the Don, and he invites Zerlina to his castle, where, he says, he will marry her at once.

The duet that follows is so charming that it had to be sung over three times at the opera's *première*. Thereafter encores were forbidden. The Don, without too much difficulty, persuades Zerlina that his intentions are honorable, and she agrees to give them a try. Toward the close of the duet, Donna Elvira comes on the scene and sees what is going on. Just as the couple are about to go to the castle, Elvira dramatically interrupts and denounces the Don and his intentions, of which, as she points out, she has had firsthand experience. He tries to whisper to Elvira that this is only a pastime, and to Zerlina that Elvira is only a poor wretch suffering from jealousy. A short, dramatic—almost melodramatic—aria by Elvira, however, prevents his getting away with it this time, and Zerlina allows herself to be saved for the moment. With both women off the stage, the Don remarks that the Devil himself seems to be getting in the way of everything he's doing today.

And speaking of the Devil, in come Donna Anna and Don Ottavio, still discussing the revenge they have sworn on her father's murderer (whose identity they still, of course, do not know). Ironically, they appeal to Don Giovanni himself for help, which he is delighted to promise them. But now Elvira comes back on the scene and urges them not to trust in the Don. A remarkable quartet follows in which Donna Anna and Don Ottavio are impressed by Donna Elvira's protests. They are particularly impressed by her being a member of the nobility. Meanwhile, Elvira continues her denunciations while Don Giovanni tries alternately to persuade her to behave in a less spectacular fashion and to assure the other two that the lady is slightly out of her mind. Finally he manages to lead her away. The poor thing, is his parting comment to the others, needs someone to keep her from suicide.[9]

Suddenly the truth dawns on Donna Anna. In agitated accents she describes to Don Ottavio the invasion of her bedroom by an unknown man whom she at first took for Ottavio himself. A violent struggle ended (to Ottavio's evident relief) in her frightening the intruder away; but her father followed him and was murdered. Now, she says, she has recognized the man: he was Don Giovanni. Then, in an aria of great strength and nobility, she calls upon Don Ottavio once more to swear vengeance and leaves the stage.

The rather one-track mind of Don Ottavio can scarcely believe that a nobleman could behave so badly; but he swears, nevertheless, to help Donna Anna and sings the serene aria "Dalla sua pace," a beautiful melody that Mozart added after the initial performance in order to make the leading tenor look a little less like a superficial ornament.

Leporello now comes back, again resolving to leave the service of his master; but as soon as Don Giovanni appears, he reports that though matters couldn't have been going much worse with the peasants, he has handled them rather ingeniously. The Don congratulates him enthusiastically. It seems that Leporello had considerable difficulty with the jealous Masetto; but he got them all to eating and drinking, when who should come in but—as Don Giovanni guesses—Zerlina; and who should be with her but (the Don guesses correctly again) Elvira. Elvira was still at the business of cursing out the Don, but somehow Leporello managed to get her out of the house and lock the door on her.

Don Giovanni is so much delighted with this report of progress that he bursts into the light, mercurial patter song sometimes called the "Champagne" Aria. In it he instructs Leporello to invite all the prettiest girls he can find to his party for drinking, dancing, and nonsense unconfined. By morning, he grandiosely deludes himself, he shall have added ten more names to his list of feminine conquests.

---

[9] Presumably as an exercise in dramatic vocal composition in preparation for *Fidelio,* Beethoven copied out the vocal lines of this quartet. Beethoven's holograph is now owned by Walter Slezak, the actor, son of Leo Slezak, the tenor.

Scene 4: The next change of scene brings us, that evening, to the garden outside of Don Giovanni's castle, with a wing of the castle itself and its balcony visible on one side. Zerlina and Masetto are there, among the rosebushes, and they are still quarreling about the Don's outrageous prenuptial attentions to another's bride. Zerlina is all contrition and pleads that she really isn't to blame. If she was misled for a moment, she didn't *really* succumb to the nobleman. Won't Masetto believe her? He may kill her if it isn't so—and she sings the aria "Batti, batti," which is so tender a compound of innocence and flirtatiousness that a much more adamant swain than Masetto would be moved by it.

Masetto has scarcely been won over when Zerlina hears the Don giving directions for the reception of his guests, and she has a sinking feeling that maybe—just maybe—she had better hide herself. But it is Masetto who hides, deliberately leaving the reluctant Zerlina in the dangerous Don's path and retiring to an arbor to watch. The villain enters still pursuing her, though giving directions to four servants at the same time. Zerlina tries to hide from him, but he catches her by the hand and starts pressing his suit once more. The technique this time is to draw Zerlina with him into the privacy of the arbor, where, of course, he bumps right into Masetto. Nonplused for only a moment, he tells the young man that his poor little girl has been pining away for him. Masetto is hardly convinced, but the Don, gallantly and diplomatically taking an arm of each of the lovers, escorts them into the castle as he invites them to his party, and they accept in a gay little trio.

Scarcely have they left when three figures in masks come on the darkening scene. They are the Donnas Elvira and Anna with Don Ottavio. Elvira and Ottavio sing of the rather indefinite revenge they hope to get on Giovanni, and Anna sings of her fears for the other two. Inside, the famous Minuet is quietly played as Leporello and Don Giovanni appear on the balcony and notice the maskers. The Don instructs his servant to invite these strangers to the party; and while the music of the minuet continues, the invitation is delivered from the balcony and courteously accepted by Don Ottavio.

Then, just before entering the castle, the three masked figures come to the footlights to sing a soft prayer that they may achieve a just revenge. The voices weave in and out in transparent and beautifully flowing lines of close harmony, creating at once the loveliest and most solemn moment in the act.

Scene 5: The last scene of the first act brings us right into the castle of Don Giovanni, where there is apparently nothing going on but brilliant gaiety everywhere. No fewer than three separate orchestras are playing in as many little balconies of the main hall; two other rooms for dancing are observable on the sides; while in back, doors open onto the garden, which is also illuminated with lamps and gaily decorated.

The party is in full swing, with Don Giovanni and Leporello offering refreshments to everyone. Masetto and Zerlina are rather nervous —and with good reason, for the Don starts flirting with Zerlina almost at once. She cannot help responding a little; and as Masetto gets angrier and angrier, Leporello and the Don promise that he will be punished for his jealousy. The entrance of the three maskers temporarily puts a stop to the growing tension. They are cordially welcomed, and the Don calls for more music. As the minuet is again struck up, he picks Zerlina for his partner; the maskers consult together; and Leporello pursues and annoys the jealous Masetto, finally forcing the poor fellow to dance with him.

The musical and dramatic effect here is extraordinarily ingenious when it is well done, but practically impossible to reproduce on a single piano. Mozart has three different dances going on at once, each of the stage orchestras playing a different tune in a different rhythm. The minuet, on the top line, is for the nobles, the contradance for the peasants, and the waltz for Leporello and Masetto. In the general excitement the Don still pursues Zerlina, who tries (not too violently) to escape him, and finally he manages to draw her off to a room on the right. Masetto meanwhile has managed to shake off Leporello, who follows his master into the next room. A moment later, the dancing is interrupted by a cry from Zerlina off stage, and everyone turns to the door, which is locked. They try to force it and are about to break it down when the Don comes out, prodding Leporello in before him at the point of his sword (carefully kept in the scabbard).

No one is fooled. They all angrily attack their host, Don Ottavio even threatening him with a pistol. But in the general confusion of the exciting ensemble number that follows, Giovanni never once loses his coolness. His sword now drawn, he makes his way through the crowd and gets away from all of them through the window into the garden in back.

ACT II—*Scene* 1: The second act starts with formulas that are already familiar. It is evening on a square in Seville with Donna Elvira's house and balcony on one side—though we are not told whose address it is till a little later on. Don Giovanni is arguing with Leporello on their pet theme: Leporello wants to leave this service, and the Don wants to keep him in it. A large tip—four doubloons (about sixteen dollars)—makes Leporello begin to see reason, provided the Don will only leave the women alone. "Give up the women?" cries the Don. "Why, they're more necessary to me than bread and breath!" As for what Leporello calls "deceiving," it is all done for love. How could one be faithful to just one woman without being cruel to all the others? No, the Don's expanse of sentiment is far too wide for any such niggardly ideas: he wishes well for all women.

And now to business. If Leporello will kindly lend the Don his costume, he'd like to try his luck with Donna Elvira's lovely little maid. And why the exchange of cloaks? Well, says the Don—possibly remembering Masetto and Zerlina—common folk sometimes have suspicions about the motives of noblemen; and, angrily silencing Leporello's protests, he exchanges hats and cloaks with him.

But it is Donna Elvira herself, and not the maid, who appears on the balcony, still breathing romantic revenge. The Don takes cruel advantage of the situation. He stands behind Leporello (who, in the dark of the night, can easily be mistaken for the Don) and with his own voice pleads to be taken back by Elvira. At the same time, he moves Leporello's arms for him in appropriately romantic gestures—a bit of low comedy that few actors can resist from overindulging to the extent of spoiling some very lovely music. The foolish Elvira succumbs almost at once, and after a trio, in which the Don and his servant laugh at her, she comes down to them. As she descends inside the house, the Don instructs the reluctant Leporello to impersonate him in the dark and persuade Elvira to leave with him so that the coast may be clear again for Giovanni's own love-making.

Leporello is at first afraid to try this deception, but he has no choice; and when he finds the job easier than he thought, with Elvira practically melting in his arms, he rather warms up to the business. He is swearing eternal fidelity when the Don, who has been watching on the side, jumps out and makes believe he is a holdup man about to kill them both. Elvira and Leporello run away.

Don Giovanni now sets the stage for himself—even to a mandolin that he had brought along and leant carefully against the side of the house. He picks up the instrument and, to a tune that he had already begun a few moments earlier when serenading Elvira, he now serenades her maid. He thinks he hears the girl coming onto the balcony; but just at this point a group of armed peasants, led by Masetto, come in, looking for the Don, whom they fully intend to murder. Seeing there are quite a few of them, Giovanni makes believe he is Leporello, disguising his voice just as skillfully as Leporello disguised his own when wooing Elvira. He tells the rustics that he fully agrees in their low opinion of Don Giovanni, and he instructs them how to find him: half must go this way, half the other way, and should they run across a man in such a cloak and such a hat (and here he describes the costume he had forced on poor Leporello), making love to a lady, that will be Don Giovanni. He gets the rest to leave, and Masetto to stay with him.

"Won't just a beating do for the Don?" he asks.

"No," says Masetto, "I want to kill him, to cut him up into a hundred pieces."

"Do you have good weapons?" asks the Don in friendly anxiety.

"Well, just look," says Masetto, and hands over his musket and pistol.

Whereupon the Don takes them from him, beats the poor fellow with the flat of his sword, and runs off. Masetto sets up a great cry, but Zerlina comes on the stage and discovers that he is not nearly so badly hurt as he thinks he is. She sings to him with Mozartean magic about the remedy she has for him—a most pleasant medicine that she carries with her. Doesn't he guess what it is? And she lays his hand on her heart as he hobbles off the stage with her, already half cured.

Scene 2: In the next scene, Leporello and Donna Elvira have accidentally strayed into the garden of the Commandant, where Donna Anna lives. It is still dark; Elvira still thinks she is with Don Giovanni; and Donna Anna and Don Ottavio, who enter on the other side, are still busy mourning her father. While Donna Anna laments and Ottavio tries to comfort her, Leporello gropes along the wall for an exit. He thinks he has it, when he is suddenly confronted by Zerlina and Masetto. Everyone, of course, mistakes him for his master, whose clothes he is wearing, and they are about to murder him when Donna Elvira intervenes and pleads for "her husband," as she calls him. Leporello, in desperation, now shows his face. They are first astonished and then angrily determined to punish him too; but he has learned enough from his master to talk himself out of harder spots than this one. He kneels before them, apologizes to each in succession, blames the Don, pleads to be allowed to go, and suddenly darts out.

Don Ottavio now says he is sure that Don Giovanni is the murderer of the Commandant (though his reasoning is not quite clear), and he will go and get some help from the law. For a Spanish don, this would appear to be a sin against romantic tradition, but he makes up for it by singing one of the loveliest arias Mozart ever wrote—the fluent and enormously difficult "Il mio tesoro."

(A low-comedy scene follows in the score, but it is almost always omitted in modern productions. Zerlina catches up with Leporello once more, drags him around the stage, ties him up in a chair, threatens him with a razor, and then goes off for the others. While they are gone, the window to which Zerlina had tied the rope drops, and she returns with the others to find that Leporello has hopped out. I have never seen this scene done, but I have no deep regrets about it. This scene is followed by the aria "Mi tardi," in which Donna Elvira once again voices her grief over Don Giovanni's betrayal of her. It is a very fine aria and in American productions usually is sung before a drop curtain.)

Scene 3: It is now two o'clock in the morning, as Don Giovanni tells us in the next scene. Still in Leporello's cloak, he has just climbed over the wall of a churchyard whose chief ornament is a large equestrian statue of the Commandant. The Don is in high spirits, wondering what has happened to Leporello and rubbing his hands over another little adventure he has had in the meantime. Leporello, escaping from his tormentors, comes the same way; but he is naturally in poorer spirits. Those spirits are not improved by the little tale the Don tells. He had met a pretty little miss in the street, made up to her, and been very tenderly received because—and here's the joke—she mistook the Don for Leporello himself. It was one of Leporello's girls.

"But suppose she had been my wife?" objects the servant.

"All the better," laughs the Don.

Just then the moon breaks through the clouds, the statue is flooded with a ghostly light, and a voice solemnly says, "Your joking will end before dawn."

For a moment the Don thinks it must be someone hiding in the churchyard. Then the voice speaks again, and he suspects it may be the statue. He forces the terror-stricken Leporello to read the inscription on the base. This is what it says:

> **"Here I wait for Vengeance on the Impious**
> **Man who Killed Me."**

Leporello can scarcely read for fright, but the Don apparently remains unmoved. He calls it a great joke and instructs Leporello to invite the statue to dinner. Poor Leporello does his best to get out of this impiety, and only after a few threats of sudden death at the end of the Don's sword does he manage to sputter out the invitation— adding that this is strictly the Don's invitation, not his own. Leporello sees the statue nod its head in acceptance and reports the phenomenon to his master. Finally the Don sees it too, but he insists that the statue should answer his invitation orally. It does, with one "Yes."

The Don still tries to appear unafraid. He remarks that this is certainly bizarre and instructs Leporello to get ready to receive their guest. But his voice (the passage is marked *mezza voce*) shows that he is moved underneath his cold exterior. As for Leporello, he can hardly stand for fright, and he makes no bones about saying so as he runs off.

Scene 4: In the brief scene that follows, Don Ottavio tries to persuade Donna Anna to forget her sorrow, now that Don Giovanni will soon be brought to justice, and to marry him. In an aria full of tenderness—and also of difficult, florid passages—Donna Anna tells him that she cannot do so now, while her sorrow is still fresh, but that she loves him and some day heaven will bless their union. This is the famous "Non mi dir."

Scene 5: The last scene of all—and the most dramatic—takes place in Don Giovanni's banqueting hall, which is brightly lighted, richly furnished, and blessed with a private orchestra that plays in a gallery. The tunes it plays include some of the hits of Mozart's day—an air each from Martín y Soler's *Una cosa rara,* Sarti's *Fra due litiganti,* and Mozart's own *Le Nozze di Figaro,* which was an enormous hit in Prague at the time of the *première* of *Don Giovanni.* Leporello comments on this last (it is the "Non più andrai") with: "I know that thing only too well."

Meantime, the Don is eating away, served dish after dish by his dining-room staff, and calling on Leporello to amuse him. Just as the meal is about over, Donna Elvira rushes in in a frenzied mood and begs the Don to change his manner of living. Giovanni thinks this is a good joke, mockingly kneels beside her, and makes fun of her while Leporello marvels at the lady's persistence. No one seems to notice the sound of approaching thunder. When the Don has had enough of his joke, he sits down again to eat—and that is more than even the long-suffering Elvira can stand. She curses him and starts to rush out of the center door in back.

At once, she jumps back and screams. Leporello follows her and, just outside the door, also lets out a shout. He comes back to report in quaking accents that the white stone man is there. Don Giovanni refuses to believe him, and when a knocking begins at the door, he orders Leporello to open. The poor fellow just can't do it: he can barely stand for fright, and he hides under the table.

The Don himself takes up a light, opens the door, and there stands the great marble figure of the statue, announcing—to the accompaniment of thunder—that he has come to dinner, as he was invited to. Still the perfect gentleman, Don Giovanni orders Leporello to lay another cover, but the statue saves him this trouble. "Whoever has eaten in heaven," he says, "does not need earthly food." On the contrary, he has come to invite the Don to dine with him. Does he accept?

Leporello, still under the table, begs his master not to accept and even tries to assure the statue that there's a previous engagement which will interfere. But the Don, protesting—perhaps too much—

that he doesn't even know the meaning of fear, accepts the invitation, if not exactly with pleasure. At once, the statue reaches out his hand to seal the compact, and Don Giovanni finds himself held in a terrible stony clasp. The statue urges him—even at this late hour—to repent, but the Don proudly refuses and orders his guest away. Finally, he wrests his hand free as the statue, in deep tones, tells him his time is up.

Flames start leaping up everywhere, a chorus of hollow voices announces the Don's eternal damnation, and he himself at last cries out in agony as fire consumes the whole house.[10]

The curtain goes down on this scene of destruction, and before it step Elvira, Anna, Zerlina, Ottavio, and Masetto, accompanied by the ministers of justice, whose job has been anticipated for them. Leporello, who somehow has managed to escape the conflagration, comes in and, still all but incoherent with fright, tells what he has seen. Anna then promises to marry Ottavio after a year of mourning; Zerlina and Masetto plan prompter nuptials; while Elvira declares she will enter a convent, and Leporello that he will seek a better master.

And the opera closes on a moral little sextet in which all agree that Don Giovanni has come to a most appropriate end.

H. W. S.

THE CHARACTERS

Leporello is the central figure of the opera. In the fantastic world in which it is played, he is the one real person, the firm rock of reality in the midst of a dream. He is the reasonable man, the man on the Clapham omnibus, as Lord Justice Bowen put it. If the audience is too prone to be carried away by Don Giovanni's gallantry or by Elvira's misery, it is Leporello who brings it back to earth. The whole opera may be regarded as Leporello's dream; where in a real world would such figures appear as Don Giovanni or the Statue? He goes through the most extraordinary experiences for the sake of his master, never questioning the latter's authority to others, only

---

[10] In Europe many opera houses end *Don Giovanni* at this point. They fear that what follows will be an anticlimax. Mozart apparently wanted only to lower the tragic tone of the previous action and to point the moral to his tale.

grumbling to himself or to Don Giovanni. He is ready to deal with each situation as it arises, coping in turn with an irate husband, a deserted wife, a dead man's statue, and he even survives the shock of witnessing Don Giovanni's descent into Hell. Through each of these experiences his reactions are those of the normal man. He is genuinely terrified by the Statue, for instance, and quails beneath the table in the presence of Hell! At the end, however, he throws off the past without any difficulty. He has not suffered by his master's downfall, and even hell fire has not left him a nervous wreck. Having recounted the details of Don Giovanni's end to the others, he picks up his bag and announces his intention of finding a new master. The whole thing was a dream. He is too sane to let it affect him deeply. Leporello is almost the hero. The opera rests more on his shoulders than on those of his master.

Don Giovanni himself is the reckless libertine, who has brought dangerous living to a fine art, and absolutely refuses to know the meaning of fear until actually faced with death. What is his motive for pursuing women? It must be something more than mere physical lust. Perhaps it is ambition, or the insatiable desire to conquer new fields, or the thrill of adventure. It seems strange that his enthusiasm should have survived the number of conquests recorded in Leporello's catalogue. Will he never be disillusioned, never tired? Will he always imagine that his newest adventure will be more thrilling than any previous one? Ambition and pride probably more truly represent his motives. He has never yet failed to subject a woman by his charms, and admission of failure in any given case would be a recognition of the approach of middle age, the waning of his star. There is apparently no question of social ambition. All types of women are potential conquests. He flouts conventions and defies the institutions of an ordered life. His dreadful end is the victory of stable society over one who will not conform to its standards. That is why the story is immortal, for the conflict between society and the individual occurs in all ages. He who sets himself against society and its conventions will always go under in the end. This is the fate of Don Giovanni. The rules and institutions of society are too strong even for him, and since he will not conform to them, there is no place for him in the world.

Apart from Leporello, the other normal person among the men

of the opera is Masetto. He is an honest peasant and sees through Don Giovanni's attempts to seduce his bride, but is ready enough to forgive her afterwards. Who would not forgive such a charming person, particularly as her affair with Don Giovanni does not survive their first encounter? Masetto has often been made to appear as a complete clown, but his music shows that he has great strength of character. He may be simple, but he is no mere fool, or he would offer no resistance to Don Giovanni. It is interesting to note that Masetto's aria in Act I, "Ho capito," was apparently the last part of the score to be written before the Prague performance. In his introduction to the score, Einstein refers to the different parts of the opera that were written by Mozart in Vienna before he arrived at Prague, and suggests that he was able to write most of the opera in advance because he knew, from his visit in February, 1787, the singers who would take part. Einstein suggests that the only one whom he did not know was Giuseppe Lolli, who doubled the parts of the Commendatore and of Masetto. Hence the aria was left to the end until he knew his singer. It is also possible that Mozart may have wished to strengthen the part of Masetto by making him resist Don Giovanni's brutality, and added the aria for this purpose.

Ottavio is the most difficult of the men; he has to sing the formal music of a leading lyric tenor, and behave as a spineless operatic hero. He scarcely seems to come to life throughout the opera, but some attempt must be made to turn him into a convincing character. E. T. A. Hoffmann has some valuable suggestions to make in his fanciful story *Don Juan*. At one stage in his career, in 1808, Hoffmann became musical director in Bamberg, where the inn "Zur Rose" was connected with the theatre by a private entrance to one of the boxes. Hoffmann's story tells of a visitor to the inn who attends a performance of the opera in the adjoining theatre. After the performance he returns to the theatre, and sits in the box writing a letter to a friend. The letter contains Hoffmann's own interpretation of the opera. It is a romantic interpretation, and as such has been freely criticized, but his observations on some of the characters are useful. His description of Ottavio is worth reproducing:

A tender, well-groomed dandy, at the most twenty-one years of age. As Anna's betrothed he can be called up so quickly because he probably lives in the house; at the first cry, which he certainly must have heard, he could have hurried out and saved her father; but he has to tidy himself, and is reluctant to be called out in the night at all.

The character of Anna presents many difficulties. Although infused with great fire and determination, her music is essentially typical of a dramatic soprano. She is scarcely human, and even when her father's murder has been satisfactorily avenged, she insists on waiting a year before considering Ottavio's suit. Here again, Hoffmann is illuminating. He has come in for a lot of criticism because he assumes, as the basis of his remarks about Anna, that she was actually seduced by Don Giovanni. From the text there is nothing to justify this assumption, and many writers have taken upon themselves the task of defending Anna's honour against Hoffmann's charges! His thesis, which certainly makes Anna's motives psychologically real, can stand just as well without the seduction. His idea is that Anna, a voluptuous woman at heart, has been roused for the first and only time in her life by Don Giovanni. He alone could awaken her dormant passion, and beside him, the great romantic lover, her own Ottavio cuts a poor figure. Before Don Giovanni appeared, she knew no better than to believe that she loved Ottavio; but once awakened to the greater overpowering passion which she feels for Don Giovanni, all else fades. "She feels that only Don Giovanni's end can bring peace to her tortured spirit; but this peace is her own earthly end." It follows from this, as Hoffmann points out, that she will never marry Ottavio.

The same passion consumed Elvira, though she alone succeeded in marrying Don Giovanni. He has deserted her, and moved by the same overwhelming thirst for his downfall, she warns the world of his infamy. Jealousy is her real motive. No one else shall have him, if she may not. Such conduct is a thin disguise. She is still desperately in love with the man, and would take him back to-morrow if he would come; but knowing that she can no longer hold him she determines that no one else shall take her place. If Anna is the lady, the nobleman's daughter, Elvira belongs to the middle class. She had great beauty in her day, but once cast aside, all poise is gone, and her natural character reveals itself. She behaves like any other disappointed parvenue, and Leporello's aside—"Pare un libro stampato" (She's like a printed book)—sums her up, for she is essentially the bore of the opera. She continually pursues Don Giovanni, for ever reminding him that she is his wife. In a sense she is the only one who has defeated him. In order to conquer her, he had to satisfy her middle-class outlook by going through some form of marriage with her! She never ceases to "nag" at him, and her music is all in the same tragic vein. A healthy sense of humour would have stood her in good stead. Apart from Don Giovanni she has no status in the world, and unless she can establish her claim to be his wife she has no reason to live.

A tradition seems to have grown up that Anna, and not Elvira, is the principal lady in the opera. The *prima donna* of the opera company is usually cast as Anna, and Elvira is left to a singer of less experience. But the claims of both parts, from the musical point of view, are equal, and Elvira is surely the more difficult part to act. A fine actress can make little of the part of Anna however hard she tries, but her experience and technique can find ample scope in the part of Elvira.

Zerlina is the most normal woman of the opera. She is not a co-quette, nor an inexperienced country girl. Don Giovanni is not the first man with whom she has had to deal, nor the first of the aristocracy who has paid attention to her. But she has never before been handled with such deference, or treated as an equal by one of them. In the normal run of things, Masetto, as the peasant husband, would have to swallow such attentions as part of the lot of all men in his position. But after her first encounter with Don Giovanni, Zerlina has had enough of him. Not because of anything which she has been told by Elvira, but because she realizes that the glamour of that first meeting will not last and that her real happiness in life is to be found with Masetto. She does not, like the others, allow Don Giovanni to ruin her whole life, for she is endowed with a fuller measure of common sense.

C. B.

Così fan tutte

[*Thus Do All Women*]

Opera buffa in two acts.
Book by Lorenzo Da Ponte.
First performance: Burgtheater, Vienna, January 26, 1790.

CHARACTERS

Fiordiligi, a lady of Ferrara, SOPRANO
Dorabella, her sister, SOPRANO OR
  MEZZO-SOPRANO
Despina, their waiting maid, SOPRANO
Ferrando, an officer, in love with
  Dorabella, TENOR

Guglielmo, an officer, in love with
  Fiordiligi, BARITONE
Don Alfonso, a cynical old bachelor,
  BASSO BUFFO
  Soldiers, Servants, Musicians,
  Boatmen, Wedding Guests, etc.

The action takes place in Naples during the eighteenth century

THE BACKGROUND

ONE MIGHT say that *Così fan tutte* has always been the Cinderella of Mozart's three Italian comic operas; though it is hardly fair to call *The Marriage of Figaro* and *Don Giovanni* "ugly sisters." But they made their way throughout the world in the course of time, whereas *Così fan tutte* was almost completely neglected until the great Mozart revival which took place at Munich about 1895. Even then it would hardly have attracted much notice if it had not been enthusiastically encouraged by Richard Strauss, who in those days was a young conductor hardly known at all as a composer.

The three operas really may be said to form a kind of trilogy, for they are all in the same style, composed for a small theatre and a small company—it might almost be said that they were composed for the same singers; and what is more important, they all three had librettos written by the same poet, the Abbé Lorenzo Da Ponte. All three are described on the title-pages of their librettos as *dramma giocoso;* the same word is used too in Mozart's own private manuscript catalogue for his own works. Comic opera of this type, written for perhaps six or seven characters with a minimum of chorus, was a flourishing commercial industry, centered mainly on Venice after the rise of the partnership between the Venetian playwright, Goldoni, and the Venetian composer, Galuppi, who might be called the Gilbert and Sullivan of the eighteenth century. Goldoni wrote not only the spoken comedies which have since made him world famous in the history of the theatre, but also some fifty or sixty librettos for comic operas, set by various composers. They are often trivial and foolish in plot—after all, their one and only object is to amuse—but they are never clumsy or awkward in style; they are written in good conversational Italian, neat in versification and rhyme, admirably suited to musical setting and cleverly constructed for the stage, as long as one accepts the conventions of the time. Da Ponte learned a good deal from Goldoni as regards technique, but he struck out new lines as regards subject; his Italian style is always elegant and natural, and he is marvellously skilful at adapting French plays, such as those of Molière and Beaumarchais, to the requirements of the Italian comic opera stage.

The Marriage of Figaro is a landmark in operatic history because of its libretto, a play which combined an unusual amount of vigorous action on the stage with a background of social and political satire. The original play of Beaumarchais had started as a comic opera based on the older traditions of the comedy of masks. Figaro is a sort of Harlequin, the link between the stage and the audience, ready to talk informally to the spectators at any moment, and to be the mouthpiece for the author's opinions on life in general. Compared with many operas, *Figaro* is conspicuously full of action, but it is really a play of talk. Modern critics have sometimes praised Mozart (for all good points Mozart gets the credit, and for all the short-comings the librettist is invariably blamed) for eliminating all the political satire in the play and converting it into a banquet of pure melody, others have blamed Da Ponte for presenting his audience with nothing but a sordid comedy of illicit love. Beethoven seems to have taken that view, for he said that he himself could never write music for such immoral stories as those of *Figaro* and *Don Giovanni*. But in 1786, when Mozart's *Figaro* first came out, the play was still forbidden in Vienna, although translations of it were on sale in the bookshops. It has been said of Beaumarchais that he taught the aristocrats themselves to scoff at the old *régime,* and even in Vienna, which was always more reactionary (because more devout and less intelligent) than Paris, there must have been intellectuals who, when they went to see Mozart's opera, could easily supply from memory all that Da Ponte had been obliged to remove either from consideration for the censorship, or—what was more important—consideration for the stage.

Don Giovanni can hardly be called a revolutionary opera, but it could be interpreted in a revolutionary sense. We must never forget that both Da Ponte and Mozart were writing for the practical needs of the moment, and a given cast of singers; they were not consciously creating one of the world's masterpieces for the joy and admiration of eternity. *Don Giovanni* was commissioned by Prague because *Figaro* had been a success there; the Czechs were always, as they are still, immeasurably more musical than the Viennese. It was obvious at once that the new opera would have to follow the general lines of its predecessor, all the more as most of the same singers were to take part in it. *Figaro* had been laid out in four acts because the usual three, or even two, of comic opera were not enough to hold all the material which Da Ponte borrowed from Beaumarchais' five. Da Ponte and Mozart therefore planned *Don Giovanni* on the same lines—the same sort of songs, duets, and ensembles, and in four acts. For some unknown reason the opera was given in two, as it is still. The same unknown reason must have dictated the arrangement of *Così fan tutte* in two acts, although they are exceedingly long ones. In every commercial theatre such matters are decided by extraneous authority; we know how in England the hours of beginning and ending, the distribution into acts, and the length of the intervals depend on the hours of normal meal-times, the hours of last trains to the suburbs, as well as of those during which chocolates may be sold in the theatre or drinks in the bar. The construction of Mozart's operas was pretty certainly dictated by similar considerations.

Don Giovanni derives a good deal from Molière, a little from Goldoni, and most of all from Giovanni Bertati, a contemporary librettist. But these sources could only supply isolated incidents and phrases of dialogue; for the general plan and the big ensembles Da Ponte had to make use of his own invention and routine. The chief difference between *Figaro* and *Don Giovanni* is that the former is mostly a drama of talk and the latter entirely a drama of action. Social satire is apparent only in Masetto's song, and in the scene where Masetto collects the peasants to murder Don Giovanni; there is also the very important satirical aspect—derived directly from Molière—of Don Giovanni's complete cynicism as regards morality and religion. We can at any rate say that this opera brings us one step nearer to the revolution year of 1789.

By the time Così fan tutte was put on the stage the Revolution had started in Paris, and there could be no more open satire on the operatic stage in Vienna. Yet satire there is, and on the eternal subject of female frailty. To Mozart's own public there could be nothing in the least shocking about that. Both Figaro and Don Giovanni dealt undisguisedly with seduction and adultery; the libretto of Così fan tutte is as chaste as a novel of Miss Yonge. There is in it not the faintest suggestion of "impropriety," except perhaps for Despina's hints at the way in which the military behave on active service. We may perhaps accept the legend that the plot was suggested by an actual fact of recent date, and it is fairly clear that Da Ponte was influenced by the general scheme of La Grotta di Trofonio, an opera by Casti and Salieri (1785) in which the characters of two pairs of lovers are completely changed by the spells of a magician. But apart from these sources, Da Ponte's libretto is entirely his own invention, and it is a singularly accomplished piece of formal craftsmanship.

From a realistic standpoint the plot may be absurd; accept its deliberate artificiality, and the factual details do not matter. Was there a war going on in 1789 between Naples and some other maritime power? Ought not Nelson and Lady Hamilton—such admirable operatic figures, too—to have been brought in? They would have been a great nuisance. The imbecility of the two young ladies may indeed astonish us; but all that is quite subsidiary to the real motive of the opera—the mental processes by which they shift their affections from one lover to another. We see in this libretto what we are to see eventually in The Magic Flute, and what we did not see at all in either Figaro or Don Giovanni—psychological development. In The Magic Flute we see Tamino and Pamina going through all sorts of experiences and growing up to maturity thereby; and in that opera everything is perfectly serious as far as these two are concerned. In Così fan tutte nothing is serious, except perhaps Don Alfonso's hatred of the whole race of women; and it is curious to note that in both two previous operas the women have little claim on our respect. Da Ponte was a Catholic priest, but he had a considerable knowledge of the female sex. He was a great friend of Casanova, and he eventually died in New York as the father of a family.

The musical planning is masterly. Mozart is allowed an unusually large number of ensembles, and some of them are unusually extended; a great deal of the drama really takes place in the course of these "conversation-pieces." It is quite possible that Mozart may have talked the whole problem out with Da Ponte from the first, telling him exactly what he wanted in the way of musical numbers; even so, we must admire the incredible skill with which Da Ponte has constructed and arranged them. *Così fan tutte,* in fact, so far from being what many German and other critics have called it, the worst libretto ever written, is really about the nearest approach to perfection that any musical dramatist has ever achieved. It is fundamentally a comic opera; but Mozart's singers wanted grand arias in which they could show off all their virtuosity. Da Ponte provides them, with recitatives to introduce them too. But as the singers' art is artificial and formal, he makes all these grand arias and recitatives caricatures of the grand arias of the past; and this is all the better for the singers, for it enables them not merely to show off, but to exaggerate their exhibitionism to the very utmost.

Later generations took all these things with a deadly seriousness. Having no acquaintance with genuine *opera seria,* which after all had been dead for some thirty or forty years when *Così fan tutte* first came out, they could not appreciate the caricature for want of knowledge of the thing caricatured. Audiences of to-day are altogether more sophisticated than their grandparents as regards music and drama, and as regards morals and marriage as well. *Così fan tutte* is an opera for highly sophisticated people; it is the last expression of eighteenth-century artificialism.

Così fan tutte did not have much of a success at Vienna; but what could one expect from a city that had failed to appreciate both *Figaro* and *Don Giovanni?* Prague brought it out in Italian in 1791, before Mozart's death; in the same year it was performed in Italian at Leipzig and Dresden, probably by the same singers. After that, its fate depended on its German translations, and as Dr. Loewenberg says, "No other opera, perhaps, has been subjected to so many different versions and attempts to 'improve' the libretto." Needless to say, it had no success in Italy. It was given at a few Italian towns early in the next century, but it never reached Venice—where it ought to have been at home from the first—until 1934, when it was performed in German by the Vienna State Opera Company. Its first German performance in Vienna had been in 1794. In Paris it was first given in Italian, and afterwards, at widely separated dates, in all sorts of new versions, one being an adaptation of *Love's Labour's Lost.*

When *Così fan tutte* was performed for the first time in 1790, Italian *opera buffa* was on its last legs. The general repertory at all the musical theatres of Vienna became increasingly French, and the tendency of French Revolution opera was to what we should call melodrama. Melodrama (in the ordinary English sense of the word) did in fact grow out of opera, and started in France before it was imported into England. The Revolution took the theatre, including opera, very seriously, and both melodrama and melodramatic opera were designed to be powerful influences for moral education. Beethoven's *Fidelio* is the nearest thing to it that modern opera-goers are acquainted with. German native opera was modelling itself more and more on the French type, inclining towards either *bourgeois* stories, melodrama, or wild romantic supernaturalism. The ideal German heroine began to appear, the type of Agathe in *Der Frei-schütz,* the pure-minded and virtuous *Deutsches Mädchen,* with fair hair in two plaits. We know her as Marguerite in *Faust;* her first appearance was as Pamina in *The Magic Flute.* Her characteristics were simplicity and desperate seriousness, unless she was of the light soprano type, like Annette in *Der Freischütz.* Singers of these types had to do their best with *Figaro* and *Don Giovanni* in German trans-lations, but the result was to make these operas much too serious and generally too clumsy, too, in their interpretations. One might just possibly conceive of Zerlina as a *Deutsches Mädchen,* but there is no part for her in *Così fan tutte.* The romantic German stage wanted to take opera seriously, and to take *Così fan tutte* seriously is to misunderstand it from top to bottom.

E. J. D.

After *Don Giovanni* we are magically transported into yet another world: that of *Così fan tutte.* Well, scarcely a world at all; only a show of marionettes. For nothing could be more ridiculous than to pretend that the preposterous people, the still more preposterous situations of this utterly artificial intrigue, were meant to be believed in, and nothing more absurd than to take Da Ponte and Mozart to task for believing in them, which of course they never did. The philistinism of the nineteenth century which professed to take umbrage at this story of two girls who become enamoured of each other's lovers disguised as outlandish adventurers (a disguise which could not take in anybody for a moment) and which led either to the banishment of this fascinating work from the stage or to disastrous attempts at providing it with an expurgated libretto of some kind, was due to the confusion of moral and artistic values that was one of the gross immoralities of that century, with Ruskin presiding as high priest over the orgies held by addicts to aesthetic perversion. The supreme joke is that one cannot possibly help seeing the utter harmlessness of this mildly amusing piece, which contains nothing so seriously unpleasant as the Count's pursuit of Susanna in *Figaro*. Nor is it possible to see how any one could fail to be captivated by its deliberately and delectably artificial music. For once again Mozart achieved the miraculous feat of writing a score which, consistent in style from start to finish, could not by any conceivable chance lend a single one of its numbers to any other work of his. The whole perfume and flavour of the music is new and unique.

Artifice is the keynote of it. What else could it have been? But then again, who else could have made it as unfailingly charming as the master who remains the finest artificer as well as the greatest artist whose services music ever enjoyed? At the same time, of course, he infallibly hits upon the truth of his characters—the truth of their stage existences, which is all there is to them. And he does it by means of parody that has both infinite gusto and endless sympathy in it. Laughing at them, he is never cruel, and takes away the sting of his satire by making game, at the same time, of the musical mannerisms of his time, including his own.

E. B.

This brilliant lyric comedy reached America only on March 24, 1922, at the Metropolitan Opera House, New York. So much of an event was the belated *première* that, in the interest of scenic effect, a small revolving stage was superimposed on the actual Metropolitan stage, and, in the interest of musical effect, special care was taken with the casting. Artur Bodanzky, the musical director of the production, deleted from the score, however, the two arias for tenor. The cast included Florence Easton (Fiordiligi), Frances Peralta (Dorabella), Lucrezia Bori (Despina), George Meader (Ferrando), Giuseppe de Luca (Guglielmo), and Adamo Didur (Don Alfonso).

[Alfred Lunt, the noted American actor and stage director, was engaged by the Metropolitan to direct a revival of the Mozart comedy during the season of 1951–52. Ruth and Thomas Martin supplied a new English version for the bright and sumptuous production, which was conducted by Fritz Stiedry.]

P. S.

THE STORY

ACT I: The curtain rises on a café where are seated the three men, in the middle apparently of a heated argument, or so one assumes from the vigorous defence of Dorabella, his fiancée, that Ferrando is making as the music begins. There are three trios, the first for the two lovers answering the sceptical Alfonso, the second in the form of an accompanied solo for Alfonso, the third consisting of jubilation on the part of the lovers at the prospect of winning the bet which they enter upon with Alfonso. It is a scene of the purest comedy and the music matches the artificiality of the mood, culminating in a tune of bubbling, infectious gaiety such as even Mozart himself could not duplicate. The scene changes, the clarinets play in thirds over the strings,[1] and we can be sure we are with Fiordiligi and Dorabella, the paragons of faithfulness on whose constancy so much has just been wagered. They are discussing the respective merits of their young men as evinced in their portraits, and their sentimental rapture at what they see is conveyed in music of exquisitely exaggerated cast, which dissolves in the middle into a cadenza in thirds on the word "Amore." This day-dreaming is interrupted by the precipitate arrival of Don Alfonso, who makes obvious his distress

---

[1] The richness of the wind writing is unusual, even for Mozart, and there is more than a hint here and elsewhere of the great B flat major Serenade (K. 361) for thirteen wind instruments.

at the news he is only too anxious to break to the two young ladies: their lovers are ordered to the wars and are to leave immediately. It is Alfonso's nearest approach to an aria in the whole opera—is in fact described as one in the score; but its *allegro agitato* perfectly reflects the breathless agitation he counterfeits so well. The situation is admirably summed up in two quintets, which are separated by a short duet for the two officers and a military chorus. In "Sento, oh Dio" (Courage fails me)[2] the ladies are inconsolable, Don Alfonso builds up the situation, while Guglielmo is inclined to leave specific consolation to Ferrando and himself joins with Alfonso in a more general comment. Twice the two men cannot help nudging the sceptic: "There, you see now," but he remains quite unconvinced. Ferrando and Guglielmo say good-bye, soldiers march across the stage singing of the joys of a military existence, but the farewells are not complete until all four have sung a protracted and beautiful farewell, to pungent comment from Alfonso ("Di scirvermi ogni giorno": You'll write long letters often).

Their lovers departed, Fiordiligi and Dorabella show real feelings so that even Alfonso joins them in a wonderfully evocative trio, "Soave sia il vento," as they pray for calm sea and gentle breezes for the travellers. The idyllic mood does not for one bar survive their joint exit. Alfonso muses in *secco* recitative on his plans, but as he grows animated at the thought of woman's changeability he launches into an accompanied tirade against the whole sex, the one inescapably bitter moment of the score.

The scene changes, and we meet the chattering Despina, maid to the two sisters, who soon show that their loss has left them in no mood for chocolate or any other such consolation. Dorabella is the first to give vent to her feelings, in an aria of exaggeratedly tragic order, "Smanie implacabili," a parody one may think of the consciously tragic Donna Elvira or even of the wholly serious Electra in *Idomeneo*. Despina advises a more moderate line; she is the female counterpart of Don Alfonso, and in her philosophy lovers' absence affords an opportunity for sport, not for lamentation: "In uomini, in soldati." The ladies go out in disgust, and Alfonso seizes the opportunity to enlist Despina as an ally in his attempt to win the wager. Enter the two supposedly departed officers, disguised as Al-

[2] Translations throughout by the Rev. Marmaduke Browne.

banians; they are introduced to Despina, who laughs at them but does not recognise them, and is quite prepared to help them in their attempt to win the affections of her mistresses. In a moment, the two are back on the stage, indignant at finding two strange men in their house and demanding their withdrawal. Alfonso stays in hiding but comments on the situation, and emerges to embrace the Albanians as old friends of his; will the ladies not be kind to them—for his sake? Fiordiligi makes it quite clear that their protestations of love are entirely unavailing: she and her sister are each of them "firm as a rock" ("Come scoglio"). The aria is parodistic in tone, and, with its wide intervals and absurd jumps from the top to the bottom of the soprano range, seems likely to have been at any rate partly intended to poke fun at the phenomenal range and technique of Ferrarese del Bene, the original singer of Fiordiligi, who was Da Ponte's mistress at the time of the première but seems to have been no favourite of Mozart's either artistically or personally. Guglielmo answers for Ferrando as well as himself and is given music of such delicacy and charm—"Non siate ritrosi"[3] (O vision so charming)— that one cannot but be surprised that the objects of the two young men's affections turn on their respective heels and leave the room before he has had time to finish the aria, which dissolves in laughter. The rapid laughing trio is charming, but Don Alfonso has his work cut out to persuade his young friends that he has by no means lost his bet at this early juncture. Let them be ready to meet him in the garden in a few minutes time. Ferrando is left alone to sing of his love in a beautiful aria, in type romantic or even sentimental but hardly comic ("Un' aura amorosa": Her eyes so alluring). Alfonso and Despina reassure themselves that this is only a pair of women, and that there is as yet no danger of losing the bet.

For the finale we are back in the garden, under the blue Neapolitan sky and with the bay of Naples as background. Small wonder that Fiordiligi and Dorabella reflect jointly on the mutability of pleasure in music of exquisite tenderness, whose end is hardly reached before Ferrando and Guglielmo rush on to the stage brandishing bottles of poison which Alfonso is unable to prevent them drinking.

---

[3] A magnificent buffo aria, "Rivolgeti a lui lo sguardo" (K. 584), was originally planned here, but the slighter piece was substituted, one may imagine, as being more in keeping with this situation.

The situation is sufficiently complicated to provide Mozart with exactly what he wanted for an extended finale. As the Albanians sink into a coma, pandemonium breaks loose, and when Alfonso and Despina rush for the doctor, there is even an opportunity for Ferrando and Guglielmo to join in the ensemble. Alfonso returns with a doctor (Despina in disguise) who proceeds to give the corpses the benefit of the most recent scientific discovery, Mesmerism—as much the latest thing in 1790 one may imagine as Psychiatry was in the 1940's and as likely to raise a laugh, particularly when compressed, as here, into the outward form of an oversize, all-healing magnet. The corpses revive, think at first they are in the Elysian Fields, and demand a kiss from the goddesses to set the seal on their cure. In spite of the promptings of Alfonso and Despina this is denied them, and the curtain falls with the sisters defending what they appear to regard as nothing less than honour itself, to a background of derisive exclamations from Despina and Alfonso, and approving comments of "Great would be my indignation were they not to answer No" from the Albanians themselves. The music of the finale ranges from the purest beauty—the opening, for instance—to sheer farce—Despina in disguise and her trilling, omnipractic magnet. If there is in this finale less incident than in, for instance, that of Act II of *Le Nozze di Figaro,* there is nonetheless a musical variety and invention which places it in the very highest rank.

ACT II: Despina loses her patience with her virtuous employers. Make hay while the sun shines, she says, and behave like normal women when men are around; she rounds off her point in an aria, "Una donna a quindici anni." The process of persuasion so well begun is completed by the ladies themselves, who agree that there can be no harm in something so innocent as talk with the strangers. Their minds made up, each selects the appropriate partner—"Prenderò quel brunettino" (Give me then the gentle dark one)—in typically melodious fashion, to find at the end of the duet that they are invited to the garden where an entertainment is planned for their delectation. In truth, Alfonso has not exaggerated: nature has never so well imitated art—not even in the case of Cosima Wagner and the *Siegfried Idyll*—as to serenade a loved one with music as entrancing as the duet and chorus, "Secondate aurette amiche" (Gentle zephyr, softly sighing), which Ferrando and Guglielmo now combine to sing them. I have seen it made the subject of a producer's whims—the singers exchanging copies of the music, dropping them, fumbling, doing in fact everything except sing— but nothing was hindrance enough to stand in the way of the entrancing, seductive melody. If this is Mozart's most hedonistically inclined opera, no other number so perfectly illustrates its prevailing characteristic.

But, the serenade over, neither Albanian seems able to pursue the advantage gained, and, in disgust, Alfonso and Despina enact the scene for them. Neither seems a very apt pupil, but the teachers steal away at the end of their duet (the few phrases from Ferrando and Guglielmo make it technically into a quartet), leaving two rather embarrassed couples behind them talking animatedly about the weather. Ferrando is led off by Fiordiligi, and, after some tentative compliments, Guglielmo succeeds in giving Dorabella a heart-shaped locket, in return for which she removes the medallion (with its portrait of Ferrando) from her neck. Their duet, "Il core vi dono" (This heart that I give you), is charmingly light in texture and sentiment, and particularly delightful are the references to the pit-a-pat of their hearts.

The outer defences of Dorabella's constancy have been rather easily breached; Fiordiligi's are to prove much harder to carry. She turns a deaf ear to Ferrando's advances, and he is given a magnificent aria, "Ah lo veggio, quell' anima bella" (Well I knew that a maid so enchanting) in which he alternately expresses doubts and confidence as to the eventual outcome of his suit. Although it is one of the highest pieces Mozart wrote for tenor voice, perhaps it owes its frequent omission from contemporary performances not only to this high *tessitura* and its extended form, but also to the fact that it is immediately followed by an even longer aria for Fiordiligi which is much too well known to be omitted under any circumstances. Still, Ferrando's aria is far too good to be neglected as is present practice. Fiordiligi's great rondo, "Per pietà, ben mio, perdona" (Ah, my love, forgive my madness), is the principal show-piece of the opera; the extensive range, sudden and precipitous leaps from high soprano to contralto and back again, the passages of exacting coloratura, the taxing length—all combine to show off the singer's technique, which is mocked at the same time as it is used to express the turmoil of conflicting emotions in Fiordiligi's mind. A horn *obbligato* adds to the effect.

Ferrando and Guglielmo meet to compare notes on their progress to date. Guglielmo is suitably smug about the apparent constancy of Fiordiligi, but Ferrando is furiously indignant when he hears of Dorabella's conduct and sees the proof in the shape of the locket he himself had given her. He will have revenge; but, he asks Guglielmo, in what form? Don't take it so much to heart, replies his friend: "Ladies have such variations, permutations, combinations" ("Donne mie la fate a tanti"). It is a wonderful example of an *opera buffa* aria, and one of the most delightful moments in the score, as light of touch and delicate in style as the best of Mozart's own chamber music. Symmetry being the thing it is, there follows an aria for Ferrando, less formidable and shorter than "Ah, lo veggio," although by no means easy to sing; it is sometimes omitted, as is almost invariably the aria for Dorabella, "E' Amore un ladroncello" (Young love is unrelenting), in the next scene.

Fiordiligi resolves to make a last effort to extract herself and maybe Dorabella as well from the intolerable situation in which they find themselves. She sends for a couple of old suits of uniform belonging to Ferrando and Guglielmo which happen to be conveniently in the house, and announces her intention of going off to the wars taking her equally disguised sister. She launches into the opening measures of a big aria, but she has hardly started to express her determination to reach her lover's side when she is interrupted by Ferrando, still in his Albanian disguise, and protesting that before she leave him she should run her sword through his heart and end his agony for ever. Once more he protests his love, and, in response to a meltingly beautiful tune, resistance crumbles and she falls into his arms; they sing of their future happiness. Is it Mozart or the romantic Ferrando who has over-reached himself in this love duet? There is a school of thought which denies to genius the subtleties which are incidental to the main issue—there is no indication that he ever actually thought of *that,* they say, ignoring presumably the part played by the instinctive and the subconscious in the creative process. If Ferrando is in love with love as well as with Dorabella, he will be no less shattered by his new and involuntary success with her sister than he was by news of her own infidelity. The joke in fact has gone too far, and has involved too many emotional ties, old and new, for detachment to be any more a possibility—which is exactly what is conveyed by the uneasiness of the music. Granted that the lovers who began as puppets have suddenly become warm and real; perhaps it is one of music's (and therefore opera's) fascinations that such a transformation is possible, and, when achieved, is so moving.

The whole scene is watched by Guglielmo from the side, and Alfonso has his work cut out to keep him quiet until it is over. "What about your fond Fiordiligi now?" asks Ferrando; "Fior di Diavolo!" answers the discomfited Guglielmo. They are no worse than all the other women, affirms Alfonso: "Tutti accusan le donne" (Everyone berates the ladies), and at the end of his short solo, he makes the crestfallen lovers repeat the motto with him: "Così fan tutte." Despina brings the news that her mistresses have made up their minds to make their Albanian suitors happy and marry them on the spot.

The finale carries the plot one stage further and provides the expected dénouement. Servants make ready for the wedding under the direction of Despina, and hail the bridal couples when they appear. The lovers' toast is introduced by one of those unforgettable tunes such as Mozart has a habit of producing at just the moment when abundance has seemed to be sated, and the toast itself is an enchanting canon, led by Fiordiligi, which goes harmoniously on its way until it is the turn of Guglielmo to take up the tune. He contents himself with a cross aside to the effect that nothing would please him more than that the wine should turn to poison on their lips. It has been suggested that the device, which helps to lend variety to the quartet, was dictated to Mozart for the obvious reason that the tune which goes up to A flat was too high for the bass Guglielmo to sing. Alfonso brings in a notary (Despina in yet another costume) who is to take care of the legal side of the weddings, and, with much vocal disguise and a spate of pseudo-legal patter (including a punning reference to these "dame Ferraresi"), the contract is prepared and signed. This is the signal for a burst of military music from outside, which is immediately recognised by the female signatories as the march to which Ferrando and Guglielmo went off to the wars. Their suspicion turns to consternation when Alfonso confirms that Ferrando and Guglielmo are on their way up to the house at that very moment. The Albanians are bundled out, the sisters try to compose themselves, and their military lovers make an entrance to music which refers back unmistakably to the early part of Act I. Despina is discovered in an ante-room, Alfonso conveniently lets the marriage contracts fall where the young men cannot fail to see them, and they are told that proof of the inconstancy can be found in the next-door room. In a moment they re-appear, bringing with them bits of the Albanian costumes, and moreover singing snatches of the music that helped to bring the wooing to its successful conclusion. Here is a curious anomaly, which I have never yet seen explained. Guglielmo quotes from "Il ritrattino" and he and Ferrando sing the music associated with Despina's mesmerism in the finale to Act I; but before either of these, Ferrando has quoted something which he in fact never sings at any moment during the opera. Was one of Ferrando's arias changed at rehearsal, and did the second thoughts never get as far as this finale, or is there some deeper explanation?

Everything is forgiven, the four lovers are reunited—whether in the original or Albanian combination we are not told—and the six characters sing a valedictory in praise of him who is able to take the rough with the smooth and who can fall back on reason however the world treats him.

L. H.

THE CHARACTERS

An examination of the characters will make this clear at once. Don Alfonso and Despina are straightforward. They are real people, and they only appear to be cynical because they are seen against an artificial background. Their counsel is worldly, but none the less human, and the success of their schemings depends upon the age-old truth that everyone must learn for himself.

At the beginning of the opera the men will not listen to Don Alfonso nor the ladies to Despina, and it is only in the hard school of practical experience that their views are upheld. They only venture to point out that human nature has its weaknesses, advice that cannot, of course, appeal to headstrong youth!

The officers are seen at the beginning of the opera as ardent lovers. Naturally Don Alfonso's observations fall on deaf ears, for they are living in the clouds. In the throes of blind adoration—it is not to be described as love—they pay no heed to his devil's advocacy. In the first scene, their youth and inexperience are perfectly portrayed. Their music is heroic and full of purpose, but their feelings are seen to be empty enough against the saner background of Don Alfonso's experience. There is nothing to underline here. As the opera proceeds they awaken, all too slowly at first, to the realities of the situation. At the end, they have ceased to be mere boys, full of the overbearing pride of youth, and have grown into saner and more experienced men. All the different shades of their feelings in their progress between these two extremes are drawn with the reality of a drama in the grand manner. Their very seriousness in the face of what are, after all, trivial experiences shows their artificiality. Who would really be so moved by "love" such as this? They are the essence of an elegant society, caring all for pleasure, having no conception of their own emptiness. Their schooling is a bitter one; as will be seen at the turning-point of the opera, when the joke begins to have alarming consequences, they are overcome with grief—but only momentarily. As soon as they have both suffered the unfortunate experience of having their eyes opened to the infidelity of their lovers, they are at once ready to accept such conduct as normal. How quickly the pangs of remorse disappear! Clearly this was no very deep-rooted love, which can thus lightly be forgotten. The supreme subtlety of the drawing of the characters of these officers is seen when it is realized that on their own personalities are superimposed the personalities of the Albanian merchants! After the first scene, the officers are living one part and playing another!

The ladies, too, endure a bitter schooling in the opera. They start as a pair of flippant and irresponsible girls, wrapped up in themselves, engrossed in a blissful love-affair. Nothing can disturb their rosy horizon or upset their peace of mind. Then all of a sudden comes the bitter blow of their lovers' departure for the war. That alone, for the moment, is sufficient to shatter their dream and to reduce them to utter misery. Worse experiences are in store for them, and in the course of their wooing by the "Albanians" they learn of mental strife and anguish of a kind unknown to them before. For

Fiordiligi the struggle is terrific; after her first agreement to accept the suit of her "Albanian" admirer, she wildly regrets her decision. The realization that her fidelity could so easily be shaken is terrifying to her. Dorabella is more light-hearted, and her forwardness is set off against Fiordiligi's greater depth of character.

Where is the justification in this story for the high-sounding words and ardent feelings which these ladies express? How petty and how thoroughly cheap they are. Guglielmo is right when in the heat of the moment he speaks of Dorabella as a woman who is not worth two sous. What a travesty to talk of this as love; here is nothing but a story of stupid infidelity.

All this might be taken to imply that the opera is a sordid story of immorality, and so it sounds. But its artificiality saves it from any such charge. It is so delicately contrived and so artificial that there is absolutely nothing that can be regarded as immoral.

Così fan tutte is essentially a miniature; it is beautifully rounded off, and worked out from scene to scene in extraordinary detail. Of the three librettos which Da Ponte wrote for Mozart, *Così fan tutte* is his only original work. As we have seen, *Figaro* was freely taken from Beaumarchais' play, and *Don Giovanni* from Bertati's version of the story. Even *Così fan tutte* is popularly supposed to be based on true occurrences, and to have been suggested to the authors as a suitable subject for an opera by the Emperor. Further, Da Ponte's handling of the subject follows well-established lines. As Jahn points out, it is little more than a hotch-pot of all the elements which went to make up the conventional *opera buffa*. When all is said, however, Da Ponte's libretto emerges triumphant. His conception is unpretentious and essentially artificial, but his pattern is perfectly symmetrical. There are six characters, three men and three women, and every possible combination of these is exploited to the full. Each character is seen, not so much by himself, as in relation to all the others. This pattern is merely the foundation upon which Da Ponte builds an incredible series of situations, providing an opportunity for the expression of the whole gamut of human emotion.

C. B.

La Clemenza di Tito

[The Clemency of Titus]

Grand Opera in two acts.
Book by Mazzolà, adapted from Metastasio.
First performance: National Theatre, Prague, September 6, 1791.

CHARACTERS

Titus, Roman Emperor (A.D. 79–81), TENOR
Vitellia, daughter of the deposed Emperor, Vitellius, SOPRANO
Sextus ⎱ young Roman patricians ⎰ CONTRALTO
Annius ⎰   ⎱ MEZZO-SOPRANO
Servilia, sister of Sextus, SOPRANO
Publius, Captain of the Praetorian Guard, BASS

THE BACKGROUND

IT WAS IN July that a mysterious messenger presented Mozart with an anonymous letter inviting him to compose a Requiem Mass, and to name his own price for it. He accepted the offer, as he was anxious to show the world what he could do in the ecclesiastical style, now that Leopold II had reinstated the church orchestras which Joseph had abolished. In August came a more pressing invitation. The Emperor was to be crowned King of Bohemia at Prague on 6 September, and the local authorities decided at the last moment to celebrate the occasion with an opera by Mozart. The libretto chosen was an old one of Metastasio's, remodelled for this festivity, *La Clemenza di Tito,* a pompous and frigid drama of Roman history such as had always been chosen for court festivities in the first half of the century. Mozart was obliged to set off at once for Prague, accompanied by his wife and his pupil Süssmayr, composing in the carriage and writing out his ideas with Süssmayr's help wherever they stopped for the night. The opera was finished in eighteen days, rehearsed, and finally performed with all possible magnificence after the coronation banquet. It was a complete failure, and the Empress Maria Luisa, who was a daughter of the King of Naples, called it *una porcheria tedesca*. Later on it achieved what was almost popularity. It was repeated at Prague and much applauded; it was the first opera of Mozart to be performed in London (1806). For the stage of to-day it can only be considered as a museum piece.

It is obvious that the libretto was chosen by the authorities to present the monarchy in the most favourable light. The French Revolution of 1789 had struck terror in all reactionary states, and it was urgent, first, that the principle of absolute monarchy should be reasserted, and, secondly, that it should be held up to the advocates of liberty as tempering justice with mercy. The story turns on the unfailing and therefore rather monotonous clemency of the Roman Emperor Titus. . . .

The remodelling of the libretto was done by Da Ponte's old friend, Caterino Mazzolà. He removed a good many of the solo arias on which every drama of Metastasio depends, and replaced them by duets, trios, and ensembles to suit the taste of a more modern audience. The result is a rather shapeless opera, and one feels its shapelessness the more becaue its only *raison d'être* as a coronation opera is to be formal. Here is Mozart, definitely in his "third period," being forced to revert to the style of his first. It was impossible. *Idomeneo* is the work of a young man at the height of his powers, anxious above all things to express his emotions and to put in everything that he could give; *La Clemenza di Tito* was written by a man in broken health, exhausted by overwork, and forced to write in haste against his will. He knew, too, what sort of an audience he had to expect; remembering Joseph II's remark, "Too many notes, my dear Mozart!" he purposely adopted a plain and easy style with obvious melodies of old-fashioned cut, the simplest harmonies, and the thinnest orchestration. The arias, which ought to be long and stately, he cuts down to the shortest proportions; he invents a new form for them, based on Gluck's French operas, with a slow introduction and a quick movement to follow. We have met with it in Fiordiligi's aria, "Come scoglio," and indeed in *Idomeneo,* but in both of these he could take his time. In *La Clemenza di Tito* he takes his time only in the two great arias that have now become favourite concert-pieces, partly for the opportunity given to the singer and perhaps still more for the elaborate instrumental *obbligato* parts, one for clarinet, the other for basset-horn, both played at Prague by Anton Stadler. In the opera both arias stand out as concert-pieces, just like "Martern aller Arten" (which also has elaborate instrumental *obbligati*) in *Die Entführung*. There are two charming little duets, and the second—"Ah perdona"—is one of Mozart's loveliest inspirations.[1] In the concerted numbers Mozart allows his dramatic genius more freedom, and we meet with modulations and other complexities which may well have bewildered the Empress. The finest movement of all is the finale to Act I, in which the conflicting emotions of Sextus and Vitellia, Servilia and Annius are painted against a choral background. This finale has great importance because it is the first in which Mozart has combined both solo voices and chorus too in a great ensemble. The comic operas never employ the chorus in a finale at all, except for short isolated passages (as in *Figaro,* Act III, and *Così fan tutte,* Act II); each act of *Idomeneo* ends with a chorus on a large scale, but the soloists take no part in them. Here the chorus is a factor in the drama. We begin with the agonized perplexity of the principal characters; suddenly the cry of the terrified people, still far distant, tells us and tells them too that Rome is in flames. This idea must have been entirely Mozart's own invention, since the chorus have nothing to sing except horribly dramatic cries of "Ah!" until the principals join together to sum up the situation in four short lines—a procedure hitherto confined to *opera buffa*—the last two of which are repeated by the chorus. But the chorus is not brought in just to make more noise. In fact, it is not brought in at all; it remains permanently *in lontananza,* though obviously it must have been drawing nearer and nearer all the time. The chorus sings antiphonally with the group of soloists, and it is most carefully planned never to overpower them. But the mixture of formality and a certain modernity produces effects which are very curious to ears of to-day. Anyone coming across this passage in ignorance of its context might well be tempted to ascribe it to some English organist of about 1861 than to a composer of Italian opera. But we must train our minds to forget such disturbing associations and try to approach Mozart's opera from the point of view of those who heard it first performed.

E. J. D.

---

[1] Mr. H. Buxton Forman discovered that it was to this melody that Shelley wrote the song, "I arise from dreams of thee" (see *The Athenaeum* of 31 August and 2 November, 1907). But it cannot be said that the words go well with the tune.

As far as available records show, "La Clemenza di Tito" was first staged in America as part of the Berkshire Festival at Tanglewood, Massachusetts, on August 4, 1952. There had, however, been a radio performance, conducted by Alfred Wallenstein, in June, 1940. The opera was brought into the repertory of the Little Orchestra Society, Thomas Scherman conducting, at Town Hall, New York, on October 13, 1952.

THE STORY

The story is dominated by two considerations: the determination of Vitellia, who is in love with Titus, to have revenge on him when he seems disposed to marry another; and the inclination of Titus to show clemency no matter what provocation may be offered him.

Vitellia knows of Titus's plan to marry Berenice, daughter of Agrippa I of Judaea, and she urges Sextus, who is madly in love with her, to fall in with her plans and lead a conspiracy against Titus. No sooner has he agreed than she hears that Berenice has been sent home and that Titus now plans to marry a Roman. Annius asks his friend Sextus to intercede with the Emperor in the matter of his (Annius's) marriage to Servilia, Sextus's sister, but Sextus is forestalled in his plan when Titus tells him that he has chosen none other than Servilia to be Empress. Servilia herself tells the Emperor that she is in love with Annius, and he renounces her, deciding instead to take Vitellia to wife. Vitellia has no knowledge of this change of plans, and sends Sextus off to set fire to the Capitol and murder Titus, only to hear, the moment he is gone, that she is now the destined bride of Titus. Sextus succeeds in the first part of his plan, but the conspiracy against Titus's life fails when someone else, wearing his mantle, is killed in his stead. The act ends in general confusion.

It is known at the beginning of Act II that Titus has escaped death, and moreover that the details of the plot have been revealed to him. Annius advises Sextus to throw himself on the mercy of the Emperor and to show renewed zeal in his cause. Vitellia in contrast is anxious to avoid any risk that her connection with the plot may be discovered, and she urges Sextus to fly the country. Publius, however, settles the matter by arriving to arrest Sextus, who is tried by the Senate and condemned to death. Titus confronts him with proof of his guilt, but when Sextus has left him, tears up the death sentence he has just signed. As Sextus and the other conspirators are about to be thrown to the wild beasts in the arena, Vitellia can bear the load of guilt no longer and confesses her share in the plot, only in her turn to be forgiven by the clement Emperor.

L. H.

Die Zauberflöte

[*The Magic Flute*]

Opera in two acts.
Book by Emanuel Schikaneder.
First performance: Theater auf der Wieden, Vienna, September 30, 1791.

CHARACTERS

Sarastro, high priest of Isis, BASS
Tamino, an Egyptian prince, TENOR
Papageno, a birdcatcher, BARITONE
The Queen of the Night, SOPRANO
Pamina, her daughter, SOPRANO
Monostatos, a Moor, chief of the slaves of the temple, TENOR
Papagena, SOPRANO

First Lady, SOPRANO; *Second Lady*, MEZZO-SOPRANO; *Third Lady*, CONTRALTO; attendants of the Queen of the Night
First Boy, SOPRANO; *Second Boy*, MEZZO-SOPRANO; *Third Boy*, CONTRALTO; belonging to the Temple and fulfilling the designs of Sarastro

Priests and Priestesses of the Temple of Isis; Male and Female Slaves, Warriors of the Temple; Attendants, etc.

The action takes place in the Temple of Isis at Memphis and its vicinity about the time of Rameses I

THE BACKGROUND

THE LIBRETTO of *The Magic Flute* has long been regarded as an achievement in confusion and a handicap to Mozart's magnificent score. The reasons behind the composition of the opera, the choice of subject, are peculiar enough; when to that is added the fact that the motivation of the plot was reversed after the second scene had been completed, it will be seen how inevitable was its complexity.

The original suggestion for the opera came from Mozart's sometime friend, Emanuel Johann Schikaneder (1748–1812), an itinerant producer, singer, actor, and literary hack, who later performed a similar service when he commissioned from Beethoven what was to become *Fidelio*. Schikaneder had known Mozart from his Salzburg days and had even worked with him as early as the late 1770's, when the impresario, having produced Gebler's play, *Thamos, King of Egypt,* persuaded Mozart to revise and add to the incidental music he had already composed.

Early in 1789 Schikaneder, in financial straits, came to Vienna where he found his wife, from whom he had been separated, struggling to make a go of the Theater auf der Wieden. Seeing an opportunity to recoup his fortune with a Viennese success, he returned to his wife and became manager of the theater. At that time the public of the Austrian capital was especially partial to fairy tales of Oriental background and comic operas. The chief purveyor of these popular spectacles was a certain Marinelli, Schikaneder's greatest rival. Marinelli's chief stock in trade was a comic character, Kasperl, who appeared in a whole series of farces.

Schikaneder, in his efforts to find sufficiently fantastic vehicles, turned to a popular collection of Oriental tales gathered by Christoph Martin Wieland (1733–1813), entitled *Dschinnistan,* containing a story by one Liebeskind called "Lulu," or "The Magic Flute." With his practical experience in the theater, Schikaneder saw in this romance the ingredients for a fairy opera, replete with all the stock characters from the evil magician and the wronged queen to a comic Kasperl-ish role for himself. Since Mozart's sister-in-law, Josefa Hofer, who later created the Queen of the Night, was a member of his troupe, it was natural that Schikaneder should have persuaded his old friend and former colleague Mozart to write the score for his proposed production based upon the "Lulu" tale.

It is almost conclusively evident that Mozart began to set Schikaneder's libretto in May, 1791. Schikaneder probably was supplying his text piecemeal—a scene or a song at a time, and he had no scruples about having lines reset until they satisfied him. By the middle of June they had reached a point in what we know as the second scene just before the "Bei Männern" duet, when an event occurred which drastically affected the Mozart-Schikaneder project. This was the production, by the rival Marinelli, of a work entitled *Kaspar der Fagottist; oder, die Zauberzither (Kaspar the Bassoonist;*

or, the Magic Zither) with music by Wenzel Müller and text drawn from the "Lulu" of Liebeskind. To make matters worse, it was a howling success. Schikaneder was keenly aware of the folly of continuing with his original plan and, being a man of resource and ingenuity, he resolved to salvage his work by changing it in such a way that it would not only differ from the Müller opus but would also, if possible, eclipse it.

It is not difficult to estimate how much Schikaneder and Mozart had accomplished when they were forced to change their course. In addition to the first two scenes as they are generally produced today, there exists in the original libretto another episode which precedes the second scene. It notably contains a trio for three slaves wherein they discuss the relationship between Pamina, Monostatos and Sarastro. If Schikaneder had at this time written anything after the dialogue between Pamina and Papageno which precedes "Bei Männern" there is no record of it, because the whole direction of the plot makes a full turn at this point. It is doubtful if Schikaneder had had time to accomplish more with *The Magic Flute* project, for his many other activities as manager and actor kept him continually busy.

Schikaneder and Mozart, in their dilemma to make their opera different from Müller's *Magic Zither,* hit upon the idea of introducing the ideals of Freemasonry into their plot. It should be remembered that the Masonic order in the eighteenth century was colored by controversial political implications which far outran its benevolent functions. The Masonic ideal of the "regeneration of humanity by moral means" appealed strongly to the liberal-minded men of the time. It was opposed, however, by reactionary factions and clerical parties, especially the Jesuits, as being inimical to the well-being of both Church and State. During the long reign of Maria Theresa the Masons had been persistently persecuted, notwithstanding the fact her husband, Francis I, was a member of a lodge. Under her sons, Joseph II and Leopold II, Freemasonry was encouraged, but an active suppression began again in 1792 under the Emperor Francis II.

Since Schikaneder and Mozart were both active Masons, they found it both timely and dramatically appropriate to cast Masonic ideals into a quasi-allegory. They thereupon proceeded to employ

Masonic ritual and symbolism, coupling them with the "Egyptian" mysteries propounded in that extraordinary book *Sethos* by Abbé Terrasson (1670–1750) which was regarded as authentic by eighteenth century Freemasons.

After "Lulu" underwent this transmogrification, it became possible to identify the chief characters of the Schikaneder plot as contemporary figures. In the Liebeskind original, the prototype of the Queen of the Night is a "radiant fairy" called Perifirime. At her first appearance in the completed opera the Queen is still closely allied with that sympathetic character, and it is only when she assumes the personality of Maria Theresa, the bigoted enemy of the Masonic Ideal, that she becomes a maleficent force. Sarastro, the high priest, stems from a wicked magician with the fancy name of Dilsenghuin, but in the altered version he represents either Freemasonry or, according to Ernest Newman, Ignaz von Born, an eminent and enlightened Austrian scientist and Freemason. And thus Tamino, ambiguously described at his first appearance as a Japanese prince, comes to stand for Joseph II instead of the prototype of Prince Lulu, son of the King of Cashmere, while Pamina is no longer merely the fairy's daughter Sidi, but embraces the attributes of the Austrian people.

Considering the mixed sources from which *The Magic Flute* sprang, it is no surprise to learn that some years after Mozart's death a man named Giesecke came forward with the claim that he and not Schikaneder was the author of *The Magic Flute* libretto. Giesecke, whose real name was Johann Georg Metzler (1761–1833), was a member of Schikaneder's company at the time of the opera's first performance, and was entrusted with the minor role of First Slave for the première. Giesecke was a man of unusual parts and it is somewhat surprising to find him in such a relatively unimportant position. He had first studied law, which he gave up for the stage, becoming intimate with Goethe, Schiller, and their circle, and he is supposed to be the original of Wilhelm Meister. It would seem, however, that his chief interest was mineralogy which took him from the Viennese stage for a seven-year survey of Greenland and then to a professorship in Dublin, a post which he held until his death.

It would seem likely that Giesecke's claim to the authorship of the libretto was based on his skill as collaborator. Schikaneder was perfectly competent to arrange Oriental romances and to lace them with comic parts for himself, but it is more than probable that he was not up to coping with the metaphysical implications of the Masonic scenes and, therefore, had recourse to the talents of his bit-part actor. As a friend of Goethe who had translated *Hamlet,* it is probable that Giesecke could handle such sequences as the dialogue between Tamino and the aged priest as well as that of the ordeal by fire and water. The hand of Schikaneder is apparent in much of the opera; the characters of Papageno and Papagena are undoubtedly wholly his, and his happily ingenuous couplets are to be found in many scenes.

The unifying influence in this opera of many sources is the music of Mozart. It is the scope of Mozart's genius, his instinct for form, and his sympathetic grasp of human idealism which makes *The Magic Flute* a great masterwork.

W. S. A.

Legend dies hard, particularly theatrical or musical legend. One of the most pertinacious fables that ever bedevilled the history of an opera has to do with the libretto of *The Magic Flute*. Almost since the day the work was launched this book has been ridiculed and slandered with a devastation of mockery which ought by all rules of the game to have killed it generations ago.

Actually, the libretto of *The Magic Flute* is one of the best ever written. If Mozart harbored some misgivings when his old friend and brother Mason, Emmanuel Schikaneder, first approached him with the project it was much less the absurdities, the illogic, or the complications of the piece which gave him pause than the idea that he might fail in the attempt to write a so-called magic opera—a type of thing he had never undertaken before. As for Schikaneder, whatever else he may have been he was no fool. For years an itinerant barnstormer, singer, playwright, he had the barnstormer's instinct for what will make an effect in the theatre and what will not. He had acted in his time all sorts of things from Shakespeare (he was even famous for his Hamlet) to musical farces and he had the sense of the stage in his blood. If he saw nothing ridiculous in magic operas, magic farces, and other magic spectacles of the kind it was for the excellent reason that he knew his audiences and understood their reactions to nonsense however fantastic and extravagant.

For Schikaneder's public was not that of the grandiose opera house. It was the naive public of the suburb, as distinguished from the sophisticated public of the city proper. The fun and tomfoolery which we find in the comic scenes of *The Magic Flute* are substantially duplicates of the sort of entertainment the patrons of the Viennese *Vorstadt,* or suburban theatre, delighted in and accepted as readily as young children do Punch and Judy. There were a number of these suburban places of entertainment and when one of them had a success—whether in the shape of a spectacular magic piece, with comic scenes jostling more serious ones, or some other form of show—the others made haste to produce something of the identical nature, indeed, if possible, carrying those features which exerted a particular appeal to a point beyond their rivals. Nobody in those days worried about plagiarism, either musical or dramatic. Hence the absurdity of some of the tales which have grown up about *The Magic Flute* and the need which its creators are supposed to have felt of altering it in this or that respect when they discovered that another theatre had, with some other magic piece of similar content, stolen a march on them. If Schikaneder was so particular about certain of the comic portions of his role (Papageno) that he required Mozart to rewrite some of his songs several times it was only because he understood what would take best with the audiences to which he catered.

The Magic Flute, it must be remembered, is not an outright opera but a *Singspiel.* The French equivalent of the *Singspiel* is the *opéra-comique.* Neither the one nor the other is necessarily comic, as we may judge from the example of an *opéra-comique* like *Carmen,* with its tragic outcome. *Carmen,* in its original state and as always given in France, has spoken dialogue in place of recitative. This substitution of the spoken word for recitative is the distinguishing feature of both *Singspiel* and *opéra-comique.* And it is, of course, a hall mark of *The Magic Flute.*

Beethoven prized *The Magic Flute* above all other operas of Mozart not only because its plot, with its elevated, humanitarian sentiments, appealed to him far more than the morally questionable intrigues of *The Marriage of Figaro* and *Don Giovanni,* but because it contained the greatest variety of music—lofty and noble pages, such as the air of Sarastro, "Within These Hallowed Dwellings," and "O Isis and Osiris"; the uplifting choruses of the priests; tender love songs and duets, like the meltingly sentimental expressions of the lovers, Pamina and Tamino; songs of a popular, almost folk-like character (Papageno's bird-catcher song and the pretty songs with an *obbligato* of tinkling bells); figured chorale, dramatic bravura, and much else. The listener who hears *The Magic Flute* without being an actual spectator at the performance can scarcely fail to be struck by that extraordinary musical copiousness and diversity of content which caused Beethoven to value Mozart's last opera above all his others. Every scene may be said to have its typical frame and background, its characteristic color and matter.

H. F. P.

The music itself is much more diversified than that of any opera of Mozart's; yet unlike other works of the kind—Strauss's *Frau ohne Schatten,* for instance, which is a kind of modern *Magic Flute*— the disparity of its styles miraculously results in one single and wholly new style. The flashy Italian arias of the Queen of Night next to Sarastro's solemn utterances in Mozart's "masonic" manner; the popular ditties of Papageno side by side with the profound humanity of Pamina's tear-compelling G minor lament and the wonderful dramatic truth of her brief mad scene; the noble classical strains expressing Tamino's love and fortitude; the comic melodrama villainy of Monostatos; the lightly touched-in fairy-tale seriousness of the three genii; the high-minded fugal craft displayed in the overture and the fire-and-water scene contrasted with the easy fun of the Viennese suburban theatre in the incidents of the slaves bewitched by Papageno's bells and the latter's light-hearted scene of pretended suicide; the intrigues of the three ladies-in-waiting outlined in two cunningly devised and most beautiful quintets and in their dark conspirators' music with the queen and the blackamoor just before the end; all this and more is by some marvel of genius fashioned into a single gem of many facets—and of inestimable value.

For all that, it is unjustifiable to say that *The Magic Flute* is

Mozart's greatest opera, and none the less so because it is one of the commonplaces of German criticism, to which one must ever pay deference for its scholarship and immensely painstaking research, but by which it is not therefore necessary to let oneself be overawed in the matter of aesthetic apprehension. Where Mozart's operas are concerned, at any rate, German critics, who to begin with can seldom quite reconcile themselves to the vexing fact that Mozart could be as much inspired by the Italian language as by their own, have over and over again fallen into the error of the kind of moral judgment which is capable of leading to so serious a blunder as that of imagining that the music of *Così fan tutte* could possibly be vitiated by its libretto, and it is the same attitude which is responsible for the false notion that because *The Magic Flute* contains elements of greater idealistic aspiration than any other stage work of Mozart's, it necessarily also contains his greatest music. Is it not enough that it should be in its own way as great as the composer's other supreme masterpieces?

To Mozart it was all the same: religious aspiration or amorous pursuits—there was no difference between such extremes for him as an artist. And it was as an artist and nothing else that he approached his opera subjects, though we may be sure that he would not have succeeded so wonderfully had he not understood life from top to bottom as a human being. He could not specialize in any one emotion. His artistic intuition had taught him too much about life as a whole, and it was his mission to pour his knowledge into his work, to be the possession neither of ascetics nor of rakes, but of those in whom the multiform phases of existence had found some sort of balance.

This is his title to lasting glory. It was his tragedy too, no doubt, while he lived, for the conviction grows as one studies him that, occupied as he was with all human experience, he was incapable of devoting himself particularly to one. The happiness that passes all understanding did not come anywhere into his short life, so that it is perhaps a consolation to know how short that life was. But he has had his compensation ever since, for although other great composers have been more admired, more exclusively worshipped, and during some phases of musical life more assiduously cultivated, none has ever been so adored as Mozart is by those who apprehend his music. Such apprehension is not easy, and the whole mystery of him is never to be grasped, for his art too passes understanding.

E. B.

Mozart died shortly after the production of *The Magic Flute,* in deep distress. This opera, with the music of his Requiem, was in his mind until the final delirium. While the opera was performing he would take his watch from under his pillow and follow the performance in imagination: "We are now at the end of the act," or "Now comes the grand aria for the Queen of Night." The day before he died, he sang with his weak voice the opening measures of "Der Vogelfänger bin ich ja," and endeavored to beat the time with his hands. The frivolous and audacious Schikaneder, "sensualist, parasite, spendthrift," filled his purse by this opera: in 1798 he built the Theatre an der Wien. On the roof he put his own statue, clothed in the feather costume of Papageno. His luck was not constant; in 1812 he died in poverty.

P. H.

The American *première* of *The Magic Flute* occurred at the Park Theater, New York, April 17, 1833, in an English adaptation. In an Italian version, the work was given at the Academy of Music, New York, November 21, 1859, and in an uncut German version it was brought out at the German Opera House, New York, November 10, 1862. At the New York Academy of Music it was again heard January 27, 1886, in English.

The first performance at the Metropolitan Opera House, in Italian, took place March 30, 1900, with one of the most remarkable casts ever assembled, including Marcella Sembrich (Queen of the Night), Emma Eames (Pamina), Andreas Dippel (Tamino), Giuseppe Campanari (Papageno), Zélie de Lussan (Papagena), and Pol Plançon (Sarastro), besides Milka Ternina, Eugenia Mantelli, Carrie Bridewell, Suzanne Adams, Eleanore Broadfoot, Rosa Olitzka, Antonio Pini-Corsi, and Adolf Mühlmann in less conspicuous roles. Luigi Mancinelli conducted.

P. S.

EMANUEL SCHIKANEDER: *Librettist*

Schikaneder was an altogether extraordinary character. His life and his general behaviour were so grotesque that one could only imagine him to have been invented by a German Dickens as the German original of Mr. Crummles; at the same time he was in many ways a man of singular ability, invention, and foresight, who contributed much to the history of the German stage. Born at Regensburg in 1751 in the most miserable circumstances, he had spent his childhood as an itinerant fiddler; later he became an actor, and although devoid of education had sufficient natural talent to achieve a decided success by the time he was twenty-four. At twenty-seven he was managing a company of his own and touring South Germany and Austria with a repertory that included *King Lear, Hamlet,* and *Macbeth,* as well as plays by Lessing and Schiller. He was musician enough to perform Gluck's *Orpheus,* besides all sorts of patriotic pieces, ballets, spectacular entertainments, and German comic operas, some of which he composed himself. He was a capable manager, very popular with his subordinates, a passably good singer, and clever enough to see that an energetic appeal to German national sentiment was a sure road to success at a time when his countrymen were growing tired of the tyranny of French and Italian taste and preparing subconsciously for the romantic outburst of the early nineteenth century. He gave a season of German *Singspiel* (comic opera) at Vienna in the winter of 1784–85, often patronized by the Emperor; a season mainly of patriotic and spectacular pieces, interspersed with comic operas, at Regensburg in 1787. In 1789 he came back to Vienna to begin a long series of successes at the Theater im Starhembergischen Freihause auf der Wieden, a flimsy erection which had been run up in one of the numerous courtyards of what is still called the "Freihaus," a huge block of low yellow buildings south of the Naschmarkt. In those days it was outside the fortifications of the city, just on the right hand of the road leading out of the Kärntnerthor. The whole position of both Schikaneder and his theatre is not unlike that of the Royal Cobourg Theatre in Lambeth a generation later.

After the collapse of German opera that followed Mozart's *Ent-*

führung, Joseph had reinstated Italian opera at court; but the people of Vienna were only too glad to support some sort of popular musical entertainment in their own language. One Marinelli had obtained considerable success with comic operas, burlesques, fairy plays, and topical pieces during the last eight years; and Schikaneder, seeing what the public wanted, set himself to beat Marinelli at his own trade. He began with simple *Singspiel,* but soon saw that what drew the largest audiences were operas on Oriental subjects and romantic fairy tales, in both of which the local Viennese comic character "Kasperl" or one of his tribe could be introduced. His first "magic" opera was *Oberon,* libretto by C. L. Giesecke, music by Paul Wranitzky, produced 7 November, 1789. He now came to Mozart with the offer of a similar kind of libretto.

E. J. D.

THE STORY

ACT I—*Scene* 1: *A Lonely Landscape.* Rugged cliffs loom on all sides. To the left, in the foreground, is a cave. In the background the Temple of the Queen of the Night is visible. Alone and unarmed, Tamino, an Egyptian prince separated from his traveling companions, is being pursued by a serpent. Overcome by fright and fatigue, he collapses at the entrance to the cave. Three veiled ladies, attendants of the Queen of the Night, fly from the Temple, armed with silver javelins, and with the cry, "Die, monster!" they pierce the serpent with their weapons. The three ladies gaze admiringly on the unconscious youth, then hurry off to tell the Queen of the occurrence.

At the sound of a flute, Tamino revives, sees the dead serpent, and hides himself. Papageno, a roguish birdcatcher and would-be ladies' man, enters. Prepared to strike a bargain with the Queen's attendants, he places his bird cage on the ground and announces his presence by blowing on his pipes. The roguishness of the man may be gathered from his merry song, "Der Vogelfänger bin ich ja" (The birdcatcher am I). Though birdcatching is his occupation, he would much rather be catching pretty girls, confesses Papageno the fowler. Tamino steps from his hiding place and, assuming that Papageno killed the serpent, thanks him for saving his life. As Papageno

showily accepts the honor, the three veiled ladies, who have over-
heard the falsehood, step forward and rebuke him. One of them
places a padlock on his lips, reducing his vocabulary to "hm, hm,
hm." The three ladies turn to Prince Tamino, one of them offering
him a picture of the Queen's beautiful daughter. In a suavely tender
song—"Dies Bildnis ist bezaubernd schön" (This picture is be-
witchingly lovely)—Tamino rhapsodizes on the girl's beauty, ending
with a vow to make her his forever.

On that pledge there is a loud clap of thunder, and as the scene
darkens the mountains open and show the star-bedecked throne of
the Queen of the Night. In anxious tones the Queen informs Tamino
of her daughter's plight, and the purpose of the picture now becomes
clear. The lovely Pamina has been abducted by a scoundrel, and
the Queen can still hear her helpless screams. Tamino is to recover
the girl and avenge the Queen, for which he will be rewarded with
Pamina's hand. There is another thunderclap as the Queen with-
draws, leaving Tamino deeply moved by her plea. From the three
ladies, Tamino learns that the abductor was none other than Sarastro, high priest of Isis. His interest excited by Pamina's beauty and
the mother's words, Tamino promptly agrees to undertake the rescue. A magic flute is given Tamino, one capable of protecting its
bearer in all dangers. Papageno is instructed to accompany him on
his adventure. Before the two men leave, the ladies remove the
padlock from the birdcatcher's lips, with a warning about future
lying. Papageno is now given a casket containing chimes whose
magic power will offer them further protection. The ladies take
leave of Tamino and Papageno, who set out on their mission, guided
by three boys.

Scene 2: *A Room in Sarastro's Palace.* Pamina is being guarded by
Monostatos, a Moor, who has been using his position to force his
attentions on her. Papageno breaks into the room while the Moor
is absorbed in watching the captive princess. True to form, the
birdcatcher is entranced by the girl's beauty. The Moor, turning
around, starts up in fright, and for his part Papageno is just as frightened by the Moor's appearance. Each takes the other for the devil,
and they scurry off in opposite directions. Remembering Tamino's
instructions, Papageno finally overcomes his fear and returns to
Pamina's chamber. Once back, he tells her the purpose of his visit

and proceeds to compare her, itemizing all details, with the portrait that he wears on a ribbon around his neck. He urges Pamina to place her trust in him. When Pamina learns that Papageno has neither wife nor sweetheart, she counsels him to have patience, and the pair join in a duet of infinite grace and rippling gaiety on the theme that "men who are in love cannot fail to be good-hearted"—"Bei Männern, welche Liebe fühlen, fehlt auch ein gutes Herze nicht." The melody of this duet is from an old German folk song. After some hesitation, Pamina leaves the castle in Papageno's company.

Scene 3: *A Grove and Entrance to the Temples.* Led by three boys carrying silver palm branches, Tamino has reached Sarastro's castle and is now in a secret grove in the middle of which stand three temples. At two of the entrances Tamino is denied admittance. At the third a priest of Isis appears, and for the first time Tamino hears of the true character of Sarastro. He is a man of lofty ideals, governing with virtue and truth. Still incredulous, Tamino sneeringly reminds the priest of Pamina's abduction. The priest refuses to explain, mysteriously promising an answer to the riddle when "the hand of friendship" will lead Tamino into "the sanctuary of eternal union." The priest disappears through the same portal from which he emerged.

Alone, Tamino is a prey to conflicting thoughts. Love for the Pamina of the portrait and pity for the Queen still dominate his heart, but a yearning for true wisdom and a desire to know the real nature of Sarastro have gripped him, too. A mysterious voice assures him that Pamina still lives and that soon—or never—his eyes will find the light. As Tamino puts the magic flute to his lips and plays, its effect is truly magical! The panpipes of Papageno immediately answer, and Tamino rushes off to find his lost companion. Misled by echoes, he takes the wrong direction. He has scarcely left when Pamina and Papageno appear before the castle. Papageno silences the terrified girl when she thoughtlessly calls aloud for Tamino. Papageno tries his panpipes, and promptly comes the response of the magic flute. But Pamina's outcry has brought Monostatos and a troop of slaves upon them. When all hope seems lost, Papageno remembers the casket of chimes. As the cover flies open and the magic bells begin to play, a spell is cast over the slaves, whose enchanted limbs move only in time with the music.

Pamina and Papageno again set out to find Tamino, but it is too late! A brilliant flourish of trumpets and drums is heard, and to the cry, "Long live Sarastro!" the high priest of Isis makes a majestic entrance, followed by a host of celebrants. Throwing herself at Sarastro's feet, Pamina admits her guilt for trying to escape, but accuses the Moor of evil designs upon her. Sarastro urges her to rise and tells her that he knows what is in her heart, but warns her that only evil can come from her mother. At that moment Monostatos and his slaves bring in the captured prince. As they catch sight of one another, Tamino and Pamina rush into each other's arms. Sarastro orders Monostatos whipped; then, turning to two of his priests, he instructs them to bring veils for Pamina and Tamino. The lovers are then conducted into the temple of probation, to be purified by the secret rites.

ACT II—*Scene* 1: *A Palm Grove.* In the Temple of Wisdom the priests of Isis have assembled to consider whether Tamino is ready to be initiated into the final mysteries. Sarastro pleads warmly for the youth and reveals that the gods have ordained his marriage to Pamina. All signify their approval by blowing into their horns. Sarastro now leads the priestly gathering in a solemn invocation to the gods, "O Isis und Osiris!" begging them to grant the worthy couple strength and courage for their impending trials. Sarastro and the priests then depart in a solemn procession.

Scene 2: *Courtyard of the Temple.* Tamino and Papageno are led out by priests, who warn them that they are to be subjected to severe tests of faith and fortitude. Tamino will see Pamina, but he must not speak to her, for the probation will have begun. Papageno is undecided, but his hesitation vanishes when a priest announces that Sarastro has reserved a beautiful bride—appropriately named Papagena—for him. But he, too, is not to speak to her till the appointed time. Before they leave, the priests caution the companions against the wiles of women. Silence must be maintained at all costs! It now grows dark. Suddenly three torches, borne by the three veiled ladies of the Queen of the Night, flash in the dark, and Tamino's trial begins. Expressing horror at finding the prince and his companion in this den of evil, the ladies implore him to flee before it is too late. They warn them that their death is already ordained and remind Tamino of his vow to help the Queen, who has herself stolen into Sarastro's temple in search of her kidnaped daughter. Tamino listens unmoved, then rebukes Papageno for speaking out and breaking his oath of silence. The three ladies flee in terror as a burst of thunder is heard and priests rush in, wrathfully condemning the intruders to perdition for defiling the sacred threshold.

Scene 3: *A Garden.* Moonlight falls upon Pamina, who lies sleeping on a bench overhung with roses. Monostatos steals in cautiously and, ravished by the sight of Pamina, attempts to steal a kiss. As he approaches the sleeping girl, the Queen of the Night appears and cries out, "Back!" In imperious tones she bursts into a magnificent soliloquy, "Der Hölle Rache kocht in meinem Herzen" (The vengeance of hell seethes in my heart), the delivery of which demands great dramatic power and supreme vocal technique in handling the brilliant flurry of staccati in the high soprano register. The Queen addresses the sleeping girl in dire tones. Avenge your mother, she cries, or be forever disowned as her daughter! Pamina awakens, and with a cry of "Mother! Mother!" falls into the Queen's arms. Pamina recoils, however, when the Queen hands her a dagger. "You must kill Sarastro and bring me back the mighty zodiac!" demands the Queen. Before Pamina can protest, there is a roar of thunder and the Queen disappears. Monostatos again approaches the anxious girl, promising a way out for mother and daughter if she will yield to him. Pamina draws back horrified, and as the Moor comes nearer Sarastro appears and steps between them. Angrily, the high priest orders Monostatos out. As Pamina pleads for her mother's safety, Sarastro in a noble and moving cavatina—"In diesen heil'gen Hallen" (Within these sacred halls)—assures her that in this holy place vengeance is a stranger and enemies are forgiven.

Scene 4: *A Hall in the Temple of Probation.* Though Sarastro is satisfied with their behavior thus far, the ordeal has only begun for Tamino and Papageno. Led in once more by the priests, the companions are again warned about keeping their lips sealed. But Papageno, unable to restrain himself, begins chattering away with an old woman who brings him a drink of water. A menacing roar of thunder speedily frightens her away and reminds Papageno of his vow. Presently the three youths reappear, bringing with them the flute, the bells, and a table covered with food. Papageno applies himself diligently to a repast as Tamino plays on his flute. Drawn by the magic tones, Pamina appears and greets Tamino rapturously, only to be met by a stony silence. Certain now that Tamino no longer loves her, the girl expresses her sadness in a touching aria, "Ach, ich fühl's, es ist verschwunden, ewig hin mein ganzes Glück!" (Ah, I feel it, love's happiness has vanished forever!)—an aria calling for infinite grace of phrasing and delicacy of style. Hoping now only for death, Pamina leaves, with Tamino gazing sorrowfully after her. At that point the priestly trumpets ring out again, and Tamino wrenches Papageno away from his feasting, reminding him of the tests still to come.

Scene 5: *A Place Near the Pyramids*. Still obliged to keep silent, Tamino is brought in, veiled by the priests, to be subjected to further trials of faith and endurance. Pamina, also wearing a veil, follows him, and is soon informed that Tamino is waiting to bid her good-by. Hopefully Pamina rushes to him, only to be motioned away in apparent coldness. Again Pamina reproaches him on his apathy, declaring that her love is stronger than his. Sarastro assures them both of a happy outcome to the trial if they will only be patient, and as he accompanies Tamino, two priests lead the despairing Pamina away. As they all depart, Papageno enters, thirsty and bewildered. Angrily, he cries out to the Speaker that he would renounce all hope of heavenly bliss for one glass of wine. A huge wine goblet appears, and as Papageno drinks and grows gay, he plays his magic chimes and chants merrily of the tender little wife he would like to have. Suddenly his wish comes true. In comes the old woman again, announcing herself as the coveted bride and swearing eternal constancy to him. Papageno is warned that to spurn her will mean an everlasting diet of bread and water for him. With the whispered reservation of remaining true to her "as long as I see no fairer one," Papageno accepts, and the old woman is suddenly transformed into a young beauty. With a cry of "Papagena!" the bird-catcher tries to embrace her, but the Speaker intervenes, and, taking the young woman by the hand, drags her off with the words: "He is not yet worthy of you!"

Scene 6: *A Garden With a Lake in the Background*. The three youths meet Pamina, who is delirious in her grief. Her mother's command to murder Sarastro and Tamino's apparent coldness are too much for her. Her mind is beginning to snap, and Pamina raises the dagger to kill herself, when the three youths stop her, warning her gravely that suicide is punished by God. They assure her that Tamino loves her dearly and would be driven insane were he to witness this rash act of hers. Pamina rejoices over this assurance and asks to be led to Tamino.

Scene 7: A Wild Mountain Spot. A huge iron gate stands between two caves on a mountainside. On one side is a roaring stream, on the other a brightly glowing fire. It is twilight. Tamino appears with two priests. From outside comes the sound of Pamina's voice. The priests tell Tamino that he who overcomes dangers in pursuing his ideals will conquer death and become godlike. Tamino attests his fearlessness, and as a reward the priests bring out Pamina. The lovers embrace ardently. Tamino points to the deadly caverns through which they must venture as a final test. Pamina, certain that love will smooth the way, takes him by the hand and urges him to play the magic flute for protection—the flute that she now reveals was fashioned by her father from a thousand-year-old oak. The lovers emerge from probation of fire unscathed. Once more with the help of the flute's protective tones, they brave the cavern of water. As they reappear, again unharmed, the gathered priests hail them in an exultant chorus on their consecration to Isis. Pamina and Tamino now wend their way to the temple.

Scene 8: A Small Garden. Despairing over his unrequited love for Papagena, Papageno resolves to kill himself by hanging. As he sallies out dramatically with a rope, a near-by tree beckons conveniently. Just then the three youths hurry in, chiding Papageno on his rashness and asking him why he does not use his magic chimes to help him out of his misery. Papageno jumps at the suggestion, and now the bells peal cheerily as he wishes out loud for the little maiden. The three youths vanish, and presto! they are back with Papagena. The two greet each other ecstatically and chatter gaily about the lovely little Papagenos and Papagenas that will be theirs once they are wed. They leave arm in arm.

Scene 9: Rugged Cliffs. It is night. Monostatos, the Queen of the Night, and the three ladies steal silently toward Sarastro's temple, all bearing torches. These creatures of evil are making one final effort to destroy Sarastro's power. For his connivance Monostatos

has been promised Pamina as bride. Thunder and the roar of rushing water reach the ears of the conspirators. There is a flash of
lightning as the earth opens and wraps the villainous crew in eternal
night.

Scene 10: *The Temple of the Sun.* Sarastro is presiding over a solemn conclave of priests and priestesses. As the three youths stand by
with flowers in their hands, Tamino and Pamina appear before him
in priestly robes. In a majestic address, Sarastro pronounces the
couple consecrated in the worship of Isis. The sun's rays have banished
night and the forces of darkness. And now the celebrants raise their
voices in homage to Isis and Osiris, chanting, "The strong have conquered, and may beauty and wisdom be their eternal reward!"

L. B.

THE CHARACTERS

Die Zauberflöte resembles a parable. At first sight, it is a simple
magic story, exactly what was required by Schikaneder. Underneath
the surface, however, this simple magic story has a depth of meaning
which remains to-day as significant as ever it was to Mozart himself.

Each element of the opera, and each character, when examined,
seems to fit in with this view. The Magic Flute itself, on the face
of it an ordinary property in a magic entertainment, is surely conclusive evidence that the story underwent a change. This Flute
emanates from the Queen, given to Tamino to help him to overcome Sarastro, and yet it becomes, as the opera proceeds, a touchstone for Tamino, a sure guide to him throughout all the trials, and
a solace in adversity. Is this a mere magic contrivance? Rather has
it become a symbol, almost a sacred rite, whereby Tamino may com-
mune with the Divine. Throughout his trials, when oppressed by
the petty things of the world, when faced with jealousy or hatred,
it is the Flute which comes to his aid, and reminds him of the
ideals of humanity and love which Sarastro and his priests put before
him as life's goal.

What of Papageno, a part devised for Schikaneder himself, whose
music was to be as popular as possible, and who was to provide
the comic relief in the midst of the terrors of the Temple? Again,
on the face of it, Papageno fulfils these functions, and yet how much

deeper is the significance which the part assumes in the higher view of the opera. Papageno, "Naturmensch," as he describes himself, is the personification of the flesh, to whom all the higher spiritual values in life mean nothing. He is incapable of understanding the meaning of the trials, and he can never aspire to the perfect life. Throughout the opera he provides a complete contrast to Tamino, whose manly courage and spiritual triumph would not be seen so clearly, were it not for the background provided by Papageno. It is true that he achieves his desires, such as they are, without passing through any of the trials successfully, but his desires and their ultimate fulfilment are limited to the material things of life. Papageno is a pathetic and unsophisticated, but certainly not a purely farcical figure.

The Three Boys are another indication of the change of story. They are mentioned in the first place as the servants of the Queen, who will conduct Tamino and Papageno to the Temple and, presumably, assist in the rescue of Pamina. And yet their later appearances reveal them as the agents of Sarastro, in each case furthering his purpose. From them Tamino and Papageno receive back the Magic Flute and Bells, which have been taken away. By them Pamina and Papageno in turn are rescued from suicide, and brought back to the life which Sarastro has prepared for them. Instead of being merely part of the usual trappings of a magic entertainment, they have become, in a sense, divine messengers. In the production at Glyndebourne, the celestial character of the Three Boys was emphasized by keeping them behind a gauze veil. Each time they appeared they were thus seen only vaguely, as if they were figures in some dream or fantasy. It is to be observed that they have no individual existence. They always sing together and should therefore always move in a group upon the stage.

Tamino himself begins the opera as the ordinary Prince, the standard character of the fairy story, who rescues and, of course, marries the Princess in distress. He falls in love with her picture, another familiar feature of a fairy story, and sets off at once with high ideas for the overthrow of the wicked Sarastro. In his long interview with the Orator he is shown as the obstinate and impetuous youth who is satisfied that his ideas are right. But here at once his role in the opera has changed. In contrast to his impetuosity, the patience and restraint of the Orator show that Sarastro and his order are not the wicked tyrants which they were at first portrayed to be. From now on Tamino appears to be convinced of his mistake. At the end of his conversation with the priest he has ceased to question, and has come to accept the authority of Sarastro. All his arrogance has gone, and he willingly submits himself to the trials which Sarastro imposes upon him. He humbles himself, and prepares to make himself worthy for the higher life, worthy to grasp the hand of friendship which the Orator has promised shall be extended to him, worthy in the end to win Pamina and to succeed Sarastro as head of the order of the priests of Isis and Osiris.

The trials to which he must submit himself, and the rites of the priestly order, represent the ceremonies of initiation of the Freemasons, as is shown by the continual reference throughout the opera to the mystic number three. Tamino is no ordinary fairy prince. He becomes the novice, dedicating his life to the sacred priesthood of the gods, a calling of which he shows himself to be worthy.

This Priesthood cannot have played any part in the original conception of the story. When first mentioned by the Queen, Sarastro is spoken of as a villain and the impression is that he is a neighbouring ruler who has carried Pamina off to his castle. Tamino and Papageno ask the Three Ladies how they shall find Sarastro's castle (Burg). But as the possibilities of the story developed in Mozart's mind, the Priests came to play an important part. They are the initiates of the order, and have themselves passed through the trials and achieved that peace of mind and serenity which is Tamino's goal. In the opera they are in the background, imparting an atmosphere of dignity and peace to the scenes in the Temple.

In the final form of the opera the Queen and the Three Ladies become the representatives of evil, definitely opposed to all that Sarastro and his Priests uphold. No such significance attached to them originally, for at the beginning the Queen appears as the sorrowing mother, robbed of her daughter, and the Ladies as her attendants. In the second Act, however, it is the Ladies who become the temptresses, trying to induce Tamino to break his vow of silence; and in the penultimate scene of all, the Queen and the Ladies make an ineffective assult upon the Temple. It is interesting to see how the Queen's importance dwindles as the opera proceeds. At the beginning she appears as the great Queen who dominates the whole region. Papageno has his livelihood from her, but she is too great for him ever to have seen. Tamino at once accepts her commission to rescue her daughter, and does not for a moment question her authority. At this stage it is clear that she was intended to be the central figure of the opera, and that the conclusion of the story would see her daughter safely returned, rescued from the evil-doer's clutches. By the time she next appears, she has already lost all her character, and her injunctions to Pamina are the backbitings of an embittered spirit. At her third and last appearance she has ceased to be effective at all, and her attack on the Temple serves, by contrast, to emphasize the glory of Tamino's triumph, and the greatness of Sarastro and the Priests.

One more simple instance of the higher significance of the story is to be found in Papageno's duet with Pamina in the first Act. He finds her alone and tells her of Tamino, who has fallen in love with her picture and who will come to win her as his bride. In the magic story it is natural that they should join together in a song in praise of love. Mozart, however, has infused their simple, almost doggerel words with such a sense of divinity as to take the duet right out of the atmosphere of a fairy story. The result is a prayer, expressing the perfect conception of man's love for woman, for through love alone can man approach the infinite.

C. B.

POSTSCRIPT

LORENZO DA PONTE

LORENZO DA PONTE is so important a factor in Mozart's development that it is worth while studying his personality in some detail. He was born on 10 March, 1749, at Ceneda, at the foot of the mountains to the north of Venice. His father was a Jew, by name Geremia Conegliano, by trade a *cordovaniere,* which may mean a leather-dresser or a shoemaker.

Wishing in 1763 to take a Catholic as his second wife, he had himself baptized with great solemnity along with his three sons

Emmanuel, Baruch, and Ananias, who received the Christian names of Lorenzo, Girolamo, and Luigi respectively. According to some custom of the time, Geremia, now Gasparo, assumed the surname of the bishop who administered the sacrament, Monsignor Lorenzo Da Ponte. Our future poet was then fourteen; his education till then seems to have been rather haphazard, and he was known as *lo spiritoso ignorante*. Foreseeing that their father's second marriage would probably lead to financial difficulties, he and his brother Girolamo applied to the Bishop for admission to the local seminary; not only were they admitted, but the Bishop generously undertook to bear the cost of their maintenance. In two years the brothers had made such rapid progress in Latin that their father determined to make priests of them, although, as Lorenzo tells us, "this was utterly contrary to my vocation and my character." At seventeen he was still incapable of expressing himself in Italian,[1] but he had considerable fluency in writing Latin verse. Those who have had an English public school education will probably agree that this was no bad introduction to the study of Dante, Petrarch, Ariosto, and Tasso to which he was encouraged by one of his younger instructors. He quickly developed a passion for poetry; he translated from Latin into Italian and from Italian into Latin, acquiring a remarkable facility in dealing with any kind of style or metre. On the death of Monsignor Da Ponte he was sent to the seminary at Portogruaro, where he tells us that he began the study of mathematics and philosophy, but did not take much pleasure in them. In 1772 he was appointed professor of rhetoric and vice-rector of the seminary; on 27 March, 1773, he was ordained priest. Some six months later he left the seminary and went to Venice to seek his fortune.

Venice at that date was an international pleasure-resort comparable with Monte Carlo in recent times; and it must further be remembered that in those days the ecclesiastical habit did not necessarily imply any great strictness of morals even in Rome itself. Peter Beckford, writing from Rome a generation later, says:

> As for the Abbés, they are not only men of intrigue themselves, but, as Falstaff says of his wit, are the cause of it in others.

---

[1] At home and in the seminary he would have talked the Venetian dialect; possibly Hebrew to some extent at home and Latin in school.

They are excellent at carrying a *billet-doux,* or presenting you
to a female of easy virtue. (*Familiar Letters from Italy,* London, 1805.[2]

Lorenzo remained a year at Venice, and became involved in a
series of disreputable adventures; in the autumn of 1774, he and his
brother were summoned to Treviso to teach "humanity," rhetoric, and
grammar at the local seminary.

A poem which he wrote for public recitation, inspired by the
doctrines of Rousseau, caused a scandal and he was dismissed in
December, 1776. The next two or three years were spent in Venice;
he continued both his profligacy and his priestly functions until the
autumn of 1779, when he was advised to fly from Venetian territory,
and escaped just in time to Gorizia, where he stayed a little over a
year. Here he saw an old friend, the poet Caterino Mazzolà, who was
on his way from Venice to Dresden to be poet to the Italian opera
at the Saxon court. Da Ponte asked Mazzolà to find a post there for
himself too, and on receipt of an encouraging letter left Gorizia for
Dresden probably in December, 1780. On the way he stopped at
Vienna, where he found the city in mourning for the death of Maria
Theresa. This gives us an approximate date, as she died on 29 November of that year. Finding that there were no entertainments going on,
he stayed no more than three days. On arriving at Dresden, he discovered that the letter of invitation was a forgery; an enemy in
Gorizia had intercepted Mazzolà's genuine letter saying that there
was no opening for him, and in order to get him out of the way
had substituted a letter promising an appointment. Da Ponte remained about a year in Dresden and went to Vienna probably early
in 1782. This is dated by the fact that he was introduced to Metastasio, who read a poem of Da Ponte's aloud at an evening party.
Metastasio died 12 April, 1782. Mazzolà had given him a cordial
introduction to Salieri, and he even aspired to succeed Metastasio as
poeta cesareo; but he never achieved this honour. At this moment
he had never even attempted to write an opera libretto; but Salieri
evidently tested his powers by giving him plenty of work in the way
of adapting other operas for performance. In 1783 he wrote *Il Ricco*

---

[2] An experienced friend of mine said to me some fifty years ago, "If you want
a woman in Rome, follow a priest."

d'un Giorno for Salieri, but Salieri put off the performance till December, 1784, on account of the arrival in Vienna of Paisiello and the Abbé Giambattista Casti, who had written the brilliant libretto of *Il Re Teodoro in Venezia* for him. Paisiello was a formidable rival for both Salieri and Mozart, and Casti an even more formidable rival for Da Ponte. They had spent some time at St. Petersburg in the service of the Empress Catherine and were on their way back to Italy.

Salieri was a pupil of Gluck, and his tragic opera, *Les Danaïdes,* which was produced in Paris in 1783, was at first announced as by Gluck himself, Gluck having been unable to fulfill his contract through ill-health and wishing at the same time to give Salieri the chance of making a name for himself in Paris. His best work probably is *Axur,* composed first to a French libretto by Beaumarchais and afterwards remodelled for Vienna by Da Ponte. *Il Ricco d'un Giorno* was not successful and of course the blame was thrown on the librettist. . . .

The first act ends with an enormous finale which is very spirited. The scene is Venice; two lovers are serenading the same lady; they quarrel, start their serenades again, and are finally discomfited by a storm, with choruses of gondoliers and frightened people. Salieri was hardly equal to dealing with this anticipation of *Die Meistersinger*. Salieri said that he would sooner cut off his fingers than set another line of Da Ponte's to music; his next opera was *La Grotta di Trofonio,* on an amusing libretto by Casti. Da Ponte tried his luck with the Spaniard Vicente Martín y Solar, generally known as Martini,[3] for whom he adapted a play of Goldoni (*Le Bourru bienfaisant*) written originally in French for Paris and successfully performed in a German translation at Vienna in 1772. This must have shown him the advantage of using a successful play as a basis for an opera-book. He did the same thing for Gazzaniga in 1786, adapting a French play.

But it was Mozart himself who first suggested turning *Le Mariage*

---

[3] Vincenzo Martini must be distinguished from Padre G. B. Martini of Bologna, the learned theorist and historian, also from G. B. San Martini or Sammartini of Milan, composer of instrumental music, and from Martini il Tedesco, composer of the popular song, "Plaisir d'amour," whose real name was Aegidius Schwarzendorf.

de Figaro into an opera. The idea was partly due to the success which
Paisiello had obtained with his *Barbiere di Siviglia* and in all proba-
bility still more to the public scandal which the second comedy had
aroused both in Paris and in Vienna. It had been produced in Paris
in 1784 after three years of the best possible advertisement—prohibi-
tion by the authorities. The play was still prohibited in Vienna
as politically subversive, but Mozart probably foresaw that it might
be possible to get permission for it in the shape of an Italian opera,
and that as long as the play was forbidden, the opera would be certain to arouse curiosity.

Da Ponte and Mozart have been blamed, on the one side, for
depriving one of the greatest of French comedies of all its savour,
and turning a prophecy of revolution into a sordid intrigue; on the
other, they have been commended for eliminating all that was political, satirical, and erotic in the original and turning all things to
chastity, favour, and prettiness. It is easy for those to whom both
works are classics to pronounce such judgements. But in 1786 neither
Beaumarchais nor Mozart were classics; to that Vienna audience,
Figaro was a play of modern life, and although the scene was laid in
Spain there was no great effort wasted on trying to obtain local
colour. Anyone who takes the trouble to compare Da Ponte's libretto
page by page with the original play will be surprised to see how
closely the two correspond. One reason for this is that Beaumarchais
himself had had some experience of opera, both as librettist and
as composer. *Le Barbier de Séville* was orginally intended as a comic
opera, with music arranged by the author from his recollections of
the songs and dances he had heard in Spain. It was refused by the
Opéra-Comique and required very little alteration to transform it
into a *comédie en prose mêlée d'ariettes* such as at that date was
quite admissible at the Comédie-Française. The main outline of the
story is stated in its simplest terms by Beaumarchais himself:

> Un grand Seigneur espagnol, amoureux d'une jeune fille
> qu'il veut séduire, et les efforts que cette fiancée, celui qu'elle
> doit épouser, et la femme du Seigneur réunissent pour faire
> échouer dans son dessein un maître absolu que son rang, sa
> fortune, et sa prodigalité rendent tout-puissant pour l'accomplir.
> Voilà tout, rien de plus.

Beaumarchais's plan was to take an old-fashioned type of comic opera plot as a foundation and embroider satirical dialogue upon it, the conventional stage tricks appearing deliberately ridiculous in their new garb of fine literary artifice. It is a device with which the modern theatre has been made familiar enough, both in England and abroad. The danger of converting a play of this kind into a comic opera was that while the old tricks would remain as the foundation of the work, the flavour of the new dialogue, and, more important still, the new social point of view, would disappear entirely. But what Da Ponte was often obliged to sacrifice, Mozart could to some extent reconstitute in another medium; and in any case a dozen German translations of the play had been published by 1785, so that the audience which listened to Mozart could easily supply from their own recollection such matter as Da Ponte had thought it more prudent to omit.

Da Ponte as a librettist deserves to be taken seriously. The general tendency of English musicians is to take it for granted that all opera librettos are rubbish, and they can always quote the well-known remark of Figaro himself—*ce qui ne vaut pas la peine d'être dit, on le chante*. Historians of literature almost invariably run away in horror from any drama written for the purpose of musical setting, even when the poet is eminent enough to command general respect. The three librettos which Da Ponte wrote for Mozart are masterpieces of their own category, and his work for other composers is no less interesting. To remodel Beaumarchais's *Tarare* for performance at Vienna under the name of *Axur* was no small accomplishment; there again it is worth while going through the French and the Italian page by page. Da Ponte was evidently quite seriously interested in his task as a librettist and it is quite clear that he selected and planned his librettos with a subtle understanding of the different temperaments and abilities of the composers for whom he worked. . . .

With *Così fan Tutte* we bid farewell to Lorenzo Da Ponte as Mozart's librettist, and the reader may like to know what became of this curius and fascinating character. The death of Joseph II in February, 1790, left him without a protector. His enemies were too strong for him, and the result of intrigue and calumny was that he was obliged to take flight to Trieste, glad to escape from Vienna with his life, as we learn from the verses in which he dedicates to Byron his Italian translation of *The Prophecy of Dante*. At Trieste he made the acquaintance of an English merchant, and fell violently in love with his daughter, whose name was Nancy. The father's name was Grahl, and he was born at Dresden, but Nancy always maintained firmly that she was an Englishwoman. She had been asked in marriage by an Italian who was in business at Vienna, but he demanded too large a dowry, and the father, furious at the idea of giving his daughter to a man who only wanted her money—Mr. Grahl must indeed have been English if he was so much surprised at the normal Italian outlook on matrimony—handed her over to Da Ponte. It has been suggested that Nancy was a Jewess, and that Da Ponte married her by the Jewish rite, although he was a Catholic priest.[4]

He left Trieste with Nancy in August, 1792, with the idea of seeking his fortune in Paris. Casanova, whom he met in Prague, recommended him to go to London instead, and gave him two pieces of sound advice: "When you are in London, never set foot inside the Italian café, and never sign your name to a bill." In London he obtained the post of poet to the Italian Opera. On 1 March, 1794, Bertati's *Don Giovanni* was given there, with music put together from Gazzaniga, Sarti, and others, Mozart being represented by Leporello's catalogue aria. In 1797 Da Ponte was sent to Italy to engage singers, and seized the opportunity of visiting his old home at Ceneda. He arrived quite unexpectedly on All Souls' Eve, just as his old father, aged eighty, was drinking the health of his long-absent son, surrounded by Lorenzo's seven sisters and two brothers, with numerous other relatives. Lamartine wrote of this episode:

> Même dans les confidences de Saint-Augustin, si tendre et pieux pour sa mère, il n'y a pas beaucoup de pages en littérature intime supérieures à ce retour d'un fils aventurier dans la maison paternelle.

---

[4] Paul Nettl, "Da Ponte, Casanova, und Böhmen," in *Alt-Prager Almanach*, 1927, points out that it was not until after Nancy's death that Da Ponte took steps to reconcile himself with the Catholic Church.

He came back to London, but his inexperience seems to have been taken advantage of both by Taylor, the manager of the King's Theatre in the Haymarket, and by Messrs. Corri and Dussek, the composers and music publishers with whom he went into partnership. It need hardly be said that he disregarded both the wise counsels given him by Casanova. In 1805 he fled from his creditors and made his escape to America. He arrived first at Philadelphia, but about 1807 he settled in New York, where he taught Italian and entered into various unfortunate business ventures. The great event of his life in America was the visit of Garcia to New York in 1825 with an Italian opera company which performed *Don Giovanni*—Mozart's this time. In 1832, when he was eighty-three, he lost his Nancy. It was about this time that he entered into correspondence with the Patriarch of Venice, who had formerly been Bishop of Ceneda. He sent the Patriarch some poems, and received a kindly letter of thanks, in which the worthy prelate begged him to make his peace with Holy Church. He died on 17 August, 1838, in his ninetieth year, having made his confession and received extreme unction. A document quoted by one of his biographers, Monsignor Bernardi, from the ecclesiastical archives of New York, says that since it was not generally known that Da Ponte was a priest, it was considered advisable not to draw attention to the fact either on the occasion of his reconciliation with the Church or on that of his funeral.[5]

E. J. D.

At noon 115 years ago yesterday [August 20, 1953] some of the town's most distinguished citizens followed to the Catholic Cemetery in East Eleventh Street, between what is now Avenue A and First Avenue, the body of Lorenzo Da Ponte, who wrote the libretto for the Mozart opera, *Don Giovanni*.

The librettist, something of a spendthrift and eccentric, had been a grocer in town. He had been Columbia University's first Professor of Italian Literature, too, but death had come when he was an improverished dodderer in his ninetieth year. The body was put in a vault while friends tried to raise funds for a monument.

They never got the money. The body was forgotten. When his native Ceneda, near Venice in Italy, asked for it years later, no one

---

[5] Jacopo Bernardi, *Memorie di Lorenzo Da Ponte,* Florence, 1871.

could locate it. His family, which had lived with him at 91 Spring Street, searched for it in vain; they finally gave up. Years later, even the cemetery vanished.

The most fantastic opera libretto could not match the mysterious evanishment of Lorenzo Da Ponte—for this reason: Mozart, with whom he had worked in Vienna in the late eighteenth century on *Don Giovanni, The Marriage of Figaro,* and *Così fan tutte,* had vanished in almost exactly the same way after his burial in December, 1791, in a Viennese graveyard.

M. B.

3

The Symphonies

THE BACKGROUND

THE EARLY symphonies followed, as a rule, the formal principles of the Italian theatre-symphony, and these principles remained fixed from the time of Alessandro Scarlatti (1659–1725) to that of Mozart, who in his earlier symphonies was not inclined to break away from them. The Italian theatre-symphony had three movements: two lively movements were separated by a third, slower and of a contrasting character. It was thus distinguished from the French overture or theatre-symphony, which brought a fugued allegro between two grave movements, and was of a more solemn and imposing character. As the Italian was better suited to the technique of amateurs—princes and citizens who were fond of music and themselves wished to play—the theatre-symphony grew gradually of less theatrical importance: it no longer had a close connection with the subject of the music-drama that followed; it became mere superficial, decorative music, which sank to "organized instrumental noise," to cover the din of the assembling and chattering audience. The form survived. In the first movement noisy phrases and figures took the place of true musical thought, and if a thought occurred it was ornamented in the taste of the period. The slow movement was after the manner of the rococo pastoral song, or it was a sentimental lament. The finale was gay, generally with the character of a dance, but conventional and without any true emotional feeling. The slow movement and the finale were occasionally connected. The first movement was generally in 4/4 or 3/4; the second, in 2/4, 3/4, or

319

3/8; the third, in simple time or in 6/8. The first movement and the finale were in the same and major key. They were scored for two oboes, two horns, and strings, to which trumpets and drums were added on extraordinary occasions. The slow movement was, as a rule, in the subdominant or in the minor of the prevailing tonality, sometimes in the superdominant or in a parallel key. It was scored chiefly for string quartet, to which flutes were added, and, less frequently, oboes and horns. The cembalo was for a long time an indispensable instrument in the three movements.

In the slow movement of the conventional theatre-symphony the melody was played by the first violin to the simplest accompaniment in the bass. The middle voices were often not written in the score. The second violin went in unison or in thirds with the first violin, and the viola in octaves with the bass.

P. H.

It is still sometimes asked by those who, for instance, regard Mozart as falling short of Wagner in "range" or of Brahms in "profundity" what the qualities may be that are supposed to make him one of the greatest composers. That question cannot be answered here, though, given adequate space, it is quite capable of being settled to the satisfaction of all but those who have no wish to be satisfied. But an essay on the best of his symphonies must begin with some attempt at accounting for his greatness particularly as a symphonist.

That greatness, it should be obvious, is not a matter of quantity, for, although he wrote over forty full-sized symphonies, Haydn wrote more than twice as many—and Beethoven only nine. Nor is it a matter of Mozart's doing anything to establish the symphonic form as he established that of the piano concerto. That had been done before him, mainly by Haydn, and Mozart did not contribute nearly as much to its modification and expansion as Beethoven did after him, and Schubert too, if it comes to that—to mention no others.

Not that the mere shaping of musical forms, although great composers have often had a hand in it, is in itself an achievement making for greatness. Minor musicians all through history have often done most of the pioneering in that direction. "Interesting historical figures," Tovey called them, the inverted commas indicating a certain amount of scorn, as a sweeping Toveyan remark to the effect that "I.H.F.s cannot compose" unequivocally confirms. Be that as it may —and the I.H.F.s have at any rate written great quantities of music, whether we choose to call it composition or not—what concerns us here is to see what it is that a great master like Mozart does with a form like the symphony which he has neither invented nor greatly advanced for the benefit of later exponents. There must, we tell ourselves as we listen spellbound to a Mozart symphony, be something else than the contrivance and manipulation of structure about the creation of music in this or any other form.

There is indeed something else, and that something, hard as it is to define, is perhaps best called individuality. Mozart's handling of the symphony as a form differs from Haydn's only in the incidental details of procedure, and that does not mean a great deal if we consider that Haydn's own symphonies differ quite as much from each other in formal management. But no listener with any sort of ear trained to distinguish between styles—personal as distinct from mere period styles—could possibly for more than a moment mistake a symphony by Mozart for one by Haydn. The language may be the same, or nearly the same with some variants that amount merely to those of dialect; but what is expressed in that language belongs to different worlds of feeling, of spiritual attitude, and of mental shape.

But if Mozart's individuality is easily enough apprehended by a listener with some kind of discrimination, it becomes tantalizingly elusive directly one tries to describe it on paper. Who is to say why exactly the opening of the great G minor Symphony gives a peculiar impression of just that apprehensive agitation, just that foreboding of tragedy? A technical explanation, that the movement is fast and the key is minor, does not help, for someone may remind us that the scherzo in Mendlessohn's *Midsummer Night's Dream* music is also fast and in a minor key (in fact the very same key, as it happens) without sounding in the least apprehensively agitated or tragic. When all is said, great inspiration remains a mystery, and formal analysis can help us only to see how that inspiration has been outwardly organized by the composer without accounting for its nature and quality.

Yet, though we may feel all sorts of things on hearing Mozart and respond to his music with an intuitive understanding that goes a long way towards meeting him in his own mental and emotional sphere, we are bound to fall back on technical discussion directly we try to write about his work. This cannot help to account for his artistic individuality, but it can at least show something of the ways and means by which that individuality communicates itself to others.

Mozart's way of reaching his listeners is to make use of a faultless technical equipment. His is so smooth and natural a technique as to be very easily overlooked. In fact we are not intended to be made aware of it or to admire it for its own sake: it is merely the means to an end, and in the case of one so supremely gifted a perfectly convenient and untroublesome means, even where it involves appalling difficulties. No parade is ever made of skill or learning. Sometimes, it is true, as in the finale of the Jupiter Symphony, sheer pleasure in the exercise of a staggering virtuosity takes hold of Mozart irresistibly; but even there the music remains clear, its surface undisturbed by the polyphonic problems he tackles, so that the hearer who remains unaware of them still enjoys the incomparable flow and polish of the music.

Mozart's sovereign ease in the handling of counterpoint is the very foundation of his style and one of the great differences between him and Beethoven, who happened to find counterpoint difficult—which is not to say that he eschewed it or that, when he faced it, he failed to do justice to his own peculiar genius. What distinguishes Mozart is the fact that he always applied this gift of his, whether he intended to write polyphonically or not, and that, considering how readily contrapuntal writing came to him, he made conscious use of polyphonic skill surprisingly rarely. But it was at the very root of his technique, even where he simply wrote accompanied melody. It is this which explains why his part-writing and his spacing are always, whatever the nature of the musical texture may be at the moment, superbly lucid and limpid. It is a mistake to suppose that great contrapuntists are at their greatest only where they use counterpoint ostentatiously. Even Bach by no means always did so. Besides, there have been very highly skilled masters of counterpoint who were dry and lifeless composers—who were in fact I.H.F.s and, in at any rate one sense of Tovey's dictum, could not compose. On the other hand Schubert was misguided when he thought, at the end of his short life, that he stood in need of lessons in academic counterpoint from Sechter, who is not much of an historical figure and certainly not an interesting one. A young genius who could write such a good continually moving bass against a vital theme as that in the finale of the Octet, or bring tunes that have any amount of value and character by themselves into such perfect combination as in the slow movement of the great C major Symphony, lacked nothing as a contrapuntist that a great composer of his sort could possibly require. And in this respect Schubert resembled Mozart, whose technique is that of a great symphonist because it is fundamentally that of a great contrapuntist. So much at least of his genius we can account for technically; but he would not have been the supreme personality he was if he had not also possessed gifts of imagination which it is beyond verbal analysis to expound.

E. B. (2)

"The musical milieu of Salzburg had sufficed to turn Mozart aside from the Italianism of the preceding years; but it had not the means to substitute a new artistic pattern of a cut to satisfy a genius grown so mature and profound as Mozart's. And under these conditions one can understand the immense import at this juncture for the young Mozart of the visit to what Burney rightly calls 'the capital of the musical world,' to the city of Vienna, where he was to find an answer to the questions that were troubling him, and a clear indication of the route he was to follow."[1] Although the Mozarts had stayed in Vienna during the summer season of 1773, that is, in the vacation period, they would have had the opportunity of hearing much instrumental music—the best in the world for stimulating in Wolfgang a renewal of his symphonic art, which is to make itself felt, not during the few months' stay in Vienna, but, in due course, after his return to Salzburg.

The English traveler Burney notes the presence in Vienna during the autumn of 1772—that is, a little before the arrival of Mozart— of so many masters of music that we can easily imagine how im-

---

[1] T. de Wyzewa and G. de Saint-Foix, *W. A. Mozart*, Vol. II, p. 43.

portant this visit would be to the young and enthusiastic musician. "It will suffice," says Burney, "only to mention the names of Hasse, Gluck, Gassmann, Wagenseil, Salieri, Hoffmann, Haydn, Ditters, Vanhall, and Huber, who have all greatly distinguished themselves as composers; the symphonies and quartets of the five last mentioned composers are perhaps among the first full pieces and compositions, for violins, that have ever been produced."[2] In contact with these works Mozart set about acquiring a complete professional mastery, which remained with him all his life. Counterpoint is reawakened in his work with a new vigor, for Haydn had just written a magnificent set of quartets, several of which ended in fugues; and the same applies to those, then quite recent, of the scholar Gassmann, who had been a pupil of the venerable Padre Martini. So we must not be surprised to see the youth, scarcely arrived in Vienna, dashing off a set of six string quartets, two of which likewise end with fugues! But this is not all. The first work he wrote in Vienna was a grand Serenade, intended for the marriage of a Salzburg notability, Herr von Andretter; and in this work we can see Haydn's style reigning supreme. Mozart has perhaps never written a work in which he so closely followed the teaching of his illustrious elder. We must allow that he could not better have chosen his model from among the remarkable set of composers then in vogue in Vienna, and from now on the prodigy of 1762 and 1768 takes up his place among them. "We may say that from summer of 1773 until his arrival in Mannheim, toward the end of 1777, Mozart, in short, remains a true composer of the Viennese school."[3]

It is impossible, then, to overemphasize the importance to Mozart of the lessons learned in Vienna. It is clearly in Vienna that he became acquainted with Haydn's symphonies of 1772, which, with or without such characteristic titles as *"La Passione"* or "The Farewell" or the *Symphonie funèbre,* all reflect the intense crisis of romanticism Haydn went through in that year; to these must be added several symphonies of Vanhall, an artist of similar temperament though unequal inspiration. On the other hand, such masters as Gassmann and Ditters, smitten by *opera buffa,* are in process of creating a

[2] Charles Burney, *The Present State of Music in France and Germany,* Vol. I, p. 364.
[3] Wyzewa and Saint-Foix, *op. cit.,* Vol. II, p. 45.

Viennese instrumental style that, light and lively, is to have the sharpest reaction on Mozart.

After Vienna, then, we shall see his developments lengthening, his codas becoming weighty résumés of his first movements and finales, ths finales themselves rivaling the first movements in importance and assuming the sonata form; in a word, a more elaborate workmanship, a language more clearly symphonic, a more pronounced breadth given to all his instrumental compositions. As almost always happens with Mozart, this serious style is not going to last very long, for *"la galanterie"* is about to overrun the whole of music. But we can say that Mozart in his symphonies of 1773–74 has reached the end of a period, and that after it he will not do better, but different things.

Afterward there will be Mannheim, and Paris; his orchestral masses will be more powerful, the horizon will be wider; but, for all that, something of great intimacy and charm will have disappeared; the subtle perfume of Vienna, combined with the Italian flavor, will have vanished. Mozart's incomparable youth, as evidenced in his 1773–74 symphonies (though, alas, too rarely experienced), will be over.

G. de St.-F.

Symphony in G minor, No. 25 (K. 183)

I.	Allegro con brio	III.	Menuetto
II.	Andante	IV.	Allegro

OFTEN CALLED the "little G minor Symphony," to distinguish it from the masterpiece in the same key written in the summer of 1788, this work dates from Mozart's seventeenth year and marks an important development in style and emotional power. It is usually assigned to the year 1773 and belongs with a group of five symphonies bearing many traits in common, which the young master composed in Salzburg between his visits to Vienna and Munich. Of the five only the D major (K. 202) is dated, May 5, 1774, being specified.

As Abert points out, the five symphonies in question differ radically from Mozart's previous efforts in this form. Outwardly, they show greater logic and necessity of development. The themes are more significant and more fully and broadly expounded. The goal is kept steadily in mind, and there is a maturer striving toward an ideal of unity through all four movements, especially notable in the G minor and A major (K. 201). Inwardly they clearly reveal a new spirit of romantic fervor and passionate energy, a deeper poetry, and a higher capacity for tragic expression. This fresh vein of romantic utterance has caused scholars like Wyzewa and St.-Foix to regard the early G minor as a prototype, even an early draft, at least stylistically, of the later work.

The new development proclaimed by the G minor sprang from many sources. In the first place, Mozart had broken away from his Italian models in composition and come more directly under the influence of the Viennese school, where a robuster romanticism had begun to flourish. During his visit to Vienna, he had heard symphonies by Joseph Haydn, and one in particular, the so-called "Funeral" or "Mourning" Symphony, in E minor, probably deeply impressed him. Very possibly the Haydn work not only suggested the mood and romantic character of the G minor, but prompted Mozart to make his first symphonic essay in the minor mode. Then, too, the literary *Sturm und Drang* of romanticism was getting under way, and Goethe was launching its first fiery manifestos. Viennese music was already feeling the crisis in art and beginning to echo the new currents.

According to Wyzewa and St.-Foix, who have a passion for hunting sources, the Haydn symphony, with its marked romantic character as a single factor, best explains the G minor Symphony. "It is the same tragic pain," they say, "full of nobility, to be sure; the same consuming fire . . . the same tendency to make the symphony nothing but a great song of feverish anguish, interrupted by the sweet repose of the Andante." As further resemblances the French collaborators point to the dramatic and double exposition of the opening subject, the alternation of unison and counterpoint, the same large conception of codas. Consciously or unconsciously, they conclude, Mozart was influenced by this Haydn symphony.

Wyzewa and St.-Foix also attach great importance to another symphony, that in D major, of Vanhall, belonging, like the Haydn work, to the year 1772. The "romantic ardor" of Vanhall's music had drawn warm praise from Dr. Burney. If the G minor Symphony bears "the general line and spirit of Haydn," say the French sleuths, "it resembles Vanhall in its language, the trembling allure of its song, its syncopated rhythms and whole instrumental fabric." However, they admit that the strangest thing of all about this work is that, while clearly deriving from other sources, it remains one of Mozart's most personal expressions, bearing the "stamp of his heart and genius."

Apthorp detected further derivations from Bach and Gluck. In the style and thematic material of the Andante, he discerned traces of the Leipzig master, whose works Mozart studied eagerly whenever the chance offered. The American analyst directed special attention to the F minor Prelude in the second book of *The Well-tempered Clavier* as a probable source. In the Menuetto he found "unmistakable tokens" of the influence of Gluck.

Of course, apart from all these outside influences, there was Mozart's own inner urge to express his feelings of the moment. That these were not feelings of passionate joy the Symphony makes clear. Despondency over the increasingly oppressive atmosphere in the Archbishop of Salzburg's palace, where he was employed, may be reflected in its pages. Then, too, the letters hint of a romantic attachment which came to nothing. As Eric Blom points out, Mozart's rare use of the minor mode is like "the sudden shedding of a repression," and he agrees that the first and last movements "express an unhappy restlessness." Even the minuet has astonished many because of its "gloomy discontent and agitation." In short, Mozart, at seventeen, was quite normally experiencing the stresses and strains of adolescence.

One of the remarkable features of this Symphony is the unison announcement of chief themes in the first and last movements. Another is the fact that Mozart employs four horns, a rarity in the eighteenth century. Haydn seldom uses more than two, and Beethoven employs four only once in his symphonies, in the Ninth. The number is unusual even with Mozart, who employs four horns only in four of his symphonies, and never in the operas.

L. B.

I. The theme of the first Allegro gives a definitely somber minor cast to the opening, although it is relieved by the tripping counter-theme in B flat major. The development is brief (thirty-four bars only) but interesting. It enters on a new subject which is mingled with the principal one. There is a full return, the second subject appearing in the minor, and a short coda.

II. Commentators have found brightness and relief from the dark colorings of this symphony in the short, lyric Andante in E flat major. But if there is a romantic movement in the symphony it is this one—if the "Wertherleiden" found their affecting echo in the sensitive and receptive Mozart, it is surely here. The voice of the violins, muted, is arresting as they give forth their plaintive melody of accented, falling half-tones—the symbol of pathos with Mozart. Interwoven are dark thirds of the bassoons, here first heard. In contrast to this plaintive song there is a brief countertheme in shimmering ornamental notes from the violins—a fleeting recollection of Mozartian elegance. The melody returns to dominate the development and becomes more impassioned, shading into minor.

III. The minuet brings us back to G minor and the full orchestra. Again in contrast is the G major trio for the winds only. We imagine a peasantlike German dance, which none but an Austrian could have composed.

IV. The finale is again in sonata form in a brilliant ferocity of G minor, once more relieved by a lilting second subject in the relative B flat major. The development is as short as that of the first movement—shorter if the fast tempo be taken into account. The movement scintillates in its progress, displaying twists and turns of its composer's wit along the way.

The symphony is scored for two oboes, two bassoons, four horns, and strings.

J. N. B.

Symphony in A major, No. 29 (K. 201)

i. Allegro	iii. Minuet
ii. Andante	iv. Allegro con spirito

THERE is here a new feeling for the necessity of intensifying the symphony through imitation, and of rescuing it from the domain of the purely decorative through a refinement of detail such as is characteristic of chamber music. The instruments change character: the strings become wittier, the winds lose everything that is simply noisy, the figuration drops everything merely conventional. The new spirit shows itself in all the movements: in the Andante, which has the delicate formation of a string-quartet movement, enriched by the two pairs of wind instruments; in the Minuet, with its contrasts of grace and almost Beethoven-like violence; in the Finale, an *allegro con spirito* that is really *con spirito,* and which contains the richest and most dramatic development section Mozart had written up to this time. It is understandable that these symphonies satisfied Mozart even in his Vienna period, and that he produced them at his "academies" with only slight changes in the scoring. What an immense distance he had traveled from the Italian *sinfonia!* Who in Italy would have written such a work, and where would it have found its audience?

A. E.

Of the inscription on the score of the A major, the year 1774 alone is legible, and that faintly. The rest has been scratched out. However, internal and circumstantial evidence would date the work as of 1774 even if the year were lacking. The style alone, as Wyzewa and St.-Foix point out, would reveal it as a continuation of the C major and G minor Symphonies preceding. The A major is part of the "revolution" which overtook Mozart's outlook and method in the spring and summer of 1774.

Wyzewa and St.-Foix were convinced that a direct model for the A major existed in a symphony in the same key by Joseph Haydn's brother Michael, then a neighbor of the Mozarts in Salzburg. Though first written in 1763, the alleged prototype is dated March 4,

1774, in the revised manuscript in the Munich Library. Mozart is supposed to have heard the work in Salzburg in its later form and promptly set to work on a similar one. The many resemblances would seem to bear out the Wyzewa-St.-Foix claim. The rhythms of the opening sections are parallel. In both Mozart and Haydn the second subject is in E, and the contrast between the first and second themes is similar. The codas are long in both works and not so formalized. The double exposition of the first subject is another novel feature in Mozart, as is the return of fragments of the first theme after the announcement of the second. Also to be noted in Mozart's work is the greater part played by the basses in discoursing counterpoint with the violins. The new melodic richness and maturer orchestral patterning of the four movements speak for themselves.

"In point of invention and scope," wrote the French collaborators, "this symphony is the most perfect product of the whole first period of Mozart's career, ending with his departure for Mannheim and Paris." It is curious to find two Mozart biographers like Dyneley Hussey and Otto Jahn at opposite poles in defining the dominant mood of the symphony: "Tragic nobility," according to the British scholar; "full of cheerful humor from beginning to end," insists Jahn.

Aside from two oboes and two horns, used largely for doubling and strengthening, the symphony is scored only for strings.

L. B.

Symphony in D major, No. 31 ("Paris") (K. 297)

I. Allegro assai   II. Andante   III. Allegro

THE GRAND TOUR undertaken by Mozart in company with his mother in September, 1777, which was to be prolonged until the early part of 1779, marks an epoch of capital importance in his short life. From this time he ceased in some measure to be the Salzburg musician, to become the universal master. It is not the practical result of the journey that should be considered, but rather the considerable enrichment, the broadening, if one may say so, of his art. The young man tasted independence, wider horizons opened before him, grave events ripened him prematurely. The young and agreeable musician of Salzburg was to become, in a few months, the great, the immortal, Mozart.

One feels clearly, moreover, that he had need of a change of air, that the atmosphere of his native town was inadequate, from the sole point of view of instrumental music, to slake his thirst for novelty. So we behold him in Germany's "symphonic" town *par excellence,* that old Palatinate city wherein instrumental music had acquired a more weighty importance than anywhere else. At Mannheim, in fact, each member of the orchestra seemed to fulfill an official mission, so seriously did he take his functions; the wind, notably, attained a perfection that made an immediate and vivid impression on Mozart. But—a curious and almost inexplicable fact—he did not write a symphony! It is only much later, in Paris, that he turns to account the essentially "Mannheimist" resources of the orchestra. In the meantime he writes only for piano, violin, voice, or flute, and his music betrays strong French influences.

It is indeed very surprising that a musician such as Cannabich, whose friend and guest he was, and who kept him in constant touch with every detail of his own compositions, never encouraged him to confide to the admirable orchestra anything more substantial than his praises. It is true that, if musical interpretation there was superior, it cannot be said that Mannheim, at the particular time that Mozart was there, could boast of anyone to rival Michael Haydn, the Salzburg master, in musical worth or personal genius. For Mozart the only person who really counted in this school was old Ignace Holzbauer, another Viennese, whose *Günther von Schwarzburg* founded German opera and re-echoed in the very depths of his soul. This art, strongly tinged with Italianism, was very much more likely to please him than that of a Vogler or a Schweitzer, or even—dare one say it?—a Gluck. And as for the symphonists past and present of Mannheim, he gives scarcely any details as to the real value of their works. But he remains struck in particular by the admirable instrumental ensemble, by the timbres and their effects; especially we can say that the clarinet was revealed to Mozart during his stay in Mannheim, and that he was then granted a prophetic glimpse of the marvelous resources it was to offer him in the future.

It is now no longer to be a question of charming Salzburg *divertimenti;* his music henceforward will work toward two main ends: solidity of writing and, especially, a sort of delicately graded precision in the expression of feeling. Until then he had been content to interpret these feelings in general rather than in detail. The new elements absorbed during Mozart's five months at Mannheim are to serve as excellent preparation; he is still in close touch with the prevailing French taste, for the Palatinate was, in fact, a French colony. Karl Theodor, the Elector and reigning sovereign, was a man of entirely French culture; his architects more or less always took their lead from Versailles; all the great "Mannheim" symphonies of Toëschi and Cannabich, without exception, were sold, published, and played in Paris, so much so that Mozart on arriving in the French capital found himself hearing the Mannheim repertoire all over again at the Concert Spirituel. At the outset of his journey he had made contact with "some quite charming pieces" of the Alsatian Edelmann; then in Paris he renewed acquaintance with Schobert's sonatas and got to know those of Hullmandel. The French influence was therefore at work before his arrival in that country; and before actually arriving in Paris he even wrote some ariettas to French words.

The programs of the great Paris orchestra during the early spring of 1778 were composed mainly of the symphonies of Gossec, whom Mozart had the opportunity of meeting, and of the Abbé Sterkel, whom he reproached for playing too fast; but these programs also included Mannheim symphonies, by Toeschi and Cannabich, with in addition numerous *concertantes* designed to group the most diverse virtuosos together and show off their talents to the best advantage.

This latter is a genre that we can almost say was born in Paris, about 1770; public demand was for "solo" instruments in the symphonies, and the growing taste for virtuosity especially favored all soloists. Thus, the first proposition made to Mozart, the day after his arrival in Paris, concerned Mannheim's four most famous wind virtuosos, who had come to Paris at the same time as Mozart. The suggestion was that he should write a *"symphonie concertante pour la flute de Wendling, le hautbois de Ramm, le cor de Punto, et le basson de Ritter."*[1] But, I must add, he changed his mind and substituted for the flute a clarinet, the instrument he was so captivated by at Mannheim.

This, which, like the choruses he had written for Holzbauer's *Miserere,* was prevented from performance by some rather shady intrigues, is a monumental work, showing no evidence of the haste with which Mozart confessed he wrote it. It enormously overshadows all the *sinfonie concertante* of the age and even, by its working out, former ones by Mozart himself, and never again will he give us such an example of the art of Mannheim. The spacious designs of this great work, one of the longest he wrote, the marvelous understanding of the resources of the wind instruments, stamp it as an altogether unique work, a landmark in the history of both the symphony and the concerto. It is a direct consequence of his Mannheim visit, and in it we can see the beginnings of the grand manner of so many of his masterpieces for wind instruments. It is noteworthy that the three movements of this symphony or quartet *concertante* are all in the same key; their length, with Mozart, indicates importance, according to the popular taste at Mannheim, and shows him presenting himself to Paris with a sort of *concerto grosso,* rejuvenated and brought up to date. There is still no decisive French influence; the work remains German in both conception and working out. If Mozart wrote it in Paris, it seems to have been conceived in Mannheim, and at a time when he had as yet had no direct contact with any specifically French art; there is in the serenity of the Adagio a kind of religious sentiment akin to Beethoven, and it is no exaggeration to claim this as one of the greatest moments in all Mozart. The way the ten variations of the final Andantino follow one another, with the intercalated tuttis which never play the theme, but only the refrain, is itself an inspiration; but the penultimate one, leading to an adagio recitative that prepares the way for the final acceleration, once more carries us toward Beethoven, while the unexpectedness of the calm before the end removes us from, or rather lifts us above, the *"thème populaire"* that is the main theme of this remarkable finale. After all, perhaps the work as a whole was

---

[1] This work was replaced by a *symphonia concertante* by Cambini (1746–1823), played by the same quartet (Concert Spirituel, April 12 and 19, 1778).

deemed too different from what the subscribers to the Concert Spirituel were accustomed to hear, and no doubt this is the sole reason why this vast *concerto grosso* with which Mozart hoped to make his Paris debut was never heard.

A compensation for this first failure was not long in coming. In fact, the performance, in June, of his Symphony in D, called the "Paris" Symphony (K. 297), concerning which Mozart sent his father some details, seems to have been a great success. However, in order probably the more completely to satisfy French tastes, he entirely remodeled the Andante (in G), replacing it by a new movement, in my opinion more facile and less banal than the first. This second version has been preserved, and was even published in Sieber's edition.[2]

It must be said at once that at first glance this symphony marks a striking progress from the point of view of scoring; the Mannheim influence is undeniable. In this work Mozart, solely to please us, adopts the methods of the later "Mannheimists," in particular those of his friend Cannabich. This is a question of the precise attack by the whole orchestra, what was known then as *"le premier coup d'archet,"* a phrase which has aroused much sarcasm; of the constant repetition of themes; of the absence of repeat marks; and of an essentially brilliant veneer to the whole work; it seems to me that real French symphonic music had still not reacted on him at the time when he favored us with this "Paris" Symphony. For who was most frequently performed at the Concert Spirituel during his visit? Gossec unquestionably, whom he met, but who seems to have influenced him only during the latter part of his stay in Paris. The symphonies of the Abbé Sterkel were also frequently played, as I have remarked above, also those of Cannabich and Toëschi—without counting the numerous *concertanti* of which the public remained very fond, offering as they did such opportunities to virtuosos of renown.

The conception and composition of the "Paris" Symphony were clearly influenced by the joy he felt in having at his disposal an

---

[2] *Bibliothèque du Conservatoire Paris, Recueil No. 32 (Symphonies) "Du Répertoire du Concert Spirituel: chez le Sr Sieber, musicien, rue St-Honoré entre celle des Vielles-Etuves* [sic] *et celle d'Orléans, chez l'Apothicaire, n° 92."* This was the first edition.

admirable body of wind players, in being able worthily to employ each one, drawing from them the effects he so reveled in while at Mannheim. These effects were not used by him until his arrival in Paris, to which the leading players from Mannheim had moved at about the same time. The importance of this orchestra and its resources, which Mozart himself has enumerated,[3] led him to write for a stronger and more compact group than that of Salzburg, moreover a group of players who were often also renowned composers. The symphonic result achieved by Mozart in this, his first composition "for grand orchestra," remains, in fact, quite superficial. The admirable unity I have striven so often to emphasize, especially in the symphonies of 1772–73, does not strike us here; there is not that inward relationship between the different subjects, nor the exquisite originality of invention and working out; they follow one another without amalgamating, and it must certainly be conceded that they are somewhat ordinary. Mozart is so sensitive to every influence that he goes to the extent of impoverishing his own natural inventiveness in order to adopt the imposing but quite empty framework that distinguishes the greater number of the Mannheim symphonies; when it was a question of showing off instrumentalists of the first order he created a work infinitely greater and more original; his symphony or quartet *concertante* described above seems to me much more important than the "Paris" Symphony. Only the finale of the latter, opening piano, with the two violins announcing a *fugato,* greatly heightens the whole of the symphony; and this anticipation of the *fugato* is not wholly deceptive, for the second subject is ranged in a series of imitations; the repeated antiphonal effects between wind and strings certainly make for variety, and, also, the passage following the second subject contains a few bars in which we recognize joyfully that abrupt change of key so frequent in Mozart's rapid finales, a sudden veer of the Mozartian fancy which gives to these few disturbing moments a psychological value perhaps superior to all the rest of the work.

G. de St.-F.

---

[3] In a letter to his father, November 4, 1777. "10 or 11 firsts, the same number of seconds, 4 violas, 2 oboes, 2 flutes, 2 clarinets, 2 horns, 4 cellos, 4 bassoons, 4 double basses, trumpets and drums."

1. The first movement (Allegro assai, D major, 4/4) opens with the "premier coup d'archet," once famous in Paris orchestras—a strong *forte* chord for the full orchestra, allowing all the strings to show their accuracy of attack by coming in sharply together. In this particular instance, all the strings, brass, and kettledrums strike the tonic D in unison and octaves, the woodwind filling in the harmony. This brilliant exordium is part of the first theme, which is briefly exposed by the violins, accompanied by the woodwind and horns, and followed by a short subsidiary passage for full orchestra, ending on the tonic chord. Then follows an episodic period, still in the tonic, in which a bright little squiblike figure is developed in the first violins, against running counterpoint in triplets in the second, and a staccato bass in the violas and basses, followed by some brilliant tutti passage work which ends in the key of the dominant. This passage might be called a first subsidiary; but the thematic material upon which it is based is really a sort of anticipatory hint at the second theme of the movement. The second theme now appears in the dominant: not the quasi-sentimental cantilena (the "Adagio in the midst of an Allegro," as Wagner puts it) almost invariably used as a second theme by post-Mozartian symphonic writers, but a series of bright little fusées and descending runs in thirds in the violins, answered by little sighing figures in thirds in the woodwind. The concluding portion (antithesis) of the theme consists of some graceful developments on an arpeggio figure by the violins and violas in octaves, against sustained harmonies in the woodwind and a *pizzicato* bass. Next follows a long and fully developed second subsidiary of contrapuntal passage work for the full orchestra in *forte,* interrupted by some lighter, more playful passages in the violins and violas; the dominant is still the reigning tonality. A brief conclusion theme, in which the triplet rhythm predominates, brings the first part of the movement to a brilliant close; there is no repeat.

This first part merges immediately into the free fantasia, the opening measures of the one (first theme in the dominant) being also the closing measures of the other. This free fantasia, beginning as has been said with a re-exposition of the first theme in the dominant, soon assumes the shape of an imitative contrapuntal working out of a figure taken from the second theme, but so transformed as to seem a new theme in itself. This working out soon changes to free passage work, and the short fantasia soon ends with a return to the tonic, leading immediately to the beginning of the third part of the movement.

The third part bears quite the regular relations to the first, save that the episode on the "squib" figure is now omitted, and that both the second subsidiary and the conclusion theme are more fully developed than before—somewhat after the fashion of a free coda. The movement ends with a strong restatement of the *coup d'archet* figure of the first theme in the tonic, this time in bare unisons and octaves.

ii. The form of the second movement (Andante, G major, 6/8) is of the simplest. A long cantabile theme is developed, the melody being now in the first violins, now in the flute, and now in both together; this whole theme is then repeated, with but little change in the development or orchestration, and in the same key. Then follows a short coda, beginning with another repetition of the first part of the theme. Yet, with all this apparent simplicity, the movement is seen, upon closer examination, to have essentially the character of the sonata form. Its single theme is really tripartite, consisting of three successive periods: thesis, antithesis, and conclusion, which three periods play the part of the regular first theme, second theme, and conclusion theme of a sonata movement. One wonders, however, what the first version of this movement can have been; this, its second version, being so unusually simple.

iii. The third, and last, movement (Allegro, D major, 4/4) is also in the sonata form. The thesis of the first theme—staccato running counterpoint in the second violins, against a syncopated figure in the first—is given out *piano,* and followed by a dashing *forte* antithesis in the full orchestra. The whole theme is then repeated, exactly as before, save for a slightly more extended development of the thesis. Next follows a period of tutti subsidiary passage work, leading to a modulation to the key of the dominant, and closing with a half-cadence. Then comes the second theme, in the dominant: a brief passage in imitative contrapuntal writing, followed by an equally short subsidiary of tutti passage work. The conclusion theme, also partaking largely of the character of passagework, is considerably more extended, the first part of the movement closing in the dominant with a reminiscence of the antithesis of the first theme. The free fantasia consists of some free fugato work on the second theme; it is short, and soon leads to the return of the first theme in the tonic at the beginning of the third part of the movement. This third part is a rather incomplete reproduction of the first, the whole second theme being omitted; on the other hand, the first and conclusion themes are somewhat more extendedly developed.

The whole symphony is brilliant, and speaks more of vivacity and high animal spirits than of profound feeling. It is also conspicuous for the curious persistence with which it adheres to the keys of the tonic and dominant, with exceedingly few, and only passing, modulations to other keys. One feels that, in it, Mozart meant to write something at once simple and finely wrought, to please the Parisian taste.

The symphony is scored for two flutes, two oboes, two clarinets, two bassoons, two horns, two trumpets, one pair of kettledrums, and the usual strings. In the first and last movements the bassoon parts are written on the same staff with the cellos and double basses; now and then, on any staff left vacant for the nonce by other wind instruments.

W. F. A.

Symphony in C major, No. 34 (K. 338)

I. Allegro vivace   II. Andante di molto   III. Finale: Allegro vivace

SINCE MOZART during the years 1775 to 1777, both before his great Mannheim tour and while he was in France, wrote no symphonies properly so called, one may well feel some astonishment on finding him, once more returned to Salzburg, applying rapidly the techniques that have just revealed to him a school very different from that of his native town. Whether this unexpected recrudescence of his symphonic productivity was the result of an order from the Archbishop, or whether it was simply one more indication of his interest in orchestration, we cannot say; but we may well believe that, back in this narrow and backward town that he disliked, he could not resist the temptation to give his compatriots some idea of both Parisian tastes and his own improved abilities. From all the

memories seething in his brain he chooses first of all something
heroic, pathetic, something at the same time very frank and clean in
expression, with new and very varied nuances. This something was
the outcome of a very real intercourse with the French masters and,
although he remains absolutely silent on the subject, probably also
with the opera or the comic opera. All the projects he had cherished
in this regard in France came to nothing, and these frustrations
must undoubtedly have helped to embitter him and indispose him
toward the French: Mozart owed us, in fact, a lyric tragedy, *Alexandre et Roxane,* both poet and libretto of which remained unknown
to him. But we can console ourselves with the fact that these prepara-
tory studies of Mozart and his father's counsel on the subject of
French taste led up to Wolfgang's first dramatic masterpiece, the
lyric tragedy *Idomeneo.* . . .

One might almost call the present the symphonic period of
Mozart's life: the period of the *sinfonia concertante.* In fact, the
effect of all that he had learned at Mannheim or Paris was chiefly
a stressing of some one instrument, or category of instruments, in
the ensemble. And then the opportunity to write for a whole series
of eminent soloists tended to emphasize the *concertante* spirit, which
shows itself in a variety of manners, in a variety of instrumental
groupings. Later all will be used; the musical ensemble will absorb
technical innovations, and once more the development of instrumental virtuosity will be found to have made a notable contribution,
to have enriched and enlarged the whole field of music. . . .

If we now inquire what were Mozart's varied tendencies during
this period, we must recognize that the French influence is in general the dominant one, despite the Viennese style and the survival
of the Italian form. Sometimes, too, the master seems to draw near
to Haydn, but at the same time decidedly following his own bent,
and we feel from now on that Mozart's genius is already so sure
of itself, so powerful, that he can be content to borrow a procedure
or a form from one or the other, but that his language and technique
are now definitely formed, that the unshakable foundations of this
language are already laid.

This period of mellowing and deepening, spent entirely in the
calm of Salzburg, gave him the opportunity to absorb and fuse forever in one crucible all the new instrumental devices, all the impres-

sions gained in Mannheim and Paris. He is to turn them to account
and give us the true meaning and right application in the tragedy
Idomeneo, already in his head; this is the goal to which all the striving, all the experiments—in a nutshell, all the riches and inventions
gained from the most memorable of all his travels—are leading.

G. de St.-F.

The year 1780 marks a fresh stage in the development of Mozart's
genius. Within a few months of each other he composed the C major
Symphony (K. 338) and the opera *Idomeneo,* each in its own way
representing a brisk stride forward in creative power and expression.
Moreover, the C major is the earliest of Mozart's symphonies to
achieve "any degree of permanence, as far as concert practice goes,"
as Eric Blom puts it.

The work belongs to the Salzburg period of 1799–81, following
his return from Paris and Mannheim. The final break with his
employer, the Archbishop of Salzburg, a stern and irascible task-
master, came a few months later in the spring of 1781. The episode
is worth recounting as an example of Mozart's independent spirit.
He had tired of playing flunky to the Austrian dignitary, had dis-
obeyed a command to return instantly from Vienna, and was called
a "knave," "a scoundrel," and a "scurvy fellow" for his rebuff.
The doughty twenty-five-year-old composer finally braved the storm.
He brought his formal resignation in person to the archbishop's
palace. Hot words were exchanged. A well-aimed pontifical kick cut
short the interview. "Except as a visitor, Salzburg was to know him
no more," says Mr. Blom.

Shortly before the humiliating clash with the Salzburg potentate,
we find Mozart writing from Vienna to his father about the performance of one of his symphonies: "I forgot to tell you the other
day that at the concert the symphony went *magnifique* and had the
greatest *succès*—40 violins played—the wind instruments all doubled—10 violas—10 double-basses, 8 violoncellos, and 6 bassoons."
It has been long assumed that the symphony in question was the
C major (K. 338). The late Sir Donald Francis Tovey warned
against making any such facile identification. "Apart from the bassoons," he pointed out, "the symphony has no wind to double except
the oboes and horns, for nobody could suppose that the trumpets

wanted doubling. Mozart may have been writing of a revival of the "Paris" Symphony, which has full wind, including clarinets."

The symphony is scored for two oboes, two bassoons, two horns, two trumpets, kettledrums, and strings. Tovey refers specifically to the omission of flutes and clarinets as proof enough that the symphony mentioned in Mozart's letter was not the C major. Yet, the omission need not clash with the loose reference to wind instruments. The word "all" is inconclusive. Tovey also was convinced that what he termed "the substance of the first movement" had caused the oversight on the part of Otto Jahn, Mozart's biographer. It was Jahn who first made the identification.

Of course the striking thing about the symphony is its three-movement division, a departure from contemporary usage. Mozart began sketching a Minuet movement, but never completed it. Oddly enough, it was intended for second place in the symphonic scheme, right after the opening Allegro, rather than as the usual third movement. Fourteen measures (Allegro, C major) of the discarded Minuet exist, typically Mozartean in their natural beauty. They are shown crossed out in the surviving autograph. Mozart nowhere explains why he decided to omit it, though in masterly unity and compact texture the tripartite plan sufficiently explains itself. Mozart left a record of the date of completion on the score reading: *"Di Wolfgango Amadeo Mozart li 29 d'Agosto, Salisburgo, 1780."*

Three Mozart operas have been mentioned as bearing family resemblances to the C major Symphony. Eduard Hanslick heard unmistakable birth cries of motives used in *The Marriage of Figaro* and *Così fan tutte* overtures. In fact, he thought either of the end Allegros could serve intact as overture to an *opera buffa* by Mozart. Then, Eric Blom discerns foreshadowings of the music allotted a chief character in *The Escape from the Seraglio,* written two years after the C major Symphony. "Osmin already peeps out of it," writes Mozart's English biographer.

L. B.

1. The first movement of this symphony seems to mark a definite step toward that complete awareness of the problem which is shown in the three amazing symphonies of 1788. Its principal theme (Allegro vivace, C major, 4/4) is firm and tense—two sturdy chords

on strong beats followed by active, sometimes twitching energy. There follows a variant of this opening in the subdominant (this, in itself, a heightening of the tension), and the *piano* passages that follow continue the same note. The second theme is a descending phrase, somewhat chromatic, which features, in its continuation, the "twitch" that appeared in the fourth bar of the main theme. No repetition of the exposition is indicated—an unusual detail, to our eye wholly in accord with the nature of the thought so far expressed. (Jahn suggests that the Salzburgers disliked the repetition.) The development is mostly concerned with the four even quarter-notes of the third bar of the main theme, to which the strings supply a background of excited triplet figures. The development, however, is short, and almost wholly on this one thought. The recapitulation is somewhat intensified.

II. The Andante di molto (F major, 2/4) is scored only for strings and bassoon. The main theme is presented as a kind of subject and answer by the two violins and by the divided violas. There is presently a sort of second subject, not very highly contrasted (whence the homogeneous orchestration), and the whole movement, which is without a development section, thus has the general form AB, AB.

(There is no Minuet. Mozart began one, a year later, which is thought to have been intended for this piece, but discarded it. Jahn says the Salzburg audiences did not care for minuets in symphonies. But other audiences must have been of the same mind, for the early examples of the form mostly have but three movements.)

III. The finale (Allegro vivace, 6/8) has as principal theme a lively jig tune, gaily continued for some time. The second subject, in G, offers but little contrast, the dance character of the movement being so marked that no great departure would have been possible. Although the movement approximates to the sonata form, with the exposition marked to be repeated, there is no elaborate development, the recapitulation is regular, and there is no elaborate coda.

D. F.

The symphony is scored for two oboes, two bassoons, two horns, two trumpets, timpani, and strings.

The minuet was not first introduced into the symphony by Haydn, as is often stated. There is one in a symphony in D major by Georg Matthias Monn composed before 1740. Haydn's first symphony was composed in 1759. Gossec's first symphonies were published in 1754. Sammartini (1734) and others had written symphonies before Gossec; but the date of Gossec's introduction of the minuet has not been determined. There were some who thought that a symphony worthy the name should be without a minuet. The learned Hofrath Johann Gottlieb Carl Spazier of Berlin wrote a strong protest which appeared in the number of the *Musikalisches Wochenblatt* after the issue that announced Mozart's death. He characterized the minuet as a destroyer of unity and coherence.

In a dignified work there should be no discordant mirth. If a minuet be allowed, why not a polonaise or a gavotte? The first movement should be in some prevailing mood, joyful, uplifted, proud, solemn, etc. A slow and gentle movement brings relief, and prepares the hearer for the finale or still stronger presentation of the first mood. The minuet is disturbing: it reminds one of the dance hall and the misuse of music: "When it is caricatured, as is often the case in minuets by Haydn or Pleyel, it excites laughter. The minuet retards the flow of the symphony, and it should never be found in a passionate work or in one that induces meditation." Thus the Hofrath Spazier of Berlin.

P. H.

Symphony in D major, No. 35 ("Haffner") (K. 385)

| I. Allegro con spirito | III. Menuetto |
| II. Andante | IV. Finale: Presto |

MORE THAN a year after he finally settled in Vienna,[1] Mozart made the acquaintance of a rich amateur, Baron van Swieten, through whom he gradually came to know and understand the principal masterpieces of the old masters. Van Swieten not only

---

[1] Mozart arrived in Vienna on March 16, 1781, having been summoned there from Salzburg by the Archbishop.

implanted an admiration for Bach and Handel that was to last
to the end of his days, but charged him with the thankless task of
"reorchestrating" several of the latter's most celebrated works.
Mozart was also expected to take part in performances at the house
of his new patron; he had to direct many a choral or instrumental
work of Handel or Bach, and no more was needed to make him an
immediate convert to these two great men. The moment had arrived
when counterpoint and fugue were to give rise to numerous attempts
at elaboration and rejuvenation; and while their beauty and grandeur
are revived in him, counterpoint and fugue become his favorite
modes of expression. His contrapuntal haste and fever is so great
that a number of works remain unfinished, and looking over them
one cannot help bitterly regretting this incomplete state. Moreover,
another revelation, equally important artistically, led to a fresh
conception of rondo form and incited him to throw off some admirable fantasias, which show him freely improvising at the piano;
a result, this, of reading Emanuel Bach, which we can also attribute
to the new intimacy with van Swieten. One can see how during this
period of his life he was leaving Viennese taste behind him, and can
realize the value for him of this enthusiastic study of great classical
music.

G. de St.-F.

A festivity in the home of Burgomaster Sigmund Haffner of Salzburg occasioned the writing of Mozart's D major Symphony, No.
35, in the summer of 1782. Hence the title. The worthy Burgomaster
wanted music to go with his party. He so apprised Mozart's father,
Leopold, who was still in Salzburg. Leopold relayed the request to
Vienna, where Mozart had been rooming with his bride-to-be's
family, the Webers.

The request only added to Mozart's mounting woes. Life was
growing complicated for the young genius. He was writing volu-
minously for Vienna's garden fetes and concerts. Orders arrived
almost daily for more music. Intrigues and alterations were holding
up a planned première of his opera *The Escape from the Seraglio.*
Then, Papa Leopold was against his marriage to Constanze Weber
and long withheld his consent. The Webers, on their side, did not
make life and brighter for Mozart. Frau Weber was becoming, to

quote Eric Blom, "alcoholically abusive." She expected the couple, when wedded, to come to live with her and pay board. To cap it all, the lovers had a stormy clash, over a trifle. During a game of "forfeits" Constanze allowed a young gallant to measure her leg— a quaint Viennese parlor practice of the time. Mozart, ordinarily a good sport, was furious. The lovers exchanged outbursts of temper, wept, and patched up. Mozart, a bit wiser and sadder for the episode, went back to his music. Constanze and he were finally married on August 4, 1782. On August 5, Leopold's belated consent arrived from Salzburg.

Early in July, while still tangled up with private and professional commitments, Mozart received his father's note conveying the Burgomaster's request for a "Serenade." Herr Haffner, it seemed, was in a frightful hurry. Mozart at first thought of refusing. "How is such a thing possible?" he wrote back. "You have no idea of the difficulty of arranging a work of this kind for an orchestra. Well, all that I can do is to devote the night to the task, for it cannot be managed otherwise. You may count on having something from me by every post, and I will write as quickly as I can, and as well as haste will permit." Six years before, Mozart, while in Salzburg, had composed a March and a D major Serenade for the wedding of Haffner's daughter. The Salzburg merchant and official had paid well. There is also evidence of a loan from him.

Leopold received the Serenade piecemeal, the opening Allegro arriving in Salzburg seven days after Mozart's reply. Between sections Mozart dashed off a new C minor Serenade for wind instruments (K. 388). In a final communication, Mozart, pleading lack of time, suggests that the Burgomaster's Serenade be submitted minus a March. The March from the earlier wedding music of 1776 might easily do as a substitute, he adds. Later, however, we find him writing to Leopold: "I sent you a short March yesterday. I only hope that it will arrive in time and be to your taste." He also emphasizes that the first Allegro "must go in a fiery manner and the last as fast as possible."

When the Serenade came back from Salzburg, Mozart added parts for flute and clarinet, dropped one of the two minuets, as well as the March, and launched it afresh as the D major Symphony. Its première occurred in Vienna on March 3, 1783. The concert was part of the all-Mozart series, with the Emperor himself present. "What gratified me most was the presence of the Emperor," Mozart writes to his father six days later. "He gave me great applause. It is his usual custom to send the money to the box office of the theater before going there; otherwise I might justly have hoped for a larger sum, for his delight was beyond all bounds." The imperial tightwad sent twenty-five ducats. Mozart appeared as soloist in a piano concerto and also played a short fugue and a set of variations alone. Among the works on the program he mentions "my new symphony for the Haffner festival."

Blom writes in the Master Musicians Series:

> The serenade character of the work comes out in the slow movement and in the minuet with its lovely pastoral trio. In the final rondo, which Mozart said ought to go as fast as possible, he sent the Haffners a little personal message by using as his subject what is as nearly as makes no odds a quotation from Osmin's great aria of malicious triumph in *The Elopement,* the opera he had finished just before this serenade symphony.
>
> All the spirited frolic of comic opera is here blended with the grace of the two women in the stage work he wrote so lovingly in the year of his wedding (one feels that he was more deeply attached to Belmonte's Constanze than to his own), and he fell so much in love with the enchanting first episode of his rondo that he could not let it go, but developed and restated it until it became a second sonata subject.

Another striking feature of the Symphony is the use of a single theme as basis for the entire first movement. While frequent in Haydn's music, none of Mozart's other opening movements shows this monothematic pattern. The manuscript score of the D major Symphony carries the words: *"Synfonia di Amadeo Wolfgango Mozart a Vienna nel mese di Luglio,* 1782."

L. B.

1. Allegro con spirito, D major, 2/2. The principal subject opens without introduction in the full orchestra *forte*. Another idea is set

forth in A major—the orthodox key for the second theme—its material given out by the first and second violins, but this merely serves
as a countersubject to the principal theme which is heard in the
violas. Soon the material of the opening subject returns in the full
orchestra, ushering in the real second theme, presented by the strings
and woodwind in A major. There is no repetition of the exposition,
as was usual in works in the sonata form in Mozart's day. The development begins at once with a working out of the principal subject in the strings. The section is short, only thirty-six measures being
devoted to it. The second theme is not worked out at all. The recapitulation presents the principal subject in the full orchestra, as
in the exposition. The second theme now appears in D major.

ii. Andante, G major, 2/4. The subject opens in the first violins,
a sixteenth-note figure being set against it in the second violins.
The second theme follows quickly, its material in D major being
allotted to the second violins, the first violins playing repeated A's
above them. The exposition is repeated. The development section
does not consist of working out of the material in the exposition, but
rather of episodical matter, and this very short. There is a recapitulation in which the principal subject is set forth as at the beginning
of the movement. The second subject now is played in G major
but the instrumentation is practically the same as that in the
exposition.

iii. Menuetto, D major, 3/4 time. The form of this movement is
that of nearly all minuets and other pieces of their kind. It is in three
parts, of which the first and the third are of the same material. The
trio, its subject given to the first violins and the woodwind, is in A
major. The last part is an exact repetition of the first.

iv. Finale: Presto, D major, 4/4 time. The principal theme opens,
piano, in the strings. The second subject, heard in A major in the
strings—the bassoons merely double the bass part—is succeeded by
a short coda leading to a resumption of the principal subject, scored
as at the beginning of the movement. There is a repetition of the
second theme now, however, in the key of B minor, which in its
turn is followed by another repetition of the first, once more presented as at the commencement of the exposition. The second subject
makes another appearance, this time in G major. A coda concludes
the work.

The symphony is scored for two flutes, two oboes, two clarinets, two bassoons, two horns, two trumpets, timpani, and strings.

F. B.

Symphony in C major, No. 36 ("Linz") (K. 425)

I. Adagio–Allegro spiritoso	III. Menuetto
II. Poco adagio	IV. Presto

IT IS CLEAR that at this particular moment of his sojourn in Vienna Mozart had no other model so far as the orchestra was concerned, and it must be stated once more that Haydn was then reigning in Vienna with almost unrivaled glory. Moreover, 1782 was the year in which the younger master set to work composing the first of the six quartets, to be offered three years later to his illustrious confrere and elder; so his ears would certainly, and very naturally, be full of Haydn's latest compositions. And the relations between the two great men had become, or were about to become, much more cordial; Leopold Mozart's visit to his son in 1785, and the dedication of the six quartets to Josef Haydn, helped to reinforce the existing bonds, and to make Haydn's influence much more noticeable; while for the same reason Mozart's influence on Haydn continued to grow.

It is the general opinion that in the C major Symphony (K. 425), composed at Linz and dated November 3, 1783, the acme of Haydn's influence is reached. The character of the introductory Adagio, the theme and the march rhythms of the succeeding Allegro spiritoso, the development section of the final Presto, and so forth, are instanced as direct reflections of the art of the Esterház master. It is certain that this symphony, which truly opens the period of Mozart's great orchestral compositions, is akin to Haydn's symphonies in certain obvious ways, if one wished to find an absolute model for it— notably in the prevailing mood of the finale, and also in the working-out of the development of this entrancing movement. All this is indisputable. But, to my mind, Mozart's individuality is so overwhelmingly apparent in the symphony as a whole that it is scarcely possible, at this stage of his growth, to imagine any inspiration from without; to Mozart, and to Mozart alone, belong the varied shades of feeling in the first movement—nuances often attributable to the well-managed use of contrast between wind and strings; his, too, is the march that runs through this movement, at once warlike and dreamy. And to what, if not the profound genius of Mozart, do we owe the wonderful and touching beauty of the Poco adagio? The somber clouds that momentarily tarnish its pure and serene inspiration neither form nor dissolve in the manner of Haydn; in its complexity it is already the grand adagio of the classical symphony in which one feels that the last word has been said. It is certainly not easy to understand how Mozart, taken unprepared by old Count Thun on his arrival at Linz, could in the space of a few short days have accomplished such a feat; it seems likely that the conception of the symphony was an accomplished fact before he left Salzburg, where he had just spent a holiday, and that he had to do no more than write it down some time between his departure and his return.

The Minuet is one of the most celebrated; one is liable to find it anywhere. We have seen it figuring in what is called the "ballet" in *Don Giovanni,* and in the short dances in *Figaro.* The fact is, it is more suitable for dancing than symphonic minuets in general are; and even in the trio, also in C major, its charming, soft light is maintained; the way the theme of this trio is taken up in imitation is unrivaled in any similar passage of Mozart. As for the finale, I willingly concede that the shadow of the great Haydn is discernible, but I must add at once that the variety of emotions and the undercurrent of passionate uneasiness give it so Mozartian a quality as soon as the composer gets into his subject that the very intention of following a model is effaced, and all previous suggestions become subject to an inner world of his own. It cannot be denied, however, that the treatment of the development section and the rapid passages preceding the ends of both parts derive from Haydn; these passages apart, the whole symphony stands as a pure and noble creation of Mozart, now in the full bloom of his maturity.

If, moreover, the chronological list of Haydn's symphonies is examined with any care, one cannot but be struck by the very small number of those dated between 1780 and 1782 whose introduction gives rise to a slow movement, and in general the symphonies of the Esterház master scarcely show any clear points of comparison with the "Linz" Symphony before those that he wrote for Paris and London. In comparing the "Linz" Symphony with Haydn's works, no one has envisaged the much more probable case of the reaction of this symphony on the elder composer's art. And, frankly, who knows to what ideals the young master was wedded in the autumn of this year 1783? When he returned to Vienna and had to write this Symphony in C major on his Linz visit, he most certainly had with him a symphony by his old master and Salzburg friend, Michael Haydn, who, delighted to meet his erstwhile pupil again, gave him, as a souvenir of past times, one of his latest symphonies, written in the spring of the same year. Until recent times this symphony was attributed to Mozart, who had taken the trouble to copy out the parts himself with a view to its performance at one of his Vienna concerts, or perhaps even at Linz to meet the immediate needs of a concert organized by Count Thun, the dedicatee of the Symphony in C we are dealing with. At this period in his artistic career Mozart seems to have regarded a slow introduction as almost indispensable for the opening of a grand symphony; and in fact he wrote an adagio to serve as an introduction to this symphony of Michael Haydn. The result is that people have believed themselves faced with an authentic Mozart symphony. The symphony in question is that in G, bearing the number 444 of Köchel's catalogue.

G. de St.-F.

1. The main movement is preceded by an introduction (Adagio, C major, 3/4), its opening measures being given out *forte* by the full orchestra. At the nineteenth measure there is a *fortissimo* chord of G followed by a pause, and the Allegro spiritoso (C major, 4/4 time) begins. Its principal subject is announced *piano* by the strings, afterward to be taken up *forte* by the full orchestra. A transitional passage follows with a busy figure in the lower strings. The second subject, in G major, enters quietly in the strings, oboe, and bassoon. Rather more extended than second subjects of eighteenth-century symphonies, this one closes with the customary flourish in the form of a coda. The exposition having been repeated the development begins, forty measures being devoted to the working out of material

which had been presented in the opening division, just described. The recapitulation begins with the principal theme in the strings, as in the exposition. The transitional passage leads to the second subject, now in C instead of G major. The coda, beginning with the same material as before, is extended.

II. Poco adagio, F major, 6/8. The principal subject opens at once in the strings, the wind entering at the second phrase. The strings announce a new idea (in C major) leading to the second subject proper, which opens with its melody in the first violins, in C minor, but returning to C major at the close. The exposition is repeated and, following it, the development begins. The recapitulation brings forward the principal theme in the strings, as before. The second subject is slightly modified. A short coda concludes the movement.

III. Menuetto, C major, 3/4. This movement is simply constructed in the three-part form peculiar to the minuets of Mozart's day. The first division opens *forte* in the full orchestra in C major. The second (trio) is written in the same key but with a more suave subject given to the oboe and first violins. The third division is an exact repetition of the first.

IV. Presto, C major, 2/4 time. The principal subject is given out *piano* by the strings. The transitional passage opens with a bustling figure in the full orchestra which leads to the second theme, allotted to the strings. There are several sections of this, which concludes with a sixteen-measure coda based on the principal subject. The exposition having been repeated, the second division of the movement is announced, its material being a development of the opening measures of the transitional passage. The recapitulation brings forward the principal subject in the strings. The transitional passage follows as before, leading to the second theme, given to the strings, but now in C major. The coda begins with its material drawn from the principal theme, as in the exposition, but here it is extended.

The score calls for two oboes, two bassoons, two horns, two trumpets, timpani, and strings.

F. B.

Symphony in D major, No. 38 ("Prague") (K. 504)

I. Adagio–Allegro   II. Andante   III. Presto

"PRAGUE IS indeed a very beautiful and agreeable place," wrote Mozart on his arrival there [early in 1787]. And he had good cause to be gratified with the more than friendly reception which he found awaiting him. *Figaro,* produced there in the previous season, had been an immense success, and its tunes were sung and whistled on all sides. A bid was to come for another opera, and *Don Giovanni* was to be written and produced there within a year, and to cause another furore of enthusiasm. The composer of *Figaro,* as might be expected, was applauded loud and long at the two concerts of his visit in 1787, and after the D major Symphony at the first of them, he could not appease the audience until he had improvised upon the piano for half an hour. At length a voice shouted the word "Figaro!" and Mozart, interrupting the phrase he had begun to play, captured all hearts by improvising variations from the air "Non più andrai."

Writing on January 15 to his friend Gottfried von Jacquin, Mozart related how a round of entertainment mostly connected with music-making was awaiting him. On the evening of his arrival, he went with Count Canal to the "Breitfeld Ball, where the flower of the Prague beauties assemble. You ought to have been there, my dear friend; I think I see you running, or rather limping, after all those pretty creatures, married and single. I neither danced nor flirted with any of them—the former because I was too tired, and the latter from my natural bashfulness. I saw, however, with the greatest pleasure, all these people flying about with such delight to the music of my *Figaro,* transformed into quadrilles and waltzes; for here nothing is talked of but *Figaro,* nothing played but *Figaro,* nothing but *Figaro* —very flattering to me, certainly."

Franz Němetschek, a Bohemian who wrote a biography of Mozart in 1798, said of the concert of January 19: "The symphonies which he chose for this occasion are true masterpieces of instru-

mental composition, full of surprising transitions. They have a swift
and fiery bearing, so that they at once tune the soul to the expectation of something superior. This is especially true of the great symphony in D major, which is still a favorite of the Prague public,
although it has been heard here nearly a hundred times."

J. N. B.

Some months after *Le Nozze di Figaro* Mozart entered on a period
of artistic growth that was to yield fruits so numerous and so rich
that it is astonishing to see the majority of biographies so little impressed with the fact. Both the expression and the form of his work
will grow and intensify; they will give to his work a range infinitely
greater and higher, with more force and bolder relief; and one can
say that this period, closing with *Don Giovanni* and the great symphonies, marks the most truly "romantic" epoch of his career. For
freedom, originality, and poetry it compares with that of his last
visit to Italy, in 1773, with the addition, naturally, of the ripening
of a genius that has attained, or is shortly to attain, its fullest radiance. But to reach the middle of this period Mozart must go through
some months of transition when, perhaps under the influence of
a man too unjustly disdained by him, Muzio Clementi, he will be
striving to elaborate long movements built on a single subject, unit-
ing consummate science with the divine fire of his genius. It is particularly noteworthy that, in this transitory period, it is principally
the works for piano that benefit by this newly acquired power, which
makes it all the more probable that the Italian master's influence was
then acting on him with peculiar force. The piano sonatas, trios, and
concertos particularly show this sort of progress, visible, one might
say, at the very first glance.

It was at the end of these few months that he had to write, for an
occasion that has remained unknown, the Symphony in D (K. 504)
known as the "Prague" Symphony. It would seem that everything
Mozart intended for the inhabitants and connoisseurs of that city
was invested with a quite peculiar fire and animation; he felt almost
certain of being thoroughly and profoundly understood there. And
this is no small encouragement to the artist, nor is it less a merit in
those who bring it about. We know, too, in what enthusiastic terms
he spoke of his Prague friends after *Don Giovanni*.

His first knock on their door was with the Symphony in D, re-echoing with a rough, a solid assurance. The success was equal to its anticipation. In listening to this symphony one has sometimes—nay, often—the impression of being in the presence of Beethoven, so closely are the grandeur of design and the vigor with which it is realized bound together; that enormous prelude with its intensifying rising phrases, and the modulations of the little *"gruppetti"* motif, herald events so solemn that one is almost astonished on hearing the principal theme of the Allegro, passionately "modern" in character, its feverish syncopations contrasting with the heroic interruptions from the brass. One has a striking impression of novelty, as much in the inpiration as in the scoring and harmony of all this movement. Mozart here no longer speaks the language we have met in his former compositions; we get the impression that this language is entirely his own creation, and we know of no musician who might have been able to reveal its elements to him. Perhaps if we were forced to choose one the name of Clementi would again present itself most readily to our mind. We have a foreshadowing of *Die Zauberflöte,* not only in the cast of the ideas themselves but in the effects obtained by means of counterpoint; and this symphony would be memorable if only from this point of view. The whole of the development is significant in this respect and, I would say, unique as a precursor of things to come; and the way in which the recapitulation is modulated and varied is also absolutely characteristic in its astonishing modernism. The romantic criticism of Mozart that sees in him nothing but an Olympic god, eternally serene, never experiencing the troubles or anxieties of mortal uneasiness, seems to me quite incomprehensible, the more so since this D major Symphony is by no means an isolated phenomenon in his work.

Another matter for surprise awaits us in this first movement, which we might readily expect to see built entirely on the first subject, followed by rhythmic figures on the brass and vigorous contrapuntal designs; it is the presence, nevertheless, of a second subject, but relegated to the very end of the first part and then quickly hurried through. Mozart, after some months during which, probably under Clementi's influence, he schooled himself to build his first allegros on a single subject, returned gradually to the contrast of two subjects; and thus the D major Symphony clearly marks the end of the transition period I mentioned above.

It would be difficult to employ chromaticisms and counterpoint with a more constant subtlety than in the Andante (in G major), in which feelings of such variety are so intermingled that a new and enchanted world seems to open before our eyes for the first time. I feel myself quite powerless to describe it; we recognize in this marvelous and most musical reverie something pastoral or idyllic; but for all the singing of birds and the murmuring of waters, fleeting clouds often come to darken the landscape. There are sometimes even cries of anguish to be heard; but nature's all-pervading peace soon regains the mastery, and, despite most intense and modern dissonances, despite modulations that vary the first subject at each repetition during the development, the movement ends on a note of inward peace, of poetic repose. Perhaps it is permissible to find here something akin to the feeling, not easily definable, that emerges from the "scene by the brook," a feeling that only the very greatest poets have been able to suggest; and it is certainly not the much vaunted simplicity of Mozart that reigns here! This movement proves the richness and variety of his inner life; it also proves him to have been intensely moved by the most intimate and subtle poetry of nature.

The finale, whose initial rhythm recalls the short duet in *Figaro* where Cherubino escapes by jumping through a window, is, like the other two movements, built with the rigorous symmetry of sonata form. To my mind, whatever one may say, it is again one wherein joy is not unalloyed; a burning, ardent passion creeps in and, despite its opening, it is rather of the ardors of the almost contemporary *Don Giovanni* that this finale reminds us. There are, moreover, certain aspects in which this symphony is akin to the famous overture to *Don Giovanni*. Elements of drama and joy are, in fact, closely intermingled; the symphony certainly ends on the latter note, but on some abrupt, almost lacerating rhythms that suggest more of struggle and energy than of real happiness. We do not know what hindered Mozart from writing a Minuet for this symphony; perhaps the total exclusion of dancing is deliberate or, in any case, more usual in Prague than in Vienna.

G. de St.-F.

The portentous and extended slow introduction of the "Prague" Symphony is charged with the graver aspects of *Don Giovanni;* the half-close leading to the Allegro is practically identical with that at a similar juncture in the great sextet of the opera, and an ominous figure in the *finale* almost makes one think of the stone guest appearing among a riot of mirth, though the grace and the laughter of Susanna are there too. The slow movement makes us dream of the idyllic summer-night stillness in Count Almaviva's invitingly artificial garden. The wonder of the Symphony is, however, that in spite of the variety of the visions it may suggest to the hearer, it is a perfect whole. Every structural part and every thematic feature is exquisitely proportioned. No separate incident is allowed to engage attention independently of the scheme in which it is assigned its function, even where it is as incredibly beautiful as the second subject of the first movement, which is surreptitiously introduced by a passage that is apparently merely transitional, or as engagingly spritely as the second subject of the *finale* with its bubbling bassoon accompaniment.

E. B.

1. The movement opens with an introduction (Adagio, D major, 4/4) thirty-six measures long. Although the introduction was a common feature of Haydn's symphonies and the symphonies of Beethoven, only four of Mozart's symphonies are provided with these prefatory movements. The principal subject of the main movement (Allegro, D major, 4/4) opens in the strings. There is that in the rhythmical figure in the second violins which is suggestive of the opening of the fugal subject in the overture to *The Magic Flute,* composed five years later. The second theme, in A major, is given to the strings, *piano.* Its opening sentence is repeated in A minor, the bassons being added to the strings. There is a more vigorous section, followed by a coda, based on the opening theme. The whole exposition is then repeated. The development works out, in imitation between the first and second violins, a scale figure that had originally figured in the sixth and seventh measures of the principal subject, where it had been given to the flutes and oboes. The scale figure is transferred to the lower strings, with a little trill motive above it in the violins. There is combined with it the first portion of the prin-

cipal subject. Development is now given to a vigorous figure which, in the exposition, had followed the first theme. There is no development of the second subject. The recapitulation presents the first theme as in the exposition. The second subject, given to the strings as before, now appears in D major. The coda is the same length and of the same material as that in the opening division of the main movement, but it is scored somewhat differently.

II. Andante, G major, 6/8. In the scoring of this movement, the trumpets and drums are omitted. The sonata form is employed for its design. The principal subject opens, as to its first phrase, in the strings, the wind instruments entering at the second phrase. A new idea, in E minor, more vigorously conceived, is employed as a transitional passage leading to the second subject, which is given to the first violins in D major. There is a short codetta of four measures, and the exposition is repeated. The development begins with a working out—for six measures—of the codetta, and then takes up the principal theme. The second subject is not worked out at all. The recapitulation presents the first theme as in the exposition. The transitional passage appears as before, and leads to the second subject in G major. The coda is six measures long, closing with a reminiscence of a portion of the principal theme.

III. Finale. Presto, D major, 2/4. This movement, like the two which preceded it, is written in the sonata form. It opens gaily, but not boisterously, with the principal subject in the first violins. The woodwind take up the theme in D minor, and a *forte* passage for the full orchestra leads to the second theme, in A major, allotted to the strings, its second phrase appearing in the woodwind. The coda, rather lengthy, begins with the material of the opening subject in the woodwind, answered by the strings. At the close of this the exposition is repeated. The development is concerned entirely with the first theme, and, for the most part, with its first four notes. The recapitulation brings forward the first subject as in the exposition; it is, however, modified in later portions. The second subject, in the strings as before, is now in D major, and the coda is made of the same material as in the first division of the movement.

The symphony is scored for two flutes, two oboes, two bassoons, two horns, two trumpets, timpani, and strings.

F. B.

THE GREAT TRILOGY

IN BESTOWING the title "trilogy" on this famous set of masterpieces the suggestion of a bond between them is intentional; this trinity, we may be sure, has not come about by chance. Never since he arrived at maturity had he produced, at intervals of a few days only, a succession of compositions of the same caliber; the E flat Symphony represents an immense portico through which the composer reveals to us all the warm and poetic beauty thronging his mind, before surrendering himself before our eyes to a struggle of exalted passion, to be manifest in the Symphony in G minor; and finally he invites our presence at a sort of apotheosis of his musical genius, freed from all shackles, in what has come to be known as the "Jupiter" Symphony. This imposing triple aspect that he gives to his symphonic testament in some measure sums up for us his inmost soul, and one can well understand that the production of the first should be followed so closely by the other two. But one surely ought not to imagine that Mozart intended to interpret all the vicissitudes he was going through at the time of writing; the sorry happenings of his daily round have nothing in common with the blossoming of his secret soul. And when all is said, it is to the hidden energy of his genius more than to any other cause that we must ascribe the creation of those three monumental works, dominating as they do his own instrumental work and, we may say, the whole of the instrumental output of the eighteenth century.

G. de St.-F.

"The three symphonies," according to Professor Tovey, "express the healthiest of reactions on each other, and the very fact that they are all in Mozart's ripest style makes the full range of that style appear more vividly than in any other circumstances. Consequently, they make an ideal program when played in their chronological order. The E flat Symphony has always been known as the *locus classicus* for euphony; the G minor accurately defines the range of passion comprehended in the terms of Mozart's art; and the C major ends his symphonic career with the youthful majesty of a

Greek god. Within these three types each individual movement is no less distinctive, while, of course, the contrasts within the individual symphony are expressly designed for vividness and coherence. Even in the treatment of the orchestra, where Mozart's material resources would mean starvation to any but the most spiritual of modern composers, each symphony has its own special colouring: and that colouring is none the less vivid in that it is most easily defined by stating what instruments of the normal orchestra are absent."

Mozart wrote his three greatest symphonies in 1788. The one in E flat is dated June 26, the one in G minor July 25, the one in C major with the fugue-finale, August 10.

His other works of that year are of little importance with the exception of a piano Concerto in D major which he played at the coronation festivities of Leopold II at Frankfort in 1790. There are canons and piano pieces, there is the orchestration of Handel's *Acis and Galatea,* and there are six German dances and twelve minuets for orchestra. Nor are the works composed in 1789 of interest, with the exception of the clarinet Quintet and a string Quartet dedicated to the King of Prussia. Again we find dances for orchestra— twelve minuets and twelve German dances.

Why is this? 1787 was the year of *Don Giovanni;* 1790, the year of *Così fan tutte.* Was Mozart, as some say, exhausted by the feat of producing three symphonies in such a short time? Or was there some reason for discouragement and consequent idleness?

The Ritter Gluck, composer to the Emperor Joseph II, died November 15, 1787, and thus resigned his position with salary of two thousand florins. Mozart was appointed his successor, but the thrifty Joseph cut down the salary to eight hundred florins. And Mozart at this time was sadly in need of money, as his letters show. In a letter of June, 1788, he tells of his new lodgings, where he could have better air, a garden, quiet. In another, dated June 27, he says: "I have done more work in the ten days that I have lived here than in two months in my other lodgings, and I should be much better here, were it not for dismal thoughts that often come to me. I must drive them resolutely away; for I am living comfortably, pleasantly, and cheaply." He borrowed from Puchberg, a merchant with whom he became acquainted at a Masonic lodge: the letter with Puchberg's memorandum of the amount is in the collection edited by Nohl, and later by Hans Mersmann.

Mozart could not reasonably expect help from the Emperor. The composer of *Don Giovanni* and the "Jupiter" Symphony was unfortunate in his Emperors.

The Emperor Joseph was in the habit of getting up at five o'clock; he dined on boiled bacon at 3:15 P.M.; he preferred water as a beverage, but would drink a glass of Tokay; he was continually putting chocolate drops from his waistcoat pocket into his mouth; he gave gold coins to the poor; he was unwilling to sit for his portrait; he had remarkably fine teeth; he disliked sycophantic fuss; he patronized the English who introduced horse-racing; and Michael Kelly, who tells us many things, says that Joseph was "passionately fond of music and a most excellent and accurate judge of it." We know that he did not like the music of Mozart.[1]

Joseph commanded from his composer Mozart no opera, cantata, symphony, or piece of chamber music, although he was paying him eight hundred florins a year. He did order dances, the dances named above. For the dwellers in Vienna were dancing mad. Kelly, who knew Mozart and sang in the first performance of *Le Nozze di Figaro* in 1786 says in his memoirs (written by Theodore Hook): "The ridotto rooms, where the masquerade took place were in the palace; and, spacious and commodious as they were, they were actually crammed with masqueraders. I never saw or indeed heard of any suite of rooms where elegance and convenience were more considered, for the propensity of the Vienna ladies for dancing and going to carnival masquerades was so determined that nothing was permitted to interfere with their enjoyment of their favorite amusement. . . . The ladies of Vienna are particularly celebrated for their grace and movements in waltzing, of which they never tire. For

---

[1] For a description of Joseph going to Versailles, sleeping there on a straw mattress and covered with a wolfskin, in order to give his sister Marie Antoinette lessons in the simple life "and of philosophical detachment," leaving with her on his departure a long homily to serve her as a moral guide, see *Marie Antoinette*, by the Marquis de Ségur (Chapter IV, "The Era of Folly").

my own part, I thought waltzing from ten at night until seven in the morning a continual whirligig, most tiresome to the eye and ear, to say nothing of any worse consequences." Mozart wrote for these dances, as did Haydn, Hummel, Beethoven.

Mozart was never fully appreciated in Vienna during his last wretched yet glorious years. It is not necessary to tell the story of the loneliness of his last days, the indifference of court and city, the insignificant burial. This lack of appreciation was wondered at in other towns. See, for instance, *Studien für Tonkünstler und Musikfreunde,* a musical journal published at Berlin in 1792. The Prague correspondent wrote on December 12, 1791: "Because his body swelled after death, the story arose that he had been poisoned. . . . Now that he is dead the Viennese will indeed find out what they have lost. While he was alive he always had much to do with the cabal, which he occasionally irritated through his *sans souci* ways. Neither his *Figaro* nor his *Don Giovanni* met with any luck at Vienna, yet the more in Prague. Peace be with his ashes!"

As Mr. John F. Runciman says: "It may well be doubted whether Vienna thought even so much of Capellmeister Mozart as Leipsig thought of Capellmeister Bach. Bach, it is true, was merely Capellmeister: he hardly dared to claim social equality with the citizens who tanned hides or slaughtered pigs. . . . Still he was a burgher, even as the killers of pigs and the tanners of hides. He was thoroughly respectable, and probably paid his taxes as they came due. If only by necessity of his office he went to church with regularity, and on the whole we may suppose that he got enough of respect to make life tolerable. But Mozart was only one of a crowd who provided amusement for a gay population; and a gay population, always a heartless master, holds none in such contempt as the servants who provide it with amusement. So Mozart got no respect from those he served, and his Bohemianism lost him the respect of the eminently respectable. He lived in the eighteenth-century equivalent of a 'loose set'; he was miserably poor, and presumably never paid his taxes; we may doubt whether he often went to church; he composed for the theatre; and he lacked the self-assertion which enabled Handel, Beethoven, and Wagner to hold their own. Treated as of no account, cheated by those he worked for, hardly permitted to earn his bread, he found life wholly intolerable, and as he grew older he lived more and more within himself, and gave his thoughts only to the composition of masterpieces. The crowd of mediocrities dimly felt him to be their master, and the greater the masterpieces he achieved the more vehemently did Salieri and his attendants protest that he was not a composer to compare with Salieri."

Mozart in 1788 was unappreciated save by a few, among whom was Frederick William II, King of Prussia; he was wretchedly poor; he was snubbed by his own Emperor, whom he would not leave to go into foreign, honorable, lucrative service. This was the Mozart of 1788 and 1789.

We know little or nothing concerning the first years of the three symphonies. Gerber's *Lexicon der Tonkünstler* (1790) speaks appreciatively of him: the erroneous statement is made that the Emperor fixed his salary in 1788 at six thousand florins; the varied ariettas for piano are praised especially; but there is no mention whatever of any symphony.

The enlarged edition of Gerber's work (1813) contains an extended notice of Mozart's last years, and we find in the summing up of his career: "If one knew only one of his noble symphonies, as the overpoweringly great, fiery, perfect, pathetic, sublime symphony in C." And this reference is undoubtedly to the "Jupiter."

Mozart gave a concert at Leipsig in May, 1789. The programme was made up wholly of pieces by him, and among them were two symphonies in manuscript. A story that has come down might easily lead us to believe that one of them was the one in G minor. At a rehearsal for this concert Mozart took the first Allegro of a symphony at a very fast pace, so that the orchestra soon was unable to keep up with him. He stopped the players and began again at the same speed, and he stamped the time so furiously that his steel shoe buckle flew into pieces. He laughed, and, as the players still dragged, he began the Allegro a third time. The musicians, by this time exasperated, played to suit him. Mozart afterward said to some who wondered at his conduct, because he had on other occasions protested against undue speed: "It was not caprice on my part. I saw that the majority of the players were well along in years. They would have dragged everything beyond endurance if I had not set fire to them and made them angry, so that out of sheer spite they did their best." Later in the rehearsal he praised the orchestra, and said that it was unnecessary for it to rehearse the accompaniment to the pianoforte concerto: "The parts are correct, you play well, and so do I." This concert, by the way, was poorly attended, and half of those who were present had received free tickets from Mozart, who was generous in such matters.

Mozart also gave a concert of his own works at Frankfort, October 14, 1790. Symphonies were played in Vienna in 1788, but they were by Haydn; and one by Mozart was played in 1791. In 1792 a symphony by Mozart was played at Hamburg.

The early programmes, even when they have been preserved, seldom determine the date of a first performance. It was the custom to print: "Symphonie von Wranitzky," "Sinfonie von Mozart," "Sinfonia di Haydn." Furthermore, it should be remembered that "Sinfonie" was then a term often applied to any work in three or more movements written for strings, or strings and wind instruments.

The two symphonies played at Leipsig were "unpublished." The two symphonies that preceded the great three were composed in 1783 and 1786. The latter one, in D, was performed in Prague with extraordinary success. The publishers were not slow in publishing Mozart's compositions, if they were as niggardly as Joseph II himself. The two symphonies played were probably of the three composed in 1788. Even this conclusion is a guess.

P. H.

Symphony in E flat major, No. 39 (K. 543)

I.	Adagio; Allegro	III.	Minuetto; Trio
II.	Andante	IV.	Finale: Allegro

E.T.A. HOFFMANN called this symphony the "swan song" of Mozart's youth. "Love and melancholy breathe forth in purest spirit tones; we feel ourselves drawn with inexpressible longing towards the forms which beckon as the clouds to another sphere." Wagner's more factual imagination seems to acknowledge Mozart as a primary source of his own emotional art: "The longing sigh of the great human voice, drawn to him by the loving power of his genius, breathes from his instruments. He leads the irresistible stream of richest harmony into the heart of his melody, as though with anxious care he sought to give it, by way of compensation for its delivery by mere instruments, the depth of feeling and ardour which lies at the source of the human voice as the expression of the un-fathomable depths of the heart."

Wagner also discerned a "marked relationship" between this symphony and the Seventh of Beethoven. "In both," he wrote, "the clear human consciousness of an existence meant for rejoicing is beautifully transfigured by the presage of a higher world beyond. The only distinction I would make is that in Mozart's music the language of the heart is shaped to graceful longing, whereas in Beethoven's conception this longing reaches out a bolder hand to seize the Infinite. In Mozart's symphony the fullness of feeling pre-dominates, in Beethoven's the manly consciousness of strength."

Mozart uses no oboes in his E flat Symphony, only one flute, and clarinets, bassoons, horns, and trumpets in twos. Jahn finds the blend-ing of clarinets with horns and bassoons productive of "a full, mellow tone" requisite for his special purpose, while "the addition of the flutes [flute] gives it clearness and light, and trumpets endow it with brilliancy and freshness." The delicate exploitation of the clarinets is in many parts evident, particularly in the trio of the Minuet, where the first carries the melody and the second comple-ments it with arpeggios in the deeper register.

J. N. B.

1. The symphony opens with an introduction (Adagio, E flat major, 4/4) twenty-five measures long. Much use is made in it of a dotted figure, first given out on the second beat of the second meas-ure. The introduction leads without pause into the main movement (Allegro, E flat major, 3/4), its theme announced by the first violins. The cellos and basses take up the theme. A transitional passage opens with the following idea in the full orchestra, *forte*. The second

subject, in B flat major, is given partly to the strings and partly to the woodwind. The thematic material having been set forth, the exposition is repeated, and following this repetition—which, it may be said, is not often made in modern performances—the development begins, its contents being largely concerned with the working out of the second theme and a little figure which had occurred at the close of the exposition. The recapitulation opens with the principal theme scored as at the beginning of the exposition. The transitional passage also makes its entrance as before, but the second subject is now in E flat instead of B flat major.

II. Andante con moto, A flat major, 2/4. The principal theme is allotted to the strings. Two measures for wind instruments prepare the way for another subject of more impetuous character than the first, also given to the strings. The passage which had been given to the wind instruments alone is developed, and there is a return of the first subject in the woodwind, with a countertheme against it in the strings. Development takes place, and the opening subject reappears in the strings, as at first, this repetition bringing the movement to a close.

III. Menuetto. Allegro, E flat major, 3/4. The subject is announced at once, *forte*. This is worked out, as to form, in accordance with the traditional method of constructing minuets and other pieces of their kind. The minuet proper contains two parts, each repeated, and the trio follows with its theme in the clarinet. This, too, is in two parts—each repeated—and at the close the minuet is heard once more.

IV. Finale: Allegro, E flat major, 2/4. The movement opens with a jolly theme in the first violins, the accompaniment for the first eight measures being given only to the second violins. The theme having been repeated *forte* by the full orchestra, a bustling sixteenth-note figure leads to the second subject, in B flat major, announced by the first violins. The coda is based on the first theme. On the first theme, too, the development is based. The recapitulation brings forward the first subject, more fully scored than at the beginning of the movement. The second theme is now in E flat, but scored as in the exposition. The coda is eight measures longer than that which closed the first division of the movement, but its material is the same.

The orchestration calls for one flute, two clarinets, two bassoons, two horns, two trumpets, timpani, and strings.

F. B.

Symphony in G minor, No. 40 (K. 550)

I. Allegro molto	III. Minuetto; Trio
II. Andante	IV. Finale: Allegro assai

THOUGH ALL of us might not go so far, there is no doubt that this symphony is touched with the ineffable sadness that sometimes crosses like a summer cloud the radiance of Mozart's sun-god temperament. And along with this there are moments of a celestial tenderness. Yet, at the same time, this symphony has its capricious and spritelike quality, which comes out in the ascending and descending pairs of thirty-second notes in the Andante, echoed distantly in the whimsicality and waywardness of certain measures of the Finale.

P. S.

The form of the G minor Symphony is as clear as crystal; about its mood musicians have been at considerable variance. When Professor Tovey found in it "the range of passion," as the artist Mozart saw fit to express passion, he was concurring with an authority of traditional opinion. Against him may be set, surprisingly enough, the opinion of Berlioz, who, addicted as he was to emotional interpretations, found in this symphony nothing more deep-felt than "grace, delicacy, melodic charm, and fineness of workmanship." It is difficult, of course, for a listener accustomed to the lusher music of two later centuries (outpourings never dreamt of in Mozart's philosophy) to project himself into the pristine simplicity of the eighteenth century and respond adequately to what was in its day taken as a new precedent in pathetic utterance. If one is to move discriminately within those smaller confines, receive what is fresh, personal, and humanly revealing, one must surely familiarize oneself with the run-of-the-mill music of Mozart's time. Then only will Mozart's innovations, little matters of formal sequence, modulation or instrumental coloring, become immediately outstanding, as they were not only outstanding but startling to a listener of 1790. It has required a scholar like Georges de Saint-Foix to make himself so conversant with Mozart's contemporary style that he could perceive in all its force "points where Mozart in the ardor of his subject was led to new boldness." That the G minor Symphony seemed in its day a radical expression of emotion can be readily confirmed by an examination of early commentaries. It will be interesting to review such commentaries through the century and a half which has followed the writing of the G minor Symphony.

Hans Georg Nägeli in his *Vorlesungen über Musik* (1826) took Mozart to task for his excessive melodiousness *(Cantabilität)* which, according to this writer, put a decadence of emotional ferment upon all music. Among all of Mozart's instrumental works Nägeli found only the piano concertos undistorted by this quality.

F. J. Fetis, reviewing the Symphony in Paris (*Revue Musicale,* May 11, 1828) wrote that, "although Mozart has not used formidable orchestral forces in his G minor Symphony, none of the sweeping and massive effects one meets in a symphony of Beethoven, the invention which flames in this work, the accents of passion and energy that pervade and the melancholy color that dominates it result in one of the most beautiful manifestations of the human spirit."

The Chevalier Georg Nikolaus von Nissen, who married Mozart's widow and wrote his first biography (published in 1828), there called the G minor Symphony "the expression of a moving and restless passion, a struggle, a combat against a powerful penetrating agitation."

In 1843 there appeared the biography by Alexandre Dimitrivitch Oulibicheff in which this flowery writer of a flowery epoch wrote of the slow movement of the G minor Symphony as "the divine balm applied to the wounds of the soul" and said of the last movement, "I doubt whether music contains anything more profoundly incisive, more cruelly sorrowful, more violently abandoned, more completely impassioned, than the reprise of the Finale."

Richard Wagner, hearing the symphony at a concert of the Odeon in Munich, perceived through a heavy and wooden performance, which he deplored, "a beauty so indestructible that even such mutilation could not obscure it." He found the Andante "exuberant with rapture and audacity" and "the beatitude of its last measures" reminded him of his favorite concept of "death through love." Wagner did not have occasion to describe at length the G minor Symphony, but he wrote thus of Mozart's symphonies in general with his usual clairvoyance in setting down the essential nature of an artist with a perception unobscured by the formal style of another epoch antipathetic to his own:

> The longing sigh of the great human voice, drawn to him by the loving power of his genius, breathes from his instruments. He leads the irresistible stream of richest harmony into the heart of his melody, as though with anxious care he sought to give it, by way of compensation for its delivery by mere instruments, the depth of feeling and ardour which lies at the source of the human voice as the expression of the unfathomable depths of the heart.

While Wagner sensed and pointed out the universal beauty in Mozart, the era which Wagner dominated neither remembered nor performed Mozart to any appreciable degree.

It was in 1856 that Otto Jahn brought out his penetrating biography of Mozart (which is still unsuperseded). Jahn was hardly outdone in his extravagant characterization of the G minor Symphony. He called it a symphony "of pain and lamentation" (*"Schmerz und Klage"*) in which "sorrow rises in a continuous climax to wild merriment, as if to stifle care." The "soft plaint" of the opening subject grows in the development to a "piercing cry of anguish." The Andante and Minuet strive but vainly to establish an inward calm, and the Finale brings a frenzy which "seeks to drown sorrow and goes on its course in restless excitement." Jahn calls this "the most passionate of all Mozart symphonies" and is reminded of Goethe's praise of the Laocoön as grandeur and dignity encompassing the most violent human passions "and in the same sense in which Goethe ventured to call Laocoön graceful, none can deny the grace of the Symphony, in spite of much powerful sharpness and harshness" (*"starken Schärfen und Harten"*).

Coming to our own century, one can do no better than examine the emotional interpretation of the G minor Symphony by one of its most eminent Mozart scholars, Georges de Saint-Foix, who analyzed it in detail in his *Les Symphonies de Mozart* (1932). De Saint-Foix found in the first movement a "feverish precipitousness," an "intense poignancy," a "concentrated energy which rises in the last pages to a ferocious exultation, yielding only at the end to a resigned lassitude." In the development of the Andante he found "expressive depths scarcely matched in Mozart." "The character of the Minuet," he says, "is a bitter and relentless struggle." The counterpoint produces "a sort of paroxysm and nervous tension." Only the Trio is "gentle, placid, illuminated, truly idyllic." Its second part is "so Elysian that it dispels in a few measures the tragic cast of the whole symphony." M. de Saint-Foix holds that the Finale shows "a fury of abandon" which Mozart touched nowhere else in his music. "All the resources of his art, rhythm, harmony, counterpoint, are as if pushed to the limit. A force thrilling, demoniacal, is released from him and gives the hearer no respite. Boldness such as this makes for a paroxysm of exaltation rather than free artistic creation. His art is no longer free but grips the artist himself so that he cannot breathe, and in spite of the sharpness of such a paroxysm it brings to pass a true Mozartean miracle."

Eric Blom in his life of Mozart (1935) goes so far as to call the G minor Symphony "Mozart's Pathetic Symphony," finding it full of "unhappy agitation."

Sir George Grove had long since expressed his inability to see in the repeated notes at the end of each step in the opening theme "those depths of agony ascribed to the opening by some critics." Tovey supports Grove's objection: "Just so: it is not only difficult to see depths of agony in the rhythms and idioms of comedy, but it is dangerous and not very delicate to attempt to see them. Comedy uses the language of real life; and people in real life often find the language of comedy the only dignified expression for their deepest feelings. They do not want the sympathy of sentimentalists who would be hard put to it to tell tragedy from burlesque; and the misconceptions of people who would imagine their situation and language to be merely funny are altogether below their horizon. They rise to the height of human dignity by treating the ordinary language of their fellow-mortals as if it were good enough for their troubles; and Mozart and Moliére are not fundamentally at variance with

Sophocles and Wagner in the different ways in which they immortal-ize this meaning of the word 'reserve.'"

J. N. B.

1. The first movement (Allegro molto, G minor, 4/4) opens im-mediately with the exposition of the first theme in the strings; the melody is sung by the first and second violins in octaves over a simple, but strongly rhythmic, accompaniment in the violas and basses.[1] This theme is the regulation sixteen measures long, and ends by half-cadence on the dominant. Four measures of conclusion, also ending on the dominant, are added in the full orchestra. Then the first eight measures of the theme are repeated by the strings, with sus-tained harmonies in the oboes and bassoons, with the difference, however, that, whereas it remained steadily in G minor in its first exposition, it now makes a wondrously beautiful modulation to B flat major. It is immediately followed by the first subsidiary in this key: sixteen measures of passage work for the full orchestra, also ending by half-cadence on the dominant (F major chord). Next follows the second theme, in the relative B flat major, a chromatic, sighing motive, given out by the strings and woodwind, and devel-oped for twenty-three measures, closing with a definite authentic cadence in B flat major. A short second subsidiary leads over to some contrapuntal work on the initial figure of the first theme, against

---

[1] An anecdote is told of one of Liszt's concerts in Munich, in the days when he still appeared in public as a pianist. He had just played his own matchless transcription of Beethoven's "Pastoral" Symphony, as only he could play it. It should be remembered that the "Pastoral," though homely enough in its thematic material, and generally simple in its development and working out, is, as a piece of orchestration, one of Beethoven's most complicated scores; it thus presents quite peculiar difficulties to the piano transcriber, difficulties which Liszt has conquered in a way that can only be called marvellous. After Liszt had played it at the concert in question, Franz Lachner stepped up to him in the greenroom and said: "You are a perfect magician! Think of playing literally everything in that second movement and with only ten fingers! But I can tell you one thing even you can't play with all your magicianship." "What's that?" asked Liszt. "The first sixteen measures of Mozart's little G minor Symphony, simple as they are." Liszt thought a moment, and then said with a laugh: "I think you are right; I should need a third hand. I should need both my hands for the accompaniment alone, with that viola figure in it!"

a new counterfigure, which here comes in as a conclusion theme, the first part of the movement closing in B flat major with the characteristically Mozartian winding-up passage for full orchestra, something like the tutti of a concerto. This first part is then repeated.

The free fantasia begins with the first theme, now in F sharp minor, but developed on a new plan, with frequent modulations. The working out soon begins in earnest, and is carried forward with great contrapuntal elaboration, and at greater length than is usual with Mozart.

The third part of the movement is quite regular. The most noticeable variations from the form of the first part being that, where the first theme modulates from G minor to the relative B flat major (on its second repetition) in the first part, it now modulates to E flat major (sixth degree of the principal key), and that the first subsidiary, entering in this key, is far more extendedly developed than in the first part, even to the point of imitative contrapuntal working out, the development ending by half-cadence on the dominant of the principal key (G minor). From this point on, the movement keeps steadily in the tonic key, the presentation and development of second theme, second subsidiary, and conclusion period being virtually the same as in the first part. A very short coda, beginning with the second subsidiary, and then bringing in some play on the initial figure of the first theme in four-part canon, brings the movement to a close.

II. The second movement (Andante, E flat major, 6/8) is also in the sonata form. It begins with the presentation and development of the first theme, the construction of which is peculiar. It is given out for the most part by the strings, the horns forming a background of richer tone color. The thesis of the melody comes first in the cellos and double basses, the phrase ending in the violins; then comes the antithesis, a sighing figure in the violins in octaves, closing with a little descending chromatic passage in thirds. Thesis and antithesis are now repeated, but in a considerably altered shape. The thesis now comes in the first violins, but with the eighth-notes in its original shape now lengthened to dotted quarter-notes; the antithesis comes in the cellos and double basses, against a new counterfigure in the violins in octaves. Then comes a conclusion period of three measures, with the melody in the woodwind, over a little fluttering accompaniment in the strings. The second theme follows, in the dominant (B flat major); it consists mostly of passage work, in which we find that the little fluttering figure of the accompaniment of the concluding period of the first theme now assumes a marked thematic importance.[2] A more melodious conclusion theme follows (in B flat major), and closes the first part of the movement. Even here the little fluttering figure is not quite absent.

The free fantasia is short, and consists of imitative passage work on the second theme, rather than of working out, properly so called.

The third part of the movement stands in regular relation to the first, saving that the development of the first theme is somewhat more extended.

III. The third movement (Menuetto: Allegro, G minor, 3/4) is strictly regular in form, if rather stern and elaborately contrapuntal in character. The trio (in G major) is in strong contrast to this, being light, simple, and almost waltz-like.

IV. The fourth movement (Finale: Allegro assai, G minor, 4/4) is, like the first and second, in the sonata form. It begins with the exposition of the first theme, a theme so regular in its dancelike cut (thesis and antithesis being each eight measures long, and each repeated) that it seems as if it were to be made the motive of a rondo.[3] It is immediately followed by a first subsidiary, which is developed at great length in rushing contrapuntal passage work, beginning in the tonic (G minor) and ending by half-cadence on the dominant of the relative B flat major. A more cantabile second theme follows (in B flat major), and is developed at first by the strings, then by the woodwind; it leads to some strong passage work on a figure taken

---

[2] It is to be noted that when the classic masters applied the sonata-form to a quick movement (that is, in its regular application in first movements of symphonies or sonatas), the second theme is usually of a more cantabile character than the first. In slow movements, however, we often find this reversed; the first theme being a melodious cantilena, and the second partaking more of the nature of quasi-contrapuntal passage work. This is the case in the present Andante.

[3] Commentators have noticed the coincidence that the first seven notes of the theme of the scherzo in Beethoven's C minor Symphony are (allowance being made for difference of key) identical with the corresponding notes of this theme; but the rhythm is so totally different that no similarity between the two themes can be detected by the ear.

from the first theme, which, though having apparently all the character of a second subsidiary, really takes the place of a conclusion theme, and closes the first part of the movement, which is then repeated. This first part ends in the relative B flat major.

The free fantasia, which is pretty long, is devoted entirely to an elaborate working out of the first theme in imitative counterpoint. The third part of the movement is little, if anything, more than a repetition of the first, save that the second theme and what follows it are in the tonic G minor—not G major, as might have been expected from the second theme's coming in B flat major in the first part.

The symphony is scored for one flute, two oboes, two clarinets (added for the second edition), two bassoons, two horns, and strings.

W. F. A.

Symphony in C major, No. 41 ("Jupiter") (K. 551)

I.   Allegro vivace
II. Andante cantabile

III. Minuetto; Allegro; Trio
IV. Finale: Allegro molto

THERE is nothing in the music that reminds one of Jupiter Tonans, Jupiter Fulgurator, Jupiter Pluvius; or of the god who, assuming various disguises, came down to earth, where by his adventures with women semi-divine or mortals of common clay he excited the jealous rage of Juno. The music is not of an Olympian mood. It is intensely human in its loveliness and its gayety. . . .

Nor do we know who gave the title "Jupiter" to this symphony. Some say it was applied by J. B. Cramer, to express his admiration for the loftiness of ideas and nobility of treatment. Some maintain that the triplets in the first measure suggest the thunder-bolts of Jove. Some think that the "calm, godlike beauty" of the music compelled the title. Others are satisfied with the belief that the title was given to the symphony as it might be to any masterpiece or any impressively beautiful or strong or big thing. To them "Jupiter" expresses the power and brilliance of the work.

The eulogies pronounced on this symphony are familiar to all,—

from Schumann's "There are things in the world about which nothing can be said, as Mozart's C major Symphony with the fugue,
much of Shakespeare, and pages of Beethoven," to von Bülow's "I
call Brahms's First Symphony the Tenth, not because it should be
placed after the Ninth: I should put it between the Second and the
'Eroica,' just as I think the First not the symphony of Beethoven but
the one composed by Mozart and known by the name 'Jupiter.' "
But there were decriers early in the nineteenth century. Thus Hans
Georg Nägeli (1773–1836) attacked this symphony bitterly on account of its well-defined and long-lined melody, "which Mozart
mingled and confounded with a free instrumental play of ideas, and
his very wealth of fancy and emotional gifts led to a sort of fermenta-
tion in the whole province of art, and caused it to retrograde rather
than to advance." He found fault with certain harmonic progressions
which he characterized as trivial. He allowed the composer originality and a certain power of combination, but he found him without
style, often shallow and confused. He ascribed these qualities to the
personal qualities of the man himself: "He was too hasty, when not
too frivolous, and he wrote as he himself was." Nägeli was not the
last to judge a work according to the alleged morality or immorality
of the maker.

P. H.

The amalgamation of the *galant* and the "learned," which in a
thousand features of the Symphonies in E-flat and G minor is more
hidden than displayed, is revealed in the Finale of the "Jupiter"
Symphony. This work has been somewhat mistakenly called the symphony with the fugue finale. For that movement is not a fugue, but
simply a sonata movement with fugato passages in the exposition, the
development, and the coda, like the finale of the great G major
Quartet. The complete fusion of the *galant* and "learned" styles here
achieved constitutes a moment unique in the history of music. The
sinfonia—once a subsidiary form, intended to induce the audience
to stop their conversation before the beginning of an act, or to open
or close a concert—had now become the very center of a concert
program. The slow movement—once an intermezzo—was now a
broad and deep outpouring of the soul; not yet an adagio or a largo,
as in the works of Beethoven, but nevertheless an *andante cantabile*.

The symphonic style—once, even in Mozart's own work, and not more than a few years earlier, full of the *buffo* spirit—still had something of the *buffo* character: it is significant that Mozart used in the closing theme of the first movement a motive from his arietta "Un bacio di mano" (K. 541). But the symphonic style was now also clearly stamped with what Mozart felt to be the most serious element in music: the contrapuntal. In this work of the utmost harmony and balance, there is tension, too, but it nowhere "loses its way." And perhaps it is most appropriate, after all, that this work should be the third of those composed in 1788, and the last symphony Mozart wrote.

A. E.

i. Allegro vivace, C major, 4/4. The movement opens immediately with the announcement of the first theme. The theme is in two sections: imposing triplets (full orchestra), alternating with gentle, melodious passages for strings; the section of a martial nature, with strongly marked rhythm for trumpets and drums. There is extensive development of the figures, with some new counter ones. The strings have the second theme, of which William Foster Apthorp wrote: "A yearning phrase, ascending by two successive semitones, followed by a brighter, almost a rollicking one—is it Jove laughing at lovers' perjuries?—the bassoon and flute soon adding richness to the coloring by doubling the melody of the first violins in the lower and upper octaves." This theme is in G major. There is a cheerful conclusion theme. The first part of the movement ends with a return of the martial rhythm of the second section of the first theme. The free fantasia is long and elaborate. The third part is almost like the first, but with changes of key.

ii. Andante cantabile, F major, 3/4. The first part presents the development in turn of three themes so joined that there is apparent melodic continuity. The second part consists of some more elaborate development of the same material.

iii. Menuetto: Allegro, E major, 3/4. The movement is in the traditional minuet form. The chief theme begins with the inversion of the first figure, the "chromatic sigh" of the second theme in the first movement. This "sigh" is hinted at in the trio, which is in C major.

IV. Finale: Allegro molto, C major, 4/4. It is often described as a fugue on four subjects.

Mr. Apthorp wrote: "Like the first movement, it is really in 2/2 (*alla breve*) time; but Mozart, as was not unusual with him, has omitted the hair stroke through the C of common time—a detail in the use of which he was extremely lax. As far as the fugue on four subjects goes, the movement can hardly be called a fugue; it is a brilliant rondo on four themes, and the treatment of this thematic material is for the most part of a fugal character—the responses are generally 'real' instead of 'tonal.' Ever and anon come brilliant passages for the full orchestra which savor more of the characteristically Mozartish tutti cadences to the separate divisions of a rondo, or other symphonic movement, than they do of the ordinary 'diversions' in a fugue. Still, fugal writing of a sufficiently strict character certainly predominates in the movement. For eviscerating elaborateness of working out—all the devices of *motus rectus* and *motus contrarius* being resorted to, at one time even the old *canon cancrizans*—this movement may be said almost to seek its fellow. It is at once one of the most learned and one of the most spontaneously brilliant things Mozart ever wrote."

Let us add to Mr. Apthorp's comment:

The opening theme of four measures is an old church tune that has been used by many—Bach, and no doubt many before him, Purcell, Michael Haydn, Handel, Beethoven, Croft, Schubert, Goss, Mendelssohn, Arthur Sullivan, and others. It was a favorite theme of Mozart. It appears in the Credo of the Missa Brevis in F (1774), in the Sanctus of the Mass in C (1776), in the development of the first movement of the Symphony in B flat (1779), in the development of the first movement of the Sonata in E flat for piano and violin (1785).

In the *Tablettes de Polymnie* (Paris, April, 1810) a writer observed that the fugue finale of the "Jupiter" Symphony "is understood only by a very small number of connoisseurs; but the public, which wishes to pass for a connoisseur, applauds it with the greater fury because it is absolutely ignorant in the matter."

The symphony is scored for flute, two oboes, two bassoons, two horns, two trumpets, timpani, and strings.

P. H.

Mozart's last symphonies, then, form a whole that in my opinion dominates all the production of the classical period, including the remarkable work—often unique in its own genre—of Josef Haydn. I have no doubt whatever that Mozart's last symphonies aim at a higher mark than any others that were written in the period of his maturity; not by any means that they speak a different language, or that they were conceived in a revolutionary spirit, tending to repudiate the past and erect something in its place. They spring solely from a brilliant mind, from a man whose inner world surpassed all in richness, in expression, and in beauty; Mozart's power of clothing all things from the greatest to the smallest in this beauty remained essentially the privilege of the poet he always was. And he had no need to turn things topsy-turvy, putting the end before the beginning, in order to create novelty; it was only necessary for him to fill the framework with his own thought for everything to be rejuvenated. In the same way the richness and variety of the contrasts with which his work is filled come out more and more clearly today, completely reversing the usual judgments relative to his art conceded by the romantic age: they proceed from his very special aptitude for observing mankind in all the varied manifestations of life, for grasping a foreign tongue, down to the least inflection, with an alertness and delicacy rare among his compatriots. This is not the least of our surprises in the presence of Mozart; it is evident that throughout almost the whole of his life he had the clearest appreciation of Italian *buffa* art, whose technique was appropriated by him to a degree unexampled and unforseeable; it was not only the formal beauty of the Italian musical phrase as adopted sentimentally by a Christian Bach, but a leaning toward the most biting and delicate satire, which, indeed, was quite in keeping with his own character. On reflection one realizes that he even surpasses his model by the full extent of his own genius, and, as Abert had so justly remarked, Mozart seems to smile on the personages he creates, but who, one feels, are so very different from him.

Commentators have been specially led to analyze these marvelous gifts in the stage works. I have wished to be sufficiently discerning to attempt to illustrate them from his instrumental works, and particularly here in his great symphonies. The latter seem to me the most absolute witness, the most intimate revelations of his "ego"; and I

feel that a long companionship with such masterpieces has not sufficed to reveal all the treasures of their profound and moving beauty.
As with all great creators, the secret of this beauty is not fully revealed at first sight; however, we cannot help being astonished that
it has needed nearly a century and a half for people to discover in
Mozart anything other than grace and charming elegance. This
miraculous artist, as Téodor de Wyzewa used to style him, in his last
symphonies does in fact reveal to us the true world inhabited by his
soul at the moment when it is turning toward other regions. The
fact is that from 1789 or 1790 the very source of Mozart's inspiration
changes; a sort of purification, accompanied often by a feeling of
resigned lassitude, gives to his work a beauty removed from all
passion, purged of all anxiety, testifying to an almost celestial calm.
His last three symphonies seem definitely to set the seal on the most
"romantic" period of all his career, in which the ardent tumult of
life is quelled only to allow him time to ascend to even higher
regions.

G. de St.-F.

4

The Concertos

THE PIANO CONCERTOS
THE VIOLIN CONCERTOS AND THE
SINFONIA CONCERTANTE FOR
VIOLIN AND VIOLA
CONCERTOS FOR WIND INSTRUMENTS

1. THE PIANO CONCERTOS

SPLENDID AS are the examples of the concerto form for string
and wind instruments, it was only in the piano concertos that Mozart
achieved his ideal. They are the peak of all his instrumental achievement, at least in the orchestral domain. Mozart cultivated the concerto for violin industriously, but only for a short time; to the concerto for single wind instruments—flute, oboe, bassoon, horn, clarinet—and the *sinfonia concertante,* he devoted only intermittent,
though at times very serious, attention; but with the piano concerto
he concerned himself from earliest youth until the end, and undoubtedly we should have had more than just two pianos concertos
dating from the last four years of his life—we might have had ten
or twelve such masterpieces—if the Vienna public had paid greater
attention to Mozart than it did. For of course Mozart wrote no new
concertos when he had no opportunity to play them. Of the more
than fifty symphonies by Mozart there are, strictly speaking, four

that belong among the eternal treasures of music; of the thirty-odd string quartets, ten. But among the twenty-three concertos for piano and orchestra, there is only one that is below the highest level—the concerto for three pianos (K. 242), written to be played not by Mozart himself or any capable soloist, but by three lady amateurs. One reason for the high quality of the piano concertos is the innate superiority of the piano over the other solo instruments, even when these instruments unite to form a *concertino* as in the *Sinfonia Concertante* for four wind instruments or the Double Concerto for violin and viola. Only in the piano concerto are two forces opposed that really balance each other, with neither one necessarily subordinate to the other. The piano is the only instrument that is not at a disadvantage either by reason of its limited tonal volume, like the violin, flute, or clarinet, or because of any limitations in respect to intonation and modulation, like the horn. It is just as powerful as the orchestra, to which it forms a worthy opponent because of the variety of tone production it possesses, as a highly developed percussion instrument. It should be remarked here again that Mozart wrote all his clavier works, including the concertos, not for the harpsichord but for the pianoforte, and that we should banish from the platform all those ladies and gentlemen who would like to claim the C minor Concerto, for example, or the C major, K. 503, for the harpsichord. We should also, of course, banish conductors who accompany a Mozart concerto with a string orchestra padded with ten double basses, forcing the pianist to produce a volume of tone that is possible only on our present-day mammoth instruments.

It was in the piano concerto that Mozart said the last word in respect to the fusion of the *concertante* and symphonic elements—a fusion resulting in a higher unity beyond which no progress was possible, because perfection is imperfectible. The penetrating monograph by C. M. Girdlestone, *Mozart et ses concertos pour piano* (Paris, 1939), rightly emphasizes the fact that the "emancipation of the orchestra," often attributed to Beethoven in his concerto-writing, was completely accomplished by Mozart. Beethoven perhaps juxtaposed the two forces more dramatically, and he pursued an ideal of virtuosity different from Mozart's; but at bottom he developed only one type among Mozart's concertos, which we may call for the present the "military" or "martial" type. Mozart's concerto form

is a vessel of far richer, finer, and more subline content. It is one of
the perfections of Mozart's music that its dramatic element remains
latent, and that it contains more profound depths than the struggle
between opposing forces. Sometimes the contest in Mozart's works
goes very far, but never so far that it could not be called a duality
in unity. His piano concerto is really his most characteristic creation.
It is the ideal and the realization of that which in some of his piano
trios and in the two piano quartets fails of complete expression only
because the piano in them is always the more powerful participant,
and the strings always remain partially eclipsed by it. Mozart's piano
concerto is the apotheosis of the piano—placing the instrument in the
broad frame in which it belongs—and at the same time the apotheosis of the *concertante* element is embedded in the symphonic. Or
one might even say: the symphonic element creates for itself a protag-
onist, the piano; it thus creates a dualism that endangers its unity;
and then it conquers this danger. Mozart's piano concerto never
seems to overstep the bounds of society music—how could it, since
it was always intended for performance in public, and thus was
prevented from having any quality of intimacy? And yet it always
leaves the door open to the expression of the darkest and the brightest, the most serious, the gayest, the deepest feelings. It presses forward from the *galant* world into the symphonic; it lifts the listener
to a higher level. Listeners who can really appreciate Mozart's piano
concertos are the best audience there is.

A. E.

Even Beethoven (who made a profound study of Mozart's pianoforte concertos) cannot be said to have surpassed him in this combination from within of different instrumental forces. The superiority of his great pianoforte concertos rests upon other grounds.

It must not be supposed, however, that Mozart had no higher
qualities than a finely cultivated sense for the blending of tone
colours. The invention, elaboration, and distribution of the *motifs*
were governed by the nature of the resources at his command; these
had to be taken into account in the first sketch of the work, so that
justice might be done them in its completed form; the germ must
contain the capacity for development under the most varied conditions. There is scarcely one instance in the concertos of an important

motif confided to the orchestra or the pianoforte alone; they are all shared in common. But when a subject is broadly and elaborately treated by the orchestra, it is naturally kept in the background by the pianoforte, while other *motifs,* merely announced by the orchestra, are rendered with their full effect and embellishments by the solo instrument. This competition of the two forces is most evident in the alternating effects given to the working-out of the different subjects. Of the twenty-five works more directly in question the author has heard a bare half-dozen, and his ignorance has had to be supplemented by reference to all the available published accounts of them. But it may be taken for a certainty, that, if all are delightful, at least a dozen of these pianoforte concertos are works of the very highest possible quality, are, in fact, undisputed masterpieces of their sort. It is, therefore, the more remarkable that they are so seldom performed, since more of the Mozart that the world loves lies concealed in them than in any other branch of his protean activity.

O. J.

Certainly it is amusing to trace the transformation which has come over the relations between solo instrument and orchestra since the many æsthetic problems these present were first authoritatively set out by Mozart, who had to make his way in by no means a solemn world. We can hardly have a more striking object lesson in the decay of politeness than that contained in the chapter of musical history written by the piano concerto. (I say piano advisedly, for the violin has never altogether lost the grand manner of its early prime despite Paganini's attempt to rob it of its silks and periwig. And what is true of the violin, is still more true of the 'cello.) When Mozart established the type, he made reasonable concessions to freedom. It was through his early concertos that he learnt to handle the still refractory sonata form with fluent ease. But he laid down canons of conduct governing piano and orchestra, based on the mutual respect arising from a well-defined comprehension of one another's functions, which his successors have never been quite able to enforce.

In the well-ordered Mozartian musicogony both know their place. There is no jostling, no shouting down, no recrimination. The piano does not cavil at the material provided by the orchestra; it can listen patiently through long tuttis, and never even clear its throat. Its good temper is unfailing; its breeding enables it to withstand the temptations of immoderate bravura; it indulges no mood to extremes. The orchestra, for its part, allows the pre-eminence of the piano as a general proposition, and keeps its own more unruly members in restraint. Etiquette may not prevent the bassoon from sly humour, nor the horn from becoming on occasion slightly sentimental. But all subscribe to a certain standard of decorous behaviour, and when we come to the end of those delicious finales which breathe the essence of the Viennese spirit, the soloist, in Mozart's own words, may be sweating, but it will be with the gentle perspiration of the drawing-room, not with the dripping exudation of the arena. Our pleasure, meanwhile, will have been the result of listening to a flow of ideas, expressed with the polish of a man of the world who is also a poet with a twinkle in his melancholy eye.

H. E. W.

This is one of the most delightful of the forms in which Mozart's genius asserted itself. Freedom of imagination, neatness, and poetry could go no further. These things are apparent at the first hearing of a Mozart concerto, and deeper acquaintance with them leaves this impression unimpaired, while it discovers a much greater difference in style than would be thought possible when the quantity of his work in this direction is considered. Perhaps the reason for this is that his personal contact with the music was much closer than in, for instance, one of his own symphonies. In fact, he played the solo part in both his violin and pianoforte concertos, and his very evident personal fastidiousness made him as careful of the effect he produced as if it was a question of the suit of clothes he was wearing at the concert. Of course his own actual playing of the solo part was designed to show off his particular talents of execution. We have, therefore, in the concertos Mozart, himself, as though these beautiful compositions were a set of frames for his own portrait.

But they were much more than a mere machinery of display for the instrument. Some of them may be described as copious patterns of decoration in the manner of the very finest Rococo stucchi, but such comparative easiness is only to be remarked in the least good of them. In others of them there is work on his very best level. There are pastoral, Arcadian scenes of an indescribable poetry, and so apparently simple that they are the very breath of inspiration itself. In some instances he has given a military turn to the finale so that it has all the stir and clang of martial music with the colours of bright uniforms. Then, again, with a flourish or two of the *cor-de-chasse* he evokes all the romance of hunting in the autumn woods; the winding of horns through the trees, the burnished leaves, even the early frost and the bonfire-smoke. Other movements may be more serious, like intellectual problems, set and solved of themselves with all the ease of a successful card-trick. In the later of his concertos the atmosphere becomes grave and solemn, charged with tragedy. On the lighter side there are delightful moments like a brilliant conversation in a charming room; and, to end with, there are often enough his rondos, which, alone, and in themselves, embody so many different forms of gaiety.

S. S.

In 1765, during his ninth year, Mozart arranged three sonata movements by J. C. Bach for harpsichord and orchestra (K. 107): this was his first work in concerto form. The last was the clarinet concerto of 1791, composed two months before his death. In the twenty-six intervening years he wrote over forty concertos. It was to Mozart more than to any other composer that this form owed its growth to a stature comparable with that of the symphony. Of all the instruments then in general use, only the violoncello and trombone did not receive some contribution from him, as the following brief summary will show.

Besides twenty-three works for keyboard, Mozart wrote for the violin five concertos (1775), and two rondos (1776, 1781); one *concertone* for two violins (1773); one *sinfonia concertante* for violin and viola (1779); one concerto for bassoon (1774), one for flute (K. 314, 1778); one for oboe (K. 313, 1778); four concertos and one rondo for French horn (1781–86); one concerto for flute and harp (1778), and one for clarinet (1791). Mozart's earliest original concerto was one for the trumpet (1768), which has unfortunately disappeared. Several other important works he left unfinished: we have a long fragment of a magnificent concerto for harpsichord and violin (1778), another of a work for violin, viola, and violoncello (1779), and another of a second concerto for oboe (1783).

Mozart was the prince of concerto writers. No other composer has ever combined such variety and quantity with such a generally high range of quality. One common characteristic of all these works is the remarkable understanding they display of the true nature of each and every solo instrument, even when it was not an especial favourite, or one which he played himself. The tale of Mozart's concertos might have been very different had he not enjoyed the friendship of many professional musicians—such as Leutgeb and Stadler, outstanding virtuosos on horn and clarinet respectively—and of noble patrons of ability and taste such as Baron Dürnitz, a lover of the bassoon, and the Duc de Guines, a flautist of distinction. But nearly all the keyboard concertos were written by Mozart for himself, partly to display his very fine technique, and partly to secure himself a livelihood. These masterly creations, spread over his whole lifetime, form the most important single group in all his prodigious output, and constitute his most original contribution to musical evolution. Limitation of space precludes analysis of all twenty-three within the present chapter, but we may briefly review them as a chronological series, before passing to matters of principle and style.

Mozart's first six original concertos were all composed at Salzburg between 1773 and 1779—the D major (K. 175), the B flat major (K. 238), the F major for three harpsichords (K. 242), the C major (K. 246), the E flat major (K. 271), and another (K. 365) in the same key for two harpsichords. While K. 175 is the best of the first four, with its effective contrapuntal finale, there is nothing in any of them to foreshadow the astonishing genius revealed in K. 271. As subsequent analysis will show, it is hardly an exaggeration to claim that this work forms a landmark in the history of the concerto comparable to the *Eroica* in that of the symphony.

The qualities of the first three concertos which Mozart composed in Vienna, all in 1782—the F major (K. 413), the A major (K. 414), and the C major (K. 415)—are, if less startling than those of K. 271, certainly more subtle. This trilogy leads logically to the phenomenal series of really great works which Mozart produced throughout 1784 in an effort to establish himself in his adopted city. From February to December in this *annus mirabilis,* he composed six concertos, as follows: E flat major (K. 449), B flat major (K. 450), D major (K. 451), G major (K. 453), B flat major (K. 456), F major (K. 459). Next year, 1785, came three more: D minor (K. 466), C major (K. 467), E flat major (K. 482). The year of *Figaro,* 1786, brought another three, the finest so far: A major (K. 488), C minor (K. 491), C major (K. 503). But as one hope after another failed him, his urge for self-exploitation as a performer grew less, and only two more pianoforte concertos came from his pen, the D major (K. 537, 1788) and the B flat major (K. 595, 1791). He also wrote, during 1782, two separate rondos for pianoforte and orchestra, one in D major (K. 382), most probably for his own use as an alternative to the finale of K. 175, and one in A major (K. 386), which seems to have served as the original version of the finale of K. 414.

The prodigious creative effort underlying the twelve masterpieces of 1784–86 is all the more remarkable if we remember that simultaneously Mozart was composing a continual stream of chamber works, songs and operas. ...

Up till the end of 1786, he used a steadily growing range of orchestral volume and colour, but the transformation which he brought about lay principally in the structural expansion of the first movements, of which no two are exactly alike. Their variety defies analysis on "textbook principles" exactly as do the fugues of Bach's "48" or the first movements of Beethoven's sonatas.

Mozart's achievement can be briefly summed up by saying that he combined a totally new conception of the concerto principle—fundamentally still one of contrast in timbre and volume—with the maximum of tonal and structural flexibility. He did not wholly jettison the older idea of two principal subjects in related keys, stated, developed, recapitulated, and rounded off. He expanded his thematic material so that each "subject" might include a group of two or more themes, sometimes making six or seven in all. Almost any two of them might be woven into kaleidoscopic patterns by the orchestra and soloist in combination and opposition. Mozart often went still further and allotted the soloist one or more wholly new melodies, whose entry gains in dramatic power through not having been stated in the orchestral exposition.

These movements are, in fact, voiceless dramas, full of tension, nobility, and pathos. Their melodies are just as alive and individual as Mozart's operatic characters. It is just this sense of dramatic values, re-created in instrumental terms, which enhances the revolutionary power of many of these concertos, as the expression of profound personal emotion. From K. 271 onwards, Mozart gradually turned his back on the older conception of the pianoforte concerto as entertainment music designed for social occasions. And herein lay, partly, the reason why this noble series failed to bring him security and a well-paid position—the fashionable public wanted to be entertained, not moved.

The subtlety of these creations makes verbal analysis an unsatisfactory substitute for knowledge of the actual scores, which the lover of concertos will find an inexhaustible treasure. Without the scores, the modern listener may often find himself in agreement with Mozart's friend and contemporary, Dittersdorf, who wrote, "I have never yet met with a composer who had such an amazing wealth of ideas: I could almost wish he were not so lavish in using them. He leaves his hearer out of breath; for hardly has he grasped one beautiful thought when one of greater fascination dispels the first, and this goes on throughout, so that in the end it is impossible to retain any of these beautiful melodies."

But even if analysis cannot explore all the complex bypaths of Mozart's first movements, it can indicate the broad pattern of his thought. While still a marked advance on any earlier concertos, the other movements are relatively simpler, the second chiefly consisting either of a simple sonata or *arioso* structure, or of theme and variations, and the third being either an elaborate rondo or, again, variations. Many of these second and third movements are embellished with long and important passages in which wood-wind and horns play with little or no support from the strings. It is hardly fanciful to see in these the natural successors of the serenades and divertimenti on which Mozart lavished loving care during his years at Salzburg.

A. H. K.

One of the finest analyses of Mozart's keyboard style, reconstructed from the composer's own statements and the testimony of qualified contemporaries, was that written by Philip Hale many years ago for one of Schirmer's collections of Mozart's piano music. After reviewing

Mozart's development as pianist, from the time he picked out thirds at the age of three to his last public appearance on March 4, 1791, the year of his death, Hale begins his appraisal:

The fame of the virtuoso is often an unreal thing, magnified or distorted by the testimony of prejudiced contemporaries; in the case of Mozart we not only have the unanimous testimony of skilled musicians of his day, we have also the personal record of his ideas concerning pianoforte playing. His hands were small, and the spectator wondered that they could grasp full chords; his system of fingering, derived from the study of Ph. Em. Bach, cured natural limitations.

The hands were beautiful; they pleased the eye, although they were useless in the cutting of his meat. He avoided all facial and bodily movements that smacked of affectation. According to him the player should have quiet hands; their lightness, suppleness, their unhindered speed should turn difficult passages into "flowing oil." He warned constantly against undue speed and hurrying; for they result only in slovenliness and bungling; and he knew how easy it was to play rapidly and with brilliant inaccuracy.

He insisted on a strict observance of time, and he kept with the beat so strictly that even in the free use of tempo rubato in an adagio the hands preserved unity in rhythm. He laid special stress on accuracy, the sure and easy conquering of technical difficulties, fineness of taste in the delivery, force regulated by the expression. So in reading at sight he demanded the observance of the proper tempo, the careful elaboration of the ornaments, the fitting expression: the player should seem to be the composer.

It is not surprising then that Rochlitz spoke of the "heavenly pleasure given by the elegance and the heart-melting tenderness of his performance"; that Haydn wept at the remembrance of his "incomparable playing."

As a teacher of the pianoforte he was not methodical in his instruction, and he taught rather by playing to his pupils than by listening and correcting. His most celebrated pupil was Hummel, who lived in his house two years and learned there the pure touch, the rounding of the phrase, the finish and the elegance, the facility in improvising that distinguished the performance of his master.

L. B.

Concerto for Piano and Orchestra in C major (K. 415)

I. Allegro   II. Andante   III. Allegro

THIS COMPOSITION belongs to a group of three piano concertos written by Mozart in Vienna during the autumn and winter months of 1782–83. All three largely reflect a happy period in the composer's life, a period ushered in by his marriage to Constanze Weber in August, 1782. Of the F major Concerto (K. 413), the earliest in the set, Wanda Landowska has written that "it breathes pure joy from beginning to end" and may be described as one long Minuet: "We know how much Mozart loved to dance and what a good dancer he was!"

Mme. Landowska also reminds us that the three concertos have long suffered from the unjust designation of "small." This misconception, she feels, stems partly from Mozart's own reference to the concertos in a letter to his father Leopold dated December 28, 1782:

> These concertos are a happy medium between what is too easy and too difficult; they are very brilliant, pleasing to the ear and natural, without being vapid. There are passages here and there from which connoisseurs alone can derive satisfaction; but these passages are written in such a way that the less learned cannot fail to be pleased, though without knowing why.

Concerning this amazingly candid statement, Mme. Landowska has this to say:

> It has been concluded from this letter that Mozart attributed

little importance to these concertos and consequently they have been underestimated. The irony of Mozart's "modest" remarks is too apparent to require further explanation, although we might still ask why these concertos have been relegated to oblivion. *Probably because they—and the K. 415 in particular—require more extensive extemporization on the performer's part than any other concerto.*

Continuing, Mme. Landowska makes the following remarks about the C major Concerto:

The first movement of this concerto is a type of alla marcia which advances in canonic imitations. Tranquil at first, it augments little by little and overflows into the same triplet motif which marks the opening of the *Jupiter Symphony*. Thus, this concerto, which has so long been neglected and ignored, contains from its first notes the elements of grandeur and dramatic power.

The Andante is a tender and lyrical dialogue between the soloist and strings, the latter supported from time to time by oboes, bassoons, and horns.

But it is, above all, the finale, a frolicsome dance in 6/8, which merits our fullest attention. While so much importance has been attached to the letter quoted above, another letter to his father (Vienna, January 22, 1783) throws a much more penetrating and informative light on the subject:

"I shall send the cadenzas and *Eingange*—(short introductory passages announcing the approach of new moods and extemporized like the cadenzas and organ points, although they are three utterly different aspects of improvisation) to my dear sister at the first opportunity. I have not yet altered the *Eingange* in the rondo, for whenever I play this concerto, I always play whatever occurs to me at the moment. . . ."

The use of cadenzas[1] at the end of each movement is still common today, while the small organ points, which we come upon expectedly here and there, and, most significantly the *Eingange,* which twice announce the approach of the sublime

---

[1] See below, "Mozart's Cadenzas," p. 392.

adagio in C minor, have been virtually ignored since the performance of Mozart himself and the musicians of his time.

At the end of the rondo Mozart introduces, against the murmuring of the strings, a popular folk song, ingratiating and fresh in mood.

When this concerto entered the New York Philharmonic-Symphony repertory on October 24, 1946, Mme. Landowska, the soloist, improvised the cadenzas, organ points, and *Eingange,* or entrance passages.

In connection with the C minor episode which appears twice in the Allegro finale, it is interesting to learn that Mozart originally planned the whole second movement in the minor key. Alfred Einstein, in his study of Mozart's music, suggests Mozart gave up the idea when he realized that a slow movement in C minor "would have made it much too serious for the character of these works."

Of the three concertos, the C major is the amplest in scoring, calling for two oboes, two bassoons, two horns, two trumpets, and two tympani. Both the F major (K. 413) and the A major (K. 414) lack trumpets and tympani. Slightest of the three in this respect is the A major, which also omits bassoons. All three concertos were played by Mozart at concerts for his own benefit in the National Theater of Vienna. These events were called "academies." Two of the three concertos—there is no way of determining which two—were rendered at the "academy" of March 22, 1783, quaintly reported by *Cramers Magazin* (as quoted in Mr. Einstein's *Mozart*):

Today the celebrated Chevalier Mozart gave a music academy for his own benefit at the National Theater in which pieces of his own composition, which was already very popular, were performed. The academy was honored by the presence of an extraordinarily large audience, and the *two new concertos* and other fantasies which Mr. Mozart played on the Forte Piano were received with the loudest approval.

Our Monarch, who contrary to his custom honored the whole academy with his presence, joined in the applause of the public so heartily that one can think of no similar example. The proceeds of the academy are estimated at 600 gulden.

L. B.

MOZART'S CADENZAS

Something must be said about the cadenzas. Many of Mozart's own are preserved, enough to be used for a good number of the concertos and to provide models for other people to work on. For most of the cadenzas played by pianists in the concert-room are, in association with the music they draw upon, so much rubbish, even those by otherwise reputable composers. Nearly all of them are far too long and all without exception do a great deal too much in the way of thematic developing. This is neither historically nor aesthetically the function of a cadenza, and concert-giving suffers from no abuse more offensive than these pretentious excrescences. There was originally no difference, as etymologically there is none, between the cadenza and the cadence. The former was simply an ornamental extension of the latter, inserted at first into arias and later, by analogy, into concertos as a concession to the technically gifted performer. It must therefore be a decorative feature and nothing else. The composer, at any rate a great composer like Mozart, has already worked out his thematic material exactly as much as he wished, and later musicians who take it upon themselves to show what more might have been done in that direction are guilty of an impertinence even when, as happens very rarely, they do not plaster a monstrous stylistic incongruity upon a perfectly organized structure. A glance at Mozart's own cadenzas shows that they are only very slightly thematic and tactfully keep to the subsidiary function of a desirable but not fundamentally vital embellishment.

E. B.

Concerto for Piano and Orchestra in B flat major (K. 450)

I. Allegro   II. Andante   III. Allegro

ON 9 February, 1784, Mozart began to enter in a little notebook of forty-four leaves—perhaps a bit too large to have served as a pocket notebook—all his works as he completed them, giving in each case the date, the type, and the beginning of the work written on two staves. He kept up this book until a few weeks before his death, filling fifty-eight pages. The first work he listed is a Concerto for piano in E flat major (K. 449), with accompaniment for strings, and oboes and horns *ad libitum*. The fact that the participation of the winds is made optional seems to connect this concerto with the three written in 1782–83; but the connection is only apparent. Mozart dedicated the work to his pupil Barbara Ployer, the daughter of a fellow-native of Salzburg then living in Vienna, and evidently did not wish to deprive her of the possibility of playing it with a small combination of instruments in a drawing-room. Actually, however, the wind instruments, although they seem sparingly used, can hardly be omitted; and this concerto is not really a continuation of the type of the Salzburg concertos and the first three composed in Vienna, but a new beginning—the beginning of a new series comprising no less than twelve great concertos, written between 9 February, 1784, and 4 December, 1786, and constituting the high-point of Mozart's instrumental composition. This series is followed by only the Coronation Concerto in D major and the last one, in B flat major, written in January of the year of Mozart's death.

Immediately after the concerto for Fräulein Ployer, he composed two more, in B flat (K. 450) and in D (K. 451), and then, after the Piano Quintet (K. 452), still another, in G major (K. 453), a miracle of productivity in no way less extraordinary than the miracle of the three symphonies of 1788. For all these works are as different from one another as can be imagined. In an illuminating passage in a letter to his father, dated 26 May, 1784, Mozart expressed himself briefly about them. He mentioned the two concertos in B flat and D, and continued:

> I really cannot choose between the two of them, but I regard them both as concertos that are bound to make the performer sweat. From the point of view of difficulty the B♭ concerto beats the one in D. Well, I am very curious to hear which of the three, in B♭, D, and G, you and my sister prefer. The one in E♭ does not belong at all to the same category. It is one of a

quite peculiar kind, composed rather for a small orchestra than for a large one . . .

A. E.

K. 450 is, indeed, one of the most difficult of the whole series, and gives quite exceptional prominence to the soloist, in long sections of *bravura* which are calculated as part of the organic growth, and not inserted as mere display. In many passages of quickly changing rhythms the pianoforte conflicts with the steady beat of the modest orchestra, comprising strings, oboes, bassoons, and horn, with one flute in the finale. This is a cheerful, intimate concerto, not without seriousness, in very much the same mood as the contemporary B flat "Hunt" Quartet (K. 458).

A. H. K.

I. The orchestra takes in hand unassisted the expository matter, which devolves upon an up-sliding chromatic figure. The soloist, assuming at last the burden of discourse, makes up for a long delayed entrance by dominating the situation with a sparkling bombardment of scale passages and sixteenth-notes in a rippling legato.

II. Again in the Andante (in E flat, 3/8), the piano delivers an uninterrupted and ornate obbligato, the orchestra for the most part merely fortifying the melody, which comes often from the pianist's left hand.

III. In the final rondo, the composer sees fit to give his tutti an additional edge of brilliance by the inclusion of a flute (hitherto silent). The cadenzas in the first and last movements are Mozart's own.

The orchestration consists of one flute, two oboes, two bassoons, two horns, and strings.

J. N. B.

Concerto for Piano and Orchestra in G major (K. 453)

I. Allegro   II. Andante   III. Allegretto–Presto

MOZART CROWNED the series of piano concertos written in this astonishing winter of 1784 with one in G major (K. 453), again intended *per la Signora Barbara Ployer,* as the inscription on the autograph tells us. On 10 June there was an "academy" in the country, at Ployer's house in Döbling—"a concert, where Fräulein Babette is playing her new concerto in G, and I am performing the quintet [K. 452]; we are then playing together the grand sonata for two claviers." This concerto, too, is unique. It is more intimate than its three predecessors; it welds the solo and orchestra parts into a closer unity, its friendly key is full of hidden laughter and hidden sadness. No words can describe the continuous iridescence of feeling of the first movement, or the passionate tenderness of the second. The fact that this C major movement goes as far afield as G sharp major is only an external sign of its passionate quality. The finale consists of variations on a naive, birdlike, Papageno sort of theme with a grandiose, polyphonic conclusion. Mr. Girdlestone has rightly remarked that Beethoven's most amiable concerto, in the same key, takes its departure from this work of Mozart's. But the concerto of Beethoven, who could not be naive, is powerful and robust in comparison with the delicate shadings of this unique work, which has no parallel even among Mozart's other compositions.

A. E.

I. There is the usual orchestral tutti by way of exposition. It presents two subjects, in the usual key relation of tonic-dominant, but the second subject, beginning in D, shows a wayward disposition to wander from its orthodox key center. There is also a fairly definite "closing subject." The solo then enters, dealing in the usual orderly way with the subject matter set forth in the tutti, but adding the invariable charm of Mozart's pianistic figurations. The development section is initiated by the tutti, the solo presently adding triplet figurations that finally hasten into passages of sixteenths. There is a regular recapitulation that at last burgeons into a cadenza; then a brief tutti for conclusion.

II. The Andante (C major, 3/4) begins with a short strain in the strings that ends with a fermata or "hold." Then there is a little trio for winds with a string accompaniment, after which the solo enters with the brief strain of the opening. Suddenly it bursts into a more excited strain in G minor, the first beat of the measure being strongly accentuated. The following section becomes much more florid, and leads to another subject in E flat. After a brief coda there is an end on the first theme.

III. The last movement (Allegretto, G major, 2/4) has as its principal subject a gay little tune that was learned, to Mozart's vast delight, by a starling he bought a month or so after the concerto was written. He describes how the bird sang a G sharp instead of the G flat in the theme, and comments "that was lovely!" Of this beginning there are three short sections, each repeated, after which the movement really "gets going." There is considerable elaboration with flighty triplet figures in the solo; and thereafter a second theme, prepared for by a few hints in oboe and flute, is given to the solo. There appears presently a section in G minor, first in the tutti, then in the solo, that may be taken as the third subject in a rather loosely constructed rondo form. The development is considerably extended.

The orchestration calls for flute, two oboes, two bassoons, two horns, strings, and solo piano.

D. F.

Concerto for Piano and Orchestra
in B flat major (K. 456)

I. Allegro vivace   II. Andante un poco sostenuto   III. Allegro vivace

THE YEAR 1784 brought forth two more concertos still, very different from the preceding ones and from each other. The first, again in B flat (K. 456), which Mozart completed after recovering from a very heavy cold caught at the première of *Il Rè Teodoro* by Casti and

Paisiello, is distinguished by the fact that he wrote it neither for himself nor for a pupil as talented and close to him as Babette Ployer (for himself or for Babette he would certainly not have chosen B flat again) but for another Vienna virtuoso, Maria Theresa Paradis. This young lady, who had been blind since childhood, and was at that time twenty-five years old, was the daughter of a State Councilor of Lower Austria, and a godchild of the Empress. She was a pupil of Leopold Kozeluch, and she could play, according to Gerber, "more than sixty clavier concertos [by Kozeluch] with the greatest accuracy and the finest expression, in every way worthy of her teacher." It is evidence of Mozart's broadmindedness, or of his indifference, that he wrote a new concerto for the pupil of his deadly enemy to perform in Paris, whither a concert tour brought her in the autumn of 1784. For Paris, obviously, Kozeluch's concertos did not suffice. Kozeluch was, again quoting Gerber, "without doubt, among young and old, the most generally popular of all composers now living, and that quite rightly. His works are characterized by cheerfulness and grace, the noblest melody combined with the purest harmony and the most pleasing arrangement in respect to rhythm and modulation."

Now Mozart gave even the Parisians, whom he so hated, credit for desiring something more than that. So he harked back a little to Schobert, Johann Christian Bach, and Schröter. The relations of the solo part and the orchestra in this work are, to be sure, purely Mozartean, characteristic only of him, and perhaps even closer than ever before; but the solo part has a different, more "feminine," more sensuous character than the preceding concertos, and that iridescence of expression characteristic of the second Ployer Concerto is almost completely absent. In the Ployer Concerto there is nothing like the modulation to B minor in this Parisian one, emphasized as it is by the combination of 6/8 and 2/4 meters. But Schröter, too, had indulged in such pseudo-drama, and the Parisians were fond of that sort of thing. The slow movement consists of variations with coda, in G minor. Their tearful character already has something to do with the loss of Barbarina's pin in *Figaro*; it is very French. The work is full of miracles of sonority, but it contains none of the "surprises," great or small, of the great concertos.

A. E.

Leopold may well have marveled at the daring and original use of the wind instruments in the comparatively large orchestra his son chose for this concerto, which includes a flute, and pairs of oboes, bassoons, and horns, in addition to the strings. The wind instruments are used consistently as a choir of equal, and often of greater, importance than the strings. One is struck by their prominence, and by the fact that this prominence gives a new dimension to the structure of the piano concerto. Here is a distinct feeling of three main protagonists: wind, strings, and piano, with importance in that order. Never must the piano part be given an unequal emphasis, or the subtle balance of the work will collapse. If the solo part has the first place, it is first only among equals.

I. The opening movement (Allegro vivace, 4/4) begins quietly with the first theme in the strings—soon to be echoed by the wind choir. The orchestral exposition includes all the important themes of the movement. When the piano enters it is content to repeat or to decorate these themes, adding here or there a characteristic figure of its own. Even such a passage as that of the wonderfully sustained transitional measures before the entrance of the second subject is unchanged by the addition of the piano, which merely adds color and body to the harmonies of strings and wind. The piano opens and closes the development with new melodic improvisations, but the main part of this section is devoted to a fantasia upon the closing theme of the exposition. The glory of the recapitulation is the exquisite blending of piano and wind instruments. There is a brief coda following the pause for the cadenza. Mozart left two cadenzas for this movement, by the way.

II. The slow movement (Andante un poco sostenuto, G minor, 2/4) takes the form, rather unusual in Mozart's piano concertos, of a theme and variations. The theme, given out at once by strings and wind instruments, is in the strongest contrast to the even temper of the first movement. It is full of despair, yet without passion and without hope. Alfred Einstein considers it "very French," which is appropriate enough in a work written for Paris, and perhaps it is; it is certainly ideally suited to its purpose in the work, and the five variations that follow, together with the extended coda in which the theme is mercilessly torn to shreds, are among Mozart's most moving and prophetic pages.

III. The piano opens the finale (Allegro vivace, B flat, 6/8) in the mood of the first movement. The orchestra soon takes possession of the theme and begins to develop it in Mozart's typically resourceful rondo-sonata manner, with various subsidiary themes and motives. The piano does not enter again until the beginning of the first episode, but this time it perseveres to announce both the two new subjects of this division. A trill on a chord of the dominant seventh introduces the return of the rondo theme. Again the orchestra takes possession of it, and soon modulates to B minor. There is a pause. The three main elements of the concerto, wind, strings, and piano, now unite to project the stormy music of the second episode. Against the 6/8 rhythms of the strings, the piano sings a desolate song, 2/4. The tempestuous measures reappear and are suddenly calmed. There is a return to the tonic key and the easy-going themes of the first episode—the expected repetition of the rondo theme being entirely omitted. This is the most striking passage of the work, unexpected and strangely moving, recapitulating the despairing mood of the slow movement amid a finale similar in character and themes to the first movement. A cadenza introduces the final appearance of the rondo theme and the spirited coda.

The score calls for one flute, two oboes, two bassoons, two horns, solo piano, and strings.

G. H. L. S.

Concerto for Piano and Orchestra in D minor (K. 466)

I. Allegro   II. Romanze   III. Allegro assai

STORIES of Mozart's feats of memory and technique at the piano are so plenteous that we are scarcely surprised to learn that the little man performed the première of the D minor Concerto not only without a rehearsal but without having played the rondo finale through once. This was in Vienna on February 11, 1785. We have Leopold Mozart's word for it that his son was busy at the copyist's before rushing off to the concert hall. "Wolfgang played an excellent new concerto," wrote Leopold to his daughter Marianne in Salzburg. Mozart repeated the performance on February 15. *"Magnifique!"* exclaims Leopold in a second letter to Marianne. Generations of music lovers have echoed the proud father's outburst.

The première of the D minor occurred in the Mehlgrube at one of Mozart's subscription concerts held during Lent, a lucrative season for such events in the Vienna of his time. Later to become the Hotel Münch, the Mehlgrube was a popular hall for concerts and balls. It seems flour was stored in the cellar, which accounts for its name, Mehlgrube, literally a "flour pit." We owe what information we have on the proceeds of Mozart's subscription series to his father's famous taste for finance. The series lured 150 subscribers. Wolfgang netted 559 florins, roughly $275. This was a staggering figure to the whole family, especially since Leopold's fabulous son "had often played at other people's concerts for nothing." Only when we compare the figure with the meager sums paid Mozart for the use and publication of some of his scores can we understand the family's jubilation.

Reverting to Mozart's not having rehearsed the D minor Concerto, it was Edward Holmes who advanced an intriguing theory about the première at the Mehlgrube. In the impromptu cadenzas, he suggests, "extemporary invention of the fingers of Mozart may have scattered even greater beauties than he has left in that great work." Holmes also makes the pertinent remark: "If the idea of a concerto played without a single rehearsal or trial be surprising, how much more must it appear when we remember the quantity the player wrote, and the little time that his fingers, cramped and contracted by holding the pen, had to recover their wonted freedom and agility."

At the time of the subscription concerts, Leopold Mozart was spending some months in Vienna with his son and daughter-in-law Constanze in their dwelling on the Schulerstrasse. Letters to his daughter contain frequent references to Wolfgang's triumphs. When the Piano Concerto in C major (K. 467) was played at the following concert, Leopold reported that many listeners were moved to tears by its beauty and that the applause was deafening. There was another great thrill in store for Papa Leopold during his Viennese sojourn.

One day, Joseph Haydn came to the house on the Schulerstrasse to play first violin in three new quartets by Mozart dedicated to himself. After the performance Haydn declared to the elder Mozart: "I tell you before God, and as an honest man, that your son is the greatest composer I know, either personally or by name. He has taste and apart from that the greatest science in composition." Haydn was then directing musical evenings in the town residence of Prince Nicholas Esterházy. On his invitation Mozart often participated in the musical entertainment. A great admirer of Haydn's string quartets, Mozart had earlier planned dedicating six of his own to the senior composer. The last three of the set were completed on January 14, 1785, less than a month before the rush subscription season at the Mehlgrube got under way. Haydn had become a frequent guest of the Mozarts. In the quartet sessions, Mozart himself played the viola.

The D minor is one of fifteen piano concertos composed by Mozart between 1782 and 1786. Mozart had now found fresh ways of enlarging the scope of the concerto and enriching its contents. Integrating the solo instrument and orchestra in more vital form was one of them. Through this medium he was achieving a new poetry and individuality. The D minor stands out in impassioned speech. The fervid note of tragic unrest, accentuated by the minor key, is stronger than in the others. The next concerto (C major), with its showy sequences and gay flourishes of trumpets and drums, is a far cry from the gloom and romantic despair that brood fitfully through the pages of the D minor.

L. B.

The D minor Concerto is Mozart's first piano concerto in the minor mode, and the one best known, one might almost say the only one known, in the nineteenth century. That fact reveals a great deal about the nineteenth century, which did not understand the sublime humor of the F major Concerto, but well understood what distinguished the D minor among all the piano concertos of Mozart: passion, pathos, drama. This concerto made it possible to stamp Mozart as a forerunner of Beethoven, and it is indeed no accident that for this very concerto Beethoven wrote cadenzas—a splendid one, fusing the Mozart and Beethoven styles, for the first movement, and a rather weaker one for the last. This is the first work in which the tutti and the solo in the Allegro are sharply contrasted, in a dualism there is no attempt to overcome. The orchestra represents an anonymous threatening power, and the solo instrument voices an eloquent lament. The orchestra never takes over the first theme of the solo part, a *recitativo in tempo,* or the second half of the second theme. The opposition of the two permits of no reconciliation; it is only intensified in the development section. Nor does the reprise offer any solution: the *pianissimo* conclusion of the movement is as if the furies had simply become tired out and had lain down to rest, still grumbling, and ready at any instant to take up the fight again. And they do take it up again, in the middle section (in G minor) of the Romanze, which begins and ends in such heavenly tranquillity. Mozart never included stronger contrasts within a single work, contrasts among the three movements as well as within each movement individually. The choice of key for the Andante is revealing: not F major, or D major, but the subdominant of the relative major, just as in the G minor Symphony three years later. The finale contains chromatically intensified and refined passion and drama, announced at the very beginning in the rocket-like principal motive. But this time Mozart wishes to conquer his pessimism and despair. After the cadenza, he turns towards the major, in a coda of enchanting sweetness, which represents at the same time an affecting ray of light and, in slight degree, a return to the social atmosphere of earlier works, the courtly gesture of a grand seigneur who wishes to leave his guests with a friendly impression. But this is not at all the childlike or grandiose optimism of Haydn or Beethoven.

A. E.

i. Allegro, D minor, 4/4. The somberness of a minor key and the syncopation of the first theme give the opening of the movement an almost tragic atmosphere. It starts softly in the strings and only gradually admits the support of the rest of the orchestra. Although remaining in the minor, the mood lightens a bit for the continuation of the first subject—beginning with a dialogue between violins and oboes and ending with a martial pronouncement in which the wind and the kettledrums are prominent. A transitional theme, which will be heard twice more, and always in the key of F major, entrusts a phrase to oboe and bassoon which is answered by the flute and continued in a graceful descending pattern on the violins. Back to D minor, a new note of agitation is sounded in the rising tremolo line of the violins and its declamatory continuation, but the concluding theme—an elaborately graceful counterpoint in the strings—is quieter and prepares the way for the solo's entrance. This is made on a new theme which will be most important in the subsequent development. Following this, the piano, together with the orchestra, reviews the first subject and the transitional theme, to which latter the piano adds an unexpected and beautiful countermelody. Now, with the key still in F, the real second subject, which the orchestral exposition was nôt allowed to broach, is proposed by the solo and then by the woodwind. Thereafter the second subject continues with the agitated theme of the introduction, and closes in F, in which key the development begins. This is concerned chiefly, but not exclusively, with the interplay of the orchestra's first theme and the piano's first theme. What follows is regular enough, but the recapitulation of the second subject in minor instead of the original major greatly alters its meaning. The recapitulation is followed by a short orchestral passage leading to the usual cadenza, and the orchestra's final comments make effective use of the closing themes of its exposition, to bring the movement to a soft end.

II. Romanze, B flat major, 4/4. The spacious lines on which this movement is conceived render possible the projection of a number of contrasting ideas. The first consists of two regular phrases, both announced by the solo and repeated by the orchestra. The second repetition is lengthened by an ingratiating little questioning phrase. Immediately the piano enters with an extended cantabile in a somewhat florid single line and with a simple accompaniment of strings. The questioning phrase serves to bring back the initial idea, of which only the first half is given. A middle section is introduced in G minor, with an agitated character which is the antithesis of the calmly graceful first part. The piano begins a triplet pattern and is sustained by the woodwinds in the broken melodic phrases which are set against this pattern. Like the first theme of the movement, this section consists of two regular and repeated phrases. A bridge passage on the pattern of the middle section leads back to the first theme, given in full but with only the second half repeated by the orchestra. The coda presents a final theme, first in the woodwinds and then on the piano, and ends with the questioning phrase supplemented by the piano's charmingly hesitant close.

III. Allegro assai, D minor, 2/2. The solo announces the theme and the orchestra takes it up and develops it with the aid of new material. When the piano returns, it returns with a new idea which, however, soon passes back into that of the beginning. Now again the solo announces another idea, this time in F minor, and again the orchestra takes it up and develops it, modulates to the major, and, in that key, gives out a more carefree theme of its own, on woodwinds in octaves—the only idea in the whole movement not previously given to the piano. The piano, however, does get a chance to restate it at length and to bring back the rondo theme. This and its sequel are given an extensive development before the repetition of the themes first heard in F, now both in D and both in the minor. The coda gives opportunity for a cadenza following which the key turns to major, and a sextet of oboes, horns, and bassoons restate the orchestra's carefree theme. The piano takes over and engages in a contest with the orchestra until the theme comes back. This time it is wonderfully altered as woodwinds ask a question and are gently but firmly answered by a determined little phrase of trumpets and horns. This answer furnishes the material from which the final measures are constructed.

The orchestral accompaniment calls for flute, two oboes, two bassoons, two horns, two trumpets, timpani, and strings.

B. E.

Concerto for Piano and Orchestra in C major (K. 467)

I. Allegro maestoso   II. Andante   III. Allegro vivace assai

COMPLETED ON March 9, 1785, the C major Concerto was first played three days later at a concert given by Mozart in Vienna. Leopold Mozart was then spending some months with his son and daughter-in-law Constanze in their dwelling on the Schulerstrasse. Writing to his daughter Nannerl, he described the warm reception accorded the new work. Many listeners were moved to tears by its beauty, according to the proud father, and the applause was deafening. Such behavior spoke well for the audience because, as Eric Blom points out, the Andante "must have made Mozart's hearers sit up by its daring modernities." Among such audacities were "a diminished seventh and a sweeping skip in the first bar, an unexpected transition to the tonic minor in the second, discordant suspensions in the next three, and a grinding false relation (B flat against B natural) in the last."

Whether goaded by debts and efforts to meet the high rent and expenses of the Schulerstrasse residence or merely by a feverish creative urge, the period of the C major Concerto hummed with composition, particularly for piano. Six concertos, two sonatas, and two sets of variations, all for piano, were the count by the end of 1784. Three more piano concertos followed in 1785, besides the C minor Fantasy and the sonata for violin and piano in the same key. By then the concerto form in Mozart's hands had become a "medium in which . . . he succeeded in combining perfect aptness to its special requirements with inexhaustible poetry and originality," according to Mr. Blom.

With its showy sequences and gay flourishes of trumpets and drums, the C major Concerto contrasts sharply with its predecessor, the D minor Concerto (K. 466). The change in mood is as from night to day. After glimpsing the romantic future and flinging off hints of Beethoven and Schumann to come, Mozart again slips back into the period groove of a "normal display concerto."

L. B.

Both this concerto and K. 466 are scored for exactly the same orchestra, yet they are diametrically opposed in mood and character. The fact that barely a month separates their respective entries (10th February and 9th March, 1785) in Mozart's own thematic catalogue, strongly suggests that he must have been working on both simultaneously, and provides a notable instance of his ingrained habit of producing contrasted pieces in pairs. (The string quintets in C major and G minor, of 19 April and 16 May, 1787, furnish another instance.) K. 467 is Mozart's third pianoforte concerto in C, this choice of a neutral key here serving as a basis for exhilarating freedom of modulation which, for Mozart, was far less compatible with such key signatures—admittedly infrequent—as F minor or E major. Mozart left no cadenzas to this concerto.

A. H. K.

I. The opening movement begins with the principal subject (Allegro maestoso, C major, 4/4) in the strings. This subject makes frequent appearances in the course of the movement. It should be said that the tempo indication is absent in the autograph score, which, until the end of the nineteenth century at least, was in the possession of Wilhelm Taubert. Toward the end the customary cadenza for the solo instrument is introduced.

II. Andante, F major, 4/4. The movement opens with the principal subject in the orchestra, the piano entering with the theme twenty-three measures later. A continuing section is set forth by the solo instrument, this leading to the second subject in C major.

III. Allegro vivace assai, C major, 2/4. The orchestra announces the principal theme. At its conclusion, and before the entrance of the subject in the piano, opportunity was given in the autograph score for a cadenza. The solo instrument plays the theme, which is followed by a tutti. A second subject, in G major, is introduced, first in the orchestra and then in the piano. The first theme returns and there is episodical material. A recapitulation follows, with a cadenza for the piano toward the close, the movement ending with the material of the opening theme.

The orchestral portion of the concerto is scored for flute, two oboes, two bassoons, two horns, two trumpets, timpani, and strings.

F. B.

Concerto for Piano and Orchestra
in E flat (K. 482)

I. Allegro   II. Andante   III. Allegro

THOUGH COMPOSED in December, 1785, and premiered the same month with Mozart as soloist, the E flat Concerto was one of a group of three intended for subscription concerts during Lent. Its companions, the A flat (K. 488) and the C minor (K. 491), were completed in March, 1786.

The advance première of the E flat went to a worthy cause. Vienna, then housing some 400 orchestral players, had a welfare organization that contributed to the support of musicians' widows. Like similar societies of today, it kept up a pension fund, and concerts were held regularly to add to it. Although it was a time of small ensembles, the orchestras at these concerts often consisted of Vienna's entire instrumental colony. When Dittersdorf's oratorio *Esther* was presented at an earlier pension fund concert, the personnel was 200 strong. Kisbeck reported that all 400 players frequently got together and played "as precisely and clearly as if they were only twenty or thirty." He observed proudly, "Surely this is the only concert of the kind in the world." When Mozart appeared in his E flat Concerto, the society's orchestra numbered 108 men. The announcement of the benefit concert merely stated that "During the entr'acte, a newly composed clavier concerto will be played by W. A. Mozart."

The three concertos belong to a period of feverish activity in Mozart's life. Not that there was ever a letup in his crowded career. But the winter of 1785–86 is fairly staggering in sheer work. Besides the concertos, he was "up to his ears," as his father put it, in *The Marriage of Figaro,* produced the following May. That alone makes a dismal tale of worry, conflict, and frantic last-minute changes. He wrote a violin sonata, completed December 12, the E flat Piano Concerto coming four days later. He devised a cantata, *Davidde penitente,* from the earlier unfinished Mass in C minor. On the Emperor's commission, he completed a one-act comedy, *Der Schauspieldirektor* (*The Impresario*), for the reception of the Netherlands governors held in the orangery at Schönbrunn on February 7. There were revisions and additions to make for a performance of *Idomeneo* in March. And when he could, he worked at smaller instrumental pieces.

But the composing was only one small part of Mozart's routine. He had pupils at all hours of the day, though for a time he limited the lessons to a strict afternoon schedule, so that he could give his mornings to *The Marriage of Figaro*. Since there was no hope of defraying household expenses from royalties and teaching fees alone, he made frequent appearances as soloist at public and private concerts. Yet, we have Michael Kelly's word for it that in spite of the hectic daily rounds, Mozart found time for dancing and a good game of billiards.

L. B.

By common consent, this ranks as the most queenly of all Mozart's pianoforte concertos, combining affability with dignity—"vera incessu patuit dea." Warmth of colouring comes partly from the omission of oboes and the use of clarinets for the first time in this keyboard series. Trumpets and drums are retained. In the first and last movements Mozart relies for contrast more on changes in the shape and rhythm of his themes than on tonal fluidity. It might be thought that this broadly urbane character, coming after the rather forceful asperities of K. 466 and K. 467, denoted a return to the earlier conception of concertos as "entertainment music," were this not belied by the personal intensity of the Andante. But it was this movement which had to be repeated at the first performance, given, admittedly, before a select, private audience. There are, indeed, some strong parallels between this work and Mozart's earliest E flat concerto, K. 271, but for K. 482, unfortunately, he left no cadenzas.

A. H. K.

1. Allegro. A typical Mozart opening, with its striking contrast between the bold opening notes for orchestra and the gentler continuation for horns and bassoons. The same contrast again, but this time strings have the continuation, which winds onward gracefully. Soon the mood returns to strength. A graceful interlude is assigned

to woodwinds. Then the strings pulsate rapidly. Wide leaps, and descending scale passages, herald the end of the orchestral exposition.

The piano enters with graceful variants of the subjects, at first completely alone. Soon the orchestra re-enters with the thematic material against soft and lovely arpeggios and runs for the piano. After some time the piano shifts into a more somber color, with more stubborn rhythms. This too changes to flowing figures, and then to the second subject, again for piano alone. A long series of flowing passages, and then the more willful ending of the exposition for orchestra. Again passage work for the piano, figures from the main subject lightly etched against it by strings and woodwinds in alternation. This leads to a return of the main theme, now treated together with piano runs, and some lovely melodic interludes. A sturdy section for orchestra, and liquid and symmetrical melodic passage for piano, more passage work for the solo instrument, and then a jubilant ending, much as the first time.

II. Andante. The second movement begins with a meditative subject for muted strings alone. This done, the piano sings it in variation, at first alone and then to the accompaniment of the strings. This is followed by the second verse of the song, for woodwinds, in graceful chorus. The piano re-enters, with another variation on the main song, this time with a more rapidly figured bass. Thereafter comes a new variation, moving from shadow into light, from minor into major, and with the melody in playful dialogue between flute and bassoon. The next variation is for orchestra, with interpolated phrases by the piano. Then there follows an episode which spins out the material into a lovely continuation, based upon both parts of the song. The piano winds upward very softly, and there are some soft chords for the close.

III. Allegro. Mozart usually ends gaily. And this is no exception. The piano begins at once with the joyous theme, a carefree dance, with a lightly sketched accompaniment of strings. First violins take over the dance somewhat more boisterously. The piano goes on with the second stanza, culminating in trills and a gyrating run. This brings back the first dance, scored much as before. The orchestra continues with a more powerful passage first, and then with a lovely song for clarinet and horn. It tapers off for bassoon, and then flute.

A few bars of powerful rhythm by the orchestra, and then the piano has this new theme. As usual it ends in delicate embellishment, the lovely curve of piano arabesquerie flowing ever onward. Once more alone, the piano has a new dance. Woodwinds trip it next. The piano re-enters with a more ornate version. A transitional passage leads to a return of the main dance, as before. But there is a pause, a new section (Andantino cantabile) follows, with the most luscious combinations for woodwinds. The piano too sings it very simply. At the very end it goes into soft, staccato arpeggios for the piano against plucked strings. Then there is a return to the main dance, as gay as ever. The other melodies follow in order. A cadenza is introduced into the movement. A final reference to the main theme rising to a splendid climax at the conclusion.

The orchestral part is scored for a flute, two clarinets, two bassoons, two horns, timpani, and strings.

J. G. H.

Concerto for Piano and Orchestra in A major (K. 488)

I. Allegro　　　　II. Andante　　　　III. Presto

THE MANUSCRIPTS give March as the month of composition for both the A major and the C minor concertos (K. 488 and K. 491)— a feat in speed and genius surpassed only by Mozart himself when he later wrote his three greatest symphonies in the space of six weeks! Mozart, of course, was his own soloist at the première of the A major Concerto. It may have been that concert, or some similar event, that Ambros Rieder recalled in his memoirs many years after Mozart's death:

> I cannot describe my astonishment when I happened to be so fortunate as to hear the immortal W. A. Mozart. . . . I had never been accustomed to hear anything so great or so wonderful. Such bold flights of fancy, that seem to attain the highest regions, were alike a marvel and a delight to the most experienced of

musicians. Even to this day, although a very old man, I can still hear those heavenly harmonies, and die in the firm conviction that there has only been one Mozart.

Rossini's own conviction was even more sweeping: "There is *only* Mozart."

The A major Concerto is one of fifteen such works composed by Mozart between 1782 and 1786. Constantly experimenting and developing, he had achieved a new synthesis in this medium. The solo piano had moved toward closer intimacy and teamwork with the orchestra. Solo instrument and orchestra were now more firmly integrated in a scheme of common endeavor. And with this new fusion appeared a fresh fund of expressive power. The emotional range had widened, and a brooding poetry often filled the slow movements. There was a new depth and a new sense of stress and conflict in these concertos. One has only to read Mozart's letters—the grim record of mounting bills, the drab chronicles of intrigue and chill reception, the growing domestic turmoil, the sharpening sense of fatalism—to surmise what lies behind this deepening vein. The piano concerto had become, perhaps, the favored medium for expressing his innermost feelings.

Whatever personal secret lies embedded in the Andante of the A major Concerto, there is no escaping its troubled mood. There is subdued passion here and a haunting pathos. Mozart seems preoccupied with some tragic line of thought.

L. B.

The first of the new trilogy, the Concerto in A major (K. 488), is in many respects unique among his last period works. Reading extramusical significances into a Mozart concerto is a foolish sort of business, yet one cannot help but feel a profoundly human maturity in every bar of the music, a serenity and a pathos which comes from something more than long experience in putting notes on paper. Apart from the slow movement, which is a passionate *siciliana* totally plunged into the most heart-gripping melancholy, the mood of the concerto is difficult to define. It is neither wholly nor in part a comedy or a tragedy or something in between, a tragicomedy like *Don Giovanni*. It does not conveniently alternate its cogitations between the troubled midnight and the noon's repose. Rather, like the late Shakespearean plays, its essence lies in an elusive series of emotional contradictions: a calm inquietude, a reflective laughter, and a strange sort of late autumn indulgence toward the gallant gestures and the elegant phraseology of his adolescence and early manhood. It is easier to describe what this concerto is not. It is not a sentimentalist's cliché done in the image of a wise old man gently reflecting on the joys and sorrows of his species; nor is it a jovial and sunny middle age grown a bit crotchety under the inevitably encroaching winter of his discontent; nor, once again, is there an ounce of that calm resignation, that hypocritical long patience which Shakespeare knew as a mask for despair. It is simply that this engaging, ingenuous, and often vivacious music discovers, every now and again, like a character in *The Winter's Tale,* that the "heart dances, but not for joy."

A. V. (2)

In the A major Concerto Mozart again succeeded in meeting his public halfway without sacrificing anything of his own individuality. He never wrote another first movement so simple in its structure, so "normal" in its thematic relations between tutti and solo, or so clear in its thematic invention, even where it makes excursions into the realm of counterpoint, or contains rhythmic peculiarities. The key of A major is for Mozart the key of many colors. It has the transparency of a stained-glass window.

    I. There are relations between the first movement of this concerto and the Clarinet Quintet. Not without reason are there no trumpets and timpani. But there are also darker shadings and concealed intensities, which the listener interested only in pleasant entertainment misses altogether. Already in this movement there is a threatening touch of F sharp minor, and the whole Andante is in that key, which Mozart otherwise avoided.

    II. The second movement is short, but it contains the soul of the work. It is the minor counterpart of the Andante of the "Prague" Symphony, even in the way it dissolves all polyphonic elements in a new style. In this movement there appears in veiled form that passion which in the Andante of the preceding concerto had revealed itself nakedly; the resignation and the hopelessness are the same.

III. And when Mozart overcomes this impression with the entrance of the rondo theme, he is a true magician. This Presto seems to introduce a breath of fresh air and a ray of sunlight into a dark and musty room. The gaiety of this uninterrupted stream of melody and rhythm is irresistible. But this is no ordinary gaiety. Again, as in the E flat major Piano Quartet, or the B flat major Piano Trio, the clarinet introduces one of those "unrelated" themes (in D major) in which the world seems perfectly balanced, and the scheme of things is fully justified. The work reverses the course of another work in A major, the violin sonata (K. 526), in which the Andante is the movement of tranquillity, and the finale sets loose a whole world of demons—another evidence of the breadth of Mozart's conception of the individuality of keys.

The orchestral portion is scored for flute, two clarinets, two bassoons, two horns, and strings.

A. E.

Concerto for Piano and Orchestra in C minor (K. 491)

I. Allegro   II. Larghetto   III. Allegretto

WHEN MOZART entered this work in his catalogue on 24 March, 1786, he completed a creative effort scarcely surpassed by that of his three last symphonies of 1788. For only twenty-two days before, on 2nd March, he had entered K. 488, and during that same month the opera *Figaro* was making heavy demands on his time. This C minor Concerto is not only the most sublime of the whole series but also one of the greatest pianoforte concertos ever composed. In its sustained imaginative power, in unity of conception, and in the amazing structure of its first movement, devised to contain and resolve stark and tragic passions within formal bounds, it reaches heights of Sophoclean grandeur. Here Mozart included in his orchestra both oboes and clarinets, as well as trumpets and drums, the largest force used in any of these concertos. Study of the autograph is most rewarding, for it reveals a great number of corrections, including two and even three drafts of certain passages. Here, as often, the perfecting of details assuredly cost Mozart much trouble.

A. H. K.

The passion that is veiled in the Andante of the A major Concerto breaks out again vehemently in the Concerto in C minor, which bears the Köchel number immediately preceding that of *Figaro*. It seems as if Mozart wished to exhaust the key that he had previously, in the Andante of the E flat major Concerto, used for an effect not quite legitimate, according to his conception of art as a heightened expression of feeling. At the same time there is a secret connection between this great, somber work and the C minor Serenade for Wind Instruments, of 1782. The concerto is related to *Figaro* as the serenade is to *Die Entführung,* even though the serenade was not finished until shortly after the completion of the *Singspiel*. But in March, 1786, *Figaro* was also practically finished. In both instances, Mozart evidently needed to indulge in an explosion of the dark, tragic, passionate emotions. There is a connection of a different sort with the Clavier Concerto in D minor, which shows Mozart's concerto form at its most dramatic. This C minor Concerto is another one that is a little Beethovenish; at least Beethoven admired it, and paid a certain homage to it in his own C minor Concerto, Op. 37. But Mozart's C minor Concerto is superior to the one in D minor. It is symphonic rather than simply in dialogue form, and the use of the richest orchestration Mozart had ever employed in a concerto—including both oboes and clarinets and with the wind instruments, both soli and as a body, taking a more prominent part than ever—is only external evidence of this fact. The passion in this work is deeper. Its affirmations of the key—all the modulations, no matter how far they wander, seem only to confirm the principal key—are more inevitable, more inexorable. Even when E flat major is arrived at, the way remains strait and thorny.

Nothing is left of the ideal march; this first movement is in 3/4 meter. Nothing is left of any compromise with social music, as in the finale of the D minor Concerto; this finale is an uncanny, revolutionary quick-march consisting of variations with free "episodes" (actually anything but episodes), which represent glimpses of Elysian fields—but the conclusion is a return to the inevitable.

It is hard to imagine the expression on the faces of the Viennese public when on 7 April, 1786, Mozart played this work at one of his subscription concerts. Perhaps they contented themselves with the Larghetto, which moves in regions of the purest and most moving tranquillity, and has a transcendent simplicity of expression.

A. E.

That he [Mozart] can be quite gloomy, though without ever sacrificing the most limpid euphony, is shown by the next concerto, in C minor (K. 491), the work immediately preceding *Figaro* and as different from it as a rainy day from a cloudless one. However, it is almost equally unlike the only other concerto in a minor key Mozart ever wrote. Less dramatic than the D minor, it is more declamatory. It has a more classical repose of gesture, more poise and shape, more unity of atmosphere. There is nothing like the unexpected ending of the earlier work: it closes, as it began, in the dark key of C minor. The one resemblance is the rondo form of the slow movement, with rather too frequent recurrences of a subject of very much the same type. There is no dramatic episode here, however, for Mozart again takes to a serenading tone with concertizing wind instruments, and there is another *Così fan tutti*-ish episode in A flat major. The finale is a set of very original variations on a shapely and sorrowfully elegant C minor allegretto theme. If tunes really can be portraits, as Couperin wished them to be, this would be one of a well-dressed and perfectly mannered widow who lets the world guess her grief without consciously showing it. There are two beautiful incidents in major keys, but the final variation in 6/8 not only keeps to the minor to the end, but has Neapolitan depressions.

The orchestral part of the score calls for flute, two oboes, two clarinets, two bassoons, two horns, two trumpets, timpani, and strings.

E. B.

Concerto for Piano and Orchestra in C major (K. 503)

ı. Allegro maestoso   ıı. Andante   ııı. Allegretto

THIS work reverts to the rather earlier type in which Mozart concentrated the principal interest in the first movement. Despite the sparkle of the finale, the whole has a certain statuesque quality and an unimpassioned aloofness which have prevented it from winning wide popularity. Clarinets are lacking, but the scoring is bold and powerful, and the apparent reserve masks a magnificence of conception which only repeated hearings or a study of the score can fully reveal. From its position, almost midway between *Figaro* and *Don Giovanni,* K. 503 forms an epilogue to the eleven concertos written in the preceding two and a quarter years. No original cadenzas for it are extant.

A. H. K.

Chronologically, the C major Concerto nestles midway between Mozart's two operatic masterpieces, *The Marriage of Figaro,* produced in May, 1786, and *Don Giovanni,* produced late in 1787. Mozart's autograph gives December 4, 1786, as the date of completion. Like many of the other fourteen piano concertos Mozart had composed in Vienna since 1782, the C major was written for a concert series given by him during Advent, a season rivaling Lent in lucrative returns for a pianist composer in Vienna who was also a genius. As usual, Mozart was heavily in debt. The dwelling on the Schulerstrasse was expensive. Medical bills were mounting. The *Figaro* opera proved a disappointment as an immediate revenue raiser. To add to the emotional stress, Mozart's latest son, Johann Thomas Leopold, born on October 18, died less than a month later. The concert series was a sure way to raise quick funds—and, possibly, to forget. Composition came easily; performance even more easily. On December 6, only two days after finishing the C major Concerto, we find the busy little man inscribing a fresh date of completion on the manuscript of the D major Symphony (K. 504)! "As soon as he set pen to paper, the usual miracle happened," writes Eric Blom; "trouble forsook him." Could anyone begrudge Mozart this avenue of escape?

The ill luck that hounded Mozart during those bleak December days of 1786 did not stop there. Something of a curse has lain on the C major Concerto. Despite the ardent espousal of specialists, the public, until recently, scarcely knew this work. When Artur Schnabel and George Szell first collaborated in the concerto with the Vienna Symphony at the Grosser Konzerthaussaal in May, 1934, they made an astounding discovery. There was no record of a previous performance in Vienna since Mozart's time!

As for America, research among the program files for major orchestras in the Music Room of the New York Public Library revealed one definite listing—a pair of performances by Webster Aitken with Eugene Goossens and the Cincinnati Symphony on January 30 and 31, 1942. In recent years Nadia Reisenberg, in a WOR broadcast series, and Clarence Adler, on WQXR and at the Town Hall, have included it in their Mozart surveys. The rest is silence—always barring, of course, possible private and unlisted renderings.

Just why the C major has been a dark horse among Mozart's twenty-seven piano concertos it is hard to say. No less an authority than Professor Tovey ranked it with the "Jupiter" Symphony in "triumphant majesty and contrapuntal display." Perhaps one reason may be found in the treacherous rondo finale. There Mozart, exceeding himself, demands the utmost dexterity in what amounts to an endurance test for the right hand. But, then, whoever heard of fright in these days of intrepid virtuosity?

Almost alone among Mozart specialists, Blom has refused to grant the C major's claims to first rank. Ordinarily writing in highly laudatory vein about Mozart's music, the British scholar reserves some of his harshest judgments for the C major. He agrees that its technical problems make it "on the whole" the most difficult of the Mozart piano concertos. "But the performer is not sufficiently repaid by the effort of overcoming them," he insists. "For it is all rather frigid and comparatively unoriginal." Compare Professor Tovey's words about the concerto's "breadth" and "boldness and richness of style." To Blom, the C major was the one work of this period betraying "a certain laxity of spirits." To Tovey it represented Mozart at the highest maturity of his powers. Of the first movement he wrote:

"The music carries us out with its tide, and we realize that we have indeed begun a grand voyage of discovery."

The few earlier references in Mozart literature to the C major would seem to uphold Professor Tovey rather than his learned colleague. Carl Reinicke speaks of its "lively brilliance and dramatic excitement" (*"lebhafter Glanz und dramatische Erregung"*). Abert, in his revised and amplified edition of Jahn's biography, noted a quality common to all three of the late C major concertos (K. 415, K. 467, and K. 503): "A powerful, at times taut dignity, which in the last of the three is constantly struggling with all kinds of dark undercurrents, thanks to the characteristic changes of major and minor." Jahn himself described the concerto as *glänzend und prächtig*— another reference to its brilliance and splendor. Abraham Veinus's phrase for the score is suggestive: "A bit impersonal in a towering sort of way"—on the whole, though, "an inscrutable work."

What strikes one particularly is the amazing polyphonic wealth of the score, its myriad-hued texture, yielding, on closer scrutiny, ever-growing design in its intricacy of detail. The orchestration is typical of Mozart's maturest style in the imagination and resource with which he utilizes every instrument. In these later scores of Mozart, integration of piano and orchestra in a fresh and vital unity had become an established fact in concerto writing. The accompaniment is no longer merely a prop. A new reciprocal play of themes, novel coloring, and rich counterpoint serve to heighten the effect of the whole fabric, besides setting off the solo voice more vividly. In short, a new teamwork between piano and orchestra had been found.

Another remarkable feature is the way the three movements are strongly differentiated. Despite its tender second subject, a majestic spirit sweeps through the opening Allegro maestoso. Contrastingly, the second movement (Andante) is of a "celestial placidity" rarely equalled even by Mozart himself. Special vigilance is needed in the sustained song of the Andante since the performer "must express very much with very few notes." The finale (Allegretto) again leaps to a sharply divergent mood, being witty, joyous, and exuberant. Here a *perpetuum mobile* is suggested in an almost continuous span of sixteenth-note triplets. While the writing is difficult for both hands, the right is subjected to a sharper test of staying power. Special note has been taken of the development section of the opening Allegro maestoso, built on a march theme in E minor. Of it Professor Tovey writes:

> The concerto has been grand and surprising, leaving us continually mystified as to what is to happen, and now it takes shape. This theme that so happily pulls the whole design together all the way back from its single appearance in the ritornello, now moves calmly through a long series of very straightforward sequences through various keys.

> But though the sequences are simple in their steps, they are infinitely varied in coloring, and they rapidly increase in complexity until, to the surprise of any one who still believes that Mozart is a childishly simple composer, they move in eight real parts. These eight parts are in triple, or, if we count added thirds, quadruple canon, two in the strings, four in the wind with the added thirds, and two of light antiphonal scales in the pianoforte. *No such polyphony has occurred since in any concerto, except one passage in the middle of the finale of Brahms' D minor* [author's italics].

In the Andante the big moment comes when the piano builds up the second subject and returns "by a really colossal passage on a dominant pedal to the main theme in the tonic." In the rondo finale Mozart achieves a breadth of style in the free-rhythmed connecting passages between the main sections "that was never approached until surpassed by Beethoven," according to Professor Tovey.

The work was first published by Mozart's widow Constanze at her own expense in 1798. This is indicated in an Italian inscription found in that edition: *"Nr. 1 del retaggio del defunto publicato alle spese della vedova."* The *retaggio,* or legacy, alluded to was the huge mass of manuscript scores left by Mozart. The subsequent story of these posthumous publications is involved and at times dismal. There was the expected bargaining and bickering. Even Constanze's new husband, the Danish diplomat George N. Nissen, felt called upon to play a part in the transactions. He suspected chicanery on the part of the first publisher to buy up the priceless bequest. "Don't attach too much importance to his fussiness and preciseness," Constanze mollifies Johann A. André, the buyer, after casually mentioning her husband's suspicions. "See that you preserve your present good will, which, indeed, I merit in return for what I feel as your most devoted friend and servant." It seems Nissen, who kept a careful tally of successive opus issues, thought he had detected a sinister discrepancy in André's numbering.

While one of the world's greatest artistic legacies was making its way into profitable circulation, what still remained of the legator lay buried in a pauper's grave.

Besides the piano, the C major Concerto is scored for one flute, two oboes, two bassoons, two horns, two trumpets, tympani, and strings. Trumpets and timpani are omitted from the second movement.

L. B.

Concerto for Piano and Orchestra in D major ("Coronation") (K. 537)

I. Allegro   II. Larghetto   III. Allegretto

WE ARE NOW virtually at the end of Mozart's career as a concerto composer. His intensive preoccupation with the form had ceased. During 1787 he was occupied with *Don Giovanni,* but in February, 1788, he produced a solitary Piano Concerto in D major (K. 537). The tide of passion which had engulfed the concertos of 1785–86 had now swept beyond the confines of the concerto form. The D major is a splendid and mature work but not a deeply moving one. It is planned on a grand scale, brilliant pianistically, harmonically full and solid, and studded with rich though coolly woven counterpoints. There are, as in every Mozart concerto, moments of stress and introspective tenderness, but on the whole it is the objective workmanship which most consistently engages our attention. There has been a needless tendency to decry the concerto, largely, it would seem, because it makes none of the overt dramatic gestures of its immediate predecessors. This is a completely personal matter and is determined entirely by what any particular listener believes he has a right to expect from a Mozart concerto. If our expectation is always to enjoy the particular values which Mozart chooses to stress, then the fact that this work lives on a less passionate level of emotion will not hamper our pleasure in its superb craftsmanship and in the objective nobility of its style. *Coriolanus* is less dramatically compelling than *King Lear,* yet only an insensitive reader will fail to find pleasure in the play.

Mozart's own performances of this concerto are bound up with two desperate attempts to stem the flood of financial misfortune which embittered his last years. In April, 1789, he undertook a journey to Dresden, where he played the D major Concerto before the Elector of Saxony. In September, 1790, he went to Frankfort for the festivities attending the coronation of Leopold II. Although not a member of the official court retinue of composers and performers, he hoped that, among the festive crowds that had gathered from all Europe for the coronation, his music would find receptive ears and generous purses. In Dresden he was rewarded with "a very handsome snuffbox" and some money. In Frankfort he achieved a Pyrrhic victory with his concerto. "It was a splendid success," he wrote to his wife, "from the point of view of honor and glory, but a failure as far as money was concerned." It is this performance, nearly three years after the composition of the work, which has given it its misleading title as the "Coronation" Concerto. A second piano concerto was also performed for the occasion, probably the one in F major (K. 459).

A. V. (2)

There is no question that it was the proper work for festive occasions. It is very Mozartean, while at the same time it does not express the whole or even the half of Mozart. It is, in fact, so "Mozartesque" that one might say that in it Mozart imitated himself—no difficult task for him. It is both brilliant and amiable, especially in the slow movement; it is very simple, even primitive, in its relation between the solo and the tutti, and so completely easy to understand that even the nineteenth century always grasped it without difficulty. It has become, along with the D minor, the best known of Mozart's piano concertos. This popularity illustrates once again the strange fact that those works are often held to be particularly characteristic which do not survive in wholly authentic form. For Mozart left the solo part of this concerto in an especially sketchy state. Now, we do not know exactly how he played any of his concertos. Only four were published during his lifetime, and while in his autographs he wrote out the orchestra parts with complete care, he did not do the same with the solo parts; indeed it would have been in his interest not to write them out at all, so as not to lead unscrupulous copyists into temptation. For he knew perfectly well what he had to play. The solo parts in the form in which they survive are always only a suggestion of the actual performance, and a constant invitation to read the breath of life into them. But the solo part of this D major Concerto in particular is no more than a bare sketch, obviously entered into the score by Mozart simply to refresh his memory, consisting mostly of a single line with only the more polyphonic passages written out for both hands. Suffice it to say that only the accompaniment of the rondo theme survives in Mozart's own authentic version. Who was responsible for the version of the solo part that is accepted by pianists without questions? I suspect that it was Johann André, who brought out the first edition of the work, in parts, in 1794. For the most part, this version is extremely simple and not too offensive, but at times—for example in the accompaniment of the Larghetto theme—it is very clumsy, and the whole solo part would gain infinitely by revision and refinement in Mozart's own style. No other work—unless it be the score of *Figaro*—shows more clearly how badly we need a new edition of Mozart's works.

Besides piano, the scoring of the "Coronation" Concerto calls for one flute, two oboes, two bassoons, two horns, two trumpets, timpani, and strings.

A. E.

Concerto for Piano and Orchestra in B flat major (K. 595)

I. Allegro   II. Larghetto   III. Allegro

ANOTHER *hors d'oeuvre*, though in quite a different sense, is the piano Concerto in B flat (K. 595), Mozart's last, completed on January 5 of the year of which he did not live to see the end. He played it on March 4, 1791—not in an "academy" of his own, which the Viennese public would no longer support, but at a concert of the clarinetist Joseph Bähr, in the concert hall of the Court-Caterer Jahn in the Himmelpfortgasse (Gate-of-Heaven-Road). Indeed, the work stands "at the gate of heaven," at the door of eternity. But when we term this concerto a work of farewell we do so not at all from sentimentality, or from any misconception of this "last concerto for clavier." In the eleven months that remained to him, Mozart wrote a great deal of various kinds of music; it was not in the Requiem that he said his last word, however, but in this work, which belongs to a species in which he also said his greatest. This is the musical counterpart to the confession he made in his letters to the effect that life had lost attraction for him. When he wrote this concerto, he had two terrible years behind him, years of disappointment in every sense, and 1790 had been even more terrible than 1789. He no longer rebelled against his fate, as he had in the G minor Symphony, to which, not only in key, but in other ways as well, this concerto is a sort of complement. Both these works, and only these, begin with a prefatory measure that established the "atmosphere" of the key, like the *Eroica* or a symphony by Bruckner. The mood of resignation no longer expresses itself loudly or emphatically; every stirring of energy is rejected or suppressed; and this fact makes all the more uncanny the depths of sadness that are touched in the shadings and modulations of the harmony. The Larghetto is full of a religious, or, as Mr. Girdlestone calls it, a "Franciscan" mildness; the finale breathes a veiled joyfulness, as if blessed children were playing in Elysian fields, joyful, but without hate and without love. Mozart used the theme of this rondo a few days later for a song entitled "Sehnsucht nach dem Frühlinge" (Longing for Spring). The theme has the resigned cheerfulness that comes from the knowledge that this is the last spring. But the most moving thing about it is that in it Mozart received the divine gift of being able *zu sagen was er leide* (to tell the fullness of his suffering). This last piano concerto is also a work of the highest mastery in invention—invention that has the quality of that "second naïveté" of which we have spoken, welding the solo and tutti parts into the richest, closest relation, speaking in the most transparent sonority, and fusing perfectly the galant and "learned" styles. It is so perfect that the question of style has become meaningless. The very act of parting from life achieves immortality.

A. E.

For some of its material, Mozart seems to have drawn, unconsciously or not, upon ideas in certain of his earlier scores. Thus the subject for the first violins which, beginning at the second bar, opens the first movement (Allegro, B flat major, 4/4), bears an unmistakable likeness to the opening subject to the Romanze of the D minor Piano Concerto, composed six years earlier. The two melodies are not, of course, in their entirety, identical; but the second bar of the violin melody of the B flat Allegro contains a phrase of half a dozen notes which is virtually the same as a phrase in the famous melody of the earlier Romanze—though the difference between the tempi of the two movements tends to disguise the resemblance. There is also a likeness, less marked, between the first measure of the theme for the piano which begins the Larghetto of the B flat Concerto and the opening subject of the Andante of the E flat Symphony composed three years before. But a more striking resemblance is that between the ascending chromatic phrase which forms the fourth measure of the opening theme of the Larghetto and the ascending chromatic phrase that is so memorable a feature of the Andante of the "Prague" Symphony (K. 504, composed in 1786). The two phrases are most nearly alike in the fourth bar of the Larghetto of the concerto and the seventh bar of the Andante of the symphony. In both cases, this phrase is an important element in the melodic texture of the respective movements.

i. The opening theme of the first Allegro of the concerto—a theme noteworthy for its romantic lyricism—is enunciated by the strings alone. It is soon broken in upon by an energetic motive for the wind (flute, oboes, bassoons, and horns), which intrudes at the fifth bar upon the quiet flow of the strings.

After this material has been developed for seventy-three measures, the piano enters with a solo based upon the chief theme, but exquisitely adorned with a gruppetto. Four bars later, the orchestra enters with an accompaniment figure based on the formerly energetic wind motive, now uttered quietly by the strings. In the *Durch-*

führung, the chief subject achieves a warmly lyrical expansiveness
that is rare even for Mozart (one of the remarkable features of this
development section is the appearance of the chief theme in the
irrubrically distant tonality of B minor!).

II. The Larghetto (E flat major, 4/4) opens with an eight-bar solo
for the piano, introducing the theme alluded to above. The orchestra
takes it up, in a *forte;* the piano is again heard in a longer solo; and
then the strings and wind bring forward a more vigorous theme.

III. The final movement is a captivating rondo (Allegro, B flat
major, 6/8), begun by the piano alone, and evolved with brilliant
and exhilarating vitality and resourcefulness. In the middle section
we encounter, surprisingly enough, what seems to be a reminiscence
of the ascending chromatic phrase from the Larghetto, extended and
intensified.

The instrumentation of the concerto is for flute, two oboes, two
bassons, two horns, and strings.

L. G.

Concerto for Two Pianos in E flat major (K. 365)

I. Allegro   II. Andante   III. Rondo

THE TWO concertos Mozart composed in 1779 after his return to
Salzburg from Paris are both for two soloists. The *Sinfonia Concertante* (K. 364) for violin and viola is no doubt the greater of the
two, a restless and deeply emotional work into which Mozart poured
some of his most profoundly moving music. This concerto for two
pianos is a companion piece to it. They were written the same year
and they are in the same key. But the dark coloration of the *Sinfonia
Concertante* is only occasionally in evidence here; e.g., the recapitulation in the first movement, the middle episodes of the second and
third movements. For the most part, the disappointments Mozart
had experienced on his trip and the aggravations of an unwilling
return to Salzburg are not reflected. The work was written for himself and his sister Nannerl, a domestic piece, so to speak, and one

of his most enjoyable concertos both to listen to and to perform. It has a lean vigor, a supple graciousness of melodic line, and a wonderful felicitousness in the handling of both the relationship of the two soloists to each other and their joint relationship to the orchestra.

A. V. (1)

Not a great work, but technically a most attractive one by reason of the composer's joy in the special problem of co-ordinating two keyboards. His effects are sometimes quite unlike what could have been obtained from any other combination, as though they came from some transfigured, heavenly barrel-organ.

This double concerto is a joy for two pianists to play even without an orchestra: it is singularly engaging to participate in those surprisingly rich figurations one seems apparently to be producing all oneself without any corresponding effort.[1] It is also pleasant to change over parts, as the two instruments by no means play exactly the same themes. The slow movement is fastidiously ornamented, and the final rondo abounds in good humour. The way in which Mozart makes the cadential phrase at the end of the subject take different harmonic turns is irresistibly comic as well as infallibly artistic.

E. B.

1. Allegro, E flat major, 4/4. The orchestral exposition opens at once with the principal theme in the full orchestra *forte*. After a pause on the chord of B flat major, the second subject of this first exposition enters *piano* in the second violins and violas, its opening phrase being repeated with fuller scoring. The exposition for the solo instruments is, as to its first phrase, introduced with the principal subject in both pianos. A dialogue between the two solo instruments leads to the second theme—different to that in the orchestral exposition—given to the first piano, in B flat, and then repeated by the second. There is another section of the subject, also alternating in the two pianos, and followed by a tutti six bars long, based on a portion of the first exposition. The pianos also take up a figure originally employed in the orchestral exposition, and there is passage

---

[1] All the concertos, it may be said here, are delightful to play on two pianos with a second piano part arranged from the full score.

work for both. A tutti brings forward what had previously been the second theme in the opening exposition; this orchestral matter alternates with material for the pianos, and finally leads into the recapitulation, in which the first phrase of the principal subject is given out, as before, by the full orchestra *forte*. The remainder of the theme is allotted to the pianos. The second subject now appears (in the first piano) in E flat major. At the close of this there are suggestions of the opening theme, and passage work for the pianos leads to a tutti, which, in its turn, paves the way for a cadenza for the solo instruments. The cadenza is succeeded by a final tutti constructed of material taken from the first exposition.

II. Andante, B flat major, 3/4. The principal subject is announced by the strings, oboe, and bassoon. At the eleventh measure it is taken up by the pianos. A new idea is introduced in the piano parts in E flat major, and this is followed by a return to the first theme in B flat. A quiet coda closes the movement.

III. Rondo. Allegro. E flat major, 2/4. The principal theme is announced by the first violins. The first piano enters with an episode, which is repeated an octave lower by the second. A suggestion of the first subject is played by the orchestra, and passage work for the pianos follows. The principal theme now finds repetition in the first piano part, and it is taken up by a tutti. A second episode in C minor is allotted to the pianos. The principal theme returns in the second piano, and is continued by the orchestra. Development of it follows, with a triplet accompaniment, in the two pianos alternately. Scale passages for these instruments lead to a tutti, which serves as an introduction to a cadenza. The first piano, accompanied by triplets in the second, gives out the principal theme for the last time, and a tutti brings the concerto to a close.

The orchestral accompaniment is scored for two oboes (two clarinets), bassoon, two horns, and strings.

F. B.

2. THE VIOLIN CONCERTOS

FIVE VIOLIN concertos (K. 207, 211, 216, 218, and 219), his most notable contribution to this specific form, were composed in 1775, his nineteenth year. Taken all in all, this series is an amazing performance. It would seem that nineteen is hardly the age for the production of earth-shaking masterpieces. In all truth, there have been greater wonders than these concertos known in the world, some of them the productions of the maturer Mozart; yet many a reputable composer thrice his age would have fallen over his academic shoelaces for a chance to claim as his own the incredible fluency of musical speech, the richness of texture, and the sheer beauty of melodic line that pervades this music. A genius at any age, nineteen or ninety, is one of the earth's unaccountable eccentricities, and it takes a long-standing experience in believing, like the Red Queen, "six impossible things before breakfast" to credit, on the one hand, a Titian in his nineties painting with the fresh exuberance of a young man first discovering the manifold wonders of a colorful world, and, on the other, a youth of nineteen maneuvering through the infinite complexities of the sound-world with a surety and a wisdom which he lacked years enough to derive from experience. It is the surety, the conscious command of his craft, which is most astonishing. These five concertos are, as Eric Blom has noted, the earliest of his music to maintain itself permanently in the world's concert repertoire; nor are the reasons hard to find, for Mozart's style at this period is the last word in elegance and refinement. Lest these much-maligned adjectives be misconstrued, let it be understood that at no time was Mozart capable of simulating the hard elegance, the inanimate refinement of polished enamel or carved ivory. There are moments of self-conscious "gallantry" in the concertos, just as there are moments of genuine tenderness. The elegance of the concertos is at no point a factor of shallowness of feeling, but a component rather of the mobile grace, the conscious sophistication which we associate naturally with all that is youthful, living, and lovely. To be sure, the profound agitations and the exalted sorrows of the G minor Symphony, the D minor piano Concerto, the great Requiem, will not be found in the five violin concertos, for such difficult emotions presuppose, in addition to a knowledge of the craft of composition, both the personal experience and the inner mastery of profound misfortune. Part of the groundwork for this was being laid in Mozart's service to the Salzburg Archbishop, but at the moment this undercurrent of unhappiness had broken to the surface neither in his life nor in his music.

While each of the five is an entity in itself, there are a few basic resemblances in general technique which may be noted. Purely for its sheer abundance of melody this series deserves to be ranked among the richest contributions to the violinist's repertoire. Melodies of surpassing loveliness are piled thick and fast one upon the other; so much so that often Mozart bothers not even to write in a little transitional fanfare or a scale sequence to bridge the distance from one melody to another. Even for the main melodies in a sonata-form movement he does little more than spare the time and space for their repetitions in the necessary places. In the first movement of the fourth Concerto in D major (K. 218), where the embarrassment of riches is especially evident, the music becomes so crowded with new ideas that the main subject of the movement is soon lost sight of completely and fails to reappear even in the final recapitulation of all leading melodies. So far as the development of themes is concerned, more often than not, in place of the extension of an already established subject we are given a group of new ideas with only a general feeling of kinship with the old. Mozart's creative genius was truly at a fever pitch. Beautiful melodies evolved with too much spontaneous rapidity for him to have been overly concerned with extracting the ultimate amount of flavor from any one of them. Structurally, if not emotionally, these concertos are rhapsodies controlled by an innate refinement of expression and an unerring sense of inner form. The counterpoints of the previous period are wholly forgotten. These works are ruled by an expansive spirit, by a continual sense of the imminent discovery of a new melodic kingdom. While in the last three concertos the orchestration is quite substantial, in the first two (K. 207, 211) the orchestral load is noticeably lightened to speed the voyage of discovery. There is little time for a tourist's meditation on the swiftly passing landscape. The time had not yet come when, as in the G minor Symphony, Mozart could probe with a passionate and single-minded concentration the ultimate depths of the profoundly tender little motive which opens the work. The world, at nineteen, is too full of wonderful variety, and these concertos, for all their maturity, are an eager reflection of this world.

The concertos were designed principally for Mozart's own use, and also for Gaetano Brunetti, who served as concertmaster in the Salzburg court orchestra. They are undoubtedly an accurate reflection of Mozart's style of violin playing. In one of his letters he tells us that, when he performed the fourth Concerto in D major (K. 218), it "went like oil," adding that "everyone praised my beautiful, pure tone." If this describes his violin technique, it also describes the quality of the concertos. They should go like oil, and a violinist needs to bring to this music not so much an extravagant virtuoso technique as a pure and beautiful tone. As a concession to Brunetti, Mozart composed two alternate movements to the concertos. One was an Adagio (K. 261) to replace the slow movement of the fifth Concerto in A major (K. 219). Leopold Mozart subsequently recalled it to his son's memory by describing it as the Adagio "which you wrote specially for Brunetti, because he found the other one too artificial." Brunetti certainly had peculiar taste. It is interesting that Mozart did not stalk off in outraged dignity, as we are told geniuses are supposed to do when the value of their work is questioned. Music was then a commodity intended primarily for use, not for gathering dust in attics or library cellars where it might enjoy only the ceremonial obeisances of the elite. Mozart found it inconsistent neither with his integrity nor his genius to indulge the limitations of a colleague's taste, although one can only wish that for the sake of such work as *Don Giovanni,* for example, Mozart had not felt compelled to humor the whims of his singers with the odds and ends which now stand interpolated in the score. The other alternate movement composed for Brunetti is a Rondo Concertante (K. 269) to replace the final movement of the first Concerto in B flat major (K. 207). Both alternate movements date from 1776, the year following the composition of the concertos. The substitution of a rondo finale in the first violin concerto brings it in line with the second, third, and fourth concertos, each of which concludes with a rondo movement. The fact that Mozart used the French form of the word, "rondeau," has been taken, along with general stylistic considerations, as evidence of the influence of the French *galant* violin concerto upon Mozart. Be that as it may—and the point is not an unlikely one—the final movement of the fifth concerto (K. 219) is blessed by a trio section which is an uninhibited Hungarian rhapsody, the kind of wonderful folkish outburst one expects to find in Haydn rather than in Mozart.

The fourth violin concerto (K. 218) has a close analogue in a Concerto in D major by Luigi Boccherini (1743–1805).[1] The Boccherini work was composed in 1768, seven years prior to the Mozart concerto, and intended for Fillipino Manfredi, a noted violinist and a friend of the composer. Despite the general thematic similarity between the two works, the influence of the Boccherini concerto can easily be exaggerated. Mozart's indebtedness to Boccherini is of much the same variety as the indebtedness of a creative portrait painter to the physical features of the subject who poses for him. There is a decided resemblance in the physical outline of the melodies, but in the spirit which animates the Mozart concerto we recognize only Mozart and positively no one else. For example, the opening theme in the second movement of the Mozart concerto is taken over verbatim from Boccherini. Yet in Boccherini this theme is merely an inner voice accompaniment taken in the tenor part of the harmony, whereas in Mozart it is elevated note for note to the position of the first theme of the movement: a pearl that Boccherini neglected and Mozart seized upon. This melody appears, incidentally, in an ingenious rhythmic disguise in the final movement of the Mozart concerto, and curiously enough in still another rhythmic variant also in the finale of a *concertone* in C major (K. 190) composed by Mozart in 1773. The resemblance to Boccherini in this particular case may be accidental; just as the resemblance between the opening of Mozart's fifth violin Concerto in A major (K. 219) and the opening of the Vivaldi violin concerto, Op. 6, No. 4, undoubtedly is. The fourth Mozart Concerto in D major (K. 218) was referred to by Mozart and his father as the "Strassburg" Concerto. A theme in the final rondo is reminiscent of a Strassburg dance.

The remaining works for violin and orchestra can only be summarized here. They comprise mainly compositions whose authenticity is doubtful. The first is the famous "Adelaide" Concerto, which Mozart supposedly composed at the age of ten. It is a joyously naïve little work and has been edited by Casadesus with three cadenzas by

---

[1] Boccherini is the composer of several lovely 'cello concertos. The best known, the 'cello concerto in B flat, is still often heard in our concert halls. It combines a nicety and precision of detail with a type of warm Italianate melody rich in sentiment and devoid of sentimentality.

Paul Hindemith. Whether or not its creation would be beyond the capacity of a ten-year-old is an irrelevant question in Mozart's case. The concerto was supposed to have been written at Versailles for the French Princess Adélaïde. A dedicatory letter from Mozart to the Princess is extant, but for a variety of reasons both the letter and the concerto are open to question. The *concertone* (K. 190) for two violins and orchestra is authentic Mozart. It was composed in 1773 and bears, in its first movement, abundant evidence of the contrapuntal writing characteristic of Mozart's "serious" style that year. It is a minor contemporary of the first Piano Concerto in D major (K. 175), and much smaller in stature than the violin concertos of 1775. The other violin concertos (K. 268 and 271a) have been doubtfully attributed to Mozart, although it is probable that they are in part his work. It has been suggested, for example, for the E flat major Violin Concerto (K. 268) that the form in which it now survives is a reworking of Mozartean material by Johann Friedrich Eck, a Munich violinist who had heard the work performed by Mozart. The authenticity of the D major Concerto (K. 271a) is likewise doubtful, although the finale contains a motive also used by Mozart in his ballet *Les Petits Riens*. There has been no general agreement among scholars on the two concertos as they now stand. From a musical and technical standpoint they are markedly different from the five violin concertos of 1775, although they fall comfortably enough within the general framework of what one may call a Mozartean style. While the two concertos contain much worth-while music, they are dominated by a virtuoso spirit foreign to the five clearly authentic violin concertos. In the case of the D major Concerto (K. 271a) this has been explained on the basis of Mozart's need for a display piece during his Paris visit. The enlarged proportions of the two concertos are, unlike his later piano concertos, not a result of the greater scope of his musical ideas, but principally a matter of making room for a brilliant virtuosity which is spread-eagled over the broad surface of the music. The last work for violin and orchestra is a Rondo (K. 373) which Mozart composed for Brunetti in April, 1781, and which also appeared in a flute transcription (K. Anh. 184).

A. V. (2)

Dyneley Hussey considered the five concertos "magnificent examples" of Mozart's work of the Salzburg period, though he conceded that they are not completely faultless in the matter of style, noting what he called the "routinier working out." Whereas Hussey found them largely French in form and style, Pitts Sanborn maintained they revealed the nineteen-year-old Mozart as "an accomplished cosmopolitan." To the former Philharmonic-Symphony annotator the concertos were "German in melody and Italian in the violin technic and to a lesser degree in the melody."

A. Hyatt King has also written discerningly of these concertos: "To pass from the pianoforte concertos to those for violin, is rather like a descent from a great range of mountains to the lower slopes along their foothills. But here the air is just as fresh as on the majestic peaks, and the surroundings gain not a little by being more intimate. It is, emphatically, transition—not anticlimax, for the violin concertos contain better music than the harpsichord concertos (except K. 271) of nearly the same period. Indeed, Mozart, being a good enough violinist to appear as soloist in public, and fully competent to take the viola in quartet playing, could write his concertos with an expert hand, and though not always as difficult as the first violin parts in some of his divertimenti, they do not fall far short of the highest standards of that day. . . . All these works for violin bear eloquent testimony to the cosmopolitan nature of his style at this period. In the first and second movements the smooth cantilena shows strong influence of the northern Italian composers such as Sammartini. Most of the finales are headed 'rondeau,' a spelling which fully accords with the French style in which, broadly, these delightful movements are written. Where an element of seriousness breaks in, it is in that finely-drawn Germanic mood which lends such an intimate, personal quality to many of Mozart's works at this time."

Joining in the international hunt, Eric Blom traced Hungarian gypsy influences in the A major Concerto, a theory later sustained by Abraham Veinus, who caught Magyar echoes in the middle section of the finale. One passage in the Rondo, a kind of "alla turca," admits Turkey to the conference table of this polyglot concerto.

The five concertos have many points in common. They are in

three movements:—an opening Allegro, in which the solo violin and accompanying instruments alternate in elaborating the themes; a slow movement (either Andante or Adagio), in which a central melody is woven in the style of a romanza or "pastoral arioso" and a gay Rondo finale. The accompaniment is usually modest.

Concerto for Violin and Orchestra in G major (K. 216)

I. Allegro   II. Adagio   III. Rondeau: Allegro

WE KNOW from the manuscript of the G major Concerto that it was completed by Mozart on September 12, 1775. The autograph reads: "Concerto di Violino di Wolfgango Amadeo Mozart mp. Salisburgo li 12 di Septembre 1775." As the third in the series of five it represents a bold stride forward from the preceding two, an astonishing advance that has long puzzled the Mozart scholars, among them Alfred Einstein who expresses his bewilderment in these words:

"What had happened in the three months that separate the second concerto from the third? We do not know. Suddenly there is a new depth and richness to Mozart's whole language. Instead of an Andante there is an Adagio that seems to have fallen straight from heaven, in which flutes take the place of oboes, and in which the key of D major has a quite new character. All three movements, besides being on a higher level, contain the surprises of which we have previously spoken, and in a double sense: as when, in the Adagio, the solo returns once more to speak with poignant intensity; or when, in the Rondo, the ending comes in the winds . . . or when the recapitulation of the magnificent first movement is introduced by an eloquent recitative. Suddenly the whole orchestra begins to speak and to enter into a new, intimate relation with the solo part. Nothing is more miraculous in Mozart's work than the appearance of this concerto at this stage in his development. . . ."

I. In the opening Allegro (G major, 4/4), the first and second themes are expounded by the orchestra before the solo instrument makes its appearance. There is a key shift in D major when the violin takes up the second theme. Towards the end there is a cadenza followed by a brief coda.

II. Accompanying strings begin the main theme of the Adagio (D major, 4/4). Soon the solo violin steps in to complete the statement of this theme, out of which the movement is largely constructed.

III. The finale (Rondeau: Allegro, G major, 3/8) offers the sprightly first theme among the strings, the violin later introducing the second subject in D major. There are graceful shifts from Allegro to Andante to Allegretto in the course of the movement. A courtly episode in G minor occurs about midway, where the violin and accompanying instruments gracefully step in and out of a dance-like ceremony.

Both Joseph Joachim and Eugene Ysaye devised cadenzas for the G major Concerto.

In the original, the G major Concerto calls for two violins, viola, bass, two oboes (two flutes), and two horns.

L. B.

Concerto for Violin and Orchestra in D major (K. 218)

I. Allegro   II. Andante cantabile   III. Rondo: Andante grazioso; Allegro ma non troppo

THE CONCERTO in D major is very different from its predecessor in G. It is much more sensuous in sonority, and this quality springs not only from the choice of the more brilliant key, but also from the nature of the model Mozart undoubtedly had in mind. This model is the violin concerto in the same key of Boccherini, written about ten years earlier; the two works have almost the same structure, and their thematic relations are palpable. But the saying *Facile inventis addere* is just as little applicable here as in many another case. It took Mozart to add spirit and wit to the sensuousness of Boccherini's work. The Andante cantabile is in reality an uninterrupted song for the violin, and an avowal of love. The Rondo combines Italian and French elements, in that, as in the third concerto, it interpolates little humorous episodes containing references familiar to its listeners: a gavotte, and a musette mentioned several times in the Mozart correspondence as being of Strassburg. This concerto too ends in a *pianissimo* whisper. It is a work of the spirit, not one intended to have a great effect.

A. E.

Mozart's own nickname for the D major was "the Strassburg Concerto." That information comes from a letter he wrote to his father on October 23, 1777. Mozart had had lunch [on the 19th] at the Heiligkreuz Monastery, it seems, and he spoke of the occasion as follows:

> During the meal we had some music. In spite of their poor fiddling, I prefer the monastery players to the Augsburg orchestra. I performed a symphony and played Vanhall's Violin Concerto in B flat, which was unanimously applauded. The Dean, who is a cousin of Eberlin, by name Zeschinger, is a fine, jolly fellow and knows Papa quite well. In the evening at supper I played my Strassburg Concerto, which went like oil. Everyone praised my beautiful, pure tone.

I. Allegro, D major, 4/4. The movement opens with the orchestral exposition usual in Mozart's day. The principal subject is announced in octaves by the full orchestra. The second theme is brought forward in D major by the strings. The solo instrument enters with the principal subject, which is in two sections. Passage work for the violin leads to the second theme, in A major, which is also played by the solo instrument. A short tutti follows, leading to the development section, which is, however, largely occupied by passage work for the violin. The recapitulation omits the first, vigorous section of the principal theme, and begins with the second. The second subject, now in D major, is given to the violin, as before. A tutti five measures long leads to a cadenza, and at the conclusion of this movement comes to an end with a short coda.

II. Andante cantabile, A major, 3/4. The first theme is given out by the orchestra, the solo instrument taking its share of it eleven measures later. The second subject is introduced by the violin in E major. The first theme returns in the original key, and it is followed by a repetition of the second, again given to the solo instrument, and now in A major. A cadenza is followed by a short coda.

III. Rondo: Andante grazioso, D major, 2/4. The solo violin announces the first theme. At its conclusion there is a pause, and the tempo changes to Allegro ma non troppo, and the time to 6/8. The violin brings forward the subject of this section, and also a new idea in A major. The Andante grazioso material returns, followed again by that of the Allegro ma non troppo. In the middle of this there is an episode for the solo instrument consisting of passage work in B minor (Andante grazioso, 2/2 time). A new subject is presented in G major by the violin, lightly accompanied by the strings (Allegro ma non troppo). A portion of this former material is developed, and, ending in a pause, is followed by a cadenza. The Andante grazioso returns, to be succeeded by a final presentation of the subject originally heard in the Allegro ma non troppo.

The concerto in D is scored as to its accompaniment for orchestra for two oboes, two horns, and strings.

F. B.

Concerto for Violin and Orchestra in A major (K. 219)

I. Allegro aperto   II. Adagio   III. Rondo: Tempo di menuetto

IN WIT and rhythmical variety, in elegance and imaginative power, this work not only excels Mozart's four other concertos for violin, but has no rival throughout the second half of the eighteenth century. Even if he had returned to this form during the years of his Viennese maturity it is doubtful if he could have surpassed the freshness and gracious beauty of this crowning masterpiece of 1775.

A. H. K.

This concerto is unsurpassed for brilliance, tenderness, and wit. Even a new middle movement (K. 261), which Mozart wrote late in 1776 "especially" for the violinist Brunetti, "because he found the other one too studied" (letter of Leopold, 9 October, 1777), despite its tenderness and its enchanted, shimmering sonority, cannot match the simplicity and innocence of the original Adagio. The first and last movements are full of surprises: in the first movement, the half improvisatory way in which the violin makes its appearance, possibly inspired by a clavier concerto of Philipp Emanuel Bach in D, published in 1772, and the alternation between gracefulness in march tempo, good-natured roughness, and cajolery; in the last movement, instead of quotations such as had occurred in the rondos of the two preceding works, a humorous outbreak of sound and fury in "Turkish" style. Mozart borrowed the noisy tutti in A minor of this "Turkish" intermezzo from himself: it had originally occurred in the ballet *Le Gelosie del serraglio,* which he wrote in 1773 in Milan for his *Lucio Silla.* It is in duple meter, and contrasts as naturally as it combines with the irresistible *Tempo di minuetto* of the main portion of the movement.

A. E.

1. Allegro aperto, A major, 4/4. The opening movement of the concerto differs slightly, as to the handling of the material which begins it, from other concertos by Mozart and by masters of his day. The double exposition is made up of two movements, only the first of which has any connection with the material of the main movement which follows them. The first of these is an Allegro thirty-nine measures long; the second—separated from the first by a pause—is an Adagio in which the subject is given out by the solo violin, accompanied by a thirty-second note figure in the first and second violins. This slow section is only six measures in length and is followed by the principal theme of the main movement, stated by the solo instrument accompanied by the strings. The subject in the orchestra is that which began the first exposition, but above it there is allotted to the solo violin a new theme. A transitional passage leads to the second subject, played by the solo instrument in E major, lightly accompanied by the first and second violins. A tutti is followed by the development section—a division which is short and which is succeeded by the recapitulation in which the principal subject is presented as at the opening of the second exposition. The

second theme now is in A major. Toward the close of the movement
a cadenza is introduced, and this is followed by a coda seven measures long.

II. Adagio, E major, 2/4. The principal subject is heard first in
the orchestra, the actual theme being set forth by the first violins.
At the twenty-second measure the solo instrument enters with the
same theme, which almost immediately is followed by the second
subject—now in B major—also given to the solo violin. There is a
tutti leading into the development section, which is short and concerned principally with the opening theme. The recapitulation has
the first theme stated by the solo violin, which also sets forth the
second, now in E major. There is a cadenza at the end.

III. Rondo: Tempo di menuetto, A major, 3/4. This movement is
a minuet having the construction of a rondo. Its principal theme
begins without introduction in the solo part, accompanied by the
strings. At the eighth measure it is taken up by the orchestra. Following this presentation there is a transitional passage leading to the
second subject, given out in E major by the violin. The principal
theme returns and is succeeded by an episode whose subject is announced in F sharp minor by the solo instrument. The first theme
reappears, once again in the violin, and this leads to an entirely new
section (Allegro, A minor, 2/4) whose material is extensively developed. At the close of this, the original theme, time and key are
restated and the movement closes softly.

Besides the strings, the accompaniment calls only for two oboes
and two horns.

F. B.

Sinfonia Concertante for Violin, Viola, and Orchestra in E flat major (K. 364)

I. Allegro maestoso   II. Andante   III. Presto

A SHROUD of silence and mystery covers the origin of this composition. That it dates from the summer or late summer of 1779,
while Mozart was still in the service of the Archbishop of Salzburg,

seems fairly certain. There is no surviving manuscript to give us the precise date and no reference in Mozart's voluminous correspondence to indicate the occasion of the première. Sketches of the few final bars of the first movement are extant, with fragments of cadenza writing on the other side. Johann André brought out the first edition of this "double concerto" in 1801. Subsequent editions include arrangements for piano (four hands), and for violin, viola, and piano (Breitkopf and Härtel). There is a strong possibility that Mozart wrote the viola part with himself in mind as soloist. Although he was a facile violinist, he began to favor the viola during the Salzburg period, a switch in allegiance that infuriated his father Leopold. Later, when Joseph Haydn used to visit him in Vienna, Mozart would play the viola in the frequent quartet sessions. Haydn would be first violinist, his friend Karl Dittersdorf second violinist, and Johann Wanhal cellist. Dittersdorf, a brilliant virtuoso, is assumed to have trained Haydn in the violin, though Haydn's first love, of course, like Mozart's, was the keyboard.

Mozart's special feeling for the viola may be noted in the writing for the solo part of the *Sinfonia Concertante*. The part for viola is written a half-tone lower, i.e., in D, instead of E flat. There was good reason for this. By tuning the viola a half-tone up, the soloist would achieve greater brightness and clarity against the supporting violas of the orchestra. Mozart probably wanted the friendly rivalry of the solo instruments to run on an evener plane. One notes this impartiality throughout the work in the treatment of the solo voices. The solo instruments move in chatty emulation, almost the precise way they do in Mozart's Concerto for Two Pianos (K. 365), which is in the same key and dates from the same period. In the allotment of melodies the basis is also one of strict equality. Shortly after composing the *Sinfonia Concertante,* Mozart tackled another for violin, viola, and cello, but never finished it. Alfred Einstein refers to this second *Concertante* as a "mighty torso" and lists it in an appendix of his monumental edition of the Köchel catalogue as No. 104.

Despite the scant hearings accorded the *Sinfonia Concertante* for violin and viola, the Mozart scholars all hail it as a creative summit of Mozart's Salzburg period. Alfred Einstein goes so far as to call it Mozart's "crowning achievement in the field of the violin concerto." Another keen Mozart student, Noel Straus, frankly affirmed in a recent review that the *Sinfonia Concertante* excelled Beethoven's triple concerto and Brahms's double concerto in its "unification and fusion of the symphonic and concertolike factors involved," Abert speaks of its "proud, dark splendor," and Eric Blom returns to this theme of dim luster by sensing still darker things:

> A beautiful, dark-colored work in which a passion not at all suited to an archiepiscopal court, and perhaps disclosing active revolt against it, seems to smolder under a perfectly decorous style and exquisite proportions.

Mr. Blom's suspicion that the *Sinfonia Concertante* hides a secret aim under its suave mantle is not so far-fetched. Mozart was not happy in the oppressive atmosphere of the Salzburg court. He had returned from triumphs in Paris and Mannheim a maturer artist with a new sense of freedom and independence. There had been stormy sessions with his employer over the court rules and regulations that bound down the young genius. Requests for leaves of absence and even complete release led to fresh unpleasantness. The final break with the Archbishop of Salzburg was to come in the spring of 1781, when Mozart appeared one day with a formal resignation. Employer and employee exchanged some candid thoughts, and the interview came to an abrupt end with the celebrated episcopal kick. The revolt that was smoldering in the *Sinfonia Concertante* of two years before had finally come to a furious and perhaps inglorious climax.

The fresh power that Mozart brought back with him from his tours throbs through all three movements of the *Sinfonia Concertante*. The work seems an epitome of Mozart's resources during those summer months of 1779. The style is broader, the feeling richer. The orchestra is no mere support, but a highly articulate participant in this symposium of theme and development. Though the solo instruments have right of way, the other instruments insist on rights of their own. There is a closer rapport between the violin and viola and the orchestra, and the emotional focus is stronger. As Einstein points out, the *Sinfonia Concertante* has broken away from the diverting gallantries of "entertainment" music. Something deeper and graver has replaced the light chatter and rippling laughter of earlier serenades. Each of the movements reveals a firmer unity of structure, the orchestra is continuously alive with fresh details, and wind instruments are assigned major thematic roles in the orchestral scheme. Mozart seems to have concentrated his strongest feelings in the first two movements, but the finale has a driving power of its own. As Abert puts it, "the dark spirits have vanished, but the strength remains."

Notable in the first movement, too, is the use of the "Mannheim crescendo," another souvenir of Mozart's recent travels. The effect of orchestral unity is also enhanced by the single tonality. Both end movements are in E flat, the Andante being in the relative key of C minor. Even the side theme brought in by the winds in the first movement is in E flat. The three movements of the *Sinfonia Concertante* are: I. Allegro maestoso, 4/4, E flat major; II. Andante, 3/4, C minor; III. Presto, 2/4, E flat major.

Mozart wrote out the cadenzas for the *Sinfonia Concertante*. The story is that the copy used by André for the first edition contained the cadenzas in Mozart's handwriting. This edition was used at the Mozart Festival in Salzburg in 1856, which Otto Jahn refers to in his biography of Mozart.

The original scoring calls for two violins, two violas, bass, two oboes, and two horns, besides the solo violin and viola.

L. B.

3. CONCERTOS FOR WIND INSTRUMENTS

AS REGARDS Mozart's concertos for wind instruments, we can deal with them in short order. They are for the most part occasional works in the narrower sense, intended to make a pleasant impression, and since it is in the very nature of wind instruments that their players must be treated with consideration, all these works are simpler in structure, and the character of their melodic invention is determined by the limitations of the instruments. Not that Mozart himself felt in any way cramped. He always moved comfortably and freely within any limitations, and turned them into positive advantages. Wind instrument players are usually naive, with something very individual about them—quite different from violinists or pianists. Accordingly all these concertos have something special and personal about them, and when one hears them in a concert hall, which is seldom enough, one has the feeling that the windows have suddenly been opened and a breath of fresh air has been let in.

Thus the very first of these concertos, K. 191, written in June, 1774, is a work unmistakably conceived for a wind instrument, a real bassoon concerto, which could not be arranged, say, for violoncello. (The latter instrument, unfortunately, Mozart treated like a stepchild, or rather he never thought of it at all.) The solo portions are full of leaps, runs, and singing passages completely suited to the instrument. The work was written *con amore* from beginning to end, as is particularly evident in the lively participation of the orchestra. This is even truer of the Flute Concerto in G major (K. 313), written in Mannheim early in 1778, on commission for the Dutch amateur and patron of music, De Jean. We know that Mozart approached the task of writing it without pleasure, since he did not like the flute. But the longer one knows the work, the less trace one can find of his dislike. The slow movement (in D major) is, in fact, so personal, one might say even so fantastic, so completely individual in character, that the man who had commissioned the work evidently did not know what to do with it. Mozart then presumably had to replace it with a simpler, more pastoral or idyllic Andante in C (K. 315). The Rondo of this G major concerto, a *Tempo di minuetto,* is a veritable fountain of good spirits and fresh invention. Since the concerto is for flute and not for violin, Mozart naturally renounced any such quotations as had characterized the last Salzburg violin concertos and concerto-like serenade movements, for, as we have seen, he did not like to overstep the bounds of a given species. A second Flute Concerto, in D major (K. 314), apparently written in Mannheim, is almost certainly the same as the Oboe Concerto written for the Salzburg oboist, Giuseppe Ferlendis, in 1777, and often mentioned in the Mozart correspondence. Mozart re-wrote it, out of sheer lack of time and money, for the impatient De Jean, transposing it from C major to D major. (Almost conclusive evidence that the original key was C major is the fact that in the transposition to D the violins never go below the A on the G-string.) The lighter tone of this work, and the fact that it was written earlier than the one in G major, are obvious. It is significant that Mozart later returned to the Rondo theme in composing

THE MOZART HANDBOOK

Blonde's aria "Welche Wonne, welche Lust" in *Die Entführung aus dem Serail*. Early in the Vienna period, Mozart asked his father to send him the original form of this concerto (15 February, 1783):

> Please send me at once the little book which contains the oboe concerto I wrote for Ramm, or rather for Ferlendis. Prince Esterházy's oboist is giving me three ducats for it, and has offered me six if I will compose a new concerto for him . . .

The oboist referred to was probably Franz Joseph Czerwenka, an excellent player, and two beginnings of oboe concertos have been preserved that are undoubtedly connected with the reference in Mozart's letter, both in F major: a shorter one (K. 416g), and a longer one, of 61 measures (K. 293), of which the former proves to be simply a variant of the entry of the oboe after the tutti in the latter. Why the work was never finished and Mozart never received the six ducats we do not know, but we must regret the fact, for the tutti is full of energy and vitality.

The concertos for horn, with one significant exception, are works intended to please, and nothing more. Mozart wrote them mostly for the Salzburg horn player, Leitgeb, who seems to have been the perpetual butt of his good-natured jokes. There are evidences of this in the autographs, as for example in that of the manuscript fragment of the last concerto (K. 495), which is written in a gay variety of blue, red, green, and black inks, to confuse the poor performer; or in another (the Rondo of K. 412), in which the soloist's part bears a succession of remarks such as *adagio—a lei Signor Asino. Animo—presto—su via—da bravo—Coraggio—bestia—o che stonatura—Ahi!—ohime—bravo poveretto—*and at the end: *grazia al Ciel! basta, basta!* The first of these pieces, a Rondo (K. 371), composed in Vienna while Mozart was still in the service of the Archbishop (21 March, 1781), survives only in the form of a sketch, although a complete one, and fragments of a first movement to go with it are also preserved. The Rondo is, of course, a comparatively primitive concerto movement, judged from the point of view of the rondos of the piano or violin concertos. But it is full of spontaneity and freshness. Its most striking feature is the appearance of the motive that is to play so great a role in the first finale of *Figaro* ("Susanna, son morta"). A Concerto for Horn (K. 412) has been made out of two movements, an Allegro and a Rondo in D, which cannot belong altogether if for no better reason than that the bassoons employed in the first of them are missing in the second. Mozart's joking with the soloist, in the first movement, sometimes carries over into the musical invention also; an accompaniment figure which occurs in the violins is not ordinarily to be found in Mozart's works in serious mood. The movement is *gemütlich* (homely, comfortable)—undoubtedly fitting the phlegmatic soloist to a T. And even the Rondo, which Mozart wrote out again 17 April, 1787, changing it considerably on that occasion, has something of the same character, although it was apparently written for a different virtuoso.

The first complete concerto (K. 417, in E flat, like all the others) represents Mozart "taking pity on that ass, ox, and fool of a Leitgeb, in Vienna, 27 May, 1783"; it was a work in which, in the *Maestoso* of the first movement (which also ventures into darker regions), in the cantabile of the second, and in the hunting fanfares of the third, Leitgeb could do himself proud. This work has a strange connection with the last two concertos (K. 447 and K. 495). The later of these, written "für den Leitgeb" on 26 June, 1786, is like a duplicate of the 1783 work but on a higher level, for a work of Mozart's written after a lapse of three years is always on a higher level than its predecessor. The first theme bears a strange relation to the cantata *Die Maurerfreude* (K. 471), dating from the preceding year. This Concerto offers opportunities for cadenzas. The middle movement is a Romanza. As for the earlier work, K. 447, one would be tempted to attribute it to a later date if it were conceivable that Mozart should have omitted such a work from his thematic catalogue. It is a unique composition, and makes demands of the soloist that Mozart would not have made of "that ass Leitgeb." The instrumentation, too, is unusual and subtler than before: clarinets and bassoons take the place of oboes and horns. It is significant that the middle movement, a Romanza, is in the subdominant; here we have a precedent and counterpart for the depth of expression, if not for the length, of the Adagio in the Piano and Violin Sonata K. 481. Even in the opening and closing movements, although there is a relation to the "Leitgeb" style (the Finale being again a hunting scene), there is a depth and earnestness quite different from anything in the earlier works. Perhaps some day the discovery of the autograph will contribute to the solution of this puzzle.

One final wind concerto remains to be discussed—the one for clarinet and orchestra (flutes, bassoons, horns, and strings), K. 622. This is the last concerto of any kind that Mozart wrote. He had originally sketched the first movement (K. 584b) for basset horn, presumably at the end of 1789, and then took it up again in October, 1791, transposed it from G to A, and completed it for his clarinetist friend, "Mr. Stadler, the elder." The greatness and the transcendent beauty of this work are such as its high Köchel number would lead us to expect. One almost has the impression that Mozart felt impelled to express again, in greater and dramatically animated form, what he had already expressed in more lyric form in the domain of chamber music, in the Stadler Quintet. The first movement is from beginning to end in Mozart's last style, informed throughout by the closest relation between the soloist and the orchestra, and by the utmost possible vitality in the orchestral portion itself, as may be observed by following simply the play of the two violins in dialogue. Significantly, in this work the basses are sometimes separated from the 'cellos: in the Adagio, a counterpart to the Larghetto of the Quintet, there are passages of transparent sonority in which the contrabass is silent. And how all the registers of the solo instrument are exploited, yet without any exhibition of virtuosity! There is no opportunity for free cadenzas. One need only compare this work with similar compositions by another great lover of the clarinet and master in writing for it, Carl Maria von Weber, such as his "great Quintet," Op. 34, or his "great Concertos," Opp. 73 and 74, to see the difference between the supreme effectiveness of simplicity and mere virtuoso exhibition.

A. E.

Concerto in B flat major for Bassoon and Orchestra (K. 191)

ı. Allegro   ıı. Andante ma adagio   ııı. Rondo: Tempo di menuetto

WHEN STRAVINSKY discovered the loveliness of the high bassoon register in the opening of his *Sacre,* the members of his Parisian audience promptly beat each other over the head with their umbrellas and started the finest riot in recent music history. Usually there is supposed to be something funny about a solo bassoon. It is a natural-born comedian, a character actor, a kind of Bottom among the fairies or a Dopey among the Seven Dwarfs. Yet, a well-developed sense of humor often goes with a sensitive taste for lyric poetry. This the greatest of orchestrators understood, and lyrical episodes for the solo bassoon are sometimes among the most appealing passages in a Beethoven or a Stravinsky score.

The Mozart Bassoon Concerto is a suave, sophisticated, and delicately lyrical work. It is one of his earliest concertos, composed (June, 1774), when he was eighteen, for a Baron Thaddäus von Dürnitz. The Baron was one of the aristocratic dilettantes to whom composers of the period were often indebted for commissions, and for him Mozart composed three bassoon concertos and a sonata for bassoon and 'cello. At this particular period Mozart's music began to show traces of the elegance and refinement which characterized the so-called *galant* style of the period. His later music never lost its delicacy or nicety of phrasing, but it was deepened by profounder passions and a wider vision. Even in this work, the air of suave elegance and youthful gallantry is moderated by deeply lyrical episodes in minor and by a virile orchestration. The bassoon's witticisms are consequently refined rather than Rabelaisian, and Mozart avoids the kind of cavorting in the low bassoon register which always seems a sort of indelicate joke.

The orchestra's opening themes are spirited and gracious. The bassoon takes them up, adding ornamental runs and testing its range in wide leaps. An episode in minor intervenes, for even the most sophisticated young men have a predilection for melancholy moods. Orchestra and bassoon are exquisitely balanced during this episode. Mozart was a consummate master even at eighteen. His orchestra sacrifices neither its sharpness nor it strength, while the bassoon matches the orchestra without committing itself to a dramatic range it is by nature not equipped to explore. The opening themes with the bassoon's figurations and leaps are then resumed, and the movement concludes with a Mozartean blend of energy and elegance.

In the Andante, the bassoon is given its opportunity for sustained and sensitive lyricism. It moves quietly, absorbed in its gentle melodies and the coloraturas that weave naturally around them. The Rondo finale is in the tempo of a minuet. Mozart is singularly felicitous in such movements, for despite the courtly dance figures, his music nowhere suggests prim, enervated aristocrats pirouetting in faded brocades. His rhythms have always an innate virility, and his melodies an incomparable simplicity and strength.

A. V. (1)

THE FLUTE CONCERTOS

THE STRAINED relations between Mozart and his employer, the Archbishop of Salzburg, came to a breaking point during the middle of 1777. After interminable wranglings, the Archbishop finally dismissed his difficult, albeit talented, "servant," and Mozart was free to travel. With his mother as chaperon, the twenty-one-year-old genius tried Munich first and then Augsburg. Mannheim, a city with a fine orchestra and a flourishing musical life, was reached on October 30, 1777. But in none of these cities had anything worthwhile materialized. As his father, who remained behind, continued to remind him, the purpose of the journey was "either to get a good permanent appointment, or . . . to go off to some big city where large sums of money can be earned." Old Leopold was frankly worried. The trip had proved an unrewarded expense. His letters grew a bit frantic, and he was soon accusing his son of idleness and extravagance. He was oppressed by the thought of the debts he had incurred to pay for his son's journey, and he even speculated nervously on what might happen to his daughter Nannerl if he were to die.

Mozart soon decided that the solution was a trip to Paris, "the only place," he wrote his father, "where one can still make money and a great reputation." However, since the projected journey was still two months off, he had, in the meantime, to meet current living expenses for himself and his mother and to build up a reserve for the trip to Paris. At this point a most welcome commission arrived from an amateur Dutch flutist named De Jean (or Deschamps), "a gentleman of means and a lover of all the sciences," who offered two hundred gulden for "three short, simple concertos and a couple of quartets for the flute." Mozart reported this to his father in December, 1777, but the following February he wrote to say that De Jean had not paid up in full. "M. De Jean is also leaving for Paris tomorrow," wrote Mozart, "and, because I have only finished two concertos and three quartets for him, has sent me ninety-six gulden (this is four gulden too little, evidently supposing that this was the half of two hundred); but he must pay me in full . . . and I can send him the other pieces later."

It does not appear that Mozart ever received further satisfaction from De Jean. In any case, he had still to explain why he had failed to produce all the flute music he had promised. "It is not surprising," he wrote his father, "that I have not been able to finish them, for I never have a single quiet hour here. I can compose only at night, so that I can't get up early as well; besides, one is not always in the mood for working. I could, to be sure, scribble off things the whole day long, but a composition of this kind goes out into the world, and naturally I do not want to have cause to be ashamed of my name on the title page. Moreover, you know that I become quite powerless whenever I am obliged to write for an instrument [the flute] which I cannot bear. Hence, as a diversion, I compose something else such as duets for clavier and piano, or I work at my Mass."

It would be a pity if this irritated outburst against the flute were thought cause, by any critic, to belittle the concertos he wrote for the instrument. Obiously he was in a bad frame of mind, badgered by unaccustomed responsibilities, worried by letters from a nervous father. Moreover, he wanted above all else to compose an opera, which under the circumstances was wholly impracticable. Thus far he had sought in vain for an opportunity to display the fullness of his genius. Wearily, and quite naturally, he made a scapegoat of what lay closest to hand—the flute. It is difficult to believe that these beautiful concertos, and the many sensitive passages for the flute in his operas and symphonies, were products of an inveterate antipathy. A sense of self-criticism and a deep personal integrity are both strongly evident in the letter. He would permit no work to bear his name unless it contained the very best music he was, at that moment, capable of writing.

A. V. (1)

Concerto in C major for Flute, Harp, and Orchestra (K. 299)

I. Allegro   II. Andantino   III. Rondo: Allegro

SINCE MOZART failed to secure full payment for his flute concertos, fifty more gulden were sent from home to help cover the trip from Mannheim to Paris. He arrived on March 23, 1778, and found the moment a rather inauspicious one. An operatic feud was on between Gluck and Piccini. Paris, the traditional battleground for rival musical ideologies, was characteristically engaged in a public quarrel which seems to have been strangely modelled after one of our domestic election campaigns. Mozart was no partisan. He had only himself to present; and since his appearance was unheralded by even a tidbit of interesting personal scandal, the great ladies who ruled Parisian society could scarcely be expected to show enthusiasm.

The Parisian socialites whom Mozart dutifully visited were either not at home or else imagined that a few phrases of astonishment were recompense enough for his performances. "People pay plenty of compliments, it is true," he reported ruefully, "but there it ends." Meanwhile, hiring carriages to go visiting was proving an expense— "four to five livres a day and all for nothing." The cost of living in Paris was high, and his mother, who was with him, soon wrote home that "our capital has become very small and won't go very far."

Several pupils eventually appeared, and also a few commissions. "I think I told you in my last letter," wrote Mozart to his father, "that the Duc de Guines, whose daughter is my pupil in composition, plays the flute extremely well, and that she plays the harp *magnifique*." A concerto for flute and harp was duly composed in April, 1778, for father and daughter.

Mozart seems always to have had trouble collecting payment for his commissions. In one age composers were servants; in another, unworldly creatures—in either case, not the sort of people one had to bother paying. The Duke went off to the country, and his daughter was busy getting married. Mozart found only the housekeeper, who offered him a sum too paltry to accept. "It amounts to this," declared Mozart, "that the Duke wanted to pay me for one hour instead of two—and that from *égard*. For he has already had, for the last four months, a concerto of mine for flute and harp, for which he has not yet paid me."

This is one Mozart's soft-spoken concertos. The harp for Mozart was a deft and delicate instrument, and the color relationships between the two solos are mainly of a sweet and subtle pastel variety. To offset the gentle duet, Mozart makes more use of his orchestral oboes and horns than he did in his previous flute concertos. Despite the quiet and relaxed tone of this work, it is remarkably rich in color and entrancingly subtle in its sonorities.

There are more melodies in this short work than can conveniently be quoted. In the opening movement the continuations of the main themes are themselves beautiful melodic motives. Even the transitional passages are contrived as casual little melodies leading to longer and more important themes. Only in the development section (the middle of the movement) is the subtle and relaxed interplay of instruments disturbed. There are no sharp dramatic exchanges, but the soloists lapse into a lyrical melancholia all the more touching because of the subdued tone that is maintained.

The slow movement (Andantino) is serene and evenly paced. Flute and harp are in complete accord. They serenade each other gracefully, echoing a phrase between them, each extending the other's theme into a new melodic discovery. The oboes and the horns are omitted in this movement, the strings alone assuming the orchestral burden.

The Rondo is an irresistible bit of musicmaking. It maintains a sense of eager spontaneity from beginning to end, and it is furnished with enough melodies to fit out at least two ordinary concerto rondos. If the movement were not so carefully organized, one would suspect the performers of perpetrating an eighteenth-century jam session, each challenging the other to outdo its latest melodic inspiration.

The concerto is not one of Mozart's simplest creations but surely it is one of his most engaging.

A. V. (1)

Concerto in E flat major for Horn and Orchestra (K. 447)

ɪ. Allegro   ɪɪ. Romanza: Larghetto   ɪɪɪ. Allegro

MOZART wrote four concertos for horn and orchestra: 1782 (K. 412), 1783 (K. 417), 1783 (K. 447), 1786 (K. 495); also Rondo in 1787 (K. 514). They were all written for a horn player named Leitgeb, who was a member of the Salzburg orchestra. Mozart had known him there. Leitgeb is said to have been an excellent hornist in solos, but otherwise an uneducated musician. The Rondo was from beginning to end enriched with bantering remarks in Mozart handwriting; where the solo enters is written: *Adagio—A lei Signor Asino. Animo—presto*—while the accompaniment is Allegro. There is reference to Leitgeb's tendency to drag; for after the remark at the end of the ritornelle—*A lei Signor Asino*—one finds by the theme *Animo—presto—su via—da bravo—Coraggio—e finisci già*—at the end. Mozart jokes in this way throughout the Rondo: *bestia—oh, che stonatura—chi—oimé—bravo poveretto!—Oh seccatura di coglioni!* (as the theme returns)—*Ah che mi fai ridere!—ajuto* (by a repetition)—*respira un poco!* (by some rests) *avanti, avanti!—questo poi va al meglio* (when the theme appeared again)—*e non finisci nemmeno?—ah porco infame! Oh come sei grazioso! Carino! Asinino! hahaha—respira!—Ma intoni almeno una, cazzo—bravo, evviva!—e vieni à reccarmi per la quarta, e Dio sia benedetto per l'ultima volta* (by the fourth repetition of the theme)—*ah termina,*

ti prego! ah maledetto—anche bravura? (by a short leap) *bravo—*
ah! trillo di pecore (by a trill)—*finisci? grazie al ciel!—basta, basta!*

How Leitgeb stood this raillery is not told. Mozart had met him
in Milan in 1773. Leitgeb had gone there to give a concert, without
marked success. Leopold Mozart thought this was due to the con-
cert-giver's lack of skill. Leitgeb owed Leopold money, which he
asked Wolfgang to see was repaid; but the latter asked his father
to be indulgent; things were not going well with Leitgeb in Vienna,
but he would certainly repay him little by little.

P. H.

This is the most exceptional of the four horn concertos which
Mozart composed for his friend Leitgeb, and because of its unique
qualities it has remained a puzzle to Mozart scholars. . . . There
existed between [Mozart and the horn player] an easy good humor,
and in all the horn concertos except this one Leitgeb acted as a
good-natured butt for Mozart's extravagant pleasantries. One of the
horn concertos (K. 417) bears Mozart's inscription that it was
composed out of pity "for that ass, ox, and fool of a Leitgeb." Another (K. 495) was written in an alternation of black, red, green,
and blue ink to perplex the performer. A wild little scene is appended to the rondo of the K. 412 concerto, in which Mozart exclaims in mock desperation over his friend's incompetence.

There are no such pleasantries in this horn concerto. It is written
with a range and a power quite removed from the pleasant "fool
of a Leitgeb" style of the others. It is this difference in temperament
and style which has caused confusion among Mozart scholars. The
date of its composition has usually been given as 1783. However,
Georges Saint-Foix, one of the finest of Mozart scholars, has pushed
the date forward to 1788 or 1789. The point of dissatisfaction with
the earlier date hinges on the nobility of the music, the unusual
orchestration (two clarinets and two bassoons replace the oboes and
horns customary in the earlier concertos), and on the mature,
romantic loveliness of the slow movement. These are traits which
distinguish it from the other horn concertos and seem to place it
in the latest period of Mozart's creative career. However, Mozart
began a thematic catalogue of his own music beginning with February, 1784, and this concerto is not listed. Dr. Einstein, another emi-

nent Mozart authority, would willingly subscribe to a late date for this concerto "if it were conceivable that Mozart should have omitted such a .work from his thematic catalogue." "Perhaps," continues Dr. Einstein, "some day the discovery of the autograph will contribute to the solution of this puzzle." What emerges clearly in this scholarly dispute over dates is the fact that this horn concerto is a unique creation.

Range and size are by no means synonymous concepts in music, and in a Mozart concerto the former is often in inverse proportion to the latter. Range is a matter of the emotional distance between leading ideas, while size depends upon how long the composer feels these ideas may profitably be discussed. This concerto is a very short one, but at the outset Mozart establishes a sense of the remarkable distances it will negotiate.

A. V. (1)

Concerto in A major for Clarinet and Orchestra (K. 622)

I. Allegro   II. Adagio   III. Rondo: Allegro

THIS CONCERTO was composed in October, 1791, about two months before Mozart's death. Aside from the Requiem which he did not live to finish, and a short Masonic cantata (K. 623) written in November, 1791, this concerto is Mozart's last composition. Among his concertos, it is closest in time to the beautiful one in B flat for piano (K. 595) composed the previous January, although it is distantly removed from it in spirit. Commentators have read into the Piano Concerto a valedictory mood, a last gesture of resignation and farewell. But no such attitude can be (or has been) construed in the Clarinet Concerto. His last years were filled with heartbreaking bitterness, poverty, and poor health; and "his precarious state," writes Blom, "seems to be reflected in the hectic beauty" of the Clarinet Concerto.

Nearly everything one can find in his instrumental music seems condensed into this unassuming work. It has youthful eagerness and bright charm. Yet as in an Elizabethan tragedy, so metaphorically sometimes in a Mozart score, the specter of the slain king wanders in distant corridors, and the living participants in a tranquil or festive scene are transfixed in an unreal and irrevocable loneliness. Mozart knew, even in his early concertos, that elegance of phraseology was not incompatible with eloquence of feeling. This knowledge he imparts again here, more quietly and more firmly than ever. But one thing he adds in the finale which one will not find in the earlier works—a strangely deliberate mockery of one of the most poignant melodies in the movement.

A. V. (1)

Miscellaneous Concert Music

1. OVERTURES
2. DIVERTIMENTI, SERENADES
3. GERMAN DANCES

1. THE OVERTURES

Overture to *The Abduction from the Seraglio* (*Die Entführung aus dem Serail*) CONCERT ENDING BY BUSONI

OF THIS introduction to the opera Mozart wrote "that it was short," and that "it alternates between *forte* and *piano,* the Turkish music being always *forte,* modulated by changes of key, and I do not think anyone can go to sleep over it, even if they have lain awake all the night before."

In its original form the overture leads directly into the opening scene of the opera—Belmont's air "Hier soll ich dich denn sehen, Constanze"—but in order to fit it for concert performance endings have been made by various editors.

The principal theme (Presto, C major, 2/2) is given out by the strings. After eight measures the full orchestra enters *forte* with the "Turkish music," the two divisions of the theme being then repeated. What answers to the second theme appears later with the bassoon and cellos in G major. This subject is, however, derived from the "Turkish music," and Mozart does not give it the usual recapitulation at the close. The section ordinarily devoted to development is employed for an entirely new theme (Andante, C minor, 3/8), four
456

measures of which are given out by the strings, followed by another and similar phrase presented by the woodwind. The subject of this part is drawn from the aria—previously referred to—with which the first scene of the opera opens. There, however, it is in a major and not in a minor key. The third part of the overture commences with a recapitulation of the opening theme.

The overture is scored for piccolo, two oboes, two clarinets, two bassoons, two horns, two trumpets, timpani, bass drum, cymbals, triangle, and strings.

F. B.

Overture to *The Marriage of Figaro* (*Le Nozze di Figaro*)

THE OVERTURE to the *Nozze* is a work of pure sparkle, which it is interesting to compare with the overtures to the two other masterpieces [*Don Giovanni* and *The Magic Flute*]. Lacking the tragic suggestions of the one and the solemn overtones of the other, it is all liveliness and good humor. It is marked *Presto* and is written in the key of D major. The hurried passage in soft octaves with which it opens leads to another theme in the woodwinds and horns which suddenly explodes into a rollicking tutti. All three ideas are repeated, the flutes and oboes adding a new melodic interest to the first one. The continuation furnishes breathless scales for strings and irreverent hallelujahs from the whole orchestra. The group of second subjects in A starts with a sharply accentuated theme for strings rounded off with dizzying turns for oboes and flutes. Another tutti builds up and quiets down, and, preceded by humorous tootlings on the bassoon, the movement reaches its nearest approach to a purely lyric theme. There is no development, but, following the last theme, the animation begins again and descending violins lead to a recapitulation, with the second subjects now in the tonic key. In the coda, descending scales flash down, echoed by woodwinds in thirds, sometimes a bit hard to hear against the general rejoicing of the rest of the orchestra.

The overture is scored for two flutes, two oboes, two clarinets, two bassoons, two horns, two trumpets, timpani, and strings.

B. E.

Overture to *Don Giovanni*

THE OVERTURE begins *Andante* with solemn chords by the full orchestra. The string choir chants them next, blending into a poignant phrase of the first violins. The agitation increases, bursting into powerful runs for first violins and flutes. Out of this emerges the main body of the movement (*Molto allegro*), the theme carried at first by strings alone, a restless, straining subject. Winds answer with shaken chords, the theme is resumed, climaxing in one of those powerful passages which Mozart usually appended to the enunciation of his subjects, and which serves as bridge. Graceful runs for violins are followed by softly moving chords of oboes and clarinets. The orchestra rouses itself from its slumbers and launches into a boldly rhythmic figure for first violins backed by the entire orchestra. Now comes the second theme, consisting—as do many of Mozart's— of two strongly contrasting phrases, a brief downward march of strings and woodwinds, and a graceful tripping of first violins, very lightly scored. For some time this subject is toyed with, ingenious imitations of woodwinds over the soft wavering of strings. Now follows much imaginative play upon this last and the preceding subjects, until at last we return to the original subject of the *Allegro,* transposed to G major. It is pursued at once by the second subject, in which the contrast of its two sections is exhibited again and again. After a short time this leads to the recapitulation, which is entirely regular, with some minor variations in scoring.

After the conclusion of the *Allegro,* which has been developed in full sonata form, there is a sudden intrusion, *Andante* (*quasi adagio*), of mighty chords, like the introduction, which represent the stony figure of the Commendatore. But now the continuing chords are carried by the trombones, with mysterious and ominous ponderosity. And now Busoni has appended a *Presto,* taken, he tells us, from the final scene of the opera. A fugal subject is announced by first violins against a running accompaniment by second violins. Second violins have it next, then string basses and bassoons. A Mozartian cadence, and runs in all the strings introduce a new section (*Un poco tranquillo*). A gentle figure is imitated by many voices of the orchestra. Then a phrase built on the fugal theme is danced gracefully by first violins. This descends to wild runs of strings and bassoons, a soft singing of a version of the fugal subject, a powerful downward run, and the end.

The score calls for two flutes, two oboes, two clarinets, two bassoons, two horns, two trumpets, timpani, and strings.

J. G. H.

The nineteenth century—particularly the German analysts following the lead of the fantastic E.T.A. Hoffmann—found programmatic references in the overture which Mozart probably never imagined. Hermann Abert, however, who edited the revision of Jahn's Mozart biography, maintains that the piece "is no program overture either in the old Venetian sense or in the later romantic tradition; and if Mozart utilized for its *Andante* the music of the apparition scene he did so not to introduce the Stone Guest in person but because it seemed to him the most natural way to symbolize that supernatural power" here shown in opposition to human defiance. Manifestly, however, the portentous D minor *Andante* with which it begins has a programmatic meaning of a sort. The solemn and menacing opening chords are those to which the stone statue of the murdered Commendatore stalks into the banquet hall of Don Giovanni in the last scene of the second act. These harmonies are supplemented by a momentary echo, sounding from the low strings. There follow a syncopated melody associated with the uncertainty of Don Giovanni's greeting to his uncanny visitor; and the shivering phrases depicting the agitation of the unnerved Leporello. Then come several measures of sinister ascending and descending scales in flutes and violins, with shuddersome *crescendos* and *diminuendos* which, in the opera, accompany the Statue's admonition to the unrepentant libertine. The main body of the overture is launched in D major (*Molto allegro*). "This may be taken to represent in general terms the swirl of life that accompanies Don Giovanni wherever he goes. . . . A later passage, based on the alternation of an impressive octave figure (in imitation) and a chattering one in the violins may or may not be intended to point the contrast between morality and the sternness of Fate, as represented by the Commandant, and the irreligion and levity of Don Giovanni. A fair proportion of the overture is devoted to this antithesis and a striding figure . . . plays so large a part in the development that we may be pardoned for believing it to have had some special association in Mozart's mind. Though the overture is in D minor and D major, it ends, curiously enough, in C major, from which an easy transition is made into F major, in which key the opera begins" (Ernest Newman). Abert alludes to the "unsparing energy" of the music, "which creates in the listener a demonic sense of tension and of constantly whipped-up passion. . . . The composer avoids disturbing the artistic illusion and so leads the overture into the first scene, as if a veil softly descended. . . ."

Mozart did, however, write a concert ending for this overture. It is thirteen bars long and ends in D. The page on which it was written was with the autograph score of the original. Dr. Alfred Einstein states that the occasion for which Mozart composed it is unknown. However, he takes issue with Abert's claim that this ending is "hasty, too short or unworthy of a classic overture," finding it, on the contrary, "a truly inspired piece of work." Other concert endings for the *Don Giovanni* overture were made by Christian Cannabich, by A. E. Marschner, by J. P. Schmidt; also by unnamed arrangers in the piano editions published by Granz, Bosworth, Litolff, and Breitkopf und Härtel, and in later days by Ferruccio Busoni. Conductors often use the one made by Johann Anton André, of Offenbach-am-Main.

H. F. P. (2)

Overture to *The Magic Flute* (*Die Zauberflöte*)

THE MAIN movement is preceded by an introduction (Adagio, E flat major, 2/2). The great chords with which it opens are those heard in the body of the opera itself (Act II), where they appear between the Priests' March and the aria of Sarastro—"O Isis and Osiris." There has always been supposed to have been a definite intention on Mozart's part to associate these chords, and much else in the opera, with Masonic symbolism. Edgar Istel wrote interestingly of the connection between *The Magic Flute* and Freemasonry in *The Musical Quarterly* (October, 1927): "Significant and mysterious is the motive of the introductory measures, three trombone blasts in a rhythm intelligible only to the initiated. This means that the portal to Freemasonry does not open by itself, that we are not accepted into the temple of humanity without striving on our own part. We must gain entrance to the temple by means of three strong blows, which signify, Seek, and ye shall find; Ask, and it shall be given you; Knock, and it shall be opened unto you. Zeal, faithfulness and constancy are the requisites. Entrance into the fraternity, however, is voluntary, a result of one's own intention, endeavor and strength, aimed at arriving at truth. Therefore, these three trombone blasts (in a somewhat altered shape) form the significant opening of the overture, whose secret meaning is simply and solely the portrayal of the Freemasonic ceremonial in the form of a grandiose fugato."

The Allegro which follows the slow introduction is a combination of sonata form and fugue. The subject with which it begins in the second violins, and which is heard more or less continually throughout the overture, is curiously like the opening theme of a sonata by Clementi, which Mozart had heard its composer play for the emperor some nine years before *The Magic Flute* had been set down. Sir George Grove also pointed out that the subject bears more than a passing resemblance to a passage in the fugue in E flat major in Bach's *Well-tempered Clavichord*—a work which Mozart himself arranged for stringed instruments.

The second theme, in B flat major, is given out by the flute, but with the material of the first subject appearing with it. The first division of the overture closes in B flat major, and there then follow six measures of Adagio, the three trombone chords recurring in it. The Allegro is then resumed in the development section, the latter comprising contrapuntal treatment of the thematic material of almost unbelievable ingenuity and skill. This division, which is short, is followed by the customary recapitulation, and the overture closes with a brief coda.

The overture is scored for two flutes, two oboes, two clarinets, two bassoons, two horns, two trumpets, three trombones, timpani, and strings.

F. B.

Overture to *Der Schauspieldirektor* (*The Impresario*) (K. 486)

THOUGH OFTEN included among Mozart's operas, *Der Schauspieldirektor* (*The Impresario*) is a slight one-act farce with incidental music consisting, in all, of five numbers, the bright and bustling Overture included. Gottlieb Stephanie, actor, librettist, and Burgtheater inspector, wrote the winding and witless text, which Mozart adorned with four vocal gems: two arias and two trios.

The comedy was commissioned by the Emperor Joseph II and produced at the orangery in Schönbrunn on February 7, 1786, less than two months before the première in Vienna of Mozart's comic masterpiece *Le Nozze di Figaro.* The occasion was a reception in honor of visiting Netherlands officials. Both the German and Italian troupes earlier organized by the Emperor took part in the festivities, the Italians concentrating on Salieri's *Prima la Musica e Poi le Parole* (*First the Music and Then the Words*). The Germans apparently did most of the talking, since the rambling dialogue between the Mozart arias runs to absurd lengths.

Eric Blom maintains that the vocal music, meager though it be, ranks with Mozart's maturest dramatic and psychological style. The arias are full of tenderness and delineative power, besides demanding great technical skill. The real marvel is the trio, in which the buffo tenor (the Impresario) tries to mollify two claimants for a primadonna role. In the finale—actually a somewhat modified rondo—all three agree that singers should forget their petty squabbles and jealousies and serve only art, or, as freely adapted by Blom:

> *Artists, it is true, must ever*
> *Hold in high esteem their fame;*
> *But that each alone is clever*
> *Is a thought that must forever*
> *Be redounding to the shame*
> *Of an artist with a name.*

Der Schauspieldirektor has been revived from time to time, though seldom in its original form. The plot has undergone drastic change, and Mozart and his librettist Schikaneder have been brought into the cast as key figures in a theatrical tangle. By introducing Mozart himself, adapters naturally did not overlook the chances for romantic intrigue in the plot. In the comedy the Impresario settles the issue by giving the top role to both prima donnas. Each is to depict one aspect of the character. When the singers protest that the hero cannot be in love with two heroines, the wily Impresario meets the objection with the query: "Do *I* not love you both?"

Naturally, none of the versions employing Mozart as a character was staged while Frau Constanze Mozart was still alive. Whatever the seraphic qualities of his music, Mozart was of course no saint in his private life. The stories of his amours with singers, while no doubt exaggerated, have been handed down by fairly reliable colleagues and associates of Mozart. It was rumored that while *Don Giovanni* was in rehearsal Mozart carried on love affairs with his Zerlina, Donna Anna, and Donna Elvira—"perhaps," sardonically remarks Blom, "with a view to still greater realism." It is even possible that a similar situation arose during the *Schauspieldirektor* rehearsals. The arias were such as to require arduous coaching. At any rate, Mozart in the role of romantic *intrigant* in a modified version of *The Impresario* is not far-fetched. In later revivals of the little work, arias culled from other Mozart sources have been interpolated to fill out the scant allotment of music.

What Blom, following Abert, detects as a note of "deliberate, tongue-in-the-cheek parody" in the Overture may be traceable to the presence on the Schönbrunn program of a work by Mozart's rival, Salieri. As an exponent of the Italian school, Salieri was the Emperor Joseph's favorite composer. Now, the Overture is Italian in form almost to mock imitation. If Mozart intended it as such, the parody was certainly lost on the Emperor. Salieri, however, probably got it. Did not Mozart's friend Michael Kelly speak of the Emperor's Maestro di Capella as "a clever, shrewd man possessed of crooked wisdom"?

L. B.

2. DIVERTIMENTI, SERENADES

JOHANN MATTHESON believed that a serenade should be played on the water: "Nowhere does it sound better in still weather; and one can there use all manner of instruments in their strength, which in a room would sound too violent and deafening, as trumpets, drums, horns, etc. . . . The chief characteristic of the serenade must be tenderness, la *tendresse*. . . . No melody is so small, no piece so great that in it a certain chief characteristic should not prevail and distinguish it from others; otherwise it is nothing. And when one employs a serenade out of its element—I mean effect—in congratulations, pageants, advancement of pupils in schools, etc., he goes against the peculiar nature of the thing. Things of government and military service are foreign to it; for the night is attached to nothing with such intimate friendship as it is to love" (*Kern melodischer Wissenschaft,* Hamburg, 1737, p. 101).

The first symphonies of Sammartini (1705–75?) were written for open-air performance, and Mozart wrote his father in 1782 that one Martin had obtained permission to give twelve concerts in the Augarten at Vienna and four "grand concerts of night-music" in the finest squares of the town. Volkmann planned his three serenades for concert-hall use. Brahms applied the term "serenade" to his Op. 11 and Op. 16, which were published in 1860, but Hans Volkman in his biography of Robert Volkmann (Leipsig, 1903) says that the latter did not know these works of Brahms when he composed his own serenades. Those of Brahms are more in the symphonic manner; while the purpose of Volkmann was perhaps to write music that would satisfy the dictum of the talker reported by Athenæus: "Music softens moroseness of temper; first dissipates sadness, and produces affability and a sort of gentleman-like joy." Yet Volkmann's third Serenade begins in doleful dumps.

During the sixteenth and the seventeenth centuries serenades were exceedingly popular in Germany. They were composed of vocal music or instrumental; sometimes voices and instruments were united. The vocal serenades were usually male trios, quartets, or quintets. There were serenades also of wind instruments, with music of the chase, or simple fanfares. There were "torchlight serenades." Rosseau, who defines a serenade as a concert given at night, generally with instruments, insists that the delightful effect was due largely to the darkness, and also to the silence, "which banishes all distraction." Georges Kastner comments on this statement, and adds that the celebrated viola player, the mystic Urban, would never play to his friends unless the blinds of his little room were hermetically closed. Kastner mentions ancient collections of serenades and nocturnes that might be called scholastic, written by Prætorius, Werckmeister, and others, and he classes these works with *quodlibets.*

In the eighteenth century[1] nearly every prince or rich nobleman had his own orchestra, which on summer evenings played in a park. In cities, as Vienna, there was much music in the streets, music of a complimentary or amorous nature. The music composed for these open-air and evening concerts was also performed in halls.

Short movements for one instrument or several were known in Germany as *Parthien,* and they were seldom published. Then there was the *cassazione,* or cassation, from the Latin *cassatio.* This species of music should have been a piece that brought the end of the concert, an overcoat-and-galoshes piece; but the term was applied to any piece suitable for performance in the open air at night. The serenade, which in form is much like the cassation, was performed during parties, dinners, wedding feasts, in the parlors or the gardens of princes or rich merchants. Haydn and Mozart wrote much music of this nature, but did not always distinguish between the cassation and the serenade, according to Michel Brenet, who says that the serenade always opened with a march, and that the movements were separated by Minuettos. The number of movements was from one to ten, and the instruments were from four to six. When the pieces were played in the open air, the parts were not doubled. A cassation of four instruments was played by only four musicians.

The serenade, notturno, cassation, and divertimento differed from the older suite in that all the movements were not in the same key, and the older dance forms—gavotte, sarabande, passacaglia, courante, bourrée, gigue, etc.—seldom appeared in them. "It is highly probable that compositions of this description were not intended to be played continuously, or with only such short waits between the separate

---

[1] Even in the sixteenth century princes and dukes plumed themselves upon their household musicians. The Duchess of Ferrara had her own orchestra, composed of women.

movements as are customary in symphonies or concertos: upon the whole they were not strictly concert music, but intended to be given at festive gatherings. It is most likely that the several movements were intended to be played separately, with long intervals for conversation, feasting, or other amusements between. Only in this way can the extreme length of some serenades be accounted for. We find no instance of concert compositions of such length in other forms in Mozart's and Haydn's day."

P. H.

Mozart, for four successive years, entirely abandoned the great classical ideal and yielded to a lighter, more worldly art, more in keeping with the *galant* taste which had at that time possessed the world of music. It is now a question of amusement rather than emotion. His style on the whole remains what it was, but the inspiration is slenderer, its import less. The slow movements alone—and perhaps, curiously enough, more often than in the past—will give rise to some admirably poetic reveries, infinitely surpassing the charming but unvarying gaiety of the other movements. If Mozart's present *galant* period does not permit a symphony, we cannot pass over in silence the various orchestral serenades—bulky ensembles clearly allied to the symphonic genre—which are spread over the period between 1774 and 1778.

Every summer, for wedding or anniversary feasts at the houses of the rich burghers of Salzburg, Mozart had to write one or two of these serenades, consisting of five usually very long and brilliant movements, besides a violin concerto, which was always interpolated. The prevailing mood of these serenades is decidedly the *concertante* style; the principal performers are given the opportunity for the display of a certain degree of virtuosity, which, however, is kept within reasonable bounds and as a result never runs the risk of destroying the purely musical interest of the work. But it is none the less true that these serenades, being occasional pieces, are more superficial than the symphony proper, and thus closely correspond to the *galant* ideal; so it is quite natural to find Mozart, between 1773 and 1776, occupied in midsummer in dazzling his fellow citizens with vast symphonic serenades, full at the same time of that Austro-Hungarian good humor (*Gemütlichkeit*) and of solemnity—

festive music interrupted by incomparable minuets or by melodies imprinted, or rather impregnated, with tenderness and supernatural grace. And in these serenades there is such a wealth of felicitous scoring, of dialogues between the *concertante* instruments, such a variety of sentiments (more marked perhaps than in the symphonies), that one is just astonished to see so much learning bestowed on works that, after all, were intended only for the occasion of some anniversary or festival.

Speaking generally, the new attitude is revealed in these serenades by very distinct subjects, by short and rapid imitations, by exactitude of recapitulation, and by a curtailment of the codas, lately so beautiful, which now become (except in certain of the andantes) no more than unpretentious little stretti. It was customary for the serenade to open with a march in which, in general, the first part never reappeared in the recapitulation; with Mozart the initial rhythm of the march was often recalled in the first allegro, thus giving a noticeable unity to the whole. But on the whole there was no elaboration, no really extended working out; the variety and freshness of the themes replaced the cohesion we so admired in the symphonies of preceding periods. Here, in music full of fire and brilliance, Mozart seems to concentrate his attention on the andantes, whose beautiful melodies and poetic expression compensate for the too rudimentary nature of the other movements.

In the year 1775 in particular this taste for *divertimenti* and serenades is evident on almost every page Mozart wrote. The opera he had to compose in the spring of this year was itself a pastoral serenade, *Il Rè pastore,* on a famous libretto by Metastasio. Its overture, in one movement, is to serve as the prototype of the great operatic overtures of his maturity; but, being written in 1775, it, very curiously, could not avoid being transformed into a serenade! Mozart is content to transfer the first air of the opera to the oboe, and to add a grand finale which is one of the most lively and witty rondos he has ever produced. The theme is a sort of French *contredanse,* with all the minor intermediary sections intentionally omitted, as too contrary to the prevailing *galant* ideals. But the animation of this finale and the ingenious return to its initial theme invest this work with a quite peculiar charm and give it an importance that totally escaped Mozart's first biographers, who wrongly attributed it to a period before 1770. In order that the scheme of the serenade might be complete, Mozart, on August 20, 1775, wrote a superb March in C major, opening with a bold unison *à la française* which, obviously, was intended for the opening of this curious pastoral *divertimento* (K. 214).

It should be added here that the presence of a French *contredanse* gives rise to the supposition that Mozart must have had at hand some collections of French dances at about this time, which were not without their effect on him. In fact, he used several of them in the finales of his contemporary violin concertos; and this practice could have been suggested to him not only by these collections but by the violinists of the French school, who were even then addicted to the concerto "on well-known airs."

We have no doubt that Mozart was acquainted with the works of several of the most remarkable representatives of the French violin school; neither Gaviniès nor, notably, Le Duc nor Guénin[2] were unknown. Among the concertos of these last two artists there are some striking, even disconcerting "Mozartisms," which prove the role played by the great French school in Mozart's conception of the violin concerto. We shall have moreover in a short time to consider the importance of this role in the domain of the symphony proper.

The serenade (K. 250), composed by Mozart in the middle of his twentieth year—that is to say, in the full flower of his musical inspiration, for this year, 1776, sees the full blossoming of his rarest gifts of music and poetry—this serenade marks for us the climax, not to say the apotheosis, of the period I have designated as *galant*. It is the successor of the serenades of 1773, 1774, and 1775, but with what a difference! Its exceptional length is perhaps due to the solemnity of Elisabeth Haffner's wedding (she was the daughter of the Burgomaster of Salzburg); but it is certain that on this particular day the young master was bent on making a great impression and spreading out before his fellow citizens all the richness his genius was able to produce. It is really, in every sense of the word, a musical *feast,* in which Mozart gives free rein to his fancy, creating almost new forms; where, too, rhythms to be used later in his *Don Giovanni* make their appearance before our delighted eyes. So that the late

---

[2] P. Gaviniès, 1726–1800; Marie A. Guénin, 1744–1819; Simon Le Duc, 1748–77. Grove gives some details of their lives.

Burgomaster's salon becomes as it were the antechamber of the philandering nobleman bent on some new and ephemeral conquest.

Within the limits of *galant* music, since all idea of depth and severity is banished from the musical scene, since all is effectiveness and brilliance, it seems scarcely possible to go further; not that, on the other hand, emotions at once attractive and tender are not occasionally revealed (in the long Andante, a concession to the Salzburgers' taste for prolixity), or a development of the most highly lyrical kind (in the other Andante, in the concerto). All this—the abnormal length of the movements, their variety, their brilliance, the elaboration of detail entrusted to a big orchestra—all this almost compels the adoption of the new *galant* ideal; but, on reflection, one feels all the same, both in the first movement and in the Allegro assai, the great hunting song with which the serenade concludes, how different is such a work from, for example, one of the symphonies written by Mozart a year or two earlier. Despite all the attractiveness—which is great—of this musical feast, this copious banquet, one cannot conceal the weakness of certain movements, the inordinate *longueur* of the Rondo, in G, and also of the finale. And one begins to regret the high artistic endeavor which endears the former symphonies to us, even though these may have nothing in them to equal the two amazing minuets of the Haffner Serenade, in which Mozart, with an unmatched maturity, anticipates the ballroom scene in *Don Giovanni*.

In the period we are studying, the young master, as I have shown, gives free rein to the virtuosity of his soloists, and writes concertos for most of the instruments of the orchestra calculated to show off their qualities to the best advantage—but never allowing mere brilliance to cramp the inspiration of the moment. This virtuosity, too, is ranged over a wide field; he does not content himself with opposing one performer to the orchestral mass, but divides the orchestra itself into several groups and makes them "concert" among themselves. On the other hand, he is fond of using an "echo" device, probably taking the idea from some model unknown to us; that is to say, he will write a phrase more or less long, given out by a quarter of the performers, the remainder finishing it or repeating it as an echo. But the repetition may only be partial, or even confined to quite a few bars, or the end of the phrase, or even its very last note; but always with particular care that this repetition is, like an echo, an exact textual reproduction of the preceding. This echo device, moreover, was practiced by eighteenth-century masters such as Haydn and Johann Christian Bach; the former specified that the *echo* ought to be played in *separate rooms,* but this pleasantry appertained rather, I think, to chamber music. In his symphonies for two orchestras, on the other hand, Johann Christian Bach, in the spacious rooms of the London Pantheon, used two orchestral masses responding to each other. Mozart in his *Serenata notturna* (K. 239) uses two small orchestras, one formed of two principal violins, viola, and double bass, the other of two violins, a second viola, cello, and drums. The idea here is, evidently, a dialogue exchanged between two small orchestras placed some distance from each other, as for example at each end of a room; and one can easily see that if the echo procedure is not consistent, it is employed very wittily. The other composition of the same genre is, on the contrary, a veritable "echo," entitled *Notturno* (K. 286) written for four orchestras, each of two violins, viola, two horns, and bass. As with the first, we do not know the occasion for which it was composed. The echo device is used with remarkable understanding of its effects; thus, the fine andante with which the work opens has a first subject of four bars repeated in its entirety by the "first echo," after which the other orchestras take up fragments only, getting shorter and shorter.

Sometimes, to give the effect of a more distant echo, the reply is reproduced only after a period of silence; sometimes, again, in a stretto the repetitions appear, first at a bar's interval, then a beat apart, then two beats, in canon; and thus we see the final perfection bestowed by Mozart on a phenomenon of nature known to us all.

G. de St-.F.

Serenata Notturna (Serenade No. 6) for Two Small Orchestras in D major (K. 239)

I. March   II. Menuetto   III. Rondo

TITLE AND music alike would establish this Serenade, which dates from January, 1776, as an "occasional" offering, though no clue to the occasion inspiring it is available. The possibilities are many. Mozart, at the time, was in the employ of the Archbishop of Salzburg. Divertimentos and cassations flowed from the young genius's pen for the amusement of the Archbishop's entourage during repasts and celebrations. As a rule the Archbishop encouraged only the composition of religious music. There were exceptions. The *Serenata notturna* could have been written for a gala occasion in the reception hall of the palace, though it is unlikely. The time of the year would dismiss its having been designed for outdoor use at a garden party. Other serenades of Mozart were so destined.

If the *Serenata* was composed during the last days of December, 1775, it might possibly have been intended as a New Year's Day surprise. In that case his sister Nannerl should be numbered among the likely beneficiaries. Later, in July, 1776, Nannerl received the Divertimento in D as a birthday gift from her brother. Again, Mozart's own birthday occurred on January 27. Could he have impishly intended the serenade as a self-bestowed memento? Perhaps the likeliest theory of all is to ascribe the serenade to the request of a Salzburg merchant or titled aristocrat. Mozart rarely turned down a commission. He was soon to compose his Serenade in D for the marriage of Elisabeth Haffner, daughter of Salzburg's burgomaster, and later the larger scale *Notturno* for the Countess Lodron. Music's marvellous boy could shake "occasional" tunes from his coat sleeve at a moment's notice. Accordingly, the "occasion" may have been a ball in sumptuous surroundings, with the division of the playing personnel into two detached units imparting a special note of swank.

There have been two ways of regarding this music. One was typically Eduard Hanslick's: that its charm vanished with the occasion it served and that its courtly fragrance evaporates in a concert hall. The other has been to welcome sunshine even when it beams from a *Night Serenade*. The *Serenata* is scored for two orchestras, one consisting of two violins, viola, and contrabass, the other of a string quartet and tympani (later Mozart went himself two better by composing the *Notturno*, K. 286, for four orchestras, as if sketching out plans for the ballroom scene in *Don Giovanni*). Fascinating effects of light and shade abound, and the obvious possibilities of contrast are fully exploited. Often orchestra No. 1 acts as soloist against orchestra No. 2, with a resulting richness in tonal coloring. The percussion heightens the contrast, and pizzicati are worked in deftly to extend the color scheme.

L. B.

Serenade in D major (K. 320)

I.	Adagio maestoso; Allegro con spirito	IV.	Rondo: Allegro ma non troppo
II.	Minuetto	V.	Andantino
III.	Concertante: Andante grazioso	VI.	Finale: Presto

THIS SERENADE is inscribed "1779," and therefore belongs to its composer's twenty-third year, to the last part of his residence at Salzburg, for which town indeed he wrote the larger part of his suites of this sort. It was an unhappy year for him. He had just lost his mother. His love for Aloysia Weber had come to naught. Nevertheless, when he returned to his native town from Paris, his father received him in the new abode he had found, and the family feasted as cheerfully as they might upon roast capons. Mozart continued to produce music industriously, although, having seen something of the large capitals, he was restive under the provincialism of Salzburg. "When I play in Salzburg, or when any of my compositions are performed," so he wrote to his father a little later, "the audience might just as well be chairs or tables." And Mozart went on to say that, loving work far more than idleness, nevertheless the want of congenial intercourse and inspiring surroundings made it often impossible for him to begin upon a composition. "And why? Because my mind is not at ease." In another letter he wrote, "To dawdle away one's youth in such a wretched hole is sad enough and harmful besides." His surroundings at Salzburg certainly did not prevent Mozart from composing quantities of beautiful music. Most of the serenades and divertimenti were written for Salzburg. In Vienna there seems to have been less frequent call for pieces of this kind, although the wealthier families would often keep a band for such purposes, and the Emperor Joseph liked to have music played during those meals which he held in the imperial pleasure gardens. Hostelries of the better class also retained groups of musicians for *"harmonie-musik,"* with which their guests were entertained at table. Generally speaking, Mozart must have found far better musicians to perform this sort of music after he had moved to Vienna.

The way in which serenade-making fitted into Mozart's life is illustrated by the following letter which he wrote to his father from Vienna (November 3, 1781): "I must apologise for not writing by the last post; it fell just on my birthday [October 31], and the early part of the day was given to my devotions. Afterwards, when I should have written, a shower of congratulations came and prevented me. At twelve o'clock I drove to the Leopoldstadt, to the Baroness Waldstädten, where I spent the day. At eleven o'clock at night I was greeted by a serenade for two clarinets, two horns, and two bassoons, of my own composition. I had composed it on St. Theresa's Day [October 15] for the sister of Frau von Hickl (the portrait-painter's wife), and it was then performed for the first time. The six gentlemen who execute such pieces are poor fellows, but they play very well together, especially the first clarinet and the two horns. The chief reason I wrote it was to let Herr von Strack (who goes there daily) hear something of mine, and on this account I made it rather serious. It was very much admired. It was played in three different places on St. Theresa's Night. When people had had enough of it in one place they went to another, and got paid over again."

The distinction between serenades, divertimenti, and cassations seems to have consisted mainly in the purpose for which they were intended. Each was a loosely strung together suite of movements, mostly in dance form and often beginning with a march. The movements are often symphonically developed. The successive numbers may have been intended to fill in the recurring pauses in the particular festivity for which they were written. The serenade was usually intended to be played in the evening, and in the open air (the piece which Mozart named *Eine Kleine Nachtmusik* is of the same character). The serenade was a time-honored form allied with the *Ständchen,* which was performed under a window in honor of the person who dwelt within. The group was usually wind instruments, and often limited to six players.

H. E. Krehbiel has written with discernment on this department of Mozart's art. "The divertimenti and cassations were written for indoors as well as outdoor entertainment by day, the serenades for outdoor entertainment by night. In the last part of the eighteenth century it was still as customary as it had been in the sixteenth, for a lover to bring the tribute of a musical performance to his mistress. . . . Frequently musicians were hired, and the tribute took the form of a nocturnal concert. In Shakespeare's *Two Gentlemen of Verona,* Proteus, prompting Thurio what to do to win Silvia's love, says:

> *Visit by night your lady's chamber window*
> *With some sweet concert; to their instruments*
> *Tune a deploring dump; the night's dead silence*
> *Will well become such sweet complaining grievance.*

"It was for such purposes that the serenade was invented as an instrumental form. Sir Thurio's musicians were to play out of doors, and therefore they would have used wind instruments. The oldest serenades were composed for oboes and bassoons. Afterward viols were added, and, as may be guessed from the example before us, if the occasion called for it, strings alone were thought to suffice. The serenades, down to the time of Beethoven, as we may observe in his Trio Op. 8, opened with a march, to the strains of which we may imagine the musicians approaching the lady's chamber window. Then came a minuet, to prepare her ear for the 'deploring dump' which followed—the dump of Shakespeare's day, like the dumka of ours (with which it may have etymological association), being a mournful or pathetic piece of music happily characterized by the poet as a 'sweet complaining grievance.' Then followed another piece, in merry tempo and rhythm; then a second *adagio,* and the entertainment ended with an *allegro,* generally in march rhythm, to which we fancy the musicians departing."

Mozart used varying combinations, sometimes scoring his pieces for winds only, sometimes for strings, and sometimes—as here—for wind and strings combined. This serenade requires two flutes, two oboes, two bassoons, two horns, two trumpets, timpani, two violins, and a single part each for viola and string bass. The first movement and the *finale* utilize all the instruments in a brilliant ensemble save for the flutes which are reserved for individual treatment in the first minuet, the *concertante,* and the rondo.

The first Allegro is introduced by six bars, *adagio maestoso.* The second minuet (which in the present performances replaces the first in this position) is without flutes, with the exception that in the first of the two trios there is a part indicated for flautino, with the staff left blank. It is a matter for conjecture whether the player of this instrument was allowed to fill in this part at his own discretion. The first trio is in notation for strings only; the second trio adds oboes, and a "post" horn: the only instance in the *Serenade* where the horn has other than a merely sustaining part.

After this are two movements in *concertante* form. The usual doubling between wood winds and strings ceases. In the Andante grazioso, entitled *"concertante,"* the two flutes, two oboes, and bassoons are treated with great freedom in five independently moving parts, at times contrapuntal, at times matched in thirds. An episode of the Andante grazioso is a cadenza in five voices. Otto Jahn notes that the two *concertante* movements "are elaborated with great care and accuracy, and are clear and perspicuous as well as tender and graceful; the rondo is somewhat lighter in tone than the first movement. Of bravura, properly so called, there is none to be found, and the ornamental passages are confined to moderate amplifications of the melodies. The instruments are solo in that they bear the principal part throughout, *concertante* in that they emulate each other in manifold and changing combinations; their strife is playful, with sometimes almost a mischievous tone."

The Andantino is also written freely in voice motion, but omits the flutes and gives a leading rôle to the stringed instruments, while the wind instruments are used for the etching in of detail. Jahn further notes a contrast of mood in the Andantino, in which he discerns a "serious melancholy" following upon the "light and sunshiny mood of the two previous movements."

The closing Presto, like the opening movement, is developed at length.

J. N. B.

The melodies and subjects of these works show unmistakable progress; they are of maturer invention, have more musical substance, if the expression may be allowed, more delicacy and nobility of apprehension. Technical progress is visible in the greater freedom of the contrapuntal treatment, which had already been fully developed in Mozart's vocal compositions. This is most obvious in those parts where thematic elaboration predominates, which are richer and freer than hitherto. But, above all, we recognize Mozart's sure tact in preserving the limits that prevent the interest in the different combinations of counterpoint to which a motive can be subjected from becoming essentially technical, and losing its artistic character.

O. J.

THE DIVERTIMENTO

MOZART'S CONTEMPORARIES expected from him, as from any musician of high standing, an inexhaustible fertility in deft music, which could be ordered at will by the prosperous citizens, for their entertainments. The *Unterhaltungsmusik* would grace the festivities at a wedding, or offer pleasing interludes to the good wine and conversation at table. It might help celebrate the "name day" of some prominent personage, with perhaps a serenade in a garden where a small group of wind players, with *Nachtmusik* composed for the occasion, would make an evening party quite charming. Divertimenti, serenades, cassations, Mozart provided on the shortest notice (Köchel's catalogue lists thirty-three of them as surviving). A standing wonder of Mozart's genius was that he often gave something infinitely better than was asked of him—that he now and then squandered on these frequent and passing gaieties some of his truly precious and undying musical thoughts.

J. N. B.

Divertimento in D major (K. 334)

I. Allegro
II. Theme with variations

III. Menuetto
IV. Rondo

THE DIVERTIMENTO in D major was composed in the spring or summer of 1779 for string quartet and two horns. Mozart, then twenty-three years of age, was still living with his father at Salzburg and both this divertimento and a previous one in B flat major, for the same combination of instruments, must have been written—as to the first violin part—for a performer of more than the ordinary executive skill that was possessed by the majority of violinists of that day.

The Divertimento in D major contains six movements, of which the opening Allegro, the Andante (theme and variations), the Minuet, and Rondo are usually played.

I. Allegro, D major, 4/4. The first violins, which throughout are given much brilliant passage work, present the principal theme. The second subject, in A major, is first announced by the second violins, the first violins then taking it up in embroidered form. A codetta, beginning in the second violins, makes use of a bustling sixteenth-note figure. The second division of the movement brings forward (in F major) episodical material in the first violins. The recapitulation presents the principal subject as at the beginning of the movement. The second theme is in the second violins as before, but now in D major. A coda, similar to that already heard, closes the movement brilliantly.

II. Theme with Variations. Andante, D minor, 2/4. The theme, sixteen measures long, consists of two divisions of eight measures each, both repeated. The subject is given out by the first violins. Variation I. The first violins play a triplet variation, this being divided between the other strings in the second part. Variation II. The variation is again in the first violins. Variation III. The first violins play the theme, the basses imitating it in the second half of the measure. Variation IV. The key changes to D major, and in this variation the two horns have the most important part. Variation V. D minor. The second violins open the variation, the first violins taking it up at the fifth measure. Variation VI. A figuration in thirty-second notes is played by the first violins, accompanied by the other strings *pizzicato*.

III. Menuetto, D major, 3/4. This movement scarcely requires comment. It is written in the usual three part form peculiar to the minuet, its principal theme opening gracefully in the first violins.

IV. Rondo. Allegro, D major, 6/8. The first violins set forth the gay principal theme without introduction. Following a pause, the violins give out a new idea, still, however, in D major. This is developed and brilliant passage work for the first violins leads to a theme in A major allotted to the second violins. Following more passage work, the first violins present a second division of the subject, first on the E string, then repeating it on the G string. The principal theme returns, but soon the music goes into B minor and development takes place. The first subject again recurs, as does the second, now in the first violins, in D major and in two sections as before. Keeping the rondo principle in view, Mozart returns (for the last time) to his principal theme, the movement then closing with a bustling coda.

F. B.

Eine Kleine Nachtmusik, Serenade for String Orchestra (K. 525)

I.	Allegro	III.	Menuetto; Allegretto
II.	Romanze	IV.	Rondo: Allegro

THE MOST widely played and popular of Mozart's works for orchestra, *Eine Kleine Nachtmusik,* dates from 1787. It was a crucial period for Mozart. *Don Giovanni* was composed that year, along with two of his finest string quintets, in C major and G minor (K. 515, 516), and the brilliant A major Violin Sonata (K. 526). In February his little Viennese circle of friends broke up, with the Storaces, Kelly, and Attwood all returning home to England. Mozart almost went along. On May 28 his father died. Then one day a rough-looking lad of seventeen, with a heavy Rhenish accent, came in for an audition. Mozart listened, at first politely, then sharply. The visitor showed startling gifts at the piano. Later Mozart remarked to others present in the room: "This young man should be watched. He will soon make a noise in the world." The boy's name was Ludwig van Beethoven.

The manuscript score of *Eine Kleine Nachtmusik* carries August 10, 1787, as the date of completion. It is a compact and faultlessly balanced work, with beautiful melodies woven into a highly polished fabric. The theme of the bright and chattery Rondo finale is "the naïve Viennese popular song to the very life of Schikaneder's Papageno in *The Magic Flute*," to quote Eric Blom.

L. B.

I. Allegro, G major, 4/4 time. The opening movement is in regularly constructed sonata form. The vigorous first theme in G major is followed by a contrasted subject in D. The development is slight, and concerned only with the principal theme. The usual recapitulation follows, and the movement ends with a short coda.

II. Romanze. Andante, C major, 2/2. The simple theme with which the movement opens is given extensive repetition. In the middle of the piece, a new subject (in C minor) is introduced, in which the first violins and the basses answer each other imitatively. Following this the material of the first part returns.

III. Menuetto. Allegretto, G major, 3/4. This is written in the three-part form peculiar to all minuets. The first part begins with a vigorous subject, *forte*. The second (trio) appears in D major, and the third part repeats the first without change.

IV. Rondo. Allegro, G major, 2/2. The principal theme with which this, the last division of the serenade, begins is heard five times in the course of the movement, although not always in the same key. There is a second subject which appears first in D major and in three-part harmony sixteen measures after the commencement of the piece. It is brought back later on in G major. The coda begins with a repetition of the principal theme.

The serenade is scored for first and second violins, violas, cellos, and double basses.

F. B.

3. "SIX GERMAN DANCES" (K.571)

WHEN GLUCK died on November 15, 1787, Emperor Joseph II cast about for a successor to the court composer. The choice fell on Mozart. Thus, on December 7 of that year the Salzburg genius became "court chamber musician" at a salary of 800 florins a year, a saving of 1,200 florins for the economical Joseph, who had paid Gluck 2,000. But, then, Joseph II never professed to like Mozart's music, despite Michael Kelly's statement that he was "passionately fond of music and a most excellent and accurate judge of it." Still, the money came in handy, what with Mozart's haphazard budgeting, an increasing family, and mounting doctor's bills. This was the period of the repeated borrowings from the merchant Puchberg.

Mozart's imperial duties boiled down to writing dance music for the masked balls held in the Redoutensaale, located in a wing of the Hofburg on the right side of the Josephplatz in Vienna. Quite philosophically he regarded the pay as "too high for what he did."

"What he did" in the next few years reads like a ballroom dance catalogue. The emperor ordered no operas or symphonies, only dance music for the gay celebrants of the Redoutensaale. The year 1788 brought six *Deutsche* (or *Teutsche*) and twelve minuets. Twelve *Deutsche* and a fresh dozen of minuets followed the next year. The year 1790 yielded none. In respectful observance of Joseph II's death (February 20), the Redoutensaale festivities were suspended. Leopold II ascended the throne on March 13. When the masquerades were resumed the following year, Mozart's pen again got busy, and dances poured out afresh. First came six additional minuets, then six more *Deutsche,* followed by four minuets, two country dances, two more minuets, and three more *Deutsche.* The record also includes six *Ländler* and later that year a half dozen more country dances, beside *Ein Deutscher mit Leirer-Trio,* the *Leirer* being the hurdy-gurdy man.

Viennese from all classes were invited to the Redoutensaale "masked balls," the Emperor delighting in the spectacle of democratic mingling. They usually took place on Sundays during the Carnival season, on Shrove Tuesday, and on the last three days of the carnival. As may be gathered from the Mozart inventory, minuets, waltzes (*Deutsche*), and country dances were alternately played.

Hence the waltz—the *Deutscher Tanz*—was already the rage of Vienna. Because of the huge crowds drawn to the affairs, it is said only the "lower classes danced the waltz." After the Emperor's death the director of the Court Theater went on purchasing dances from local composers. Hummel, Haydn, and Beethoven all earned a few ducats filling the director's orders.

In Mozart's time the Viennese waltz, the *Deutscher,* was a lilting, gliding dance, "a more popular Ländler," with the beat sharply marked and the dance divided into two parts, each generally eight measures long. A *Deutscher* figures in Weber's *Der Freischütz.* In the elaborate finale of the first act of Mozart's *Don Giovanni,* the stage directions call on Leporello and Masetto to dance a *Teutscher,* one of the three dances running simultaneously in the contrapuntal web. The spirit of the "German dance" was strongly folkish, alike in its sentimental strains as in its brusquer aspects. The minuet, of course, was more elegant. Thus, in the opera the Don assigns the minuet to his more distinguished guests. He himself dances a country dance with Zerlina, and Leporello drags the duped Masetto into the whirl of a *Deutscher Tanz.*

Abert, in his monumental revision of Jahn's biography of Mozart, observes that the most striking thing about these Mozart dances is their "inexhaustible inventiveness," despite the fact that the simple pattern offers little scope for marked individuality. A trio section, often containing snatches of folk music, is usually in the minor key, and Abert speaks of the delightful little touches of orchestral wit often occurring in the codas, giving as an instance the "Mannheim crescendo and finale of the K. 571 group." He mentions, too, the curiously tart chromatics of the concluding dance. In the K. 568 to 586 sets he detects Hungarian and Spanish echoes.

The Mozart *Verzeichnis* gives 1789 as the year of composition of the K. 571 group, and the place Vienna. A manuscript containing only the parts for wind instruments in pairs reposes in the Malherbe Collection in the library of the Paris Conservatory. The autograph reads "6 *teutsches.*" The corresponding manuscript of the string parts (two violins and bass) has been in the Vienna National Library since 1927. It bears the words "6 *teutsche di Wolfgango Amadeo Mozart.*" The catalogue points out that the autograph was "previously in the possession of the Emperor Maximilian in the Miramar Castle." On another copy of the score appear the words "6 *Deutsche Tänze aus dem k. k. [königlichenkaiserlichen] kleinen Redoutensaale* 1790."

L. B.

"Three German Dances" (K. 605)

Most famous of the three "German Dances" of K. 605 is the third and last, often referred to as "The Sleighride" ("Die Schlittenfahrt") because of a middle Trio section with descriptive bell effects. We have Kelly's word for it, that what Mozart had in mind was the sumptuous *course des traîneaux*—or procession of sledges—sponsored by the imperial court during the winter months. Richly caparisoned sleighs, bearing elegantly garbed courtiers and their ladies, moved by torchlight down the boulevard to the Emperor's palace. In the Trio the *Schellen*—or little bells—sound in A, F, E, and C; towards the end they fade away in a delicate diminuendo. Besides bells, the original scoring of the C major "German Dance" calls for two violins, bass, two flutes, two oboes, two bassoons, two horns (two posthorns in Trio), two trumpets, and tympani. The three dances that constitute K. 605 were completed in Vienna on February 12, 1791.

Michael Kelly, in his *Reminiscences* published in London in 1826, describes the Viennese as "in my time dancing mad." The ladies of Vienna who attended the Redoutensaale masquerades were "particularly celebrated for their grace and movements in waltzing, of which they never tire." He confessed that for his part he found waltzing from ten at night until seven in the morning "a continual whirligig most tiresome to the eye and ear, to say nothing of any worse consequences."

Kelly, who was Mozart's first Basilio in Vienna, speaks of his friend and patron as "an enthusiast in dancing." Mozart's wife went even further. "His taste," she maintained, "lay in that art rather than in music."

L. B.

6

The Chamber Music

THE BACKGROUND

TO WHAT extent the early Italian composers anticipated the coming of the form that was to represent the ideal in chamber music—that of the string quartet—will always be a matter of dispute among the erudite, for it is not easy to discern the intention of the scoring. A plausible case has been made out for a piece by Gregorio Allegri, the composer of the famous *Miserere* which Mozart wrote down from memory when in Rome in 1770. The piece in question, dating from about 1630, is certainly written in four parts, but so are some of his concertos. A much stronger claim is put forward by Professor Dent on behalf of the elder Scarlatti. He writes: "The first real string quartets were written within a few years of Corelli's death (certainly under his influence), by a composer who was traditionally his personal friend—Alessandro Scarlatti." Certainly the form was not unknown to the Italians, whether Scarlatti or another was the first to use it. But the point is not of great importance, since the credit for having developed it must be given to the German-speaking countries. Meanwhile the Italians divided their attention between the solo sonata and the concerto, which very soon became incontestably orchestral music. Thus Tartini, although he wrote quartets that dispensed with a continuo, still has access to our concert-rooms solely with his sonatas, as Geminiani, Locatelli, and others have with their concertos. Of those who concerned themselves mainly with chamber music the most prolific was a comparative late-comer, Felice de Giardini, composer of eighteen string quartets, but as he outlived Mozart he clearly belongs to a later phase of our subject.

The influence of the Italian violinists was widespread. They travelled to all musical countries and set a fashion, not only in playing, but in composition. In each country they had their imitators. In Germany there were many, few of whom achieved any noteworthy success. Although Bach himself was attracted, as is evidenced by the many Italian works he arranged, the robust art of North Germany was too firmly entrenched to go down before the invader. To that art is sometimes ascribed the first music for string quartet composed in Germany. The reference is to the *Hortus Musicus* of Johann Adam Reinken, the Hamburg organist whom Bach as a young man tramped many miles afoot to hear. It would, however, be stretching a point to regard this work, published in 1704 and consisting of six suites, as a prototype of the string quartet. It is laid out for two violins, viol da gamba, and figured bass, and is rarely in more than three independent parts. The position of Bach is better defined. A considerable portion of his music comes under the wider application of the term "chamber music," but the circumstance that it consists largely of solo and duo sonatas excludes most of it from our purview here. In the narrower sense his chamber music consists of a trio for two violins and continuo, and two for violin, flute, and continuo, the second of which forms part of the *Musikalisches Opfer* that he wrote for Frederick the Great in 1747. This was the second of two works based on a theme supplied by the King himself, the first being the *Art of Fugue*. It exploits some of the theme's yet remaining possibilities. As the continuo part has been worked out by Bach's pupil Kirnberger, his version presents the nearest approach to chamber music in the modern sense to be found in his works. His contemporary Telemann is another German composer credited with having forestalled the coming of the string quartet. His Tafelmusik is certainly an anticipation of the spirit of chamber music, but as to the form the evidence is contradictory. Finally Evaristo dall' Abaco, musical director to Max Emanuel of Bavaria, another claimant, and an interesting composer to boot, can be left out of account as he did not dispense with the continuo. The birth of the new art must be dated after his time.

Its birthplace can almost definitely be stated to have been Mannheim, where Johann Wenzel Stamitz, the founder of the Mannheim School of violinists, began giving chamber concerts in 1743. Among his pupils were his two sons, Carl, who remained at Mannheim, and Anton, who went to Paris, as well as Cannabich, who succeeded him as conductor. Others associated with the Mannheim group were Franz Xavier Richter, Anton Filtz, and Carlo Toëschi. Meanwhile Jan Zach, a Czech like Stamitz, Georg Matthias Monn, and Georg Christoph Wagenseil were producing chamber music in Vienna, and Placidus von Camerloher was doing the same at Munich. Most of these wrote quartets, and more than one of them has been put forward as having done so before Haydn, but a whole army of precursors in the form would not detract from his merit in having endowed it with substance, as none did before him. There is therefore no interest in investigating the claims of composers none of whom, save Stamitz, who seems to have the best title, produced music of sufficiently outstanding merit to endure.

Curiously enough, Haydn himself would almost appear to have unconsciously stumbled upon the form. In his young days he acquired a reputation for writing cassations, divertimenti, serenades, and the like for any instruments that happened to be available, often to be played in the open air. On the strength of that reputation he was invited in 1755 to a country-house at Weinzirl, near Melk, whose owner, von Fürnberg, was accustomed to have such music played. Haydn wrote a number of these compositions and at first made so little distinction between them that what was undoubtedly his first symphony has somehow got among his quartets, where it figures as Op. 1, No. 5! Others appear to have been played at first indiscriminately by string quartet or string orchestra. The idea of the string quartet as a form seems to have emerged gradually at some stage of the writing of the first two sets of six, which have five movements apiece, except the one that is a symphony in disguise. But he came away from Weinzirl with eighteen of these compositions in his portfolio, and it seems beyond doubt that the third set of six, apart from their having the four movements that were to establish the tradition, can only have been intended as quartets.

Hitherto, on the authority of the Paris edition begun in 1764, the Quartet in B flat which opens the first set has been accepted as Haydn's first string quartet, but recently Miss Marion Scott made the discovery that the Hummel edition, published in Amsterdam, opened with a different quartet altogether, in E flat; this is plainly inscribed Op. 1, No. 1, but disappeared from later editions. It is of course just possible that Haydn himself arranged its withdrawal, as composers will, deeming their early works no longer worthy of them, but that seems both unlike him and unlike the age in which he lived. In any case it appears that we must accept this E flat Quartet as the starting-point of modern chamber music; if we have any sentimental regard for eighty-three as the long-established number of Haydn's progeny in this form, we can retain it by discarding the Symphony in E flat which figures as No. 5. This first quartet may have been one of the works Haydn took with him to Weinzirl, in which case the traditional date of 1750 may be vindicated, or it may have been composed there, in which case Pohl's date of 1755 for this historic event stands proved. The former date has a fascination for historians. In that year Bach died, and his death is the landmark dividing his era from that of modern music, of which "Papa" Haydn is acclaimed the father.

Having now reached the threshold of chamber music as it is understood by the modern world, it behooves us perhaps to pause and take stock of what it comprises. Strictly speaking, it includes all concerted music for any number of performers from two upwards to the point at which the orchestra begins. That point is commonly understood to be the one at which individual instrumental parts are duplicated, as is the practice in orchestral music. But there is an intermediate point at which a combination, without duplicated parts, is called a chamber orchestra, and that really transcends the ordinary limits of chamber music. Although, for instance, Schönberg's Chamber Symphony really conforms to the definition, few people would be disposed to regard it as chamber music, because the number of players is too large for the intimacy that is the true characteristic of the "music of friends." At the other end of the scale it is not customary to include music for voice and piano, or even pianoforte duets, the former constituting the domain of the *Lied,* and the latter being essentially piano music, though shared between partners. For the purposes of this book all duet sonatas have been similarly excluded, and chamber music is taken as beginning with works for three performers. Although the pleasure of duet-playing is essentially that derived from chamber music, there is a certain logic in this, for the same reasons which elsewhere ordain that two are company and three none would operate here in the opposite direction, two being somewhat exclusive, and real company commencing with three. We will therefore begin by defining chamber music as consisting, for our purposes, of works performed by not fewer than three players and, except in very rare cases, not more than nine.

The majority of this music is for strings. Long experience has established the string quartet as the most perfect, concise, and self-contained combination in all music, consisting as it does of four instruments of similar hue, whose collective range is comprehensive in the sense that they can reach every part of the scale except the extreme bass, which is not required with so small a volume of tone, and that they are sufficient for four-part harmony. Almost all composers—even opera-writers like Rossini, Auber, or Verdi—have experienced the desire at some time to write for this ideal combination. But it is a treacherous field. Precisely because it is so self-contained it demands scrupulous musicianship. In the turmoil of the orchestra a composer can "get away" with workmanship that would be mercilessly exposed in a string quartet. That is why so many composers have either preferred to keep out of this field until comparatively late in life or have abandoned it, temporarily or permanently, after an early venture that brought them little satisfaction. If a composer is honest with himself, the writing of a string quartet is a searching test.

Works for fewer strings than four are not common. Most of those for two violins and 'cello are a legacy of the continuo period, but from Mozart and Beethoven to modern writers, such as Hindemith, composers have gradually furnished an attractive selection of trios for violin, viola, and 'cello, to which others, such as Kodály, have added trios for two violins and 'cello. In fact one might say that if any member of a quartet party disappoints, there is no reason why, with an adequate library at hand, the other three should not console themselves for his absence. For upwards of four players there exists ample material: quintets (some with two violas, some with two 'cellos), sextets, and octets, which are double quartets. Some combinations include a double-bass, but the unwieldiness of that instrument makes it really unsuitable for chamber use, and the depths to which its range extends belong more properly to the orchestra.

The instrument most frequently associated with the strings in chamber music is of course the piano. We have seen how the keyboard instrument entrusted with the continuo performed purely ancillary functions, but, with the advent of chamber music as we understand it, it was not long before the keyboard was reinstated in a more honourable position. The process was begun by Haydn in his trios, but more than any one work it was Mozart's G minor Quartet that established the piano in its new functions as a partner, later to become sometimes a predominant partner. Musical purists occasionally demur at the blend of piano and strings as not perfectly harmonious. It is a fact that whereas string-players use natural intonation in enharmonics, the "well-tempered" piano substitutes a compromise, but only the most sensitive ear can be incommoded by the difference. On the other hand it may be admitted that the percussive quality of the piano gives it an advantage which is foreign to the real freemasonry of chamber music and that, especially in late romantic works, the pianist is readily tempted to regard himself as playing a concerto with stringed accompaniment. There are, in fact, many modern chamber works weighted with piano parts that make as heavy demands on virtuosity as any concerto. On the whole the combinations with piano have not the same purity as those of strings only, but in practice that has not deterred the greatest composers from writing splendid chamber music in which the piano is prominent. It consists in the main of trios for piano, violin, and 'cello, quartets for piano, violin, viola, and 'cello, and quintets for piano and string quartet. For convenience these are commonly referred to as piano trios, piano quartets, and piano quintets. Piano sextets are relatively uncommon.

The association of one wind instrument with strings is usually successful, the piquancy of contrast compensating for the disturbed balance of tone. Such works are numerous, the wind instrument being the flute, oboe, clarinet, or horn. One calls to mind Brahms's horn trio, the clarinet quintets of Mozart and Brahms, the recent oboe quintets of Bax and Bliss, and many other charming compositions of this class. A larger admixture of wind instruments produces good effects, but of a more orchestral timbre, and as the wind

Salzburg in the nineteenth century.

Emanuel Schikaneder as Papageno in *The Magic Flute*. The librettist of the opera shown in his feather costume. From the first edition of *Die Zauberflöte*. In the Mozarteum, Salzburg.

element increases in importance we seem, illogically but instinctively, to be moving away from the essential quality of chamber music. When we reach combinations for wind instruments alone—generally wind quintets for flute, oboe, clarinet, bassoon, and horn—the quality of tone produced demands a greater space than a private room, in which it is apt to prove overpowering, and since it sounds far more satisfactory in a concert-hall, it partakes more of the nature of concert music than of chamber music. There is a large literature of such music, but for this reason we propose to touch upon it more sparingly.

There is one other combination that has contact with chamber music. It is that of one or more voices with a small combination of instruments. It ranges from songs with string-quartet accompaniment to chamber operas, such as Holst's memorably beautiful *Savitri*. But for practical reasons we prefer to regard the former as belonging more properly to the domain of song, and the latter to that of opera.

By far the greatest bulk of chamber music, particularly in classical and romantic times, is composed in sonata form. At the end of the eighteenth century there were divertimenti, and occasionally in the nineteenth some composer would venture to write a suite, but for practically the whole of that century the string quartet was so closely associated with sonata form that to mention one was to imply the other. The devotees of chamber music were so imbued with this tradition that it was difficult for them to take seriously any work not in sonata form. Friedrich Kiel must have been a very venturesome fellow indeed to write two sets of waltzes for string quartet, and when, later, the Russians began to write agreeable sets of pieces for that sacrosanct combination, it was taken almost as a mark of self-confessed inferiority to German standards. This priggish attitude has done chamber music an incredible amount of harm. It was peculiar to the nineteenth century. The eighteenth liked its music crisp, clear, and on occasion gay, the twentieth likes it pungent, concise, and on occasion ironic. But it is the nineteenth that has contributed the bulk of the repertoire, and that is the reason why to the man in the street—or, let us say, the radio listener—the term "chamber music" is commonly accepted as indicating lengthy, erudite works for the consumption of the few. It is a misconception that time alone can eradicate, by enriching the repertoire with works of lighter calibre to restore the balance. Meanwhile, if chamber music is to regain the hold it had on the musical public, it behooves the organizers to leaven their programs in accordance with modern taste, and flank the greater classics with music affording relaxation by contrast.

If the Mannheim School is most probably to be given the credit for launching upon the world in its definitive form the institution we know as the string quartet, the shape of the music written for it was determined by the new symphonic form, the introduction of which is generally attributed to Carl Philipp Emanuel Bach. He it was who gave sonata form its new direction, and though Haydn does not appear to have been associated with him at any time, there can be little doubt that in his search for the ideal form he was influenced by the elder master. C. P. E. Bach wrote a quantity of chamber music, as did also two of Johann Sebastian's younger sons, Johann Christoph and Johann Christian, the latter known as the English Bach, from his long residence in England. These younger Bachs were, however, Haydn's contemporaries, not his precursors.

Haydn's large output of chamber music is conveniently divided into two periods by an interval of ten years between two consecutive sets of quartets: Op. 20, composed in 1771, and Op. 33, composed in 1781. Of the latter he has himself said, in a letter, that they are in an "entirely new style." This interval also corresponds with a period of great activity in Mozart's career, from his fifteenth to his twenty-fifth year. Haydn was destined to outlive Mozart by many years, and if the younger composer benefited at first from the elder's example, there can be no doubt that the debt was amply repaid in the end, Haydn's later works, such as the well-known Salomon Symphonies, being distinctly influenced by Mozart. Although this influence is not conspicuous in the first quartets that followed the ten-year interval, it asserted itself also in these before the last of them were penned. This gives an added significance to the subdivision of Haydn's chamber music. The earlier period was one not so much of experiment, for which Haydn had little need after the experience gained in the first dozen quartets, as of quest—search for the most congenial mode of expression. As Professor Tovey has said, "If Haydn's career had ended there (after Op. 20) nobody would have guessed which of some half-dozen different lines he would have followed up," and he proceeds to enumerate them, but begins the next paragraph with: "Something different happened."

This first period of Haydn's chamber music itself permits of sub-division into two groups, each comprising three sets of six quartets each. The first eighteen quartets were composed, as we have seen, consecutively, though possibly incorporating some earlier material. Of these the first twelve could equally well be described as consisting of eleven divertimenti and a symphony. Yet they contain some highly characteristic and even prophetic movements, such as, for instance, the Andante of the F minor Quartet, Op. 2, No. 4, and some of those that are in variation form. The third set, however, shows such progress as to make it appear probable that the two earlier sets represent the accumulated material he had by him at the time, and the third the outcome of his experience at Weinzirl. One of this set, Op. 3, No. 5, in F major, with a serenade for its slow movement, ranks with his most popular quartets and the minuet from Op. 3, No. 3, nicknamed the *Dudelsack* or Bagpipes Minuet, is a universal favourite. In these three sets Haydn has definitely found the solution of the problems that confronted him at the out-set. The first of these, the distribution of the functions formerly filled by the continuo, was very early disposed of, and the others, mainly formal, were brought to the stage where principles were established and only amplification remained for the future. In fact, in these three sets the modern string quartet not only was born, but reached adolescence.

An interval divides them from the next three sets. Haydn had meanwhile entered the service of Prince Esterházy, written a large quantity of music for his band, and generally broadened his experi-ence. This shows in the next set, Op. 9, one of which, No. 4, in D minor, is fairly well known. The six comprised in Op. 17 are more important. It is here that we begin to encounter the regular concert repertoire, which may be said to include most of the six quartets comprised in Op. 20, the first to be known in the literature of cham-ber music as "great" quartets. They bore another description, being known as the "Sun" quartets, though one of them, the fifth, in F minor, is anything but sunny. With this set Haydn's development period is completed. Not only had he, so to speak, put the string quartet on its feet, but in certain movements he had attained to a height not often surpassed in his later works. It is the sustained quality of these and their maturity of thought that constitute their superiority.

Whilst Haydn gave the continuo its quietus so far as the quartet was concerned, he was at the same time paving the way for the modern use of the keyboard instrument in chamber music. The majority of his numerous piano trios belong to this early period, and though few of them approach the quartets in musical value, there is a special interest in the manner of their progress. At first the 'cello part is almost limited to duplicating the essential notes of the bass already present in the piano part. Such trios form the connecting link with the continuo period. Nor can it be said that subsequent emancipation proceeds very far, but it proceeds far enough to afford an inkling of the rôle the keyboard is to fill in later chamber music. It was left for Mozart to give a clearer indication, but not until he had won his spurs in quartet writing.

E. E.

THE MUSIC

Mozart's earliest chamber-music work was written during the first of three visits to Italy. It is a string quartet (K. 80) in G major; the manuscript is dated: Lodi, March 15, 1770, 7 p.m. In its original form it contained three movements: adagio, allegro, and minuet with trio. A rondo, as fourth movement, was added late in 1773. This quartet is not a distinguished work, nor does it differ greatly from similar works written by Mozart's Italian contemporaries. The violins move in thirds and sixths much of the time, the lower instruments are confined to an accompanying role, and kinship with the old trio sonata is not remote. While the formal details are well handled and the writing is clear and precise, the general effect is not one of maturity. The work is influenced by Italian love of melody; one short tune follows another, transitions between themes are composed of new material, and one is reminded of a potpourri. The prevailing style is homophonic; the few contrapuntal passages serve only to remind one that Mozart was a well-educated young musician, trained in all styles.

After two successful trips to Italy, Mozart returned to Salzburg. His stay at home, from December, 1771, to October, 1772, was the longest since his travels had begun, almost ten years earlier. Among the fruits of this stay at home were three quartets or, as they are called on the manuscript, divertimentos (K. 136–138). But these are not the usual kind of divertimento, for they are three-movement works without minuets; a divertimento of this time almost always contained at least one minuet.

The Italian influence prominent in K. 80 is here noticeably absent. In its place one finds the ingratiating qualities and clichés of the Rococo period. Broken chords and scale passages give rise to a feeling of restlessness. Rapid pulsations in eighth-notes, usually carried by either the viola or the cello, are characteristic throughout these three quartets and serve to disguise lack of harmonic movement. But even in these early works there are premonitions of the genius Mozart was to show in later life; they are best seen in the sonata-form movements, at the transition from first to second theme in the recapitulation. In that section (the recapitulation) the musical intention is to present both themes in the tonic key, but to approach the second theme as though it were still in the dominant, as it had been in the exposition. The problem of balancing exposition and recapitulation sections, one containing themes on tonic and dominant, the other on tonic and tonic, was apparently a fascinating one for Mozart. Nowhere did he show his genius so clearly and so often as in these transitions. An early example of that skill is seen in the first movement of the B flat Quartet (K. 137); a series of chromatic bass sequences leads to the return of the second theme in a highly original way. In other respects these quartets are not noteworthy. Developments are short, and the typical Mozartean device of introducing a new subject in the development is seen (K. 138). The first violin dominates in these quartets; the second has the dual role of accompanying the first violin in thirds or in imitations and of adding its voice to the purely harmonic accompaniment provided by the viola and the cello.

A few months after these quartets were written the Mozarts were again on the road to Italy, to remain from October, 1772, to March, 1773. On the way to Milan, Mozart composed a quartet (Jahn hints at boredom during a stop-over at Bozen, before returning home

he wrote five more. These six quartets (K. 155–160), although written within a few months of the K. 136–138 set, show again with
what giant strides Mozart approached artistic maturity. Each of the
six contains three movements, but there all similarity with the earlier
set ceases.

There is first of all a greater degree of freedom in Mozart's handling of the lower voices. In K. 155 the second violin emerges with
a charming melody; in K. 159 it announces the first theme, while the
first violin rests. The cello is given a part in imitative developments
in K. 157, and in K. 158 all three lower instruments share honors
with the first violin. Formal details, also, are treated with comparable
freedom. Transitions hint at forthcoming themes; a second theme
on occasion (K. 155) modulates throughout its entire course; an increasing competence in contrapuntal technique is recognized (K.
158).

Mozart has also grown wiser in his choice of themes. First and
second themes contrast to a greater degree than they do in the earlier
quartets and, for that matter, than they do in many of the Haydn
quartets up to Opus 20. The consequences of thematic contrast were
not yet realized by Mozart; the vivid interplay of diverse dramatic
and lyric bits, as we find it twenty-five years later in Beethoven,
was seldom to become a factor of Mozart's style. Perhaps we do
the latter an injustice in pointing out the absence of this useful and
expressive device in the early works. We should be content that
Mozart wrote these cheerful works and be glad that they pave the
way for the great quartets of the following decade.

There are evidences of growth, of changes leading toward a mature style, in almost every major composer. A late work, when
compared with an earlier one, reveals how the composer has acquired
a more sensitive feeling for melody, has found a new use for counterpoint, has changed his rhythmic habits, or has altered his style in
general. Such growth is typical of Mozart, too, as we have seen above.
But what sets Mozart apart from other composers is the rapidity
with which major changes in style take place. Almost a decade was
required for Haydn to progress from counterpoint to imitative
development; seven years went by before the Classical Beethoven
became the Romantic Beethoven. Comparable changes took place in
Mozart after a few months had elapsed. He too suffered the growing

pains which are the lot of every composer, be he child prodigy or not, but his rate was much faster than anyone else's. His year encompassed another man's decade.

A case in point is provided by the next set of six quartets (K. 168–173), written in 1773, the year which also saw the writing of the K. 155–160 set. Mozart spent the summer of that year in Vienna, where he became acquainted with Haydn's quartets of Opus 20 (published in 1772), those in which Haydn rediscovered counterpoint and wrote fugues. What is the result? Mozart discovers that counterpoint is admirably suited to quartet writing, and composes fugues: two of the quartets (the first and the sixth) contain fugal last movements, and for the first time he employs the four-movement form, a form found in Haydn ever since his Opus 3, about 1755–60.

Nor does the resemblance end at this point. K. 168 begins with a nine-measure period composed of one three-measure phrase and three of two measures—an irregularity typical of Haydn. The second movement begins with the intervals found in Haydn's Opus 20, No. 5. Likewise in the others of this set; the fugal finales, mentioned above, and the first movement of K. 170, which is an andante with variations, as in Haydn, give further evidence of direct influence. Einstein, in his account of these quartets, lists several other similarities, and points out how directly and unashamedly Mozart leaned on his older contemporary. It could not have been otherwise, Mozart being what he was. Throughout his lifetime he was the perfect assimilator: he borrowed, to discard after one use or to refine on a higher level, from every composer with whom he had any feeling of kinship. His genius shows most clearly in the uses he made of other men's innovations. Having once seen or heard a new device, a new texture or style, or even a new melody, Mozart was able to estimate its worth accurately, alter it to conform to his needs, and make it an element of his style. Thus, his music becomes in a sense the synthesis of all he heard and experienced, but purified and brought into order through his immaculate taste and musical perception.

Mozart left Salzburg only once between the fall of 1773 and September, 1777: a four-month trip to Munich in the winter of 1774. For the first time since early childhood he stayed at home long enough to taste the real flavor of his native city. He had never liked Salzburg; he found its society dull and his court duties boring. And of especial significance here, he found little interest in string quartets, and he received no commissions to write for that medium. Being a practical musician, he wrote none.

Nor did he write string quartets on the almost two-year visit to Mannheim and Paris, September, 1777, to June, 1779, during the course of which his mother died. He did compose four quartets for flute and strings: K. 285, K. 285a, K. Anh. 171, and K. 298. The first three were written at Mannheim as the result of a commission. Several facts indicate that Mozart considered these works off the beaten path: the first contains only three movements, the second and third only two; Mozart had adopted the four-movement form for his string quartets several years earlier, in the K. 168–173 set. Again, the flute predominates to a large extent, while the strings merely accompany. The first quartet, in D major, is on the whole a charm-ing work, typically Mannheim in its graciousness, melodiousness, and absence of deeply felt sentiment. The second and third, K. 285a and K. Anh. 171, not being included in the *Complete Works,* are not available. Einstein reports that "they are in good style and 'tender,' nothing more." The fourth of the flute quartets (K. 298), written at Paris in 1778, is, again according to Einstein, a parody. Exuberant, perfunctory, at times almost inspid, it is not among the important works of Mozart.

After the Paris-Mannheim visit, Mozart returned home for a year and a half. Salzburg offered no more stimulation than it had earlier, and he felt no compulsion to compose string quartets during that stay. Late in 1780 Mozart went to Munich, and there, early in 1781, the quartet for oboe and strings (K. 370) was written. Un-like the flute quartets, this work deserves a high place in the music of that period. It embodies many of the stylistic elements that were later to become so characteristic. The oboe is treated in general as one of four equal instruments; it no longer dominates as the flute had done in the earlier works. And while it too contains only three movements (the minuet is omitted), the quartet provides for great contrasts of expression. A graceful yet sturdy first movement is followed by a moving adagio in which the oboe is given full oppor-tunity to exhibit its possibilities. The final rondo, in 6/8 meter, contains a unique passage in which the oboe proceeds with an embellished melody in 4/4 while the strings continue in 6/8, a device most unusual in Mozart.

In 1781 came the eventful move to Vienna. Mozart, summoned from Munich by his archbishop employer, arrived in a resentful mood, was greatly dissatisfied with the conditions of his employment, and succeeded in breaking away from the disliked archbishop. He was free, without prospects, without funds, and he was twenty-five. Secure in the knowledge of his own gifts, confident of his future, and glad to be rid of Salzburg, Mozart decided to remain in Vienna. From that time, from June, 1781, his activities were centered in that most musical, therefore most stimulating, of cities. But still no string quartets!

At about the same time Haydn was completing his Opus 33 quartets, those written "in an entirely new manner." In the winter of 1781 Haydn came to Vienna to supervise the performance of the quartets at the Austrian court; there is a strong likelihood that Mozart met the older man during that winter. Here began the ten years of friendship and mutual esteem, years full of reciprocal influence and stimulation. Mozart modeled his works on those of Haydn; yet Haydn "learned from Mozart how to compose quartets." With the stimulation provided by Vienna, the encouragement and respect offered by Haydn, and the Opus 33 quartets available as models, Mozart returned to the path he had left almost ten years earlier. He began to write quartets again in December, 1782.

It was not Mozart's custom to compose without an external reason. A great number of his works were written to complete his commissions. Many were designed to demonstrate his fitness for a particular position. Others he wrote as material for his own concerts; with some Mozart hoped, through appropriate dedications, to influence prospective employers. Only a few seem to have been composed for inner reasons, to fill some need in Mozart's life. The six quartets written at Vienna between December, 1782, and January, 1785, fall into the latter class. They were not commissioned, Mozart had no professional need for them, nor were they directed toward a particular nobleman. They arose solely out of the desire to write for musical Vienna, to demonstrate his prowess in the long-neglected field of quartet writing, and to pay homage to Haydn. The six are: K. 387, in G major; K. 421, in D minor; K. 428, in E flat; K. 458, in

B flat ("The Hunt"); K. 464, in A major; and K. 465, in C major. These six, together with four later quartets, which will be discussed below, are usually published together as the "ten famous quartets."

The first three were written within a year of December, 1782; the last three between November, 1784, and January, 1785. Published in September, 1785, they carried a dedication to Haydn in which Mozart spoke of them as being the "fruit of a long and laborious work." But no trace of effort appears in the music; only the autograph gives evidence of how Mozart altered, erased, discarded, and substituted. And the results are models of perfection: not a false gesture; not a faulty proportion. The six quartets stand as the finest examples of Mozart's genius.

We have seen that Mozart had been greatly influenced by Haydn's quartets of Opus 20 a decade earlier; he had imitated the older man's style, his counterpoint, and even his melodies. He was, perhaps, even more strongly influenced by Haydn's Opus 33, with which he became acquainted in 1782; but this time he was stimulated to go in other directions. With Haydn's Opus 33, the quartet's structure and style were virtually completed; the "new manner" of Haydn had provided the bridge between *galant* melody and "learned" counterpoint, and sonata form was fully established. Mozart, ever willing to build on another man's achievements, immediately seized upon that new manner and made it his own—with what difficulty the autographs and the dedication give evidence.

If one is to characterize the Mozart of these quartets, one must use the terms "restraint" and "subtlety." On a fabric that is in turn gloomy, pensive, resigned, and gay the designs, usually in the darker shades, are laid in a variety of patterns that defies description. Mozart does not brood, although he is aware of life's sternness; his gloomier moments are subtly lightened by contrasting passages which restore one's optimism. He does not laugh uproariously, although he is gay by temperament; his humor is always tinged with the knowledge that comedy and tragedy are a short step apart. His sunlight carries with it the promise that it will soon be cloudy, but, miraculously, one is glad to accept whatever weather Mozart ordains. Therein lies one of the great delights of these quartets. We are in the hands of a great guide, seeing through his eyes the components of human emotion. And though we may look into the darker pools, we are not plunged into them—as we will be by Tschaikowsky. Though we may observe the unrestrained humor of peasants, we do not ourselves take part in it—as we did with Haydn. Mozart in an impersonal way shows us what exists, reflects upon it with us, and returns us, moved but unimpaired, to our own worlds. That is the essence of Classical music.

It is one thing to point out the restraint and impersonal nature of these quartets; it is quite another to describe the musical means whereby they are achieved. One could quote this passage and trace the subtle overlapping of phrases; one could quote that passage and compare its effect with a similar one. One could point to a sequence of chords, to this turn of a melody, to that combination of motives. All this would be true and relevant, and yet it would not "prove" anything. A sensitiveness to untheatrical music, an appreciation of musical refinement, and an awareness of the myriad facets of human life and emotion are necessary properly to evaluate these six quartets.

One technical detail may be singled out, however: the chromatic scale or, more accurately, the fragment of chromatic melody. Mozart had often used chromatics before 1782; after that date they became characteristic. From the G major Quartet (K. 387) of that year to the Requiem (K. 626) of 1791, they are almost constantly in evidence. The half-poignant, half-resigned tone of Mozart's late works is due in no small part to the use of short chromatic lines.

For two centuries before Mozart, composers had turned to chromatic melody to depict intensities of emotion not easily achieved through the diatonic scale. Purcell, in *Dido and Aeneas,* and Bach, in the B Minor Mass, surrounded some of their most pathetic utterances with chromatic lines. But Mozart found that intensity need not be restricted to pathos. He arrived at a concentration of emotion in fast-moving passages and in minuets as well. The presence of a series of half-steps lends a conciseness, a weight, and a drive to melodic passages that a diatonic series cannot always supply. Mozart uses the chromatic line most often in transitional passages where contrast is needed or where a change of mood is anticipated; the first movement of the G major Quartet is an example. The device is used subtly to intensify a moving bass line, as in the minuet of the D minor. And in one of the most masterful of all passages, the introduction of the C major, it brings a mood of despair and resignation unequaled in all of Mozart's works. Chromatics appear numberless times in the six quartets; often they are concealed, but their effect is felt nonetheless. Several themes in the E flat Quartet are based upon chromatics; the A major, despite its bright key, is melancholy in part, and chromatic passages are largely responsible.

One finds a noticeable lack of chromaticism in the Haydn quartets before 1785 and in those after 1791, but finds the device used extensively in the period between those dates. And that is precisely the period during which Haydn and Mozart were mutually influential, and Haydn learned to know the six quartets of his younger friend. Between 1785 and 1791 Haydn wrote his quartets from Opus 50 through Opus 64; in them he made use of the chromatic elements whose effectiveness Mozart had demonstrated. But Haydn was not by nature as intense or as pensive a man as Mozart; the concentrated style was not natural to him. Small wonder, then, that during his London visits and in his later years, after Mozart's direct personal influence was no longer available, Haydn returned to the direct, expansive, and open style which was innate. The element of intensity, introduced by Mozart, was to await further use at the hands of Beethoven.

A second difference between the quartets of Mozart and those which influenced them comes to light when the element of subtlety is examined. Haydn, a simple man, was honest with himself and his listeners. His music is a reflection of a mind that was serene and strong in religious faith. Mozart, during the last ten years of his life, gave us music in which unrest, a degree of pessimism, and some concern over the prospect of death are reflected, however faintly. Even in the minuet, in the form which Haydn had filled with sly wit or outspoken humor, Mozart remained aloof, dignified, and reflective. Haydn's finales are full of boisterousness and unrestrained animal spirits. Mozart's are occasionally gay, as in the B flat Quartet, or serene, as in the C major; but the humor and the liveliness are seen as though from a distance.

Finally, a basic difference between the character of the two men is seen when formal aspects of the quartets are examined, notably the recapitulations of the sonata-form movements. Haydn was a master of the unexpected. His themes often recur in an unorthodox fashion; occasionally, when their return has been prepared for in the

usual way, they do not reappear at all. Mozart was not given to
shocking or surprising his listeners. The expected thing takes place,
but in ever new and interesting ways—therein lie the surprises in
Mozart. The transitions between development and recapitulation
and the transitions between main themes best show his genius and
marvelous subtlety. It is fair to say that Haydn had his listeners in
mind when he composed, that he chuckled at the thought of their
reactions to this effect or to that, but that Mozart remained divinely
aloof from the world, preferred to write music that expressed what
was in his mind and heart, and concerned himself only slightly
with the reactions of individual listeners. In that sense Mozart was
an aristocrat.

In variety of mood, quality of workmanship, and musical excellence the six quartets of 1785 are among Mozart's great works. The
composer had taken all possible pains with them and felt that they
were quartets to be proud of. Haydn, as we know, was enthusiastic
about them; the playing of the last three occasioned his famous
remark about Mozart's being the greatest composer of whom he
had any knowledge. But public reaction to them was not satisfactory; they attracted no great attention, nor did they lead to commissions. More than a year elapsed before Mozart again tried his
hand at quartet writing: a single Quartet in D major (K. 499) was
the result. The work was published about 1788 with a dedication
to Franz Anton Hoffmeister, publisher and Mozart's friend. Jahn
surmises that in this quartet Mozart tried to approach public taste
without lowering the standards of quartet style. But there is no
trace of such popularizing in the music.

It is first of all a gracious work, clear and direct in its first movement, strong in its minuet, and deeply moving in its adagio. Only in
the last movement are there traces of the melancholy tone which
pervades so many works of these years. And even there it is manfully
concealed under the outward signs of brightness: D major tonality,
bustling vitality in the themes, incisive pauses between phrases. Perhaps this general restlessness contributes to the feeling that all was
not well with Mozart when he wrote the quartet.

The *Adagio and Fugue* for string quartet (or string orchestra),
K. 546, has an interesting history. In December, 1783, Mozart completed a fugue for two pianos, one of the only two works which he

wrote for that pair of instruments. About a year earlier Mozart had first become acquainted with the music of Johann Sebastian Bach. Deeply impressed with the grandeur of that music, he had arranged some of Bach's music for string groups, had written other works in the style of that master, and finally, according to his established custom, had made elements of that style his own. The fugue for two pianos (K. 426) is one of the results. In June, 1788, he arranged that work for strings and added a prelude. In the latter form it is known as K. 546. The prelude, appropriately enough, is somewhat like an old French overture. A slow, stately section with dotted rhythms, in the style of Handel and Bach, alternates with quiet lyric bits typical of the pensive Mozart. The fugue is a masterpiece. The style, in a technical sense, is that of Bach: all the contrapuntal arts of inversion, expansion, and overlapping of phrases are present. Yet the piece is unmistakably by Mozart. Sinuous chromatic lines, characteristic melodic figures, and Mozartian phrase structure provide the trademarks. In all respects the piece is worthy of a high place in Mozart's works.[1]

In the spring of 1789 Mozart visited at the court of Frederick William II, king of Prussia, the sovereign to whom Haydn had dedicated his Opus 50 quartets two years earlier. One result of the visit was a commission to compose some quartets—apparently the first time that an actual request for quartets had come to Mozart. The commission seems to have pleased him greatly, for the first quartet was completed and sent to the King during the month following his return to Vienna. Financial worries arising out of dire poverty hindered the completion of the commission: the two remaining quartets were delayed almost a year, until May and June, 1790. Mozart's letters of that year indicate his troubled state of mind and his serious concern for the future; but no traces of that worry and gloom are found in the music. The three quartets are in D major, K. 575; in B flat, K. 589; and in F major, K. 590. They were published late in 1791, a few weeks after Mozart's death.

Few late works of Mozart's are as unburdened and free from

---

[1] The Adagio and Fugue, along with K. 155–160, K. 168–173, the two flute quartets, and the one for oboe, are contained in an American edition published by Kalmus (New York) as Vol. II of Mozart's Quartets.

doubt as these three quartets. If reserve and pensiveness are characteristic of the six "Haydn" quartets of 1785, then sheer beauty and serenity describe the three of 1789–90. Hardly a single moody passage is found anywhere in the quartets; the few turns into minor and the few excursions into darker keys only serve to emphasize the optimism present everywhere else. One melody flows out of another and gives way to a third—all under an unbroken, cloudless sky. Not that Mozart loses his dignity and becomes merely tuneful. But the inner soul-searching, the reflective moodiness so characteristic of the 1785 set is no longer present.

And a new element appears in these quartets: virtuosity. Frederick William was a competent cellist; as Mozart's patron in this instance, he deserved richer cello parts than the chamber music of that time usually afforded. And Mozart provided them. Themes are about equally divided between first violin and cello, and occasionally the cello is given a solo, as in the trio of the D major Quartet's minuet. Nor is the cello spared in the figurations and passage work with which these quartets are replete. Brilliant scale passages, rapid string crossings, and a full share of development episodes fall to that instrument, all without destroying the balance of the four instruments. Mozart achieves this quite simply by first raising the cello to a dominating position and providing it with glorious melodies, then lifting the other instruments proportionately high and restoring the balance. As a consequence, the whole level is raised, and new standards of brilliance are set. Only in one or two movements, notably in the minuet of the F major Quartet, does Mozart forget that his cello part is for a king of Prussia. There he writes in the accustomed simpler vein.

The line of string quartets which began in 1770 with K. 80 breaks off with the F major Quartet (K. 590) of 1790. We have in these twenty-six works a complete record of changes in Mozart's style. Italian characteristics, the warm sentiment of Johann Christian Bach, the mannerisms of the Mannheimers, and the benign influence of Haydn—all appear in turn. Changes in Mozart's temperament, or rather in his outlook, are observed, and the development of his genius is laid down for all to see. The other series of chamber-music works, notably the string quintets and the piano trios, are not nearly as complete; they illustrate now one, now another aspect of Mozart's style. Only in the quartets has he left a complete record of his growth as a chamber-music composer.

The majority of string quintets contain a part for second viola added to the usual string quartet.[2] Exactly who first contrived this instrumentation is not known. There are several quintets among the works of the Mannheim composers, but most of these include two or three wind instruments. Some of Mozart's early symphonies contain parts for two violas; perhaps the idea of string quintet originated there. The quintets of Luigi Boccherini (1743–1805) were known to Mozart in the 1770's; Michael Haydn (1737–1806), Mozart's fellow townsman and friend, wrote several quintets during those years. But no composer before Mozart had invested the medium with such a wealth of musical ideas, profundity, and charm. The obvious rejoinder is that Mozart was the first major composer to be interested in that medium. Only one or two of Mozart's eight quintets are believed to have been ordered; various other reasons contributed to his choice of the quintet medium. The first, in B flat (K. 174), written late in 1773 at Salzburg,[3] may have been modeled upon the quintets of Michael Haydn.

The year 1773 had seen the writing of the six string quartets K. 155–160, those in which Mozart progressed far beyond Rococo mannerisms; it had seen also the emergence of the K. 168–173 set, in which Mozart made use of Haydn's rediscovery of counterpoint. And the very next work was the quintet. But the contrapuntal treatment, which Mozart had so wholeheartedly appropriated a short time before, is noticeably absent in the quintet. Except for a few bits of imitation in development sections, the music goes on for page after page in a melodious, homophonic style. Only in the finale, a long, fast, sonata-form movement, does Mozart allow himself to write contrapuntally; yet even there extended passages based on busy-work in the middle voices tend to remove the piece from the

---

[2] Einstein believes that Boccherini's 113 quintets with two cellos are actually for two violins, two violas, and one cello; the "alto violoncello" part is written in viola clef throughout.

[3] Jahn states that the work was written following Mozart's return from Vienna in the fall of 1773; Einstein declares that it was written in the spring of that year (i.e., before Mozart became acquainted with Haydn's Opus 20), and was revised in December.

category of pure counterpoint. On the whole, the quintet is a diverse work, full of episodes of orchestral weight, of others replete with virtuoso brilliance, and still others which are in the tradition of chamber music.

Fourteen years elapsed between the writing of the B flat Quintet and the two following ones, in C major (K. 515) and G minor (K. 516), respectively.[4] In the interval, Mozart had written the moody "Haydn" quartets and the ingratiating "Hoffmeister" quartet (K. 499). The intensity and charm of those works are found again in the quintets of 1787.

The C major Quintet begins with a rising arpeggio figure in the cello, a graceful lyric comment in the first violin, and a light, pulsating accompaniment in the inner voices. These simple elements, plus a scale fragment in broken thirds, are enough to enable Mozart to construct a movement unequaled for strength, dramatic concentration, and excitement. And the stage is set for three other movements equal to the first, but in contrasting directions. A sturdy minuet is followed by a charming slow movement with beautifully ornamented lyric melodies. The quintet ends with a finale whose deceptive simplicity conceals a wealth of contrapuntal subtleties and imaginative developments.

The following quintet, in G minor, is a direct antithesis of the C major work. Here all is dark and hopeless; the resignation of the "Haydn" quartets has turned to despair. The concentration of mood in the first movement is scarcely duplicated anywhere in the literature. A short phrase with the inevitable chromaticism and a downward inflection, another phrase which rises and falls—these are the elements out of which this most pathetic of movements is created; both themes appear in G minor, and the piece ends in that key. The minuet gives the impression of one stumbling in the gloom; the adagio is a rich movement in which the stumbling is replaced by groping—but still in the darkness. After three such intense, almost desperate movements, the final rondo is disappointing. It does not measure up to the others, either in content or in style.

In September, 1789, a short time after the first quartet for the King of Prussia was written, Mozart composed a Quintet in A major

---

[4] K. 515 is unaccountably missing from the list in *Cobbett's Cyclopedic Survey of Chamber Music,* II, 151.

for clarinet and strings (K. 581). It was designed for his friend Anton Stadler, an excellent Viennese clarinetist. The combination of wind and string instruments in chamber music was not new. We have seen dozens of trio sonatas for flute and violin; we have mentioned Mozart's own quartets in which flute and oboe, respectively, are used; we shall shortly hear about this trio, quintet, and sextet for combinations of winds and strings. What is new in the K. 581 quintet is the way in which the five instruments are combined. Mozart was faced with the possibilities of treating the clarinet as a solo instrument, thus writing non-chamber music, or of ignoring its special characteristics and treating it as just another voice in a five-voice texture, thus writing dull chamber music. He made neither mistake, but evolved a texture in which the beauties of the wind instrument shine through, in which no instrument is slighted, and in which tonal balance is achieved perfectly. First violin and clarinet alternate in the first announcement of the themes; but lest that practice seem too ordinary, Mozart writes so that all the instruments share in subsequent thematic statements. The result is a piece of music whose charm and delicacy are difficult to duplicate in the literature for strings and winds.

Two more string quintets were written during the last year of Mozart's life: the D major (K. 593) in December, 1790, and the E flat (K. 614) in April, 1791. The feeling of oppression, so characteristic of the G minor Quintet and the six "Haydn" quartets, is completely missing in both the D major and the E flat quintets. Such darker moments as exist are full of noble sentiment and great feeling rather than pensiveness or gloom. The fast movements incline toward Haydn's type of humor. Light, bustling figures are characteristic, and an air of openness and naïveté takes the place of subtle turns toward dark moods. Both quintets are alive and sparkling, in a manner reminiscent of the Prussian quartets of 1789, and are on the same level of brilliance and virtuosity.

There remain for discussion four works in different categories and in different styles. About 1782 Mozart wrote an octet for wind instruments (K. 388): two each of oboes, clarinets, horns, and bassoons. In that form it is one of his finest works; the title "Serenade" is misleading, for this is no occasional piece to be performed out of doors, even though it was commissioned for such a purpose. The

work contains the four movements usually found only in the more
serious quartets and symphonies. Its dark color, its many gloomy
moments, the contrapuntal genius shown especially in the minuet,
the flares of passion—all these make it unsuited as a serenade. Why
Mozart later arranged the work for string quintet is not known with
certainty. Einstein assumes that the four quintets of 1787–91 (K. 515,
516, 593, 614) were written with an eye to dedicating a set of six
to Frederick William II (hence the prominence of the cello part in
several of these works), and "to hasten the achievement of that goal
he even arranged one of his own wind serenades as a quintet—
surely against his artistic conscience." The quintet version, known
as K. 406, can hold a place with any of the regularly conceived
chamber music. The slight loss of instrumental color is more than
compensated for by the greater expressive flexibility of the string
version.

The Peters edition of Mozart's quintets contains several other
works in addition to the seven quintets discussed above. Vol. II of
that edition begins with two quintets labeled K.S. (supplement?)
515 and K. 46, respectively. Now, Einstein declares that K. 46 is
spurious. But K. 46 consists of four movements which Mozart
used in a divertimento for thirteen wind instruments, K. 361, written
in 1780 or 1781. The latter work consists of seven movements; there
is, in the minds of the authorities, no question of its authenticity.
The editor of Mozart's *Complete Works,* Vol. IV₁, says of this work:
"movements 1, 2, 3, and 7 are arrangements of a string quintet composed in 1768." Obviously, if the content of K. 361 is genuine, then
K. 46 must be. To a lesser degree this is true also of the quintet
labeled K.S. 515 in the Peters edition. This work, of four movements,
contains a first and a third movement which are identical with the
fifth and sixth, respectively, of K. 361 again. The second and the
fourth movements of K.S. 515 do not appear in the latter work, nor
is their original status made clear elsewhere. It would appear, then,
that K. 361 is composed of all of K. 46, two movements of K.S. 515,
and one movement all its own. Questions of priority and arranger
remain; but if K. 361 is Mozart, then K. 46 and at least half of
K.S. 515 are likewise.

Vol. II of the Peters edition includes an arrangement of the clarinet quintet K. 581, which has been discussed above, and of a quintet

for horn and strings, K. 407. The latter three-movement work in E flat, written about 1782, is for violin, two violas, horn, and cello. It is an unassuming piece which is part serenade, part concerto for horn, and part chamber music. The overweight of low-register instruments accounts for a certain lack of sprightliness, to which the general emptiness of melody and figuration contributes.

Before discussing the seven piano trios and the two piano quartets of Mozart one does well to recall the place of the keyboard instrument in chamber music in the decades before 1770. The trio sonata was a vehicle dominated by the two violins; the harpsichord (later, the piano) supplied missing chord tones, provided a degree of rhythmic movement, and augmented the musical structure in general. And the bass or cello merely amplified the keyboard instrument's lowest voice. Thus the piano served only in an accompanying role. With the emergence of the string quartet the piano was cast out of its relationship with the strings, only to develop its own solo literature in the field of the piano sonata. Then arose the strange medium of piano solo accompanied by violin and/or cello. And out of these grew the modern violin sonata, cello sonata, and piano trio.

In the early years of the piano trio's life, notably in the works of Haydn, the concept was retained that the piano should dominate. Many of the Haydn trios can dispense with violin and cello without great loss to the performance. Were we to investigate the almost three dozen violin sonatas of Mozart, we would find that the violin is, in the main, really unessential—at least in the early works. In the later ones, of course, this is not true.

In the first of the Mozart piano trios, in B flat (K. 254), written in the summer of 1776, when Mozart was twenty, a similar concept prevails. The violin part in the first of the three movements contains nothing more than a few accompanying figures and a few doublings of the piano's upper voice; the cello is tied to the bass line throughout. In other movements the violin is used more individually. Seen as a balanced trio, the work is at an elementary stage. As a piece of music, on the other hand, it holds its own with other works of that period. The first movement is light and entertaining; the last is graceful. The slow movement contains an aria-like, broad melody over a running accompaniment, in Mozart's most romantic vein.

Ten years elapsed before Mozart again turned to the piano trio. (One work, K. 422, in D minor, begun about 1783, had remained unfinished.) In 1786 he composed three in quick succession: one in G major, K. 496; one in E flat for clarinet, viola, and piano, K. 498; one in B flat, K. 502. Two years later, in 1788, three more issued from his pen: the E major Trio, K. 542; the C major, K. 548; and the G major, K. 564. Taking them in order, one feels a rising level of quality when approaching the E major Trio and a rather quick falling off afterward. The first G major (K. 496) is no longer of the type which K. 254 represents. The violin and the cello are responsible individuals; they are no longer confined to accompanying roles, but have important parts to play in the creation of the musical structure. And near the beginning of the first movement one realizes that a new texture is about to be born: a texture composed of two dissimilar tonal bodies. Violin and cello, working together, are opposed by the piano; a duality of intention results. This division of textures becomes important in Beethoven and reaches its peak in Brahms. But without doubt it begins with Mozart.

The G major Trio is an excellent and satisfying piece of chamber music in all respects. But it is overshadowed by the unique tone color, peculiar charm, and complete perfection of the E flat Trio, K. 498. The choice of instruments is unusual: both clarinet and viola are on the dark side, and both are essentially in the alto range. These facts, coupled with the fact that the trio's first movement is an andante, should go far to establish a melancholy mood in the music. But, miraculously enough, a mood of well-being, of melodic serenity, pervades all three movements. The final rondo is a marvelous example of musical sensitivity and takes a place high among Mozart's finest works.

The rising level of quality continues in the B flat Trio, K. 502, of 1786. That work contains everything that Mozart had achieved up to this point: an air of gentle brooding, combined with moments of brilliant display; perfection of form with daring and unexpected turns of phrase; sublime melodies with roughly dramatic contrasts. The trio as a whole is a great musical achievement and is perhaps equaled only by the E major Trio, K. 542, written in the summer of the year (1788) that saw the three great symphonies come to light —the E flat, the G minor, and the "Jupiter." If the E major Trio seems more brilliant than the B flat, it is only because of its brighter tonality. If it seems richer, it may be because of remote and colorful modulations. Drama, lyric beauty, charm, repose, fire—everything is there. One cannot choose between these two masterworks; they remain among the great music of the Classical period.

Quite differently placed are the two remaining trios of 1788: the C major, K. 548, and the G major, K. 564. The C major Trio has about it an air of reserve, of seeming unwillingness to be brilliant or dramatic or even lyric. It is "correct," and moves along in expected, traditional fashion. But beyond that, it leaves one unenthusiastic, and it provides a good example of the untutored layman's idea of "classical music." The G major Trio was, according to Einstein, originally a piano sonata, "obviously intended for beginners." Although it contains charming movements and would undoubtedly rank high among the piano sonatas, the trio version leaves much to be desired. The texture is rather thin; the string instruments add nothing really essential to the structure. If these two trios are disappointing, we must remember that "the yardstick of perfection against which we measure these two works was put into our hands by Mozart himself."

Two piano quartets, in G minor, K. 478, and in E flat, K. 493, were composed in 1785 and 1786, respectively. These are among the first examples of a vehicle that was to become important in the nineteenth century. It may be recalled that Haydn wrote no piano quartets; that when the Mannheim composers (among whom we may include their spiritual brother, Johann Christian Bach) wrote for piano and other instruments they turned out either piano concertos or *galant* pieces in which the piano dominated. The G minor Piano Quartet is completely different from such earlier works; it is a piece of true chamber music, making virtuoso demands upon the pianist, but allowing the strings full responsibility in establishing a real ensemble texture. The E flat Quartet is like its companion except for the differences brought about by the tonality. Where the G minor is pensive, dark, or morbid, the E flat is energetic, dramatic, and straightforward. Einstein calls attention to the influence on the latter work of a quartet by Schobert which Mozart had first heard two decades earlier and whose sweeping power "enriches Mozart's fantasy years later." Such other piano quartets as are attributed to

Mozart are arrangements: the quintet for piano and winds, K. 452, and the string quintets K. 581 and 593.

The last two works to be discussed are completely different from each other. The sextet, K. 522, for string quartet and two horns, written in 1787, is a *musikalischer Spass*—a musical joke. Full of wrong notes, structural defects, uncalled-for cadenzas, and the like, the piece represents a playful, practical-joking vein in Mozart of which his biography gives ample evidence, but which his music seldom exhibits.

The Divertimento in E flat, K. 563, for violin, viola, and cello, is a serious and profound work. Again the title is misleading. For while this trio contains six movements in the manner of a divertimento (allegro, adagio, minuetto and trio, andante, minuetto and two trios, allegro), it is not music written to be merely diverting. This is sincere, heart-felt, and deeply moving music, whose variety of effects is astounding. That Mozart was able to draw so many different textures and so great a variety of colors from three instruments is a never-ending source of astonishment. No feeling that an instrument is missing, no feeling of incompleteness or of hampered resources exists. Rather one receives an impression of intensity and concentrated power; seldom does a work achieve so much with such limited means. The contrasts between the powerful first movement and the beautiful adagio, between the comfortable andante with variations and the happy finale—these are only part of the picture. Moments of concentration and dramatic power, details of counterpoint—all these add to the completeness of the work and make it one of Mozart's most satisfying chamber-music compositions.

H. U.

7

Music for the Piano

THE BACKGROUND

THERE CAME a time in the history of music when a revulsion against polyphony set in. No composer arose of a stature to excel the counterpoint of Palestrina and Bach. Less gifted writers made canon ridiculous by unmusical essays in eight and nine voices and barren ingenuities like "table" and "riddle" canons. The world yearned for a new, a simpler and more direct medium of tonal expression. Hence the rise and triumph of what we call homophony, in which preference is given to a single melodic line with harmonic accompaniment.

The period of transition is best exemplified in Carl Philipp Emanuel Bach, best known of the Leipzig cantor's sons. Some of his smaller pieces are perennial classroom favorites; the Solfeggietto, the Allegro in F minor, and the Rondo in B minor may confidently be recommended. You must look farther, however, for a just estimate of his importance. Examine the six sonatas edited by Bülow in the Peters Edition, or say the two in A minor and G minor, and you will realize that C. P. E. Bach was the pathfinder of the classic sonata form, blazing a trail that was broadened by Haydn to a thoroughfare and by Mozart and Beethoven to a highway. He wrote over two hundred solo pieces, fifty-two concertos, and many sonatas for piano. His *Essay on the True Method of Playing the Clavier* is deservedly famous as the first orderly exposition of the art.

The other sons of the great Bach, even Wilhelm Friedemann, most talented of them all in the estimation of his father, but the prodigal and disgrace of the family, did little to further the course of piano history. Some of their works will always be found in collections of old music. Wilhelm Friedemann wrote one or two excellent concertos. He stole so unblushingly from Vivaldi that he incurred odium even in a day when liberal borrowing from other composers was generally condoned. The Organ Concerto in D minor that became popular in a piano arrangement by Stradal is now ascribed to Vivaldi. His sonatas and fugues offer little of interest to modern students, but the twelve polonaises contain beautiful numbers. Johann Christian Bach deserves passing mention, if only for his finely developed Prelude and Fugue in C minor, contained in Isidor Philipp's *Clavecinistes allemands* (Durand Edition).

It was left for Haydn to establish the sonata and symphony as unmistakable, universally recognized new forms of homophonic composition.

Many of us are still apt, perhaps, to think of Haydn principally as an amiable, rather unsophisticated forerunner of Mozart and Beethoven. This is a complete misconception of his genius, only to be accounted for by the fact that the effortlessness and spontaneity of his writing easily delude us into an impression of naïveté. In truth he was a greater originator than either Mozart or Beethoven: he created the sonata form; they adopted it, expanded it, and experimented with it. It may be thought extravagant to claim the creation of an art form for any one individual, yet in the case of Haydn the assertion seems irrefutable, for it is impossible to discover in earlier writers (including Carl Philipp Emanuel Bach) a true parallel to the structure of his symphonies, sonatas, and quartets. His grouping of measures into periodic units was freer than that of Mozart and Beethoven; [2] they stabilized the eight-bar period, and in the end it threatened a rigidity from which modern composers were driven to rebel. The first section of the double theme of Haydn's F minor Variations, for instance, divides into five periods of six, six, five, five, and seven measures respectively; while the themes of Beethoven's variations from the sonatas Opus 26, Opus 109, and Opus 111 are composed entirely of eight-bar periods, each subdivided into two four-bar phrases, excepting only the third period of the theme in Opus 26, which is extended to ten measures. Again, Haydn's range of keys was far wider than that of Mozart, whose sonatas and concertos rarely venture as far as signatures of three sharps or flats, whereas Haydn is undaunted by tonalities like A flat, D flat, and C sharp major and minor. He is equally bold in modulation and in direct leaps from key to key by simply moving a semitone up or down, as Beethoven afterwards loved to do. In sufficient proof of this harmonic daring I need only refer to the first of the thirty-four sonatas, with its three movements in E flat, E major (*sic*) and E flat. In the first movement he introduces his second theme in the conventional dominant, B flat, but in the development section he springs surprises on us. Twice he comes to a pause on a G major triad, thence proceeding to entrances of the second theme, first, with happy effect, in C major and then, most astonishingly, in the utterly remote key of E major, eventually stealing back to E flat for the recapitulation by gliding chromatically from the dominant seventh of B minor to that of E flat major. The whole passage merits close study. The C major Fantasia, too, furnishes several examples of abrupt and effective key transitions. One may safely believe that Haydn took delight in unexpected effects of every kind; not to speak of the "Surprise" Symphony with the jolt of its famous forte chord, what is the finale of the "Farewell" Symphony but one long-drawn-out mystification?

The term "sonata form" may be somewhat misleading to the uninitiated, for it is used both in reference to the sonata as a whole and, more strictly, to describe the structure of what is usually the first movement. In both senses sonata form is the basis of the sonata itself, of the symphony and classical concerto, and of the trios, quartets, and so on, of chamber music. The concert overture, in addition, is written in the first-movement form, omitting the repetition of the first section. In these pages I shall try to preserve a distinction by writing "sonata form" in two words when the entire work is concerned and "sonata-form" (hyphenated) when the structure of the first movement only is referred to.

A general definition of the sonata cannot be given. It may have two, three, or four movements, very rarely one or five. Typically, however, it consists of three movements, the first (usually an allegro) in sonata-form, the second a slow movement, variable as to form, the last another fast movement, often in rondo or again in sonata-form. When a fourth movement is added, it will be a minuet or scherzo in dance form, following or occasionally preceding the slow movement. This arrangement is primarily due to Haydn, who gave the first-movement form its modern shape and selected from the known

favorites of his time the rondo, the minuet, and the variation form
as best suited for possible if not invariable use in the later movements.
The rondo was found to be appropriate as a finale; the minuet acquired distinction as the only dance to survive, at least temporarily,
in the symphony; and the errant theme with variations served
equally well as slow movement or finale, at times even usurping the
place of the regular first movement.

Haydn's immense service to music in molding its greatest instrumental form would have availed comparatively little had he not
been able to endow the form with beauty, interest, and variety. One
may expatiate on his achievement as a pioneer, then, without in any
way slighting his creative genius. On both counts his title to fame
rests secure. . . .

It has been said above that Haydn was a bolder innovator than
his immediate successors in the establishment of homophonic music.
Mozart was content, with one striking exception, to accept forms
already provided, to use the orchestra and the piano as he found
them, and to write even his most elaborate arias for the voices of
singers whom he knew personally. His piano works, accordingly,
rarely transcend the limitations of the instrument as it existed in his
day, when the harpsichord had not yet been definitely displaced for
public performance. If you turn the pages of his piano sonatas in an
authentic edition, you will see that they abound in the dynamic
directions of forte, piano, *sforzando,* and crescendos of short dura-
tion. Fortissimo and pianissimo occur very seldom indeed, for the
excellent reason that while it was easy to make clean distinctions
between loud and soft and to inflect the tone at will within that
range, it was still difficult to achieve gradations between forte and
fortissimo, piano and pianissimo, or to sustain a crescendo for more
than a measure or two.

Now, if you will, turn the pages once more and note the exactness
of Mozart's markings of legato and staccato. In this respect he is
often more accurate than Beethoven. If you wish to study touch in
all its variety and modulation, go to Mozart and make him the
model of your phrasing. You need take only one precaution, namely,
to remember that the classics were accustomed to close their slurs at
the end of the measure, or even at the end of the beat, without intending a break in the legato. They used the legato slur, in other

words, much as they used it in writing for strings, where it merely indicates the notes to be played with a single bow, not necessarily ending a phrase. . . .

E. H.

Ernest Hutcheson

From Mozart's letters, one learns something about his own manner of playing the piano:

"Herr Stein sees and hears that I am more of a player than Beecke —that without making grimaces of any kind I play so expressively that, according to his own confession, no one shows off his pianoforte as well as I. That I always remain strictly in time surprises everyone; they cannot understand that the left hand should not in the least be concerned in a tempo rubato. When they play, the left hand always follows." (1777.)

About Nannette Stein's playing: "She sits opposite the treble instead of in the middle of the instrument, so that there may be greater opportunities for swaying about and making grimaces. Then she rolls up her eyes and smirks. If a passage occurs twice, it is played slower the second time; if three times, still slower. When a passage comes, up goes the arm, and, if there is to be an emphasis it must come from the arm, heavily and clumsily, not from the fingers. But the best of all is that when there comes a passage (which ought to flow like oil) in which there necessarily occurs a change of fingers, there is no need of taking care: when the time comes you stop, lift the hand and nonchalantly begin again. This helps one the better to catch a false note, and the effect is frequently curious." (1777.) Nannette was then eight years old.

At Aurnhammer's: "The young woman[1] is a fright, but she plays ravishingly, though she lacks the true singing style in her cantabile; she is too jerky." (1781.)[2]

"Whenever I played for him [Richter, a pianist], he looked immovably at my fingers, and one day he said, 'My God! how I am obliged to torment myself and sweat, and yet without obtaining applause; and for you, my friend, it is mere play!' 'Yes,' said I, 'I had to labor once in order not to show labor now.'" (1784.)

---

[1] Josepha Aurnhammer, famous pianist in her day, composer of piano pieces, maried one Bösinhönig of Vienna in 1796.
[2] Beethoven found this fault with Mozart's playing.

"It is much easier to play rapidly than slowly; you can drop a few notes in passages without any one noticing it. But is it beautiful? At such speed you can use the hands indiscriminately; but is that beautiful?" (1778.)

"Give me the best clavier in Europe and at the same time hearers who understand nothing or want to understand nothing, and who do not feel what I play with me, and all my joy is gone." (1778.)

"The Andante is going to give us the most trouble, for it is full of expression and must be played with taste. . . . If I were her [Rose Cannabich's] regular teacher, I would lock up all her music, cover the keyboard with a handkerchief, and make her practice on nothing but passages, trills, mordents, etc., until the difficulty with the left hand was remedied."

"I must say a few words to my sister about Clementi's sonatas. . . . There are in them no remarkable or striking passages, with the exception of those in sixths and octaves, and I beg my sister not to devote too much time to these lest she spoil her quiet and steady hand and make it lose its natural lightness, suppleness, and fluent rapidity. What, after all, is the use? She is expected to play the sixths and octaves with the greatest velocity (which no man will accomplish, not even Clementi), and if she tries she will produce a frightful zig-zag and nothing more. Clementi is a *ciarlatáno* like all Italians. He writes upon a sonata *Presto,* or even *Prestissimo* and *alla breve,* and plays it *Allegro* in 4/4 time. I know it because I have heard him! What he does well is his playing of passages in thirds; but he sweated over these day and night in London. Aside from this he has nothing—absolutely nothing; not excellence in reading, nor taste, nor sentiment." This splenetic outburst is in a letter to Mozart's father and sister written in 1783. This harsh criticism was undoubtedly unjust. Mozart disliked Italians because they were highly esteemed in Vienna and were often in his way. That there was some truth in the criticism is shown by what Clementi said to his pupil Ludwig Berger[3]: "I asked Clementi whether in 1781 he had begun to treat the instrument in his present [1806] style. He answered *no,* and added that in those early days he had

---

[3] Berger (1777–1839) of Berlin was a famous pianist and teacher in his day. Mendelssohn and Henselt were among his pupils; nor are his compositions, from operas to piano pieces, negligible.

cultivated a brilliant execution, especially in double notes, hardly known then, and in extemporized cadenzas, and that he had subsequently achieved a more melodic and noble style of performance after listening attentively to famous singers, and also by means of the perfected mechanism of the English pianos, the construction of which formerly stood in the way of a cantabile and legato style of playing." Clementi, born at Rome in 1752, died at Evershane, England, in 1832. Even shortly before his death, his hearers, among them Cramer and Moscheles, were enthusiastic over his playing and improvisations. Clementi, who played a-vie with Mozart in 1781, was more generous than his rival. He always spoke admiringly of Mozart's singing touch and exquisite taste.

Saint-Saëns, lover of irony and paradox, wrote a preface to his edition of Mozart's Pianoforte Sonatas, published at Paris in 1915, in which, after a discussion of the ornaments, he has this to say:

"One is accustomed in modern editions to be prodigal with *liaisons*, to indicate constantly legato, molto legato, sempre legato. There is nothing of this in the manuscripts and the old editions. Everything leads us to believe that this music should be performed lightly, that the figures should produce an effect analogous to that obtained on the violin by giving a stroke to each note without leaving the string. When Mozart wished the legato, he indicated it. In the middle of the last century, pianists were still found whose playing was singularly leaping (as one may say). The old non-legato, being exaggerated, became a staccato. This exaggeration brought a reaction in the contrary sense, and this was pushed too far. . . .

"This music of Mozart during his early years is destitute of nuances; occasionally a *piano* or a *forte;* nothing more. The reason for this abstinence is because these pieces were written for the clavecin, and its sonority could not be modified by a pressure of the finger. Clavecins with two keyboards could alternate with *forte* and *piano,* but nuances, properly speaking, were unknown to them.

"In the eighteenth century, one lived more quietly than to-day, nor were there in music our modern habits of speed, which is often inflicted on ancient compositions to their great injury. It is necessary to shun in the case of Mozart this tendency to hurry the movements, as too often happens. His *presto* corresponds to our *allegro;* his *allegro* to our *allegro moderato*. His adagios are extremely slow, as is shown by the multiplicity of notes sometimes contained in a single beat. The *andante* is not very slow.

"It was the rule, in his time, not to put the thumb on a black key except from absolute necessity. This method of fingering gives to the hand great restfulness, precious for the performance of old music that demands perfect equality of the fingers.

"The first pianofortes were far from having the powerful sonority of the great modern instruments. Therefore, it is not always necessary to take Mozart's *forte* literally; it is often the equivalent of our *mezzo forte*."

Compare with Saint-Saëns's definitions of various tempi, J. G. Walther's in his *Musikalisches Lexicon* (Leipsig, 1732):

"*Andante,* to go with equal steps. Somewhat faster than *adagio.*

"*Adagio.* Comfortably; slow.

"*Allegro.* Joyfully, in a lively manner; very often fast and flitting; but also, often, moderate, though gay and lively.

"*Presto.* Fast."

The indication *Allegro moderato* is not in Walther's *Lexicon,* nor in Brossard's *Dictionnaire de Musique* (first edition, 1703; freely used by Walther). They define "moderato." Brossard: "With moderation, discretion, wisdom, etc.; not too loud, not too soft, not too quick, not too slow, etc."

P. H.

Mozart was, as we know, a great clavier player, one of the greatest clavier virtuosi of his time, although not a virtuoso in the sense that term came to have in the following generation. He lived long enough to begin to know that type and to reject it—in the person of Clementi. His judgment of Clementi, with whom he had to compete late in 1781 or early in 1782 before the Emperor Joseph, was very harsh (letter of 16 January, 1782):

> He is an excellent cembalo-player, but that is all. He has great facility with his right hand. His star passages are thirds. Apart from this, he has not a farthing's worth of taste or feeling; he is a mere *mechanicus.*

Now, Clementi was much more than a mere "mechanicus," and in many important respects he was the prototype of a whole generation of pianists and composers for the piano, the generation to which Beethoven belonged. Mozart would have had to pronounce the same verdict if Beethoven had played one of his own sonatas *à la* Clementi (as he may have done on the occasion of their famous meeting in 1787)—such for example as the C major Sonata, Op. 2, No. 3. Perhaps on that occasion Mozart did not credit even Beethoven with either taste or feeling. The ideals of his clavier style were very different from those of the early nineteenth century. Yet it should be noted that he wrote for the same instrument as Beethoven, Weber, or Chopin—not for the clavichord or the harpsichord, but for the pianoforte, although of course not for the powerful instrument we know in the products of Erard or Steinway. The only works that can have been conceived and written for harpsichord are the early concerto arrangements after Johann Christian Bach and minor "French" composers (K. 107, and K. 37, 39, 40, 41). One must not be misled by the fact that even in the last years of Mozart's life he used the word *cembalo* to indicate the clavier part in his scores—or because some famous harpsichordist gains ovations by playing the *Rondo alla turca* from the A major Sonata on his or her instrument. In the Mozart household there were one or more pianofortes constructed by the Regensburg clavier-builder, Franz Jacob Späth, but when Mozart made the acquaintance of the instruments of Johann Andreas Stein of Augsburg (who was to become the father-in-law and teacher of Johann Andreas Streicher, who worked for Beethoven), the latter became his favorites. He gave his reasons in detail (letter of 17 October, 1777):

> This time I shall begin at once with Stein's pianofortes. Before I had seen any of his make, Späth's claviers has always been my favorites. But now I much prefer Stein's, for they damp ever so much better than the Regensburg instruments. When I strike hard, I can keep my finger on the note or raise it, but the sound ceases the moment I have produced it. In whatever way I touch the keys, the tone is always even. It never jars, it is never stronger or weaker or entirely absent; in a word, it is always even. It is true that he does not sell a pianoforte of this kind for less than three hundred gulden, but the trouble and the labor that Stein

English Tea at the Contis, painted (1763) by Michel Barthelemy Ollivier, showing Mozart at the Clavier in the Salon des Quatre Glaces of the Temple. In the Louvre, Paris.

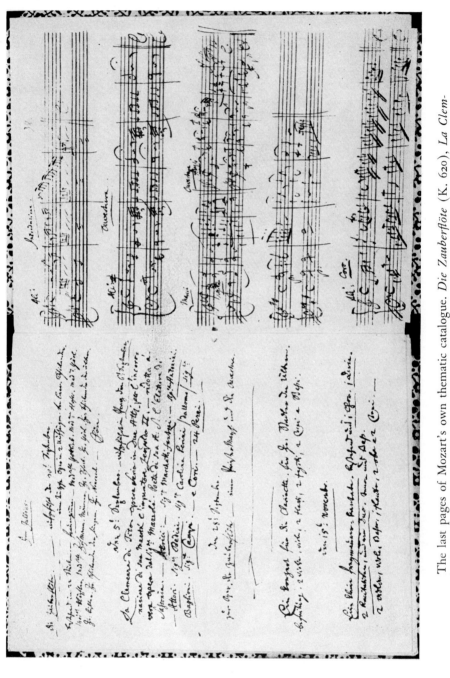

The last pages of Mozart's own thematic catalogue. *Die Zauberflöte* (K. 620), *La Clemenza di Tito* (K. 621), the march of the priests and overture from *The Magic Flute*

puts into the making of it cannot be paid for. His instruments have this splendid advantage over others, that they are made with escape action. Only one maker in a hundred bothers about this. But without an escapement it is impossible to avoid jangling and vibration after the note is struck. When you touch the keys, the hammers fall back again the moment after they have struck the strings, whether you hold down the keys or release them.

It was for such an instrument that Mozart wrote his sonatas, variations, and concertos.

What Mozart did for the development of this instrument can be appreciated only when one remembers that while certain virtuosi played the instrument, it was in general use mainly by amateurs. And this fact had a considerable influence on the music written for it. A work for piano, or for a group of instruments including piano, was usually not taken so seriously as a quartet or quintet for strings, which was intended for performance by professional musicians or by the more serious type of amateurs. A work for quartet or quintet of strings had four movements, while a piano sonata had only three. A string quartet was for connoisseurs (*Kenner*); a piano sonata, a sonata for piano and violin, a piano trio or piano quartet was for amateurs (*Liebhaber*), masculine or feminine. "For piano and violin," not "for violin and piano": the striking fact, from the point of view of the nineteenth or twentieth century, is that in these works the keyboard instrument has the dominant role, and thus is responsible for their lighter character. From about 1750 on, the role of the keyboard instrument became very different from what it had been previously. In an early classic work—say, a "solo sonata" for violin and harpsichord—everything of importance was in the violin part, which was at times even written in chordal or polyphonic form, and the harpsichord part was relatively unimportant, containing only the bass-line, the support or accompaniment for a solo instrument. But after 1750 the keyboard instrument became the dominant partner, and the violin part became so insignificant, so completely *ad libitum,* that in most cases it could actually be omitted without much loss. Before 1750 there were violin sonatas with *basso-continuo;* after 1750 came clavier sonatas with accompanying violin part. It was a long time before the violin was again treated in truly obbligato fashion, so that both instruments were essential to the musical whole, as we know them to be in the violin and piano sonatas of Beethoven; and it was Mozart first and foremost who achieved a balance between the two instruments and created a true dialogue between them.

A. E.

THE MISCELLANEOUS PIECES AND VARIATIONS

Every pianist should own a copy of the miscellaneous pieces of Mozart, a volume small but worth its weight in gold. It contains three fantasias, three rondos, an *Overture in the Style of Handel,* an adagio, a minuet, and a gigue. Commendable editions are those of Peters, Augener, and the Universal Edition. The three fantasias are included in the Breitkopf & Härtel *Urtext* of the sonatas and the Kalmus reprint.

The three fantasias differ widely from each other in form. In mood they are among Mozart's most serious compositions. The shortest, in D minor, deserves a better fate than to be used, as it mostly is, as a teaching piece. An artist can make much even of the unassuming slow arpeggios of the introductory Andante. The second, in C minor, must not be confused with the *Fantasia and Sonata* in the same key always printed in the collection of sonatas. This C minor Fantasia is an adagio written in regular sonata-form with an extended development section. The rather florid ornamentation does not detract from its grave majesty. The player's style and powers of expression are put to a severe test if he would do it justice. The third fantasia, in C major, bears considerable resemblance in outline to the toccatas of Bach. A short Adagio leads to a rather long improvisational Andante ending on the dominant; the finale is a splendid fugue adorned with strettos, augmentation, and abbreviated diminutions. Though the influence of Bach is apparent, there is nothing imitative of his manner. In this respect the piece contrasts with the *Overture in the Style of Handel,* which is obviously an imitation and perhaps for that reason one of the least valued of Mozart's works.

The pleasant Rondo in D major is peculiar in that it goes through all the motions of the sonata-form while keeping throughout to one main theme. This form is rare. A distinct analogy may be traced in the first movement of Schumann's *Piano Concerto.* The second rondo, in A minor, far the finest of the three, might be selected as truly representative of Mozart's piano idiom at its best, touchingly beautiful, perfect alike in form and content, and wonderfully rounded out by the deep emotion of the coda. As for the last rondo, in F major, I must confess that to me its *galanterie* seems overdone.

Another lovely piece is the Adagio in B minor, too important to serve as the slow movement of a sonata and therefore rightly thought as an independent work. Two small pieces, a Menuetto in D and a Gigue in G, complete the list of miscellaneous compositions.[1] Both are gems, the minuet unusually serious for its type, the gigue sparkling and full of finesse.

No one who examines with care the three fantasias, the Rondo in A minor, the B minor Adagio, and the minuet will make the mistake of considering this piano music essentially light or shallow. Mozart was not a *Jupiter tonans,* and it would be vain to seek in him the heaven-storming tragedy of Beethoven, the impetuosity of Schumann, the turbulence of Chopin's scherzos, the orchestral sonorities of Liszt. Nevertheless he excels in accents of profound emotion and brings tears to the eye more often, perhaps, than they—the tears that well up in us when we are stirred by pure beauty, deep pathos, or superlative joy.

Mozart wrote many sets of variations for piano. Seventeen of them are authentic, and four more by other composers (one by E. A. Förster, two by Anton Eberl, one by an unknown writer) are commonly ascribed to him and included in his published works. Incidentally, at least three of the supposititious sets are remarkably good and might easily deceive an expert. On the other hand, the popular *Pastorale variée,* from the pen of Franz Bendel, is obviously spurious to any reader conversant with Mozart's style.

Speaking of the variations in general, it may be noted that, apart from the usual artifices of ringing changes on a theme by elaborations of melodic line or accompanying figuration, Mozart often resorts to more marked contrasts. Sometimes he will shift from tonic major to tonic minor or vice versa. He often introduces an adagio for relief, usually highly ornamented or expanded to greater length.

---

[1] Some editions add a march and a waltz, assumedly genuine but hardly worthy of the master's genius.

Again he may prolong the last variation to a coda or finale of larger proportion, perhaps altering the time signature for additional novelty. None of these devices is original with Mozart or peculiar to him; Haydn anticipated some and Beethoven adopted all of them. Still, they are characteristically Mozartean. The paradoxical difficulty in composing variations is to secure variety, and evidently Mozart was well aware of the danger of monotony inherent in the form.

The best sets of variations are the following:

1. *On the air, "Je suis Lindor," E flat.* We have remarked on Mozart's small range of tonalities; here, quite exceptionally, he inserts a variation in E flat minor.

2. *On the air, "Ah! vous dirais-je, Maman," C major.* Simple but charming.

3. *On Paisiello's air, "Salve tu, Domine," F major.* Rather less simple than the last and still more charming. Note the cadenzas in variations 5 and 6.

4. *On an (original?) Allegretto, F major.* A delight to the ear.

5. *From the Clarinet Quintet, A major.* Beautiful, but heard to more advantage in the original setting.

6. *On the air "Unser dummer Pöbel meint," G major.* The best of all, rich in humor and perfect in workmanship. Observe the long Adagio and the enlarged Finale, the latter varying between 3/8 and common time.

THE SONATAS

Coming now to the sonatas we are confronted with an annoying difficulty in identifying them accurately. Mozart's works are not designated by opus numbers, and the sequence of sonatas is different in the various editions. Add to this that there are four sonatas in C, four in F, three or four in B flat, and three in D, and we see that it is meaningless to speak of a Sonata in F, No. 12, unless we refer to a particular edition probably not owned by the reader. The only means of positive identification is the invaluable *Thematic Catalogue* of Köchel, an expensive book hard to procure and confusing to any but an expert and a German scholar, since it, too, uses two different numberings and has not yet been translated into English. Köchel, be it noted, follows the chronological order of composition.

The comparative table on page 527 may clarify the matter: at least, I hope it will not further confound it. The key and the Köchel number (K) of each sonata are given first, then the serial number of the various editions is indicated thus:

Ur. = *Urtext,* Breitkopf & Härtel (the best edition, reprinted by Kalmus)

U.E. = Universal Edition

D. = Durand (*Édition classique*)

(These three follow the order of the Köchel catalogue.)

P. = Peters

C + S I = Cotta and the first Schirmer Edition. In these the sonatas are arranged in a supposed order of difficulty.

S II = the second Schirmer Edition, revised by Richard Epstein.

In commenting on the sonatas individually I shall follow the order of the *Urtext,* an edition available in America through the exact reprint of Edwin F. Kalmus. To describe the form briefly, I shall call it regular whenever a sonata contains three movements, the first in sonata-form, the second a slow movement, and the third in rondo or condensed sonata-form.

No. 1, K. 279, C major. Form regular. One of the larger sonatas, though not very well known nor of remarkable importance; somewhat formal, except for the expressive slow movement.

No. 2, K. 280, F major. Form regular. A truly Mozartean piece, possibly the best of the easier sonatas. The pathetic Adagio is rarely touching.

No. 3, K. 281, B flat major. Form regular. The first movement may be thought a trifle dry; the Andante and Rondo are musically superior.

No. 4, K. 282, E flat major. This sonata opens with a slow movement, followed by a Minuet and Rondo. It is seldom played and certainly not one of Mozart's best works. The Cotta and the first Schirmer Edition omit it.

No. 5, K. 283, G major. Form regular. Despite its small proportions this graceful piece is one of the most attractive of the early sonatas. Myra Hess has meritoriously acquainted the concert-going public with its elegance.

No. 6, K. 284, D major. First movement in sonata-form; second movement entitled *Rondeau en Polonaise;* last movement a set of variations. Mozart makes a great stride forward in the first movement, rejecting the ornamental style for something far more meaningful and virile. The slow movement holds its own, if not conspicuously beautiful, but the variations, agreeable as is their theme, make a rather weak ending to a work that started out with high promise.

No. 7, K. 309, C major. Form regular. One of the greater sonatas, faultless in structure, well balanced in its moods, pianistically and musically effective.

No. 8, K. 310, A minor. Form regular. A work of genius in which every movement is masterly. Excepting the *Fantasia and Sonata* this is Mozart's only sonata in the minor mode. A gripping composition, dramatically conceived and calling for an impassioned interpretation. Even the final Rondo has a touch of *Weltschmerz* and must not be taken playfully.

No. 9, K. 311, D major. Form regular.

No. 10, K. 330, C major. Form regular. Mozart has now attained full control of the sonata form. These two works and all their successors are perfect alike in construction, content, and symmetrical alternation of mood.

No. 11, K. 331, A major. Form irregular. The first movement is a Theme with Variations, the second a Minuet, the last the famous *alla Turca* march. The Variations and Minuet are in Mozart's best style, and the Turkish March when played with the needed *élan* is irresistibly exciting. Mozart had a pronounced fondness for the Turkish idiom and the Janizary band; witness many of the numbers in *Die Entführung aus dem Serail,* where piccolo, triangle, cymbals, and bass drum lend oriental color to the score. This piece should be played as if it were a piano transcription of Janizary music.

No. 12, K. 332, F major. Form regular. A work of outstanding beauty, peculiarly suitable for concert performance because of its grateful pianistic quality, culminating in an exceptionally brilliant finale. The slow movement wears its lavish ornamentation with grace, and the additional embellishments of early editions on the repetition of the themes, though not present in the autograph, have been adopted by pianists without hesitation.

No. 13, K. 333, B flat major. Form regular. Another work of fin-

THE PIANO SONATAS OF MOZART
as numbered in various editions

KEY	K.	UR.	U.E.	D.	P.	C+S I	S II	DATE
			[abbreviations explained on page 525]					
C	279	1	1	1	16	5	8	1774
F	280	2	2	2	11	6	2	1774
B♭	281	3	3	3	17	8	6	1774
E♭	282	4	4	4	9	—	17	1774
G	283	5	5	5	14	2	5	1774
D	284	6	6	6	10	15	9	1775
C	309	7	7	7	8	11	10	1777
A minor	310	8	8	8	7	16	14	1778
D	311	9	9	9	3	13	12	1788
C	330	10	10	10	2	3	11	1779
A	331	11	11	11	12	9	16	1779
F	332	12	12	12	6	7	1	1779
B♭	333	13	13	13	4	10	7	1779
⎰ C minor[1]	475	14A	14A					1785
				18	18	18	18	
⎱ C minor	457	14B	14B					1784
C	545	15	15	14	15	1	3	1788
B♭	570	16	16	—	—	—	—	1789
D	576	17	17	17	13	14	15	1789
⎰ FA[2]	547	—	18	—	—	—	—	1788
⎱ FB[2]	547A	—	—	16	5	4	13	1788
B♭	498A[3]	—	—	—	—	12	19	1776
F	533[4]	—	—	15	1	17	4	1788

[1] This is the Fantasia and Sonata.

[2] An arrangement of a sonata for piano and violin. The figuration of the first three measures is the same as that of the Violin Sonata in FA (K. 547A) but slightly different in FB.

[3] Described in Appendix 136 as "Sonata movement and Minuet," but as printed has four movements.

[4] Described in K. as "Allegro and Andante," but as printed has a third movement (Rondo) antedating the others by two years but added posthumously.

E. H.

ished perfection. The Rondo is unusually important in thematic material and development.

No. 14A and 14B, Fantasia (K. 475) and Sonata (K. 457) in C minor. Though the Sonata was composed two years before the Fantasia, they were published together in the first authorized edition, and Mozart's own title proves that he regarded them as a single work. While it is permissible to play each separately, the spiritual affinity is obvious. Together they constitute Mozart's *magnum opus* for piano solo. The plan of the Fantasia is singularly symmetrical. There are five sections: a tragic Adagio, a dramatic interruption, a lyrical Intermezzo (Andantino), a second dramatic passage, and a return to the tragic opening. *De Profundis* would be a fitting name for this eloquent piece. The modulations are astonishingly rich and adventurous: after passing in the first ten measures from C minor through B flat minor, D flat, and E flat minor to B major, Mozart reaches a wonderful succession of harmonies. The Sonata is regular in form. Less grave in feeling than the Fantasia, it is intensely dramatic in the first and last movements; in the last (*Molto allegro* according to the autograph, *Allegro assai* in Artaria's early edition), the syncopations of the main theme create an impression of disquietude. The Adagio is pure song. In the middle section of this movement we discover an anticipation of the *Adagio cantabile* from Beethoven's *Sonate pathétique;* even the key and pitch are the same.

No. 15, K. 545, C major. Form regular. Known the world over as the "Easy" Sonata in C, this little jewel is as perfect in its tiny form as any symphony in all its grandeur. I can think of few things more enchanting than to hear it well played by a talented child. A mature mind is apt either to "play down" to it or to load its fragile frame with greater pretension than it can bear; therefore, it should be learned in early youth.

No. 16, K. 570, B flat major. Form regular. Here is a golden opportunity for the amateur to acquire merit by taking into his repertory a piece at once unhackneyed, charming, and not difficult. It appears only in the *Urtext,* the Universal, and the Augener editions. There is an inferior version with an unauthentic violin part added.

No. 17, K. 576, D major. Form regular. Another valuable concert number, difficult but remunerating. As usual, it contains a lovely slow movement. The imitative treatment in the first movement is uncommon in the sonatas and doubly interesting on that account.

Sonata in F, K. 547 and 547A. This and two other sonatas still to be mentioned are not printed in the *Urtext*. It is an arrangement by Mozart himself of a sonata for piano and violin in the same key. K. 547 follows the reading of the violin sonata for the beginning of the first movement. There are only two movements (Allegro and Rondo) as always printed, but there is little doubt that Mozart intended the Variations on an Allegretto in F to add a third movement to the piece. The Allegro and the Variations appear also in the Sonatina for piano and violin, K. 547. The Rondo had already been used by Mozart as the finale of the "Easy" Sonata in C. An animated work, useful in the classroom but not of special importance.

Sonata in B flat, K. 498A. (See note to the table of sonatas, page 527). Printed only in the Cotta, Schirmer, and Augener editions. Four movements (Allegro, Andante, Minuet, Rondo). Only the Allegro and the dainty Minuet are genuine. The Andante is a much abbreviated version by another hand of the slow movement of the Piano Concerto in B flat, K. 450. The Rondo, an unauthentic medley of themes from three different concertos in B flat, is not even clever patchwork.

Sonata in F, K. 533. The Allegro and Andante cited by Köchel were completed by the Rondo in F, K. 494. All movements are genuine. Though the form in general is regular, the Rondo departs from convention by presenting no fewer than four distinct themes, with four appearances of the main subject in addition to its re-entry in the coda. From its length and elaborate form we may well believe that the Rondo was originally written as an independent piece. The sonata is among Mozart's best and contains much interesting contrapuntal and imitative treatment. Yet I have never heard it played publicly.

E. H.

A word must be said about the original compositions for piano duet, which make ideal home music—indeed a kind of keyboard chamber music. There are six sonatas, four of which are usually found in the published collections. Of these the works in B flat major (K. 358) and D major (K. 381) are pleasant, entertaining music without any particular depth. The late Sonata in C major

(K. 521) is a more mature work of the same kind, with a pouncingly brilliant first movement, a finely elaborated Andante and one of those friendly Allegretto finales that seem so characteristic of classical music but are in fact rare in it. That in spite of their mildness they should be effective in Mozart's work when they do occur is surely due to their infrequency.

The F major Sonata (K. 497) removes us to another world—the world of the great chamber music, especially of the string quintets. Indeed an arrangement of some sort for a combination of instruments would make a magnificent concert work of this almost uncomfortably great piece of domestic music, though the writing is at times splendidly suited to the keyboard. It is a tempting idea to transfer the sonata to the medium for which Schubert wrote his octet. A performance of it with that work would make an evening's programme enough to draw one anywhere on the wettest of nights. Sir Donald Tovey, to whom we are indebted for a masterly note on this sonata in the first volume of his *Essays in Musical Analysis,* suggests a string quintet with two cellos.

There is also a set of four-hand variations (K. 501) on an Andante theme of the most enchanting shape and expression: light and luminous music of perfect behaviour. Nor must one forget the two arrangements—one possibly the composer's own, the other, or both, by Johann Mederitsch—of his two great pieces in F minor (K. 594, 608) written for that mechanical organ that bored him so much and for which he wrote what are masterpieces in that amazing late style of his which allows him to use contrapuntal feats with apparent unconcern to make music of extraordinary emotional significance.

The short and very intricate Fugue in G minor (K. 401) is again one of the polyphonic works Constanze urged him to write after she had been smitten by Bach and Handel at van Swieten's. But he seems hardly to have had his heart in it: like the C minor Fugue for two pianos (K. 426) it is very ingenious, but rather dry. Not so the Sonata in D major for two pianos (K. 448), an elegant and endearing work, beautifully devised for its special medium. Once again one notices that emotional detachment in Mozart when it came to matters of life and even of love: he wrote better music for the ugly and exasperating Miss Aurnhammer than for his dear Constanze.

E. B.

Music for Violin and Piano

THE SONATAS for violin and pianoforte (or harpsichord at first) are more properly reviewed with those for keyboard alone than with the chamber music. The eighteenth-century convention was that such works should be essentially keyboard music. Sonatas were written for clavier. The violin could join in if it was available,[1] but the composer was not going to have the popularity of his domestic music threatened by the comparative rarity of players on that instrument. Every household had a harpsichord or clavichord, displaced some time during the second half of the century by the rapidly spreading pianoforte, and sonatas were so devised that they could be played just as well without a second instrument, though their effect was heightened by its participation.

Mozart himself started out by adhering to this fashion without questioning its justification. His early sonatas for violin and clavier dating from 1762 to 1766, only sixteen of which are now regarded as genuine, all show this tendency towards a subordinate violin part very distinctly. They are thus of small interest to the modern player, quite apart from their immaturity as music, which makes them merely historically worthy of study nowadays. They are very properly published in the complete Mozart edition, but as rightly omitted by modern editors from the ordinary collections for home and concert use.

Such collections usually begin with the Sonata in C major (K. 296), written at Mannheim in 1778 and dedicated to Therese Pierron Serrarius, a girl of fifteen whom Mozart taught the clavier during

[1] Or in England the alternative "German flute."

his visit there. That is perhaps why the violin part here is still largely
an accompaniment. Pretty well the whole sonata might be played
on the piano alone without loss of many essential melodic features,
though certainly with a distinct lessening of those charming effects
produced by the collaboration of two antagonistic instruments. The
opening of the work will show at once how the violin part is made
merely to fill in, and this is typical of much of Mozart's writing, not
only in this composition, but in the later ones for the same two instruments. The old habit persisted, and it is significant that so late
a work of his as a piano Sonata in B flat major (K. 570) is better
known with an accompanying violin part which did not come from
his pen at all. All the same, these participations of the violin, even if
they happen to be only a supplementing of the melody a third or a
sixth below or a tiny echo phrase, are becoming astonishingly attractive, and when the violin does suddenly blossom out into a melody
of its own, the surprise is peculiarly appealing. Mozart's method in
this C major Sonata has the touching appeal of adolescence: an
anxious clinging to the support of the conventions in which the violin sonata had been brought up, with little shy outbursts of independence.

The six sonatas (K. 301–306), written for the Electress Palatine,
apparently at Mannheim on his return from Paris, begin to show
greater freedom in the violin parts, though the delightful element
of chamber-musicianly collaboration between the two instruments
remains. Note, for instance, how a purely accompanying figure in
the sixth of these sonatas suddenly flowers into a melody that may
be merely supplementary, but without which the bloom would be
stripped off.

These six works show that surprising maturity in a young man
of twenty-two which one notices that his music reflects very strikingly at the time of his falling in love with Aloysia and the death of
his mother. There is something of a new, chastened tone about the
gentle gravity of the *andante grazioso* rondo of the E flat major
Sonata (K. 302), which makes a slow middle movement superfluous.
The C major Sonata (K. 303) for the first time has a slow introduction and, more curiously, an *adagio* interruption in the middle of the
first *allegro*. The A major (K. 305) boldly presents the first subject
turned upside down and in a minor key at the beginning of the

working-out section, and there is a set of variations for a second movement. The D major (K. 306) is the only one of these works in three fully developed movements.

The most arresting, however, is the fourth, in E minor (K. 304). Once again we find Mozart surprisingly daring, dramatic and individual on taking to a minor key, as he did so strikingly seldom but scarcely ever without producing what in a less fastidious composer one would be tempted to call a sensation. In the proper sense of the term it certainly is that here. This sonata is startling in its emotional tension and ripeness. From the very opening, with its hollow unison, we are held spellbound by the tragic force of the music. The second subject, in the relative major at first, has a kind of sorrowful grace, and the presentation of the first subject in canon, but without any extra harmony, makes a positively grisly climax to the exposition. The working-out heightens the dramatic tension by a new, ingeniously interlaced figure in answer to the main theme, and there is almost a touch of horror when at the recapitulation the subject breaks in surprisingly harmonized. A coda of almost Beethovenish breadth and importance, quite strange in Mozart at this period, concludes the movement. The second, which is also the last, is slighter, yet far more portentous than its minuet time would seem to indicate. There is an episode in E major of heavenly loveliness, pointing ten years ahead to the major trio of the Minuet in the great G minor Symphony, and indeed to Schubert's favourite device for bringing the hearer to the edge of tears, too easily at times, but irresistibly.

Three years later, in 1781, came another set of violin sonatas, five in number, but apparently intended for a half-dozen, for there is an Allegro of a B flat major Sonata (K. 372) which for some reason remained detached. The second, F major (K. 377), and the fourth, G major-minor (K. 379), have sets of variations as second movements, and the latter is particularly interesting by reason of its large slow introduction in G major, followed by a passionate G minor Allegro. The former makes use, at the start and elsewhere, of effective repeated triplets for the violin.

The third sonata of this set, in B flat major (K. 378), has a first movement of concerto-like brilliance. It opens in the old accompanying style, the violin suddenly emerging into prominence with delightful unobtrusiveness, and there is a second subject that must be counted among Mozart's prettiest inventions. It is introduced by the piano alone and then continued by both instruments in a whole long chain of charming ideas, perfectly strung together in a sort of happy inevitability of sequence. The final Rondeau has a showy episode in a different tempo in the manner of the violin concertos. The E flat major Sonata (K. 380) is another piece designed for display, but display of the true Mozartian quality, enhancing the musical value, not smothering it under meaningless ornaments. There is a fine, spacious slow movement in G minor and a well-developed rondo.

The next sonata is the work in B flat major (K. 454) written for Regina Strinasacchi in 1784, on a scale similar to that of the preceding, and not unlike it in character. The famous soloist is given plenty of opportunities, but even here there is give and take between the players, so that if the work is a concerto, it is a *concerto da camera*. If Mozart really did play the piano part from memory just as he wrote it out afterwards, there can have been no vestige of improvisation about the performance, for as usual everything is inevitable, everything comes at the right moment and stands in the right position. If anything, the working-out is perhaps unduly free of thematic allusions; but then it often is, even in mature works of Mozart's, showing clearly that his sonata movements have their root in the old *da capo* aria of Alessandro Scarlatti and Handel, to mention only two exponents who are well known, one by reputation and the other from practice. Even where the development is intended to be elaborately thematic, as here it is not, Mozart often slyly begins his workings-out as though he were going to wander casually away from the matter in hand, only to spring the sudden surprise of an extraordinarily rich and subtle allusiveness. The Andante is a long and exquisite dialogue between the two instruments, with stabbing accents of passion here and there. One cannot resist the thought that if the composer and his young Italian performer did not fall in love with each other while they played this movement, it can only have been that they both possessed the imagination which is the perfect artist's substitute for experience. Only the second-rate, both among creators and interpreters, feel that they must have personally touched everything before they attain to the insight they need.

The E flat major Sonata (K. 481) of the following year is a somewhat less important work. At any rate the final variations come near insignificance. Although it could not be played without the violin part, the old habit of the accompanying manner makes itself felt in the first and last movements. The Adagio, however, is a grand piece of work, full of suppressed temperamental expressions and twice boldly taking the roundabout way of enharmonic modulation, an effect which, like that of the diminished seventh, had not become stale by abuse and certainly was not overworked by Mozart himself.

Grand all through is the Sonata in A major (K. 526) of 1787—just before *Don Giovanni*. The first movement is, rather exceptionally, in 6/8 time. It receives a very close development, with a scrupulously thematic working-out section this time. The violin part is most artfully interlaced with the right-hand piano part and the cadential ends of phrases are extended by harmonic circumlocutions which somehow retain their quality of surprise however often one has heard the music. But expansion here is wonderfully made amends for by concentration elsewhere. In the slow movement a similar balance by compensation is effected, but this time by harmonic means. Mozart goes out of his way to keep his texture bare almost to the point of bleakness here and there. Apart from that, this is one of the most original slow movements he ever wrote. The final Presto is akin in character to that of the greater of the two piano concertos in the same key (K. 488), and scarcely less difficult for the keyboard player, the violin part requiring some very neat fitting in. The movement is one of those, not infrequent in Mozart, in which animation makes an impression of stress, not of gaiety. The whole is perfectly organized, spun out at great length without letting the interest drop for an instant, and an extraordinary richness is gained by a minimum of harmonic filling-in. The movement goes by so fast that, as in Domenico Scarlatti's sonatas, the witty dryness of which it somewhat resembles, a greater number of notes would inevitably mean an effect of redundancy.

The F major Sonata (K. 547) is only a curious kind of appendix. Like the little piano Sonata in C major (K. 545), it is supposed to be an easy piece for beginners, though any hopeful pianist or fiddler might be only too glad to begin like this. It is so oddly arranged that one wonders whether the Allegro in the middle ought not to have come before the Andante cantabile at the beginning, or indeed whether the whole work is not merely jumbled together at random.

At any rate it is suspicious that the Allegro exists also in an arrangement for piano alone, with a little rondo of K. 545, transposed into
F major, as a finale, and that the final variations, with a modestly
accompanying violin part, got into Köchel's catalogue as a piano
solo with the very early number 54.

Two separate sets of variations for violin and piano (K. 359, 360)
are agreeably entertaining. Of much greater interest is the fragment
of a Sonata in A major-minor (K. 402), which even as finished by
Maximilian Stadler still remains a torso, for it was not like Mozart
to write a prelude in A major for a fugue in A minor and leave it at
that. The introduction is a very powerful piece of work, the fugue
rather dry and crabbed. It dates from the time (1782) when Constanze urged fugal writing upon Mozart, and it is not the only
work of the kind written in the year of their marriage which shows
a certain lack of interest.[2] To judge from this that he was not a
contrapuntist would be the height of absurdity. At the most it might
be said that he was a contrapuntist by nature rather than by taste.
To write a fugue for fugue's sake meant nothing to him, but when
one was required of him—in a mass, let us say—he could produce
it with Bach's own facility and triumphant skill. More than that, he
could turn out the most elaborate fugal fabrics where they were
not particularly required, as in the G major string Quartet (K. 387),
in the "Jupiter" Symphony, in *The Magic Flute,* and so on. But it
is curious that Constanze could not induce him to give himself at
least the pleasure of pleasing her by writing fugues unapplied to any
other purpose. However, he may have been too busy with other
things in 1782. He certainly left two other violin sonatas, both in
C major (K. 403–404), incomplete as well as one for piano in B
flat major (K. 400).

E. B.

---

[2] Can it be doubted that the unfinished *Overture in the style of Handel* (K. 399)
was intended to finish with a fugue?

9

Church Music

THE REQUIEM

CHURCH MUSIC

WHEN THE romantic nineteenth century began to discover the Middle Ages, not only the Gothic cathedrals and the Pre-Raphaelites, but also what it considered medieval in music—the alleged *a cappella* style of the Gabrielis, Lasso, and Palestrina—the church music of the seventeenth and eighteenth centuries became an object of contempt. Not only the lesser masters were included in this disdain, but also, and particularly, Joseph Haydn and Wolfgang Amadeus Mozart. As early as in Otto Jahn's biography of Mozart, the first in a scientific sense, there was cited and refuted the passage that may be found in *Über Reinheit der Tonkunst* (1824), a singular book by Anton Friedrich Justus Thibaut, jurist, professor at the University of Heidelberg, and Privy Councilor:

Thus our more recent masses and other ecclesiastical compositions have degenerated to the extent that they have become purely amorous and emotional and bear the absolute stamp of secular opera and even of that type of opera which is most in demand, that is, downright vulgar opera [What does Thibaut mean? *Opera buffa?*], in which, to be sure, the crowd feels most at home, and people of quality even more so than the common herd. Even the church music of Mozart and Haydn deserves that reproach, and both masters have even expressed it themselves. Mozart openly smiled at his masses, and several

537

times, when he was commissioned to write a mass, protested, on the ground that he was only made for the opera. But since he was offered 100 louis d'or for each mass, he could not refuse, but explained laughingly that anything good in his masses would be taken out later for use in his operas. . . .

Now Mozart wrote hardly more than two Masses "on commission": the solemn one in C minor for the consecration of the Waisenhaus-Kirche am Rennweg in Vienna, when he was a lad of thirteen, and the Requiem in D minor; and in both cases he neither protested nor smiled, either secretly or openly. His Salzburg church music was written not to order but "in service," or out of friendship, or to accommodate someone, and his finest church composition, the great C minor Mass, was composed in fulfilment of a vow. Mozart utilize his Masses for his operas? Mozart, who had the most sensitive feeling for the limitations of forms, for the tradition within those limitations? It is certainly true that ecclesiastical texts were set to music from Mozart's operas, for example from Così fan tutte; this was not Mozart's fault, however, but that of the nineteenth century.

The scorn on the part of the nineteenth-century Romantic purists and "Cecilians" for the church style of Haydn and Mozart is the more comical because their admiration for the church music of the Palestrina period rests upon a historical fallacy. If they had had a better knowledge of the secular music of Palestrina and Lasso and the Gabrielis, they would have had to reject the church music of these masters and their contemporaries also, as being too similar to the secular music and flowing from the same spirit. They regarded as eminently churchly works that in reality were full of an eminently secular symbolism of expression, or at least were full of a symbolism common to both secular and sacred music. If they had known more, nothing would have remained to the Cecilians à la Thibaut but to go back to plainsong or the antiphonal chants of the early Christians. Creative centuries do not think in terms of history. It never occurred to the architects of Chartres or Rheims or Notre Dame to build in the Romanesque style, any more than it occurred to Bramante or Michelangelo to return to the Gothic style for Saint Peter's, although the Gothic style is supposed to be "more pious" than that of the Renaissance. We have already compared Mozart's

Catholicism in his church music with the jubilant Rococo churches in Southern Bavaria and Upper and Lower Austria, which are no less pious and no more secular than San Vitale in Ravenna. If Mozart's church music is to be criticized, then, it must be on the ground not of being too "worldly," but because it is not worldly enough. There was no historical reminiscence, no remnant of a heterogeneous past, in the style of those builders who created the Wies-Kirche or the Klosterkirche of Ettal in Upper Bavaria. Unfortunately, in music, and especially in eighteenth-century church music, there was such a remnant: what Mozart's contemporaries called the "strict" style, the *stile osservato*. Mozart's church works are written partly in a mixed style. As we have seen, tradition demanded that individual sections of the Mass—the "Cum sancto spiritu" or "Et vitam venturi"—and the concluding parts of other liturgical texts be treated "fugally," in an archaic, polyphonic style; and Mozart was a traditionalist. As a traditionalist and an ambitious musician he attached particular value to such contrapuntal show-pieces, and the more he did so, the more strongly he emphasized the stylistic dualism of his church compositions. Not in all his church compositions; but he never completely overcame this dualism, even in the Requiem—in striking contrast to his success in doing so in his instrumental works and operas. *This* is the esthetic reproach, if any, that may be leveled against his church music.

But not the reproach that this music is too worldly, not devout or Catholic enough; that it does not fit the requirements for ecclesiastical music laid down in the *Motu proprio* of Pope Pius X of 22 November, 1903. It surely cannot be called unliturgical. It always employs the full text of the Mass or litany; and only in individual cases does it becloud the understanding of the text by its use of "polytexture"—that is, by a simultaneous singing of different textual passages that according to liturgical precept should properly follow in succession. Mozart's church music, we repeat, is "Catholic" in a higher sense—namely, in the sense that it is pious as a work of art, and the piety of an artist can consist only in his desire to give his utmost. Otherwise the devout little pictures, the imitation Lourdes grottoes, the besugared "Christ-childs" of the religious-goods industry would be more Catholic than Giotto's frescoes or Duccio's panels, and one of the boring "Nazarene" Masses or hymns by Ett or

Aiblinger more Catholic than Mozart's "Misericordias" or "Ave verum." Furthermore, the Catholic quality of Mozart's church music, in the higher sense, consists not perhaps in any so-called and questionable dignity—a fitness for the interior of a Romanesque or Gothic church—but in its humanity, in its appeal to all devout and childlike hearts, in its directness. If one wishes to be "pure in style," one should certainly not perform it in a Gothic church and least of all in a nineteenth- or twentieth-century church; just as one should not perform the Organa of Perotin or the Masses of Obrecht in a Rococo church. One can no more find fault with Mozart for writing Masses, vespers, offertories, motets, litanies, and hymns in the spirit of his time than one can find fault with Giambatista Tiepolo for approaching his church pictures with the same artistic assumptions as those with which he approached his mythological or historical scenes. It was the ultracultured and Alexandrian nineteenth century that first cast this stone.

A. E.

THE REQUIEM

Die Zauberflöte was produced on September 30, 1791, but in the meantime its composition had been interrupted by two other important commissions. In July "a stranger, a tall, thin, grave-looking man," says Jahn, "dressed from head to foot in grey, and calculated from his very appearance to make a striking and weird impression, presented Mozart with an anonymous letter begging him, with many flattering allusions to his accomplishments as an artist, to name his price for composing a *Requiem,* and the shortest time in which he could undertake to complete it." Mozart . . . was anxious to prove his capacity as a Church-composer to the new Emperor, who had abolished the innovations in Church music instituted by the Emperor Joseph and re-established the orchestras. So he accepted this commission readily, the more so as he was specifically allowed to compose the *Requiem* according to his own ideas and was to be subject to no restrictions, saving that he must not seek to discover the identity of his mysterious patron. . . .

The mysterious manner in which the *Requiem* was commissioned has already been related. The oddness of it made a deep impression on Mozart's imagination, and when, at the very moment of his departure to Prague for the production of *La Clemenza di Tito,* the stranger reappeared to enquire how the work was progressing, it seemed to Mozart, already overwought mentally and physically, that here was in very truth a visitant from another world come to summon him away. The idea became an obsession, and he could not banish from his mind the conviction that he was composing the *Requiem* against his own death.

The explanation of the mystery was simple, though strange enough. The messenger was the steward of Count Franz von Walsegg, a minor nobleman who had a small Court at Stuppach. This gentleman had ambitions in the direction of musical composition. But since he had the good sense to realize his own inability to write music, he commissioned others, who had the necessary training, to supply him with compositions, which were well paid for and then passed off on his Court as the products of his own genius. His wife had died recently, and he evidently felt that this was an occasion on which he would be expected to turn out, under the stimulus of his grief, a really first-rate work. So he had the further good sense to apply for a *Requiem* in her honour to one who had the reputation of being a first-rate composer. He seems to have been disappointed at the low price of fifty ducats which Mozart demanded; for he promised him a further sum on the completion of the work. Perhaps, like many art-patrons, he could not believe that a work was good unless it was also expensive.

In the present instance the deceiver—if we suppose his Court was really taken in by him—was himself deceived. For of the *Requiem,* which was handed to him some time after Mozart's death, a part is not of his composition. Count von Walsegg was, indeed, the victim of a clever forgery. Constanze, left destitute with two children, did not scruple to get the balance of the money promised by delivering to von Walsegg a score completed by Süssmayr in a hand almost indistinguishable from his master's. Then, much to the discomfiture of the amateur, who had the *Requiem* performed as a work of his own composition in December, 1793, she allowed it to be given under her husband's name. When she further arranged for its publication by Messrs. Breitkopf and Härtel, the Count, who had at any rate bought and paid for the rights of the work, felt that this was going too far and brought an action against Mozart's widow. However, the action was settled out of court and the Count even allowed his copy to be used for the revision of the proofs.

There is, indeed, no more romantic story in the whole history of music than that connected with the *Requiem* Mass. It has all the materials for imaginative embroidery—a dying composer, a mysterious visitant, an uncompleted work. There is, too, for those who like scandal, the double deception practised by Constanze on the Count and by the Count upon the world—that is to say his own little Court. No wonder that legends grew about the already fantastic facts like barnacles upon a moored hulk! It took an inquest by experts to sift the true from the false, and to find some common measure in the various conflicting statements made by Constanze and by Süssmayr. The experts pronounced for the authenticity of the greater part of the work, wherein they had the support of Beethoven, whose sole comment upon the essay of its chief detractor was to scribble upon it the words: "Oh! you arch ass!"

But there are even now some who do not accept this decision. Messrs. de Wyzewa and de Saint-Foix state categorically and without argument, since the *Requiem* does not come within the scope of the main part of their book, that the "Requiem" and "Kyrie" are the only movements which Mozart certainly completed. "As to the rest of the work," they continue, "everything tends to the belief that Mozart wrote only the 'Recordare,' the 'Confutatis,' and the first notes of the 'Lacrimosa,' which themselves must have been revised and scored by his pupil." Similarly Mr. William Watson seeks to prove that Mozart's share in the work was negligible, though he admits somewhat inconsistently that Süssmayr was incapable of writing the music, which is consequently attributed to him.

The facts are, briefly, that on his return from Prague in September Mozart completed *Die Zauberflöte* by writing the overture, the march and chorus of the Priests, Papageno's song in Act II, and the finale, besides orchestrating the whole, and then started work on the *Requiem*. The first two numbers were completed and exist in Mozart's handwriting. There also exist sketches for all but four of the remaining numbers, which consist of the whole of the voice-parts together with the figured bass and sufficient indications of the instrumentation for a capable musician, with whom the composer had discussed his ideas many times over, to complete them in accordance with his intentions. Of the four other numbers, the beginning of one (the "Lacrimosa") is admittedly by Mozart, while the final section of the work has been set to the music of the "Requiem" and "Kyrie." This leaves to Süssmayr's credit three whole numbers ("Sanctus," "Benedictus," and "Agnus Dei") and part of one other ("Lacrimosa"), besides the completion of Mozart's sketches. An examination of the sketches in detail proves that all the things which strike us in a performance of the *Requiem* as being most remarkable, were either fully worked out or at least clearly indicated in Mozart's own hand. For example, in the "Confutatis," the whole of the first violin part of the latter half of the movement (from the words "oro supplex et acclinis"), which is one of the most arresting passages in the whole work, is complete in the sketch, and the entry of the basset-horns and bassoons is cued in. While, therefore, a large part of the actual score is Süssmayr's handiwork, the essential things, those which make it great music, are indisputably Mozart's own.

Of the movements of which no sketches by Mozart are in existence, the "Sanctus" and "Osanna" may be certainly attributed to Süssmayr. This number is competent and mediocre. If it appeared in a work about which there was no dispute, it might pass for authentic Mozart in an uninspired moment. The same may be said of the "Benedictus." But here a doubt arises, for the first five notes of its theme appear in the first of the exercises set by Mozart for a niece of the Abbé Stadler in 1784, while there is also a resemblance to it in the fifth of the pianoforte variations (K. 500) written in 1786. Mr. Oldman, who has kindly supplied me with this information, adds: "But there is not much in this. The thematic figure itself may well have been a commonplace of the time. Judged as a whole the three pieces of music are as different as they well could be." So I think this resemblance may be set down as fortuitous and the "Benedictus" safely judged to be genuine Süssmayr.

The "Agnus Dei," alone of the movements which do not appear in Mozart's sketches, reaches the level of the authentic parts of the work, and long before I had examined the evidence in any detail I was convinced by hearing the music that no one but Mozart himself could have written the opening section of the movement. It is not unreasonable to suppose that Süssmayr had before him some sketches which have not survived. At least it is certain that nothing in Süssmayr's acknowledged works warrants the opposite supposition that he was capable of writing the first part of the "Agnus Dei." Even Gottfried Weber, Bethoven's "arch ass," who first seriously disputed the authenticity of the *Requiem,* confessed that in the parts which are with reason attributed to Süssmayr, "there were flowers which never grew in Süssmayr's garden." Personally I believe—and I have found, since I first expressed this opinion, more support for it from various sources than I expected—that Mozart wrote the first strain of the "Agnus," even as he wrote the first few bars of the "Lacrimosa." It is altogether so typically Mozartian in feeling, and the figure of the violin accompaniment is so characteristic and original that it is almost impossible to accept it as a brilliant imitation. Süssmayr may very well, on the other hand, be responsible for the sickly-sweet sentimentality of the second strain ("dona eis requiem"). My conjecture has further support from the way in which the movement proceeds. For the subsequent treatment of the first strain is of the ordinary kind, which might be expected of the pupil, and is devoid of those surprising turns which the master alone could imagine. All this is, of course, mere conjecture and is not susceptible of proof, for Süssmayr may, like many another third-rate composer, have risen for once above his normal level.

Yet even when we deny to Süssmayr the credit for all those things which impress us most deeply in the *Requiem,* we must acknowledge our admiration for the way in which he carried out his task. No one but Joseph! Yet, while the debt to Handel is clear at any rate in the general style—if not in the conscious choice of the subjects, which are after all of the ordinary kinds that suggest themselves for fugal treatment—the manner of working out the material is entirely original, and, in this context, the first subject seems to look forward into the next century towards the first movement of Beethoven's last pianoforte sonata. The development of the music leads to a climax of the greatest agitation by way of a series of extraordinary chromatic passages, which Gottfried Weber contemptuously and expressively termed "Gurgeleien," before sinking to a more resigned and dignified mood at the close.

It is quite possible that in choosing to follow the conventional practise in his treatment of these opening movements, Mozart was influenced as much by artistic motives as by the desire to show his mastery of the old Church style. He may, in fact, have seen that the "Dies Irae," which follows, required the contrast of a formal introduction in order to set off to the fullest possible extent the more brutish emotions aroused by its verses as compared with those of the Liturgy proper. For this poem, which dates to the middle of the thirteenth century, is an interpolation in the Mass for the Dead. It embodies all those terrible ideas of the pains of Hell and the tortures of the eternally damned contrasted with the hardly won bliss of the righteous, which were so vivid to the mediaeval imagination and proved the chief mainstay of the Church's power. The "Dies Irae" is, indeed, the counterpart in words of those strange pictures of the Last Judgement, which still awe the spectator by the crude violence of their horrors, even though he may be amused by the blue and yellow devils pitch-forking emaciated bodies in every contortion of physical anguish into the fiery mouths of enormous dragons. You may still see these scenes enacted in the stained glass windows of many churches, notably at Fairford, whose windows must be among the latest to be installed while the belief in this kind of physical torment after death was still a living reality to all good Christians.

But when this belief had waned, at least among the more thoughtful, it still held its power to stimulate the artist. One cannot believe that Rubens accepted the facts, which he depicted with such magnificent gusto in his "Fall of the Damned," as anything more than the material for a fine decoration. So the "Dies Irae" appeared to Mozart an opportunity for a splendid and terrible musical design, in which, as in Ruben's picture, the horrible details, relics of a past tradition, would be subordinate to the unity of the whole and would, therefore, sink into insignificance and so lose their brutality. But there entered another factor—the delusions under which Mozart laboured concerning the work on which he was engaged. For once, a note of hysterical passion sounded in his music, ordinarily so disciplined and so detached from any morbid reference to his own personal feelings. It is this note of hysteria which makes the *Requiem* one of the most painful works to contemplate, painful in the way that the cry of an animal caught in a snare or the Pathetic Symphony of Tchaikovsky, who was expert in the expression of self-pity, are painful.

The contrast between the *Requiem* and the serene nobility of *Die Zauberflöte* is as remarkable as their resemblances. Both works treat of the same supreme ordeal which mankind has to face; the one with the calm and intellectual philosophy of the Mason, the other with the more emotional faith, with its complement of troubling doubts, of the Catholic. Their common factors are in the general style of the music as well as in the predominance in the orchestration of the basset-horn and trombones, although the instrumentation of the opera is far more elaborate than that of the Mass. The *Requiem* shows a falling-off, if not always from the musical standard, at least from the untroubled confidence of *Die Zauberflöte,* which is not unnatural in a man wasted by disease and face to face with the inevitable foe whom in better days he had been able to regard with an unflinching eye.

The words of the "Dies Irae" insist upon the very terrors of death, which that noble profession of faith denies. The sick man fell under their spell and his music became filled with the agony of death as no other work has been, with the possible exception of "The Dream of Gerontius." Moving and wonderful though the *Requiem* is, and the more moving on account of the circumstances in which it was composed, it is to *Die Zauberflöte* that we should look for the true expression of Mozart's philosophy of life and death.

D. H.

10

Mozart and the Critics

NO GREAT musical genius was simpler, more modest, or more human than Haydn. Where the music of other great composers tried to raise the audience to its own lofty heights, Haydn's seemed to remain firmly rooted in the earth, kindly and familiar as Haydn's own character. His happiness, humor, and religious feeling conspired with his delight in composing, as well as with his clarity and friendly urbanity, to make music that was closely connected with the feelings of the common man. His music was not at all difficult to understand—not even the music critics found it hard.

It was otherwise with Mozart, whose music was more complex, more aristocratic, a precious mixture of tragic and comic mood. There was, of course, sensual beauty in his music; splendor of sound and angelic purity; but it was neither so simple nor so healthy as Haydn's music. Mozart was a nervous child, easily brought to tears. He lived in a world of fairy tales, and all his life he remained a child who enjoyed the gaiety of masked balls, and who, when there was no fire, danced with his wife around the stove as two children dance around a Christmas tree. When he composed, his wife had to sit beside him and tell him tales of Snow White and Cinderella. The mood of Mozart's music is the mood of fairy tales. The listener moves into a world where lights are brighter and colors more vivid than those on earth. Like Shelley, he had "luminous wings."

Mozart, like Haydn, arrived at the summit of musical achievement without the help of musical criticism. Criticisms of his

547

work were infrequent before the *Marriage of Figaro* appeared. When *Idomeneo* was first performed in Munich on January 29, 1781, the report of the *Münchener Staats gelehrten und vermischten Nachrichten* (*"Munich News of the State, Science, and Various Matters"*) consisted of these few lines: "On the 29th of the past month, the opera *Idomeneo* was performed for the first time in our new opera house. Libretto, music, and translation originated in Salzburg. The decorations—of which the most inspiring are the view of the seaport and the temple of Neptune—are masterpieces by our theater architect, Mr. Corent Quaglio, and aroused the admiration of all." That is the entire text of the notice. The first real criticisms of Mozart appeared after the first night of his great masterpiece, *The Abduction from the Seraglio*. This opera, the monument to Mozart's love for Constanza Weber, was first performed on July 19, 1782, in the National Theater of Vienna, where Gluck had once been conductor and where *Orfeo* and *Alceste* had been performed for the first time. The theater, small but high, with the Emperor in the first box on the right, flanked by all the aristocrats, was overcrowded. "The opera," reported Cramer's *Magazin der Musik,* "is full of beautiful music. It surpassed the expectation of the public. The striking taste and ideas of the author enjoyed the loudest applause of all." The same magazine also published a detailed, highly laudatory article on the opera. Another flattering article written by B. A. Weber in 1788, appeared in the *Dramaturgische Blätter* (*"Dramatic Magazine"*). Weber, noted as pianist, composer, and conductor, had been visiting Vienna and was present at a performance of the opera. Mozart, who liked the sweet smell of praise as well as any other artist, was so pleased with both these articles that he kept copies of them. After his death they were found in his small library.

In 1783 Mozart gave a subscription concert in the National Theater, playing two new piano concertos of his own composition. His success as a pianist is well documented. Haydn said with tears in his eyes that Mozart's playing was unforgettable because it touched the heart. Clementi testified that nobody else could play with as much spirit and grace as Mozart, and Dittersdorf found an unequaled fusion of art and taste in his playing. "Mozart is the best, the most accomplished pianist I ever heard," reported the Vienna correspondent of Cramer's *Magazin der Musik* in 1787.

And Rochlitz wrote in the *Allgemeine musikalische Zeitung* that he would never forget "the heavenly delight that Mozart evoked with the spirit of his compositions and the splendor and heart-affecting delicacy of his rendition."

On March 29, 1783, Mozart wrote to his father about the concert in the National Theater. He was happy—he said—that His Majesty the Emperor was present and that he enjoyed the concert and that he applauded so enthusiastically. . . . The concert was reviewed in Cramer's magazine:

> Today the famous Chevalier Mozart[1] gave a musical concert for his own benefit in which some of his favorite compositions were performed. The concert was distinguished by an unusually large audience, and the two new concertos and other fantasias which Mozart played on the piano were given much applause. Our Emperor, contrary to his habit, honored the concert with his presence, and the whole audience applauded so unanimously that no similar case comes to mind.

The clarinetist Stadler, for whom Mozart had composed the charming clarinet quintet, gave a concert in Vienna in 1784. On the program was Mozart's serenade for two oboes, two clarinets, two basset horns, four horns, two bassoons, violoncello, and double bass. The Hamburg music critic Schink expressed his opinion of the concert in a series of exclamations: "Today I heard a piece for wind instruments composed by Mr. Mozart, in four movements . . . wonderful and splendid! . . . Every instrument was played by a master. . . . Oh, it makes an effect! . . . wonderful and great, excellent and magnificent!" The concert was reviewed by the Vienna *Zeitung*. The critic wrote, "A great composition for wind instruments of quite a special kind was performed, composed by Mr. Mozart."

From 1785 on, the laudatory criticisms of Mozart were intermingled with unfavorable and malevolent criticisms. It almost seems as if the dullest critics had a fine feeling for the exact point at which an artist begins to develop the new and personal forces of his genius. When Beethoven began to expand Haydn's sym-

[1] Mozart was a Knight of the Golden Spur. The order had been conferred upon him by the Pope when the boy visited Rome in 1770.

phonic framework, or Wagner to free himself from the romantic operatic form of Weber, Marschner, and Meyerbeer, the music critics scented that something new was in the air, and began to shout that the future of music was imperiled. So the critics scented—and they were right—that the Mozart of 1785 was about to reach heights from which his view of the world was wider. They suspected that he was leaving the sunny, happy days of youth for a different world, where his mastery would become more conscious. Three new accomplishments proved Mozart's new outlook on life and art. The first was his use of the full symphonic orchestra for the first time in *The Marriage of Figaro*. The second was his new use of chromatic harmonies and of dissonances on a chromatic basis. And the third was his Shakespearean mixture of tragedy and comedy. The critics of Mozart's time smelled a rat; and the more conservative they were, the more they cautioned the public against Mozart's innovations. Their unfavorable and indignant criticisms were merely their own way of saying that a genius was beginning to create new art forms. Their intuition was correct.

Criticism turned really sour in 1785 when Mozart published his six string quartets dedicated to Haydn. These quartets had not been composed to order. Mozart wrote them to try out the strengthened forces of his imagination, and his mature technical mastery. This was music to please his own sense of beauty and to meet his own highest ideas of art. In the touching dedication to Haydn by which Mozart introduces these compositions, his children, to the "famous man and dearest friend," he speaks of "his long and industrious work." As a matter of fact, Mozart worked over five years on these quartets. They were written for himself, and this explains the boldness of their style, the novelty of their harmonies, and the joy in experiment which is so evident in them.

The last of these six string quartets is in C major. Sharp dissonances are used in the introduction, and major and minor clash. Dissonant anticipations are so cutting that at each hearing one feels that one is being struck with a knife. Never before had tragic pain been expressed in music with such directness. The artistic expression is almost naturalistic.

It stands to reason that these dissonances met with opposition. Boldness of harmony has always been exciting. Neither eccentric melodies nor strange rhythms are as stirring as new harmonies. To Hanslick, for example, the opening bars of the Prelude to *Tristan and Isolde* were only "chromatic whining." In point of fact they were the heralds of a new age of harmony. Mozart's chromaticism met with the same opposition—and with reason, for Mozart was daring. He used chromatic turns and changes of harmony to express differentiated mental states, to give slight shades and delicate colors. These chromatic mixtures and oscillations impart rich coloring to his harmonies. Even Haydn could learn from Mozart. Witness the chromatic chords that conclude the prelude to *The Creation* and so strikingly anticipate the harmonies of *Tristan*. Even today the dissonances of the introductory measures of the Quartet in C major prick the ears of the critics.[2]

In January, 1787, the Viennese correspondent of the *Magazin der Musik* reported of Mozart: "He is the best and cleverest piano player I have ever heard; but it is a pity that in his ingenious and really beautiful compositions he goes too far in his attempt to be new, so that feeling and sentiment are little cared for. His new quartets, dedicated to Haydn, are too strongly spiced—and what palate can stand that for long?" Another guardian of the public taste wrote in the same magazine, "The works of Kozeluch [a forgotten composer] remain alive and are welcomed everywhere, but Mozart's compositions do not unanimously please. It is true, and his new quartets dedicated to Haydn prove it, that he has a decided inclination for the grave and unusual."

The main characteristic that impressed the critics of the day seems to have been his daring harmonies. The *Allgemeine musikalische Zeitung* advises its readers to regard a composition as Mozart's "especially when one audacious transition closely follows another." As late as 1809 J. B. Schaul[3] found Mozart's harmonies "hard and sophisticated"; Mozart led his hearers "between steep rocks into a thorny forest in which flowers grow but thinly," whereas Boccherini led one "into serene country with flowering meadows, clear,

---

[2] One finds them stinging the ears of such an intelligent and witty critic as Ernest Newman, who defends his fellow critics as a good uncle defends the conduct of his naughty nephews. See his book, *A Musical Critic's Holiday*.

[3] Court musician in Stuttgart and a writer whose book, *Letters on Taste in Music* (1809), enjoyed considerable authority.

rushing brooks, and thick groves"; Mozart was "a musical Daedalus" who knew "how to construct great, impenetrable labyrinths" but the writer lamented that he knew no Ariadne to provide the thread which should guide him out through the tortuous passages.

How bizarre some critics found Mozart's music is demonstrated by J. G. K. Spazier's review of a concert by the pianist Rick. The review appeared in Reichardt's *Musikalisches Wochenblatt ("Musical Weekly")* in 1791. The reviewer wrote: "He played a concerto by Mozart and brought out effectively the sensitive passages and the peculiar traits of this rich artist, who like every great genius must command the most bizarre flights of the soul and who often indulges in the strangest paradoxical turns." Even as late as 1826 Nägeli was lamenting "the exaggerated, debauching contrasts" in Mozart's music. In this last case, it was the Prelude to *Don Giovanni* that aroused the critic to protest.

Mozart's harmonies were not the only elements of his art which offended critical ears. His use of the symphonic orchestra in the opera weighed heavily upon them. This new orchestra was not mere accompaniment, as the orchestras of the earlier Italian *opera buffa* had been. It was the painter of all moods and of all the details of the dramatic action. Out of the orchestra rose Cherubino's enamored sighs, the Countess's noble laments, and the clear laugh of Susanna. The orchestra contained the possibility of the merry movement of a musical comedy as well as the calm of the night where only whispers thronged the air. The voices of the orchestra, as in the symphony, were richly tinted. The strings sang tender melodies, or perhaps chirped and chattered like a guitar, scurrying and running, laughing or joking. The wind instruments uttered only a breath, the delicate sound of longing. The horns shouted in mockery. Dittersdorf writes in his autobiography that the Emperor Joseph II said after a performance of *The Marriage of Figaro* that Mozart completely blanketed the singers with his full orchestra. In the *Journal des Luxus und der Moden* of 1791, we read that Mozart's operatic orchestra is "artificial, weighty, and overloaded with instruments."

No other reproach is so often met with in contemporary criticisms of Mozart as the charge that his music is overloaded and overstuffed. The impact of this music on indolent ears must have been similar to that which the music of Richard Strauss made on conservative hearers between 1890 and 1910. When *Don Giovanni* was performed in Berlin in 1790, Spazier wrote in the *Musikalisches Wochenblatt* that Mozart was hurling such large masses of sound at his audience that it was almost impossible to survey "the excellent whole." And B. A. Weber maintained in the same journal that if Mozart were to be reproached, "this would be the only blame: that the wealth of beautiful detail almost crushes the soul."

The mighty stride which carried Mozart from *The Marriage of Figaro* to *Don Giovanni* left the critics far behind. They attacked both the immorality of the libretto and the complexity of the music. After the first performance of *Don Giovanni* in Berlin, the *Chronik von Berlin* (*"Berlin Chronicle"*) thundered from the critical pulpit that in this opera the eye was satiated, the ear charmed, reason grieved, morality offended, and virtue and feeling trampled upon by vice. "Oh!" cried the critic to unperturbed Mozart, "had you not so greatly wasted the power of your mind! Had your feeling been more in correspondence with your fancy!" The Munich censor even prohibited the showing of the opera. Other critics took exception to the overloading of the music. The *Chronik von Berlin* declaimed to the effect that

> music for the theater knows no other rule, and no other judge than the heart. . . . What the composer must express is, not an overloaded orchestra, but heart, feeling, and passion. Only as he writes in a great style, only then will his name be given to posterity. Grétry, Monsigny, and Philidor prove this. Mozart in his *Don Giovanni* intended to write something uncommonly, inimitably great. There is no doubt: the uncommon is here, but not the inimitably great! Whim, caprice, ambition but not heart created *Don Giovanni*.

Again and again the critics chant their theme song, that Mozart is not a tasteful composer. In 1793, the *Allgemeine musikalische Zeitung* carried an article that said among other things: "Mozart was a great genius, but he had no real taste, and little or perhaps no cultivated taste. He missed, of course, any effect in his original operas." The critic challenges anyone to come forward and "prove that Mozart understood how to treat a libretto correctly!" When B. A.

Weber expressed his admiration for Mozart in the columns of the *Musikalisches Wochenblatt,* an irate reader sent a letter to the publisher, saying, "Weber's judgment on Mozart is highly exaggerated and one-sided. Nobody will overlook the talented man in Mozart and the experienced, rich, and pleasant composer. But I never heard a single profound expert praise him as a correct, much less a perfect composer. Least of all will the tasteful critic believe him to be a composer who is correct in regard to poetry, and sensitive." In 1801 the Parisian correspondent of the Leipzig *Allgemeine musikalische Zeitung* wrote of Mozart as Haydn's rival, but not a serious rival since "he possesses more genius than taste."

One can eaily realize how the libretto of *The Magic Flute,* which fused popular humor with nonsense and wisdom and raised the Viennese popular theater to its greatest heights, displeased the tasteful critics. Like Shakespeare's *Winter's Tale,* the opera combined colorful imagination, naïve jokes, and solemnity. Jack Pudding jested before temple walls ornamented with magic signs, while behind them sounded the choruses of the priests. Sublime symbols of light and darkness were to be seen in the background, while in front the animals listened enchanted to the magic flute and wagged their tails. No rationalist could understand this free play of imagination, which so charmed the mind of Goethe. Hence we see in Koch's *Journal der Tonkunst* (*"Journal of Music"*) of 1795, a critic lamenting that one "has in this very century to see the fugue, the greatest masterpiece of art, parodied in an opera intended to be half comical and half serious. In that opera, clowns and sages, together with animals and all the other elements, form a chaos in order (as I suppose) to make the miraculous in the serious part of the opera comprehensible, and to make war on good taste and sane reason in a spectacle that dishonors the poetry of our age." Rationalism has here come to the border line beyond which begins the realm of free imagination, where the comedies of Aristophanes, the *commedia dell' arte, A Midsummer Night's Dream, The Winter's Tale,* and *The Tempest* of Shakespeare, and *The Magic Flute* of Mozart are all at home.

Men like Reichardt and Rochlitz, around 1800, began to inaugurate new and serious forms of musical criticism in their magazines, and began to do justice to Mozart as they had already done to Haydn. The new, enthusiastic style of Rochlitz may be seen in one of his articles, published in the *Allgemeine musikalische Zeitung* in 1800, which praised the quartets for piano, violin, viola, and violoncello that Mozart had composed between 1795 and 1786.

That these quartets enjoyed an immediate success and were played both in drawing rooms and in concerts, we learn from an article entitled "On the Newest Favorite Music Played in the Great Concerts," written in 1788 by a Viennese correspondent of the *Journal des Luxus und der Moden.* This article is of the greatest interest. It shows not only the wide circulation obtained by new music without the benefit of present-day advertising methods, but also that Mozart's music could not be instantly and easily understood. It was complicated music—complicated both from the player's standpoint, and the listener's.

> Some time ago there was published [wrote this Viennese correspondent] a quartet (for piano, violin, viola, and violoncello) which is very artfully composed. Its performance requires the greatest precision on the part of all four players, but even in perfect rendition the music can be enjoyed only by musical experts. . . . The rumor that "Mozart has composed a new quartet, that this and that princess owns it and plays it," spread quickly and caused this particular composition to be senselessly performed in great noisy concerts. . . . Many other pieces are impressive even in a mediocre rendition. But this work of Mozart's is intolerable . . . when carelessly executed. This happened last winter in innumerable cases. Almost everywhere I went . . . a lady, or middle-class girl, or some saucy dilettante appeared with the quartet . . . and insisted that one must enjoy the music. One could not enjoy it. Everyone was bored and yawning at the incomprehensible hodgepodge of instruments which did not harmonize in a single bar. . . . But the music had to please. It had to be praised. I can hardly describe with how great obstinacy people took pains to obtrude this music everywhere. It means nothing to dismiss this folly as a passing craze of the day, because it lasted almost the whole winter and was to be met—as I have been told—everywhere and any time.

There we have in one picture the popularity of Mozart's music around 1788, and the ambition of amateurs to play it. We see Viennese society and the difficulties of understanding this modern music. Rochlitz's criticism of these same compositions is serious, enthusiastic, and intelligent, in spite of the many flowers he puts into his critical vase.

> In those compositions [he wrote] which are intended only for select, smaller groups, the spirit of the artist appears in a strange, rare form, great and sublime like an apparition from another world. When he softens into sweet melancholy or for some moments dallies with a merry mood, they are but moments only, after which he pulls himself together—if only for moments too—to bold, sometimes wild force; or perhaps he writhes in bitter, cutting agony, triumphant after victory or dying in battle. In order not to believe these words to be mere empty enthusiasm . . . it is necessary to hear an accomplished performance (which is only attainable by persons who possess, besides the necessary great skill, a heart and mature intelligence). . . . One may hear it, then study it and hear it again.

Romantic critics produced the finest evaluations of Mozart, who was most certainly a Romantic himself. To prove the point one need cite only the veiled melancholy of the Quintet in G minor, the tragic storm of the Piano Concerto in C minor, the ghost voices in *Don Giovanni,* the ironic ball game of *Così fan tutte*. Mozart's chromatic harmonies were romantic, as were the changing colors of light and shadow that were intensified by Chopin and Debussy. Romantic likewise was his sense of the tragic meaning of life. E. T. A. Hoffmann, musician, poet, and critic, revealed Mozart's romanticism in his fantastic short story *Don Juan,* which he wrote in 1812. And in his *Phantasiestücke* he sang a hymn of praise to the Symphony in G minor. "Love and melancholy sound in the sweet voices of ghosts. Night rises in shining gleams of purple. In ineffable longing we follow the apparitions, who beckon in friendly wise. We may join their round dance and fly through the clouds in the eternal dance of the spheres." It was Hoffmann too who first uncovered the romantic irony in *Così fan tutte* in the pages of his collection of tales and novels, *Die Serapionsbrüder.* In 1792 the *Journal des Luxus und der Moden* had called the opera "the silliest thing in the world." Twenty years later, Hoffmann praised the same work as "the essence of comic opera in the fantastic mood that depends on the fanciful flights of the characters, and partly on the bizarre play of chance." The epoch of rationalistic criticism was drawing to an end. The age of poetical criticism was beginning.

M. G.

PART III

Mozart

IN HIS DEATH

INTRODUCTORY NOTE

In any attempt to reconstruct a great man's life, interest clings most tenaciously to those few last days and hours when last words are uttered and last, feverish glimpses are afforded to those hovering near in helpless anxiety. The death of Mozart at thirty-six still arouses a sense of powerless anguish, profound pity, and even incredulity. It is hard to take the impact, even at this distance, of such a magnificent endowment cut off in its opulent prime. There is, on one side, the horror of early death; there is, on the other, the horror to art of the thought of what might still have come from this divine singer so cruelly silenced. We cannot help speculating. What might Mozart have done had he lived? Because his death poses a question that has engaged professional and amateur minds for almost two centuries, I thought it best to devote the last part of this Handbook *to three aspects of it. First, the circumstances of Mozart's death as told by eye-witnesses. Second, the nature of the disease that killed Mozart. Third, the loss to music from so premature a death. The Requiem was Mozart's last artistic task—an unfinished masterpiece. Was it symbolic of an "unfinished" genius, whose work, had he lived, would have accelerated the progress of music by several decades? Or had Mozart, after thirty years of uninterrupted writing, said all he had to say?*

The Handbook *thus ends on a note of speculation: one wonders, naturally, whether every single detail is authentic in the vivid third-person report of Joseph Deiner, Hausmeister of "The Silver Serpent" restaurant where Mozart often dined. One cannot be absolutely certain that Dr. Barraut's post-mortem, made more than a century later, is right. And Dyneley Hussey's speculation of what lay ahead for Mozart and music had he survived, brilliant though it is, remains only a conjecture. With all due respect to a revered British colleague, I should think that in a fascinating game of this kind anybody's guess is as good, if not as persuasive, as his.*

L. B.

561

SOPHIE HAIBEL

(Sister-in-law of Mozart, married to Jakob Haibel, 1761–1826, musician and composer, was among those near Mozart at the time of his death. Her sister Constanze's second husband was Georg Nikolaus Nissen, a counsellor at the Danish Legation in Vienna, and first biographer of Mozart. It was while at work on the biography that Nissen, early in 1825, asked Sophie for information about the composer's last days. Her reply of April 7, 1825, from Diakovar, where her husband was choirmaster, supplies us with a few precious, intimate glimpses untouched by literary self-consciousness or artificiality.)

L. B.

. . . Now I must tell you of Mozart's last days. Well, Mozart became fonder and fonder of our dear departed mother and she of him. Indeed he often came running along in great haste to the Wieden (where she and I were lodging at the Goldner Pflug), carrying under his arm a little bag containing coffee and sugar, which he would hand to our good mother, saying,

"Here, mother dear, now you can have a little 'Jause'" [afternoon coffee].

She used to be as delighted as a child. He did this very often. In short, Mozart in the end never came to see us without bringing something.

Now when Mozart fell ill, we both made him a night-jacket which he could put on frontways, since on account of his swollen condition he was unable to turn in bed. Then, as we didn't know how seriously ill he was, we also made him a quilted dressing-gown (though indeed his dear wife, my sister, had given us the materials for both garments), so that when he got up he should have everything he needed. We often visited him and he seemed to be really looking forward to wearing his dressing-gown. I used to go into town every day to see him. Well, one Saturday when I was with him, Mozart said to me:

"Dear Sophie, do tell Mamma that I am fairly well and that I shall be able to go and congratulate her on the octave of her name-day."

Who could have been more delighted than I to bring such cheerful news to my mother, who was ever anxious to hear how he was? I hurried home therefore to comfort her, the more so as he himself really seemed to be bright and happy. The following day was a Sunday. I was young then and rather vain, I confess, and liked to dress up. But I never cared to go out walking from our suburb into town in my fine clothes, and I had no money for a drive. So I said to our good mother:

"Dear Mamma, I'm not going to see Mozart today. He was so well yesterday that surely he will be much better this morning, and one day more or less won't make much difference."

Well, my mother said: "Listen to this. Make me a bowl of coffee and then I'll tell you what you ought to do." She was rather inclined to keep me at home; and indeed my sister knows how much I had to be with her. I went into the kitchen. The fire was out. I had to light the lamp and make a fire. All the time I was thinking of Mozart. I had made the coffee and the lamp was still burning. Then I noticed how wasteful I had been with my lamp, I mean, that I had burned so much oil. It was still burning brightly. I stared into the flame and thought to myself,

"How I should love to know how Mozart is."

While I was thinking and gazing at the flame, it went out, as completely as if the lamp had never been burning. Not a spark remained on the main wick and yet there wasn't the slightest draught—that I can swear to. A horrible feeling came over me. I ran to our mother and told her all. She said:

"Well, take off your fine clothes and go into town and bring me back news of him at once. But be sure not to delay."

I hurried along as fast as I could. Alas, how frightened I was when my sister, who was almost despairing and yet trying to keep calm, came out to me, saying:

"Thank God that you have come, dear Sophie. Last night he was so ill that I thought he would not be alive this morning. Do stay with me today, for if he has another bad turn, he will pass away tonight. Go in to him for a little while and see how he is."

I tried to control myself and went to his bedside. He immediately called me to him and said:

"Ah, dear Sophie, how glad I am that you have come. You must stay here tonight and see me die."

I tried hard to be brave and to persuade him to the contrary. But to all my attempts he only replied:

"Why, I am already tasting death. And, if you do not stay, who will support my dearest Constanze when I am gone?"

"Yes, yes, dear Mozart," I assured him, "but I must first go back to our mother and tell her that you would like me to stay with you to-day. Otherwise she will think that some misfortune has befallen you."

"Yes, do so," said Mozart, "but be sure and come back soon."

Good God, how distressed I felt! My poor sister followed me to the door and begged me for Heaven's sake to go to the priests at St. Peter's and implore one of them to come to Mozart—a chance call, as it were. I did so, but for a long time they refused to come and I had a great deal of trouble to persuade one of those heartless people to go to him. Then I ran off to my mother who was anxiously awaiting me.

It was already dark. Poor soul, how shocked she was! I persuaded her to go and spend the night with her eldest daughter, the late Josefa Hofer. I then ran back as fast as I could to my distracted sister. Süssmayr was at Mozart's bedside. The well-known Requiem lay on the quilt and Mozart was explaining to him how, in his opinion, he ought to finish it, when he was gone. Further, he urged his wife to keep his death a secret until she should have informed Albrechtsberger [chief organist of the Stefanskirche], who was in charge of all the services.

A long search was made for Dr. Closset,[1] who was found at the theatre, but who had to wait for the end of the play. He came and ordered cold poultices to be placed on Mozart's burning head, which, however, affected him to such an extent that he became unconscious and remained so until he died [at fifty-five minutes past midnight on December 5].

His last movement was an attempt to express with his mouth the drum passages in the Requiem. That I can still hear. Müller[2] from

---

[1] Dr. Nikolaus Closset, who had been treating Mozart.

[2] Count Josef Deym (1750–1804), alias Müller, was the owner of a collection of wax-works and casts from the antique, which from 1797 onwards was housed

the Art Gallery came and took a cast of his pale, dead face. Words fail me, dearest brother, to describe how his devoted wife in her utter misery threw herself on her knees and implored the Almighty for His aid. She simply could not tear herself away from Mozart, however much I begged her to do so. If it was possible to increase her sorrow, this was done on the day after that distressing night, when crowds of people walked past his corpse and wept and mourned for him. All my life I never saw Mozart in a temper, still less, angry.

Translated by E. A.

JOSEPH DEINER

(During the last months of his life Mozart often had lunch at the "Zur Silbernen Schlange"— "The Silver Serpent"—a restaurant and beer-shop on the Kärntnergasse. Its Hausmeister—or steward—was a genial and obliging young man named Joseph Deiner. From Mozart's last letters we gather that a pleasant comradeship developed between the two. Mozart even had a nickname—"Don Primus"— for this attentive companion who woke him in the morning, lit the fire, attended to the mail, and brought him food. In his letters to his wife, Mozart speaks of him as "that good fellow Primus." On October 7 he tells Constanze, "Why, here is Don Primus with the cutlets! Che gusto!"—and, later in the same letter, "at half past five Primus had lit the fire and then woke me up at a quarter to six." The next day we find Mozart "thoroughly" enjoying his half of a capon "which friend Primus has brought back with him." In Mozart's very last letter, dated October 14, we have a final glimpse of the thoughtful fellow: "I have sent out my faithful comrade Primus to fetch some food." That was Joseph Deiner. His third-person account of those last days was printed in the Wiener Morgenpost *in January, 1856, on the occasion of the centenary of Mozart's birth. There would seem to be little reason to question the authen-*

---

in a building in the Stock im Eisen. Mozart's death-mask has disappeared. Acording to Nohl (*Mozart nach den Schilderungen seiner Zeitgenossen*, p. 393) Constanze, one day while cleaning, smashed the copy in her possession. She is said to have remarked that "she was glad that the ugly old thing was broken."

ticity of the bulk of these reminiscences. Even so vigilant and me-
ticulous a biographer as Paumgartner draws on them freely, and
both Prod'homme and Leitzmann have given them a conspicuous
place in their compilations of eye-witness material. . . . One cher-
ishes the memory of this "Don Primus" for the many loving little
acts of kindness and attention to that dying friend and patron of
the "Silberne Schlange" whom Sophie Haibel had never once seen
angry.

L. B.

It was a cold, unpleasant November day in 1791 when Mozart
walked into the Silver Serpent tavern, in Vienna, where he went
quite often. This *Bierhaus* was located in the Kärntnerstrasse, then
Number 1112, now Number 1074. Authors, singers and musicians
used to gather there. . . . On the day in question Mozart found
several new guests in the first *Extrazimmer,* so he immediately
passed into the next room, a smaller one, which had only three
tables. This little room had trees painted on the walls. . .

Mozart dropped wearily into a chair, propped his right arm on
the table and let his head sink into his hand. He sat this way for
rather a long time, then he ordered the waiter to bring him some
wine, although he usually drank beer. When the barkeeper had
set the wine before him, Mozart remained sitting there motionless,
without even tasting the drink.

Then Joseph Deiner, the caretaker, came in through a door leading to the little courtyard. He was a man well known to Mozart,
who always treated him with confiding familiarity. When Deiner
caught sight of the composer he stopped and looked at him attentively for a long time. Mozart was unusually pale, his powdered
blond hair was disheveled and the little braid carelessly done. He
suddenly looked up and saw the Hausmeister.

"Well, Joseph, how are things?" he asked.

"I ought to ask *you* that," answered Deiner. "You look sick and
miserable, *maestro!* I heard you were in Prague and the air of
Bohemia didn't do you any good. . . . Anyone can see that looking
at you. You're drinking wine now, that's a good idea; I suppose

you drank a lot of beer in Bohemia and spoiled your stomach. It's nothing serious, maestro!"

"My stomach is better than you think," said Mozart. "I've learned to swallow all sorts of things!"

A sigh accompanied these words.

"That's fine," Deiner replied. "All sickness starts in the stomach—that's what my General Laudon said when we stood before Belgrade and the Archduke Franz was sick for a few days too. But I don't think this is a good day to tell you about Turkish music—which you've laughed at often enough!"

"No," answered Mozart, "I have a feeling the music will be all played out soon. There's a chill come over me, and I can't understand it. Here, Deiner, drink up my wine and take this [he gave Deiner a coin]. Come to the house tomorrow morning. Winter's starting and we need wood. My wife will go with you to buy it; I'm even having a fire made up today."

He called the waiter now, pressed a silver coin into his hand and left the tavern. Hausmeister Deiner sat down to Mozart's wine in the first "extra room" and said to himself: "Such a young man thinking about dying! Well, there's plenty of time for that yet, I suppose. . . . But I mustn't forget about the wood, November is good and cold. . . ."

A crowd of Italian singers came into the Silver Serpent. Deiner hated these singers because they always tormented his beloved *maestro,* wouldn't leave him alone, so he too left the place.

The next morning at seven o'clock Deiner betook himself to No. 970 Rauhensteingasse. . . . When he knocked at the door of Mozart's apartment on the first floor, the maid opened the door; she knew him and let him in. She told him that she had had to call the doctor during the night, the Herr Kapellmeister was very sick. Nevertheless Deiner was called in by Mozart's wife. Mozart was lying in a bed with white covers which stood in a corner of the room. When he heard Deiner talking he opened his eyes and said barely audibly: "There's nothing doing today, Joseph, just doctors and druggists today!"

Joseph Deiner left the house. He remembered that the year before he had been at Mozart's discussing firewood. That time he had found Mozart with his wife in his study, which had two windows facing the Rauhensteingasse and one facing the Himmelpfortgasse. Mozart and his wife were dancing around the room in fine form. When Deiner asked if Mozart was teaching his wife to dance, he laughed and said, "We're only warming ourselves up, we're freezing and we can't buy any wood." Deiner ran right out and brought them some of his own wood. Mozart took it and promised to pay well for it when he had money.

On the 28th of November the doctors held a consultation about Mozart's condition. The then renowned Dr. Closset and Dr. Sallaba, chief physician of the general hospital, were present.

Since Mozart's illness was growing more serious every minute, his wife once again called Dr. Sallaba on December 5, 1791. He came and shortly thereafter also Kapellmeister Süssmayr, to whom Sallaba confided privately that Mozart could not survive the night. Dr. Sallaba this time also prescribed a medicine for Mozart's wife, who felt sick too. After another glance at Mozart he took his leave.

Süssmayr remained at the side of the dying composer. At twelve o'clock at night Mozart sat up in bed, his eyes fixed; then he leaned over with his head against the wall and seemed to fall asleep again. At four o'clock in the morning he was dead.

At five o'clock in the morning there came a violent knocking at the door of the Silver Serpent. Deiner opened. Mozart's maid, Elise, was standing there sobbing. The Hausmeister asked what she wanted. "Mr. Deiner," said the maid, "you're to come over and dress the master." "For a walk?" "No, he's dead; he died an hour ago—but come quick!"

Deiner found Mozart's wife weeping and so weak she could not stand on her feet. He did for Mozart what one usually does for the dead. Next day Mozart was laid on his bier in a shroud of black cloth, which was customary at the time; this practice continued until the year 1818. His body was carried into the study and placed near his piano.

The church service was held on December 6th at three o'clock in the afternoon at St. Stephan's, not inside the church but at the north side, in the Kreuzkapelle. . . . A third-class interment took place, for which eight gulden thirty-six kreuzer was paid. The hearse cost an additional three gulden.

The night of his death was dark and stormy, and even at the church service it began to howl and bluster outside. Rain and snow fell together, as if nature were angry at the great composer's contemporaries so few of whom had come to attend his burial rites. Only a few friends and three women accompanied the body. Mozart's wife was not present. These few mourners stood with their umbrellas around the bier, which was then carried through the Grand Schulerstrasse to the cemetery. Since the storm was getting worse and worse, even these few friends decided to turn back at the Stubentor (one of the city gates), and they went into the Silver Serpent. Hausmeister Deiner had also been at the service in the chapel. He then went to Mozart's wife and asked her whether she didn't intend to put a cross on his grave. "Yes, yes," she answered, "he'll get one. . . ."* (Joseph Deiner [*Translated by* P. R. C.])

MOZART'S ILLNESS

TO A French journal, *La Chronique médicale,* Paris, under the date of November 15, 1905, a French doctor, J. Barraut, contributed an article entitled "A quelle maladie a succombé Mozart?" I succeeded in obtaining a copy of this article, in which Dr. Barraut goes into the matter very thoroughly. After consideration of all the evidence available, including the account of his death and the particulars of the various illnesses from which Mozart suffered as a child, he comes to the conclusion that Mozart naturally must have had an exceedingly robust constitution, "the constitution of a centenarian." He adds that there was not the slightest trace of tuberculosis in Mozart or his family and points out that Mozart's sister lived to be an octogenarian. His final diagnosis is as follows:

"Two factors hastened Mozart's death. The first was a chronic cause, dating from his earliest years and increasing every day. This was simply excessive work, continual fatigue, and profound misery. One should be able to say of a man as of a machine: 'this machine is used up, it has been worked too much.' The word *used* applies perfectly to Mozart. Mozart arrived at the age of 35 worn out, having expended all his vital power.

---

* From *Mozart's Persönlichkerten: Urteile der Zeitgenossen und erläutert von Albert Leitzmann*. Leipzig, 1914.

"It was at that moment that the disease which carried him off laid hold of him. If we consider his rapid emaciation, his difficulty in breathing, his faintings, the swelling of his legs and hands, paresis, and if we remember that when young he had scarlatina, we are indeed led to the conclusion: nephritis. Mozart, in our opinion, died of Bright's disease. And if one considers his extreme weakness when he felt the first attacks of this malady one can readily understand that the disease only took six months, from July to December, to exterminate a man who throughout his life had been obliged to fight . . . in order to have bread to eat."

W. J. T.

CONJECTURE

LIKE THE runner who brought the news of Marathon to Athens, Mozart fell exhausted at the moment of triumph. Those who are interested in post-mortem details will find support for entering in a certificate of the cause of his death such various diseases as typhus, meningitis, influenza, phthisis, and many other items from the medical dictionary. For laymen it will be sufficient to say that Mozart died of continual overwork and only less continual under-nourishment during the twenty-five years since Leopold dragged him round Europe as a show for amateurs of the abnormal. But it matters really very little of what Mozart died. What does matter is when he died—in the thirty-sixth year of his life, in the last decade of the century. Of no man, who has been cut off thus in his prime— not of Schubert or Mendelssohn, of Shelley or Keats, not even of Purcell—can we say with so much assurance that his death deprived us of a new development in art, the nature of which cannot even be imagined. It has been argued that Mozart died, having completed his task, dried up his well of inspiration, and worked from his particular vein the last ounce of ore. How far this is from the truth will be perceived by anyone who cares to examine the works of his last year and to compare them with those of even the year or two before. He will be astonished at the new turn which Mozart's genius had taken, and at the recuperative powers of his brain, which could achieve such a development while his physical strength was quickly failing. There is no reason whatever why, if success had come a few months earlier and the composer had been able to take the rest and to obtain the food he required, he should not have lived on to an age nearer to the average span of human life. He suffered, so far as is known, from no organic complaint, only from a delicacy of physique which was unable to endure the exceptional strain upon it—a strain which made his body receptive to and unable to combat whichever of the malignant diseases it was that actually killed him. Had he not been subjected to that strain, he would have had a reasonable expectancy, as the actuaries say, of at any rate twenty-five more years of life. He would have been only seventy-one, when Beethoven died. Of that age—the age of the Wagner of *Parsifal*—it might have been reasonable to talk of an exhausted mind, a well dried up, a vein worked out—or whatever metaphor happens to fall from the florid pen of the writer. But of thirty-five it is ludicrous.

On the other hand a distinguished critic has suggested that, had Mozart lived on, the face of musical history during the last century would have been fundamentally changed. "He would have done something in opera and symphony," says this authority, "compared with which his own *Zauberflöte* and 'Jupiter' would have appeared as tentative experiments, and yet something which would have been quite independent of the hectic tone which Beethoven introduced decisively into nineteenth-century music with the 'Eroica.' It is not quite idle to speculate about this, because now, looking back over what has been essentially Beethoven's century of music, it is quite clear that something was lost from music at the beginning of it which may be fairly attributable to Mozart's untimely death. The loss seems to account for some at least of the vague groping of twentieth-century music. One cannot, for example, hear such things as the quartets of Jarnach and Hindemith, or Sibelius's sixth symphony without feeling that the composers are searching in their different ways after types of musical expression which, obliterating that lush emotionalism characteristic of all the great output of the nineteenth century, would recapture something of the pure thinking in sound which makes the finale of the 'Jupiter' one of the mountain peaks of music."

That is one, and a possible, answer to the question, What would Mozart have accomplished if he had lived to the normal span? But

I do not think it is quite the right one. Mozart was moving with the times. It is safe to say that the style of the "Jupiter" Symphony, in so far as it amounts to pure thinking in sound, would not have been adhered to without modification in any symphony Mozart might have composed after 1791. Already in such comparatively insignificant works as the Quartet in F major and the E flat Quintet the germs of a new style with a distinctly dramatic and hectic tendency are conspicuous, and if the Overture to *Die Zauberflöte* is an example of pure thinking in sound, does not that description apply also to the even more dramatic C minor Symphony of Beethoven? Indeed, the more one examines the last works of Mozart, even if the Requiem is left out of account in view of the special circumstances in which it was written—circumstances which tended to make it hectic and even hysterical—the more convinced one becomes that Mozart was rapidly approaching a point of view which would soon have brought him to a position in regard to his art similar to that of Beethoven—or, shall we say? to a definitely nineteenth-century standpoint.

For I do not wish to imply that Mozart would ever have become "another Beethoven," or that, impressionable as he was by outside influences, he would have fallen more deeply under the spell of the rising star than he had under that of Haydn—since each man of genius must always remain essentially himself and inevitably loses his claim to the title of genius when he sinks to the level of belonging to someone's school. But I do suggest that, had he lived, he would have developed his new manner in a way which we cannot indeed imagine, but which would have added to his great works in the branches of symphony, of chamber-music, and of opera, others which would have stood level in the same class as the great works of Beethoven instead of being as are the works we know, in a class distinct from and therefore not really comparable with the works of the younger man. A Mozart living on into the nineteenth century might have made the transition from the Classical to the Romantic less abrupt; he would hardly have influenced the course of musical history by perpetuating a tradition which was already passing away, even in his own works, when he died.

D. H. (2)

Appendices

THE KÖCHEL CATALOGUE

A word must be said about the numbering of Mozart's works. Mozart rarely used opus numbers and left few clues about the chronology of his many compositions. About the middle of the nineteenth century Ludwig von Köchel, an Austrian naturalist, musician, and, later, nobleman, began the process of collating the compositions with Mozart's letters, contemporary newspaper accounts, internal evidence supplied by the quality of paper and ink, and similar information. The result was the publication, in 1862, of Köchel, Chronologisch-systematisches Verzeichniss, *listing all Mozart's works. Better known as K. or K.V., it furnishes accurate chronological data on the origin of Mozart's works; reference to those works customarily includes the K. item numbers. A revision of the* Verzeichniss, *which removed certain inaccuracies and attained a greater degree of completeness, was made by Alfred Einstein in 1937.*

H.U.

WITH THE appearance of Alfred Einstein's revision of the Köchel catalogue, the Mozart literature has become immeasurably enriched. Long anxiously awaited, the new Köchel more than fulfills expectations, representing the invaluable results of a stupendous amount of research and labor on the part of its compiler. What Hermann Abert did for the superannuated Mozart tomes by Jahn, Einstein has accomplished for the catalogue, virtually rewriting it and bringing it completely up to date.

Some idea of the wealth of material added in the Bavarian musicologist's revision may be gleaned from a mere consideration of the relative size of the three editions of the catalogue to date. The original volume, prepared by Ludwig von Köchel, the Austrian naturalist and musical historian, which reached publication in 1862, consisted of 551 pages, with a short introduction of 18 pages. The second edition, revised by Paul, Count von Waldersee, and published in 1905, had 676 pages and a 24-page preface. As for the new edition, it boasts 984 pages, plus 49 more of introductory exposition. Larger in format than either of its predecessors, the Einstein-Köchel virtually doubles the first edition in voluminousness of content.

As Mr. Einstein remarks in his prefatory discussion, there was urgent need of a new Köchel, not only because the second edition had long been out of print, but also on account of the vast accumulation of data piled up by Mozart scholars since the Waldersee revamping. In truth, Waldersee feared to make any extensive alterations in the original version, being deterred by the veneration in which the work was held. His edition at first encountered little criticism. But with the passing years a growing dissatisfaction reached expression. The catalogue's lack of information concerning first editions and important later reprints was more and more deplored by serious scholars. Then came the revolutionary volumes by Wyzewa and Saint-Foix, who, leaving Jahn

575

and Köchel behind them, had gone back to Mozart's works and there traced his artistic development and the influence on him of contemporary masters. Their valuable findings necessitated a definite rift with Köchel in the chronological ordering and numbering of the composer's creations.

And when Hermann Abert issued his version of Jahn's monograph, in 1921, it was found that he too was at the parting of the ways with the Köchel enumeration. For though he employed the catalogue numbers, his own alignment of the compositions was largely influenced by that devised by Wyzewa and Saint-Foix. Quite obviously the Waldersee Köchel had become outmoded and no longer served its purpose as the prime Mozart authority.

Realizing this fully, the publishers Breitkopf & Härtel in 1925 commissioned Dr. Bernhard Paumgartner, director of the Mozarteum in Salzburg, to make the desired revision. But due to the innumerable trips involved in the undertaking, Dr. Paumgartner found it impossible to continue the necessary research, and in 1929 the entire project was turned over to Mr. Einstein.

Fortunately, Mr. Einstein was then resident in Berlin, where the world's chief collection of Mozart autograph manuscripts is assembled in the State Library. In Berlin, too, he had access to the many Mozart treasures belonging to Leo Liepmannsohn, the antiquarian. After exhausting these sources he visited the Munich State Museum, the Fürstenberg Library at Donaueschingen and the National Library of Stuttgart during his first year's activities. The next year he was in Salzburg, where he studied the material at the Mozarteum, as well as that in the remarkable collection owned by Stefan Zweig.

This was but the beginning. Later Mr. Einstein spent much time in Paris at the conservatory and the institute. There were journeys to Basle, Zurich, and Frankfort on the hunt for details, to London and Cambridge, to Bologna and Florence, and finally to Vienna. The required information from Sweden and Belgium was gained by correspondence. And Mr. Einstein was spared a voyage to America through the data supplied him by the music division of the Library of Congress. According to Harold Spivacke, assistant chief, Mr. Einstein was especially concerned with that library's original Mozart opera librettos in the Schatz collection, the largest of its kind in the world.

Inasmuch as Mr. Einstein is a highly trained musician, he had the advantage of Jahn and Köchel, both of whom were more or less deficient in that respect, so that they were forced to depend on scholarship rather than musical insight in determining the date of a composition. Mr. Einstein employed both methods of approach. His predecessors had stressed the importance of taking into account the paper on which Mozart wrote, as a determining factor in arriving at the time and place of a work's origin. But Mr. Einstein demonstrates the fallacy of this idea and also of the notion that much can be told, in either regard, from the character of Mozart's script.

As Mr. Einstein points out, Mozart wrote on thirty-five kinds of paper in the Salzburg fragments alone. The paper most frequently found in his autographs is watermarked with three half-moons. On paper of the identical kind, copies of compositions by Gluck were made for the Imperial court in Vienna from 1750 to 1760. On it, indeed, works by Gluck were printed as late as 1785, and on it, according to Mr. Einstein, Benedetto Marcello had penned his *Arianna* as far back as 1727. As a consequence, Mr. Einstein scrapped this means of making decisions except in special instances—as, for example, in the case of works written on the small notepaper which Mozart is known to have had with him on the trips to Mannheim and Paris in 1777. Mr. Einstein also found it impossible to depend on the handwriting as a criterion, because, as he discloses, Mozart's had taken on a form by 1771 from which it never afterward departed.

Although in its general appearance and format the Einstein Köchel closely resembles its two forerunners, there are many new features. The "incipits," or citations of opening bars of all compositions, have been retained, of course, but, wherever possible, Einstein has made use of the autographs and not relied on the *Gesamt-Ausgabe,* as Count Waldersee did. And, as it happens, the new Köchel is intended to form the basis of a revision of the *Gesamt-Ausgabe,* in addition to being a synthesis of the entire findings of serious Mozart research to date.

Not content with giving the "incipits," the editor also indicates the number of measures in every movement of every work, even those of the trios of minuets. He has brought the date of the location of the autographs down to the present moment wherever feasible, and has given full account of the various editions of every published composition. But, for lack of space, all esthetic opinion and attempts to pass judgments on the worth of works, such as Köchel indulged in, have been dispensed with. On the contrary, citations from the letters of Mozart and others, which give clues to the dates of compositions, are more numerous than in the former editions. Another valuable feature is the specific page reference to the literature concerning each work.

Since Mozart's compositions have been identified and referred to for decades by their Köchel number, Mr. Einstein and the publishing firm felt it incumbent upon them not to dispense with the old enumeration. So, despite the fact that much of the material which formerly stood in the appendices has been incorporated into the main body of the book (and vice versa), the numerical dilemma has been solved by printing the new Köchel numbers in light and the old in heavy type. Moreover, the number assigned to each composition by Wyzewa and Saint-Foix is indicated as well.

It is interesting to notice that Einstein puts a question mark before the note dealing with the present location of the autograph of the celebrated "Haffner" Symphony. The answer to the question is that the symphony now is owned by Charles Scribner's Sons. They bought it from a German collector who had acquired it at a Höpli-Opperman auction in 1934. This Mozart autograph undoubtedly is the most important one now [1937] in American hands. Of the slight number of others on this continent, the New York Public Library possesses the largest share. Its more significant examples include the Violin Sonata in C major (K. 296), the Overture in G major (K. 318) and the Adagio and Allegro for a Clock Organ (K. 594). The Library of Congress has the soprano aria, "Quaere Superna" and the last of the "Five Minuets" (K. 461). There are a few Mozart autographs elsewhere in the United States, mostly fragments or unidentified works of lesser consequence. All of them, however, are fully described in this new German catalogue, which is as all-embracing and thorough in its field as ingenuity, erudition and unremitting labor could well make it.

N. S.

CLASSIFIED LIST OF MOZART'S WORKS

(Prepared by Elizabeth C. Moore for Ann M. Lingg's Mozart: Genius of Harmony, and reprinted here with very slight editing and without her accompanying list of recordings)

I—INSTRUMENTAL

A—FOR ORCHESTRA

1. Symphonies

K. 16, E flat major. Composed in London, 1764–65.

K. 19, D major. London, 1765.

K. 22, B flat major. The Hague, 1765.

K. 76, F major, Vienna, 1767

K. 45, D major. Vienna, 1768.

Anh. 221, G major. Vienna, 1768.

Anh. 214, B flat major. Vienna, 1768.

K. 48, D major. Vienna, 1768

K. 81, D major. Rome, 1770.

K. 97, D major. Rome, 1770.

K. 95, D major. Rome, 1770.

K. 84, D major. Milan and Bologna, 1770.

K. 74, G major. Milan, 1770.

Anh. 216, B flat major. Salzburg, 1771.

K. 75, F major. Salzburg, 1771.

K. 73, C major. Salzburg, 1771.

K. 110, G major. Salzburg, 1771.

K. 96, C major. Milan, 1771.

K. 112, F major. Milan, 1771.

K. 114, A major. Salzburg, 1771.

K. 124, G major. Salzburg, 1772.

K. 128, C major. Salzburg, 1772.

K. 129, G major. Salzburg, 1772.

K. 130, F major. Salzburg, 1772.

K. 132, E flat major. Salzburg, 1772.

K. 133, D major. Salzburg, 1772.

K. 134, A major. Salzburg, 1772.

K. 161 and 163, D major. Salzburg, Milan, 1772.

K. 162, C major. Salzburg, 1773.

K. 199, G major. Salzburg, 1773.

K. 181, D major. Salzburg, 1773.

K. 184, E flat major. Salzburg, 1773.

K. 182, B flat major. Salzburg, 1773.

K. 200, C major. Salzburg, 1773.

K. 183, G minor (No. 25, the "little G minor"). Salzburg, 1773.

K. 201, A major. Salzburg, 1774.

K. 202, D major. Salzburg, 1774.

Anh. 9 (297b), E flat major (*Sinfonia Concertante*). Paris, 1778.

K. 297, D major (No. 31, "Paris"). Paris, 1778.

Anh. 8, B flat major. Paris, 1778.

K. 318, G major. Salzburg, 1779.

K. 319, B flat major. Salzburg, 1779.

K. 338, C major (No. 34). Salzburg, 1780.

K. 385, D major (No. 35, "Haffner"). Vienna, 1782.

K. 425, C major ("Linz"). Linz, 1783.

K. 444, G major (really by Michael Haydn, Mozart having written the Introduction only). Linz, 1783.

K. 504, D major (No. 38, "Prague," or Symphony without a Minuet). Vienna, 1786.

K. 543, E flat major (No. 39). Vienna, 1788.

K. 550, G minor (No. 40). Vienna, 1788.

K. 551, C major (No. 41, "Jupiter"). Vienna, 1788.

2. Serenades, Divertimenti, etc.

K. 62, Cassation, D major. Salzburg, 1769.

K. 99, Cassation, B flat major. Salzburg, 1769.

K. 100, Serenade, D major. Salzburg, 1769.

K. 63, Divertimento, G major. Salzburg, 1769.

K. 113, Divertimento, E flat major. Milan, 1771.

K. 131, Divertimento, D major. Salzburg, 1772.

K. 136, Divertimento, D major. Salzburg, 1772.

K. 137, Divertimento, B flat major. Salzburg, 1772.

K. 138, Divertimento, F major. Salzburg, 1772.

K. 166, Divertimento, E flat major. Salzburg, 1773.

K. 185, Serenade, D major. Vienna, 1773.

K. 186, Divertimento, B flat major. Milan, 1773.

K. 187, Divertimento, C major. Salzburg, 1773.

K. 205. Divertimento, D major. Vienna, 1773.

K. 203, Serenade, D major. Salzburg, 1774.

K. 204, Serenade, D major. Salzburg, 1775.

K. 213, Divertimento, F major. Salzburg, 1775.

Anh. 226, Divertimento, E flat major. Munich, 1775.

Anh. 227, Divertimento, B flat major. Munich, 1775.

K. 101, Serenade, F major. Salzburg, 1776.

K. 188, Divertimento, C major. Salzburg, 1776.

K. 239, *Serenata notturna,* D major. Salzburg, 1776.

K. 240, Divertimento, B flat major. Salzburg, 1776.

K. 247, Divertimento, F major. Salzburg, 1776.

K. 250, Serenade, D major ("Haffner"). Salzburg, 1776.

K. 251, Divertimento, D major (*Septett*). Salzburg, 1776.

K. 252, Divertimento, E flat major. Salzburg, 1776.

K. 253, Divertimento, F major. Salzburg, 1776.

K. 286, Divertimento, D major (*Notturno*). Salzburg, 1776–77.

K. 270, Divertimento, B flat major. Salzburg, 1777.

K. 287, Divertimento, B flat major. Salzburg, 1777.

K. 288, Divertimento, F major. Salzburg, 1777.

K. 289, Divertimento, E flat major. Salzburg, 1777.

K. 320, Serenade, D major. Salzburg, 1779.

K. 334, Divertimento, D major. Salzburg, 1779.

K. 361, Serenade, B flat major (*Gran Partita*). Munich and Vienna, 1781.

K. 375, Serenade, E flat major. Vienna, 1781.

K. 388, Serenade, C minor. Vienna, 1782.

K. 525, Serenade, G major (*Eine Kleine Nachtmusik*). Vienna, 1787.

K. 563, Divertimento, E flat major. Vienna, 1788.

3. *Dance Tunes for Orchestra*

K. 25a, Minuet.

K. 64, Minuet, D major. 1769.

K. 65a, 7 Minuets for strings. 1769.

K. 103, 19 Minuets. 1769.

K. 104, 6 Minuets. 1769.

K. 105, 6 Minuets. 1769.

K. 61g, 6 Minuets. 1769.

K. 61h, 2 Minuets. 1769.

K. 122, Minuet. 1770.

K. 123, Kontretanz. 1770.

K. 164, 6 Minuets. 1772.
K. 176, 16 Minuets. 1773.
K. 267, 4 Kontretänze. 1777.
K. 300, Gavotte. 1778.
K. 363, 3 Minuets. 1780.
K. 446, Music for a Pantomime. 1783.
K. 461, 6 Minuets. 1784.
K. 462, 6 Kontretänze. 1784.
K. 463, 2 Quadrilles. 1784.
K. 509, 6 German Dances. 1787.
K. 510, 9 Kontretänze. 1787.
K. 534, *Das Donnerwetter* (The Thunderstorm). 1788.
K. 535, Kontretanz, *The Battle.* 1788.
K. 535a, 3 Kontretänze. 1788.
K. 536, 6 German Dances. 1788.
K. 565, 2 Kontretänze. 1788.
K. 567, 6 German Dances. 1788.
K. 568, 12 Minuets. 1788.
K. 571, 6 German Dances. 1789.
K. 586, 12 German Dances. 1789.
K. 587, Kontretanz, *The Hero of Coburg.* 1789.
K. 106, Ouverture and 3 Kontretänze. 1790.
K. 599, 6 Minuets. 1791.
K. 600, 6 German Dances. 1791.
K. 601, 4 Minuets. 1791.
K. 602, 4 German Dances. 1791.
K. 603, 2 Kontretänze. 1791.
K. 604, 2 Minuets. 1791.
K. 605, 3 German Dances. 1791.
K. 606, 6 Ländler. 1791.
K. 607, Kontretanz. 1791.
K. 609, 5 Kontretänze. 1791.
K. 610, Kontretanz, *The Malicious Girls.* 1791.
K. 611, Dance. 1791.

4. *Marches, Symphonic Movements, Minor Orchestration*

K. 189, March, D major. 1773.
K. 214, March, C major. 1775.
K. 215, March, D major. 1775.

K. 237, March, D major. 1774.
K. 248, March, F major. 1776.
K. 249, March, D major. 1776.
K. 290, March, D major. 1773.
K. 335, Two Marches, D major. 1779.
K. 445, March, D major. 1779.
K. 408, Four Marches. 1782.
K. 477, Masonic Dead March, C minor. 1785.
K. 544, March, D major. 1788.
K. 32, Galimathias musicum (*Quodlibet*), D major. 1766.
K. 120, Finale for the symphony of *Ascanio in Alba.* 1771.
K. 161 and 163, Allegro and Andante for a symphony, D major. 1772.
K. 102, Finale for a symphony or divertimento, C major. 1775.
K. 121, Finale for a symphony or divertimento, D major. 1775.
Anh. 103, *La Chasse,* A major. 1779.
K. 409, Symphony Minuet, C major. 1782.
K. 410, Adagio for basson and 2 basset horns, F major. 1783.
K. 411, Adagio for 2 clarinets and 3 basset horns, B flat major. 1783.
K. 522, *Ein musikalischer Spass* (A Musical Joke), sextet for strings and horns, F major. 1787.
K. 594, Adagio and Allegro for organ, A flat major. 1790.
K. 616, Andante for a small organ, F major. 1791.

B—CONCERTOS

1. *For Violin and Orchestra*

Anh. 294a, D major ("Adelaide"). Paris, 1766.
K. 190, Concerto for two violins, C major. Salzburg, 1773.
K. 207, B flat major. Salzburg, 1775.
K. 211, D major. Salzburg, 1775.

K. 216, G major. Salzburg, 1775.

K. 218, D major. Salzburg, 1775.

K. 219, A major ("Turkish"). Salzburg, 1775.

K. 261, Adagio, E major, for a violin concerto, alternative for slow movement of K. 219. Salzburg, 1776.

K. 269, Rondo Concertante (Finale), B flat major, for a violin concerto, alternative for Finale of K. 207. Salzburg, 1776.

K. 271a, D major. Salzburg, 1777.

K. 364, Concertante Sinfonie for violin and viola with orchestra, E flat major. Salzburg, 1779.

K. 268, E flat major. Salzburg and Munich, 1780.

K. 373, Rondo for a violin concerto, C major. Vienna, 1781.

K. 470, Andante for a violin concerto, A major. Vienna, 1785.

2. *For Piano and Orchestra*

K. 107, Concerto arr. from 3 clavier sonatas by Johann Christian Bach (*Jugendkonzert*). London, 1765.

K. 37, F major. Salzburg, 1767.

K. 39, B flat major. Salzburg, 1767.

K. 40, D major. Salzburg, 1767.

K. 41, G major. Salzburg, 1767.

K. 175, D major. Salzburg, 1773.

K. 238, B flat major. Salzburg, 1776.

K. 242, Concerto for three pianos, F major (*Lodron*). Salzburg. 1776.

K. 246, C major (*Lützow*). Salzburg, Paris, 1762–4.

K. 271, E flat major (*Jeunehomme*). Salzburg, 1777.

K. 365, Concerto for two pianos, E flat major. Salzburg, 1779.

K. 382, Concerto Rondo, D major. Vienna, 1782.

K. 386, Concerto Rondo, A major. Vienna, 1782.

K. 413, F major. Vienna, 1782–83.

K. 414, A major. Vienna, 1782.

K. 415, C major. Vienna, 1782–83.

K. 449, E flat major. Vienna, 1784.

K. 450, B flat major. Vienna, 1784.

K. 451, D major. Vienna, 1784.

K. 453, G major. Vienna, 1784.

K. 456, B flat major. Vienna, 1784.

K. 459, F major. Vienna, 1784.

K. 466, D minor. Vienna, 1785.

K. 467, C major. Vienna, 1785.

K. 482, E flat major. Vienna, 1785.

K. 488, A major. Vienna, 1786.

K. 491, C minor. Vienna, 1786.

K. 503, C major. Vienna, 1786.

K. 537, D major ("Coronation"). Vienna, 1788.

K. 595, B flat major. Vienna, 1791.

3. *For Wind Instrument and Orchestra*

K. 191, for bassoon, B flat major. Salzburg, 1774.

K. 299, for flute and harp, C major. Paris, 1778.

K. 313, for flute, G major. Mannheim, 1778.

K. 314, for flute, D major. Mannheim, 1778.

K. 315, Andante for flute and orchestra, C major. Mannheim, 1778.

K. 371, Rondo finale for horn concerto, E flat major. Vienna, 1781.

K. 412, for horn, D major. Vienna, 1782.

K. 293, for oboe, F major. Vienna, 1783.

K. 417, for horn, E flat major. Vienna, 1783.

K. 447, for horn, E flat major. Vienna, 1783.

K. 495, for horn, E flat major. Vienna, 1786.

K. 622, for clarinet, A major. Vienna, 1791.

c—CHAMBER MUSIC

1. *Duo Sonatas for Piano and Violin*

K. 6, C major. Salzburg, Brussels, Paris, 1762–4.

K. 7, D major. Paris, 1763–4.

K. 8, B flat major. Paris, 1763–4.

K. 9, G major. Paris, 1764.

K. 10, B flat major (for violin or flute). London, 1764 (*"âgé de huit ans"*).

K. 11, G major (for violin or flute). London, 1764.

K. 26, E flat major. The Hague, 1766.

K. 27, G major. The Hague, 1766.

K. 28, C major. The Hague, 1766.

K. 29, D major. The Hague, 1766.

K. 30, F major. The Hague, 1766.

K. 31, B flat major. The Hague, 1766.

K. 55, F major.
K. 56, C major.
K. 57, F major.
K. 58, E flat major.⎫ Date and place
K. 59, E flat major.⎬ uncertain
K. 60, E minor.
K. 61, A major.⎭

K. 296, C major. Mannheim, 1778.

K. 301, G major. Mannheim, 1778.

K. 302, E flat major. Mannheim, 1778.

K. 303, C major. Mannheim, 1778.

K. 304, E minor. Paris, 1778.

K. 305, A major. Paris, 1778.

K. 306, D major. Paris, 1778.

K. 376, F major. Vienna, 1781.

K. 377, F major. Vienna, 1781.

K. 378, B flat major. Salzburg, 1779.

K. 379, G major. Vienna, 1781.

K. 380, E flat major. Vienna, 1781.

K. 402, A major. Vienna, 1782.

K. 403, C major. Vienna, 1782.

K. 454, B flat major. Vienna, 1784.

K. 481, E flat major. Vienna, 1785.

K. 526, A major. Vienna, 1787.

Anh. 50, A major. Vienna, 1787.

Anh. 47, G major. Vienna, 1788.

K. 359, Variations on *La Bergère Célimène*. Vienna, 1781.

K. 360, Variations on *Hélas, j'ai perdu mon amant*. Vienna, 1781.

K. 372, Allegro, B flat major, for a duo sonata. Vienna, 1781.

K. 396, Adagio, C minor, for a duo sonata. Vienna, 1782.

K. 404, Andante and Allegretto, C major, for a duo sonata. Vienna, 1783.

Anh. 48, Allegro, A major, for a duo sonata. Vienna, 1785.

K. 547, Sonatina, F major. Vienna, 1788.

2. *Duos and Trios for Strings and for Wind*

K. 46d, Duo for violin(?) and violoncello, or for clavier, C major. Vienna, 1768.

K. 46e, Duo for violin(?) and violoncello, or for clavier, F major. Vienna, 1768.

K. 423, Duo for violin and viola in G major. Salzburg, 1783.

K. 424, Duo for violin and viola in B flat major. Salzburg, 1783.

K. 292, Sonata for bassoon and violoncello, B flat major. Munich, 1775.

K. 266, Trio for 2 violins and violoncello, B flat major. Salzburg, 1777.

K. 404a, Six 3-voice (J. S.) Bach fugues arr. for violin, viola, violoncello. Vienna, 1782.

K. 443, Fugue for violin, viola, violoncello, G major. Vienna, 1783.

Anh. 229 and 229a, Five Divertimenti for clarinets and bassoon, B flat major. Vienna, 1783.

K. 487, Twelve duos for horns, C major. Vienna, 1786.

3. *String Quartets (2 violins, viola, violoncello)*[1]

K. 80, G major. Lodi and Vienna, 1770, 1773 (or Salzburg, 1774).
K. 155, D major. Bozen, 1772.
K. 156, G major. Milan, 1772.
K. 157, C major. Milan, 1772.
K. 158, F major. Milan, 1773.
K. 159, B flat major. Milan, 1773.
K. 160, E flat major. Milan and Salzburg, 1773.
K. 168, F major. Vienna, 1773.
K. 169, A major. Vienna, 1773.
K. 170, C major. Vienna, 1773.
K. 171, E flat major. Vienna, 1773.
K. 172, B flat major. Vienna, 1773.
K. 173, D minor. Vienna, 1773.
K. 387, G major. Vienna, 1782.
K. 421, D minor. Vienna, 1783.
K. 428, E flat major. Vienna, 1783.
K. 458, B flat major ("Hunting"). Vienna, 1784.
K. 464, A major. Vienna, 1785.
K. 465, C major ("Dissonant"). Vienna, 1785.
> (Note—The six quartets above, 387 through 465, are those dedicated to Haydn.)

K. 499, D major. Vienna, 1786.
K. 575, D major ('Cello). Vienna, 1789.
K. 589, B flat major. Vienna, 1790.
K. 590, F major. Vienna, 1790.
> (Note—The three quartets above, K. 575, 589, and 590, are those dedicated to King Frederick William II of Prussia.)

K. 405, Five 4-voice (J. S.) Bach fugues arr. for string quartet. Vienna, 1782–83.
K. 546, Adagio and Fugue, E flat major, for string quartet. Vienna, 1788.

4. *Quartets for Strings and Wind*

K. 285, D major, flute and strings. Mannheim, 1777.
Anh. 171, Allegro and Andantino, C major, flute and strings. Mannheim, 1778.
K. 298, A major, flute and strings. Paris, 1778.
K. 370, F major, oboe and strings. Munich, 1781.

5. *Quintets for Strings, and for Strings with Wind*

K. 174, B flat major, quartet with 2d viola. Salzburg, 1773.
K. 406, C minor, quartet with 2d viola. Vienna, 1787.
K. 407, E flat major, quartet and horn. Salzburg, 1773.
K. 515, C major, quartet with 2d viola. Vienna, 1787.
K. 516, G minor, quartet with 2d viola. Vienna, 1787.
K. 546, C minor, Adagio and Fugue, quartet with double-bass. Vienna, 1788.
K. 581, A major (*Stadler*), quartet with clarinet. Vienna, 1789.
K. 593, D major, quartet with 2d viola. Vienna, 1790.
K. 614, E flat major, quartet with 2d viola. Vienna, 1791.

6. *Piano Trios, Quartets, Quintets*

K. 12, Trio, A major, piano and strings. London, 1764.
K. 13, Trio, F major, piano and strings. London, 1764.
K. 14, Trio, C major, piano and strings. London, 1764.

---

[1] A number of Mozart's works are called either String Quartets or Divertimenti—e.g., K. 136, 137, and 138, listed above as Divertimenti, are sometimes played by the four instruments of a quartet, and sometimes by a larger number.

K. 15, Trio, B flat major, piano and strings. London, 1764.

K. 254, Divertimento, B flat major, piano and strings. Salzburg, 1776.

K. 442, Trio, D minor, piano and strings. Vienna, 1783.

K. 452, Quintet, E flat major, piano, oboe, clarinet, horn, bassoon. Vienna, 1784.

K. 478, Quartet, G minor, piano and strings. Vienna, 1785.

K. 493, Quartet, E flat major, piano and strings. Vienna, 1786.

K. 496, Trio, G major, piano and strings. Vienna, 1786.

K. 498, Trio, E flat major, piano, clarinet, viola. Vienna, 1786.

K. 502, Trio, B flat major, piano and strings. Vienna, 1786.

K. 542, Trio, E major, piano and strings. Vienna, 1788.

K. 548, Trio, C major, piano and strings. Vienna, 1788.

K. 564, Trio, G major, piano and strings. Vienna, 1788.

K. 617, Adagio and Rondo, C minor, harmonica, flute, oboe, viola, violoncello. Vienna, 1791.

D—PIANO COMPOSITIONS

1. *Sonatas and Fantasias*

K. 279, Sonata, C major. Salzburg, 1774.

K. 280, Sonata, F major. Salzburg, 1774.

K. 281, Sonata, B flat major. Salzburg, 1774.

K. 282, Sonata, E flat major. Salzburg, 1774.

K. 283, Sonata, G major. Salzburg, 1774.

K. 284, Sonata, D major (*Dürnitz*). Munich, 1775.

K. 309, Sonata, C major. Mannheim, 1777.

K. 311, Sonata, D major. Mannheim, 1777.

K. 310, Sonata, A minor. Paris, 1778.

K. 330, Sonata, C major. Paris, 1778.

K. 331, Sonata, A major (with the Rondo *alla turca*). Paris, 1778.

K. 332, Sonata, F major. Paris, 1778.

K. 333, Sonata, B flat major. Paris, 1778.

K. 395, Capriccio, C major. Paris, 1778.

K. 394, Fantasia with a Fugue, C major. Vienna, 1782.

K. 396, Sonata movement, C minor. Vienna, 1782.

K. 397, Fantasia, D minor. Vienna, 1782.

K. 457, Sonata, C minor. Vienna, 1784.

K. 475, Fantasia, C minor. Vienna, 1785.

K. 545, Sonata, C major. Vienna, 1788.

Anh. 135 and 138a, Sonata, F major. Vienna, 1788.

K. 570, Sonata, B flat major. Vienna, 1789.

K. 576, Sonata, D major. Vienna, 1789.

2. *Variations*

K. 24, Eight Variations, G major, on a Dutch song. The Hague, 1766

K. 25, Seven Variations, D major, on *Willem van Nassau*. Amsterdam, 1766.

K. 180, Six Variations, G major, on *Mio caro Adone*. Vienna, 1773.

K. 179, Twelve Variations, C major, on a Minuet by Fischer. Salzburg, 1774.

K. 354, Twelve Variations, E flat major, on the aria *Je suis Lindor* from Beaumarchais's opera *The Barber of Seville*. Paris, 1778.

K. 265, Twelve Variations, C major, on *Ah, vous dirai-je, Maman*. Paris, 1778.

K. 353, Twelve Variations, E flat major, on *La belle Françoise*. Paris, 1778.

K. 264, Nine Variations, C major, on *Lison dormait*. Paris, 1778.

K. 352, Eight Variations, F major, on the March from Grétry's opera *Les Mariages Samnites*. Vienna, 1781.

K. 398, Six Variations, F major, on *Salve tu, Domine*, from Paisiello's opera *The Astrologers*. Vienna, 1783.

K. 460, Eight Variations, A major, on the aria *Come un' agnello* by Sarti. Vienna(?), 1784.

K. 455, Ten Variations, G major, on *Unser dummer Pöbel meint* from Gluck's opera *The Pilgrim of Mecca*. Vienna, 1784.

K. 500, Twelve Variations, B flat major, on an Allegretto. Vienna, 1786.

K. 573, Nine Variations, D major, on a Minuet by Duport. Potsdam, 1789.

K. 613, Eight Variations, F major, on the song *Ein Weib ist das herrlichste Ding*. Vienna, 1791.

3. Duets for One or Two Pianos

K. 19d, Sonata, C major, for 4 hands. London, 1765.

K. 381, Sonata, D major, for 4 hands. Salzburg(?), 1772.

K. 358, Sonata, B flat major, for 4 hands. Salzburg, 1774.

K. 448, Sonata, D major, for 2 pianos. Vienna, 1781.

K. 401, Fugue, B flat major, for 2 or 4 hands. Vienna, 1782.

K. 426, Fugue, C minor, for 2 pianos. Vienna, 1783.

K. 357, Sonata, G major, for 4 hands. Vienna, 1786.

K. 497, Sonata, F major, for 4 hands. Vienna, 1786.

K. 501, Andante with five variations, G major, for 4 hands. Vienna, 1786.

K. 521, Sonata, C major, for 4 hands. Vienna, 1787.

4. Other Piano Compositions ("Einzelstücke")

K. 1, Minuet and Trio in G major, Salzburg, 1761 or 1762 (Mozart aged 5 or 6). .

K. 2, Minuet in F major. Salzburg, 1762.

K. 3, Allegro, B flat major. Salzburg, 1762.

K. 4, Minuet in F major. Salzburg, 1762.

K. 5, Minuet in F major. Salzburg, 1762.

K. 9a, Allegro, C major. 1763.

K. 9b, Andante, B flat major. 1763.

K. 15a, Allegro for clavier. London, 1764.

K. 312, Allegro for a clavier sonata, G minor. Salzburg, 1774.

K. 315a, Eight Minuets with trios. Salzburg, 1779.

K. 400, Allegro for a clavier sonata, B flat major. Vienna, 1781.

K. 153, Beginning of a fugue, E flat major. Vienna, 1782.

K. 154, Fugue, B flat major. Vienna, 1782.

K. 154a, Two little fugues for clavier or organ.

K. 399, Piano suite, C major. Vienna, 1782.

K. 453a, Little funeral march, C minor. Vienna, 1784.

K. 485, Rondo, D major. Vienna, 1786.

K. 494, Rondo, F major. Vienna, 1786.

Anh. 136, Clavier sonata, B flat major. Vienna, 1786.

K. 511, Rondo, A minor. Vienna, 1787.

K. 511a, Rondo (Beethoven), B flat major.

K. 533, Allegro and Andante, F major. Vienna, 1788.

K. 540, Adagio, B minor. Vienna, 1788.

K. 574, Little gigue, G major. Leipzig, 1789.

K. 236, Andantino, B flat major. Vienna, 1790.

K. 355, Minuet, D major. Vienna, 1790.

K. 356, Adagio, C major, for harmonica. Vienna, 1791.

K. 624. Cadenzas for the piano concertos, 1768–91.

E—ORGAN COMPOSITIONS

K. 67, Church Sonata, E flat major, for organ and strings. Salzburg, 1767.

K. 68, Church Sonata, B flat major, for organ and strings. Salzburg, 1767.

K. 69, Church Sonata, D major, for organ and strings. Salzburg, 1767.

K. 144, Church Sonata, D major, for violins and organ (or violoncello). Salzburg, 1772.

K. 145, Church Sonata, F major, for violins and organ (or violoncello). Salzburg, 1772.

K. 212, Church Sonata, B flat major, for organ and strings. Salzburg, 1775.

K. 241, Church Sonata, G major, for organ and strings. Salzburg, 1776.

K. 224, Church Sonata, F major, for organ and strings. Salzburg, 1776.

K. 225, Church Sonata, A major, for organ and strings. Salzburg, 1776.

K. 244, Church Sonata, F major, for organ and strings. Salzburg, 1776.

K. 245, Church Sonata, D major, for organ and strings. Salzburg, 1776.

K. 263, Church Sonata, C major, for organ, violins, trumpets. Salzburg, 1776.

K. 274, Church Sonata, G major, for organ and strings. Salzburg, 1777.

K. 278, Church Sonata, C major, for organ, strings, oboes, trumpets, bassoon. Salzburg, 1777.

K. 329, Church Sonata, C major, for organ, strings, oboes, horns, trumpets, bassoon. Salzburg, 1779.

K. 336, Church Sonata, C major, for organ and strings. Salzburg, 1780.

K. 608, Organ Fantasia, F minor, Vienna, 1791.

II—VOCAL

A—CHURCH MUSIC

1. *Masses*

K. 49, Missa brevis, G major. Vienna, 1768.

K. 65, Missa brevis, D minor. Salzburg, 1769.

K. 66, Missa (*Dominicus*), C major. Salzburg, 1769.

K. 116, Missa brevis, F major. Salzburg, 1771.

K. 139, Missa [solemnis], C minor. Salzburg, 1772.

K. 115, Missa brevis, C major. Salzburg, 1773.

K. 167, Missa in honorem SSmae Trinitatis, C major. Salzburg, 1773.

K. 192, Missa brevis, F major. Salzburg, 1774.

K. 194, Missa brevis, D major. Salzburg, 1774.

K. 220, Missa brevis in C major. Munich, 1775.

K. 257, Missa [*Credo*], C major. Salzburg 1776.

K. 258, Missa brevis, C major. Salzburg, 1776.

K. 262, Missa [longa], C major. Salzburg, 1776.

K. 259, Missa brevis (*Organ Solo*), C major. Salzburg, 1776.

K. 275, Missa brevis, B flat major. Salzburg, 1777.

K. 317, Missa (*Coronation*), C major. Salzburg, 1780.

K. 337, Missa solemnis (*Fagottsolomesse*), C major. Salzburg, 1780.

K. 427, Missa, C minor (unfinished). Vienna, 1782–83.

K. 626, Requiem, D minor. Vienna, 1791 (finished by Süssmayr).

(Note—The so-called "Twelfth Mass" is now known to be by a minor composer and not by Mozart.)

2. *Litanies and Vespers*

K. 109, Litaniae de B. M. V. (*Lauretanae*), B flat major. Salzburg, 1771.

K. 125, Litaniae de venerabili altaris sacramento, B flat major. Salzburg, 1772.

K. 195, Litaniae Lauretanae, D major. Salzburg, 1774.

K. 243, Litaniae de venerabili altaris sacramento, E flat major. Salzburg, 1776.

K. 193, Dixit and Magnificat, C major. Salzburg, 1774.

K. 321, Vesperae de Dominica, C major. Salzburg, 1779.

K. 339, Vesperae solennes de confessore, C major. Salzburg, 1780.

3. *Kyries, Offertories, etc.*

K. 33, Kyrie, F major, for voices and orchestra. Paris, 1766.

K. 89, Kyrie for 5 sopranos. Rome, 1770.

K. 90, Kyrie, D minor, for voices and organ. Salzburg, 1771.

K. 91, Kyrie, D major, for voices, strings, organ, 1774.

K. 221, Kyrie, C major, for voices and basso continuo. Salzburg, 1771.

K. 322, Kyrie, E flat major, for voices, orchestra, organ. Mannheim, 1778.

K. 323, Kyrie, C major, for voices, orchestra, organ. Salzburg, 1779.

K. 340, Kyrie, C major, for solo voices. 1780.

K. 341, Kyrie, D minor, for voices, orchestra, organ. Munich, 1781.

K. 20, Motet, D minor, *God Is Our Refuge.* London, 1765.

K. 34, Offertorium in festo S. Benedicti, *Scande coeli limina,* for voices, orchestra, organ. 1766–7.

K. 44, Introit *Cibavit eos* for voices and organ. Bologna, 1770.

K. 47, *Veni Sancte Spiritus,* for voices and organ. Vienna, 1768.

K. 72, Offertorium pro festo S. Joannis Baptistae, *Inter natos mulierum,* for voices, strings, organ. Salzburg, 1771.

K. 85, *Miserere,* C major. Bologna, 1770.

K. 86, Antiphon *Quaerite primum regnum Dei.* Bologna, 1770.

K. 92, *Salve Regina,* F major, for voices, orchestra, organ. 1769(?).

K. 93, Psalm *De profundis,* E flat major, for voices and organ. Salzburg, 1771.

K. 108, *Regina Coeli,* C major, for voices, orchestra, organ. Salzburg, 1771.

K. 117, Offertorium [pro omni tempore], *Benedictus sit Deus; Introibo; Jubilate*. Voices, orchestra, organ. Salzburg, 1769.

K. 127, *Regina Coeli*, B flat major, for voices, orchestra, organ. Salzburg, 1772.

K. 141, *Te Deum*, C major, for voices, strings, organ. Salzburg, 1769.

K. 142, *Tantum ergo*, B flat major, for voices, orchestra, organ.

K. 143, Soprano aria *Ergo interest* and *Quaere superna*, with strings and organ. Milan, 1770.

K. 165, Soprano motet, F major, *Exsultate, jubilate*, with orchestra and organ. Milan, 1773.

K. 197, *Tantum ergo*, D major, for voices, orchestra, organ.

K. 198, Offertorium for soprano and tenor, *Sub tuum praesidium*, F major, with strings and organ. Milan, 1773.

K. 222, Offertorium de tempore, *Misericordias Domini*, F major, for voices and organ. Munich, 1775.

K. 223, *Osanna*, C major, for voices, strings, organ. 1773(?).

K. 260, Offertorium de venerabili sacramento, *Venite, populi*, D major, for two choirs, strings, organs. Salzburg, 1776.

K. 273, Graduale ad festum B. M. V., *Sancta Maria*, F major, for voices, strings, organ. Salzburg, 1777.

K. 276, *Regina Coeli*, C major, for voices, orchestra, organ. Salzburg, 1779.

K. 277, Offertorium de B. M. V., *Alma Dei creatoris*, F major, for voices, strings, organ. Salzburg, 1777.

K. 326, Hymns, *Justum deduxit Dominus* and *O sancte*, for voices and organ. Salzburg, 1771.

K. 327, Hymn, *Adoramus te*, for voices and organ.

K. 343, Two hymns, *O Gottes Lamm* and *Als aus Ägypten*, solo with bass accompaniment. Salzburg, 1779.

K. 618, Motet, *Ave, verum corpus*, D major, for voices, strings, organ. Baden near Vienna, 1791.

B—CANTATAS

K. 42 Passion Cantata with accompaniment of strings and horns. Salzburg, 1767.

K. 118, *La Betulia liberata*, oratorio in 2 parts, text by Metastasio. Salzburg, 1771.

K. 429, *Dir, Seele des Weltalls*, cantata for tenors and bass with orchestra. Vienna, 1783.

K. 469, *Davidde penitente*, cantata for 3 solo voices, chorus, orchestra. Text by Da Ponte(?). Vienna, 1785.

K. 471, *Sehen, wie dem Starren Forscherauge*, short Masonic cantata for tenor and men's chorus with orchestra. Vienna, 1785.

K. 623, *Laut verkünde unsre Freude*, short Masonic cantata for tenors and bass with orchestra. Vienna, 1791.

C—OPERAS

K. 35, *Die Schuldigkeit des ersten Gebotes* (The Observance of the First Commandment), sacred opera in 3 parts, only the first part by Mozart. Salzburg, 1767.

K. 38, *Apollo et Hyacinthus*, a Latin comedy. Salzburg, 1767.

K. 50, *Bastien et Bastienne*, a one-act operetta. Vienna, 1768.

K. 51, *La finta semplice*, opera bouffe in 3 acts. Vienna, 1768.

K. 87, *Mitridate, Rè di Ponto*, opera in 3 acts. Milan, 1770.

K. 111, *Ascanio in Alba,* dramatic serenade in 2 acts. Milan, 1771.

K. 126, *Il sogno di Scipione,* dramatic serenade, text by Metastasio. Salzburg, 1772.

K. 135, *Lucio Silla,* drama with music in 3 acts. Salzburg, 1772.

K. 196, *La finta giardiniera,* opera bouffe in 3 acts. Salzburg and Munich, 1774–75.

K. 208, *Il Rè pastore,* drama with music in 2 acts. Salzburg, 1775.

Anh. 10, Ballet music for the pantomime *Les Petits Riens.* Paris, 1778.

K. 344, *Zaide,* opera in 2 acts. Salzburg, 1779.

K. 345, Choruses and incidental music for *Thamos, King of Egypt.* Salzburg, 1779.

K. 366, *Idomeneo, Rè di Creta,* opera in 3 acts. Salzburg and Munich, 1780–81.

K. 367, Ballet music for *Idomeneo.* Munich, 1781.

K. 384, *Die Entführung aus dem Serail* (The Abduction from the Seraglio), comic opera in 3 acts. 1781–82.

K. 422, *L'oca del Cairo,* opera bouffe in 2 acts. Salzburg, 1783.

K. 430, *Lo sposo deluso,* opera bouffe in 2 acts. Salzburg, 1783.

✓ K. 486, *Der Schauspieldirektor* (The Impresario), one-act comedy with music. Vienna, 1786.

K. 492, *Le Nozze di Figaro* (The Marriage of Figaro), opera bouffe in 4 acts. Vienna, 1786.

K. 527, *Don Giovanni,* opera bouffe in 2 acts. Prague, 1787.

K. 588, *Così fan tutte,* opera bouffe in 2 acts. Vienna, 1790.

K. 620, *Die Zauberflöte* (The Magic Flute), grand opera in 2 acts. Vienna, 1791.

K. 621, *La clemenza di Tito,* grand opera in 2 acts. Vienna and Prague, 1791.

K. 311a, Overture in B flat major.

D—SONGS FOR ONE OR MORE VOICES
WITH PIANO (OR ORGAN)
ACCOMPANIMENT

K. 53, *To Joy ("Freude, Königin der Weisen").*

K. 52, *Daphne, deine Rosenwangen.*

K. 147, *Wie unglücklich bin ich nit.*

K. 148, *O heiliges Band.*

K. 149, *Die grossmütige Gelassenheit ("Ich hab' es längst gesagt").*

K. 150, *Geheime Liebe ("Was ich in Gedanken küsse").*

K. 151, *Die Zufriedenheit im niedrigen Stande ("Ich trachte mich nach solchen Dingen").*

K. 152, Canzonetta, *Ridente la calma ("Der Sylphe des Friedens").*

K. 307, Arietta, *Oiseaux, si tous les ans ("Wohl tauscht ihr Vögelein").*

K. 308, Arietta, *Dans un bois solitaire ("Einsam ging ich jüngst").*

K. 349a and b, *Die Zufriedenheit ("Was frag ich")*—two versions.

K. 351, *Komm, liebe Zither.*

K. 390, *An die Hoffnung ("Ich würd auf meinem Pfad").*

K. 391, *An die Einsamkeit ("Sei du mein Trost").*

K. 392, *Verdankt sei es dem Glanz* and *Mich locket nicht der Schall.*

K. 393, Solfeggien.

K. 441, *Das Bandel ("Liebes Mandel, wo is 's Bandel?")*

K. 468, *Gesellenreise ("Die ihr einem neuen Grade").*

K. 472, *Der Zauberer ("Ihr Mädchen, flieht Damöten ja").*

K. 473, *Die Zufriedenheit ("Wie sanft").*

K. 474, *Die betrogene Welt ("Der reiche Tor")*.

K. 476, *Das Veilchen ("Ein Veilchen auf der Wiese stand")*.

K. 506, *Lied der Freiheit ("Wer unter eines Mädchens Hand")*.

K. 517, *Die Alte ("Zu meiner Zeit")*.

K. 518, *Die Verschweigung ("Sobald Damoetas Chloen sieht")*.

K. 519, *Das Lied der Trennung ("Die Engel Gottes weinen")*.

K. 520, *Als Luise die Briefe ihres ungetreuen Liebhabers verbrannte ("Erzeugt von heisser Phantasie")*.

K. 523, *Abendempfindung ("Abend ist's")*.

K. 524, *An Chloe ("Wenn die Lieb'")*.

K. 529, *Des kleinen Friedrichs Geburtstag ("Es war weinmal")*.

K. 530, *Das Traumbild ("Wo bist du, Bild?")*.

K. 531, *Die kleine Spinnerin ("Was spinnst du")*.

K. 552, *Beim Auszug in das Feld ("Dem hohen Kaiser-Worte treu")*.

K. 596, *Sehnsucht nach dem Frühlinge ("Komm, lieber Mai")*.

K. 597, *Im Frühlingsanfang ("Erwacht zum neuen Leben")*.

K. 598, *Das Kinderspiel ("Wir Kinder, wir schmecken")*.

K. 619, *Die ihr der unermesslichen Weltalls Schöpfer ehrt*, a little German cantata, solo.

K. 441c, *Ständchen*, trio for 2 sopranos (or tenors) and bass.

Anh. 5, *Caro mio Druck und Schluck*, comic quartet for soprano, 2 tenors, bass.

K. 483, *Zerfliesset ‖ heut', geliebte Brüder*, 3-part chorus with organ.

K. 484, *Ihr unsre neuen Leiter*, song for 3-part chorus with organ.

E—CANONS

K. 89, Canon, A major, for 4 voices (no text).

K. 89a, Five riddle-canons.

K. 228, *Ach, zu kurz ist unsers Lebens Lauf*, double canon for 4 voices.

K. 229, *Sie ist dahin*, 3 voices.

K. 230, *Selig, selig alle*, 2 voices.

K. 231, *Leck mich im Arsch*, 6 voices.

K. 232, *Lieber Freistädtler, lieber Gaulimauli*, 4 voices.

K. 223, *Leck mir den Arsch*, 3 voices.

K. 234, *Bei der Hitz im Sommer ess ich*, 3 voices.

K. 347, *Lasst uns ziehn*, 6 voices.

K. 348, *V'amo di core teneramente*, three 4-voice choruses.

K. 507, *Heiterkeit und leichtes Blut*, 3 voices.

K. 508, *Auf das Wohl aller Freunde*, 3 voices.

K. 508a, Eight canons (no text).

K. 553, *Alleluja*, 4 voices.

K. 554, *Ave Maria*, 4 voices.

K. 555, *Lacrimoso son' io*, 4 voices.

K. 556, *G'rechtelt's enk*, 4 voices.

K. 557, *Nascoso è il mio sol*, 4 voices.

K. 558, *Gehn ma in 'n Prada*, 4 voices.

K. 559, *Difficile lectu mihi mars*, 3 voices.

K. 560a and b, *O du eselhafter Peierl* and *O du eselhafter Martin*, 4 voices.

K. 561, *Bona nox, bist a rechta Ox*, 4 voices.

K. 562, *Caro, bell' idol mio*, 3 voices.

K. 562a, Canon for 4 voices (no text).

K. 562b, Study for a canon, 4 voices.

Anh. 191, Canon for 4 voices.

F—ARIAS

K. 23, Soprano air, *Conservati fedele*. 1766.

K. 21, Tenor air, *Va, dal furor portata*. 1765.

K. 36, Tenor recitative and air, *Or che il dover* and *Tali e cotanti sono*. 1766.

K. 70, Soprano recitative and air, *A Berenice* and *Sol nascente*. 1769.

K. 71, Tenor air, *Ah, più tremar non voglio*. 1769–70.

K. 74b. Soprano air, *Non curo l'affetto*. 1771.

K. 77, Soprano recitative and air, *Misero me* and *Misero pargoletto*. 1770.

K. 78, Soprano air, *Per pietà, bell' idol mio*. 1770.

K. 79, Soprano air, *O temerario Arbace* and *Per quel paterno amplesso*. 1770.

K. 82, Soprano air, *Se ardire, e speranza*. 1770.

K. 83, Soprano air, *Se tutti i mali miei*. 1770.

K. 88, Soprano air, *Fra cento affanni*. 1770.

K. 119, Soprano air, *Der liebe himmlisches Gefühl*. 1782.

K. 146, Soprano air, *Kommet her, ihr frechen Sünder*. 1779.

K. 178, Soprano air, *Ah, spiegarti, o Dio*. 1772.

K. 209, Tenor air, *Si mostra la sorte*. 1775.

K. 210, Tenor air, *Con ossequio, con rispetto*. 1775.

K. 217, Soprano air, *Voi avete cor fedele*. 1775.

K. 255. Alto recitative and air, *Ombra felice* and *Io ti lascio, e questo addio*. 1776.

K. 256, Tenor air, *Clarice cara mia sposa*. 1776.

K. 272, Soprano recitative and air, *Ah, lo previdi* and *Ah, t'invola agl' occhi mei*. 1777.

K. 294, Soprano recitative and air, *Alcandro, lo confesso* and *Non so d'onde viene*. 1778.

K. 295, Tenor air, *Se al labbro mio non credi* and *Il cor dolente*. 1778.

K. 316, Soprano recitative and air, *Popoli di Tessaglia* and *Io non chiedo, eterni dei*. 1778.

K. 368, Soprano recitative and air, *Ma, che vi fece, o stelle sperai vicino il lido*. 1781.

K. 369, Soprano scene and air, *Misera dove son!* and *Ah! non son' io che parlo*. 1781.

K. 374, Soprano recitative and air, *A questo seno deh vieni* and *Or che il cielo a me ti rende*. 1781.

K. 383, Soprano air, *Nehmt meinen Dank, ihr holden Gönner!* 1782.

K. 416, Soprano scene and rondo, *Mia speranza adorata* and *Ah, non sai, qual pena*. 1783.

K. 418, Soprano air, *Vorrei spiegarvi, oh Dio* and *Ah conte, partite*. 1783.

K. 419, Soprano air, *No, no, che non sei capace*. 1783.

K. 420, Tenor air, *Per pietà, non ricercate*. 1783.

K. 432, Bass recitative and air, *Cosi dunque tradisci* and *Aspri rimorsi atroci*. 1783.

K. 433, Bass air, *Männer suchen stets zu naschen*. 1783.

K. 434, Tenor recitative and air, *Misero! o sogno* and *Aura, che intorno*. 1783.

K. 435, Tenor air, *Müsst ich auch durch tausend Drachen*. 1783.

K. 440, Soprano air, *In te spero, o sposo*. 1782.

K. 486a, Soprano recitative and air, *Basta, vincesti* and *Ah non lasciarmi, no*. 1778.

K. 490, Soprano scene with rondo,

Non più, tutto ascoltai and *Non temer, amato bene.* 1786.

K. 505, Soprano scene with rondo, *Ch'io mi scordi di te* and *Non temer, amato bene.* 1786.

K. 512, Bass recitative and air, *Alcandro, lo confesso* and *Non so, d'onde viene.* 1787.

K. 513, Bass air, *Mentre ti lascio, o figlia.* 1787.

K. 528, Soprano scene, *Bella mia fiammi* and *Resta, o cara.* 1787.

K. 538, Soprano air, *Ah se in ciel, benigne stelle.* 1788.

K. 539, A German war song, *Ich möchte wohl der Kaiser sein.* 1788.

K. 541, Bass air, *Un bacio di mano.* 1788.

K. 569, Air, *Ohne zwang, aus eignem Triebe.* 1789.

K. 577, Soprano rondo, *Al desio, di chi t' adora.* 1789.

K. 578, Soprano air, *Alma grande e nobil core.* 1789.

K. 579, Soprano air, *Un moto di gioia mi sento.* 1789.

K. 580, Soprano air, *Schon lacht der holde Frühling.* 1789.

K. 582, Soprano air, *Chi sà, chi sà, qual sia.* 1789.

K. 583, Soprano air, *Vado, ma dove? —oh Dei!* 1789.

K. 584, Bass air, *Rivolgeti a lui lo sguardo.* 1789.

K. 584a, Soprano air, *Donne vaghe.* 1789.

K. 612, Bass air, *Per questa bella mano.* 1791.

Anh. 245, Bass air, *Io ti lascio, o cara, addio.* 1791.

G—DUETS, TRIOS, QUARTETS AND CHORUS

K. 389, Duet for 2 tenors, *Welch angstliches Beben.* 1782.

K. 436, Duet (Notturno) for soprano and bass, *Ecco quel fiero istante.* 1783.

K. 437, Duet (Notturno) for soprano and bass, *Mi lagnerò tacendo.* 1783.

K. 489, Duet for soprano and tenor, *Spiegarti non poss' io.* 1786.

K. 625, Comic duet for soprano and bass, *Nun, liebes Weibchen, ziehst mit mir.* 1790.

K. 346, Trio (Notturno) for 3 voices, *Luci care, luci belle.* 1783.

K. 438, Trio (Notturno), *Se lontan, ben mio, tu sei.* 1783.

K. 439, Trio (Notturno) for 2 sopranos and bass, *Due pupille amabile.* 1783.

K. 480, Terzett (Trio), *Mandina amabile.* 1785.

K. 532, Trio for soprano, tenor, bass, *Grazie agl' inganni tuoi.* 1787.

K. 549, Canzonetta for 2 sopranos and bass, *Più non si trovano.* 1788.

K. 479, Quartet for soprano, tenor, 2 basses, *Dite almeno, in che mancai.* 1785.

K. 615, Final Chorus, *Viviamo felici in dolce contento.* 1791.

CHRONOLOGY

(This table was prepared by Elizabeth C. Moore for Ann M. Lingg's *Mozart: Genius of Harmony.*
It is reprinted here without change.)

MOZART'S LIFE	MUSICAL EVENTS	WORLD EVENTS
1756 Born on Jan. 27 at Salzburg.	1756 B., Prince Carl Lichnowsky, friend of Mozart and Beethoven. Mozart's father Leopold publishes his *Violin Method.*	1756 B., "Light-Horse Harry" Lee, Aaron Burr. In Europe, Seven Years' War declared (in America, the French and Indian War).
	1757 D., Domenico Scarlatti, J. W. Stamitz. B., Ignaz Pleyel.	1757 B., Lafayette, Wm. Blake. Franklin goes to England to represent the Pennsylvania Colonial Assembly. British wars in India begin.
	1759 D., Handel. Joseph Haydn composes his First Symphony and is apptd. cond. of Count Morzin's orchestra.	1759 B., Burns, Pitt, Schiller. G. Washington marries Mrs. Custis. British take Quebec; Generals Montcalm and Wolfe killed.
1760 Begins clavier lessons with his father.	1760 B., Cherubini, Dussek, Rouget de Lisle. In Vienna, Gluck's opera *Tetide* is produced.	1760 George II d., George III succeeds. French surrender Canada to British. Macpherson's *Ossian* (Pt. I) pub.
1761 Composes first clavier pieces.	1761 Haydn enters service of Prince Esterházy at Eisenstadt. Gluck produces *Don Juan* ballet in Vienna.	1761 D., Samuel Richardson. B., Sir John Moore, Albert Gallatin.

MOZART'S LIFE	MUSICAL EVENTS	WORLD EVENTS
1762 With his father and sister, visits Munich, Vienna, and Pressburg.	1762 J. C. Bach (the "English Bach") goes to London to live. Gluck's finest opera, *Orfeo*, produced in Vienna.	1762 B., George IV, Fichte. Catherine II usurps Russian throne on death of Elizabeth Petrovna. In London, the "Cock Lane Ghost" affair.
1763 Returns to Salzburg. Some little clavier pieces are published. Concert tour as far as Paris.	1763 B., Méhul. At Esterházy, Haydn prod. his *Acis and Galatea* and writes first clavier sonata.	1763 B., "Jean Paul" Richter, Wm. Cobbett, Fouché. End of Seven Years' War in Europe, and of French and Indian in America.
1764 At Versailles (Court of Louis XV) where he plays. Then to London, meeting J. C. Bach and playing at court. Composes syms. and sonatas.	1764 D., Rameau, Leclair, Mattheson, Locatelli. Haydn's six "Paris" symphonies pub. In Vienna, *La Rencontre imprévue*, by Gluck.	1764 D., Hogarth. Goldsmith's *Traveller*, Walpole's *Castle of Otranto*, Voltaire's *Dictionnaire philosophique*.
1765 The Mozarts give concerts in London. On ending their visit they go on to Holland.	1765 B., Thomas Attwood, pupil of Mozart (1785) and organist at St. Paul's. Gluck ballet *Semiramide*, Vienna.	1765 B., Robt. Fulton, Eli Whitney. Watt inv. steam engine. Stamp Act passed. Blackstone's *Commentaries* pub.
1766 Concerts in Holland. Visits to Versailles, Paris. Family returns home by way of Switzerland.	1766 D., Porpora. Haydn becomes conductor of the Esterházy orchestra.	1766 Franklin goes to England to fight Stamp Act; it is repealed. Goldsmith's *Vicar of Wakefield* published.
1767 Second visit to Vienna.	1767 D., Telemann. In Vienna, Gluck's opera *Alceste* is produced.	1767 B., Andrew Jackson, John Quincy Adams. Britain imposes tea and other duties on American colonies.

MOZART'S LIFE	MUSICAL EVENTS	WORLD EVENTS
1768 Another Vienna visit. Comp. the opera *La Finta semplice*, and has *Bastien and Bastienne* produced in Dr. Mesmer's private theater.	1768 Fire at Esterházy destroys much of Haydn's music. His opera *Lo Speziale* produced. In Paris, Grétry's opera *Le Huron*.	1768 D., L. Sterne. B., Tecumseh, Charlotte Corday, Chateaubriand. Genoa cedes Corsica to France. Sterne's *Sentimental Journey* published.
1769 *La Finta semplice* is produced in Salzburg. In December, sets out for Italy with his father.	1769 B., Benjamin Carr, comp. of early American operas. Grétry produces *Le Tableau vivant* in Paris.	1769 B., Napoleon Bonaparte, Humboldt, Cuvier, Wellington, DeWitt Clinton. In Phila., Rittenhouse erects telescope to observe transit of Venus.
1770 Italian triumphs. Studies with Martini. Opera *Mitridate, Rè di Ponto* is prod. in Milan, Wolfgang conducting.	1770 D., Tartini. B., Ludwig van Beethoven. In Vienna, Gluck's opera *Paris and Helen*. Parts of *Messiah* (Handel) first heard in America.	1770 B., Wordsworth, Hegel. Boston Massacre. Capt. James Cook, on first circumnavigation, discovers Australia. Goldsmith's *Deserted Village* pub.
1771 Salzburg again. The Mozarts return to Milan in August, where *Ascanio in Alba* is produced.	1771 B., J. B. Cramer. In Paris, Grétry's *Zémire et Azor*. Dr. Burney's *Present State of Music in France and Italy* published.	1771 B., Walter Scott, Sydney Smith, Robert Owen, Mungo Park. Smollett's *Humphry Clinker* published.
1772 Salzburg. Wolfgang composes much. In October, he and his father go to Italy. *Lucio Silla* produced in Milan.	1772 D., Daquin. Haydn writes *Farewell Symphony*. Gluck makes his first visit to Paris to produce opera.	1772 D., John Woolman. B., Coleridge. First partition of Poland among powers. Cook's 2d voyage begins.

1773 From Salzburg goes to Vienna in vain quest of court position. Composes first string quintet.

1773 In Paris, Grétry's *Le Magnifique* and *Céphale et Procris*. Gossec reorganizes the Concerts Spirituels. Burney pub. *The Present State of Music in Germany.*

1773 D., Lord Chesterfield. B., Metternich, Wm. Henry Harrison. Boston Tea Party. Daniel Boone moves to Kentucky. Publication of Cook's *Voyage Round the World, 1768–71.*

1774 Salzburg. Visits Munich in December.

1774 D., Jommelli. B., Spontini. Gluck goes to Paris to live; prod. *Iphigénie en Aulide* and (revised) *Orfeo.*

1774 D., Louis XV, Goldsmith, Clive. First Continental Congress meets at Phila. British close port of Boston. Goethe's *Sorrows of Werther* pub. Warren Hastings made Governor of India.

1775 In Munich, he produces *La Finta giardiniera*, January; and in April *Il Rè pastore* at Salzburg.

1775 D., Giovanni Sammartini. B., Boieldieu. In London, J. C. Bach starts the Bach-Abel Concerts. Haydn's oratorio *Il Ritorno di Tobia* is performed in Vienna.

1775 B., Charles Lamb, Jane Austen, J. M. W. Turner, Lyman Beecher. Battles of Lexington, Concord, Bunker Hill; and Washington takes command of Continental armies. Edmund Burke's speech on conciliation of the colonies.

1776 Salzburg. *Haffner* Serenade comp. for wedding in friend's family. Increasing friction with the Archbp. of Salzburg.

1776 Vienna Natl. Theater founded. Gluck produces *Alceste* in Paris. Feud begins between his followers and Piccinni's. Haydn composes opera *La vera costanza.*

1776 Declaration of Independence. Benj. Franklin goes to Paris for 9 years. Battles of Long Island and Trenton. Nathan Hale executed. Adam Smith's *Wealth of Nations* published.

MOZART'S LIFE

1777 With his mother, starts on another tour. At Mannheim meets the Weber family.

1778 Goes on to Paris, where his mother falls ill and dies. Comp. music for ballet, *Les petits riens*. Home by way of Mannheim and Munich.

1779 In Salzburg, composing actively.

1780 Salzburg. Receives commission for opera *Idomeneo* from Munich, where he goes in November.

MUSICAL EVENTS

1777 D., G. C. Wagenseil. Gluck produces *Armide* in Paris. Erard makes first French pianoforte.

1778 D., Thomas Arne. B., J. N. Hummel. Vienna National Singspiel is founded.

1779 Gluck's *Iphigénie en Tauride* establishes his supremacy over Piccinni. At Esterházy, Haydn prod. opera *L'isola disabitata*.

1780 D., J. L. Krebs. B., famous stage soprano Angelica Catalani. Grétry's opera *Andromaque* in Paris.

WORLD EVENTS

1777 B., Henry Clay, T. Campbell, Taney, Hallam, Mme. Récamier. Battle of Saratoga; Burgoyne surrenders. Washington at Valley Forge. Articles of Confederation signed, creating the U. S. A.

1778 D., Voltaire, Rousseau, Piranesi, elder Pitt, Linnaeus. B., Brougham, Brummell, Hazlitt, Robt. Emmet, Gay-Lussac. Alliance signed between U. S. and France. Burney's *Evelina* pub.

1779 Capt. Cook killed in Hawaii by natives. B., Zebulon M. Pike, Decatur, Thomas Moore, Lord Melbourne. Naval battle between *Bonhomme Richard* and H.M.S. *Serapis*. Col. George Rogers Clark seizes British Northwest.

1780 D., Empress Maria Theresa. B., Francis Scott Key, Béranger, Mary Somerville. Rochambeau arrives in U. S. Benedict Arnold's treason; John André hanged. British defeated at King's Mountain.

MOZART'S LIFE	MUSICAL EVENTS	WORLD EVENTS
1781 January, *Idomeneo* is produced in Munich. Mozart goes to Salzburg and Vienna. Quarrels with Archbp. and leaves his service. Contest with Clementi. Meets Haydn.	1781 B., Diabelli. Haydn publishes his *Stabat Mater.* His friendship with Mozart begins. Beethoven starts lessons in organ, violin, and composition.	1781 D., Lessing, Turgot, Battle of the Cowpens, siege of Yorktown, surrender of Cornwallis. Pub. of Kant's *Critique of Pure Reason,* Schiller's *The Robbers,* Rousseau's *Confessions.*
1782 In Vienna. *Die Entführung aus dem Serail* is produced in July. On August 4 he marries Constanze Weber.	1782 D., Metastasio (librettist), J. C. Bach. B., Paganini, Auber, John Field. Rousseau's collected writings on music are published.	1782 B., Daniel Webster, John C. Calhoun, Martin Van Buren, Thomas Hart Benton. Lord North resigns. Britain signs prelim. peace with U. S. Publication of Fanny Burney's *Cecilia.*
1783 Takes his wife to Salzburg to meet his father and sister. Begins and abandons *L'Oca del Cairo.* Returns to Vienna.	1783 D., Johann Adolf Hasse, Caffarelli, Kirnberger, Padre Soler. Beethoven, aged 13, is appointed to the court orchestra at Bonn.	1783 D., Dr. Wm. Hunter, D'Alembert, Mme d'Epinay. B., Bolivar, Iturbide, Washington Irving, Stendhal, Nancy Hanks. European powers recog. independence of U. S. Treaty of Paris signed. Pitt becomes prime minister.
1784 In Vienna. Meets Paisiello and Sarti.	1784 D., Wilhelm Friedemann Bach (J. S. Bach's eldest son), Padre Martini. B., Spohr, Ferdinand Ries, Fétis. Beethoven made deputy court organist. Gossec establishes Ecole Royale de Chant in Paris.	1784 D., Diderot, Dr. Johnson. B., Leigh Hunt, Lord Palmerston. "Affair of the Diamond Necklace" begins, Paris. King's College, N. Y., becomes Columbia College. Jefferson's *Notes on the State of Virginia* published.

MOZART'S LIFE	MUSICAL EVENTS	WORLD EVENTS
1785 In Vienna. Visited by his father. Is called by Haydn "the greatest composer known to him." Begins *Le Nozze di Figaro*.	1785 D., Galuppi. In Vienna, J. H. Hummel becomes Kapellm. at Schikaneder Theater; his son takes lessons from Mozart.	1785 B., Audubon, Oliver Hazard Perry, De Quincey, the Dauphin ("Louis XVII"). Napoleon Bonaparte is commissioned lieutenant of artillery.
1786 In Vienna. In February, *Der Schauspieldirektor* is produced at Schönbrunn. On May 1, *Le Nozze di Figaro* is produced.	1786 D., Michael Arne. B., Sir Henry Bishop, Carl Maria von Weber. Cherubini leaves Italy to live in Paris.	1786 D., Fredk. the Great. Impeachment of Warren Hastings begins. World's first steamboat built by Symington at Edinburgh. Burns's *Poems* pub.
1787 Visits Prague; *Prague* Symphony given, *Don Giovanni* commissioned. In Vienna visited by Beethoven. *Don Giovanni* produced on Oct. 29, Prague.	1787 D., Gluck, Mozart's father Leopold. Haydn composes "King of Prussia" Quartets.	1787 Assembly of Notables at Versailles. U. S. Constitution signed. Shays's Rebellion in Mass. *Federalist Papers* start publication.
1788 *Don Giovanni* (revised) introduced to Vienna. During the summer composes last three Symphonies—E flat major, G minor, and C major (*Jupiter*).	1788 D., Karl Philipp Emanuel Bach. Beethoven apptd. violist in court orchestra, Bonn; friendship with the Breunings and Waldstein begins. Haydn writes *Oxford* Symphony.	1788 D., Gainsborough, Buffon, the Young Pretender (Charles Edward Stuart). B., Byron, Schopenhauer, Sir Robt. Peel. London *Times* started. Penal settlement founded in Australia.
1789 With Prince Lichnowsky, visits Dresden, Leipzig, and Berlin. In Vienna, is commissioned by Emperor Joseph II to write *Così fan tutte*.	1789 In Paris, Sarrette forms the Natl. Guard Band. Cimarosa succeeds Paisiello in St. Petersburg as court composer.	1789 B., Jas. Fenimore Cooper, Daguerre. Washington elected President. Mutiny on the *Bounty*. Paris mob seizes Bastille, French Revolution begins.

MOZART'S LIFE	MUSICAL EVENTS	WORLD EVENTS
1790 *Così fan tutte* produced. At Emperor's coronation, at Frankfort, plays *Coronation* Pf. Concerto.	1790 On death of Esterházy, Haydn retires on a pension. He meets the young Beethoven at Bonn.	1790 D., Franklin. B., Lamartine. Galvani discovers current electricity. Louis XVI accepts new Constitution.
1791 Vienna. Meets Schikaneder, composes *Die Zauberflöte*. Mysterious stranger commissions a *Requiem*. *La Clemenza di Tito* prod. in Prague. Though ill, he conducts prem. of *Die Zauberflöte*. On Dec. 5 dies, leaving *Requiem* unfinished.	1791 D., Paradies. B., Czerny, Meyerbeer. Haydn makes first visit to England; comp. new symphonies for London and Oxford performance.	1791 D., Mirabeau. B., Faraday, S. F. B. Morse. Congress passes first ten amendments (Bill of Rights). Flight of French king and queen to Varennes. Boswell's *Johnson*, Paine's *Rights of Man* pub. Bank of U. S. founded.

601

BIBLIOGRAPHY

(Books, Articles, Catalogues)

ABERT, HERMANN, *W. A. Mozart,* a revision of Otto Jahn's biography, actually a new book; two volumes, Leipzig, 1923. (*Only in German.*)

BARRAUT, DR. J., "A quelle maladie a succombé Mozart?", *in La Chronique médicale,* Paris, Nov. 15, 1905.

BARRINGTON, DAINES, "Account of a Very Remarkable Young Musician," *Philosophical Transactions of the Royal Society,* Vol. 60, London, 1770.

BENN, CHRISTOPHER, *Mozart on the Stage,* New York, 1946.

BELLAIGUE, CAMILLE, *Mozart,* Paris, 1927.

BERLIOZ, HECTOR, "Mozart, Weber, and Wagner," essay in *The Critical Writings of Hector Berlioz,* translated by Edwin Evans, London, 1918.

BLOM, ERIC, *Mozart,* London, 1935.

BLÜMML, E. K., *Aus Mozarts Freundes— und Familienkreis,* Leipzig, 1923.

BOSCHOT, ADOLPHE, *La Lumière de Mozart,* Paris, 1928.

BREAKSPEARE, EUSTACE J., *Mozart,* London, 1902.

BUENZOD, E., *Mozart,* Paris, 1930.

COHEN, HERMANN, *Die dramatische Idee in Mozarts Operntexten,* Berlin, 1915.

CURZON, HENRI DE, *Mozart,* Paris, 1914.

DAVENPORT, MARCIA, *Mozart,* New York, 1932.

DENT, EDWARD J., *Mozart's Operas: A Critical Study,* London, 1913; revised edition, 1946.

DICKINSON, A. E. F., *A Study of Mozart's Last Three Symphonies,* Oxford and London, 1927.

DUNHILL, THOMAS, *Mozart's String Quartets,* Oxford and London, 1927.

EINSTEIN, ALFRED, *Mozart, His Character, His Work,* translated by Arthur Mandel and Nathan Broder, New York, 1945.

ENGEL, CARL, "The Mozart Couple," essay in *Discords Mingled,* New York, 1931.

GHÉON, HENRI, *In Search of Mozart,* translated by Alexander Dru, New York, 1934 (original French edition, *Promenades avec Mozart,* Paris, 1932.)

GIRDLESTONE, CUTHBERT MORTON, *Mozart and His Piano Concertos,* Norman, Okla., 1952. (original French edition, *Mozart: ses concertos pour piano,* two volumes, Paris, 1939.)

GOUNOD, CHARLES, *Mozart's 'Don Giovanni,'* translated from the third French edition by Windeyer Clark and J. T. Hutchinson, London, 1895.

602

GROAG-BELMONTE, CAROLA, *Die Frauen im Leben Mozarts,* Vienna and Leipzig, 1923.

HAAS, ROBERT, *Wolfgang Amadeus Mozart,* Potsdam, 1933.

HOLMES, EDWARD, *The Life of Mozart,* London, 1845.

HUSSEY, DYNELEY, *Wolfgang Amade Mozart,* London, 1928.

HUTCHINGS, ARTHUR, *A Companion to Mozart's Piano Concertos,* Oxford, 1948.

JAHN, OTTO, *The Life of Mozart,* translated by Pauline D. Townsend, three volumes, London, 1891. (See also Abert, *supra.*)

KELLER, OTTO, *Wolfgang Amadeus Mozart: Bibliographie und Ikonographie,* Berlin and Leipzig, 1927.

KELLY, MICHAEL, *Reminiscences,* two volumes, London, 1826.

KERST, FRIEDRICH, *Mozart as Revealed in His Own Words,* translated by H. E. Krehbiel, New York, 1905.

KOLB, ANNETTE, *Mozart: Sein Leben,* Vienna, 1937.

KÖCHEL, LUDWIG VON, *Chronologisch-thematisches Verzeichnis sämtlicher Tonwerke Wolfgang Amade Mozarts,* edited and revised by Alfred Einstein, Leipzig, 1937. (reprinted by J. W. Edwards, Ann Arbor, Mich., 1947.)

KREITMEIER, JOSEF, *Mozart: Eine Charakterzeichnung des grossen Meisters,* Düsseldorf, 1919.

LACH, ROBERT, *W. A. Mozart als Theoretiker,* Vienna, 1918.

LEITZMANN, ALBERT, *Mozarts Persönlichkeit,* Leipzig, 1914.

LERT, ERNEST JOSEF MARIA, *Mozart auf dem Theater,* Berlin, 1918.

LINGG, ANN M., *Mozart: Genius of Harmony,* New York, 1946.

MARKS, F. H., *The Sonata: Its Form and Meaning as Exemplified in the Pianoforte Sonatas of Mozart,* London, 1921.

MERSMAN, HANS, *Mozart,* Berlin, 1925.

MÖRIKE, EDUARD, *Mozart auf der Reise nach Prag,* fiction (translated *Mozart on the Way to Prague,* by Walter and Catherine Alison Phillips, Oxford, 1934).

MOZART FAMILY, *Briefe,* edited by Ludwig Schiedermair, four volumes, with a fifth containing Iconography, Munich and Leipzig, 1914.

MOZART, CONSTANZE, *Briefe—Aufzeichnungen—Dokumente, 1782–1842,* edited by Arthur Schurig, Dresden, 1922.

MOZART, W. A., *Letters,* selected and edited by Hans Mersmann, translated by M. M. Bozman, London, 1928.

———, *The Letters of Mozart and His Family,* chronologically arranged, translated and edited with an introduction, notes and indices, by Emily Anderson; with extracts from the letters of Constanze Mozart to Johann Anton André, translated and edited by C. B. Oldman, three volumes, London, 1938.

NAGEL, WILLIBALD, *Gluck und Mozart,* Langensalza, 1908.

——, *Goethe und Mozart,* Langensalza, 1904.

NETTL, PAUL, *Mozart und Casanova, Eine Erzählung,* Prague, 1929.

——, "DaPonte, Casanova, und Böhmen," *Alt-Prager Almanach,* 1927; *The Other Casanova,* Philosophical Library, 1950.

NIEMETSCHEK, FRANZ, *W. A. Mozart's Leben,* Prague, 1798; new edition, 1905.

NISSEN, GEORG NIKOLAUS VON, *Biographie W. A. Mozarts,* Leipzig, 1828.

NOHL, LUDWIG, *Mozarts Leben,* Berlin, 1876.

——, *Mozart nach den Schilderungen seiner Zeitgenossen* (Mozart as described by his contemporaries), a compilation, Leipzig, 1880.

NOTTEBOHM, GUSTAV, *Mozartiana,* Leipzig, 1880.

OLDMAN, C. B., Article on Mozart in Grove's *Dictionary of Music and Musicians,* third edition, London, 1927.

——, "Mozart and Modern Research," in *Proceedings of the Musical Association,* London, 1932.

OULIBISHEV, ALEXANDER, *Mozart,* in French, Moscow, 1843; in German, Stuttgart, 1847 and 1859.

PARRY, C. HUBERT H., *Studies of Great Composers,* London, 1900.

PAUMGARTNER, BERNHARD, *Mozart,* Berlin, 1927.

PITROU, R., *La Vie de Mozart,* Paris, 1936.

POHL, C. F., *Haydn und Mozart in London,* Vienna, 1867.

PONTE, LORENZO DA, *Memoirs,* translated by L. A. Sheppard, London, 1929.

PRIEGER, KARL, *Urteile bedeutender Dichter, Philosophen und Musiker über Mozart,* gesammelt und herausgegeben von Karl Prieger, second enlarged edition, Wiesbaden, 1886. (A compilation of statements about Mozart by poets, philosophers, and musicians.)

PROCHAZKA, RUDOLF FREIHERRN, *Mozart in Prag,* Prague, 1892.

PROD'HOMME, J.-G., *Mozart, raconté par ceux qui l'ont vu* (Mozart according to those who saw and knew him), Paris, 1928.

REICH, WILLI, *Bekenntnis zu Mozart* (symposium of pieces by many authors), Lucerne, 1945.

SAINT-FOIX, GEORGES DE, *The Symphonies of Mozart,* translated by Leslie Orrey, New York, 1949.

SCHIEDERMAIR, LUDWIG, *Mozart, sein Leben und seine Werke,* Munich, 1922.

Schurig, Arthur, *Mozart, sein Leben und seine Werke,* Leipzig, 1913.

——, *Wolfgang Amade Mozart,* Leipzig, 1923.

Sitwell, Sacheverell, *Mozart,* London, 1932.

Stefan, Paul, *Don Giovanni,* Vienna, 1938.

——, *Die Zauberflöte,* Vienna, 1937.

Talbot, J. E., *Mozart,* Leipzig, 1930.

Tenschert, Roland, *Mozart,* Leipzig, 1930.

——, *Mozart, Ein Kunstlerleben in Bildern und Dokumenten* (An Artist's Life in Pictures and Documents), Amsterdam, 1931.

Turner, W. J., *Mozart: The Man and His Works.* London and New York, 1938.

——, "Wolfgang Mozart," in *The Heritage of Music,* edited by Hubert J. Foss, Oxford and London, 1927.

Waltershausen, Hermann W. von, *Die Zauberflöte, eine Operndrama-turgische Studie,* Munich, 1920.

Wurzbach, Constantin von, *Mozart-Buch,* Vienna, 1869.

Wyzewa, Téodor de, and Saint-Foix, Georges de, *W. A. Mozart: Sa vie musicale et son oeuvre de l'enfance à la pleine maturité,* essai de biographie critique, five volumes (last three by Saint-Foix alone), Paris, 1912–46. (Not available in English.)

INDEX

INDEX TO CONTRIBUTORS

ABOUT THE EDITOR

LOUIS BIANCOLLI was born in New York City in 1907. He received his B. A. and M. A. at New York University and did graduate work at Columbia. He is music critic of *The New York World-Telegram and Sun,* and for several years was co-annotator, with Robert Bagar, of the New York Philharmonic-Symphony Orchestra program books. With Mr. Bagar he has also co-authored *The Victor Book of Operas* and *The Concert Companion.*

Other books by Mr. Biancolli include *The Book of Great Conversations* (later re-issued as *From Socrates to Shaw*), *Mary Garden's Story* (with Miss Garden), *The Analytical Concert Guide, The Flagstad Manuscript, The Opera Reader,* and *Masters of the Orchestra* (with Herbert F. Peyser). Among his translations is a literal version of the libretto of Moussorgsky's opera, *Boris Godounoff.*

Mr. Biancolli is married and the father of a seventeen-year-old daughter, to whom *The Mozart Handbook* has been dedicated.